T0263431

Soft Computing and Intelligent Systems:
Theory and Applications

ACADEMIC PRESS SERIES IN ENGINEERING

Series Editor
J. David Irwin
Auburn University

Designed to bring together interdependent topics in electrical engineering, mechanical engineering, computer engineering, and manufacturing, the Academic Press Series in Engineering provides state-of-the-art handbooks, textbooks, and professional reference books for researchers, students, and engineers. This series provides readers with a comprehensive group of books essential for success in modern industry. Particular emphasis is given to the applications of cutting-edge research. Engineers, researchers, and students alike will find the Academic Press Series in engineering to be an indispensable part of their design toolkit.

Published books in the series:

Industrial Controls and Manufacturing, 1999, E. Kamen
DSP Integrated Circuits, 1999, L. Wanhammar.
Single and Multi-Chip Microcontroller Interfacing, 1999, G. J. Lipovski
Control in Robotics and Automation: Sensor-Based Integration, 1999,
    B. K. Ghosh, N. Xi, T. J. Tarn
Soft Computing and Intelligent Systems, 1999, N. K. Sinha, M. M. Gupta
Introduction to Microcontrollers, 1999, G. J. Lipovski

Soft Computing and Intelligent Systems:
Theory and Applications

NARESH K. SINHA
McMaster University, Hamilton Canada

MADAN M. GUPTA
University of Saskatchewan, Saskatoon, Canada

Honorary Editor

LOTFI A. ZADEH
University of California, Berkeley USA

ACADEMIC PRESS

A Harcourt Science and
Technology Company

SAN DIEGO / SAN FRANCISCO / NEW YORK / BOSTON / LONDON / SYDNEY / TOKYO

Requests for permission to make copies of any part of the work should be mailed to:
Permissions Department, Harcourt, Inc., 6277 Sea Harbor Drive,
Orlando, Florida, 32887-6777

ACADEMIC PRESS
A Harcourt Science and Technology Company
525 B Street, Suite 1900, San Diego, CA 92101-4495, USA
http://www.apnet.com

Academic Press
24–28 Oval Road, London NW1 7DX, UK
http://www.hbuk.co.uk/ap/

Library of Congress Catalog Card Number: 0-12-646490-1
International Standard Book Number: 99-65097

Printed and bound by CPI Group (UK) Ltd, Croydon, CR0 4YY

Transferred to Digital Print 2011

DEDICATION

To
the researchers in this global village who have made countless
contributions to this developing field of soft computing and intelligent
systems some of which is reported in these pages;

and, to

Meena Sinha, Suman Gupta, and Fay Zadeh
who have created a synergistic atmosphere at our homes
for our thirst for the knowledge.

— The Editors

इन्द्रियाणि पराण्याहुरिन्द्रयेभ्यः परं मनः।

मनसस्तु परा बुद्धिर्यो बुद्धेः परतस्तु सः ।।

They say that the senses are superior to the body, the mind is superior to the senses, and the intellect is superior to the mind; but He (the Self) is superior to the intellect.

The Bhagvad-Gita: III, 42

ज्ञानेन तु तदज्ञानं येषां नाशितमात्मनः ।

तेषामादित्यवज्ज्ञानं प्रकाशयति तत्परम् ।।

Ignorance is destroyed by knowledge, just as darkness is destroyed by the Sun.

The Bhagvad-Gita: V, 16

Contents

Part III: Implementation and Application of Intelligent Control

Part IV: Future Perspectives

Foreword

The past few years have witnessed a growing recognition of the centrality of soft computing (SC) as a principal component of methodologies that underlie the conception, design, construction and utilization of information/intelligent systems. This volume, 'Soft Computing and Intelligent Systems', edited by Professors Sinha and Gupta, makes an important contribution to a better understanding of the basics of soft computing and is an authoritative exposition of the principal tools of soft computing and their applications.

To see soft computing in a proper perspective, a bit of history is in order. In a paper published in 1981, "Possibility Theory of Soft Data Analysis," I employed the term "soft data analysis" to describe data that are partly probabilistic and partly possibilistic. Ten years later, in 1991, the Berkeley Initiative in Soft Computing (BISC) was launched. This initiative was motivated by the fact that in science, as in other realms, there is a tendency to be nationalistic—to commit oneself to a particular methodology and employ it as if it were a universal tool. This is aptly expressed as the well-known hammer principle: if the only tool you have is a hammer, everything looks like a nail.

As systems become more varied and more complex, we find that no single methodology suffices to deal with them. This is particularly true of what may be called information/intelligent systems—systems that form the core of modern technology. To conceive, design, analyze, and use such systems we frequently have to employ the totality of tools that are available. Among such tools are the techniques centered on fuzzy logic, neurocomputing, evolutionary computing, probabilistic computing, and related methodologies. It is this conclusion that formed the genesis of the concept of soft computing.

There are two aspects of SC that stand out in importance. First, SC is not a single methodology; rather, it is a consortium of methodologies that are aimed at exploiting the tolerance for imprecision, uncertainty, and partial truth to achieve tractability, robustness, and low solution cost. Second, the constituent methodologies in SC are for the most part complementary and synergistic rather than competitive. What this means is that in many applications it is advantageous to employ the constituent methodologies of SC in combination rather than in a stand-alone mode. A number of chapters in this book deal with applications of this type.

At this juncture, the principal members of the SC consortium are: fuzzy logic (FL); neurocomputing (NC); evolutionary computing (EC); probabilistic computing (PC); and parts of machine learning theory (ML). Within SC, the main contribution of FL is a machinery for dealing with imprecision and partial truth—a machinery in which the principle tools are the calculus of fuzzy if–then rules; the concept of a linguistic variable; the methodology of computing with words; and the computational theory of perceptions. The primary focus of

NC is on systems with connectionist architecture, that is, systems composed of nodes and weighted links. Such systems—which are inspired by the structure of the nervous system in humans—serve as a basis for system modeling and identification. In this perspective, the principal contribution of NC is algorithms that allow a neural network to be trained by exemplification. The primary contribution of EC, which is inspired by genetic evolution in humans and animals, is algorithms for systematized random search; and that of PC is centered on the management of uncertainty, Bayesian networks, and decision analysis.

The constituent methodologies in SC have their strengths and limitations. For example, FL is most effective when the point of departure is a human solution. In this context, fuzzy logic is employed as a programming language that serves to translate a human solution into the language of fuzzy if–then rules. The use of NC does not require the availability of a human solution, but problems in which the input and output data are complex may exceed the learning capability of a neural network. In the case of EC, it is necessary to have a model that can be used for simulation. If no such model is available, the use of EC techniques is, in general, impractical. In PC, a source of difficulty is the lack of precise knowledge of probabilities and utilities. If there is some perceptual information about them, the computational theory of perceptions—which is based on fuzzy logic—may be employed to arrive at approximate values of probabilities and utilities.

As was alluded to earlier, the guiding principle of soft computing is that, in general, it is advantageous to employ its constituent methodologies in combination. This is reflected in the contents of this book. Today, so-called neurofuzzy systems have the highest visibility. But we are beginning to see systems that are fuzzy-genetic, neuro-genetic and neuro-fuzzy-genetic. In my view, most high MIQ (Machine IQ) systems in coming years will be of hybrid type, employing various combinations of the constituent methodologies of soft computing. This is the direction charted by the editors and contributors to *Soft Computing and Intelligent Systems*. We are entering a fascinating era of machines that can make intelligent decisions in complex situations that lie beyond the reach of the human mind. It is this vision that underlies the authoritative, up-to-date and reader-friendly exposition of soft computing and its applications in this book.

Lotfi A. Zadeh
Berkeley, California

Preface

Intelligence in human beings is the creation of nature. It possesses robust attributes with distributed sensors and control mechanisms. The faculty of cognition—which is housed in our carbon-based computer, the brain—acquires information fuzzily about the environment through various natural sensory mechanisms such as vision, hearing, touch, taste, and smell. It integrates this fuzzy information and provides appropriate interpretation through the cognitive computing. The cognitive process then advances further towards some attributes, such as learning, recollection, and reasoning, which results in appropriate actions through muscular control. The mechanism of muscular control is directed by a complex neural network distributed in the central nervous system (CNS). This process of cognition takes place through neural computing that, unlike the hard computing in our present-day digital computers, is based on some sort of soft computing. It is this process of soft computing that takes place through biological neural mechanisms and that is what makes the human an intelligent animal.

The traditional mathematical concepts, the mathematics that we learn and teach, and through which we develop scientific and engineering concepts, are based upon some precise, quantitative aspects and rigorous concepts. Such quantitative aspects and rigorous concepts are beautiful, but they fail to formulate the imprecise and qualitative nature of our cognitive behaviour—*the intelligence*.

Man has learned many good things from nature. We have learned how to fly, and have created flying machines that can fly almost in synchrony with the sun.

We are also learning from nature and trying to imitate the process of cognition and intelligence into machines. Our aim is to construct an autonomous robotic system that can think and act robustly in an uncertain and unstructured environment. Robots in manufacturing, mining, agriculture, space, ocean exploration, and health sciences are just a few challenging examples of applications where human like cognitive faculty and intelligence can be used. Also, in the fields of decision making such as economics, politics, law, management sciences, health sciences, and administration, some of the mathematical tools evolving around the notions of fuzzy logic, neural networks, and soft computing may contribute to the strength of the decision making field.

The subject of this volume: *Soft Computing and Intelligent Systems* is a subset of the vast growing field of intelligent machines. The field of control, the second key word in the title, is not new. Since its mathematical inception in the early 1940s, it has gone through many phases of development. During the first phase (1940–1960), we saw the development of linear and nonlinear control mechanisms, which was mainly based upon frequency domain approaches. During the second phase of control systems (1960–1980), we saw the introduction of many innovative tools such as state-space approach, optimal control theory, and the notion of learning and adaptation. Some of these theoretical tools were applied to the process control and aerospace industries. A great deal of credit for this growth can be attributed to the efforts and synergies of international societies such as the International Federation of Automatic Control (IFAC), IEEE, ASME and others. Many new control concepts and methodologies appeared during this period. However, again these concepts relied heavily on rigorous mathematical concepts.

Since the inception of the notion of fuzzy arithmetic and fuzzy logic in 1965, which was originated by Professor Lotfi A. Zadeh, we started thinking about the *quantitative* and *qualitative* aspects of control mechanisms, and introduced the notion of intelligent systems. This logic is capable of emulating certain functional elements of human intelligence. In partnership with other mathematical tools such as neural networks, genetic algorithms, and chaos theory, the field of fuzzy arithmetic and fuzzy logic is responsible for the creation of a new field—the field of *soft computing*.

In this decade, the field of soft computing has become a new emerging discipline in providing solutions to complex industrial and management problems, problems that are deeply surrounded by both qualitative and quantitative uncertainties.

Thus, the elements of this emerging field of soft computing provide some mathematical strength in the emulation of human-like intelligence, and in the creation of systems that we call intelligent systems. The mathematics of soft computing has started making advances in this era of intelligent systems. This *artificial intelligence* in machines has started to create a profound impact in our thinking, communication processes, and industrial robotic systems, and in the development of decision making algorithms.

In 1996 (with a second printing in 1998), we published the IEEE Press book *Intelligent Control Systems: Theory and Applications*. It contains 29 chapters authored by 55 international researchers from eight countries. Since the publication of that volume, the field of intelligent control has been growing exponentially, introducing many innovative theoretical notions and practical applications. Some of these innovative theoretical notions and new applications appear in this new volume.

In designing the present book, we strove to present a pedagogically sound volume that would be useful as a supplementary or even as a main text for graduate students. Additionally, this collection of chapters authored by some world-renowned researchers in the field has conceptual and theoretical information embodying a comprehensive view of the general field of soft computing and intelligent control systems. We hope that our efforts in designing this volume will stimulate the learning and research interests of academics researchers and industrial users.

This volume on *Soft Computing and Intelligent Systems: Theory and Applications* contains 25 chapters authored by 41 invited researchers from world-renowned schools in ten countries.* These chapters are classified into the following four parts:

Part I: Foundations of Soft Computing and Intelligent Control Systems
           (Chapters 1 to 10)

Part II: Theory of Soft Computing and Intelligent Control Systems
           (Chapters 11 to 16)

Part III: Implications and Applications of Intelligent Control
           (Chapters 17 to 24)

Part IV: Future Perspectives
           (Chapter 25)

---

* Australia (2 authors, 1 chapter); Canada (5 authors, 7 chapters); Germany (4 authors, 3 chapters); India (4 authors, 4 chapters); Japan (5 authors, 2 chapters); Pakistan (1 author, 1 chapter); Singapore (4 authors, 1 chapter); Slovenia (2 authors, 1 chapter); UK (3 authors, 1 chapter); and USA (11 authors, 7 chapters).

The main technical focus of these 25 chapters is summarized in the table following this preface. It may be noted that this book covers a wide variety of topics in the fields related to soft computing and intelligent systems. The contributions made in these 25 chapters will, it is hoped, serve a wide community of students, researchers, and engineers working in the field of intelligent control.

This volume is compiled for graduate students, academic researches, and industrial users working in the field. We hope that it provides readers with a comprehensive view of the field, its problems, as well as its accomplishments, and its future potentials, and perspectives.

We also hope that this volume will provide some new challenges to readers, will generate curiosity for learning more in the field, and will arouse a desire to seek new theoretical tools and applications. We will consider our efforts successful if the reading of this book raises one's level of curiosity.

Naresh K. Sinha
Madan M. Gupta

Acknowledgements

With the evolution of a complex technological society and the introduction of new notions and innovative theoretical tools in systems science, the field of control systems is going through enormous changes. The innovative theoretical tools that are evolving are centered around the theory of *soft computing* — a theory that embodies the theory of the fields of *fuzzy logic*, *neural networks*, *evolutionary computing*, *probabilistic computing*, *genetic algorithms*. It is true that the tools of soft computing are providing some intelligence and robustness in systems similar to those seen in natural biological processes. The idea for a volume on intelligent control systems was conceived during research discussions in classrooms and at international scientific meetings. We produced the first book in this field through the IEEE Press in 1996. In the present volume, we present another 25 chapters authored by 41 researchers from 10 different countries.

We are grateful to the authors of these chapters, and to the many research colleagues and students around the globe who have inspired our thinking in this emerging field of soft computing and intelligent control systems. We wish to acknowledge the helpful feedback that we received from the reviewers. In particular, we are grateful to Professor Jay Farrell, who provided some very constructive feedback to the authors through his extensive review process, and who also designed an initial layout of the Summary Table given at the end of the Preface. We also thank Mr. Joel Claypool, Executive Editor, Academic Press, for his assistance and useful feedback during the preparation of this volume.

Finally, we are grateful to our graduate students and many research colleagues for creating a warm atmosphere through their continuous intellectual dialogues for the nourishment of this book and many similar publications over the years.

We are also much indebted to our families and our wives, Fay Zadeh, Meena Sinha, and Suman Gupta, who have a complete understanding of our spare time that we use for the exploration of knowledge.

List of Contributors

P.J. Antsaklis Dept. of Electrical Engineering, University of Notre Dame, Notre Dame, In 46556, U.S.A. Tel. 219 631 5792, Fax: 219 631 4393, e-mail: antsaklis.1@nd.edu

Fumihito Arai Department of Micro System Engineering, Graduate School of Engineering, Nagoya University, Japan

R.G.S. Asthana Vice-President, Business Standard Ltd., 5 BSZ Marg, New Delhi 110 002, India. e-mail: r.asthana@computer.org

S.K. Basu Computer Centre, Banaras Hindu University, Varanasi, 22105, India. Tel: +91 542 316680 (home), Fax: +91 542 312 059, e-mail: swapank@banaras,ernet.in

Yangquan Chen Department of Electrical Engineering, National University of Singapore, 10 Kent Ridge Crescent, Singapore 119260

Anthony Engwarda Intelligent Control Systems Laboratory, School of Microelectronic Engineering, Griffith University, Nathan, Q411, Australia. Fax: +61 7 3875 5384

M. Fischer Siemens AG, Automotive Systems, Germany

T. Fukuda Dept. of Micro System Engineering, Nagoya University, Furo-cho, Chikasua-ku, Nagoya 464-8603, Japan. E-mail: fukuda@mein.nagoya-u.ac.jp

Q. Gan Image, Speech and Intelligent Systems Group, Department of Electronics and Computer Science, University of Southampton, Southampton, U.K.

M.M. Gupta Intelligent Systems Laboratory, School of Engineering, Saskatchewan, SK S7N 5A9, Canada. Tel: 306 966 5451 (office), 306 933 0663 (home), Fax: 306 966 8710 or 306 966 5427, e-mail: guptam@sask.usask.ca

Pramod Gupta Ansoft Corporation, 669 River Drive, Suite 200, Elmwood Park, NJ 07407-1361, U.S.A., Tel: (201) 796-2003, FAX: (201) 796-6555, e-mail: gupta@comsoft.com.

C.C. Hang Department of Electrical Engineering, National University of Singapore, 10 Kent Ridge Crescent, Singapore 119260

Steven Alex Harp Honeywell Technology Center, Minneapolis, MN 55418, U.S.A.

Simon Haykin   Department of Electrical & Computer Engineering, McMaster University, Hamilton, Ontario, Canada L8S 4K1. Tel: 905 525 9140 ext. 24809, Fax: 905 521 2922, e-mail: haykin@soma.crl.mcmaster.ca

C.J. Harris   Department of Electronics & Computer Science, University of Southampton, Highfield, Southampton SO17 1BJ, U.K. Tel: +44 1703 592353, Fax: +44 1703 594498, e-mail: cjh@ecs.soton.zc.uk

X. Hong   Image, Speech and Intelligent Systems Group, Department of Electronics and Computer Science, University of Southampton, Southampton, U.K.

R. Isermann   Institute of Automatic Control, Darmstadt University of Technology, D-64283 Darmstadt, Germany. Tel: +49 6151 162114, Fax: +49 6151 293445, e-mail: RIsermann @iat.tu-darmstadt.de

Makoto Kajitani   Kajitani-Ming Laboratory of Mechatronics, Department of Mechanical & Control Engineering, The University of Electro-Communications, 1-501 Chofugaoka, Chofu, Tokyo 182, Japan. Tel: 0424 43 5421, Fax: 0424 80 2778, e-mail: kajitani@mce.uec.ac.jp

Futoshi Kobyashi   Dept. of Micro System Engineering, Nagoya University, Furo-cho, Chikasua-ku, Nagoya 464-8603, Japan. Tel: 952 789 3925, Fax: 952 789 3909, e-mail: futoshi@robo.mein.nagoya-u.ac.jp

X.D. Koutsoukos   Department of Electrical Engineering, University of Notre Dame, Notre Dame, IN 46556, U.S.A.

Tong Heng Lee   Department of Electrical Engineering, National University of Singapore, 10 Kent Ridge Crescent, Singapore 119260, Fax: +65 777-3847, e-mail: eleleeth@nus.edu.sg

William K. Lennon   Department of Electrical Engineering, The Ohio State University, 2015 Neil Avenue, Columbus, OH 43210, U.S.A.

A.H. Levis   Department of Systems Engineering, George Mason University, Fairfax, VA 22039-444, U.S.A, e-mail: alevis@gmu.edu

Frank L. Lewis   Automation & Robotics Research Institute, University of Texas at Arlington, 7300 Jack Newell Blvd, Fort Worth, TX 76119, U.S.A. Tel: 817 272 5957, Fax: 817 272 5989, e-mail: flewis@controls.uta.edu

D. Matko,   Faculty of Electrical & Computer Engineering, University of Ljubljana, Ljubljana 6100, Slovenia. e-mail: DRAGO@lsav-8.fer.uni-lj.si

Petr Musilek   Intelligent Systems Laboratory, College of Engineering, University of Saskatchewan, Saskatoon, Saskatchewan, Canada S7N 5A9

Oliver Nelles   Darmstadt University of Technology, Institute of Automatic Control, Tel: +49 6151 164524, Fax: +49 6151 293445, e-mail: Onelles@irt.tu-darmstadt.de

Kevin M. Passino   Department of Electrical Engineering, The Ohio State University, 2015 Neil Avenue, Columbus, OH 43210, U.S.A. Tel: 614-292-5716, Fax: 614-292-7596, e-mail: passino@ee.eng.ohio-state.edu

D. Popovic   Head, Institute of Automation Technology, Universität Bremen, Fachberich 1, Bibliothekstraße, 28539 Bremen, Germany. e-mail: popovic@physik.ubremen.de

Dandina H. Rao   Head, Department of Electronics & Communication Engineering, Gogte Institute of Technology, Udyambag, Belgaum 590 008, Karnataka, India. Tel: +91 831 441 104, Fax: +91 831 424 909

Tariq Samad   Honeywell Technological Center, 3660 Technology Drive, Minneapolis, MN 55418, U.S.A. Tel: 612-951-7069, Fax: 612-951-7438, e-mail: samad@htc.honeywell.com

Rastko R. Šelmić   University of Texas at Arlington, 7300 Jack Newell Blvd, Fort Worth, TX 76119, U.S.A. e-mail: rselmic@arriso4.uta.edu

Koji Shimojima   National Industrial Research Institute of Nagoya, MITI, Nagoya, Japan

K.K. Shukla   Department of Computer Engineering, I.T., Banaras Hindu University, Varanasi 221005, India. Tel: +91 542 314 401 (home), e-mail: kkshukla@banaras.ernet.in

Ramnandan P. Singh   Department of the Navy, Naval Air Warfare Center, Aircraft Division, Building 2185, Suite 1190, 22347 Cedar Point Road; Unit 16 Patuxent River, MD 20670-1161, U.S.A. e-mail: SinghRP@navair.navy.mil

Naresh, K. Sinha   Department of Electrical & Computer Engineering, McMaster University, Hamilton, Ontario, Canada L8S 4K1. Tel: 905 525 9140 ext. 24968 (office), 905 628 2750 (home), Fax: 905 523 4407 (office), e-mail: sinha@ece.eng.mcmaster.ca or naresh.sinha@ieee.org

Igor Škranjc   Faculty of Electrical & Computer Engineering, University of Ljubljana, Ljubljana 6100, Slovenia. e-mail: igor.skranjc@lsav-8.fer.uni-lj.si

Ljubo Vlacic   Intelligent Control Systems Laboratory, School of Microelectronic Engineering, Griffith University, Nathan, Q411, Australia. Tel: +61 71 3875 5024, Fax: +61 71 3875 5384, e-mail: L. Vlacic@me.gu.edu.au

Jian Xin Xu   Intelligent Systems Laboratory, College of Engineering, University of Saskatchewan, Saskatoon, Saskatchewan, Canada S7N 5A9

Lotfi A. Zadeh   Computer Science Division, University of California-Berkeley, Berkeley, CA 94720-1776, U.S.A. Tel: 510 642 4959 or 642 8271, e-mail: zadeh@cs.berkeley.edu

Abbas K. Zaidi   Department of Computer Science, University of Karachi, Karachi 75270, Pakistan.

Summary of Book Chapters with Classification of Approaches

Chapter	Authors	Title	Overview 1	Architecture 2	Soft Computing 3	Neural Networks 4	Fuzzy Logic 5	Neuro-Fuzzy Systems 6	Genetic Algorithms 7	Evolutionary Algorithms 8
PART I										
1.	Zadeh	Outline of a Computational Theory of Perception based on Computing with Words	X		X		X	X	X	X
2.	Sinha and Gupta	Introduction to Soft Computing and Intelligent Control Systems	X		X	X	X		X	
3	Koutsoukos and Antsaklis	Computational Issues in Intelligent Control							X	
4.	Haykin	Neural Networks – A Guided Tour	X		X	X				
5.	Zaidi and Levis	On Generating Variable Structure Organization Using a Genetic Algorithm							X	X
6.	Asthana	Evolutionary Algorithms and Neural Networks				X			X	X
7.	Musilek and Gupta	Neural Networks and Fuzzy Systems	X	X	X	X	X	X		
8.	Musilek and Gupta	Fuzzy Neural Networks				X	X	X		
9.	Basu	A Cursory Look at Parallel and Distributed Architectures and Biologically Inspired Computing	X	X		X			X	
10.	Xu, Lee, Hang, and Chen	Developments in Learning Control Systems								
PART II										
11.	Lennon and Passino	Techniques for Genetic Adaptive Control							X	
12.	Vlacic, Enginwirda, and Kajitani	Cooperative Behavior of Intelligent Agents: Theory and Practice								
13.	Popovic	Expert Systems in Process Diagnosis and Control								
14.	Gupta and Sinha	Neural Networks for Identification of Nonlinear Systems: An Overview	X			X				
15.	Kobayashi, Shimojima, Arai, and Fukuda	Sensor Fusion System Using Recurrent Fuzzy Inference				X	X	X		
16.	Harris, Hong, and Gan	Neurofuzzy State Estimators					X	X		

Neuro-Control Systems 9	Neuro-Vision Systems 10	Adaptive Systems 11	Learning Systems 12	Distributed Intelligent Systems 13	Hybrid Systems 14	Petri Networks 15	Robotic Systems 16	Discrete Events Systems 17	Intelligent Systems 18	Biological Computing 19	Expert Systems 20	System Identification 21
									X			
									X			
					X	X		X	X			
									X			
				X								
X												
			X						X			
									X			
					X					X		
		X	X						X			
		X	X									
		X	X	X					X			
		X									X	
												X

(*continued*)

Summary of Book Chapters with Classification of Approaches (*continued*)

Chapter	Authors	Title	Overview 1	Architecture 2	Soft Computing 3	Neural Networks 4	Fuzzy Logic 5	Neuro-Fuzzy Systems 6	Genetic Algorithms 7	Evolutionary Algorithms 8
PART III										
17.	Shukla	Soft Computing Paradigms for Artificial Vision			X	X		X	X	
18.	Popovic	Intelligent Control with Neural Networks				X				
19.	Fischer, Nelles, and Iserman	Knowledge-Based Adaptation of Neurofuzzy Models in Predictive Control of a Heat Exchanger					X	X		
20.	Selmic and Lewis	Neural Network Approximation of Piecewise Continuous Functions: Application to Friction Compensation				X				
21.	Skrjanc and Matko	Fuzzy Adaptive and Predictive Control of a Thermic Process				X				
22.	Singh	An Intelligent Approach to Positive Target Identification								
23.	Harp and Samad	Adaptive Agents and Artificial Life: Insights for the Power Industry			X	X	X			
24.	Gupta and Rao	Truck Backer-Upper Control Using Dynamic Neural Network		X	X	X				
PART IV										
25.	Gupta and Sinha	Toward Intelligent Machines: Future Perspectives	X	X						

Neuro-Control Systems 9	Neuro-Vision Systems 10	Adaptive Systems 11	Learning Systems 12	Distributed Intelligent Systems 13	Hybrid Systems 14	Petri Networks 15	Robotic Systems 16	Discrete Events Systems 17	Intelligent Systems 18	Biological Computing 19	Expert Systems 20	System Identification 21
	X											
X		X	X						X			
		Y	Y									
		X	X									
		X	X									
	X								X			X
							X	X				
									X			

PART I

FOUNDATIONS OF SOFT COMPUTING AND INTELLIGENT CONTROL SYSTEMS

CHAPTER 1

Outline of a Computational Theory of Perceptions Based on Computing with Words

L. A. ZADEH

Berkeley Initiative in Soft Computing (BISC), University of California, Berkeley, California, USA

To James Albus and Alex Meystel

INTRODUCTION

Perceptions play a pivotal role in human cognition. The literature on perceptions is enormous, encompassing thousands of papers and books in the realms of psychology, linguistics, philosophy, and brain science, among others [64]. And yet, what is not in existence is a theory in which perceptions are treated as objects of computation. A preliminary version of such a theory, called the computational theory of perceptions (CTP), is outlined in this chapter.

The computational theory of perceptions is inspired by the remarkable human capability to perform a wide variety of physical and mental tasks without any measurements and without any computations. Everyday examples of such tasks are parking a car, driving in city traffic, playing golf, cooking a meal, and summarizing a story. Underlying this remarkable capability is the brain's ability to manipulate perceptions—perceptions of time, distance, force, direction, speed, shape, color, likelihood, intent, truth and other attributes of physical and mental objects.

A basic difference between measurements and perceptions is that, in general, measurements are crisp and quantitative whereas perceptions are fuzzy and qualitative. Furthermore, the finite ability of the human brain to resolve detail and store information necessitates a partitioning of objects (points) into granules, with a granule being a clump of objects (points) drawn together by indistinguishability, similarity, proximity, or functionality [62]. For example, a perception of age

3

may be described as *young*, with *young* being a context-dependent granule of the variable *Age* (Figure 1). Thus, in general, perceptions are both fuzzy and granular, or for short, f granular. In this perspective, use of perceptions may be viewed as a human way of achieving fuzzy data compression.

One of the fundamental aims of science has been and continues to be that of progressing from perceptions to measurement. Pursuit of this aim has led to brilliant successes. We have sent men to the moon; we can build computers that are capable of performing billions of computations per second; we have constructed telescopes that can explore the far reaches of the universe; and we can date rocks that are millions of years old. But alongside the brilliant successes stand conspicuous underachievements. We cannot build robots that can move with the agility of animals or humans; we cannot automate driving in city traffic; we cannot translate from one language to another at the level of a human interpreter; we cannot create programs that can summarize nontrivial stories; our ability to model the behavior of economic systems leaves much to be desired; and we cannot build machines that can compete with children in the performance of a wide variety of physical and cognitive tasks.

It may be argued that underlying the underachievements is the lack of a machinery for manipulation of perception. A case in point is the problem of automation of driving in city traffic—a problem that is certainly not academic in nature. Human drivers do it routinely, without any measurements and any computations. Now assume that we had a limitless number of sensors to measure anything that we might want. Would this be of any help in constructing a system that would do the driving on its own? The answer is a clear no. Thus, in this instance, as in others, progressing from perceptions to measurements does not solve the problem.

To illustrate a related point, consider an example in which we have a transparent box containing black and white balls. Suppose that the question is: What is the probability that a ball drawn at random is black? Now, if I can count the balls in the box and the proportion of black balls is, say, 0.7, then my answer would be 0.7. If I cannot count the balls but my visual perception is that most are black, the traditional approach would be to draw on subjective probability theory. Using an elicitation procedure in this theory would lead to a numerical value of the desired probability, say, 0.7. By so doing, I have quantified my perception of the desired probability; but can I justify the procedure that led me to the numerical value?

Countertraditionally, employing CTP would yield the following answer: If my perception is that most balls are black, then the probability that a ball drawn at random is black is *most*, where *most* is interpreted as a fuzzy proportion (Figure 2). Thus, in the traditional approach the data are

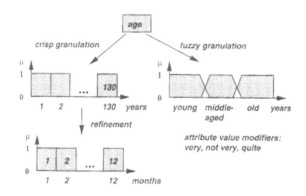

FIGURE 1
Crisp and fuzzy granulation of *Age*. Note that *young* is context-dependent.

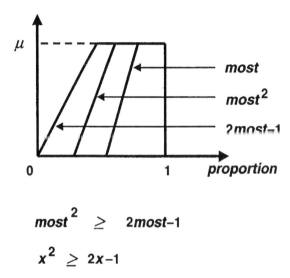

$$most^2 \geq 2most-1$$

$$x^2 \geq 2x-1$$

FIGURE 2
Definition of *most* and related perceptual quantifiers. Note that *most* is context-dependent.

imprecise but the answer is precise. In the countertraditional approach, imprecise data induce an imprecise answer [63].

An interesting point is that even if I know that 80% of the balls are black, it may suffice—for some purposes—to employ a perception of the desired probability rather than its numerical value. In this instance, we are moving, countertraditionally, from measurements to perceptions to exploit the tolerance for imprecision. This is the basic rationale for the use of words in place of numbers in many of the applications of fuzzy logic, especially in the realm of consumer products [41, 63].

An additional rationale is that for humans it is easier to base a decision on information that is presented in a graphical or pie-chart form rather than as reams of numbers. In this case, as in many others, there is a significant advantage in moving from measurements to perceptions.

An important conclusion that emerges is that, in addition to methodologies in which we follow the tradition of moving from perceptions to measurements, we need methodologies in which we move, countertraditionally, from measurements to perceptions (Figure 3). It is this

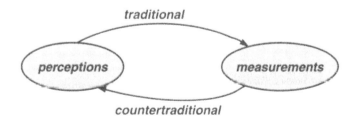

Computational theory of perceptions (CTP) is aimed at a formalization of the remarkable human capability to perform a wide variety of physical and mental tasks without any measurements and any computations

FIGURE 3
Evolution of science.

conclusion that serves as the genesis for the computational theory of perceptions. More fundamentally, it is a conclusion that has important implications for the course of the evolution of science, especially in those fields, e.g., economics, in which perceptions play an important role.

THE BASICS OF THE COMPUTATIONAL THEORY OF PERCEPTIONS

In the computational theory of perceptions, perceptions are not dealt with directly. Rather, they are dealt with through their description as words or propositions expressed in a natural or synthetic language. Simple examples of perceptions described in a natural language are the following:

- several large balls
- Mary is young
- Mary is much older than Carol
- Robert is very honest
- overeating causes obesity
- precision carries a cost
- Mary is telling the truth
- it is likely that Robert knows Mary
- it is very likely that there will be a significant increase in the price of oil in the near future

In fact, a natural language may be viewed as a system for describing perceptions. There are many ways in which perceptions can be categorized. A system that is important for our purposes is the following:

1. Perceptions that are descriptions of unary relations

   Examples: Mary is young

                   Berkeley is a lively city

2. Perceptions that are descriptions of binary relations

   Examples   Mary is much older than Carol

                   Berkeley is near San Francisco

3. Perceptions that are descriptions of functions

   Examples (see Figure 4):

                   if X is *small* then Y is *small*

                   if X is *medium* then Y is *large*

                   if X is *large* then Y is *small*

4. Perceptions that are descriptions of systems. A system is assumed to be associated with sequences of inputs $X_1, X_2, X_3, \ldots$; sequences of outputs $Y_1, Y_2, Y_3, \ldots$; sequences of states $S_1, S_2, S_3, \ldots$; the state transition function

$$S_{t+1} = f(S_t, X_t), \qquad t = 1, 2, \ldots$$

and the output function

$$Y_t = g(S_t, X_t)$$

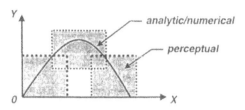

perceptual.   if X is small then Y is small

if X is medium then Y is large

if X is large then Y is small

question: what is the maximum value of Y ?

FIGURE 4
Perception-based function representation.

in which X_t, Y_t, and S_t denote the values of input, output and state at time t. The inputs, outputs, states, f and g are assumed to be perception-based.

Example: Perception-based model of a system (Figure 5)
if S_t is *small* and X_t is *small* then S_{t+1} is *medium*
if S_t is *small* and X_t is *medium* then S_{t+1} is *small*
...

if S_t is *large* and X_t is *large* then S_{t+1} is *small*
if S_t is *small* and X_t is *small* then Y_t is *large*
...

if S_t is *large* and X_t is *large* then Y_t is *medium*

Perception of dependencies involving functions and relations plays a pivotal role in human decision making. Thus, when we have to decide which action to take, we base our choice on the knowledge of a perception-based model that relates the outputs (consequences) to inputs (actions). This is what we do when we park a car, in which case what we know is a

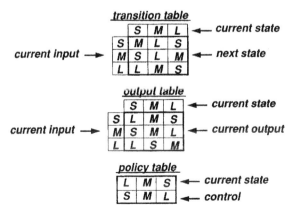

FIGURE 5
Perception-based model of a system.

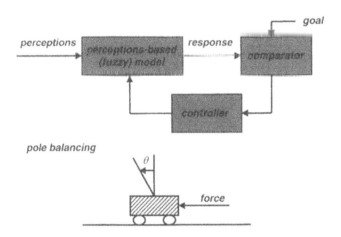

FIGURE 6
Perception-based human decision-making and control.

perception-based model of the kinematics of the car that we are parking. In a more general setting, the perception-based structure of decision making is shown in Figure 6.

By adopting as the point of departure in CTP the assumption that perceptions are described in a natural or synthetic language, we are moving the problem of manipulation of perceptions into familiar territory where we can deploy a wide variety of available methods. However, based as they are on predicate logic and various meaning-representation schemes, the available methods do not have sufficient expressive power to deal with perceptions. For example, the meaning of the simple perception *most Swedes are tall*, cannot be represented through the use of any meaning-representation scheme based on two-valued logic. If this is the case, then how could we represent the meaning of *it is very unlikely that there will be a significant increase in the price of oil in the near future?*

In CTP, what is used for purposes of meaning-representation and computing with perceptions is a fuzzy-logic-based methodology called computing with words (CW) [61]. As its name suggests, computing with words is a methodology in which words are used in place of numbers for computing and reasoning. In CW, a word is viewed as a label of a granule, that is, a clump of points (objects) drawn together by indistinguishability, similarity, proximity, or functionality. Unless otherwise specified, a granule is assumed to be a fuzzy set. In this sense, granulation may be interpreted as fuzzy partitioning. For example, when granulation is applied to a human head, the resulting granules are the nose, forehead, scalp, cheeks, chin, etc.

Basically, there are four principal rationales for the use of CW.

(a) The *don't know* rationale. In this case, the values of variables and/or parameters are not known with sufficient precision to justify the use of conventional methods of numerical computing. An example is decision-making with poorly defined probabilities and utilities.

(b) The *don't need* rationale. In this case, there is a tolerance for imprecision that can be exploited to achieve tractability, robustness, low solution cost, and better rapport with reality. An example is the problem of parking a car. Exploitation of the tolerance for imprecision is an issue of central importance in CW.

(c) The *can't solve* rationale. In this case, the problem cannot be solved through the use of numerical measurements and numerical computing. An example is the problem of automation of driving in city traffic.

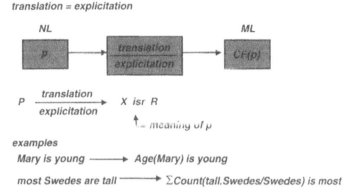

FIGURE 7
Translation/explicitation and canonical form.

(d) The *can't define* rationale. In this case, a concept that we wish to define is too complex to admit of definition in terms of a set of numerical criteria. A case in point is the concept of causality. Causality is an instance of what may be called an *amorphic* concept.

The point of departure in CW—the initial data set (IDS)—is a collection of propositions expressed in a natural language. A premise—that is, a constituent proposition in IDS—is interpreted as an implicit constraint on an implicit variable. For purposes of computation, the premises are expressed as canonical forms that serve to explicitate the implicit variables and the associated constraints. Typically, a canonical form is expressed as X isr R, where X is a variable, R is a constraining relation and isr is a variable copula in which a value of the variable r defines the way in which R constrains X (Figure 7). The constraints can assume a variety of forms, among which are possibilistic, probabilistic, veristic, functional, and random-set types [63].

In CW, the constraints are propagated from premises to conclusions through the use of rules of inference in fuzzy logic, among which the generalized extension principle plays the principal

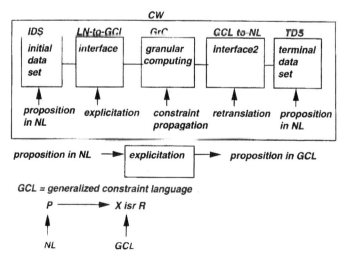

FIGURE 8
Structure of computing with words.

role. The induced constraints are retranslated into a natural language, yielding the terminal data set (TDS). The structure of CW is summarized in Figure 8.

A key component of CW is a system for representing the meaning of propositions expressed in a natural language. This system is referred to as *constraint-centered semantics of natural languages* (CSNL). A summary of CSNL is described in the following.

CONSTRAINT-CENTERED SEMANTICS OF NATURAL LANGUAGES (CSNL)

Issues related to meaning representation have long played major roles in linguistics, logic, philosophy of languages, and AI. In the literature on meaning, one can find a large number of methods of meaning representation based on two-valued logic. The problem, as was alluded to already, is that conventional methods of meaning representation do not have sufficient expressive power to represent the meaning of perceptions.

In a departure from convention, the constraint-centered semantics of natural languages is based on fuzzy logic. In essence, the need for fuzzy logic is dictated by the f-granularity of perceptions. The concept of f-granularity is pervasive in human cognition and plays a key role in fuzzy logic and its applications. By contrast, f-granularity is totally ignored in traditional logical systems. Considering the basic importance of f-granularity, it is hard to rationalize this omission.

The key idea underlying CSNL is that the meaning of a proposition is a constraint on a variable, with the understanding that a proposition is an instantiation of a relation. In the case of mathematical languages, the constraint is explicit, as in $a \leq X \leq b$. By contrast, in the case of natural languages, the constraints are, in general, implicit. Thus, meaning representation in CSNL is, in effect, a procedure that explicitates the constrained variable and the relation that constrains it. The concept of CSNL is closely related to that of test-score semantics [58].

In more specific terms, the point of departure in CSNL is a set of four basic assumptions.

1. A proposition, p, is an answer to a question, q. In general q is implicit rather than explicit in p.

2. The meaning of p is a constraint on an instantiated variable. In general, both the variable and the constraint to which it is subjected are implicit in p. The canonical form of p, $CF(p)$, places in evidence the constrained variable and the constraining relation (Figure 7).

3. A proposition, p, is viewed as a carrier of information. The canonical form of p defines the information that p carries.

4. In CTP, reasoning is viewed as a form of computation. Computation with perceptions is based on propagation of constraints from premises (antecedent propositions) to conclusions (consequent propositions).

In one form or another, manipulation of constraints plays a central role in a wide variety of methods and techniques, among which are mathematical programming, constraint programming, logic programming, and qualitative reasoning. However, in these methods and techniques, the usual assumption is that a constraint on a variable X is expressible as $X \in A$, where A is a crisp set, e.g., $a \leq X \leq b$. In other words, conventional constraints are crisp and possibilistic in the sense that what they constrain are the possible values of variables.

If our goal is to represent the meaning of a proposition drawn from a natural language as a constraint on a variable, then what is needed is a variety of constraints of different types—a variety that includes the standard constraint $X \in A$ as a special case. This is what underlies the concept of a generalized constraint [60] in constraint-centered semantics of natural languages.

A generalized constraint is represented as

$$X \text{ isr } R$$

where isr, pronounced "ezar," is a variable copula that defines the way in which R constrains X. More specifically, the role of R in relation to X is defined by the value of the discrete variable r. The values of r and their interpretations are defined below.

e:	equal	(abbreviated to $=$)
d:	disjunctive (possibilistic)	(abbreviated to blank)
v:	veristic	
p:	probabilistic	
λ:	probability value	
u:	usuality	
rs:	random set	
rfs:	random fuzzy set	
fg:	fuzzy graph	
ps:	rough set (Pawlak set)	
$\cdot$:	. . .	

As an illustration, when $r = e$, the constraint is an equality constraint and is abbreviated to $=$. When r takes the value d, the constraint is disjunctive (possibilistic) and "isd," abbreviated to "is," leads to the expression

$$X \text{ is } R$$

in which R is a fuzzy relation that constrains X by playing the role of the possibility distribution of X [17, 60]. Additional examples are shown in Figure 9.

As was alluded to already, the key idea underlying the constraint-centered semantics of natural languages is that the meaning of a proposition, p, may be represented as a generalized constraint on a variable. Schematically, this is represented as

$$p \longrightarrow X \text{ isr } R$$

examples

- $X = 5$ *(equality)*
- $5 \leq X \leq 10$ ⟶ X is [5,10] *(possibilistic, hard)*
- X is small *(possibilistic, fuzzy)*
- Fluency(Robert) isv { 1/English + 0.6/French } ⟶
  Robert is fluent to the degree 1 in English and 0.6 in French
- X isp N(m, σ^2) ⟶ X is a normally distributed random variable
  with mean m and variance σ^2
- X isu small ⟶ usually X is small
- f isfg (small x large + large x small) ⟶
  f is a function such that if X is small then Y is large and
  if X is large then Y is small

FIGURE 9
Examples of constraints.

key idea:

meaning = generalized constraint

translation = explicitation

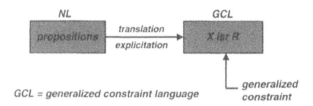

GCL = generalized constraint language

FIGURE 10
Generalized constraint language.

with the understanding that the target language of translation is the language of generalized constraints, that is, the Generalized Constraint Language (GCL) [63] (Figure 10). In this perspective, translation is viewed as an explicitation of the constrained variable, X, the defining copula variable, r, and the constraining relation, R. In general, X, r, and R are implicit rather than explicit in p. Furthermore, X, r, and R depend on the question to which p is an answer. The result of translation/explicitation is the canonical form of p.

As a very simple example, consider the proposition

$$p:\quad Mary \text{ is } young$$

Assuming that the question is: How old is Mary?, the meaning of p would be represented as the canonical form

$$P \longrightarrow Age(Mary) \text{ is } young$$

where $Age(Mary)$ is the constrained variable; *young* is the constraining relation; and the constraint defines the possibility distribution of $Age(Mary)$. If the membership function of *young* is defined as shown in Figure 1, then the same function defines the possibility distribution of $Age(Mary)$. More specifically, if the grade of membership of, say, 25 in *young* is 0.8, then the possibility that Mary is 25 given that Mary is young is 0.8.

Similarly, if

$$p:\quad Mary \text{ is } not\ very\ young$$

the constrained variable is $Age(Mary)$ but the constraining relation becomes

$$R = (^2young)'$$

where ^2young is an intensified version of *young*, that is, the result of applying the intensifier *very* to *young*, and $(^2young)'$ is the complement of (^2young), that is, the result of applying negation *not* to *very young*.

Proceeding further, consider the proposition

$$p:\quad Mary \text{ is } much\ older\ than\ Carol$$

In this case, the constrained variable is

$$X = (Age(Mary),\ Age(Carol))$$

and the canonical form of p is

$$(Age(Mary), \ Age(Carol)) \text{ is } much.older$$

where *much.older* is the constraining relation.

The constraining relation *much.older* may be interpreted as a perception that is defined by a collection of fuzzy if–then rules such as:

if *Age(Carol)* is *about 20* then *Age(Mary)* is *over* (*about 35*)

if *Age(Carol)* is *about 25* then *Age(Mary)* is *over* (*about 40*)

. . .

if *Age(Carol)* is *about 50* then *Age(Mary)* is *over* (*about 70*)

. . .

An important point that is made in this example is that, in general, the constraining relation R may be defined as a composite perception which is described by a collection of fuzzy if–then rules, with each rule playing the role of an elementary perception.

As a further example, consider the proposition (perception)

$$p: \quad \textit{most Swedes are tall}$$

In this case, the constrained variable, X, is the proportion of tall Swedes among Swedes, which is expressed as the relative sigma-count [59]:

$$X = \sum \text{Count}(tall.Swedes/Swedes)$$

More specifically, if we have a population of Swedes $\{Swede_1, \ldots, Swede_N\}$, with the height of $Swede_i, \ i = 1, \ldots, N$, being h_i and the grade of membership of h_i in *tall* being $\mu_{tall}(h_i)$, then

$$\sum \text{Count}(tall.Swedes/Swedes) = \frac{1}{N}\left(\sum_i \mu_{tall}(h_i)\right)$$

Thus, the constrained variable is

$$X - \frac{1}{N}\left(\sum_i \mu_{tall}(h_i)\right)$$

and the constraining relation is *most*. The canonical form of p may be expressed as

$$\frac{1}{N}\left(\sum_i \mu_{tall}(h_i)\right) \text{ is } \textit{most}$$

A concept that plays an important role in the representation of meaning is that of the depth of explicitation. In essence, depth of explicitation is a measure of the difficulty of representing the meaning of a proposition, p, as an explicit constraint on a variable, that is, as its canonical form $CF(p)$. As an illustration, the following propositions are listed in the order of *increasing* depth.

- *Mary is young*
- *Mary is not very young*
- *Mary is much older than Carol*
- *most Swedes are tall*

- *Carol lives in a small city near San Francisco*
- *Robert is honest*
- *high inflation causes high interest rates*
- *it is very unlikely that there will be a significant increase in the price of oil in the near future.*

For purposes of illustration, consider the problem of explicitation of the last proposition in the list,

>   *p: it is very unlikely that there will be a significant increase in the price of oil*
>   *in the near future*

Assume that the constrained variable is the probability of the event *E*, where

>   *E: significant increase in the price of oil in the near future*

Furthermore, assume that *E* contains the secondary event:

> $E_{secondary}$:   *significant increase in the price of oil*

The relationship between *E* and $E_{secondary}$ is represented as a semantic network in Figure 11.

Assuming that the labels *significant increase* and *near future* are defined by their membership functions as shown in Figure 12, we can compute, for any specified price time-function, the degree to which it fits the event *E*. In effect, this means that *E* plays the role of a fuzzy event [55]. The constraining relation is the fuzzy probability *very unlikely*, which is related to *likely* by

$$very \ unlikely = {}^2(ant(likely))$$

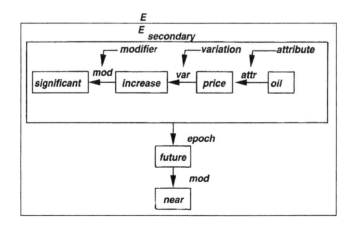

FIGURE 11
Semantic network representation of the perception *it is very unlikely that there will be a significant increase in the price of oil in the near future.*

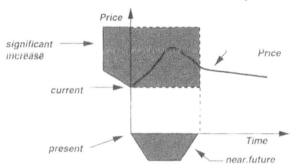

- *it is very unlikely that there will be a significant increase
  in the price of oil in the near future*

$\downarrow$ *explicitation*

Prob(E) *is* ^{2}(ant(likely))

E : Epoch([Variation(Price(oil)) is significant.increase] is near.future)

FIGURE 12
Fuzzy events E and $E_{\text{secondary}}$.

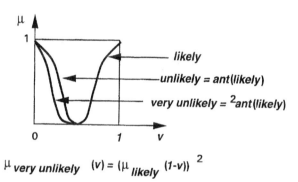

$$\mu_{very\ unlikely}\ (v) = (\mu_{likely}\ (1\text{-}v))^{2}$$

FIGURE 13
Definitions of *likely, unlikely* and *very likely.*

where *ant(likely)* is the antonym of *likely* and $^2(ant(likely))$ is the result of intensification of
ant(likely) by the intensifier *very* (Figure 13). Combining these results, the canonical form of *p*
may be expressed as

$$Prob(E) \text{ is } {}^2(ant(likely))$$

REASONING WITH PERCEPTIONS BASED ON GENERALIZED CONSTRAINT PROPAGATION

In the computational theory of perceptions, reasoning with perceptions is viewed as a process of
generalized constraint propagation from premises to a conclusion, with the conclusion playing
the role of an answer to a question.

As a very simple example, assume that the premises are the perceptions

p_2:   *Dana* is *young*

p_2:   *Tandy* is *a few years older than Dana*

and the question is

$$q. \quad \textit{How old is Tandy?}$$

Explicitation of p_1 and p_2 leads to the constraints

$$p_1 \longrightarrow \textit{Age}(\textit{Dana}) \text{ is } \textit{young}$$
$$p_2 \longrightarrow (\textit{Age}(\textit{Tandy}), \textit{Age}(\textit{Dana})) \text{ is } \textit{few.years.older}$$

Applying the rules of constraint propagation that are discussed in the following, leads to a constraint that constitutes the answer to q. Specifically,

$$\textit{Ans}(q) \longrightarrow \textit{young} + \textit{few}$$

In this expression, *young* and *few* play the role of fuzzy numbers and their sum can be computed through the use of fuzzy arithmetic [28].

The basic structure of the reasoning process in CTP is shown in Figure 14. The first step involves description of the given perceptions as propositions expressed in a natural language, resulting in the initial data set IDS. The second step involves translation of propositions in IDS into the generalized constraint language GCL, resulting in antecedent constraints. The third step involves translation of the question into GCL. The fourth step involves augmentation of antecedent constraints, resulting in the augmented data set ADS. ADS consist of constraints induced by IDS and the external knowledge base set KBS. Application of rules governing generalized constraint propagation to constraints in ADS leads to consequent constraints in the terminal data set TDS. The fifth and last step involves retranslation of consequent constraints into the answer to q.

Generalized constraint propagation is a process that involves successive application of rules of combination and modification of generalized constraints. In generic form, the principal rules

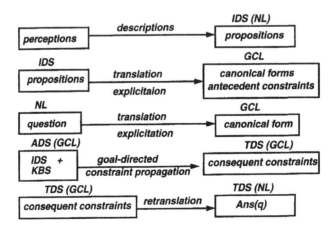

FIGURE 14
Basic structure of reasoning with perceptions.

governing constraint propagation are the following. These rules coincide with the generic form of rules of inference in fuzzy logic.

Conjunctive rule 1:

$$\frac{\begin{array}{ccc} X & \text{isr} & A \\ X & \text{iss} & B \end{array}}{\begin{array}{ccc} X & \text{ist} & C \end{array}}$$

Conjunctive rule 2:

$$\frac{\begin{array}{ccc} X & \text{isr} & A \\ Y & \text{ist} & C \end{array}}{\begin{array}{ccc} (X,Y) & \text{ist} & C \end{array}}$$

Disjunctive rule 1:

$$X \quad \text{isr} \quad A$$
$$\text{or}$$
$$\frac{X \quad \text{iss} \quad B}{X \quad \text{ist} \quad C}$$

Disjunctive rule 2:

$$X \quad \text{isr} \quad A$$
$$\text{or}$$
$$\frac{Y \quad \text{iss} \quad B}{(X,Y) \quad \text{ist} \quad C}$$

Projective rule:

$$\frac{(X,Y) \quad \text{isr} \quad A}{X \quad \text{iss} \quad B}$$

Surjective rule:

$$\frac{X \quad \text{isr} \quad A}{(X,Y) \quad \text{iss} \quad B}$$

Compositional rule:

$$\frac{\begin{array}{ccc} X & \text{isr} & A \\ (X,Y) & \text{iss} & B \end{array}}{\begin{array}{ccc} Y & \text{ist} & C \end{array}}$$

Generalized extension principle:

$$\frac{f(X) \quad \text{isr} \quad A}{g(X) \quad \text{iss} \quad B}$$

Implication rule (joint):

$$\frac{\text{if} \quad X \quad \text{isr} \quad A \quad \text{then} \quad Y \quad \text{iss} \quad B}{(X,Y) \quad \text{ist} \quad C}$$

Implication rule (conditional):

$$\frac{\text{if} \quad X \quad \text{isr} \quad A \quad \text{then} \quad Y \quad \text{iss} \quad B}{(Y\,|\,X) \quad \text{ist} \quad C}$$

In these rules, the dependence of C on A and B is determined by r, s, and t. For example, in the case of possibilistic constraints, $r = s = t = $ blank, and the compositional rule assumes the form

$$\frac{\begin{array}{ccc} X & \text{is} & A \\ (X,Y) & \text{is} & B \end{array}}{\begin{array}{ccc} Y & \text{is} & A \cdot B \end{array}}$$

where $A \cdot B$ is the composition of relations A and B. Similarly, in the case of probabilistic constraints, we have

$$
\begin{array}{rcl}
X & \text{isp} & A \\
(Y \mid X) & \text{isp} & B \\
\hline
Y & \text{isp} & A \cdot B
\end{array}
$$

where B is the conditional probability distribution of Y given X, and the consequent constraint expresses the familiar Bayesian rule of combination of probabilities.

The rules governing generalized constraint propagation become more complex when the constituent constraints are heterogeneous. For example, if the constraint on X is probabilistic:

$$X \quad \text{isp} \quad A$$

and the constraint on (X, Y) is possibilistic:

$$(X, Y) \quad \text{is} \quad B$$

then the constraint on Y is of random set type, i.e.:

$$Y \quad \text{isrs} \quad C$$

Such constraints play a central role in the Dempster–Shafer theory of evidence [48].

The principal rule of inference in the computational theory of perceptions is the *generalized extension principle* [63]. For possibilistic constraints, it may be expressed as

$$
\frac{f(X) \quad \text{is} \quad R}{g(X) \quad \text{is} \quad g(f^{-1}(R))}
$$

In this constraint-propagation rule, $f(X)$ is R plays the role of an antecedent constraint that is an explicitation of a given perception or perceptions; X is the constrained variable; f is a given function; R is a relation that constrains $f(X)$; g is a given function and $f^{-1}(R)$ is the preimage of R. In effect, $f(X)$ is R is a generalized constraint that represents the information conveyed by antecedent perception(s), while $g(X)$ is $g(f^{-1}(R))$ defines the induced generalized constraint on a specified function of X (Figure 15).

$$
\frac{f(X_1, \ldots, X_n) \ \text{is} \ R}{g(X_1, \ldots, X_n) \ \text{is} \ g(f^{-1}(R))}
\quad \longleftarrow \quad \text{antecedent constraint}
$$
$$\longleftarrow \quad \text{consequent constraint}$$

$$
\mu_{g(f^{-1}(R))}(v) = \sup_{u_1, \ldots, u_n \mid v = f(u_1, \ldots, u_n)} \mu_R(f(u_1, \ldots, u_n))
$$

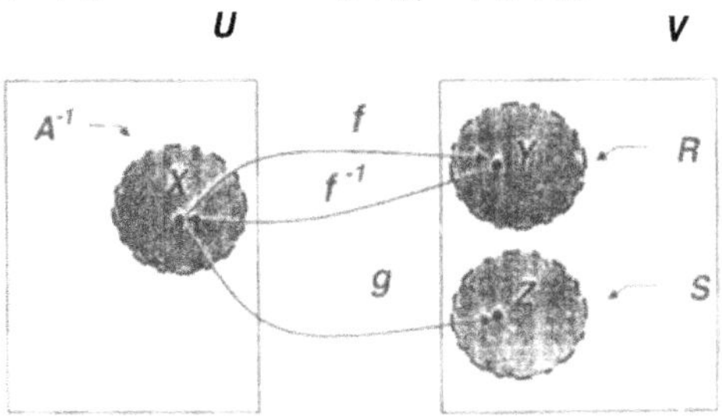

FIGURE 15
Generalized extension principle.

As a simple illustration of the generalized extension principle, assume that the initial data set is the perception

$$p: \quad \textit{most Swedes are tall}$$

and the question is

$$q: \quad \textit{what is the average height of Swedes}$$

Referring to our previous discussion of the example, we note that the canonical forms of p and q are

$$CF(p): \quad \frac{1}{N}\left(\sum_i \mu_{tall}(h_i)\right) \text{ is most}$$

$$CF(q): \quad \frac{1}{N}\sum_i h_i \text{ is } ?B$$

where $?B$ denotes the relation that constrains the answer to q.

Using the generalized extension principle reduces the determination of $?B$ to the solution of the constrained maximization problem [63]:

$$\mu_{h_{ave}}(v) = sup_{h_1,...,h_N}\left(\mu_{most}\left(\frac{1}{N}\sum_i \mu_{tall}(h_i)\right)\right)$$

subject to the constraint

$$v = \frac{1}{N}\sum_i h_i$$

The solution is a fuzzy interval since the initial data set is a proposition that describes a perception.

In a general setting, application of the generalized extension principle transforms the problem of reasoning with perceptions into the problem of constrained maximization of the membership function of a variable that is constrained by a question. The example considered above is a simple instance of this process.

CONCLUDING REMARK

The computational theory of perceptions which is outlined in this chapter may be viewed as a first step toward the development of a better understanding of ways in which the remarkable human ability to reason with perceptions may be mechanized. Eventually, the availability of a machinery for computing with perceptions may have a profound impact on theories in which human decision-making plays an important role. Furthermore, in moving countertraditionally from measurements to perceptions, we may be able to conceive and construct systems with higher MIQ (Machine IQ) than those we have today.

Acknowledgment

Research supported in part by NASA Grant NAC2-1177, ONR Grant N00014-96-1-0556, ARO Grant DAAH 04-961-0341 and the BISC Program of UC Berkeley.

REFERENCES AND RELATED PAPERS

[1] J. Albus, Outline for a theory of intelligence, *IEEE Trans. Systems, Man, and Cybernetics*, Vol. 21, pp. 473–509, 1991.

[2] J. Albus, and A. Meystel, A reference model architecture for design and implementation of intelligent control in large and complex systems, *Int. J. Intelligent Control and Systems*, Vol. 1, pp. 15–30, 1996.

[3] A.B. Baker, Nonmonotonic reasoning in the framework of situation calculus, *Artificial Intelligence*, Vol. 49, pp. 5–23, 1991.

[4] D.G. Bobrow, *Qualitative Reasoning about Physical Systems*, Bradford Books/MIT Press, Cambridge, MA, 1985.

[5] J. Bowen, R. Lai, and D. Bahler, Fuzzy semantics and fuzzy constraint networks, *Proc. 1st IEEE Conf. Fuzzy Systems, San Francisco*, pp. 1009–1016, 1992.

[6] E.W. Coiera, Qualitative superposition, *Artificial Intelligence*, Vol. 56, pp. 171–196, 1992.

[7] P. Dague, Symbolic reasoning with relative orders of magnitude, *Proc. Thirteenth Int. Joint Conf. Artificial Intelligence*. Morgan Kaufmann, San Mateo, CA, 1993.

[8] B. D'Ambrosio, Extending the mathematics in qualitative process theory, in L.E. Widman, K.A. Loparo, and N.R. Nielsen, (eds.) *Artificial Intelligence, Simulation, and Modeling*, pp. 133–158. Wiley-Interscience, New York, 1989.

[9] E. Davis, Constraint propagation with interval labels, *Artificial Intelligence*, Vol. 24, pp. 347–410, 1987.

[10] E. Davis, *Representations of Commonsense Knowledge*, Morgan Kaufmann, San Mateo, CA, 1990.

[11] J. de Kleer, Multiple representations of knowledge in a mechanics problem-solver, *Proc. 5th Int. Joint Conf. Artificial Intelligence*. pp. 299–304. Morgan Kaufmann, San Mateo, CA, 1977.

[12] J. de Kleer, and D.G. Bobrow, Qualitative reasoning with higher-order derivatives, *Proc. 4th National Conf. Artificial Intelligence*. Morgan Kaufmann, San Mateo, CA, 1984.

[13] J. de Kleer, and J.S. Brown, A qualitative physics based on confluences, *Artificial Intelligence*, Vol. 24, pp. 7–83, 1984.

[14] J. Doyle, and E. Sacks, Markov analysis of qualitative dynamics, *Computational Intelligence*, Vol. 7, pp. 1–10, 1991.

[15] D. Dubois, H. Fargier, and H. Prade, The calculus of fuzzy restrictions as a basis for flexible constraint satisfaction, *Proc. 2nd IEEE Int. Conf. Fuzzy Systems, San Francisco*, pp. 1131–1136, 1993.

[16] D. Dubois, H. Fargier, and H. Prade, Propagation and satisfaction of flexible constraints, in R.R. Yager, L.A. Zadeh (eds.) *Fuzzy Sets, Neural Networks, and Soft Computing*, pp. 166–187. Von Nostrand Reinhold, New York, 1994.

[17] D. Dubois, H. Fargier, and H. Prade, Possibility theory in constraint satisfaction problems: handling priority, preference and uncertainty, *Applied Intelligence*, pp. 287–309, 1996.

[18] B. Falkenhainer, Modeling without amnesia: making experience-sanctioned approximations, *Proc. 6th Int. Workshop Qualitative Reasoning about Physical Systems, Edinburgh, Scotland*, 1992.

[19] K.D. Forbus, and D. Gentner, Causal reasoning about quantities, *Proc. 5th Annual Conf. of the Cognitive Science Society*, pp. 196–206. Lawrence Erlbaum and Associates, Palo Alto, CA, 1983.

[20] K.D. Forbus, Qualitative process theory, *Artificial Intelligence*, Vol. 24, pp. 85–168, 1984.

[21] E.C. Freuder, Synthesizing constraint expressions, *Communications of the ACM*, Vol. 21, pp. 958–966, 1978.

[22] E.C. Freuder, and P. Snow, Improved relaxation and search methods for approximate constraint satisfaction with a maximum criterion, *Proc. 8th Biennial Conf. Canadian Society for Computational Studies of Intelligence, Ontario*, pp. 227–230, 1990.

[23] J.Z. Geng, Fuzzy CMAC neural networks, *J. Intelligent and Fuzzy Systems*, Vol. 3, pp. 87–102, 1995.

[24] P.J. Hayes, The naive physics manifesto, *Expert Systems in the Micro Electronic Age*, Edinburgh University Press, Edinburgh, 1979.

[25] P.J. Hayes, The second naive physics manifesto, in J.R. Hobbs, and R.C. Moore (eds.) *Formal theories of the Commonsense World*, pp. 1–36. Ablex Publishing Corp., Norwood, NJ, 1985.

[26] J. Kalagnanam, H.A. Simon, and Y. Iwasaki, The mathematical bases for qualitative reasoning, *IEEE Expert*, pp. 11–19, 1991.

[27] O. Katai, S. Matsubara, H. Masuichi, M. Ida, et al., Synergetic computation for constraint satisfaction problems involving continuous and fuzzy variables by using Occam, in S. Noguchi and H. Umeo (eds.) *Transputer/Occam, Proc. 4th Transputer/Occam Int. Conf.*, IOS Press, Amsterdam, 1992.

[28] A. Kaufmann, and M.M. Gupta, *Introduction to Fuzzy Arithmetic: Theory and Applications*. Von Nostrand, New York, 1985.

[29] G. Klir, and B. Yuan, *Fuzzy Sets and Fuzzy Logic*. Prentice Hall, Englewood Cliffs, NJ, 1995.

[30] B.J. Kuipers, Commonsense reasoning about causality: deriving behavior from structure, *Artificial Intelligence*, Vol. 24, pp. 169–204, 1984.

[31] B.J. Kuipers, *Qualitative Reasoning*, MIT Press, Cambridge, MA, 1994.

[32] K. Lano, A constraint-based fuzzy inference system, in P. Barahona, L.M. Pereira, and A. Porto (eds.) *EPIA 91, 5th Portuguese Conf. Artificial Intelligence*, pp. 45–59. Springer-Verlag, Berlin, 1991.

[33] D. Lenat, and R. Guha, *Building Large Knowledge-Based Systems*. Addison-Wesley, Reading, MA, 1990.

[34] M. Mares, *Computation Over Fuzzy Quantities*. CRC Press, Boca Raton, 1994.

[35] M.L. Mavrovouniotis, and G. Stephanopoulos, Reasoning with orders of magnitude and approximate relations, *Proc. 6th National Conf. Artificial Intelligence*, pp. 626–630. Morgan Kaufmann, San Mateo, CA, 1987.

[36] J. McCarthy, and P.J. Hayes, Some philosophical problems from the standpoint of artificial intelligence, in R. Meltzer and D. Michie (eds.) *Machine Intelligence 4*, pp. 463–502. Edinburgh University Press, Edinburgh, 1969.

[37] D. McDermott, A temporal logic for reasoning about processes and plans, *Cognitive Science*, Vol. 6, pp. 101–155, 1982.

[38] A. Meystel, Planning in a hierarchical nested controller for autonomous robots, *Proc. IEEE 25th Conf. Decision and Control*, Athens, Greece, 1986.

[39] V. Novak, Fuzzy logic, fuzzy sets, and natural languages, *Int. J. General Systems* Vol. 20, No. 1, pp. 83–97, 1991.

[40] V. Novak, M. Ramik, M. Cerny, and J. Nekola (eds.), *Fuzzy Approach to Reasoning and Decision-Making*. Kluwer, Boston, 1992.

[41] W. Pedrycz, and F. Gomide, *Introduction to Fuzzy Sets*, MIT Press, Cambridge, MA, 1998.

[42] C.J. Puccia, and R. Levins, *Qualitative Modeling of Complex Systems*, Harvard University Press, Cambridge, MA, 1985.

[43] O. Rainman, Order of magnitude reasoning, *Proc. 5th National Conf. Artificial Intelligence*, pp. 100–104. Morgan Kaufmann, San Mateo, CA, 1986.

[44] O. Rainman, Order of magnitude reasoning, *Artificial Intelligence*, Vol. 51, pp. 11–38, 1991.

[45] H. Rasiowa, and M. Marek, On reaching consensus by groups of intelligent agents, in Z.W. Ras, (ed.) *Methodologies for Intelligent Systems*, pp. 234–243. North-Holland, Amsterdam, 1989.

[46] M. Sakawa, K. Sawada, and M. Inuiguchi, A fuzzy satisfying method for large-scale linear programming problems with block angular structure, *European J. Operational Research*, Vol. 81, No. 2, pp. 399–409, 1995.

[47] E. Sandewall, Combining logic and differential equations for describing real-world systems, *Proc. 1st Int. Conf. Principles of Knowledge Representation and Reasoning*, pp. 412–420. Morgan Kaufmann, San Mateo, CA, 1989.

[48] G. Shafer, *A Mathematical Theory of Evidence*. Princeton University Press, Princeton, 1976.

[49] Q. Shen, and R. Leitch, Combining qualitative simulation and fuzzy sets, in B. Faltings, and P. Struss (eds.) *Recent Advances in Qualitative Physics*, MIT Press, Cambridge, MA, 1992.

[50] Y. Shoham, and D. McDermott, Problems in formal temporal reasoning, *Artificial Intelligence*, Vol. 36, pp. 49–61, 1988.

[51] P. Struss, Problems of interval-based qualitative reasoning, in D. Weld, and J. de Kleer (eds.) *Qualitative Reasoning about Physical Systems*. pp. 288–305. Morgan Kaufmann, San Mateo, CA, 1990.

[52] R. Vallee, *Cognition et Systeme*. l'Interdisciplinaire Systeme(s), Paris, 1995.

[53] D.S. Weld, and J. de Kleer, *Readings in Qualitative Reasoning about Physical Systems*. Morgan Kaufmann, San Mateo, CA, 1990.

[54] R.R. Yager, Some extensions of constraint propagation of label sets, *Int. J. Approximate Reasoning*, Vol. 3, pp. 417–435, 1989.

[55] L.A. Zadeh, Probability measures of fuzzy events, *J. Mathematical Analysis and Applications*, Vol. 23, pp. 421–427, 1968.

[56] L.A. Zadeh, A fuzzy-set-theoretic interpretation of linguistic hedges, *J. Cybernetics*, Vol. 2, pp. 4–34, 1972.

[57] L.A. Zadeh, Outline of a new approach to the analysis of complex systems and decision processes, *IEEE Trans. Systems, Man, and Cybernetics*, Vol. SMC-3, pp. 28–44, 1973.

[58] L.A. Zadeh, Test-score semantics for natural languages and nearing representation via: PRUF, *Empirical Semantics*, B. Rieger (ed.), pp. 281–349, Brockmeyer, Bochum, Germany, 1982.

[59] L.A. Zadeh, A computational approach to Fuzzy quantiless in natural languages. *Computers and Mathematics*, Vol. 9, pp. 149–184, 1983.

[60] L.A. Zadeh, Outline of a computational approach to meaning and knowledge representation based on the concept of a generalized assignment statement, in M. Thoma and A. Wyner (eds.) *Proc. Int. Seminar Artificial Intelligence and Man-Machine Systems*, pp. 198–211, Springer-Verlag, Heidelberg, 1986.

[61] L.A. Zadeh, Fuzzy logic = computing with words, *IEEE Trans. Fuzzy Systems*, Vol. 4, pp. 103–111, 1996.

[62] L.A. Zadeh, Toward a theory of fuzzy information granulation and its centrality in human reasoning and fuzzy logic, *Fuzzy Sets and Systems*, Vol. 90, pp. 111–127, 1997.

[63] L.A. Zadeh, From computing with numbers to computing with words—from manipulation of measurements to manipulation of perceptions, *IEEE Trans. Circuits and Systems*, Vol. 45, pp. 105–119, 1999

[64] L.W. Barsalou, Perceptual symbol systems, *Behavioural and Brain Sciences*, Vol. 22, pp. 577–660, 1999.

CHAPTER 2

Introduction to Soft Computing and Intelligent Control Systems

NARESH K. SINHA

Department of Electrical and Computer Engineering, McMaster University, Hamilton, Ontario, L8S 4L7, Canada

MADAN M. GUPTA

Intelligent Systems Research Laboratory, College of Engineering, University of Saskatchewan, Saskatoon, Sask. S7N 5A9, Canada

> The path that leads to scientific discovery often begins when one of us takes an adventurous step into the world of endless possibilities. Scientists intrigued by a mere glimpse of a subtle variation may uncover a clue or link, and from that fragment emerges an idea to be developed and worked into shape.

1 INTRODUCTION

Man has always dreamed of creating a portrait of himself, a machine with humanlike attributes such as locomotion, speech, vision, and cognition (memory, learning, thinking, adaptation, intelligence). Through his creative actions, he has been able to realize some of his dreams. In today's technological society, there are machines that have some of the human attributes that emulate several human functions with tremendous capacity and capabilities: human locomotion versus transportation systems, human speech and vision versus communications systems, and human low-level cognition versus computing systems. No doubt the machines that are an extension of human muscular power (cars, tractors, airplane, trains, robots, etc.), have brought luxury to human life. But who provides control to these mighty machines—human intelligence, the human cognition?

When the computer first appeared in the early fifties, we admired it as an *artificial brain*, and we thought that we were successful in creating a low-level decision making cognitive machine. We called it "artificial intelligence" and waited for many potential applications to evolve. However, after several years we realized that the so-called *artificial intelligence* (AI) was, indeed, very artificial in nature. In AI, about half of what we hear is *not true*, and the other half is *not possible*.

Now we are moving into a new era of "information technology", the technology for processing statistical information and cognitive information, the information originating from the human cognitive faculty. New computing theories with a sound biological understanding have been evolving. This new field of computing falls under the category of *neural and soft computing systems*. The new computing technology has been evolving under disciplines such as optical computing, optoelectronics, and molecular computing. This new technology seems to have the potential of surpassing the micro-, nano-, and pico-technologies. The neural computing systems have also been proven (theoretically) to supplement the enormous processing power of the von Neuman digital computer.* Hopefully, these new computing methods, with the neural architecture as a basis, will be able to provide a thinking machine—a low-level cognitive machine for which scientists have been striving for so long.

Today, we are in the process of designing neural computing-based information processing systems using the biological neural systems as a basis. The highly *parallel* processing and layered neuronal morphology with learning abilities of the human cognitive faculty—the brain— provides us with a new tool for designing a cognitive machine that can learn and recognize complicated patterns like human faces and Japanese characters. The theory of fuzzy logic, the basis for soft computing, provides mathematical power for the emulation of the higher-order cognitive functions—the thought and perception processes. A marriage between these evolving disciplines, such as neural computing, genetic algorithms and fuzzy logic, may provide a new class of computing systems—neural-fuzzy systems—for the emulation of higher-order cognitive power. The chaotic behavior inherent in biological systems—the heart and brain, for example— and the neuronal phenomena and the genetic algorithms are some of the other important subjects that promise to provide robustness to our neural computing systems.

2 INTELLIGENT CONTROL SYSTEMS

Factors that are to be understood and learned for designing an intelligent control system are primarily the process characteristics, characteristics of the disturbances, and equipment operating practices. It is desirable to acquire and store this knowledge so that it can be easily retrieved and updated. Also, the system should be able to autonomously improve its performance as experience is gained.

Apart from the standard methods in the theory of feedback control systems, papers in the area of intelligent control used ideas from several areas of artificial intelligence, such as knowledge-based systems (also known as expert systems), neural networks, learning, qualitative simulation, genetic algorithms and fuzzy control. Although these appear to be a collection of techniques that are somewhat unrelated, attempts have been made to combine two or more of these to obtain better results. It is felt that it should be possible to combine these ideas in a suitable manner to develop a framework for intelligent control. In fact, several authors have already tried to combine fuzzy logic with neural network ("neuro-fuzzy") control in their approach to intelligent control of robots.

2.1 Learning Control Systems

Some of the earliest attempts for the intelligent control of robots were based on the introduction of some form of learning. The concept of learning in control systems has been around us for

---

* In terms of memory and processing power, the carbon-based cognitive computer possessed by a "fly" is much superior to the combined power of many silicon-based supercomputers.

some time. Learning control techniques have been developed as a means of improving the performance of poorly modelled nonlinear systems by exploring the experience gained with on-line interaction with the actual plant. A very lurid description of the motivation and implementation of learning control systems has been given by Farrel and Baker in *Intelligent Control Systems: theory and Applications* (edited by M.M. Gupta and N.K. Sinha, IEEE-Press, 1996). Adaptation has been defined as the *ability to adjust to a specific situation*. On the other hand, learning can be defined as *gaining mastery through experience and storing it into memory*. Thus, a system that treats every different operating situation as new is limited to adaptive operation whereas a learning system is able to exploit past experiences by correlating them with past situations to improve its performance in the future.

The implementation of learning control requires three capabilities: (i) performance feedback; (ii) memory and (iii) training. To improve its performance, a learning system (like an adaptive control system) must receive performance feedback information, based on the cost function that is to be optimized. This information is then used to adjust the parameters of the controller to improve the process performance. The accumulated knowledge must be stored in the memory for its use in the future. The training, or memory adjustment process, is designed to automatically adjust the parameters of the controller when the process is subjected to an uncertain situation. It is evident that the main problem in the learning process is gaining the speed and efficiency.

2.2 Knowledge-based or Expert Systems

Another approach to intelligent control is through the use of a knowledge-based system, usually called an expert system. The field of automatic control has, for a long time, focused on the development of algorithms. With the availability of inexpensive digital computers, attempts are now being made to add other elements such as logic, reasoning, sequencing, and heuristics. Knowledge-based control is one alternative for obtaining controllers with improved functional features.

Knowledge-based control systems are based on the operator's heuristic knowledge of the system to be controlled. The main objective is to extend the range of conventional control algorithms by encoding knowledge and heuristics about identification and adaptation in a supervisory expert system.

An ideal expert control system should have the following objectives:

- It should be able to control in a satisfactory manner a large class of processes that may be time-varying and subject to a variety of disturbances.
- It should require minimal *a priori* knowledge about the process.
- It should be able to make intelligent use of all available prior knowledge.
- It should improve the control performance as it gathers more knowledge about the system.
- It should allow the user to enter performance specifications in simple qualitative terms like *small overshoot* and *as fast as possible*.
- It should monitor the performance of the system and detect problems with sensors, actuators, and other components.
- It should be possible for the user to get information about process dynamics, control performance, and the factors that limit the performance, in an easy manner.
- The heuristic and the underlying knowledge about the control system should be stored in a transparent manner so that it can be easily accessed, examined, and modified.

Some of these properties can also be found in many conventional control systems, but no existing control system satisfies all of these. One way to research these goals is to visualize an expert control engineer as part of the control loop and equipped with a toolbox consisting of many algorithms for control, identification, measurement, monitoring, and design.

Thus, an expert control system supports several of the functions that are traditionally performed by operators and control engineers. These functions are either fully automated or supported by a computer.

The block diagram of a typical knowledge-based system is shown in Figure 1. This system, in addition to the main feedback loop, has an outer loop involving parameter identification, supervision, and control. Also, several alternatives for controllers and identification algorithms are available. For example, the controller may be of a simple PID type, or it may involve an observer and state feedback. Similarly, it may be possible to generate special perturbation signals for system identification. There may also be fault detection algorithms and diagnostic tasks aimed at finding faults that are local to the control loop of which the expert controller is a part. These algorithms are coordinated by an expert system, which decides what algorithms should be used at a given specific time.

It can be concluded that a knowledge-based system provides an efficient approach to intelligent control as it does not require much on-line computation. However, the rule-base may become very complicated in certain cases, with the result that the expert system might not be able to handle a novel situation that has not already been included in the knowledge base.

2.3   Fuzzy Logic Controller

We shall now consider controllers based on fuzzy logic. There are many situations where classical control may not be very effective:

- A precise model for the process may not be available, or the process may be too complex to be modeled.
- Control algorithms derived from classical control techniques do not respond very well to measurement noise in sensors.

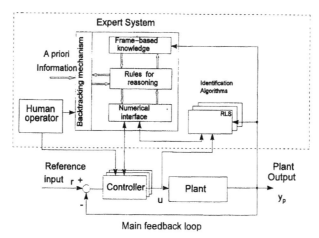

Main feedback loop

FIGURE 1
A typical knowledge-based (expert) system.

- The performance available from classical control algorithms may not be adequate for the task at hand.

Fuzzy logic-based control systems were introduced to overcome some of these problems. An example of such a fuzzy logic control system is shown in Figure 2.

The sensor readings, which are nonfuzzy, must be converted to a fuzzy form, and this occurs in a unit called the *fuzzifier*. The definitions of the fuzzy predicates are stored in a database associated with the controller. The linguistic control rules are stored as a set of fuzzy conditional statements in a rule-base and can be regarded as specifying a fuzzy relational algorithm. The control unit combines the fuzzified sensor data with the database and the rule-base generates a fuzzy control action. Finally, this is converted to specific nonfuzzy control action by the defuzzifier. One assumption behind the above model is that the conditional statements in the rule-base relate the sensor reading and their rate of change to the control parameters.

Fuzzy representations of control algorithms, as linguistic rules per se, offer a number of advantages over the conventional approach to the specification of control algorithms as algebraic formulas, particularly in ill-structured situations. The key idea is that linguistic rules describe the operation of the process of interest from the standpoint of some (human) operator of the process and capture the empirical knowledge of operation of that process that has been acquired through direct experience with the actual operation of the process. Clearly, this knowledge can be reflected in the rule set only to the extent that the operator can articulate the control action in linguistic form. It is this empirical knowledge, nonetheless, that a fuzzy controller effectively embodies, and which enables it to control the process as if it were the human operator.

It follows, therefore, that to design a fuzzy control scheme what is essentially needed is:

some prior and usually direct knowledge of the operation of the process;
the ability to articulate this knowledge in linguistic form; and
the means to represent this knowledge in a meaningful and yet in a quantitatively sound manner.

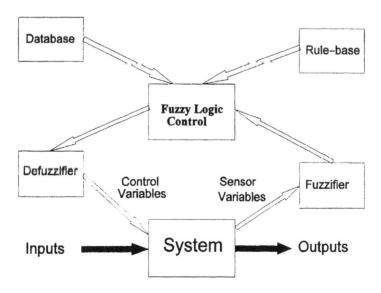

FIGURE 2
Fuzzy logic controller.

The outcome of the design process, a knowledge engineering problem, is a control algorithm that ideally mimics the control function of the human operator of the given process.

2.4 Neuro-control Systems (Figure 3)

The use of neural networks for the control of complex nonlinear systems has become very popular during the last decade. The following properties of neural networks are important from the control point of view:

- *Distributed nonlinearity*
- Ability to *learn* from experience
- Massively *parallel distributed processing*
- *Generalizing* the performance over inputs for which no training has been received
- The capability to *approximate an arbitrary function* given sufficient number of neurons

Neural networks have attracted a lot of interest because of these abilities and have been used in several applications for performing various mappings. From the control theory point of view, the ability of neural networks to deal with nonlinear systems is perhaps the most significant.

Since neural networks are not model-based, they have been recognized as viable alternatives to the traditional methods of identification and control of industrial robots. Their most important property is the ability to learn mapping, which may even be mathematical intractable. This makes them ideally suitable to mimic human thinking and decision making processes.

Neural networks have some features particularly suitable for use with robots. They can be trained to handle inverse and forward kinematics, to represent any complex relations between the inputs and the outputs of a robot arm with n joints, and to design any trajectory as a reference model for the robot. A great deal of research effort has gone into the design of neural network applications for the control of manipulators.

There are five basic paradigms of neuro-control that have been proposed in the literature. These are (i) supervised control, (ii) direct inverse control, (iii) neural adaptive control, (iv) back-propagation through time, and (v) adaptive control methods. Among these, *direct inverse control* has the most straightforward and robust applications for the control of robotic manipulators. The neural network learns the nonlinear mapping from the position of the robot arm to the actuator

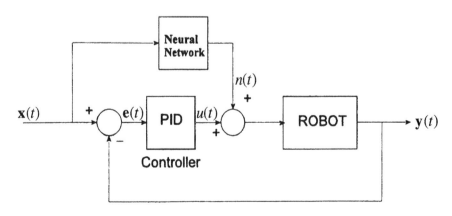

FIGURE 3
A basic structure of neuro-control system.

signals that would move the arm to that position. The neural network is then used to make the arm follow the desired trajectory.

BIBLIOGRAPHY

General Background

[1] M. Black, Vagueness: An exercise in logical analysis, *Philosophy of Science*, Vol. 4, pp. 427–455, 1937.

[2] W.S. McCulloch and W. Pitts, A logical calculus of the ideas immanent in nervous activity, *Bulletin of Mathematical Biophysics*, Vol. 5, pp. 115–133, 1943.

[3] N. Wiener, *Cybernetics*. Wiley, New York, 1948.

[4] D.O. Hebb, *The Organization of Behavior*. Wiley, New York, 1949.

[5] F. Rosenblatt, The Perceptron: A probabilistic model for information storage and organization in the brain, *Psychological Review*, Vol. 65, pp. 386–408, 1959.

[6] B. Widrow and M.E. Hoff, Adaptive switching circuits, in *IRE WESCON Convention Record*, Vol. 4, pp. 96–104, IRS, New York, 1960.

[7] M.L. Minsky and S.A. Papert, *Perceptrons*. MIT Press, Cambridge, MA, 1969.

[8] M.A. Arbib, *The Metaphorical Brain*. Wiley, New York, 1972.

[9] R.C. Conant, Laws of information which govern systems, *IEEE Trans. Systems, Man, and Cybernetics*, Vol. 6, pp. 334–338, 1976.

[10] S.I. Amari, A mathematical approach to neural systems, in J. Metzler (ed.) *Systems Neuroscience*, pp. 67–117. Academic Press, New York, 1977.

[11] A.C. Scott, *Neurophysics*. Wiley, New York, 1977.

[12] C.O. Lovejoy, The origin of man, *Science*, Vol. 211, pp. 341–350, 1981.

[13] L.A. Zadeh, Making computers think like people, *IEEE Spectrum*, Vol. 21, No. 8, pp. 26–32, Aug. 1984.

[14] E.R. Kandel and J.H. Schwartz, *Principles of Neural Science*. North-Holland, New York, 1985.

[15] V. Brooks, *The Neural Basis for Motor Control*. Oxford University Press, New York, 1986.

[16] M.L. Minsky, *The Society of Mind*. Simon and Schuster, New York, 1986.

[17] M.A. Arbib, *Brains, Machines and Mathematics*. Springer-Verlag, New York, 1987.

[18] S. Grossberg, *Neural Networks and Natural Intelligence*. MIT Press, Cambridge, MA, 1987.

[19] M.M. Gupta, On the cognitive computing: Perspectives, in M.M. Gupta and T. Yamakawa, (eds.) *Fuzzy Computing: Theory, Hardware and Applications*. North-Holland, New York, 1988.

[20] J.S. Albus, Outlines for a theory of intelligence, *IEEE Trans. Systems, Man, and Cybernetics*, Vol. 21, No. 3, pp. 473–509, May/June 1991.

[21] J. Farrell, I. Berger, and B. Appleby, Using learning techniques to accommodate unanticipated faults, *IEEE Control Systems Mag.*, pp. 40–49, June 1993.

Adaptive and Robust Control

[22] M. Vidyasagar, *Control Systems Synthesis: A Factorization Approach*. MIT Press, Cambridge, MA, 1985.

[23] M.M. Gupta (ed.), *Adaptive Methods for Control System Design*. IEEE Press, New York, 1986.

[24] K.J. Astrom and B. Wittemnark, *Adaptive Feedback Control*. Addison-Wesley, New York, 1989.

[25] K.S. Narendra and A.M. Annaswamy, *Stable Adaptive Systems*. Prentice-Hall, Englewood Cliffs, NJ, 1989.

[26] R. Ortega and Y. Tang, Robustness of adaptive controllers—A survey, *Automatica*, Vol. 25, No. 5, pp. 651–677, 1989.

[27] D.C. McFarlane and K. Glover, Robust controller design using normalized coprime factor plant descriptions, in M. Thoma, and A. Wyner, (eds.) *Lecture Notes in Control and Information Sciences* No. 38, Springer-Verlag, Berlin, 1989.

[28] P. Dorato and R.K. Yedavalli (eds.), *Recent Advances in Robust Control*. IEEE Press, New York, 1990.

[29] C. Abdallah, D. Dawson, and M. Jamshidi, Survey of robust control for rigid machines, *IEEE Control of Systems Mag.*, pp. 24–30, Feb. 1991.

Intelligent and Neuro-Control

[30] K.S. Fu, Learning control systems—Review and outlook, *IEEE Trans. Automatic Control*, Vol. 16, pp. 210–221, Apr. 1970.

[31] F. Ersu and H. Tolle, A new concept for learning control inspired by brain theory, in *Proc. Ninth World Congress IFAC*, 1984, pp. 245–250.

[32] K.M. Passino, Bridging the gap between conventional and intelligent control, *IEEE Control systems Mag.*, pp. 12–18, June 1993.

[33] M.D. Peek and P.J. Antsaklis, Parameter learning for performance adaptation, *IEEE Control Systems Mag.*, pp. 3–11, Dec. 1990.

[34] G.E. Hinton, How neural networks learn from experience, *Scientific American*, pp. 145–151, Sept. 1992.

[35] A.G. Barto, Connectionist learning for control, in T. Miller, R.S. Sutton, and P.J. Werbos (eds.) *Neural Networks for Control*. MIT Press, Cambridge, MA, pp. 6–58, 1991.

[36] A. Guez, J.L. Eilbert, and M. Kam, Neural network architecture for control, *IEEE Control Systems Mag.*, pp. 22–25, Apr. 1988.

[37] W.P. Jones and J. Hoskins, Backpropagation: A generalized delta learning rule, *Byte*, pp. 155–162, Oct. 1987.

[38] D.R. Hush and B.G. Home, Progress in supervised neural networks, *IEEE Signal Processing Mag.*, Vol. 10, No. 1, pp. 8–39, 1993.

[39] B. Widrow and M.A. Lehr, 30 Years of adaptive neural networks: Perceptron, Madaline, and backpropagation, *Proc. IEEE*, Vol. 78, No. 9, pp. 1415–1442, Sept. 1990.

[40] M.M. Gupta, Virtual cognitive systems (VCS), *Neural Network World*, Vol. 2, No. 6, pp. 621–628, 1992.

[41] Y.H. Pao, *Adaptive Pattern Recognition and Neural Networks*. Addison-Wesley, Redwood City, CA. 1989.

[42] P.D. Wasserman, *Neural Computing: Theory and Practice*. Van Nostrand Reinhold, New York, 1989.

[43] W.T. Miller III, R.S. Sutton, and R.J. Werbos (eds.), *Neural Networks for Control*. MIT Press, Cambridge, MA, 1990.

[44] J.S. Judd, *Neural Network Design and the Complexity of Learning*. MIT Press, Cambridge, MA, 1990.

[45] T. Khanna, *Foundations of Neural Networks*. Addison-Wesley, Redwood City, CA, 1990.

[46] R.K. Simpson, *Artificial Neural Systems: Foundations, Paradigms, Applications, and Implementations*, Pergamon Press, New York, 1990.

[47] S.Y. Kung, *Digital Neural Computing: From Theory to Application*. Prentice-Hall, Englewood Cliffs, NJ, 1991.

[48] R.J. Mammone and Y.Y. Zeevi, *Neural Networks: Theory and Applications*. Academic Press, San Diego, CA, 1991.

[49] K. Warwick, G.W. Irwin, and K.J. Hunt (eds.), *Neural Networks for Control and Systems*. Peter Peregrinus, London, 1992.

[50] B. Kosko, *Neural Networks for Signal Processing*. Prentice-Hall, Englewood Cliffs, NJ, 1992.

[51] J.M. Zurada, *Introduction to Artificial Neural Systems*. West Publishing Company, St. Paul, MN, 1992.

[52] M.M. Gupta and D.H. Rao (eds.), *Neuro-Control Systems: Theory and Applications*. IEEE Press, New York, 1994.

[53] M.M. Gupta and N.K. Sinha (eds.), *Intelligent Control Systems: Theory and Applications*. IEEE Press, New York, 1996.

[54] S.G. Tzafestas (ed.), *Methods and Applications of Intelligent Control*. Kluwer Academic, Dordrecht, Holland, 1997.

[55] Special Issues on Neural Networks, *IEEE Control Systems Mag.*, Apr. 1988, Apr. 1989, Apr. 1990.

Biological Motivation

[56] B. Widrow, Generalization and information storage in networks of Adaline neurons, in M. Yovitz, G. Jacobi, and C. Goldstein (eds.) *Self-Organizing Systems*. Spartan Books, Washington, DC, pp. 435–461, 1962.

[57] C.F. Stevens, Synaptic physiology, *Proc. IEEE*, Vol. 79, No. 9, pp. 916–930, June 1968.

[58] M. Ito, Neurophysiological aspects of the cerebellar motor control system, *Int. J. Neurology*, Vol. 7, No. 2.3–4, pp. 162–176, 1970.

[59] P.A. Anninos, B. Beek, T.J. Csermel, E.E. Harth, and G. Pertile, Dyanmics of neural structures, *J. Theoretical Biology*, Vol. 26, pp. 121–148, 1970.

[60] S.I. Amari, Neural theory of association and concept-formation, *Biological Cybernetics*, Vol. 26, pp. 175–185, 1977.

[61] M. Fujita, Adaptive filter model of the cerebellum, *Biological Cybernetics*, Vol. 45, pp. 195–206, 1982.

[62] D.E. Rumelhart and J.L. McClelland (eds.), *Parallel Distributed Processing: Explorations in the Microstructures of Cognition*, Vol. 1. MIT Press, Cambridge, MA, 1986.

[63] G.A. Carpenter and S. Grossberg, A massively parallel architecture for a self-organizing neural pattern recognition machine, *Computer Vision, Graphics, and Image Processing*, Vol. 37, pp. 54–115, 1987.

[64] A.C. Guyton, *Text Book of Medical Physiology*. W.B. Saunders, Philadelphia, 1987.

[65] R.P. Lipmann, An introduction to computing with neural nets, *ASSP Mag.*, Vol. 4, No. 2, pp. 4–22, 1987.

[66] D.S. Melkonian, Mathematical theory of chemical synaptic transmission, *Biological Cybernetics*, Vol. 62, pp. 539–548, 1990.

[67] J.A. Anderson and E. Rosenfield, *Neurocomputing: Foundations of Research*. MIT Press, Cambridge, MA, 1991.

[68] D.S. Touretzky (ed.), *Advances in Neural Information Processing Systems*. Morgan Kaufmann, San Mateo, CA, 1992.

[69] B. Pansky, D.J. Allen, and G.C. Budd, *Review of Neuroscience*, 2d ed. Macmillan, New York, 1992.

[70] *Scientific American*, Sept. 1992.

Neuronal Morphologies

[71] J.S. Albus, A new approach to manipulator control: The cerebellar model articulation controller (CMAC), *J. Dynamic Systems, Measurement, and Control*, pp. 220–227, Sept. 1975.

[72] K. Fukushima, S. Miyake, and T. Ito, Neocognitron: A neural network model for a mechanism of visual pattern recognition, *IEEE Trans. Systems, Man, and Cybernetics*, Vol. 13, No. 5, pp. 826–834, Sept./Oct. 1983.

[73] J.S. Denker, Neural-network models of learning and adaptation, *Physica-D*, Vol. 22, pp. 216–232, 1986.

[74] F.J. Pinda, Dynamics and architecture for neural computation, *J. Complexity*, Vol. 4, pp. 216–245, 1988.

[75] L.O. Chua and L. Yang, Cellular neural networks: Theory, *IEEE Trans. Circuits and Systems*, Vol. 35, pp. 1257–1272, 1988.

[76] G. Crick, The recent excitement about neural networks, *Nature*, Vol. 337, pp. 129–132, 1989.

[77] K.J. Lang, A.H. Waibel, and G.E. Hinton, A time-delay neural network architecture from isolated word recognition, *Neural Networks*, Vol. 3, No. 1, pp. 23–44, 1990.

[78] S.D. Wang and M.S. Yeh, Self-adaptive neural architectures for control applications, in *Proc. IEEE Int. Joint Conf. Neural Networks, (IJCNN)*, 1990, pp. 309–314.

[79] L. Tarassenko, J.N. Tombs, and J.H. Reynolds, Neural network architectures: for content-addressable memory, *IEEE Proc.-F*, Vol. 138, No. 1, pp. 33–39, Feb. 1991.

[80] G. Nagy, Neural networks—Then and now, *IEEE Trans. Neural Networks*, Vol. 2, No. 2, pp. 316–318, Mar. 1991.

[81] M.M. Gupta, Fuzzy logic and neural networks, presented at *Int. Conf. Fuzzy Logic and Neural Networks, IIZUKA, Japan*, 1992, Vol. A, pp. 157–160.

[82] M.M. Gupta and G.K. Knopf, A multitask visual information processor with a biologically motivated design, *J. Visual Communication and Image Representation*, Vol. 3, No. 3, pp. 230–246, Sept. 1992.

[83] Q. Zhang and A. Benveniste, Wavelet networks, *IEEE Trans. Neural Networks*, Vol. 3, No. 6, pp. 889–898, Nov. 1992.

[84] R. Hecht-Nielsen, Counterpropagation networks, *Applied Optics*, Vol. 26, pp. 4979–4984, 1987.

[85] J.J. Hopfield, Artificial neural networks are coming, An Interview by W. Myers, *IEEE Expert*, pp. 3–6, Apr. 1990.

[86] B. Widrow and R.G. Winter, Neural nets for adaptive filtering and adaptive pattern recognition, *IEEE Computer*, pp. 25–39, Mar. 1988.

[87] P.J. Werbos, *Beyond Regression: New Tools for Prediction and Analysis in the Behavior Sciences*. PhD. Thesis, Harvard University, 1974.

[88] D. Hammerstrom, Working with neural networks, *IEEE Spectrum*, Vol. 30, No. 6, pp. 26–32, June 1993.

[89] D. Hammerstrom, Working with neural networks, *IEEE Spectrum*, Vol. 30, No. 7, pp. 46–53, July 1993.

[90] M.M. Gupta and G.K. Knopf (eds.), *Neuro Vision Systems: Principles and Applications*, IEEE Press, New York, 1994.

Functional Approximation

[91] T. Poggio and F. Girosi, Networks for approximation and learning, *Proc. IEEE*, Vol. 78, No. 9, pp. 1481–1497, Sept. 1990.

[92] G.A. Watson, *Approximation Theory and Numerical Methods*. Wiley, New York, 1980.

[93] L.V. Kantorovich and G.R. Akilov, *Functional Analysis*, translated by H.L. Silcock. Pergamon Press, Elmsford, NY, 1982.

[94] A.N. Kolmogorov and S.V. Fornin, *Introductory Real Analysis*, translated by R.A. Silverman. Prentice-Hall, Englewood Cliffs, NJ, 1970.

[95] E.K. Blum and L.K. U, Approximation theory and feedforward networks, *Neural Networks*, Vol. 4, pp. 511–515, 1991.

[96] A.R. Gallant and H. White, Mere exists a neural network that dot not make avoidable mistakes, in *Proc. IEEE Conf. Neural Networks, San Diego*, 1988, Vol. 1, pp. 657–664.

[97] P. Cardaliaguet and G. Euvrard, Approximation of a function and its derivative with a neural network, *Neural Networks*, Vol. 5, pp. 20–220, 1992.

[98] R. Hecht-Nielsen, Kolmogorov's mapping neural network existence theorem, in *Proc. IEEE Conf. Neural Networks, San Diego*, 1987, Vol. 11, pp. 11–14.

[99] N.E. Cotter and T.J. Gullerm, The CMAC and a theorem of Kolmogorov, *Neural Networks*, Vol. 5, pp. 221–228, 1992.

[100] V. Kurkova, Kolmogorov's theorem and multilayer neural networks, *Neural Networks*, Vol. 5, pp. 501–506, 1992.

[101] F. Girosi and T. Poggio, Representation of properties of networks: Kolmogorov's theorem is irrelevant, *Neural Computation*, Vol. 63, pp. 169–176, 1990.

[102] D. Chester, Why two hidden layers are better than one, in *Proc. IEEE Int. Joint Conf. Neural Networks (IJCNN)*, pp. 265–268, 1990.

[103] D.S. Broomhead and D. Lowe, Multivariable functional interpolation and adaptive networks, *Complex Systems*, Vol. 2, pp. 321–355, 1988.

[104] W.I. Daunicht, Defanet–A deterministic approach to function approximation by neural networks, in *Proc. IEEE Int. Joint Conf. Neural Networks (IJCNN)*, 1990, pp. 161–164.

[105] P.J. Gawthrop and D.G. Sbarbo, Stochastic approximation and multilayer Perceptrons: The gain back-propagation algorithm, *Complex Systems*, Vol. 4, pp. 51–74, 1990.

[106] C.L. Giles and T. Maxwell, Learning, invariance, and generalization in higher-order neural networks, *Applied Optics*, Vol. 26, pp. 4972–4978, 1987.

[107] G. Josin, Neural-space generalization of a topological transformation, *Biological Cybernetics*, Vol. 59, pp. 238–290, 1988.

[108] E.J. Hartman, J.D. Keeler, and I.M. Kowalski, Layered neural networks with Gaussian hidden units as universal approximators, *Neural Computation*, Vol. 2, No. 2, pp. 210–215, 1990.

[109] E.D. Sontag, Sigmoids distinguish more efficiently than Heavisides, *Neural Computation*, Vol. 1, pp. 470–472, 1989.

[110] J.A. Leonard, M.A. Kramer, and L.H. Ungar, Using radial basis functions to approximate a function and its error bounds, *IEEE Trans. Neural Networks*, Vol. 3, No. 4, pp. 624–626, July 1992.

[111] K.-Y. Siu and I. Bruck, Neural computation of arithmetic functions, *Proc. IEEE*, Vol. 78, No. 10, pp. 111–120, Oct. 1990.

Neural Networks and Their Applications

[112] S.I. Amari, Mathematical foundations of neurocomputing, *Proc. IEEE*, Vol. 78, No. 9, pp. 1443–1462, Sept. 1990.

[117] W.R. Jones and J. Hoskins, Backpropagation: A generalized delta learning rule, *Byte*, pp. 155–162, Oct. 1987.

[118] A. Guez, J.L. Eilbert, and M. Kam, Neural network architecture for control, *IEEE Control Systems Mag.*, pp. 22–25, Apr. 1988.

[119] S.C. Huang and Y.F. Hyang, Bounds on the number of hidden neurons in multilayer Perceptrons, *IEEE Trans. Neural Networks*, Vol. 2, No. 1, pp. 47–55, 1991.

[120] W.Y. Huang and R.R. Lippmann, Neural net and traditional classifiers, in *Neural Information Processing Systems*. Morgan Kaufman, San Mateo, CA, pp. 387–396, 1988.

[121] A.D. Kulkarni, Solving ill-posed problems with artificial neural networks, *Neural Networks*, Vol. 4, pp. 477–484, 1991.

[122] D.F. Specht, Probabilistic neural networks, *Neural Networks*, Vol. 3, pp. 109–118, 1990.

[123] H. White, Learning in artificial neural networks. A statistical perspective, *Neural Computation*, Vol. 1, No. 4, pp. 425–464, 1989.

[124] S. Lee and R.M. Kil, A Gaussian potential function network with hierarchically self-organizing learning, *Neural Networks*, Vol. 4, pp. 207–224, 1991.

[125] M.T. Musavi, W. Ahmed, K.H. Chan, K.B. Faris, and D.M. Hummels, On the training of radial basis function classifiers, *Neural Networks*, Vol. 5, pp. 595–603, 1992.

[126] S. Chen, C.R.N. Cowan, and P.M. Grant, Orthogonal least squares learning algorithm for radial basis function networks, *IEEE Trans. Neural Networks*, Vol. 2, No. 2, pp. 302–309, Mar. 1991.

[127] LiMin Fu, *Neural Networks in Computer Intelligence*, McGraw-Hill, New York, 1994.

[128] S. Haykin, *Neural Networks: A Comprehensive Foundation*, Macmillan, New York, 1994.

System Identification and Control

[129] A. Guez and J. Selinsky, A trainable neuromorphic controller, *J. Robotic Systems*, Vol. 5, No. 4, pp. 363–388, 1988.

[130] S.-R. Chi, R. Shoureshi, and M. Tenorio, Neural networks for system identification, *IEEE Control Systems Mag.*, Vol. 10, pp. 31–34, 1990.

[131] S. Chen, S.A. Billings, and P.M. Grant, Nonlinear system identification using neural networks, *Int. J. Control*, Vol. 51, No. 6, pp. 1191–1214, 1990.

[132] S.A. Billings, H.B. Jamaluddin, and S. Chen, Properties of neural networks with applications to modeling nonlinear dynamical systems, *Int. J. Control*, Vol. 55, No. 1, pp. 193–224, 1992.

[133] S. Mukhopadbyay and K.S. Narendra, Disturbance rejection in nonlinear systems using neural networks, *IEEE Trans. Neural Networks*, Vol. 4, No. 1, pp. 63–72, 1993.

[134] A.U. Levin and K.S. Narendra, Control of nonlinear dynamical systems using neural networks: Controllability and stabilization, *IEEE Trans. Neural Networks*, Vol. 4, No. 2, pp. 192–206, Mar. 1993.

[135] J. Fu and N.K. Sinha, An iterative learning scheme for motion control of robots using neural networks: a case study, *J. Intelligent and Robotic systems*, Vol. 8, pp. 375–398, 1993.

[136] T. Yabuta and T. Yamada, Neural network controller characteristics with regard to adaptive control, *IEEE Trans. Systems, Man, and Cybernetics*, Vol. 22, No. 1, pp. 170–176, Jan./Feb. 1991.

[137] R.M. Sanner, J.-J.E. Slotine, Gaussian networks for direct adaptive control, *IEEE Trans. Neural Networks*, Vol. 3, No. 6, pp. 837–863, Nov. 1992.

[138] D.H. Rao, M.M. Gupta, and H.C. Wood, Neural networks in control systems, in *Proc. IEEE Conf. Communication, Computers, Power in Modern Environment*, Saskatoon, 1993, pp. 313–319.

[139] Y. Ichikawa and T. Sawa, Neural network applications for direct feedback controllers, *IEEE Trans. Neural Networks*, Vol. 3, No. 2, pp. 224–231, Mar. 1992.

[140] D.A. Hoskins, J.N. Hwang, and J. Vagners, Iterative inversion of neural networks and its application to adaptive control, *IEEE Trans. Neural Networks*, Vol. 3, No. 2, pp. 292–301, Mar. 1992.

[141] J.G. Kuschewski, S. Hui, and S.H. Zak, Application of feedforward neural networks to dynamical system identification and control, *IEEE Trans. Control Systems Technology*, Vol. 1, No. 1, pp. 37–49, Mar. 1993.

[142] M.M. Gupta and D.H. Rao, Adaptive control of unknown nonlinear systems using multi-stage dynamic neural networks, in *Proc. SPIE Conf. Intelligent Robots and Computer Vision XI, Boston*, 1992, pp. 130–142.

[143] M.M. Gupta, D.H. Rao, and P.N. Nikiforuk, Neuro-controller with dynamic learning and adaptation, *Int. J. Intelligent and Robotic Systems*, Vol. 7, No. 2, pp. 151–173, Apr. 1993.

[144] D.H. Rao and M.M. Gupta, Dynamic neural adaptive control schemes, in *Proceedings of American Control Conference, San Francisco*, 1993, pp. 1450–1454.

[145] D. Sbarbaro-Hofer, D. Neumerkel, and K. Hunt, Neural control of a steel rolling mill, *IEEE Control Systems Mag.*, pp. 69–76, June 1993.

[146] T. Samad, Neurocontrol: Concepts and Practical Considerations, in M.M. Gupta and N.K. Sinha (eds.) *Intelligent Control Systems: Theory and Applications*, pp. 265–294. IEEE Press, New York, 1996.

[147] M. Saerens, J. M. Renders, and H. Bersini, Neurocontrol based on the back-propagation algorithm, in M.M. Gupta and N.K. Sinha (eds.) *Intelligent Control Systems: Theory and Applications*, pp. 292–326. IEEE Press, New York, 1996.

[148] K.S. Narendra and S. Mukhopadhyay, Intelligent control using neural networks, in M.M. Gupta and N.K. Sinha (eds.) *Intelligent Control Systems: Theory and Applications*, pp. 151–186, IEEE Press, New York, 1996.

[149] P.J. Werbos, Neurocontrol and elastic fuzzy logic, in M.M. Gupta and N.K. Sinha (eds.) *Intelligent Control Systems: Theory and Applications*, pp. 327–345. IEEE Press, 1996.

Robotics

[150] H. Miyamota, M. Kawato, T. Setoyama, and R. Suzuki, Feedback-error-learning neural network for trajectory control of a robotic manipulator, *Neural Networks*, Vol. 1, pp. 251–265, 1988.

[151] M. Kawato, Y. Uno, M. Isobe, and R. Suzuki, Hierarchical neural network model for voluntary movement with application to robotics, *IEEE Control systems Mag.*, pp. 8–15, Apr. 1988.

[152] D.E. Bassi and G.A. Beckey, Decomposition of neural network model of robot dynamics: A feasibility study, *Simulation and AI*, Vol. 220, pp. 8–13, 1989.

[153] H. Wang, T.T. Lee, and W.A. Gruver, A neuromorphic controller for a three-link biped robot, *IEEE Trans. Systems, Man and Cybernetics*, Vol. 22, No. 1, pp. 164–169, Jan./Feb. 1991.

[154] A. Guez and Z. Ahmad, Solution to the inverse kinematics problem in robotics by neural networks, in *Proc. IEEE Int. Conf. Neural Networks, San Diego*, Mar. 1988, pp. 617–624.

[155] J. Barhen, S. Gulati, and M. Zak, Neural learning of constrained nonlinear transformations, *IEEE Computer*, pp. 167–76, June 1989.

[156] M.M. Gupta, D.H. Rao, and R.N. Nikiforuk, Dyanmic neural network based inverse-kinematics transformation of two- and three-linked robots, presented at *IFAC Conf., Sydney, Australia*, 1993, Vol. 3, pp. 289–296.

[157] M.M. Gupta and D.H. Rao, Neural learning of robot inverse kinematics transformations, in S. Mitra, W. Kraske, and M.M. Gupta (eds.) *Neural and Fuzzy Systems: The Emerging Science of Intelligent Computing*, pp. 85–112, SPIE Press, New York, 1994.

[158] W.J. Daunicht, Control of manipulators by neural networks, *IEE Proc.*, Vol. 136, Pt. E, No. 5, pp. 395–399, Sept. 1989.

[159] L.C. Rabelo and X.J.R. Avula, Hierarchical neurocontroller architecture for robotic manipulation, *IEEE Control Systems Mag.*, pp. 37–41, Apr. 1992.

[160] M.M. Gupta and D.H. Rao, Dynamic neural processor and its applications to robotics and control, in M.M. Gupta and N.K. Sinha (eds.) *Intelligent Control Systems: Theory and Applications*, pp. 515–545, IEEE Press, New york, 1996.

[161] P. Gupta and N.K. Sinha, Control of robotic manipulators using neural networks—A Survey, in S.G. Tzafestas (ed.) *Methods and Applications of Intelligent Control*, pp. 103–136, Kluwer Academic, Boston, 1997.

[162] F.L. Lewis, K. Liu, and A. Yesilidrek, *Neural Network Control of Robot Manipulators and Nonlinear Systems*, Taylor and Francis, Philadelphia, 1999.

Miscellaneous

[163] B.P. Yuhas, M.H. Goldstein, Jr., I.J. Sejnowski, and R.E. Jenkins, Neural network models of sensory integration for improved vowel recognition, *Proc. IEEE*, Vol. 78, No. 10, pp. 1658–1668, Oct. 1990.

[164] D.J. Burr, Experiments on neural net recognition of spoken and written text, *IEEE Trans. Acoustics, Speech and Signal Processing*, Vol. 36, No. 7, pp. 1162–1168, July 1988.

[165] R.P. Gorman and T.J. Sejnowski, Learned classification of sonar targets using a massively parallel network, *IEEE Trans. Acoustics, Speech, Signal Processing*, Vol. 36, No. 7, pp. 1135–1140, July 1988.

[166] M.J. Wdlis, G.A. Montague, C.D. Massimo, M.T. Ilam, and A.J. Morris, Artificial neural networks in process estimation and control, *Automatica*, Vol. 28, No. 6, pp. 1181–1187, 1992.

[167] D.H. Rao, P.N. Nikiforuk, M.M. Gupta, and H.C. Wood, Neural equalization of communication channels, in *Proc. IEEE Conf. Communications, Computers, and Power in the Modern Environment, Saskatoon*, 1993, pp. 282–290.

[168] D.H. Rao, P.N. Nikiforuk, and M.M. Gupta, A central pattern generator model using dynamic neural processor, presented at *World Congress on Neural Networks, Portland OR*, 1993, Vol. IV, pp. 533–536.

[169] C. Moallemi, Classifying cells for cancer diagnosis using neural networks, *IEEE Expert*, Vol. 6, No. 6, pp. 8–12, Dec. 1991.

[170] L. Udapa and S.S. Udapa, Neural networks for the classification of nondestructive evaluation signals, *IEE Proc.—F*, Vol. 138, No. 1, pp. 41–45, Feb. 1991.

[171] J. Graf, Long-term stock market forecasting using neural networks, *Neural Network World*, Vol. 2, No. 6, pp. 615–620, 1992.

[172] M. Sabourin and A. Mitiche, Optical character recognition by a neural network, *Neural Networks*, Vol. 5, pp. 943–852, 1992.

[173] B. Kosko, bidirectional associative memories, *IEEE Trans. Systems Man, and Cybernetics*, Vol. 18, No. 1, pp. 49–60, Jan./Feb. 1990.

Dynamic Neural Networks

[174] A. Waibel, T. Hanazawa, G. Hinton, K. Shikano, and K.J. Lang, Phoneme recognition using time-delay neural networks, *IEEE Trans. Acoustics, Speech and Signal Processing*, Vol. 37, No. 3, pp. 328–339, Mar. 1989.

[175] J.J. Hopfield, Neurons with graded response have collective computational properties like those of two-state neurons, *Proc. Natl. Acad. Sci.*, Vol. 81, pp. 3088–3092, 1984.

[176] P. Strumillo and T.S. Durani, Simulations of cardiac arrhythmia based on dynamical interactions between neural models of cardiac pace-makers, *Second Int. Conf. Artificial Neural Networks*, 1991, (IEEE Publication No. 349), pp. 195–199.

[177] M.M. Gupta and G.K. Knopf, A neural network with multiple hysteresis capabilities for short-term visual memory, in *Proc. Int. Joint Conf. Neural Networks, Seattle, WA*, 1991, Vol. 1, pp. 671–676.

[178] M.M. Gupta and G.K. Knopf, A Multitask visual information processor with a biologically motivated design, *J. Visual Communication and Image Representation*, Vol. 3, No. 3, pp. 230–246, Sept. 1992.

[179] G.K. Knopf and M.M. Gupta, A multi-purpose neural processor for machine vision system, *IEEE Trans. Neural Networks*, Vol. 4, No. 4, pp. 762–777, Sept. 1993.

[180] T. Sejnowski and C.R. Rosenberg, *NETtalk: A neural network that learns to read aloud*, Tech. Rep. JHU/EECS-86101, Johns Hopkins University, Baltimore, 1986.

[181] D.H. Rao and M.M. Gupta, A neural processor for coordinating multiple systems with dynamic uncertainties, in *Proc. Int. Symp. Uncertainty and Management (ISUMA), Maryland*, 1993, pp. 633–640.

[182] D.H. Rao and M.M. Gupta, Dynamic neural network with somatic adaptation, in *Proc. IEEE Conf. Neural Networks, San Francisco*, 1993, pp. 558–563.

[183] D.H. Rao and M.M. Gupta, A multi-functional dynamic neural processor for control applications, in *Proc. Amer. Control Conf., San Francisco*, 1993, pp. 2902–2906.

[184] C.L. Giles, C.B. Miller, D. Chen, G.Z. Sun, and Y.C. Lee, Learning and extracting finite state automata with second-order recurrent neural networks, *Neural Computation*, Vol. 4, No. 3, pp. 393–405, 1992.

[185] K.J. Lang, A.H. Waibel, and G.E. Hinton, A time-delay neural network architecture from isolated word recognition, *Neural Networks*, Vol. 3, No. 1, pp. 23–44, 1990.

[186] E.A. Wan, Temporal backpropagation for FIR neural networks, in *Proc. Int. Joint Conf. Neural Networks (IJCNN)*, pp. 575–580, June 1990.

[187] G. Tsutsumidani, N. Ohnishi, and N. Sugie, Properties and learning algorithm of discrete neural network with time delay, in *Proc. Int. Joint Conf. Neural Networks (IJCNN)*, 1991, pp. 529–534.

[188] S.L. Sudharsanan and M.K. Sundareshan, Training of a three-layer dynamical recurrent neural network for nonlinear input-output mapping, in *Proc. Int. Joint Conf. Neural Networks (IJCNN)*, 1991, pp. 111–115.

[189] R.J. Williams and D. Zipser, A learning algorithm for continually running fully recurrent neural networks, *Neural Computation*, Vol. 1, No. 2, pp. 270–280, 1989.

[190] S. Gardellam, T. Kumagai, R. Hashimoto, and M. Wada, On the dynamics and potentialities of a discrete-time binary neural network with time delay, in *Proc. Second Int. Conf. Fuzzy Logic and Neural Networks, Fukuoka, Japan*, 1992, pp. 493–499.

[191] F.J. Pinda, Recurrent backpropagation and the dynamical approach to adaptive neural computation, *Neural Computation*, Vol. 1, pp. 161–172, 1989.

[192] H. Li and B. Xu, A learning algorithm for MLN with dynamic neurons, in *Proc. Int. Joint Conf. Neural Networks (IJCNN)*, 1991, pp. 523–528.

[193] A. Porlon, A. Atiya, and K. Chong, Recurrent multilayer perceptron for nonlinear system identification, in *Proc. Int. Joint Conf. Neural Networks (IJCNN)*, 1991, pp. 537–540.

[194] P.A. Anninos, B. Beek, T.J. Csermal, E.E. Harth, and G. Pertile, Dynamics of neural structures, *J. Theoretical Biology*, Vol. 26, pp. 121–148, 1970.

[195] D. Zipser, A subgrouping strategy that reduces complexity and speeds up learning in recurrent neural networks, *Neural Computation*, Vol. 1, pp. 552–558, 1989.

[196] Y. Fang and T. Sejnowski, Faster learning for dynamic recurrent back-propagation, *Neural Computation*, Vol. 2, pp. 270–274, 1990.

[197] R. Krisnapuram and L.-F. Chen, Implementation of parallel thinning algorithms using recurrent neural networks, *IEEE Trans. Neural Networks*, Vol. 4, No. 1, pp. 142–147, Jan. 1993.

[198] B.C. Cragg and H.N.V. Temperley, Memory: Ile analogy with ferromagnetic hysteresis, *Brain*, Vol. 78, pp. 304–316, 1955.

[199] J. Jondies, D.E. Irwin, and S. Yantis, Integrating visual information from successive fixations, *Science*, Vol. 25, pp. 192–194, 1982.

[200] N.H. Farhat, Microwave diversity imaging and automated target identification based on models of neural wetworks, *Proc. IEEE*, Vol. 77, No. 5, pp. 670–681, 1989.

[201] J.M. Zurada, *Introduction to Artificial Neural Systems*, West Publishing Company, St. Paul, MN, 1992.

[202] G.W. Hoffmann, Neuron with hysteresis?, in R. Cotterill (ed.) *Computer Simulation in Brain Science*, pp. 74–87. Cambridge: Cambridge University Press, 1988.

[203] G.W. Hoffmann, A neural network based on the analogy with the immune system, *J. Theoretical Biology*, Vol. 122, pp. 33–67, 1986.

[204] D. Fender and B. Julesz, Extension of Panum's fusional area in binocularly stabilized vision, *J. Optical Society of America*, Vol. 57, No. 6, pp. 819–830, 1967.

[205] G.W. Hoffmann and M.W. Benson, Neurons with hysteresis from a network that can learn without any changes in synaptic connection strengths, *American Institute of Physics*, pp. 219–225, 1986.

[206] N.E. Cotter and T.J. Guillerm, The CMAC and a theorem of Kolmogorov, *Neural Networks*, Vol. 5, pp. 221–228, 1992.

Fuzzy Logic and Fuzzy Neural Networks

[207] M.E. Cohen and D.L. Hudson, An expert system on neural network techniques, in *Proc. NAFIP, Toronto*, pp. 117–122, 1990.

[208] M.M. Gupta and G.K. Knopf, Fuzzy neural network approach to control systems, in *Proc. First Int. Symp. Uncertainty Modeling and Analysis, Maryland*, pp. 483–488, 1990.

[209] D.C. Kuncicky and A. Kandel, A fuzzy interpretation of neural networks, in *Proc. Third IFSA Congress, Seattle, WA*, pp. 113–116, 1989.

[210] I. Hayashi, H. Nomura, and N. Wakami, Artificial neural network driven fuzzy control and its application to learning of inverted pendulum system, in *Proc. Third IFSA Congress, Seattle, WA*, pp. 610–613, 1989.

[211] J.B. Kiska and M.M. Gupta, Fuzzy logic neural network, *BUSE-FAL*, No. 4, pp. 104–109, 1990.

[212] S. Nakanishi, T. Takagi, K. Uehara, and Y. Gotoh, Self-organizing fuzzy controllers by neural networks, in *Proc. Int. Conf. Fuzzy Logic and Neural Networks IIZUKA '90, Japan*, pp. 187–192, 1990.

[213] J.C. Bezdek, *Pattern Recognition with Fuzzy Objective Function Algorithms*, Plenum Press, New York, 1991.

[214] M.M. Gupta and J. Qi, On fuzzy neuron models, in *Proc. Int. Joint Conf. Neural Networks (IJCNN), Seattle*, pp. 431–456, 1991.

[215] G.A. Carpenter, S. Grossberg, N. Markuzon, J.H. Reynolds, and D.B. Rosen, Fuzzy ARTMAP: A neural network architecture for incremental supervised learning of analog multidimensional maps, *IEEE Trans. Neural Networks*, Vol. 3, No. 5, pp. 698–713, Sept. 1992.

[216] P.K. Simpson, Fuzzy min-max neural networks—Part 1: Classification, *IEEE Trans. Neural Networks*, Vol. 3, No. 5, pp. 776–786, Sept. 1992.

[217] M.M. Gupta, Uncertainty and information: The emerging paradigms, *Int. J. Neuro and Mass-Parallel Computing and Information Systems*, Vol. 2, pp. 65–70, 1991.

[218] A. Kaufmann and M.M. Gupta, *Introduction to Fuzzy Arithmetic: Theory and Applications*, 2d ed. Van Nostrand Reinhold, New York, 1991.

[219] S.K. Paul and S. Mitra, Multilayer Perceptron, fuzzy sets, and classification, *IEEE Trans. Neural Networks*, Vol. 3, No. 5, pp. 683–697, Sept. 1992.

[220] M.M. Gupta and D.H. Rao, Virtual cognitive systems (VCS): Neural-fuzzy logic approach, in *Proc. IFAC Conf., Sydney, Australia*, 1993, Vol. 8, pp. 323–330.

[221] Special Issue on Fuzzy Logic and Neural Networks, *IEEE Trans. Neural Networks*, Vol. 3, No. 5, Sept. 1992.

[222] M.M. Gupta and E. Sanchez (eds.) *Fuzzy Information and Decision Processes*. North-Holland, New York, 1982.

[223] M.M. Gupta and E. Sanchez (eds.) *Approximate Reasoning in Decision Analysis*. North-Holland, New York, 1982.

[224] M.M. Gupta, A. Kandel, and W. Bandler (eds.) *Approximate Reasoning in Expert Systems*. North-Holland, New York, 1985.

[225] A. Kaufmann and M.M. Gupta, *Introduction to Fuzzy Arithmetic: Theory and Applications*, 2d ed., Van Nostrand Reinhold, New York, 1991.

[226] M.M. Gupta and T. Yamakawa (eds.) *Fuzzy Computing: Theory, Hardware and Applications*. North-Holland, New York, 1988.

[227] M.M. Gupta and T. Yamakawa (eds.) *Fuzzy Logic in Knowledge-Based Systems, Decision and Control*. North-Holland, New York, 1988.

[228] A. Kaufmann and M.M. Gupta, *Fuzzy Mathematical Models in Engineering and Management Science*. North-Holland, New York, 1992.

[229] B.M. Ayyub, M.M. Gupta, and L.N. Kanal (eds.) *Analysis and Management of Uncertainty: Theory and Application*. Kluwer Academic, Dordrecht, 1992.

[230] M.M. Gupta, Fuzzy neural computing systems, *Neural Network World*, Vol. 2, No. 6, pp. 629–648, 1992.

[231] B. Kosko, *Neural Networks and Fuzzy Systems*, Prentice-Hall, Englewood Cliffs, NJ, 1992.

[232] J. Yen, R. Langari, and L.A. Zadeh (eds.) *Industrial Applications of Fuzzy Logic and Intelligent Systems*, IEEE Press, New York, 1995.

Hardware Implementations

[233] A.M. Chiang and M.L. Chuang, A CCD programmable image processor and its neural network applications, *IEEE J. Solid-State Circuits*, Vol. 26, pp. 1894–1901, 1991.

[234] S. Kemeny, H. Torbey, H. Meadows, R. Bredthauer, M. La Shell, and E. Fossum, CCD focal-plane image reorganization processors for lossless image compression, *IEEE J. Solid-State Circuits*, Vol. 27, pp. 398–405, 1992.

[235] B.E. Boser, E. Sackinger, J. Bron-dey, Y. Le Cun, and L.D. Jackel, An analog neural network processor with programmable topology, *IEEE J. Solid-State Circuits*, Vol. 26, pp. 2017–2025, 1991.

[236] H.R. Graf, L.D. Jackel, and W.E. Hubbard, VLSI implementation of a neural network model, *IEEE Computer*, Vol. 21, No. 3, pp. 41–49, 1988.

[237] J. Hutchinson, C. Koch, J. Luo, and C. Mead, Computing motion using analog and binary resistive networks, *IEEE Computer*, Vol. 21, pp. 52–64, 1981.

[238] H. Kobayashi, J.L. White, and A.A. Abidi, An active resistor network for Gaussian filter of images, *IEEE J. Solid-State Circuits*, Vol. 26, pp. 738–748, 1991.

[239] H. Li and C.II. Chen, Simulating a function of visual peripheral processes with an analog VLSI network, *IEEE Micro*, Vol. 11, pp. 8–15, 1991.

[240] M.A. Maher, S.R. Deweerth, M.A. Mahowald, and C.A. Mead, Implementing neural architectures using analog VLSI circuits, *IEEE Trans. Circuits and Systems*, Vol. 36, No. 5, pp. 643–653, 1989.

[241] M.A. Mahowald and C. Mead, The silicon retina, *Scientific American*, pp. 76–82, 1991.

[242] B.A. White and M.I. Elmasry, The digi-Neocognitron: A digital Neocognitron neural network model for VLSI. *IEEE Trans. Neural Networks*, Vol. 3, No. 1, pp. 73–81, 1992.

[243] J. Caulfield, J. Kinser, and N.K. Rogers, Optical neural networks, *Proc. IEEE*, Vol. 77, No. 10, pp. 1573–1583, 1989.

[244] K.Y. Hsu, H.Y. Li, and D. Psaltis, Holographic implementation of a fully connected neural network, *Proc. IEEE*, Vol. 78, No. 10, pp. 1637–1645, 1990.

[245] D. Casasent, Multifunctional hybrid neural net, *Neural Networks*, Vol. 5, pp. 361–370, 1992.

[246] A.F. Murray, Silicon implementations of neural networks, *IEE Proc.—F*, Vol. 138, No. 1, pp. 3–12, Feb. 1991.

[247] H.C. Card, C.R. Schneider, and W.R. Moore, Hebbian plasticity in MOS synapses, *IEE Proc.—F*, Vol. 138, No. 1, pp. 13–16, Feb. 1991.

[248] C. Mead and M. Ismail (eds.) *Analog VLSI Implementation of Neural Systems*. Kluwer Academic, Boston, 1989.

[249] B.E. Boser, E. Sackinger, J. Bromely, Y.L. Cun, and L.D. Jackel, Hardware requirements for neural network pattern classifiers: A case study and implementation, *IEEE Micro*, pp. 32–40, Feb. 1992.

[250] D.W. Tank and J.J. Hopfield, Simple neural optimization networks: An A/D converter, signal decision circuit, and a linear programming circuit, *IEEE Trans. Circuits and Systems*, Vol. 33, No. 5, pp. 533–541, 1986.

[251] S.W. Tsay and R.W. Newcomb, VLSI implementation of ARTI memories, *IEEE Trans. Neural Networks*, Vol. 2, No. 2, pp. 214–221, 1991.

[252] Special Issues on Neural Networks Hardware, *IEEE Trans. Neural Networks*, May 1992, May 1993.

CHAPTER 3

Computational Issues in Intelligent Control: Discrete-Event and Hybrid Systems

XENOFON D. KOUTSOUKOS and PANOS J. ANTSAKLIS

Department of Electrical Engineering, University of Notre Dame, Notre Dame, IN 46556, USA

1 INTRODUCTION

The quest for machines that allow physical systems to exhibit higher autonomy has been the driving force in the development of control systems over the centuries. For systems with high degrees of autonomy, intelligent control methodologies appear to be necessary. An intelligent control system should be able to operate appropriately and with a high degree of autonomy under significant uncertainty that results from the fact that its components, control goals, plant models, and control laws are not always completely defined, either because they were not known at the time of design or because they changed unexpectedly. Intelligent and autonomous control fundamentals are discussed for example in [3, 4, 8, 26] and the references therein.

In order to control complex systems, one has to deal effectively with the issue of computational complexity. This has been on the periphery of the interests of researchers in conventional control, but it is clear that computational complexity is a central issue whenever one attempts to control complex systems. The physical processes of interest in intelligent control are usually more general and complex than the processes that appear in conventional control. They often exhibit complicated phenomena such as nonlinear behaviors and switching mechanisms. In addition, the goals of intelligent control problems are more ambitious [3]. Apart from the usual problems of conventional control, concepts such as liveness and deadlock developed in operations research and computer science arise in intelligent control. To develop tools that facilitate the use of intelligent control systems it is essential to capture the phenomena of interest accurately and in tractable mathematical form. A good mathematical description must be detailed enough to describe accurately the phenomena of interest and at the same time simple enough to be amenable to analysis and especially to design procedures.

The study of the computational issues in intelligent control is very helpful in the evaluation of the progress of the research toward building systems with higher degrees of autonomy. It is also useful in identifying specific algorithms and methodologies that appear to be computationally intractable and reconsidering their mathematical modelling. By modelling at different levels of abstraction, computationally tractable solutions for complex intelligent control problems can be identified. On the practical side, the utilization of the available computer resources can be improved by considering the computational complexity of the relevant procedures. In this work, we concentrate on computational issues in intelligent control that arise when discrete-event and hybrid models are used to describe mathematically the processes of interest. The reader, of course, should be aware of the computational results on conventional control algorithms (see for example [65]) that have appeared in the literature in recent years. These results are not studied here. The use of discrete-event and hybrid models in intelligent control systems has been discussed at length, for example, in [6, 9, 61, 63, 82]. Here, we focus on the computational issues of specific approaches that have been proposed for the analysis, synthesis, and simulation of such systems. It should be noted that the treatment of the subject it is not complete by far. The importance of studying the computational issues in discrete-event and hybrid systems is only starting to be recognized by the research community, and a number of relevant articles have appeared in the literature. For example, computational issues of supervisor control theory for discrete-event systems [70] have been addressed in [58, 60, 72, 81]. Complexity results for hybrid systems can be found in [10, 12, 32, 75]. In this chapter, we study computational issues in recent approaches to discrete-event and hybrid system analysis and design that were developed by our group using Petri nets. We also present computational issues of related analysis and synthesis problems that have appeared in the literature. A quantitative theory of intelligent control based on formal models such as discrete-event or hybrid system models may result in algorithms of high complexity. Often, there are applications for which the same algorithms can be applied efficiently. There are also cases where the designer may decide on a compromise for a "suboptimal" solution that can be computed in an efficient manner.

The modeling tool that we have selected to study the computational issues in intelligent control here is that of Petri nets. Petri nets are a powerful modeling paradigm for a variety of systems. Their basic characteristic is that they provide an excellent tool for capturing concurrency and conflict within a system. They have an appealing graphical and mathematical representation and they have been used extensively to model information processing systems, manufacturing systems, communication systems, and chemical processes, among others. Petri nets have been used extensively as a tool for modeling, analysis and synthesis for discrete-event systems [16, 54]. In this chapter, ordinary Petri nets are used in the design of supervisors for discrete-event systems [52] and a class of timed Petri nets, named programmable timed Petri nets, is used for studying hybrid systems [40]. Petri nets can be viewed as a generalization of finite automata and are used instead of finite automata for a number of reasons. The first is the expressiveness of Petri nets. Petri net languages include the regular languages described by finite automata and they can model switching policies that describe conflict, concurrency, synchro-nization, and buffer sizes. Another reason is that recent results in the supervisory control of discrete-event systems using ordinary Petri nets [52] have made possible the design of super-visors in an efficient and transparent manner. In general, a Petri net representation for a concurrent process will be more compact (fewer vertices) than its associated automaton representation, and with the use of partial order semantics it is now possible to search the Petri net's state space in a efficient manner [48]. The compactness of Petri nets may lead to algorithms of high complexity. Note that theoretical results concerning Petri net modeling power and limitations exist in the literature, as Petri nets have been used in a wide range of applications. For example, in industrial process control Petri nets have been used to implement real-time controllers, and to serve as a replacement for programmable logic controllers [18].

The aim of this chapter is to investigate computational issues in discrete-event and hybrid systems that are central in intelligent control and the importance and suitability of Petri net-based models for intelligent control by studying computational issues that arise in such contexts. Our framework for intelligent control is discussed in Section 2, where a hierarchical functional architecture that can facilitate the study of fundamental issues of a quantitative theory of autonomous intelligent control is used. Note that such architecture also offers advantages with respect to computational issues. In Section 2.2, the need for discrete-event and hybrid models in intelligent control systems is discussed as well as the levels of abstraction in the hierarchical architecture where such models frequently appear. Section 3 briefly reviews some basic notions from complexity theory that are necessary for the study of computational issues in intelligent control. Petri nets are discussed in Section 4. Some basic notions are first introduced in Section 4.1. Then, in Section 4.2, computational aspects of Petri nets are discussed including decidability issues for various analysis problems. An integer programming technique for checking properties of interest is discussed in Section 4.3 and an approach based on partial order semantics (unfolding) for searching the state space is discussed in Section 4.4. Synthesis results and supervisor control of Petri nets based on place invariants are discussed in Section 4.5. The computational aspects of hybrid models are discussed in Section 5. First in Section 5.1, computational issues in hybrid automata are discussed at length. Hybrid automata provide a general modeling formalism for the formal specification and algorithmic analysis of hybrid systems [1] and they are widely used in both the computer science and the control communities. The computational issues of some important synthesis approaches proposed, in the literature are also discussed. Programmable timed Petri nets are presented in Section 5.2, with emphasis on the computational complexity of algorithms for the analysis and supervision of hybrid systems. The computational aspects of simulating intelligent control systems are discussed in Section 6. In particular, a parallel computing architecture for intelligent control is presented. The discussion describes ongoing research for development of parallel computing tools for large, computationally demanding, irregular applications where the computational load may change during run-time. Our motivation was a parallel run-time system intended for symmetric multiprocessors (SMPs) that has been implemented on an IBM RISC 6000/SP machine. This parallel architecture, is an application-driven scheme for applications that require large computational tasks such as intelligent control systems. We discuss the suitability of this parallel computing scheme for simulation of intelligent control systems, and in Section 6.1 we illustrate its advantages by considering parallel discrete-event simulations.

2   INTELLIGENT CONTROL

2.1   General Concepts

Intelligent control describes the discipline in which the control methods developed attempt to emulate important characteristics of human intelligence. These characteristics include adaptation and learning, planning under large uncertainty, and coping with large amounts of data. Today, the area of intelligent control tends to encompass everything that is not characterized as conventional control. Intelligent control is interdisciplinary as it combines and extends theories and methods from areas such as control, computer science, and operations research. It uses theories from mathematics and seeks inspiration and ideas from biological systems. Intelligent control methodologies are being applied to robotics and automation, communications, manufacturing, and traffic control, to mention but a few areas of application. Neural networks, fuzzy control, genetic algorithms, planning systems, expert systems, and hybrid systems are all areas where related work is taking place. The areas of computer science and in particular artificial intelligence provide knowledge representation ideas, methodologies and tools such as semantic networks, frames, reasoning techniques, and computer languages such as LISP and PROLOG. Concepts and algorithms developed in the areas of adaptive control and machine learning help intelligent controllers to adapt and learn. Advances in sensors, actuators, computation technology and communication networks help provide the necessary techniques for implementation of intelligent control hardware.

Why is intelligent control needed? The fact is that there are problems of control today that cannot be formulated and studied in the conventional differential/difference equation mathematical framework using "conventional (or traditional) control" methodologies that were developed in past decades to control dynamical systems [3]. To address these complex problems in a systematic way, a number of methods have been developed in recent years that are collectively known as "intelligent control" methodologies. Intelligent control uses conventional control methods to solve "lower-level" control problems and conventional control is included in the area of intelligent control. Intelligent control attempts to build upon and enhance the conventional control methodologies to solve new, challenging control problems.

To control complex systems one has to deal effectively with the computational complexity issue. This has been peripheral in the interests of the researchers in conventional control, but it is clear that computational complexity is a central issue whenever one attempts to control complex systems. Computational complexity issues are usually addressed by using hierarchies to describe the operation of complex systems. A hierarchical functional architecture of a controller that is used to attain high degrees of autonomy has been proposed in [9] (for intelligent control architectures see also [73], the contributions in [8], and the references therein). This hierarchical architecture, which is shown in Figure 1, has three levels: the execution level, the coordination level, and the management and organization level. The architecture exhibits certain characteristics that have been shown in the literature to be necessary and desirable in autonomous

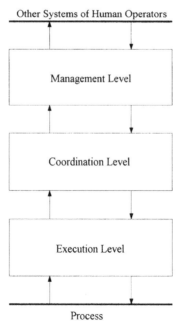

FIGURE 1
Intelligent autonomous controller functional architecture.

intelligent systems. Such a hierarchical architecture can facilitate the study of fundamental issues of a quantitative theory of autonomous intelligent control. The representation of a complex system using formal models at different levels of this hierarchy enables the researcher to use standard control-theoretic analysis (for example, conventional control or supervisor control theory of discrete event systems). More importantly, in view of the content of this chapter, it enables the study of the computational complexity of important problems in intelligent control.

We briefly outline some characteristics of the architecture. There is a successive delegation of duties from the higher to lower levels; consequently the number of distinct tasks increases as we go down the hierarchy. Higher levels are concerned with slower aspects of the system's behavior and with its larger portions, or broader aspects. There is then a smaller contextual horizon at lower levels, that is, the control decisions are made by considering less information. Also notice that higher levels are concerned with longer time horizons than are lower levels. Because of the need for high-level decision making abilities at the higher levels in the hierarchy, it has been proposed that there is increasing intelligence as one moves from the lower to the higher levels. This is reflected in the use of fewer conventional numeric–algorithmic methods at higher levels as well as the use of more symbolic–decision making methods. This is the "principle of increasing intelligence with decreasing precision" of Saridis (see also [74] and the references therein). The decreasing precision is reflected by a decrease in time scale density, decrease in bandwidth or system rate, and a decrease in the decision (control action) rate. These properties have been studied for a class of hierarchical systems in [62]. All these characteristics lead to a decrease in granularity of models used, or equivalently, to an increase in model abstractness.

2.2   Models for Intelligent Controllers

In highly autonomous control systems, the plant is sometimes so complex that it is either impossible. or inappropriate to describe it by conventional mathematical system models consisting only of differential or difference equations. Even though it might be possible to accurately describe some systems with highly complex nonlinear differential equations, such description may be inappropriate if it makes subsequent analysis too difficult or too computationally complex to be useful. The complexity of the plant model needed in design depends both on the complexity of the physical system and on how demanding the design specifications are. There is a trade-off between model complexity and our ability to perform analysis on the system via the model. Frequently, a more abstract, higher-level model can be utilized, which will make subsequent analysis simpler. This model intentionally ignores some of the system characteristics, specifically those that need not be considered in attempting to meet the particular performance specifications. For example, a simple temperature controller could ignore almost all the dynamics of the house or the office and consider only a temperature threshold model of the system to switch the furnace off or on (see also the discussion on hybrid systems later).

2.2.1   Discrete-Event System Models. Discrete-event system (DES) models that use finite automata or Petri nets, queuing network models, Markov chains, etc. are quite useful for modeling the higher-level decision making processes in an intelligent autonomous controller. The choice whether to use such models will, of course, depend on what properties of the autonomous system are to be studied. More specifically, DES models are appropriate for general expert control systems, planning systems, abstract learning control and often the higher "management and coordination levels- in the hierarchical architecture for intelligent autonomous systems. DES analysis and controller synthesis techniques (for example [70]) have been successfully developed. Other important topics for intelligent control include approaches to controllability, reachability, stability, and performance analysis. Applications of DES theoretic techniques have been reported for the modeling and analysis of AI planning systems and the stability analysis of expert control systems (see for example [63, 64]). Discrete-event systems are of course important in their own right and they have been studied using many approaches. They are also very useful in connection with hybrid systems. Recently, an efficient methodology for supervisory controller design for DES was developed using Petri nets [51, 52, 53, 85]. The approach uses the concept of place invariants of the net to design control supervisors that enforce linear constraints on the marking and firing vectors of the net. This approach is discussed later in this chapter with emphasis on its computational efficiency and simplicity. Potential applications of the approach in intelligent control include real-time control reconfiguration and planning different control tasks, for example, in manufacturing and hybrid systems. In general, when considering the application of DES theoretic techniques to intelligent control systems, it is important to study their computational aspects, particularly in problems such as reachability, liveness, and deadlock detection that arise in many intelligent control applications. Studying the computational issues of DES approaches can be very important in automated verification, controller synthesis, on-line reconfiguration, and task planning among others. Several models have been proposed in the literature to describe the dynamics of DES. An important observation is that higher expressiveness of the model typically results in algorithms of higher complexity. Petri nets provide a trade-off between expressiveness and complexity and are suitable for describing concurrent processes that appear frequently in intelligent systems. Petri nets are studied at length in this chapter with respect to their computational properties.

2.2.2 Hybrid System Models. Hybrid systems are dynamical systems whose behavior of interest is determined by interacting continuous and discrete dynamics (see for example [7]). These systems typically contain variables or signals that take values from a continuous set (e.g. the set of real numbers) and also variables that take values from a discrete, typically finite set (e.g. the set of symbols $\{a, b, c\}$). These continuous or discrete-valued variables or signals depend on independent variables such as time, which may also be continuous or discrete; some of the variables may also be discrete-event driven in an asynchronous manner.

There are several reasons for using hybrid models to represent the dynamic behavior of interest. Reducing complexity was and still is an important reason for dealing with hybrid systems; this is accomplished by incorporating models of dynamic processes having different levels of abstraction. For example, a thermostat typically sees a very simple, but adequate for the task in hand, model of the complex heat flow dynamics. As another example, in order to avoid dealing directly with a set of nonlinear equations one may choose to work with sets of simpler equations (e.g. linear), and switch among these simpler models. The advent of digital machines has made hybrid systems very common. Whenever a digital device interacts with the continuous world, the behavior involves hybrid phenomena that need to be analyzed and understood.

Hybrid control systems typically arise from computer-aided control of continuous processes in industrial processes, manufacturing and communication networks, for example. They also arise from the hierarchical organization of complex control systems. There, hierarchical organization helps manage complexity and higher levels in the hierarchy require less detailed models (discrete abstractions) of the functioning of the lower levels (continuous dynamics), necessitating the interaction of discrete and continuous components. The study of hybrid control systems is essential in designing sequential supervisory controllers for continuous systems, and it is central in designing intelligent control systems with a high degree of autonomy. Hybrid system analysis and controller synthesis techniques could provide an approach for design and verification of intelligent control systems that exhibit a truly autonomous operation.

Hybrid control systems appear in the intelligent autonomous control system framework whenever one considers the execution level together with control functions performed in the higher coordination and management levels. Examples include expert systems supervising and tuning conventional controller parameters, planning systems setting the setpoints of local control regulators, and sequential controllers deciding which one of a number of conventional controllers is to be used to control a system, to mention but a few.

The analysis, design, simulation, and verification of hybrid systems requires the development of computationally efficient algorithms and approaches. Several models have been proposed in the literature for the development of analysis and controller synthesis techniques (see for example [5]). Timed automata and hybrid automata have been used by several researchers for modeling, verification and controller synthesis techniques of hybrid systems. Although the initial results concerning the complexity of approaches based on timed and hybrid automata were negative, recent efforts have proposed systematic techniques that are applicable to a large class of problems. Because of the importance of hybrid automata-based methods, we outline some of the basic computational issues of hybrid automata based approaches later in this contribution.

Recently, a class of timed Petri nets named *programmable timed Petri nets* [42] has been used to model hybrid control systems. The main characteristic of the proposed modeling formalism is the introduction of a clock structure that consists of generalized local timers that evolve according to continuous-time vector dynamical equations. They can be seen as an extension of the approach taken in [2, 1]. They provide a simple but powerful way to annotate the Petri net graph with generalized timing constraints expressed by propositional logic formulas. It may be that the more powerful expressiveness of Petri nets will result in analysis and controller synthesis approaches of higher complexity than those based on hybrid automata. However, Petri nets may be preferable as there are complex systems that include, for example, concurrency and/or conflict and can be modeled more compactly using Petri nets than using finite automata. There are also control specifications, for example mutual exclusion constraints, that can be studied more efficiently in a Petri net framework. Moreover, there is the need to investigate the applicability of recent results in Petri nets in a hybrid framework. Stability and supervisory control design of hybrid systems modeled by programmable timed Petri nets have been studied in [40], and in Section 5.2 we briefly outline that approach and focus on its computational advantages.

3   ELEMENTS OF COMPUTATIONAL COMPLEXITY THEORY

This section contains some basic notions of complexity theory that are necessary for the study of computational issues in intelligent control. The discussion here is kept rather informal, and for precise results the reader is referred to texts in complexity theory (see for example [35, 91]. An *alphabet* is a finite set of symbols. A *string* over an alphabet Σ is a finite-length sequence of symbols from Σ. We denote the set of all strings over a fixed alphabet Σ by Σ^*. A *language L* over an alphabet Σ is a set of strings of symbols over Σ. In the following, the term *problem* is used to define a general question to be answered, which may have several parameters whose values are to be determined. A problem is usually defined by describing its parameters and specifying the properties an (optimal) solution is required to satisfy. An *instance* of a problem is a list of values, one value for each parameter of the problem. In order to give a precise definition of a problem Π, we consider a fixed alphabet Σ (e.g. $\Sigma = \{0, 1, \emptyset\}$) and an encoding scheme that translates any instance of the problem to a string of symbols over Σ. Therefore, a problem can be defined mathematically as a subset Π of $\Sigma^* \times \Sigma^*$. Each $\sigma \in \Sigma^*$ that encodes all the known parameters of the problem is called *input* of Π. A string $\tau \in \Sigma^*$ is called an *output* or *solution* of Π if $(\sigma, \tau) \in \Pi$. A *decision problem* is a problem with yes or no answer. A decision problem can be defined mathematically as a subset of Σ^*, or equivalently as a language over Σ. To solve problems, we develop procedures that utilize computing resources. The formal descriptions of these procedures are called *algorithms*. An algorithm is identified with some computer model and therefore, the study of algorithms requires the definition of a computer model. The model that more often is used to represent a real-world computer is the Turing machine.

Consider the Turing machine M with input alphabet Σ. The language accepted by M, denoted by $L(M)$, is the set of words in Σ^* that cause M to enter an accepting state. Given a Turing machine M recognizing the language M, it is assumed that M halts whenever the input is accepted. For not accepted words, it is possible that M will never halt. A language that is accepted by a Turing machine is said to be *recursively enumerable*. Another important class of languages are the - machine that halts *recursive* language, which are defined as those accepted by at least one Turing, on all inputs. An algorithm can be considered formally as a Turing machine M. The description of the parameters of the problem constitutes the input string of the Turing machine (after the application of an encoding scheme). The algorithm *solves* the problem for each input string and initial state of the machine if, after a finite number of moves of the tape head, it stops in an accepting state, while it writes a string that is a solution of the problem. Consider now a decision problem Π and encoding instances of the problem by strings of symbols over Σ. For these problems it is assumed that the answer is "yes" if the machine M halts and to be "no" otherwise. Therefore, the question whether there exists an algorithm for solving a decision problem can be transformed to whether or not a particular language is recursive.

Decidable and undecidable problems. The discussion now is focused on the existence of algorithms for decision problems. While it may seem restrictive to consider only decision problems, in fact this is not the case since many general problems can be transformed to decision problems that are provably as difficult as the general problem. A problem whose language is recursive is said to be *decidable*. Otherwise, the problem is *undecidable*. That is, a problem is undecidable if there is no algorithm that takes as input an instance of the problem and determines whether the answer to that instance is "yes" or "no". *Semi-decidable* procedures are often proposed to deal with undecidable problems. These algorithms produce the correct answer if they terminate, but their termination is not guaranteed.

Computational Complexity. It follows from the previous discussion that there are problems that are unsolvable on a Turing machine (and by Church's thesis on any computer). The following discussion is focused on decidable problems. In particular, we classify decidable problems based on the amount of time on space (or other resource) needed to solve a problem (recognize the corresponding language) on a universal computer model, such as a Turing machine. Consider a Turing machine M. If for a given string σ of length n, M makes at most $T(n)$ number of steps before halting, then M is said to be of *time complexity* $T(n)$ with *time complexity function* $T(n)$: $\mathbb{N} \to \mathbb{N}$. The language $L(M)$ accepted by M is also said to be of *time complexity* $T(n)$. Similarly, if for every input string of length n, M scans at most $S(n)$ cells, then M is said to be of *space complexity* $S(n)$ with *space complexity function* $S(n)$: $\mathbb{N} \to \mathbb{N}$. The language $L(M)$ is also said to be of *space complexity* $S(n)$.

The Classes $\mathcal{P}$ and $\mathcal{NP}$. An algorithm is said to be of *polynomial time (space) complexity* if its time (space) complexity function $f(n)$ satisfies $f(n) \le p(n)$ for some polynomial p. The class of all decision problems for which a polynomial time algorithm exists is called the class $\mathcal{P}$. Intuitively, $\mathcal{P}$ is the class of problems that can be solved efficiently. The class of decision problems that can be solved by a deterministic Turing machine by using a polynomial amount of working space is denoted by PSPACE. Similarly, EXPSPACE is used to denote the class of problems that need an exponential amount of space. A number of important problems do not appear to be in $\mathcal{P}$ but have *nondeterministic polynomial algorithms*. This class of problems is denoted by $\mathcal{NP}$. To define formally the class $\mathcal{NP}$, the nondeterministic Turing machine is used [35]. A problem belongs to the class $\mathcal{NP}$ if it can be solved by a nondeterministic polynomial algorithm (which is identified by a nondeterministic Turing machine). Of course, any attempt to execute a nondeterministic algorithm in a deterministic device will need much more time, since all possible choices have to be performed. Given a language L in the class $\mathcal{NP}$ then L is accepted by a deterministic Turing machine of time complexity $k^{p(n)}$, for some constant k and polynomial p. However, despite enormous research effort there is no language L in $\mathcal{NP}$ that has been proved not to be in $\mathcal{P}$. Finally, we close the discussion of basic notions in complexity theory with the class of $\mathcal{NP}$-complete problems. A problem Π (or language) is $\mathcal{NP}$-complete if Π belongs to the class $\mathcal{NP}$ and every other problem in $\mathcal{NP}$ can be polynomially reduced to Π. What is interesting about this class is that if a polynomial algorithm exists for any of these problems, then all problems in $\mathcal{NP}$ will be polynomial time solvable. $\mathcal{NP}$-completeness characterizes problems that are "hard" in a well-defined sense and more likely they are not in $\mathcal{P}$. Note that the notion of completeness is more general and can be applied to any class $\mathcal{C}$ of problems. We say that a problem Π is $\mathcal{C}$-complete if Π belongs to the class $\mathcal{C}$ and every Π' in $\mathcal{C}$ can be polynomially reduced to Π.

4   DES IN INTELLIGENT CONTROL USING PETRI NETS

In this section, Petri nets are used to study computational issues that appear in connection with DES in intelligent control. As was mentioned in the introduction, there are several results on computational issues of DES that use finite automata and the reader is referred to [58, 60, 72, 81] and the references therein for more information. Petri net models have a wide range of applications in intelligent control, for instance in task planning and fault diagnosis. They are especially useful in the case of concurrent systems and they can be enhanced to model various dynamical systems. In this section, several computational issues in the analysis and design of systems modeled by Petri nets are studied. Decidability issues for checking basic properties in Petri nets are discussed. The use of integer programming for checking system properties is also presented. In addition, the computational advantages of unfolding algorithms that address the state explosion problem in Petri nets are examined. Finally, a synthesis method for Petri net supervisors is briefly presented with the emphasis on its computational efficiency.

4.1   Petri Nets: Basic Notions

Petri nets are a powerful modeling paradigm for a variety of systems [54, 67, 71]. Their basic characteristic is that they provide an excellent tool for capturing concurrency and conflict within a system. They have an appealing graphical and mathematical representation and they have been used extensively to model information processing systems, manufacturing systems, communication systems, industrial processes and so forth. In the following, some basic notions of Petri nets that are necessary for the following sections are presented.

Definition. A *Petri net structure* is defined as a 3-tuple $N = (P, T, F)$ where P is a finite set of *places*, T is a finite set of *transitions*, and $F \subseteq (P \times T) \cup (T \times P)$ is the *incidence relation* representing a set of directed arcs connecting places to transitions and vice versa.

The *preset* and *postset* of a place p are defined by $\bullet p = \{t : (t, p) \in F\}$ and $p \bullet = \{t : (p, t) \in F\}$. The *preset* and *postset* of a transition t are $\bullet t = \{p : (p, t) \in F\}$ and $\bullet t = p : (P, t) \in F\}$, respectively. The *marking* of a Petri net is a mapping $\mu : P \to \mathbb{N}$ from the set of places onto the nonnegative integers which assigns to each place p a number of tokens $\mu(p)$. The dynamics of ordinary Petri nets are characterized by the evolution of the marking vector that is referred to as the *state* of the net. A *net system* $\langle N, \mu_0 \rangle$ is a net $N = (P, T, F)$ with initial marking μ_0.

The marking can be represented by an m-dimensional column vector $\mu = [\mu_1, \ldots, \mu_m]^T$, where $m = |P|$ is the number of places. The vector μ gives, for each place p_i, the number of tokens in that place, $\mu_i = \mu(p_i)$. The marking can be identified also with the multiset containing $\mu(p_i)$ copies of p_i for every $p_i \in P$. A multiset is a collection of elements over some domain that, unlike a set, allows multiple occurrences of the elements. To avoid confusion, the marking μ is interpreted as a mapping when it is appeared with an argument and as a vector of nonnegative integers otherwise. Multiset relations are frequently used. For example, the notation $\mu \subset \mu'$ is interpreted as a multiset inclusion relation and it is true if and only if $\mu(p_i) < \mu'(p_i)$ for all $p_i \in P$.

A transition t is *enabled* when each one of its input places is marked with at least one token, $\mu(p) > 0$ for all $p \in \bullet t$. An enabled transition may fire. If $\mu(p)$ and $\mu'(p)$ denote the marking of place p before and after the firing of enabled transition t, then

$$\mu'(p) = \begin{cases} \mu(p) + 1 & \text{if } p \in t\bullet \setminus \bullet t \\ \mu(p) - 1 & \text{if } p \in t\bullet \setminus \bullet t \\ \mu(p) & \text{otherwise} \end{cases} \tag{1}$$

In words, firing an enabled transition t causes one token to be removed from each place $p \in \bullet t$, and one token to be added to each $p \in t\bullet$. The firing of the transition t that is enabled at marking μ and results in the new marking μ' is denoted as $\mu[t\rangle\mu'$. A *firing sequence* from a marking μ_0 is a sequence of $\sigma = t_1 t_2 \ldots t_n$ such that $\mu_0[t_1\rangle\mu_1[t_1\rangle\mu_2 \ldots [t_n\rangle\mu_n$. A marking μ is *reachable* in the net system $\langle N, \mu_0 \rangle$ if there exists a firing sequence such that $\mu[\sigma\rangle\mu'$. The set of reachable markings from μ_0 in the Petri net N is denoted by $R(N, \mu_0)$.

State space description of Petri net. The dynamic behavior of concurrent systems modeled by Petri nets can also be described by matrix equations. These equations are similar to the difference equation that are used to describe linear discrete-time systems with the additional restriction that all parameters and vaiables involved take values only from the set of nonnegative integers. Note that the state space description can be used to represent Petri nets with weighted arcs.

Let $\mathbb{N}$ be the set of nonnegative integers and let $m = |P|$ and $n = |T|$ denote the number of places and transitions, respectively. The incidence relation can be represented using two matrices. The arcs connecting transitions to places are described by the matrix $D^+ \in \mathbb{N}^{m \times n}$ and the arcs connecting places to transitions are described by the matrix $D^- \in \mathbb{N}^{m \times n}$ with entries denoting the weights of each arc. Then the Petri net incidence matrix is defined $D = D^+ - D^-$. Recall that the marking is represented with the m-dimensional integer vector μ and describes the distribution of tokens throughout the net. Let μ_k denote the marking of the Petri net after the kth execution. Using the incidence matrix μ_{k+1} s determined by

$$\mu_{k+1} = \mu_k + Dq_k \tag{2}$$

where q_k is the n-dimensional *firing vector*. Each entry of the vector q_k represents the number of times the corresponding transition has fired during the kth execution of the net. Equation (2) is called the *state equation* of a Petri net. A given firing vector represents a valid possible firing if all of the transitions for which it contains nonzero entries are enabled. The validity of a firing vector q can be determined by checking the *enabling condition* $\mu \geq D^- q$. In the remaining of the section, both the graphical and algebraic representations of Petri nets are used to discuss the computational complexity of central analysis and synthesis problems.

4.2   Decidability Issues in Petri Nets

In spite of the large expressive power of Petri nets, most of the interesting properties for verification purposes are decidable; however, they tend to involve algorithms of high computational complexity. In the following, we review some basic decidability results for Petri nets. For more details see [20] and references therein.

Boundness. A net system is *bounded* if there exists finite $k \in \mathbb{N}$ such that $\mu(p) \leq k$ for every place p and reachable marking $\mu \in R(N, \mu_0)$. The set of reachable markings for a bounded Petri net is finite. If the net is used to model systems with buffers or registers, then the verification of the boundness property is essential to guarantee that there will be no overflows in the system. The boundness problem for Petri nets is decidable. Checking boundness requires at least space $2^{c\sqrt{n}}$ where c is a constant and n is the size of the Petri net that reflects the number of places, transitions and their interconnections. In the case when the bound k is constant $k \geq 4$, then the problem is PSPACE-complete. A net N is *structurally bounded* if it is bounded for all possible markings. It has been shown that a net is structurally bounded if and only if the system of linear inequalities $XD \leq 0$ has a solution [50].

Reachability. The reachability problem is one of the fundamental problems for Petri net analysis. Given a marking μ of the net system $\langle N, \mu_0 \rangle$, the reachability problem is the problem of deciding whether $\mu \in R(N, \mu_0)$. The reachability problem is decidable. A lower bound for its complexity is that it needs at least exponential space and exponential time. An extension of Petri nets named *extended Petri nets* has been defined to increase the expressive power of ordinary Petri nets. These nets contain *inhibitor arcs* from places to transitions. If the place p is connected with the transition t via an inhibitor arc, then t can fire only if $\mu(p) = 0$ (zero detector). It is interesting that the reachability problem of Petri nets with one inhibitor arc is decidable while, with at least two inhibitor arcs, it is undecidable [20].

Liveness. The notion of liveness is fundamental for the detection and avoidance of deadlocks. A transition t is *live* with respect to a marking μ_0 if for each $\mu \in R(N, \mu_0)$ there exists a firing sequence σ such that μ enables t. A net system is live with respect to the initial marking if every transition is live. The liveness problem is recursively equivalent to the reachability problem, and thus decidable. Relevant to the liveness notion is deadlock-freedom. A Petri net is deadlock-free with respect to μ_0 if every reachable marking $\mu \in R(N, \mu_0)$ enables a transition. The problem of deadlock-freedom can be reduced in polynomial time to the reachability problem.

Persistence. Persistence is a useful property in the verification of parallel computing protocols and asynchronous circuits [38]. It is related to conflict-freedom and is also central to identifying and allocating shared resources in manufacturing systems. A Petri net is persistent if for any marking in $R(N, \mu_0)$ an enabled transition can be disabled only by its own firing. If a Petri net is persistent, then for any two enabled transitions, the firing of the one transition will not disable the other. The problem to decide whether a given Petri net is persistent is decidable. In [38], persistence of Petri nets is efficiently analyzed using unfoldings (see discussion later in the section).

Equality problem for Petri net reachability sets. Consider two net systems $\langle N_1, \mu_1 \rangle$ and $\langle N_2, \mu_2 \rangle$, then the problem of checking whether $R(N_1, \mu_1) = R(N_2, \mu_2)$ is undecidable. Deciding whether $R(N_1, \mu_1) \subseteq R(N_2, \mu_2)$ is also undecidable. The proof of these statements is based on *Hilbert's tenth problem* [67]. It can be shown that the language inclusion problem is also undecidable for Petri nets. Assume that the system and the desired specifications have been modeled by the Petri nets N_1 and N_2, respectively. The above undecidability results prohibit the automated verification for proving that the specifications represented by the net N_2 are satisfied by the system N_1. However, there are subclasses of Petri nets for which these problems are decidable and algorithms for automated verification have been developed. An interesting special case is for bounded Petri nets where the set of reachable markings is finite.

Reachability tree. The simplest way to investigate the reachability problem of Petri nets is to expand its *reachability tree*. The reachability tree represents an exhaustive enumeration of all the reachable markings. Starting with the initial marking μ_0 all the enabled transitions are fired. This leads to a set of new possible markings. Taking each of those as a new root, the reachability tree can be constructed recursively. If the Petri net is bounded and therefore it has a finite reachability set, then this procedure will terminate. In the case of an unbounded net, it is possible that the reachability tree could grow indefinitely. However, by using a special symbol ω as pseudo-infinity to represent number of tokens that can be made arbitrarily large, it can be proved [67] that the reachability tree is finite. The analysis of Petri nets using the reachability tree has its limitations. For example, it cannot, in general, be used to solve the reachability or the liveness problems in unbounded nets because the presence of the pseudo-infinity problem leads to a loss of information. In addition, the size of the reachability tree can grow exponentially with respect to the size of the original Petri net; thus the use of the reachability tree for analysis of Petri nets is computationally inefficient. Alternative methods for avoiding the state explosion problem have been proposed; see the discussion on unfolding later in this section.

4.3 Checking Properties Using Integer Programming

As it was discussed earlier, the dynamic behavior of a Petri net can be described by a matrix equation known as *state* or *marking equation*. The use of the marking equation makes possible the application of linear algebraic techniques for the analysis and verification of Petri nets. In particular, we are interested in how integer programming can be used to check properties of interest. For more details the reader is referred to [49].

The marking equation is derived using the initial marking and the incidence matrix of the net and it can be seen as a set of linear constraints L that every reachable marking must satisfy. It is important to notice that the set of reachable markings is a subset of the solutions of the linear constraints L. Assume we want to check a property of interest P and let L_P be a set of linear constraints that specify the markings that do not satisfy P. Then if the system $L \cup L_P$, which can be solved using integer programming, does not have a solution, every reachable marking satisfies the property P. The disadvantage of this method is that the solution of $L \cup L_P$ may or may not correspond to a reachable marking.

If $\mu \in R(N, \mu_0)$, then the following problem has at least one solution with respect to the n-dimensional vector x, which corresponds to the firing sequence σ such that $\mu_0[\sigma\rangle\mu$.

$$\text{Variables} : x, \mu \text{ integer}$$
$$\mu = \mu + 0 + Dx$$
$$x, \mu \geq 0$$

It is often desirable to check a property P that corresponds to linear (or equivalently convex) constraints on the marking of the Petri net. These properties are general enough and usually correspond to generalized mutual exclusion constraints. Such a property can be described by the set of linear inequalities $L\mu \leq b$, where L, b are of appropriate dimensions and consist of integers. If the following integer programming problem does not have any solution with respect to the vectors x and μ, then every reachable marking satisfies the property $L\mu > b$.

$$\text{Variables} : x, \mu \text{ integer}$$
$$\mu = \mu_0 + Dx$$
$$L\mu \leq b$$
$$x, \mu \geq 0$$

Integer programming and mixed integer programming can be used to check other properties of Petri nets such as deadlock-freedom (see [49]). An additional disadvantage of this approach is the $\mathcal{N}P$-completeness of the integer programming problem. There are many applications in the area of intelligent control (for example, manufacturing systems or communication protocols) where it is desirable for the discrete state to satisfy convex constraints. For large-scale systems, to check if such a property holds can be computationally expensive. Another approach is to modify the system to guarantee that such constraints will be satisfied. In Section 4.5, a method for designing a supervisor to enforce linear constraints on the marking is discussed. The method is very simple and computationally efficient. The Petri net is changed by adding appropriate monitor places that are determined by a single matrix multiplication.

4.4   State Space Search Using Unfolding

Net unfolding is a well-known partial order semantics of Petri nets [19, 57] and provide a method of searching the state space without considering all the interleavings of concurrent events. An unfolding technique to avoid the state explosion problem in the verification of systems modeled by ordinary Petri nets has been proposed by McMillan [48]. Specifically, an algorithm to construct a finite prefix of the unfolding that contains full information about the reachable states is introduced and then the algorithm is used for deadlock detection. The unfolding technique has been enhanced and applied to other verification problems, see for example [21, 38]. The advantage of the unfolding technique over an exhaustive state space search is that it takes into consideration the captured conflict in the net and narrows the interleavings of concurrent transitions. This section presents briefly the basic notions and the computational advantages of Petri net unfoldings.

The first result of the unfolding algorithm is an acyclic net called occurrence net. Briefly, an occurrence net is a Petri net without backward conflict (without two transitions outputing in the same place), and without cycles. Formally, an *occurrence net* is a net $N' = (P', T', F')$ such that (i) for every $p \in P' \mid \bullet p' \mid \leq 1$; (ii) F' is acyclic, i.e., the (irreflexive) transitive closure of F' is a partial order; (iii) N' is finitely preceded, i.e., for every $x' \in P' \cup T'$, the set of elements $y' \in P' \cup T'$ such that (y', x') belongs to the transitive closure of F is finite; and (iv) no transition $t' \in T'$ is in self-conflict. In the following, $Min(N')$ denotes the set of minimal elements of $P' \cup T'$ with respect to the transitive closure of F'.

Let $N_1 = (P_1, T_1, F_1)$ and $N_2 = (P_2, T_2, F_2)$ be two nets. A *homomorphism* from N_1 to N_2 is a mapping $h : P_1 \cup T_1 \rightarrow P_2 \cup T_2$ such that: (i) $h(P_1) \subseteq P_2$ and $h(T_1) \subseteq T_2$ and (ii) for every $t \in T_1$, the restriction of h to $\bullet t$ is a bijection between $\bullet t$ (in N_1) and $\bullet h(t)$ (in N_2), and similarly for $t\bullet$ and $h(t)\bullet$.

A *branching process* of a net system $\langle N, \mu_0 \rangle$ is a pair $\beta = (N', h)$ where $N' = (P', T', F')$ is an occurrence net and h is a homomorphism from N to N' such that (i) the restriction of h to $Min(N')$ is a bijection between $Min(N')$ and μ_0 (μ_0 is interpreted as a multiset), and (ii) for every $t_1, t_2 \in T'$, if $\bullet t_1 = \bullet t_2$ and $h(t_1) = h(t_2)$ then $t_1 = t_2$. Two branching processes $\beta_1 = (N_1, h_1)$ and $\beta_2 = (N_2, h_2)$ of a net system are *isomorphic* if there is a bijective homomorphism h from N_1 to N_2 such that $h_2 \circ h = h_1$. Furthermore, (N_1, h_1) contains (N_2, h_2)if $N_2 \subseteq N_1$and the restriction of

h_1 to nodes in N_2 is identical to h_1. An *unfolding* is the maximal branching process up to isomorphism associated with a net system.

Consider the unfolding $\beta = (N', h)$ of the net system $\langle N, \mu_0 \rangle$. The homomorphism h can be seen as a label function that preserves the environment of the transitions. More specifically, the following remarks are concluded from the previous definitions. Since N' s an occurrence net, the unfolding is finitely preceded and it contains neither forward conflict ($|\bullet p'| \leq 1$) nor self-conflict. Since β is a branching process, it has no redundancy (for every $t_1, t_2 \in T'$, if $\bullet t_1 = \bullet t_2$ and $h(t_1) = h(t_2)$ then $t_1 = t_2$). Since h is a homomorphism, the labels of the preset and postset of any transition in the unfolding match the preset and postset of the corresponding transition in the original net (for every $t \in T_1$, the restriction of h to $\bullet t$ is a bijection between $\bullet t$ (in N_1) and $\bullet h(t)$ (in N_2), and similarly for, $t\bullet$ and $h(t)\bullet$). Also, the labels of the places in the unfolding with no predecessors match the initial marking of the original net system (the restriction of h to $Min(N')$ is a bijection between $Min(N')$ and μ_0).

In general, the unfolding of a net system is infinite in size. It is possible, however, to construct finite prefixes of a maximal branching process that enumerate the reachable markings in a computationally efficient manner. An important theoretical notion regarding occurrence nets is that of a *configuration*. A configuration is a set of events representing a possibly partially ordered run of the net. In an unfolding, each transition corresponds to a transition of the original net (via the mapping h). We can associate each configuration of the unfolding with a state (marking) of the original net by simply identifying those places whose tokens are produced but not consumed by the transitions in the configuration. Then, it can be shown that every marking represented in a branching process is reachable, and that every reachable marking is represented in the unfolding of the net system. The *local configuration* associated with any transition consists of that transition and all of its predecessors in the dependency order. This is the set of transitions that necessarily are contained in any configuration containing the given transition.

Consider the problem of building a fragment of the unfolding that is large enough to represent all reachable markings of the original net. The process starts with a set of places corresponding to the initial marking of the original net. The unfolding is grown by finding a set of places that correspond to the inputs (preset) of a transition in the original net, then adding a new instance of that transition to the unfolding, as well as a new set of places corresponding to its outputs (postset). If the new transition has no conflicts in its local configuration (more precisely, if it has a local configuration), it is kept, otherwise it is disregarded. This is because the existence of a conflict means that the new transition can occur in no configuration of the unfolding. The unfolding of a net system is always complete. A *complete* prefix contains as much information as the unfolding. Since a bounded net system has only finitely many reachable markings, its unfolding contains at least one complete finite prefix. The key to termination of the unfolding is to identify a set of transitions of the unfolding to act as *cutoff points*. This set must have the following property: any configuration containing a cutoff point must be equivalent (in terms of final state) to some configuration containing no cutoff points. From this, it follows that any successor of a cutoff point can be safely omitted from the unfolding without sacrificing any reachable markings of the original net. A sufficient condition for a transition to be a cutoff point is the following: The final state of its local configuration is the same as that of some other transition whose local configuration is smaller (see [21] for details).

Unfoldings of Petri nets provide a method for avoiding the state-space explosion in analysis problems. The main advantage is the reduced size of the unfolding in comparison with the reachability tree. A simple and elegant algorithm for the construction of the unfolding of a Petri net is presented in [481. The size of the produced unfolding can be exponential in the size of the Petri net. However, this is only the worst case; there are interesting applications when the size of the unfolding is linear in the size of the Petri net. In general, the size of the unfolding will be smaller than the size of the corresponding reachability tree and will depend on the degree of parallelism of the Petri net. In [48] it is also shown that the problem of existence of a marking that will result in deadlock in an occurrence net is $\mathcal{NP}$-complete. This is in agreement with the worst-case analysis for the size of the unfolding of a Petri net. However, there are cases when the exponential complexity is avoided (for example, the dining philosophers problem). An improvement of McMillan's algorithms has been presented in [21], where it is shown that a minimal complete prefix can be constructed with size polynomial in the size of the Petri net. A technique that results also in a compression of the size of the unfolding is presented in [38] Unfoldings can be used for the analysis of Petri nets to study all problems that are related to the reachability problem. Such problems include liveness, deadlock-avoidance, boundness, and persistence. In view of the time complexity of the resulting algorithms, it can easily be shown that it will be polynomial in the size of the unfolding. Therefore, the size of the unfolding is the important factor in the analysis of Petri nets following this approach.

4.5   Supervisory Control Theory of Petri Nets

The methods discussed above are concerned with the analysis and verification of systems modeled by Petri nets and in general, do not lead to computationally efficient procedures. Another approach, motivated by the supervisory control theory in [70], aims at the modification of the original Petri net model (open loop plant) so that the resulting Petri net (closed loop) will satisfy the desirable properties. If we assume that the specifications are expressed as a set of legal markings for the system, then the aim of the control is to restrict the behavior of the net so that only legal markings can be reached. In the following, we will briefly discuss approaches that rely on the linear algebraic representation of the Petri net model of the plant.

Li and Wonham [43, 44] consider the synthesis of maximally permissive feedback control policies when the legal markings are specified by a system of linear predicates. They showed that under certain assumptions the supervisory state feedback control problem can be reduced to solving a sequence of linear integer programming problems (in the presence of uncontrollable transitions). The attraction of the general linear integer programming approach to Petri nets is that the synthesis of supervisory control policies is reduced to the solution of a standard optimization problem, eliminating the need to compute the reachability graph of the Petri net.

Linear constraints on the marking vector can also be enforced by *monitor* or *controller* places. These places represent control places that are connected to existing transitions of the Petri net model. A methodology for DES control based on Petri net place invariants has been developed in [51, 52, 53, 85]. A *place invariant* of a Petri net is defined as every integer vector x that satisfies $x^T \mu = x^T \mu_0$ where μ_0 is the initial marking and μ any reachable subsequent marking. Place invariants characterize sets of places whose the weighted sum of tokens remains constant at all reachable markings and is determined only by the initial marking. Consider linear constraints of the form $L\mu_p \leq b$ on the marking vector μ_p of the plant net. This inequality can be transformed to the equality $L\mu_p + \mu_c = b$ by introducing an external Petri net controller whose places are represented by the "slack variables" μ_c. The incidence matrix of the controller is then computed by the equation $D_c = -LD_p$ and its initial marking is $\mu_{c0} = b - L\mu_{p0}$. The controller introduces place invariants in the closed loop system that enforce the linear constraint $L\mu_p \leq b$. For more details on the place invariant method for controllable transitions see [85].

The significance of invariant-based supervision techniques to Petri net controller design is that the control net can be computed very efficiently; thus the method shows promise for controlling large, complex systems, or for recomputing the control law online due to some plant failure. An invariant-based supervisor is computed very efficiently by a single matrix multiplication, and its size grows polynomially with the number of specifications. In the case when all the transitions of the plant net are controllable and observable, the invariant-based control method is shown to be maximally permissive [85].

A more challenging case arises with the presence of uncontrollable and unobservable transitions. Li and Wonham [43, 44, 45] show that optimal, or maximally permissive, control actions which account for uncontrollable transitions can be found by analytically solving an integer linear programming problem. If is not possible to solve the integer programming problem symbolically, then it is necessary for the controller to numerically solve integer programs at every iteration of the evolution of the discrete-event system. This can be computationally very expensive for large problems. The approach presented in [51] for supervising a plant with uncontrollable and/or unobservable transitions is to actually modify the constraints themselves so that the new constraints account for the difficult structures in the plant. If it is possible to obtain an analytic solution for the transformed constraints, then the controller logic itself will be very simple. Two techniques are presented in [51] for generating transformations of linear constraints that will facilitate the controller synthesis in the presence of uncontrollable and/or unobservable transitions. The first technique involves the solution of an integer linear problem and the other the triangularization of an integer matrix through constrained row operations. Although the derived supervisors are not always maximally permissive, a more restricted control policy can be easily computed and implemented with monitor places. These suboptimal controllers may be sufficient for many tasks, depending on the application. The suitability of this technique has also been examined for deadlock avoidance and liveness. These methods that apply to nets where uncontrollable and/or unobservable transitions may be present involve finding the invariants and siphons of a Petri net and reduce computationally to finding elements of the kernel of an integer matrix for which established algorithms exist (for more details see [52]).

5   HYBRID SYSTEMS IN INTELLIGENT CONTROL

Hybrid control systems typically arise from the interaction of discrete planning algorithms and continuous processes, and, as such, they provide the basic framework and methodology for the analysis and synthesis of autonomous and intelligent systems. Whenever a computer program interacts with a physical process, hybrid system methodologies are necessary to guarantee the desirable operation of the system. Hybrid automata have been proposed as a model for hybrid systems and they have been studied extensively for the verification of computer programs that involve continuous variables. Because of the importance of hybrid automata in the study of hybrid systems, we review in Section 5.1 basic computational issues concerning the analysis of such systems. Some recent results for controller synthesis are also outlined, with comments on their computational complexity. Although most of the problems are computationally very difficult and even undecidable, for many of them interesting applications efficient algorithms can be developed. In Section 5.2, programmable timed Petri nets are presented as a model for hybrid systems and some analysis and controller synthesis algorithms are described with emphasis on their computational advantages.

5.1   Computational Issues in Hybrid Automata

Hybrid automata provide a general modeling formalism for the formal specification and algorithmic analysis of hybrid systems [1]. They are used to model dynamical systems that consist of both discrete and analog components that arise when computer programs interact with an analog environment in real time. In the following we review some computational issues in the analysis and verification of hybrid systems modeled by hybrid automata.

A hybrid automaton is a finite state machine equipped with a set of real-valued variables. More specifically, a hybrid automaton consists of a finite set $X = \{x_1, \ldots, x_n\}$ of real-valued variables and a labeled directed graph (V, E). A vertex $v \in V$ is called a *control mode* or *location* and is equipped with the following labeling functions: a *flow condition* or activity described by a differential equation in the variables in X and an *invariant condition* $inv(v) \in \mathfrak{R}^n$ described by a logical formula in the variables in X. An edge $e \in E$ is called *control switch* or *transition* and is labeled with a guarded assignment in the variables in X. A transition is enabled when the associated guard is true and its execution modifies the values of the variables according to the assignment. Another labeling function assigns to each transition an event from a finite set Σ.

A *state* $\sigma = (v, x)$ of the hybrid automaton consists of a control location $v \in V$ and a valuation $x \in \mathfrak{R}^n$ of the variables in X. The state can change either by a discrete and instantaneous transition or by a time delay. A discrete transition changes both the control location and the real-valued variables, while a time delay changes only the values of the variables in X according to the flow condition. A *run* of a hybrid automaton H is a finite or infinite sequence

$$\rho = \sigma_0 \to^{t_0}_{f_0} \sigma_1 \to^{t_1}_{f_1} \sigma_2 \to^{t}_{f_2} 2 \cdots$$

where $\sigma_i = (v_i, x_i)$ are the state of H and f_i is the flow condition for the vertex v_i such that (i) $f_i(0) = x_i$, (ii) $f_i(t) = inv(v_i)$ for all $t \in \mathfrak{R} : 0 \le t \le t_i$, and (iii) σ_{i+1} is a transition successor of $\sigma'_i = (v_i, f_i(t_i))$ and σ'_i is a time successor of σ_i.

An important notion for the realizability of the hybrid automaton is the divergence of time. A hybrid automaton is said to be *nonzeno* if it cannot prevent time for diverging. If a hybrid automaton is nonzeno only finitely many transitions can be executed in every bounded time interval.

EXAMPLE [1]
The hybrid automaton of Figure 2 models a thermostat controlling the temperature of a room by turning on and off a heater. The system has two control modes *off* and *on*. When the heater is off the temperature of the room (denoted by the real valued variable x) is governed by the differential equation $\dot{x} = -Kx$ (flow condition). When the heater is on (control mode *on*) the temperature of the system evolves according to the flow condition $\dot{x} = -K(h - x)$, where h is a constant. The location invariants and the transition relation are specified by logical formulas and by guarded commands in the variables in X, respectively. These labeling functions detect when the temperature crosses the thresholds m and M and trigger an appropriate control switching.

Complex Systems can be modeled by using the parallel composition of simple hybrid automata. The basic rule for the parallel composition is that two interacting hybrid automata synchronize the execution of transitions labeled with common events (for more details see [1]).

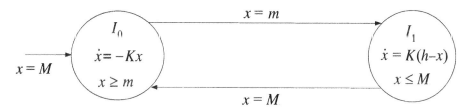

FIGURE 2
Hybrid automaton describing a thermostat [1].

Linear hybrid automata. The modeling formalism of hybrid automata is particularly useful in the case when the flow conditions, the invariants, and the transition relations are described by linear expressions in the variables in X. However, for many of significant results that have been reported in the literature, hybrid systems are modeled by more general hybrid automata [30, 47, 69].

A hybrid automaton is *linear* if its flow conditions, invariants, and transition relations can be defined by linear expressions over the set X of variables. Note the special interpretation of the term linear in this context. More specifically, for the control modes the flow condition is defined by a differential equation of the form $\dot{x} = k$ where k is a constant, one for each variable in X, and the invariant $inv(v)$ is defined by a linear predicate (which corresponds to a convex polyhedron) in X. Also, for each transition the set of guarded assignments consists of linear formulas in X, one for each variable. Note that the run of a linear hybrid automaton can be described by a piecewise linear function whose values at the points of first-order discontinuity are finite sequences of discrete changes. An interesting special case of a linear hybrid automaton is a *timed automaton* [2]. In a timed automaton each continuous variable increases uniformly with time (with slope 1) and can be considered as a *clock $\dot{x} = 1$. A discrete transition either resets the clock or leaves it unchanged.*

Another interesting case of linear hybrid automata is a rectangular automaton [29]. A hybrid automaton is rectangular if the flow conditions are independent of the control modes, and the variables are pairwise independent. In a rectangular automaton, the flow condition has the form $\dot{x} = [a, b]$ for each variable $x \in X$. The invariant condition and the transition relation are described by linear predicates that also correspond to n-dimensional rectangles. Rectangular automata are interesting because they characterize an exact boundary between the decidability and undecidability of verification problems of hybrid automata.

Decision problems. The main decision problems concerning the analysis and verification of hybrid systems are the emptiness problem, the language inclusion problem, and the reachability problem. In the following we discuss some of the decidability results reported in the literature for hybrid automata [29, 32] and timed automata [2].

The emptiness problem is concerned with the existence of a divergent run and is a fundamental task for the verification of liveness requirements in hybrid automata. The emptiness problem for rectangular hybrid automata is PSPACE-complete. Checking the emptiness of timed automata is also PSPACE-complete (see [32] and [2] for complete proofs). On the negative side, the emptiness problem is undecidable for linear hybrid automata. This follows from stronger undecidability results reported in [1] for restricted classes of linear hybrid automata.

The reachability problem is formulated as follows. Let σ and σ' be two states in the infinite state space S of a hybrid automaton H. Then, σ' is reachable from σ if there exists a run of H that starts is σ and ends in σ'. The reachability problem is central to the verification of hybrid systems. In particular, the verification of invariance properties is equivalent to the reachability problem. For example, a set $R \subset S$ is invariant if no state in $S \backslash R$ can be reached from an initial state of H. From the undecidability of the emptiness problem, it follows that the reachability problem is also undecidable for linear hybrid automata. For decidability and undecidability results for particular classes of hybrid automata see [1, 32, 33].

Timed automata. The language inclusion problem for timed automata is very important in the automatic verification of finite state real-time systems. Given two timed automata A_1 and A_2 over an alphabet Σ, the problem of checking if $L(A_1) \subseteq L(A_2)$ is undecidable. However, if A_2 is deterministic, the previous problem is PSPACE-complete [2]. (In a deterministic timed automaton all the edges that stem from the same state have mutually exclusive clock constraints). The language inclusion problem for linear hybrid automata is more general and it is studied by introducing two labeled transition systems. The *time transition system* abstracts continuous flows retaining only information for the source and the destination locations and the duration of the flow. The *time-abstract transition system* abstracts also the duration of the flows. The timed inclusion problem compares the runs of a hybrid automaton with timed specifications, and the time-abstract inclusion problem compares the runs of a hybrid automaton with a time-abstract specification. For details see [29].

Verification of linear hybrid automata. While the reachability problem is undecidable even for very restricted classes of hybrid automata, two semi-decision procedures, forward and backward analysis, have been proposed in [1] for the verification of safety specifications of linear hybrid automata. A *data region* R_v is a finite union of convex polyhedra in $\mathfrak{R}^n$. A *region* $R = (v, R_v)$ consists of a location $v \in V$ and a data region R_v and is a set of states of the linear hybrid automaton. Given a region R, the precondition of R, denoted by $pre(R)$, is the set of all states σ such that R can be reached from σ. The postcondition of R, denoted by $post(R)$ is the set of all the reachable states from R. For linear hybrid automata both $pre(R)$ and $post(R)$ are regions, that is, the corresponding data region is a finite union of convex polyhedra. given a linear hybrid automaton H, an initial region R and a target region T, the reachability problem is concerned with the existence of a run of H that drives a state from R to a state in T. Two approaches for solving the reachability problem have been proposed. The first one computes the target region $post * (R)$ of all states that can be reached from the initial state R and checks if $post^*(R) \cap T =$ (forward reachability analysis). The second approach computes the region $pre^*(T)$ of the states that can be driven to the final region T and checks if $pre^*(T) \cap R = \emptyset$ (backward reachability analysis). Since the reachability problem for linear hybrid automata is undecidable, these procedures may not terminate (semi-decision procedures). They terminate with a positive answer if T is reachable from R and a negative answer if no new states can be added and T is not reachable from R. The crucial step in these approaches is the computation of the precondition or postcondition of a region.

Controller synthesis approaches based on hybrid automata. The undecidability of the reachability problem is a fundamental obstacle in the analysis and controller synthesis for linear hybrid automata. Nevertheless, considerable research effort has been focused on developing systematic procedures for synthesizing controllers for large classes of problems.

Tittus and Egardt [79] studied control design for a class of hybrid systems with continuous dynamics described by pure integrators. Although this class of hybrid systems is rather limited, these models are very important for control of batch processes. Note that even when the continuous dynamics of the physical system are more complicated, it is efficient to use low-level continuous controllers to impose linear ramplike setpoints. By using traditional feedback control in the execution level of the hierarchical architecture, the dynamics of the low-level closed loops is abstracted by integrators in the coordination level. More specifically, the continuous dynamics in [79] are described by differential equations of the form $\dot{x}(t) = k_v$, where k_v is a constant vector associated with the control mode v of the hybrid automaton. The control specifications are represented by data regions $R_v = \{x \in \mathfrak{R}^n : A_v x + b_v \leq 0\}$ and by a set Q_f of *forbidden control modes* or *forbidden control switches*. Controllability of hybrid integrator systems is defined with respect to a pair of regions of the hybrid state space. A hybrid system is controllable with respect to (R_1, R_2) if there exists an acceptable trajectory that drives the state (v, x) from R_1 to R_2. An acceptable trajectory is a trajectory of the hybrid system that satisfies the control specifications. For example, no forbidden control mode $v \in Q_f$ is visited and for every legal control mode v the continuous state x lies in R_v. Based on the definition of controllability, a semi-decidable algorithm is described that uses backward reachability analysis. The algorithm that analyzes these integrator hybrid systems with respect to controllability generates as a by-product a set of correct control laws that switch the system between a predefined number of control modes. The semi-decidability of the algorithm is due to the undecidability of the reachability problem of linear hybrid automata. Note that an algorithm for backward reachability that can be applied in more general cases has been presented in [76].

Discrete-time control for rectangular hybrid automata has been studied in [31], where it is shown that rectangular automata form a maximal class of systems for which the sampling-controller synthesis problem can be solved algorithmically. A realistic assumption for controller synthesis is that, while the plant evolves in continuous time, the controller samples the state of the system in discrete time. The methodology for controller synthesis for hybrid automata can be seen as an extension of supervisor control theory [70]. Let Q be the set of states (v, x), $v \in V$, $x \in \Re^n$ of the hybrid automaton H. A controller C is defined as a mapping $f_c : Q \to \Sigma$ from the set of states to the set of controllable events. The coupling of the hybrid automaton H with the controller C is defined as a infinite-state transition system. given a region R of unsafe states, the basic control problem is to determine whether there exists a controller C such that the region R is unreachable in the closed loop system (H, C). In [31] this problem is called the *safety control decision problem*. In the case when the answer to this problem is affirmative, the problem of constructing a controller is referred as the *safety controller synthesis problem*. It is proven in [31] that the safety control decision problem can be solved in PSPACE and the safety controller synthesis problem can be solved in exponential time. The safety control problem can be solved by iterating a predecessor operator on regions. In particular, the operator used is called the *uncontrollable-predecessor operator U Pr e(R)* : $2^Q \to 2^Q$ and represents the set of states that no controller can keep out of R for even one transition.

A semi-decision procedure for synthesizing controllers for a larger class of linear hybrid automata has been presented in [84]. In this work, the continuous dynamics are governed by differential inclusions of the form $A\dot{x} \geq b$ where A and b are a constant matrix and vector, respectively. The control problem is formulated as a safety requirement represented as a linear region R. A controller C is *legal* if all states that can be reached from the initial states of the hybrid automaton H lie in the safe region R. The supervisor control problem is concerned with the existence and the construction of a legal controller. It is known in [84] that the controller synthesis problem for this class of linear hybrid automata with linear safety requirements is semi-decidable. The control problem in this case is also solved by iterating an appropriate predecessor operator. Controller synthesis procedures are presented under either full or partial observability and sufficient conditions for the nonzenoness of the synthesized controller are given. The efficiency of the method depends heavily on the efficiency of the algorithm implementing the predecessor operator.

A methodology for synthesizing controllers for nonlinear hybrid automata has been presented in [80]. Motivated by problems in aircraft conflict resolution, the authors developed a synthesis procedure based on game theoretic methodologies. The continuous dynamics are described by nonlinear differential equations (that satisfy appropriate conditions for the existence and uniqueness of solutions). The regions of the hybrid state space consist of arbitrary invariant conditions for the control modes and regions of the form $G = \{x \in \Re^n : l(x) < 0\}$ where $l : \Re^n \to \Re^n$ is a differentiable function. The control specifications are expressed as acceptance conditions on the system's state. The controller synthesis problem is formulated as a dynamic game between the controller and the environment. The goal is to construct the largest set of states for which the control can guarantee that the acceptance condition is met despite the action of the disturbance. The problem is solved by iterating two appropriate predecessor operators. Consider a region K of the hybrid state space. The *controllable predecessor* of K contains all states in K

for which the controllable actions can force the state to remain in K for at least one discrete step. The *uncontrollable predecessor* contains all states in K^c} (the complement of K) and all states from which the uncontrollable actions may be able to force the state outside K. The computation of the predecessor operators is carried out using an appropriate Hamilton–Jacobi–Bellman equation. The computational efficiency of the synthesis procedure depends on the ability to solve efficiently this equation.

In summary, recent research efforts towards controller synthesis results have shown that there are classes of hybrid systems for which computationally tractable procedures can be applied. Although many important problems related to hybrid automata are intrinsically difficult, there are efficient algorithms for large classes of systems. Many practical applications can be modeled accurately enough by simple hybrid models. Again, the choice of such models depend on their suitability for studying specific problems.

5.2   Programmable Timed Petri Nets

In this section, a class of timed Petri nets named *programmable timed Petri nets* (PTPN) [42] is used to model hybrid control systems. The main characteristic of the proposed modeling formalism is the introduction of a clock structure that consists of generalized local timers that evolve according to continuous-time vector dynamical equations. They can be seen as an extension of the approach taken in [2, 1]. They provide a simple, but powerful way to annotate the Petri net graph with generalized timing constraints expressed by propositional logic formulas. In contrast to previous efforts to include continuous processes in the Petri net modeling framework (for example [17, 23, 25, 41], the proposed model still consists of discrete places and transitions, and it preserves the simple structure of ordinary Petri nets. The information for the continuous dynamics of a hybrid system is embedded in the logical propositions that label the different elements of the Petri net graph. In view of result on hybrid automata, corresponding problems of PTPNs will be of the same or higher complexity. The introduction of hybrid Petri nets does not aim at solving problems similar to those presented at Section 5.1. The motivation is to develop a framework to use supervisor control design similar to the one presented in Section 4.5. Supervisor control of Petri nets based on place invariants is a special case of the general supervisor control theory for which controllers can be synthesized very efficiently. With respect to continuous dynamics, the basic idea is to follow a natural invariants approach as presented in [76]. In contrast to the hybrid automata-based approaches presented above, these considerations limit the potential problems to cases where the continuous and discrete specifications are uncoupled.

Formally, a *programmable timed Petri net* is denoted by the ordered tuple

$$(N, X, l_P, l_T, l_I, l_O)$$

where

- $N = (P, T, I, O)$ is an ordinary Petri net where P, T, I, and O denote the set of places, transitions, input arcs (from places to transitions) and output arcs (from transitions to places), respectively.
- X is a set of N *local clocks* that can be seen as a collection of continuous-time dynamical systems. The ith clock, X_i is described by $\dot{x}_i = f(x_i)$ where $x_i \in \mathfrak{R}^n$ is the continuous state (local time) and $f : \mathfrak{R}^n \to \mathfrak{R}^n$ is Lipschitz continuous automorphism over $\mathfrak{R}^n$ characterizing the local clock's rate $\dot{x}_i$.

- $l_P : P \to \mathcal{P}$, $l_T : T \to \mathcal{P}$, $l_I : I \to \mathcal{P}$, and $l_O : O \to \mathcal{P}$ are functions that label the places, transitions, input arcs, and outputs arcs (respectively) of the Petri net N. $\mathcal{P}$ is the set of the logical formulas that are constructed by applying propositional connectives between *rate constraints* $(\dot{x}_i - f(x_i))$, *time constraints* $(h(x_i) < 0$ and/or $h(x_i) = 0$, $h : \Re^n \to \Re)$, and *reset equations* $(x_i(\tau) = \bar{x}_0)$.

For more details in PTPN modeling of hybrid systems see [40, 42].

A PTPN can be used to model a hybrid dynamical system in the following manner. The network, N, is used to represent the logical dependencies between mode switches. The timers, X, of the PTPN are the dynamical equations associated with the continuous-time dynamics of the system. The label, l_P, l_T, l_I, and l_O are chosen to represent conditions on the continuous state for mode switches as well as describing the various switching behaviors within the network.

Analysis of hybrid systems modeled by PTPNs. PTPNs have been used in [40] for studying the uniform ultimate boundness of hybrid systems consisting of multiple linear time invariant plants and switching mechanisms that uses a logical rule described by a Petri net. Sufficient conditions for the stability of LTI switched systems can be found in [11, 36, 66]. Computational methods based on solving linear matrix inequalities (LMIs) for checking the sufficient conditions for switched system stability are provided in [37, 68]. The sufficient conditions that are used to compute candidate Lyapunov functionals can be very conservative, unless the structure of the switching law is explicitly accounted for. Petri net models of the switching logics can be used to extract useful information to formulate the appropriate LMIs. A sufficient condition [28] for the Lyapunov stability and ultimate bounded behavior of a switched LTI system is that a set of feasible LMIs associated only with the fundamental cycles of the system's reachability graph exist. The fundamental cycles can be found using computationally efficient techniques based on the unfoldings of the PTPN. This approach addresses the problem of identifying potential system faults that violate the specifications without having to resort to exhaustive simulation. The computational complexity of the approach depends on the complexity of the unfolding algorithms for Petri nets and on algorithms for solving LMIs.

Supervision of hybrid systems. In a hybrid control architecture, the supervisor control algorithms must guarantee the proper and safe operation of the system for a *large number* of different plans. Moreover, the algorithms should exhibit some capability to *react* to the perceived situation in order to handle unexpected events and uncertain plant behavior. Supervisor control algorithms based on invariant properties of the discrete and continuous dynamics have been proposed in [39, 40]. These algorithms are realized using state feedback control (discrete or continuous) and therefore the control action depends on the state of the system.

A methodology for DES control based on Petri net place invariants has been discussed briefly in Section 4.5. A feedback controller based on place invariants is implemented by adding control places and arcs to existing transitions in the Petri net structure. Although the method was developed for ordinary Petri nets, the introduction of time delays associated with each transition will not affect the controlled behavior of the Petri net with respect to the discrete specifications. With respect to continuous dynamics, the basic idea is to follow a natural invariants approach. The natural invariants of the system are used to partition the state space into regions. The switching policy for the hybrid system is then derived by determining the region where the continuous state lies. The basic property of these regions is that their boundaries satisfy certain conditions that preclude the state trajectories from crossing them. The resulting conditions can be embedded very efficiently in the PTPN model of the hybrid system by changing the label functions.

The underlying Petri net structure, which generates the switching policy, offers two important computational advantages. First, it makes possible to efficiently design the supervisor that satisfies specifications that frequently appear in complex systems such as generalized mutual exclusion constraints. Second, it reduces considerably the search for common flow regions, since only desirable switching strategies generated by the controlled Petri net have to be examined. The set of all invariant hypersurfaces can be found by solving analytically a partial differential equation (the characteristic equation for the vector field of the system [76]). The task of determining suitable invariant hypersurfaces is very difficult in general. For special cases (e.g integrator systems), the differential equation can be solved analytically. Otherwise, a computerized procedure for identifying the common flow regions using backtracking from the target region can be used. In this case, the computational complexity of the algorithm is of the order q^n, where q is the number of quantization levels and n is the number of the continuous states. There are also interesting cases where it is sufficient for the control objective to approximate the invariant hypersurfaces using Lyapunov functionals [40]. This approach is more efficient and can be applied to a larger class of systems; furthermore, the design based on Lyapunov functions exhibits desirable robustness properties. However, by assuming that the common flow regions are bounded by manifolds defined by Lyapunov functionals, we impose restrictive conditions on the dynamics of the continuous subsystems. In most of the cases, these conditions are quite restrictive but they provide a systematic way to compute common flow regions.

Programmable timed Petri nets provide a very powerful modeling formalism for hybrid systems. It is shown that certain problems in the analysis and synthesis of hybrid systems can be addressed using PTPNs and efficient algorithms are developed. Current research effort aims at identifying additional problems in hybrid systems where the use of Petri net will offer computational advantages.

6 PARALLEL COMPUTING ARCHITECTURE FOR INTELLIGENT CONTROL

An important requirement for the evaluation and control of intelligent systems is the availability of efficient simulations tools. A hierarchical functional architecture was used throughout this chapter to describe a number of computational issues that arise in intelligent control. Such architecture requires the availability of simulation tools at different levels of abstraction and the means to transfer efficiently useful information between the different levels. These issues have been studied for example in [13, 87]. Integration of heterogeneous mathematical models and algorithms is necessary because of the complexity of the physical processes involved and the generality of the control objectives. The simulation of intelligent control systems may require highly diverse discrete-event system simulators, optimization algorithms, on-line control reconfiguration algorithms, and task planning among others. Furthermore, because of the size of the systems of interest, simulation of intelligent control systems often requires great computational resources. It is therefore natural to consider the parallel execution of such simulations. The objective of simulations in general is to extract useful information about the system to facilitate decision making algorithms to control the system so that it exhibits desirable behavior. The aim of parallelizing techniques is to discover a set of modules that are as independent as possible in order to minimize the communication costs among the components. The purpose of parallel simulations is to reduce the execution time of a simulation by distributing the modules of a system model among a number of simulation agents running in parallel. These agents organize the simulation of the whole model by the interchange of messages among each other.

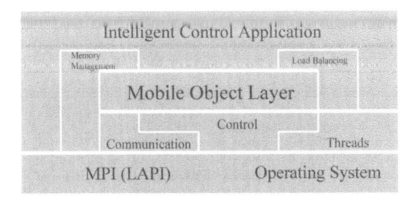

FIGURE 3
Parallel run-time system: architecture [15].

Recent advances in parallel computing have ignited considerable research effort towards exploiting the parallelization of heterogeneous simulations (see for example [34, 88]). We present now a parallel computing architecture appropriate for modeling parts of intelligent control systems. Our purpose is to take a step toward the development of an application-driven parallel computing scheme for intelligent control applications. Motivated by a parallel run-time system for the efficient implementation of adaptive applications on distributed memory machines [15], our goal is to explore recent advances in parallel computing for intelligent control applications. The architecture of the overall run-time system and its layers are depicted in Figure 3. It must be noted that this section described current research for the use of high-performance computing for large, irregular applications. Intelligent control applications have been identified as a challenging area where there is the need for the development of high-performance computing tools. We describe now the basic characteristics of this architecture.

The first layer, named Data Movement and Control Substrate (DMCS) [15], consists of the following three modules:(i) a *threads* module, (ii) a *communications* module, and (iii) a *control* module. The threads module provides machine-dependent code for creating, running, and stopping threads. It also provides an easy interface for writing and porting thread packages. The communication module is implemented on top of a generic active message implementation on an IBM RISC/6000 SP [14, 83]. The fundamental idea in active messages is that every message is sent along with a reference to a handler which is invoked on receipt of the message. DMCS provides the notion of a *global pointer* through which remote data can be accessed. A global pointer consists of a processor *id* and a pointer to the local address space. The integration of the communication module and threads takes place in the control module. The control subpackage provides support for *remote service request* and *load balancing*. A remote service request consists of a remote context (processor), a function to be executed at the remote context, and the arguments of the function. In addition, a type argument is also passed, indicating the type of the remote service request (threaded, nonthreaded) and its priority (lazy, urgent). DMCS implements a simple parametized load balancing primitive. The load on a processor is defined to be simply the number of threads on that processor. DMCS also provides a primitive that enables a processor to start a new thread on the least loaded processor within a certain window size, which can be customized.

The second layer, named Mobile Object Layer (MOL) [27], provides the tools to build distributed data structures consisting of mobile objects linked with mobile pointers. For example, a directed graph might be built using one mobile object for each node. Each node holds a list of mobile pointers to other nodes. The data structure of the mobile object can be moved from processor to processor and all the mobile pointers remain valid. MOL uses a decentralized directory and updates the local directories of each processor using a *lazy* protocol to reduce the overhead of broadcasting updates. The specific implementation is built on top of the DMCS layer to handle messages sent to objects. MOL provides the mechanisms to support mobile objects and mobile pointers, but it does not specify the policies that govern the use of mobile objects. It is the responsibility of the application to decide the migration policy. MOL supports both threaded and nonthreaded models of execution.

The parallel run-time system described above is an application-driven scheme that is general enough and uncoupled from the specific application. Its main advantages are that it hides the bookkeeping of data structures and messages from the application developer and it provides efficient tools for remote service request and load balancing. The parallel run-time system provides to the application developer a very simple but powerful interface for building application programs or libraries.

The program complexity of intelligent control applications increases due to the computation and communication requirements that are dynamic, data-dependent, and irregular. Simulations of intelligent control applications usually consist of several algorithms (for example, continuous or discrete-event simulations, task planning, feedback control, optimization algorithms, and so on) that are implemented using different models (discrete-event, continuous, hybrid). The formal models of the physical processes involved can be represented as mobile objects holding several data structures. Then the algorithms can be viewed as methods that can be invoked upon the receipt of an active message by the object. The parallel architecture discussed above offers the maintenance of complex and distributed data structures and a sophisticated run-time system for low-latency communication and load balancing. At the same time it hides the details from the application developer to allow fast and efficient programming. The run-time system automatically maintains the validity of global pointers as data migrates from one processor to another and implements a correct and efficient message forwarding and communication mechanism between the migrating objects. In intelligent control applications of large-scale systems the workload is known only at run-time. There are many heuristic algorithms for the dynamic load balancing problem and can be incorporated easily using the proposed architecture (migration policy). In summary, the parallel computing architecture outlined above provides the primitives for utilizing powerful symmetric multiprocessors (SMPs) to solve large problems and to speed up computations.

As an architecture of how such computing architecture can be used in intelligent control, consider a hybrid system described by a large programmable timed Petri net. The PTPN can be viewed as a data structure consisting of mobile objects (nodes) linked with mobile pointers. Each mobile object holds substructures representing the rate constraints (differential equations), generalized time constraints, and reset equations and methods that can be applied to these substructures describing ODE solvers, feedback control algorithms, or algorithms for solving optimization problems. Assume that we want to initiate the simulation of the continuous dynamics according to the label $l_P(p)$, that associates with the place p of the PTPN a differential equation. The place of the PTPN is considered as a mobile object that holds appropriate representations of its label functions. A message can be sent to the object using a mobile pointer. When the message reaches the object, a user-specified handler is invoked. The remote invocation call, (which can be caused, for example, by a change of the operation point of the system), can initiate the simulation of the continuous dynamics using appropriate ODE solvers, a different local feedback control algorithm, or the contribution of the local mode to a global optimization problem.

We believe that such a framework can be very useful in the design of intelligent control applications. The designer can focus on the application-specific problems and not on the implementation of the parallel computing protocols. On the other hand, the architecture is sufficiently open to allow the efficient use of existing codes for a variety of problems. The main characteristic is basically the use of the global pointer, which can easily be incorporated to existing application programs. The reader is referred to [15, 27] for issues concerning the portability of the implementation as well as other systems using similar architecture.

6.1 Parallel Discrete-Event Simulation

We have investigated the advantages of this approach for parallel discrete-event simulation (PDES). It should be clear that, in our view of intelligent control, PDES is an essential part in the design of intelligent control applications. Our intention is not to study new techniques for PDES, but rather to show that results that have appeared in the literature can be incorporated in the application development using the proposed parallel architecture. Discrete-event simulations are very useful for the evaluation of an intelligent control system at a level of abstraction where discrete-event system models or event-based control of hybrid systems [78] are used. Discrete-event system representations in intelligent control have been also used in [86]. A discrete-event simulation model assumes that the system being simulated changes state only at discrete points in simulated time. When we choose to model a real-world system using discrete-event simulation, we give up the ability to capture a degree of detail that can only be described as smooth continuous change. In return, we get simplicity that allows us to capture important features of interest that are too complex to capture with continuous simulations.

Discrete-event simulations have been studied in [22, 24, 46, 55] and typically require significant computational effort. A *discrete-event simulation* discretizes the observation of the simulated system at event occurrence instants. When executed sequentially, a discrete-event simulation repeatedly processes the occurrence of events in simulated time, often called *virtual time*, by maintaining a time-ordered *event list*, holding time-stamped events scheduled to occur in the future, and using a (global) *clock* indicating the current time and *state variables* defining the current state of the system. A *simulation engine* drives the simulation by continuously taking the first event out of the event list (i.e., the one with the lowest time-stamp), simulating the effect of the event by changing the state variables and scheduling new events in the event list. This is performed until some predefined end-time is reached, or until there are no further events to occur. The objective of parallel discrete-event simulations is to accelerate the execution of simulations using P processors. The parallelism in discrete-event simulations can be exploited at different levels. At the *function level*, the execution time of the simulation is reduced due to the distribution of the subroutines, constituting a simulation experiment, to the available processors. At the *component level* the simulation model is decomposed into submodels to reflect the inherent model parallelism. Model parallelism exploitation at the next lower level, the *event level*, aims at a distribution of single events among processors for concurrent execution. The event list can be a *centralized* data structure maintained by a master processor. A higher degree of parallelism can be exploited in strategies that allow the concurrent simulation of events with different time stamps. In this scheme, each node maintains its own *decentralized* event list. Schemes following this idea require protocols for local synchronization, which in turn may cause increased communication costs.

The main idea for all simulation strategies at the event level is to partition the discrete-event model into a set of communicating *logical processes* (LPs). The objective is to exploit the parallelism inherent among the model components with the concurrent execution of the logical processes. A parallel discrete-event simulation can be viewed as a collection of communicating and synchronizing simulations of submodels.

Using the proposed parallel architecture, most of the difficulties in parallel discrete-event simulation can be addressed very efficiently. Consider the case when timed Petri net are used for discrete-event simulation. The performance of the simulation depends on how the partition of the overall system into logical processes captures the inherited parallelism of the involved processes. To achieve high performance, automated PDES must measure workload at run-time, and perform dynamic remapping when needed; for example dynamic remapping algorithms have been proposed in [56] to address load imbalancing. It was discussed above that the nodes of the Petri net can be viewed as mobile objects connected using mobile pointers. The initial partition of the Petri net model results in a distribution of mobile objects to different processors. Several dynamic remapping algorithms can be implemented with migration policies of the mobile objects so that the designer will not have to keep track of the location of the objects. The additional communication overhead due to the remote service requests has been measured in certain applications and is only 7–10%.

7 CONCLUSIONS

In considering intelligent control of complex systems, it is necessary to address the computational complexity issue. In this chapter, computational aspects of intelligent control methodologies are discussed at length. In particular, computational issues in the analysis, controller synthesis, and simulation of discrete-event and hybrid systems were studied. Emphasis is put on computational issues in recent approaches to discrete-event and hybrid system design that have been developed by our group using Petri nets.

Acknowledgments

The authors thank Professor Nikos Chrisochoides of the Computer Science and engineering Department at the University of Notre Dame for his valuable assistance concerning the parallel computing architecture. The financial support of the National Science Foundation (ECS95-31485) and the Army Research Office (DAAG55-98-1-0199) is gratefully acknowledged.

REFERENCES

[1] R. Alur, C. Courcoubetis, N. Halbwachs, T.A. Henzinger, P-H. Ho, X. Nicollin, A. Oliveiro, J. Sifakis, and S. Yovine, The algorithmic analysis of hybrid systems, *Theoretical and Computer Science*, Vol. 138, pp. 3–34, 1995.

[2] R. Alur and D. Dill, The theory of timed automata. *Theoretical and Computer Science*, Vol. 126, pp. 183–235, 1994.

[3] P.J. Antsaklis, Defining intelligent control, *IEEE Control Systems*, pp. 4–5, 58–66, June 1994. (Report of the Task Force on Intelligent Control, P.J. Antsaklis, Chair.)

[4] P.J. Antsaklis, Intelligent control, in *Encyclopedia of Electrical and Electronics Engineering*, Wiley, New York, 1997.

[5] P.J. Antsaklis, X.D. Koutsoukos, and J. Zaytoon, On hybrid control of complex systems: A survey, *European Journal of Automation*, Vol. 32, No. 9–10, pp. 1023–1045, Dec. 1998.

[6] P.J. Antsaklis, M. Lemmon, and J.A. Stiver, Learning to be autonomous: Intelligent supervisory control, in M.M. Gupta and N.K. Sinha (eds.) *Intelligent Control Systems: Theory and Applications*, pp. 28–62. IEEE Press, New York, 1996.

[7] P.J. Antsaklis and A. Nerode, Hybrid control systems: An introductory discussion to the special issue, in P.J. Antsaklis and A. Nerode (eds.) *IEEE Trans. Automatic Control*, (Special Issue on Hybrid Control Systems), Vol. 43, pp. 457–460, Apr. 1998.

[8] P.J. Antsaklis and K.M. Passino (eds.), *An Introduction to Intelligent and Autonomous Control.* Kluwer Academic, Boston, 1993.

[9] P.J. Antsaklis and K.M. Passino, Introduction to intelligent control systems with high degrees of autonomy, in P.J. Antsaklis and K.M. Passino (eds.) *An Introduction to Intelligent and Autonomous Control*, pp. 1 26. Kluwer Academic, Boston, 1993.

[10] V.D. Blondel and J.N. Tsitsiklis, Complexity of elementary hybrid systems, in *Proc. European Control Conference 97, Brussels, Belgium*, 1997.

[11] M. Branicky, Multiple Lyapunov functions and other analysis tools for switched and hybrid systems, *IEEE Trans. Automatic Control*, Vol. 43, No. 4, pp. 475–482, 1998.

[12] M. Branicky, Universal computation and other capabilities of hybrid and continuous dynamical systems, *Theoretical and Computer Science*, Vol. 138, pp. 67–100, 1995.

[13] F.E. Cellier, Integrated continuous-system modeling and simulation environments, in D. Linkens (ed.) *CAD for Control Systems*, pp. 1–29. Marcel Dekker, New York, 1993.

[14] C. Chang, G. Gzajkowski, C. Hawblitzell, and T. von Eicken, Low-latency communication on the IBM risc system/6000 SP, in *Proc. Supercomputing '96*, 1996.

[15] N. Chrisochoides, I. Kodukula, and K. Pingali, Data movement and control substrate for parallel scientific computing, in *Lecture Notes in Computer Science*, No. 1199, pp. 256–268. Springer-Verlag, Berlin, 1997.

[16] R. David and H. Alla, Petri nets for modeling of dynamic systems: A survey, *Automatica*. Vol. 30, No. 2, pp. 175–202, 1998.

[17] L. Demongodin and N.T. Koussoulas, Differential Petri nets: Representing continuous systems in a discrete-event world, *IEEE Trans. Automatic Control*, Vol. 34, No. 4, pp. 573–579, 1998.

[18] A.A. Desrochers and P.Y. Al-Jaar, *Applications of Petri Nets in Manufacturing Systems*, IEEE Press, New York, 1995.

[19] J. Engelfriet, Branching processes of Petri nets, *Acta Informatica*, Vol. 28, pp. 575–591, 1991.

[20] J. Esparza and M. Nielsen, Decidability issues for Petri nets—a survey, *J. Information Processing and Cybernetics*, Vol. 30, No. 3, pp. 143–160, 1994.

[21] J. Esparza, S. Römer, and W. Volger, An improvement of McMillan's unfolding algorithm, in T. Margaria and B. Steffen (eds.) *Proc. TACAS '96 (Lecture Notes in Computer Science* No. 1055) pp. 87–106. Springer-Verlag, Berlin, 1996.

[22] A. Ferscha, Parallel and distributed simulation of discrete-event systems, in *Handbook of Parallel and Distributed Computing*, McGraw-Hill, New York, 1995.

[23] J-M. Flaus and H. Alla, Structural analysis of hybrid systems modelled by hybrid flow nets, in *Proc. European Control Conference 97, Brussels, Belgium*, 1997.

[24] R.M. Fuzimoto, Parallel discrete event simulation, *Communications of the ACM*, Vol. 33, No. 10, pp. 30–53, Oct. 1990.

[25] A. Giua and E. Usai, High-level hybrid Petri nets: A definition, in *Proc. 35th Conf. Decision and Control, Kobe, Japan*, 1996.

[26] M.M. Gupta and N.K. Sinha (eds.), *Intelligent Control Systems: Theory and Applications*, IEEE Press, New York, 1996.

[27] C. Hawblitzel and N. Chrisochoides, *Mobile object layer: A data migration framework for active messages communication paradigm*, Technical Report TS-98-7, Department of Computer Science and Engineering, University of Notre Dame, 1998.

[28] K.X. He and M.D. Lemmon, Lyapunov stability of continuous valued systems under the supervision of discrete event transition systems. in T.A. Henzinger and S. Sastry (eds.) *HSCC 98: Hybrid Systems—Computation and Control (Lecture Notes in Computer Science* No. 1386), pp. 175–189. Springer-Verlag, Berlin, 1998.

[29] T.A. Henzinger, The theory of hybrid automata, in *Proc. 11th Annual Symp. Logic in Computer Science*, pp. 278–292. IEEE Computer Society Press, New York, 1996.

[30] T.A. Henzinger, P-H. Ho, and H. Wong-Toi, Algorithmic analysis of nonlinear hybrid systems, *Trans. Automatic Control*, Vol. 43, No. 4, pp. 540–554, 1998.

[31] T.A. Henzinger and P.W. Kopke, Discrete-time control for rectangular hybrid automata, in P. Degano *et al.*, (eds.) *ICALP 97: Automata, Languages, and Programming (Lecture Notes in Computer Science* No. 1256), pp. 582–593. Springer-Verlag, Berlin, 1997.

[32] T.A. Henzinger, P.W. Kopke, A. Puri, and P. Varaiya, What's decidable about hybrid automata? *Journal of Computer and System Sciences*, Vol. 57, pp. 94–124, 1998.

[33] T.A. Henzinger and V. Rusu, Reachability verification for hybrid automata. In T.A. Henzinger and S. Sastry (eds.) *HSCC 98: Hybrid Systems—Computation and Control (Lecture Notes in Computer Science* No. 1386), pp. 190–204. Springer-Verlag, Berlin, 1998.

[34] P.T. Homer and R.D. Schlichting, A software platform for constructing scientific applications from heterogeneous resources, *J. Parallel and Distributed Computing*, Vol. 21, No. 3, pp. 301–315, 1994.

[35] J.E. Hopcroft and J.D. Ullman, *Introduction to Automata Theory, Languages and Computation*. Addison-Wesley, Reading, MA, 1979.

[36] L. Hou, A.N. Michel, and H. Ye, Stability analysis of switched systems, in *Proc. 35th Conf. Decision and Control, Kobe, Japan*, 1996.

[37] M. Johansson and A. Rantzer, Computation of piecewise quadratic Lyapunov functions for hybrid systems. *IEEE Trans. Automatic Control*, Vol. 43, No. 4, pp. 555–559, 1998.

[38] A. Kondratyev, M. Kishinevsky, A. Taubin, and S. Ten, A structural approach for the analysis of Petri nets by reduced unfoldings, in *Applications and Theory of Petri Nets 1996 (Lecture Notes in Computer Science* No. 1091), pp. 346–365. Springer-Verlag, Berlin, 1996.

[39] X.D. Koutsoukos and P.J. Antsaklis, Hybrid control systems using timed Petri nets: Supervisory control design based on invariant properties, in P. Antsaklis, (*Lecture Notes in Computer Science*), W. Kohn, M. Lemmon, A. Nerode, and S. Sastry, (eds.) *Hybrid Systems V*, Vol. 1567 pp. 142–162, Springer-Verlag, Berlin, 1999.

[40] X.D. Koutsoukos, K.X. He, M.D. Lemmon, and P.J. Antsaklis, Timed Petri nets in hybrid systems: Stability and supervisory control, *J. Discrete Event Dynamic Systems: Theory and Applications*, Vol. 8, No. 2, pp. 137–173, 1998.

[41] J. LeBail, H. Alla, and R. David, Hybrid Petri nets, in *Proc. 1st European Control Conference, Grenoble, France*, 1991.

[42] M.D. Lemmon, K.X. He, and C.J. Bett, Modeling hybrid control systems using programmable Petri nets, in *3rd Int. Conf. ADMP '98, Automation of Mixed Processes: Dynamic Hybrid Systems, Reims, France*, pp. 177–184, 1998.

[43] Y. Li and W.M. Wonham, Control of vector discrete-event systems I—the base model, *IEEE Trans. Automatic Control*, Vol. 38, No. 8, pp. 1214–1337, 1993.

[44] Y. Li and W.M. Wonham, Control of vector discrete-event systems II—controller synthesis, *IEEE Trans. Automatic Control*, Vol. 39, No. 3, pp. 512–531, 1994.

[45] Y. Li and W.M. Wonham, Concurrent vector discrete-event systems, *IEEE Trans. Automatic Control*, Vol. 40, No. 4, pp. 628–638, 1995.

[46] Y-B. Lin and P.A. Fischwick, Asynchronous parallel discrete event simulation, *IEEE Trans. Systems, Man, and Cybernetics*, Vol. 26, No. 4, pp. 249–286, 1996.

[47] J. Lygeros, D.N. Godbole, and S. Sastry, Multiagent hybrid system design using game theory and optimal control. in *Proc. 35th IEEE Conf. Decision and Control, Kobe, Japan*, pp. 1190–1195, 1996.

[48] K.L. McMillan, A technique of a state space search based on unfoldings, *Formal Methods in System Design*, Vol. 6, No. 1, pp. 45–65, 1995.

[49] S. Melzer and J. Esparza, Checking system properties via integer programming, in H.R. Nielson, (ed.) *Proc. ESOP '96 (Lecture Notes in Computer Science* No. 1058), pp. 250–265. Springer-Verlag, Berlin, 1996.

[50] G. Memmi and G. Roucairol, Linear algebra in net theory, in *Net Theory and Applications, (Lecture Notes in Computer Science* No. 84), pp. 213–223. Springer-Verlag, Berin, 1980

[51] J.O. Moody, *Petri Net Supervisors for Discrete Event Systems*, PhD Thesis, Department of Electrical Engineering, University of Notre Dame, Notre Dame, IN, 1997.

[52] J.O. Moody and P.J. Antsaklis, *Supervisory Control of Discrete Event Systems using Petri Nets*. Kluwer Academic, Boston, 1998.

[53] J.O. Moody and P.J. Antsaklis, Petri net supervisors for DES with uncontrollable and unobservable transitions, *IEEE Trans. Automatic Control*, accepted for publication.

[54] T. Murata, Petri nets: Properties, analysis and applications, *Proc. IEEE*, Vol. 74, No. 4, pp. 541–580, 1989.

[55] D.M. Nicol and R.M. Fuzimoto, Parallel simulation today, *Annals of Operations Research*, Vol. 53, pp. 249–286, 1994.

[56] D.M. Nicol and S. Roy, Parallel simulation of timed Petri nets, in *Proc. 1991 Winter Simulation Conference, Phoenix, Arizona* pp. 574–583, 1991.

[57] M. Nielsen, G. Plotkin, and G. Winskel, Event structures and domains, *Theoretical Computer Science*, Vol. 13, No. 1, pp. 85–108, 1980.

[58] C.M. Özveren, A.S. Willsky, and P.J. Antsaklis, Stability and stabilizability of discrete event dynamic systems, *J. ACM*, Vol. 38, No. 3, pp. 730–752, 1991.

[59] C.H. Papadimitriou, *Computational Complexity*. Addison-Wesley, Reading, MA, 1994.

[60] C.H. Papadimitriou and J. Tsitsiklis, Intractable problems in control theory, *SIAM J. Control and Optimization*, Vol. 24, No. 24, pp. 639–654, 1986.

[61] K.M. Passino, Toward bridging the perceived gap between conventional and intelligent control, in M.M. Gupta and N.K. Sinha (eds.) *Intelligent Control Systems: Theory and Applications*, pp. 3–27 IEEE Press, New York, 1996.

[62] K.M. Passino and P.J. Antsaklis, Event rates and aggregation in hierarchical discrete event systems, *Journal of Discrete Event Dynamic Systems: Theory and Applications*, Vol. 1, No. 3, pp. 271–287, 1992.

[63] K.M. Passino and P.J. Antsaklis, Modeling and analysis of artificially planning systems, in P.J. Antsaklis and K.M. Passino (eds.) *An Introduction to Intelligent and Autonomous control*, pp. 191–214, Kluwer, Boston, 1993.

[64] K.M. Passino and A.D. Lunardhi, Qualitative analysis of expert control systems, in M.M. Gupta and N.K. Sinha (eds.) *Intelligent Control Systems: Theory and Applications*, pp. 404–442. IEEE Press, New York, 1996.

[65] R.V. Patel, A.J. Laub, and P.M. Van Dooren (eds.) *Numerical Linear Algebra Techniques for Systems and Control*, IEEE Press, New York, 1994 (Selected Reprint Series.)

[66] P. Peleties and R. DeCarlo, Asymptotic stability of m-switched systems using Lyapunov-like functions, in *Proc. American Control Conference*, 1991, pp. 1679–1684.

[67] J.L. Peterson, *Petri Net Theory and the Modeling of Systems*. Prentice-Hall, Englewood Cliffs, NJ, 1981.

[68] S. Pettersson and B. Lennartson, Stability and robustness of hybrid systems, in *Proc. 35th Conference on Decision and Control, Kobe, Japan*, 1996, pp. 1202–1207.

[69] A. Puri and P. Varaiya, Verification of hybrid systems using abstractions, in Panos Antsaklis, Wolf Kohn, Anil Nerode, and Shankar Shastry (eds.) *Hybrid Systems II*, (*Lecture Notes in Computer Science* No. 999), pp. 359–369. Springer-Verlag, Berlin, 1995.

[70] P.J. Ramadge and W.M. Wonham, The control of discrete event systems, *Proc. IEEE*, Vol. 77, No. 1, pp. 81–89, Jan. 1989.

[71] W. Reisig, *Petri Nets*. Springer-Verlag, Berlin, 1985.

[72] K. Rudie and J.C. Willems, The computational complexity of decentralized discrete-event control problems, *IEEE Trans. Automatic Control*, Vol. 40, No. 7, pp. 1313–1319, 1995.

[73] G.N. Saridis, Architecture for intelligent controls, in M.M. Gupta and N.K. Sinha (eds.) *Intelligent Control Systems: Theory and Applications*, pp. 127–148. IEEE Press, New York, 1996.

[74] G.N. Saridis and K.P. Valavanis, Analytical design of intelligent machines, *Automatica*, Vol. 24, No. 2, pp. 123–133, 1988.

[75] E.D. Sontag, Interconnected automata and linear systems: A theoretical framework in discrete-time, in R. Alur, T.A. Henzinger, and E.D. Sontag, (eds.) *Hybrid Systems III, Verification and Control*, (*Lecture Notes in Computer Science* No. 1066), pp. 436–448. Springer-Verlag, Berlin, 1996.

[76] J.A. Stiver, P.J. Antsaklis, and M.D. Lemmon, Interface and controller design for hybrid control systems, in Panos Antsaklis, Wolf Kohn, Anil Nerode, and Shankar Sastry (eds.) *Hybrid Systems II*, (*Lecture Notes in Computer Science* No. 999), pp. 462–492. Springer-Verlag, Berlin, 1995.

[77] J.A. Stiver, P.J. Antsaklis, and M.D. Lemmon, An invariant based approach to the design of hybrid control systems, *Mathematical and Computer Modeling*, pp. 55–76, June 1996.

[78] J.A. Stiver, P.J. Antsaklis, and M.D. Lemmon, A logical DES approach to the design of hybrid control systems, in *IFAC 13th Triennial World Congress, San Francisco*, 1996, Vol. J, pp. 467–472.

[79] M. Tittus and B. Egardt, Control design for integrator hybrid system, *Trans. Automatic Control*, Vol. 43, No. 4, pp. 491–500, 1998.

[80] C. Tomlin, J. Lygeros, and S. Sastry, Synthesizing controllers for nonlinear hybrid systems, in T.A. Henzinger and S. Sastry, (Eds.) *HSCC 98: Hybrid Systems—Computation and Control*, (*Lecture Notes in Computer Science* No. 1386), pp. 360–373. Springer-Verlag, Berlin, 1998.

[81] J.N. Tsitsiklis, On the control of discrete-event dyanmical systems, *Mathematics of Control, Signals and Systems*, Vol. 2, No. 2, pp. 95–107, 1989.

[82] K.P. Valavanis and G.N. Saridis (eds.) *Intelligent Robotic Systems: Theory, Design and Applications*, Kluwer Academic, Boston, 1992.

[83] T. von Eicken, D.E. Culler, S.C. Goldstein, and K.E. Schauser, Active messages: A mechanism for integrated communication and computation, in *Proc. 19th Int. Symp. Computer Architecture*, ACM Press, 1992.

[84] H. Wong-Toi, The synthesis of controllers for linear hybrid automata, in *Proc. IEEE Conf. Decision and Control, San Diego*, 1997, pp. 4607–4612.

[85] K. Yamalidou, J. Moody, M. Lemmon, and P. Antsaklis, Feedback control of Petri nets based on place invariants, *Automatica*, Vol. 32, No. 1, pp. 15–28, 1996.

[86] B.P. Zeigler, DEVS representation of dynamical systems: Event-based intelligent control, *Proc. IEEE*, Vol. 77, No. 1, pp. 72–80, 1989.

[87] B.P. Zeigler, S.D. Chi, and F.E. Cellier, Model-based architecture for high autonomy systems, in S.G. Tzafestas (eds.) *Engineering Systems with Intelligence—Concepts, Tools and Applications*, pp. 3–22, Kluwer Academic, Boston, 1991.

[88] B.P. Zeigler and G. Zhang, Mapping hierarchical discrete event models to multiprocessor systems: Concepts, algorithms, and simulation, *J. Parallel and Distributed Computing*, Vol. 9, pp. 271–281, 1990.

CHAPTER 4

Neural Networks: A Guided Tour

SIMON HAYKIN

Communications Research Laboratory, McMaster University, Hamilton, Ontario, Canada L8S 4K1

1 SOME BASIC DEFINITIONS

A neural network is a massively parallel distributed processor that has a natural propensity for storing experimental knowledge and making it available for use. It resembles the brain in two respects:

- Knowledge is acquired by the network through a learning process.
- Interconnection strengths known as synaptic weights are used to store the knowledge.

Basically, learning is a process by which the free parameters (i.e., synaptic weights and bias levels) of a neural network are adapted through a continuing process of stimulation by the environment in which the network is embedded. The type of learning is determined by the manner in which the parameter changes take place. Specifically, learning machines may be classified as follows:

- Learning with a teacher, also referred to as supervised learning
- Learning without a teacher

This second class of learning machines may also be subdivided into

- Reinforcement learning
- Unsupervised learning or self-organizing learning

In the subsequent sections of this chapter, we will describe the important aspects of these learning machines and highlight the algorithms involved in their designs. For a detailed treatment of the subject, see [12], which book has an up-to-date bibliography that occupies 41 pages of references.

2   SUPERVISED LEARNING

This form of learning assumes the availability of a labeled (i.e., ground-truthed) set of training data made up of N input–output examples:

$$T = \{(\mathbf{x}_i, d_i)\}_{i=1}^{N}$$

where $\mathbf{x}_i$ = input vector of ith example; d_i = desired (target) response of ith example, assumed to be scalar for convenience of presentation; N = sample size. Given the training sample T, the requirement is to compute the free parameters of the neural network so that the actual output y_i of the neural network due to $\mathbf{x}_i$ is close enough to d_i for all i in a statistical sense. For example, we may use the mean-squared error

$$E(n) = \frac{1}{N} \sum_{i=1}^{N} (d_i - y_i)^2$$

as the index of performance to be minimized.

2.1   Multilayer Perceptrons and Back-Propagation Learning

The back-propagation algorithm has emerged as the workhorse for the design of a special class of layered feedforward networks known as multilayer perceptrons (MLP). There is an input layer of source nodes and an output layer of neurons (i.e., computation nodes); these two layers connect the network to the outside world. In addition to these two layers, the multilayer perceptron usually has one or more layers of hidden neurons, which are so called because these neurons are not directly reachable either from the input end or from the output end.

The training of an MLP is usually accomplished by using a back-propagation (BP) algorithm that involves two phases [20, 26]:

- *Forward phase.* During this phase the free parameters of the network are fixed, and the input signal is propagated through the network layer by layer. The forward phase finishes with the computation of an error signal

$$e_i = d_i - y_i$$

  where d_i is the desired response and y_i is the actual output produced by the network in response to the input $\mathbf{x}_i$.
- *Backward phase.* During this second phase, the error signal e_i is propagated through the network in the backward direction, hence the name of the algorithm. It is during this phase that adjustments are applied to the free parameters of the network so as to minimize the error e_i in a statistical sense.

Back-propagation learning may be implemented in one of two basic ways, as summarized here:

- *Sequential mode* (also referred to as the pattern mode, on-line mode, or stochastic mode). In this mode of BP learning, adjustments are made to the free parameters of the network on an example-by-example basis. The sequential mode is best suited for pattern classification.
- *Batch mode.* In this second mode of BP learning, adjustments are made to the free parameters of the network on an epoch-by-epoch basis, where each epoch consists of the entire set of training examples. The batch mode is best suited for nonlinear regression.

The back-propagation learning algorithm is simple to implement, and computationally efficient in that its complexity is linear in the synaptic weights of the network. However, a major limitation of the algorithm is that it can be excruciatingly slow, particularly when we have to deal with a difficult learning task that requires the use of a large network.

We might try to make back-propagation learning perform better by invoking the following list of neuristics:

- Use neurons with antisymmetric activation functions about the origin (e.g., hyperbolic tangent function) in preference to nonsymmetric activation functions (e.g., logistic function).
- Shuffle the training examples after the presentation of each epoch; an epoch involves the presentation of the entire set of training examples to the network.
- Follow an easy-to-learn example with a difficult one.
- Preprogress the input data so as to remove the mean and decorrelate the data.
- Arrange for the neurons in the different layers to learn at essentially the same rate. This may be achieved by assigning a learning-rate parameter to neurons in the last layers that is smaller than those at the front end.
- Incorporate prior information into the network design whenever it is available.

One other heuristic that deserves to be mentioned relates to the size of the training set, N, for a pattern classification task. Given a multilayer perceptron with a total number of synaptic weights including bias levels, denoted by W, a rule of thumb for selecting N is

$$N = O\left(\frac{W}{\epsilon}\right)$$

where O denotes "the order of," and ϵ denotes the fraction of classification errors permitted on test data. For example, with an error of 10% the number of training examples needed should be about 10 times the number of synaptic weights in the network.

Supposing that we have chosen a multilayer perceptron to be trained with the back-propagation algorithm, how do we determine when it is "best" to stop the training session? How do we select the size of individual hidden layers of the MLP? The answers to these important questions may be obtained through the use of a statistical technique known as *cross-validation*, which proceeds as follows:

- The set of training examples is split into two parts:
  (i) Estimation subset used for training of the model
  (ii) Validation subset used for evaluating the model performance
- The network is finally tuned by using the entire set of training examples and then tested on test data not seen before.

2.2 Radial-basis Function (RBF) Networks

Another popular layered feedforward network is the radial-basis function (RBF) network. RBF networks use memory-based learning for their design. Specifically, learning is viewed as a curve-fitting problem in high-dimensional space [6, 19].

(i) Learning is equivalent to finding a surface in a multidimensional space that provides a best fit to the training data.

(ii) Generalization (i.e., response of the network to input data not seen before) is equivalent to the use of this multidimensional surface to interpolate the test data.

RBF networks differ from multilayer perceptrons in some fundamental respects:

- RBF networks are local approximators, whereas multilayer perceptrons are global approximators.
- RBF networks have a single hidden layer, whereas multilayer perceptrons can have any number of hidden layers.
- The output layer of a RBF network is always linear, whereas in a multilayer perceptron it can be linear or nonlinear.
- The activation function of the hidden layer in an RBF network computes the Euclidean distance between the input signal vector and a parameter vector of the network, whereas the activation function of a multilayer perceptron computes the inner product between the input signal vector and the pertinent synaptic weight vector.

The use of a linear output layer in an RBF network may be justified in light of Cover's theorem on the separability of patterns. According to this theorem, provided that the transformation from the input space to the feature (hidden) space is nonlinear and the dimensionality of the feature space is high compared to that of the input (data) space, then there is a high likelihood that a nonseparable pattern classification task in the input space is transformed into a linearly separable one in the feature space.

Design methods for RBF networks include the following:

- Random selection of fixed centres [6]
- Self-organized selection of centres [17]
- Supervised selection of centres [19]
- Regularized interpolation exploiting the connection between an RBF network and the Watson–Nadaraya regression kernel [29]

2.3   Support Vector Machines

Support vector machine (SVM) theory provides the most principled approach to the design of neural networks, eliminating the need for domain knowledge [24]. SVM theory applies to pattern classification, regression, or density estimation using any one of the following network architectures: RBF networks, MLPs with a single hidden layer, and Polynomial machines. Unlike back-propagation learning, different cost functions are used for pattern classification and regression.

Simply stated, support vectors are those data points (for the linearly separable case) that are the most difficult to classify and optimally separated from each other. In a support vector machine, the selection of basis functions is required to satisfy Mercer's theorem: that is, each basis function is in the form of a positive definite inner-product kernel:

$$K(\mathbf{x}_i, \mathbf{x}_j) = \varphi^T(\mathbf{x}_i)\varphi(\mathbf{x}_j)$$

where $\mathbf{x}_i$ and $\mathbf{x}_j$ are input vectors for examples i and j, and φ is the vector of hidden-unit outputs for inputs $\mathbf{x}_i$. The hidden (feature) space is chosen to be of high dimensionality so as to transform a nonlinear separable pattern classification problem into a linearly separable one.

The curse-of-dimensionality problem, which can plague the design of multilayer perceptrons and RBF networks, is avoided in support vector machines through the use of quadratic programming. This technique, based directly on the input data, is used to solve for the linear weights of the output layer.

3 UNSUPERVISED LEARNING

Turning next to unsupervised learning, adjustment of synaptic weights may be carried through the use of neurobiological principles, such as Hebbian learning and competitive learning, or information-theoretic principles. In this section we will describe specific applications of these three approaches.

3.1 Principal Components Analysis

According to Hebb's postulate of learning, the change in synaptic weight Δw_{ji} of a neural network is defined by

$$\Delta w_{ji} = \eta x_i y_j$$

where $\eta =$ learning-rate parameter; $x_i =$ input (presynaptic) signal; $y_j =$ output (postsynaptic) signal.

Principal component analysis (PCA) networks use a modified form of this self-organizing learning rule. To begin with, consider a linear neuron designed to operate as a maximum eigenfilter; such a neuron it referred to as Oja's neuron [18]. It is characterized as follows:

$$\Delta w_{ji} = \eta y_j (x_i - y_j w_{ji})$$

where the term $-\eta y_j^2 w_{ji}$ is added to stabilize the learning process. As the number of iterations approaches infinity, we find the following:

(i) The synaptic weight vector of neuron j approaches the eigenvector associated with the largest eigenvalue λ_{max} of the correlation matrix of the input vector (assumed to be of zero mean).

(ii) The variance of the output of neuron j approaches the largest eigenvalue λ_{max}.

The generalized Hebbian algorithm (GHA), due to Sanger [21], is a straightforward generalization of Oja's neuron for the extraction of any desired number of principal components.

3.2 Self-organizing Maps

In a self-organizing map (SOM), due to Kohonen [30], the neurons are placed at the nodes of a lattice, and they become selectively tuned to various input patterns (vectors) in the course of a competitive learning process. The process is characterized by the formation of a topographic map in which the spatial locations (i.e., coordinates) of the neurons in the lattice correspond to intrinsic features of the input patterns.

In reality, the SOM belongs to the class of vector coding algorithms [16]. That is, a fixed number of codewords are placed into a higher-dimensional input space, thereby facilitating data compression.

An integral feature of the SOM algorithm is the neighbourhood function centred around a neuron that wins the competitive process. The neighbourhood function starts by enclosing the entire lattice initially, and is then allowed to shrink gradually until it encompasses the winning neuron.

The algorithm, exhibits two distinct phases in its operation:

1. *Ordering phase*, during which the topological ordering of the weight vectors takes place.
2. *Convergence phase*, during which the computational map is fine tuned.

The SOM algorithm exhibits the following properties:

- Approximation of the continuous input space by the weight vectors of the discrete lattice.
- Topological ordering exemplified by the fact that the spatial location of a neuron in the lattice corresponds to a particular feature of the input pattern.
- The feature map computed by the algorithm reflects variations in the statistics of the input distribution.
- SOM may be viewed as a nonlinear form of principal components analysis.

3.3   Information-theoretic Models

Mutual information, defined in accordance with Shannon's information theory, provides the basis of a powerful approach for self-organized learning. The theory is embodied in the maximum mutual information (Infomax) principle, due to Linsker [15], which may be stated as follows:

The transformation of a random vector $\mathbf{X}$ observed in the input layer of a neural network to a random vector $\mathbf{Y}$ produced in the output layer should be so chosen that the activities of the neurons in the output layer jointly maximize information about the activities in the input layer. The objective function to be maximized is the mutual information $I(\mathbf{Y}; \mathbf{X})$ between $\mathbf{X}$ and $\mathbf{Y}$.

The Infomax principle finds applications in the following areas:

- Design of self-organized models and feature maps [15].
- Discovery of properties of a noisy sensory input exhibiting coherence across both space and time (first variant of Infomax due to Becker and Hinton [3]).
- Dual image processing designed to maximize the spatial differentiation between the corresponding regions of two separate images (views) of an environment of interest, as in radar polarimetry (second variant of Infomax due to Ukrainec and Haykin [23]).
- Independent components analysis for blind source separation (due to Barlow [2]; see also Comon [7]).

4   NEURODYNAMIC PROGRAMMING

Supervised learning is a cognitive learning problem performed under the tutelage of a teacher. It requires the availability of input–output examples representative of the environment. Reinforcement learning, on the other hand, is a behavioral learning problem [22]. It is performed through the interaction of a learning system with its environment. The need for a teacher is eliminated by virtue of this interactive process.

Basically, neurodynamic programming is the modern approach to reinforcement learning, building on Bellman's classic work on dynamic programming [5]. For a formal definition of neurodynamic programming, we offer the following:

Neurodynamic programming enables a system to learn how to make good decisions by observing its own behavior, and to improve its actions by using a built-in mechanism through reinforcement.

Neurodynamic programming incorporates two primary ingredients: (i) the theoretical foundation provided by dynamic programming; (ii) The learning capabilities provided by neural networks as function approximators. An important feature of neurodynamic programming is that it solves the credit assignment problem by assigning credit or blame to each one of a set of interacting decisions in a principled manner. The credit assignment problem is also referred to as the loading problem, the problem of loading a given set of training data into the free parameters of the network.

Neurodynamic programming is a natural tool for solving planning tasks. For optimal planning it is necessary to have efficient trade-off between immediate and function costs: How can a system learn to improve long-term performance when this improvement may require sacrificing short-term performance? In particular, it can provide an elegant solution to this important problem that arises in highly diverse fields (e.g., backgammon; dynamic allocation of resources in a mobile communications environment).

5 TEMPORAL PROCESSING USING FEEDFORWARD NETWORKS

Time is an essential dimension of learning. We may incorporate time into the design of a neural network implicitly or explicitly. A straightforward method of implicit representation of time is to add a short-term memory structure at the input end of a static neural network (e.g., multilayer perceptron). This configuration is called a focused time-lagged feedforward network (TLFN). Focused TLFNs are limited to stationary dynamical processes.

To deal with nonstationary dynamical processes, we may use distributed TLFNs where the effect of time is distributed at the synaptic level throughout the network. One way in which this may be accomplished is to use finite-duration impulse response (FIR) filters to implement the synaptic connections of an MLP. The training of a distributed TLFN is naturally a more difficult proposition than the training of a focused TLFN. Whereas we may use the ordinary back-propagation algorithm to train a focused TLFN, we have to extend the back-propagation algorithm to cope with the replacement of a synaptic weight in the ordinary MLP by a synaptic weight vector. This extension is referred to as the temporal back propagation algorithm due to Wan [25].

6 DYNAMICALLY DRIVEN RECURRENT NETWORKS

Another practical way of accounting for time in a neural network is to employ feedback at the local or global level. Neural networks so configured are referred to as recurrent networks.

We may identify two classes of recurrent networks:

1. Autonomous recurrent networks exemplified by the Hopfield network [14] and brain-state-in-a-box (BSB) model. These networks are well suited for building associative memories, each with its own domain of applications.
2. Dynamically driven recurrent networks, which are well suited for input–output mapping functions that are temporal in character.

Dynamically driven recurrent network architectures include input-output recurrent model, state-space model, recurrent multilayer perceptron, and second-order network. The first three configurations build on the state-space approach of modern control theory. Second-order networks use second-order neurons where the induced local field (activation potential) of each neuron is defined by

$$v_k = \sum_i \sum_j w_{kij} x_i u_j$$

where w_{kij} denotes a weight; x_i denotes a feedback signal derived from neuron j; u_j denotes a source signal. Second-order networks (due to Giles and collaborators [10] are well suited for deterministic finite-state automata.

To design a dynamically driven recurrent network, we may use any one of the following approaches:

- Back-propagation through time (BPTT), which involves unfolding the temporal operation of the recurrent network into a layered feedforward network [27]. This unfolding facilitates the application of the ordinary back-propagation algorithm.
- Real-time recurrent learning; in which adjustments are made (using a gradient-descent method) to the synaptic weights of a fully connected recurrent network in real time [28].
- Extended Kalman filter (EKF), which builds on the classic Kalman filter theory to compute the synaptic weights of the recurrent network. Two versions of the algorithm are available [9]—decoupled EKF and global EKF. The decoupled EKF algorithm is computationally less demanding than the global EKF algorithm.

A serious problem that can arise in the design of a dynamically driven recurrent network is the vanishing gradients problem. This problem pertains to the training of a recurrent network to produce a desired response at the current time that depends on input data in the distant past [4]. It makes the learning of long-term dependencies in gradient-based training algorithms difficult if not impossible in certain cases. To overcome the problem, we may use following methods:

- Extended Kalman filter (encompassing second-order information) for training.
- Elaborate optimization methods such as pseudo-Newton and simulated annealing [4].
- Use of long time delays in the network architecture [11].
- Hierarchical structuring of the network in multiple levels associated with different time scales [8].
- Use of gating units to circumvent some of the nonlinearities [13].

7   CONCLUDING REMARKS

Neural networks constitute a multidisciplinary subject rooted in the neurosciences, psychology, statistical physics, statistics and mathematics, computer science, and engineering. Neural networks are endowed with the ability to learn from examples with or without a teacher. Moreover, they can approximate any continuous input–output mapping function, and can be designed to be fault-tolerant with respect to component failures. By virtue of these important properties, neural networks find applications in such diverse fields as model building, time series analysis, financial forecasting, signal processing, pattern classification, and control. Through a seamless integration of neural networks with other complementary smart technologies such as symbolic processors and fuzzy systems, we have the basis of a powerful hybrid approach for building intelligent machines that represent the ultimate in information processing by artificial means.

REFERENCES

[1] J.A. Anderson, *Introduction to Neural Networks*. MIT Press, Cambridge, MA, 1995.

[2] H.B. Barlow, Unsupervised learning, *Neural Computation*, Vol. 1, pp. 295–311, 1989.

[3] S. Becker and G.E. Hinton, A self-organizing neural network that discovers surfaces in random-dot stereograms, *Nature (London)*, Vol. 355, pp. 161–163, 1982.

[4] Y. Bengio, P. Simard, and P. Frasconi, Learning long-term dependencies with gradient descent is difficult, *IEEE Trans. Neural Networks*, Vol. 5, pp. 157–166, 1994.

[5] D.P. Bertsekas and J.N. Tsitsiklis, *Neuro-Dynamic Programming*. Athenas Scientific, Belmont, MA, 1996.

[6] D.S. Broomhead and D. Lowe, Multivariable functional interpolation and adaptive networks, *Complex Systems*, Vol. 2, pp. 321–355, 1988.

[7] P. Comon, Independent component analysis: A new concept?, *Signal Processing*, Vol. 36, pp. 287–314, 1994.

[8] S. El Hihi and Y. Bengio, Hierarchical recurrent neural networks for long-term dependencies, in *Advances in Neural Information Processing Systems*, Vol. 8, pp. 493–499. MIT Press, Cambridge, MA, 1996.

[9] L.A. Feldkamp and G.V. Puskorius, A signal processing framework based on dynamic neural networks with application to problems in adaptation, filtering and classification, Special issue of *Proc. IEEE Intelligent Signal Processing*, Vol. 86, Nov. 1996.

[10] C.L. Giles, C.B. Miller, D. Chen, H.H. Chen, G.Z. Sun, and Y.C. Lee, Learning and extracting finite state automata with second-order recurrent neural networks, *Neural Computation*, Vol. 4, pp. 393–405, 1992.

[11] C.L. Giles, T. Lin, and B.G. Horne, Remembering the past: The role of embedded memory in recurrent neural network architectures, *Neural Networks for Signal Processing, VII, Proceedings of the 1997 IEEE Workshop*, p. 34. IEEE Press, New York.

[12] S. Haykin, *Neural Networks: A Comprehensive Foundation*, 2d ed. Prentice-Hall, Englewood Cliffs, NJ, 1999.

[13] S. Hochreiter and J. Schmidhuber, LSTM can solve hard long time lag problems, in *Advances in Neural Information Processing Systems*, Vol. 9, pp. 473–479. MIT Press, Cambridge, MA, 1997.

[14] J.J. Hopfield, Neural networks and physical systems with emergent collective computational abilities, *Proc. National Academy of Sciences, USA*, Vol. 79, pp. 2554–2558, 1982.

[15] R. Linsker, Towards an organizing principle for a layered perceptual network, in D.Z. Anderson (ed.), *Neural Information Processing Systems*, pp. 485–494. American Institute of Physics, New York, 1988.

[16] S.P. Luttrell, Self-organization: A derivation from first principle of a class of learning algorithms, *IEEE Conf. Neural Networks, Washington, DC.*, 1989, pp. 495–498.

[17] Moody and Darken, Fast learning in networks of locally-tuned processing units, *Neural Computation*, Vol. 1, pp. 281–294, 1989.

[18] E. Oja, A simplified neuron model as a principal component analyzer, *J. Mathematical Biology*, Vol. 15, pp. 267–273, 1982.

[19] Y. Poggio and F. Girosi, Networks for approximation and learning, *Proc. IEEE*, Vol. 78, pp. 1481–1497, 1990.

[20] D.E. Rumelhart, G.E. Hinton, and R.J. Williams, Learning internal representations by error propagation, in D.E. Rumelhart and J.L. McCleland (eds.) *Parallel Distributed Processing: Explanations in the Microstructures of Cognition*, Vol. 1, Chapter 8. MIT Press, Cambridge, MA, 1986.

[21] T.D. Sanger, An optimality principle for unsupervised learning, in *Advances in Neural Information Processing Systems*, Vol. 1, pp. 11–19. Morgan Kaufmann, San Mateo, CA, 1989.

[22] R.S. Sutton and A.G. Barto, *Reinforcement Learning: An Introduction*, MIT Press, Cambridge, MA, 1998.

[23] A.M. Ukrainec and S. Haykin, A modular neural network for enhancement of cross-polar radar targets, *Neural Networks*, Vol. 9, pp. 143–168, 1996.

[24] V.N. Vapnik, *Statistical Learning Theory*, Wiley, New York, 1998.

[25] E.A. Wan, Time series prediction by using a connectionist network with internal delay lines, in A.S. Weigend and N.A. Gershenfield (eds.), *Time Series Prediction: Forecasting the Future and Understanding the Past*, pp. 195–217. Addison-Wesley, Reading, MA, 1994.

[26] P.J. Werbos, *Beyond regression: New tools for prediction and analysis in the behavioral sciences*, Ph.D. Thesis, Harvard University, Cambridge, MA.

[27] P.J. Werbos, Backpropagation through time: What it does and how to do it, *Proc. IEEE*, Vol. 78, pp. 1550–1560, 1990.

[28] R.J. Williams and D. Zipser, A learning algorithm for continually running fully recurrent neural networks, *Neural Computation*, Vol. 1, pp. 270–280, 1989.

[29] P.V. Yee, *Regularized radial basis function networks: Theory and applications to probability estimation, classification, and time series prediction*, Ph.D. Thesis, McMaster University, Hamilton, Ontario.

[30] T. Kohonen, *Self Organizing Maps*, Second edition, Springer-Verlag, 1997.

[31] R. Linsker, How to generate ordered maps by maximizing the mutual information between input and output signals, *Neural Computation*, Vol. 1, pp. 402–411, 1989.

CHAPTER 5

Variable Structure Distributed Information Systems via Genetic Algorithms

ABBAS K. ZAIDI

Department of Electrical Engineering and Computer Science, Mohammad Ali Jinnah University, Karachi 75400, Pakistan

ALEXANDER H. LEVIS

Department of Electrical and Computer Engineering, George Mason University, Fairfax, VA 22030, USA

1 BACKGROUND

Advances in information technology have resulted in organizations supported by distributed information systems of every-increasing complexity and size. The easy availability of high computational power and large communication bandwidth has tightly coupled previously isolated systems into a single integrated environment through coordinated information exchange systems on one hand, and by spreading out the functionality in a distributed manner on the other. The distributed task-performing nodes of a system, whether geographically or organizationally separated, coordinate their activities by exchanging information over communication systems. The activities assigned to each node contribute a portion of the overall functionality of the system. [20] Typical examples of such systems, as presented by Demaël and Levis [8], are to be found in Air Traffic Control, where the Airport Surface Traffic Control activity has to be coordinated with the terminal Air Traffic Control, which in turn may interact with other centers through the Traffic Flow Management system. The age of electronic governance and office automation has brought with it an explosion of such systems. The information flows in such organizations need to be coordinated to ensure timeliness, accuracy, and adaptability in response to external changes. This has resulted in a need for formal frameworks for modeling such organizations and methodologies for generating their architectures that meet certain design and coordination requirements.

The methodology presented in this paper is an addition to a long list of work on modeling, designing, and evaluating *distributed intelligence systems* (DIS). A DIS is characterized by the distributed nature of the reasoning done by the system: each function of the system is spread over a number of nodes so that each node's activity contributes a little to each of several different functions [20]. The systems characterized as DIS can carry out a number of functions in sequence and/or in parallel, making it difficult to decompose them for their allocation to available resources without violating structural, coordination, and cognitive constraints [17].

In this chapter, an organization is considered as a system performing a task; the system is modeled as an interconnection of organization nodes (decision making units or DMUs). Each organization member is represented by a multistage model [16]. The formal specification of the allowable interactions between decision makers was made by Remy and Levis [23], which led to the lattice algorithm for generating all feasible *fixed-structure* architectures that meet a number of structural and user-defined constraints. Andreadakis and Levis [1] introduced an alternative model based on the functions carried out by a resource, whether that represented a human or a machine. That model formed the basis for a different algorithm for organization design—the data flow structure (DFS) algorithm [1]. In a parallel effort, Monguillet and Levis [21] formalized the notion of *variable structure* decision making organizations for organizations that adapt their structure of interactions to the input they process. Demaël and Levis [6, 8] extended this work and developed a methodology for modeling and generating variable-structure DISs. Lu and Levis [18] presented an algorithm for checking feasibility of the coordination requirements of a variable-structure organization. Levis [16] presented a general five-stage model that subsumed all the previous ones without invalidating any of the cognitive modeling or the design algorithms. All these efforts results in methodologies for designing *flat* DIS architectures in which the system is viewed only from a single level of detail [26]. Although these methodologies used mathematical properties of the feasible structures to reduce the search of the solution space, when it comes to complex, and large-scale DIS, the methodologies are confronted by the combinatorial nature of the problem. The design methodology of Zaidi and Levis [26] presented an approach to solving this problem by defining a DIS as families of structures with each family concerned with the behavior of the system as viewed from a different level of abstraction. The description of a DIS in a hierarchical manner [19] provided an alternate way for formulating and solving the design problem, especially for large organizations. Although this approach solves the problem by reducing the search of the feasible solutions, in doing so it forces a designer to make certain structural decisions earlier in the design process, which in turn limits the degree of freedom left for the design algorithm. To avoid this limitation without encountering the combinatorial nature of the design problem, Zaidi and Levis presented an alternative approach for the generation of large-scale organizational structures using genetic algorithms (GA) [27]. The GA-based approach solved the design problem for *fixed-structure* organizations, where the structure of an organization and the functions each organization member performs do not vary with the changes in the external and internal parameters. In this chapter, the GA-based approach is extended to the design problem of variable-structure organizations or distributed information systems.

2   INTRODUCTION

An organization has a *variable* structure, if the interactions between the components that belong to the organization and the process each component performs can vary in response to external or internal changes. A fixed-structure organization can, therefore, be viewed as a particular mode-of-operation of an otherwise variable-structure organization, capable of handling some predefined situation(s) determined by the internal and external parameters. Each feasible *input situation* to the organization is associated with a unique constituent fixed structure in the variable-structure organization; the mode of operation (interactions, functions, and structure) of the organization is determined uniquely by the input it processes. The interactional structure of a variable-structure organization, therefore, can be viewed as a *folded* structure of several underlying fixed-structure organizations, as described by Lu and Levis [18]. This definition of variable-structure organization translates into a design requirement: All the components of a variable-structure organization should be capable of distinguishing among different *situations* for which they are expected to behave differently (i.e., execute different functions, etc.) as part of their coordination mechanism. Demaël [7] first identified this requirement in his work on a formal framework for the generation of variable-structure organizations. Later, Lu and Levis [18] presented an algorithm to check this requirement, termed *coordination constraint*, in a variable-structure organization. A variable structure that satisfies the coordination constraint is the feasible solution to the design problem. These methods for generating feasible organization structures employ expensive computations and perform *blind* search to identify candidate solutions in the solution space. The extended approach, presented in this chapter, combines the earlier work on generating fixed-structure organizations by genetic algorithms with the work on generating variable-structure organizations. The genetic approach views a variable organization as an *organism* with several layers of *chromosomes*, each representing a constituent fixed structure. populations of these organisms are produced using genetic operators and each individual in these generations is checked for feasibility using a fitness function, which evaluates each individual against user-defined criteria and structural and coordination constraints. Information obtained during this evaluation is used in genetic operators to direct a parallel heuristic search of the solution space for more fit individuals in the following generations.

Genetic algorithms have been demonstrated to be a promising search and optimization technique [5, 10]. The approach has been successfully applied to a wide range of application areas including system identification [9, 11, 13, 14], scheduling [25], routing [4], controls[28], distributed networks [22], and distributed system architectures [27].

A GA is a search procedure modeled on the mechanics of natural selection rather than a simulated reasoning process [3]. The approach is inspired by Darwin's theory of evolution, which is based on the survival of the fittest. According to this theory, species judged stronger have a better chance of surviving and reproducing their offspring. A solution to a problem is considered an individual in a population of solutions. Domain knowledge regarding the problem is embedded in the abstract representation of a candidate solution termed an *organism*. populations are sets of these organisms. Successive populations are called *generations*. Generations are produced by first identifying the mating partners, and then applying the *genetic operators* on them to produce their offspring. Each individual so produced is checked for feasibility using a *fitness* function. Information obtained during this evaluation may be used in genetic operators to produce more fit individuals in the next generation. The initial search space (population) of a GA usually consists of solutions (individuals) generated randomly. With the initial population as the starting point, a GA mounts a parallel heuristic search of the entire solution space for better solution(s). Figure 1 presents a top-level description of the genetic algorithm (the description in the figure describes most algorithms). A good tutorial on GA is provided in [15] and in [3]. The rest of this chapter describes the representation used to encode a candidate organizational structure, the domain knowledge that is embedded in the representation, genetic operators, namely *crossover* and *mutation*, and the evaluation mechanism for identifying better solutions.

The chapter is organized as follows. Section 3 presents a mathematical model for the representation of *input situations*, fixed-structure, and variable-structure organizations. It also,

1 Inititate a population of chromosomes.

2. Evaluate each chromosome in the population.

3. Create new chromosomes by mating current chromosomes; apply mutation and recombination as the parent chromosomes mate.

4. Delete members of the population to make room for the neq chromosomes.

5. Evaluate the new chromoasomes and insert them into the population.

6. If time is up, stop and return the best chromosome; if not, go to (3).

FIGURE 1
Top-level description of a genetic algorithm [15].

describes briefly the algorithm for checking the coordination constraint. Section 4 describes the proposed GA-based approach for the solution of the design problem. An application of the methodology to a nontrivial design problem is presented in Section 5. Section 6 concludes the discussion by outlining certain weaknesses in the current approach and proposing further extensions to the methodology.

3 MATHEMATICAL MODEL

An organization, or a distributed information system, may be viewed as an information processing system that must perform several functions to accomplish its mission. These functions are divided into individual tasks (task decomposition) and these tasks are allocated to the individual intelligent nodes (task allocation) [8]. The structure of an organization may be seen as an interconnection of several processing units capable of performing appropriate tasks. A collection of several processing units can be grouped into a single node, called a decision making unit (DMU). The inputs to the organization are data from several sources of information, called *sensors*. This sensory information determines which function is to be performed by the organization, which translates into the specific tasks that must be performed by the physical entities responsible for the DMUs.

The mathematical formulation of the design problem is based on a Petri net description of the organization architectures. This paper does not describe the Petri net formalism. Readers with no background information in Petri net theory, therefore, are advised to consult [12] or any introductory book on Petri nets to understand the Petri net models of organizations.

3.1 Sensor Model

The sensor model of an organization may be seen as a collection of several distinct sources of information S_i where each S_i, $i = [1, m]$, outputs one letter from its associated alphabet $I_i = \{v_{i1}, v_{i2}, \ldots, v_{ik}\}$. These alphabets describe the basic items of information. The elements of an alphabet can include the null element, that is, the case where no item of information is transmitted [18]. A supersource S can, therefore, be created with the associated alphabet $I = I_1 \times I_2 \times \cdots \times I_m$, which generates events [29] $v \in I$. In the Petri net formalism, an individual sensor is modeled by a place. A transition models the communication of each sensor's observations to the appropriate DMU. An event generator S is modeled by a source place. In Figure 2, source place S models the event generator. Transition T1 distributes the information sources I_i, $i = [1, m]$, from the super source to the appropriate places representing

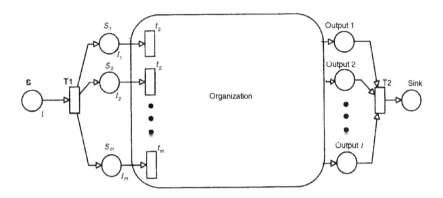

FIGURE 2
Information sources and sensors of an organization.

individual sensors, S_i, $i = [1, m]$. *The input alphabets associated with these sensors are assumed to be discrete and finite.* Places Output 1, Output 2, ..., Output I model the outputs of the organization. They converge through transition T2 into a Sink.

Definition 1: *Input event.* An input event is an m-dimensional vector $\mathbf{v} = (v_1, v_2, \ldots, v_m)$ in the input space, where $v_1 \in I_1$, $v_2 \in I_2, \ldots, v_m \in I_m$, i.e., $\mathbf{v} \in \mathbf{I} = I_1 \times I_2 \times \cdots I_m$.

Definition 2: *Feasible input domain* [18]. An input event $\mathbf{v}$ depicting an input vector processed by the organization is termed a feasible input event. The subspace $\mathbf{I}_f \subseteq \mathbf{I}$ which contains all feasible input situations is called feasible input domain.

Definition 3: *Input situation.* An input situation Ex_i is a collection of all those feasible input events for which the interactional structure of the organization and functions/tasks each processing unit performs remain unchanged. The following must hold for all the input situations associated with an organization:

$$\forall i, \; Ex_i \subseteq \mathbf{I}_f$$
$$\forall i, \forall j, \; Ex_i \cap ex_j = \Phi, \qquad i \neq j$$
$$\bigcup_i Ex_i - \mathbf{I}_f$$

A DMU in an organization may get the required input data to initiate its processing through a combination of one or more input sensors. A potential communication link from sensor S_i to DMUj can be depicted by a binary variable e_{ij}, taking values in $\{0, 1\}$, where 1 indicates the presence of the corresponding link and 0 its absence. The sensor model of an organization with m sensors and n DMUs is, therefore, represented as an $m \times n$ array $\mathbf{E}$:

$$\mathbf{E} = [e_{ij}] \qquad i = 1, 2, \ldots, m, \qquad j = 1, 2, \ldots, n$$

Figure 3 presents the sensor model of a hypothetical organization. The 3×2 matrix $\mathbf{E}$ for the organization in Figure 3 is given as:

$$\mathbf{E} = \begin{array}{c} \\ S_1 \\ S_2 \\ S_3 \end{array} \begin{array}{cc} \text{DMU1} & \text{DMU2} \\ \left[\begin{array}{cc} 1 & 0 \\ 1 & 1 \\ 0 & 1 \end{array} \right] \end{array}$$

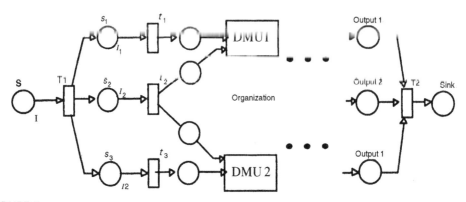

FIGURE 3
Sensor model of an organization.

3.2 Fixed-Structure Organization

The Petri net representation of the five stage decision making unit (DMU) introduced by Levis [16] is shown in Figure 4. The labels SA, IF, TP, CI and RS are generic names for the *situation assessment, information fusion, task processing, command interpretation*, and *response selection* processes, respectively. A DMU receives input or data x from the external environment (sensors). The incoming data are processed in the situation assessment (SA) stage to get the assessed situation z. This variable may be sent to other DMU. If the DMU receives assessed data from other DMU, these data z' are fused together with its own assessment z in the information fusion (IF) stage to get the revised assessed situation z''. The assessed situation is processed further in the task processing (TP) stage to determine the strategy to be used to select a response. The variable v contains both the assessed situation and the strategy to be used in the response selection stage. A particular DMU may receive a command v' from a superordinate DMU. This is depicted by the use of the command interpretation (CI) stage. The output of that stage is the variable w, which contains both the revised situation assessment data and the response selection strategy. Finally, the output or the response of the DMU, y, is generated by the response selection (RS) stage.

As mentioned and discussed in [16], only certain types of interactions make sense within the model. They are depicted in Figure 5. For the sake of clarity, only the links from the ith DMU to the jth DMU are presented. The symmetrical links from j to i are valid interactions as well. The binary variable e_i represents the *input* to a decision making node. The presence of such a link characterizes the fact that a particular DMU may receive data from the external environment, without an actual specification of the input sensor supplying the data. The binary variable s_i

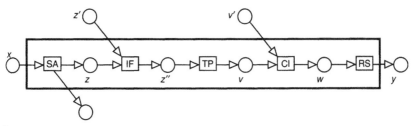

FIGURE 4
Five stage model of a DMU.

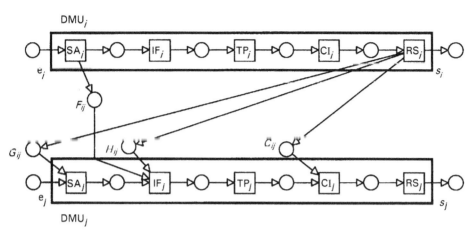

FIGURE 5
Allowable interactions.

represents the *output* of a decision making node to processes external to the organizational structure considered. The binary variable F_{ij} depicts the transmission of assessed situation from node i to node i; G_{ij} models the transmission of control from the output of a decision making node to the input of another; H_{ij} models the result or processed information sharing type of interaction between two decision making nodes, and C_{ij} represents the flow of instructions or commands from one decision making node to another.

The variables s_i, F_{ij}, G_{ij}, H_{ij}, C_{ij} in Figure 5 are binary variables taking values in $\{0, 1\}$, where 1 indicates the presence of the corresponding link in the organizational structure. Note that the value of the variable does not indicate the number of such links (or the capacity/bandwidth of the link) that actually exist. The variables are aggregated into a vectors **s**, and four matrices **F**, **G**, **H**, and **C**. The interaction structure of an organization consisting of n DMUs and m sensors is, therefore, represented by the tuple:

$$\Sigma = \{E, s, F, G, H, C\}$$

where **E** is same as defined in Section 3.1 and **s** is an $n \times 1$ array representing the interactions of the n DMUs:

$$s = [s_a], \qquad a = 1, 2, \ldots, n$$

F, **G**, **H** and **C** are four $n \times n$ arrays representing the interactions among the DMUs of the organizational structure:

$$F = [F_{ab}] \qquad G = [G_{ab}] \qquad H = [H_{ab}] \qquad C = [C_{ab}], \qquad a, b = 1, 2, \ldots, n$$

The diagonal elements of the matrices **F**, **G**, **H**, and **C** are set identically equal to zero; DMUs are not allowed to interact with themselves:

$$F_{uu} = G_{ua} - H_{aa} = C_{aa} = 0, \qquad a = 1, 2, \ldots, n$$

These relations must hold true for all solutions.

As noted earlier, each fixed organization corresponds to some input situation depicted by the feasible input event(s). When dealing with fixed structures only, the associated input situation need not be specified; however, a full description of the input situations is required, together with the corresponding fixed structures, while *folding* these structures into a variable one.

EXAMPLE 1

Let an organization, with a single input sensor and 2 DMUs be described by the following matrix representation:

$$E = [1 \quad 1] \qquad s = [1 \quad 1]$$

$$\sum_{xi} : \quad F = \begin{bmatrix} \# & 1 \\ 0 & \# \end{bmatrix} \qquad G = \begin{bmatrix} \# & 0 \\ 0 & \# \end{bmatrix}$$

$$H = \begin{bmatrix} \# & 0 \\ 0 & \# \end{bmatrix} \qquad C = \begin{bmatrix} \# & 0 \\ 0 & \# \end{bmatrix}$$

The Petri net representation of the organization is shown in Figure 6.

3.3 Variable-Structure Organization

A variable organization is considered as a set of several fixed-structure organizations where each constituent fixed structure is associated with a single input situation: the components of the variable-structure organization and its structure adapt their functionality and interactions to one of these fixed structures based on the input currently being processed. In a colored Petri net (CPN) representation, these several fixed structures, represented as Petri nets, can be *folded* into a single net. Given this CPN, and an input *token* with *color* v, $v \in I_t$, the paths that the token follows through the CPN and the task each component performs form a fixed structure. A detailed discussion on CPN representation of variable-structure organizations is presented in [8, 18]. In this chapter, we do not adhere to this CPN representation of variable organizations but rather use a slightly simpler and static representation that emphasizes the representation of the interactional and functional structures. The representation is illustrated in Example 2.

EXAMPLE 2

Consider a 2-sensor and 2-DMU variable-structure organization. For the sake of simplicity, all the processing nodes (i.e., SA, IF, TP, CI, and RS) are assumed to perform identical tasks under different input situations; the only change that occurs from one input to another is of the interactions among these processing nodes. Suppose that the feasible input space $I_t = I$ is defined as $I_t = A \times B$, $A = \{a1, a2\}$ and $B = \{b1, b2\}$ are the input alphabets associated with input sensors S1 and S2 respectively. Figure 7 shows the fixed structure $\sum x_1$ for the input situation $Ex_1 = \{(a1, b1), (a1, b2)\}$. Figure 8 presents the fixed structure $\sum x_2$ for the input situation $Ex_2 = \{(a2, b1)\}$. The fixed structure $\sum x_3$ for the remaining input situation $Ex_3 = \{(a2, b2)\}$ is given in Figure 9.

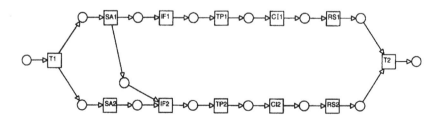

FIGURE 6
PN representation of a 1-sensor 2-DMU organization.

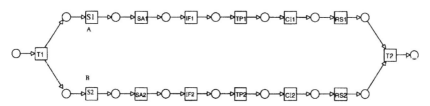

FIGURE 7
Fixed structure Σx_1 for input events $(a1, b1)$ and $(a1, b2)$.

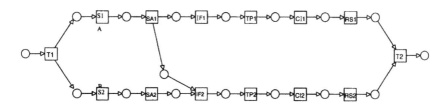

FIGURE 8
Fixed structure Σx_2 for input event $(a2, b1)$.

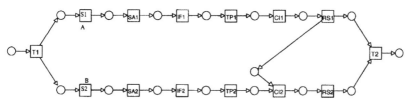

FIGURE 9
Fixed structure Σx_3 for input event $(a2, b2)$.

The variable-structure organization Π formed by folding the three fixed-structure organizations is shown in Figure 10. The variability only exists in the F-type and C-type interactions (links) of the organization. The two links are annotated with the input situation for which the corresponding links *do not* exist in the organization. For example, when an input $(a1, b1)$ is put in input place, it follows the path through the organization consisting of links *not* annotated with Ex_1. The links with Ex_1, while existing physically, are not utilized when an input $\mathbf{v} \in Ex_1$ [i.e. $(a1, b1)$ or $(a1, b2)$] is processed by the organization.

As illustrated in Example 2, a Petri net representation of a variable-structure organization is constructed by superimposing Petri nets representations of all its constituent fixed structures; the matrix representation of a variable structure Π can, therefore, be obtained by ORing corresponding elements from the matrix representations of constituent fixed structures. However, such an analytical representation is incomplete in the sense that it shows all the possible interactions among the components but hides the variations in these interactions due to different input situations. Once a matrix representation for a variable structure is obtained by the approach mentioned, an equivalent representation is constructed to incorporate the variability of the

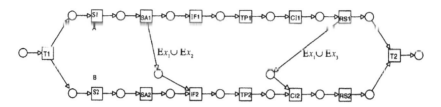

FIGURE 10
Variable-structure organization Π of Example 2.

structure. Each link (a place with an input and an output arc) and each transition in the variable structure is assigned an array of size equal to the cardinality of feasible domain. An element in an array corresponding to a link in Π corresponds to an input situation. The array elements for a link are calculated with the help of a function defined on the feasible input domain, $\mathbf{fi} : \mathbf{I}_t \rightarrow \{0, 1\}$. $\mathbf{fi(v)} = 0$ means that the fixed structure corresponding ton input event $\mathbf{v}$ does not contain this link; $\mathbf{fi(v)} = 1$ means that the link does exist for the input event $\mathbf{v}$. A transition/component in Π is also assigned an array, whose elements correspond to input events. Each element in an array associated with a transition denotes the task performed by the component under the corresponding input situation. Once all the arrays for links and transitions/components in a variable structure are specified, the structure of the organization is fully defined and represented. Therefore, we can represent the variable structure by an *incidence matrix*, except that the entries of the matrix are arrays instead of scalars.

The variable structure represented by arrays can be unfolded into a set of fixed structures with each fixed structure corresponding to one input situation. If we fold the three distinct fixed structures described in Example 2, we can obtain a variable structure with its links and transitions annotated by arrays. Figure 11 shows the Petri net for the organization in Example 2 with this alternate approach. The remaining links in the figure have arrays with all elements equal to 1.

The two representation approaches for the variable-structure organization are equivalent in the sense that one representation can be constructed uniquely from the other and vice versa. The array elements associated with a link can be determined by the presence or absence of that link in corresponding fixed structures. The matrix representation of Section 3.2 explicitly identifies the presence and absence of *external* links (links across DMUs) from or to a DMU in an organization. The *internal links* (links between stages of a single DMU) can be determined by the presence or absence of processing stages of a DMU [23]. Figure 12 outlines a simple approach for determining the participating stages of a DMU in an organizational structure, and consequently the links internal to the DMUs.

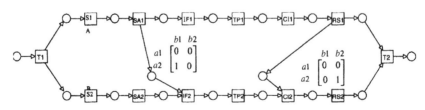

FIGURE 11
An alternate representation of the variable organization Π of Example 2.

1. If $e_i + G_{ji} < 0$ (for some j) then SAi is present.
2. If $s_i + G_{ji} + H_{ij} + C_{ij} > 0$ (for some j) then RSi is present.
3. If $C_{ji} > 0$ (for some j) then CIi is present.
4. If $F_{ji} + H_{ji} > 0$ (for some j) then IFi is present.
5. If two stages x and y are present then so are all those between these two.
6. All the links connecting the present stages are also present.

FIGURE 12
Algorithm to identify the present stages of a DMU in an organization.

3.4 Coordination Constraint

The folding of several fixed structures into a variable structure may not yield an organization that can adapt its structure to the changes in the input as perceived by the individual fixed structures. The definition of variable-structure organization as a folded structure of several fixed-structure organizations translates into a design requirement: all the components of a variable-structure organization should be capable of distinguishing among different situations for which they are supposed to behave differently (i.e., execute different functions, use different communication channels, etc.) as part of their coordination mechanism. This requirement was first identified by Demaël [7]. Later Lu and Levis [18] presented an algorithm to check this requirement, termed coordination constraint, in a variable-structure organization. A variable structure that satisfies the coordination constraint is the feasible solution to the design problem. The following is a brief description of the algorithm to check coordination constraint for the feasibility of a variable structure.

The algorithm starts with a definition of a partition process [18] associated with each input sensor. Each sensor partitions the feasible input space into subsets, where each subset contains the input events *indistinguishable* to the corresponding sensor.

Definition 4: *Distinguishable (indistinguishable) events.* Two input events $v = (v_{1i}, v_{2j}, \ldots, v_{mk})$ and $v' = (v_{10}, v_{2p}, \ldots, v_{mq})$, defined in the feasible input space $(v_{1i}, v_{10} \in I_1, v_{2j}, v_{2p} \in I_2, \ldots, v_{mk}, v_{mq} \subset I_m)$, are distinguishable with respect to I_n if and only if $n_{nr} \bullet v_{ns}(n = 1, 2, \ldots, m)$.

The concept of distinguishable input events with respect to an input alphabet induces an equivalence relation on feasible input space, which partitions the space into n subset where n is the cardinality of the corresponding input alphabet. Input events in a single partition are indistinguishable to the source, and events from different partitions are distinguishable. The partition process associated with sensor S1 in Example 2 is $P1 = \{S_{11}, S_{12}\}$, where $S_{11} = \{(a1, b1), (a1, b2)\}$ and $S_{12} = \{(a2, b1), (a2, b2)\}$. This partition can also be represented graphically as shown in Figure 13.

Once partition processes are defined for each input sensor in the sensor model, the algorithm proceeds by calculating and propagating the partition processes for each subsequent link and transition in the structure of the organization. The partition processes for the links and transitions in a structure are applied to the arrays associated with these links and transitions. Each partition thus created is checked for *consistency.*

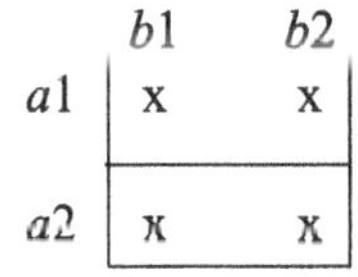

	b1	b2
a1	x	x
a2	x	x

FIGURE 13
Partition process of sensor S1 in Example 2.

The partition process for a component (transition) with single input remains that of its input link; however, for a component with multiple input links the partition process is calculated by *merging* the partition processes of all its input links. On the other hand, the partition process of a link is defined to be the *normalized* partition process of its input transition.

Definition 5: *MERGE.* Let $P1 = \{p_{11}, p_{12}, \ldots, p_{1n}\}$ and $P2 = \{p_{21}, p_{22}, \ldots, p_{2m}\}$ be two partition processes. The operation P1 EMERGE P2 results in a new partition, which is defined as

$$P3 = \left\{ p \mid j = 1, \ldots, n, \, p = p + 1j \bigcap_{i=1}^{m} p_{2i} \text{ and } p \neq \Phi \right\}$$

Definition 6: *Normalization.* A partition process $P = \{p_{11}, p_{12}, \ldots, p_{1n}\}$ is normalized by redefining its subsets as follows:

$$\text{Normalize(P)} = \{p \mid p \in P \text{ s.t. corresponding array elements in } p \text{ are all 1s, or}$$
$$p = \bigcup_j p_j \text{ s.t. all } p_j\text{s contain 0s as elements}\}$$

Figure 14 illustrates the method for calculating the partition process for the components and links in a structure.

The coordination constraint requires that the entries of arrays of output arcs and the component must be the same within a partition of the partition process of an array. The partition processes for the input links of a component with multiple inputs are dealt by with a different scheme to check the consistency. For components with multiple inputs, the entries of every array of the input links must be the same within a partition of all the partition processes associated with the input links. The process is repeated for every input link of a component with multiple inputs. Figure 15 shows examples of checking toe coordination constraint. The arrays in Figure 15 could be of a link or component. The solid lines partition each array into six partitions. The entries in each partition of the first array are the same; consequently, the coordination constraint is satisfied. In the second case, one of the partitions has two different elements. There the coordination constraint is not satisfied. Therefore, if we can find the partition processes for all the components in the organization, and find that they are consistent, a realizable or feasible variable structure is obtained.

The methodology of Lu and Levis [18] generates variable structures by arbitrarily choosing fixed structures for each input situation. The algorithm is used to check the coordination constraint for each generated variable structures. Only the variable structures that meet the coordination constraint are retained and stored as feasible solutions to the design problem.

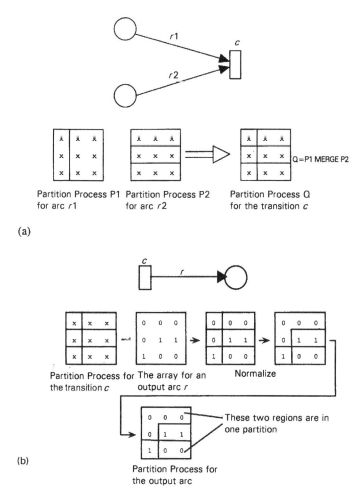

(a)

(b)

FIGURE 14
Derivation of partition processes. (a) Derivation of the partition process for a component; (b) The partition for an output link.

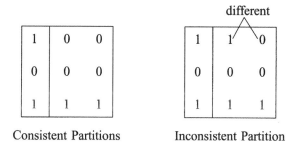

FIGURE 15
Consistency in partition process—The coordination constraint.

4   GENERATION OF STRUCTURES BY GENETIC ALGORITHM

The design procedure for generating feasible variable-structure organizations by Lu and Levis [18] is carried out in two stages: (1) sets of feasible fixed structures are generated for each input situation, (2) one element from each of these sets of fixed structures is selected arbitrarily and a variable organization is formed by folding all the selected fixed structures. Finally, the variable structure is checked for coordination constraint. The process is computationally expensive and *blind* at both of these stages; first all the feasible fixed structures are generated independent of the others with no information exchange among the processes to determine which interactional structures might result in feasible folding, and then the structures are arbitrarily selected from each set to form a variable structure. It is this that led Zaidi and Levis [27] to investigate the genetic algorithm to generate fixed structures. The genetic algorithm performs a parallel heuristic search of the solution space for feasible solutions. The same approach is extended for the generation of variable-structure organization. The rest of this section describes the approach.

4.1   Encoding

The encoding of a fixed organizational structure into a chromosome, as presented in [27], converts the matrix representation $\Sigma = \{E, s, F, G, H, C\}$ into a bit string. The encoding is illustrated in the following example.

> EXAMPLE 3
> Let the structure of an organization is given by the tuple $\Sigma_\bullet$.
>
> $$E = [0 \quad 1] \qquad s = [1 \quad 1]$$
>
> $$\Sigma_{xi}: \quad F = \begin{bmatrix} \# & 0 \\ 1 & \# \end{bmatrix} \quad G = \begin{bmatrix} \# & 0 \\ 1 & \# \end{bmatrix}$$
>
> $$H = \begin{bmatrix} \# & 0 \\ 0 & \# \end{bmatrix} \quad C = \begin{bmatrix} \# & 1 \\ 0 & \# \end{bmatrix}$$
>
> The bit string representing the chromosome, Σ, is obtained by the following encoding:
>
> $$\Sigma_{xi}: \quad \overbrace{0 \ 1}^{E} \quad \overbrace{0 \ 1}^{F} \quad \overbrace{0 \ 1}^{G} \quad \overbrace{0 \ 0}^{H} \quad \overbrace{1 \ 0}^{C} \quad \overbrace{1 \ 1}^{s}$$
>
> The diagonal elements of the matrices F, G, H, and C are ignored in the bit string representation since they remain zero throughout the design procedure.

An ith bit in the bit string representation of an organizational structure, Σ, is accessed through the notation $\Sigma[I]$ (e.g., $\Sigma[4] = 1$ in Example 3).

The length of the string representing an organizational structure Σ is denoted by $|\Sigma|$ (e.g., $|\Sigma| = 12$ in Example 3). The length of the bit string (chromosome) representing a fixed-structure organization (individual in a population) with n DMUs is given by

$$|\Sigma| = 4n^2 - (m-3)n \quad \text{where} \quad \begin{cases} n \text{ is the number of DMUs in } \sigma \\ m \text{ is the number of sensors} \end{cases}$$

Therefore, the index i in $\Sigma[i]$ takes on the values $1 \le i \le 4n^2 - (m-3)n$.

A variable organization is represented as an organism with layers of chromosomes each representing a fixed structure along with its associated input situation. Figure 16 represents an encoding of the variable structure Π of Example 2.

1	1	0	0	0	0	0	0	0	0	1	1	[for input situation {($a1, b1$), ($a1, b2$)}]
1	1	1	0	0	0	0	0	0	0	1	1	[for input situation {($a2, b1$)}]
1	1	0	0	0	0	0	0	1	0	1	1	[for input situation {($a2, b2$)}]

FIGURE 16
Organism representing a variable structure.

4.2   Design Requirements

The methodology requires a designer of an organization to specify the feasible input domain for the organization to be built. Therefore, the first requirement for the design procedure is to model the input source. Once the feasible input domain is specified, the designer is required to input the interactional requirements for each fixed structure corresponding to an input situation. The interactional requirements for a fixed structure participating in a variable organization are provided by the designer in terms of user-defined constraints, R_u. Requirements for each participating fixed structure are input to the design algorithm by putting 1s and 0s at corresponding places in the matrix representation [24]. The user-defined constraints are taken for every input event in the feasible input domain.

The user-defined constraints for a hypothetical single sensor, 2-DMU, fixed organization are given as the tuple Σ_{xi}.

$$e = [1 \quad x] \qquad s = [0 \quad x]$$

$$\Sigma_{xi}: \quad F = \begin{bmatrix} \# & 1 \\ x & \# \end{bmatrix} \qquad G = \begin{bmatrix} \# & 0 \\ 0 & \# \end{bmatrix}$$

$$H = \begin{bmatrix} \# & x \\ x & \# \end{bmatrix} \qquad C = \begin{bmatrix} \# & 0 \\ 0 & \# \end{bmatrix}$$

The bit string representation of $\bullet_{xi}$ is given as

$$\Sigma_{xi}: \quad 1 \ x \ 1 \ x \ 0 \ 0 \ x \ x \ 0 \ 0 \ 0 \ x$$

The x's in the arrays represent the unspecified elements or optional links. The optional links determine the degree of freedom left in the design process, and potentially yield a number of feasible fixed structures for the corresponding input situation.

4.3   Initial Population

An organism with each constituent chromosome representing user-defined constraints, shows the building block or *schema* for the generation of future populations of structures. A 1 or 0 at any position means that the chromosomes in future populations must have the same value at that position for them to belong to the schema. The x's represent the genes (interactions) that can be replaced by either 1s or 0s genetically to generate new populations of solutions.

The first step in the genetic algorithm approach requires an initial population of organisms to start the process. In the present approach, the bit strings representing the *universal* and the *kernel nets* corresponding to individual chromosomes are used to initialize the population; an initial population of variable structures, or organism in the genetic terminology, contains two individuals, where one individual contains all the chromosomes in its *universal net* representation and the other contains chromosomes in its *kernel net* form. This way we start the generic search at one end from the maximally connected organization and at the other end from the least-connected organization.

Definition 7: *Universal and kernel nets.* The universal net $\Omega(R_u)$ associated with the constraints R_u is the net defined by the tuple ● obtained by replacing all undetermined elements of $\{E, s, F, G, H, C\}$ by 1. Similarly, the kernel net $\omega(R_u)$ is the net obtained by replacing the same undetermined elements by zero.

Definition 8: *Universal and kernel chromosomes.* The bit strings representing $\Omega(R_u)$ and $\omega(R_u)$ are termed as universal and kernel chromosomes, respectively.

For the illustrative example in Section 4.2, the initial population is given as

$$\Omega_{xi}(R_u) : \quad 1\ 1\ 1\ 1\ 0\ 0\ 1\ 1\ 0\ 0\ 0\ 1$$
$$\Omega_{xi}(R_u) : \quad 1\ 0\ 1\ 0\ 0\ 0\ 0\ 0\ 0\ 0\ 0\ 0$$

4.4 Structural and Coordination Requirements

In order to have a feasible variable organization, or a *fit* organism in genetic terminology, each fixed structure, or chromosome in the organism, is required to be a feasible organization in terms of both structural requirements and user-defined constraints. Once we have all chromosomes in an organism represent feasible fixed organizations, the organism is checked for coordination constraint. We have already described the coordination constraint. In the present approach, each organism is converted to its array representation and partition processes are calculated for every component and interactional link in the variable organization, and partitions are checked for feasibility.

A brief description of structural constraints [24, 26] for individual fixed organization follows.

Structural Constraints

(R1)   The ordinary Petri net that corresponds to a fixed structure should be connected, that is, there should be at least one (undirected) path between any two nodes in the net. A directed path should exist from the source place to every node of the net and from every node to the sink.

The genetic implementation of R1 [27] checks each chromosome in an organism to establish the internal structure of each constituent DMU. For a connected organizational architecture the internal structures of all DMUs must fall within the following four possibilities [24].

- SA alone with $y = z$
- SA, IF, TP, CI, and RS
- IF, TP, CI, and RS with $x = z'$
- CI and RS with $x = v'$

In addition to checking the internal structures for DMUs, the following checks are also performed to ensure that each fixed organization is also connected to the external environment through inputs and outputs (sink and source places):

$$\sum_{j=1}^{n \times m} \Sigma[j] \geq 1$$

$$\sum_{j=1}^{n} \Sigma[4n^2 - (m-4)n + j] \geq 1$$

where n is the number of DMUs and m is the number of input sensors in the organization.

(R2)   The ordinary Petri net that corresponds to a fixed structure should have no loops, that is, the structure must be acyclic. An algorithm has been presented in [27] that checks for this constraint in every chromosome of an organism.

(R3)   In the ordinary Petri net that corresponds to a fixed structure, there can be at most one link from the RS stage of a DMUi to another DMUj, that is, for each i and j, only one element of the triplet $\{G_{ij}, H_{ij}, C_{ij}\}$can be nonzero. The analytical expression of this constraint is given as

$$\forall (i,j) \quad g_{ij} + h_{ij} + C_{ij} \leq 1, \quad i \neq j; j = 1, 2, \ldots, n$$

The analytical expression of this constraint, applied to the genetic representation of a fixed structure, is given as

$$\forall i \quad \Sigma[n^2 + (m-1)n + i] + \Sigma[2n^2 - (m-2)n + i] + \Sigma[3n^2 - (m-3)n + i] \leq 1,$$
$$i = 1, 2, \ldots, (n^2 - n)$$

(R4)   Information fusion can take place only at the IF and CI stages. Consequently, the SA stage of a DMU can either receive information from the external environment, or an output from another DMU. The translation of this constraint into mathematical terms follows:

$$\forall j \quad \bigvee_{k=1}^{m} e_{kj} + \sum_{i=1}^{n} G_{ij} \leq 1, \quad j = 1, 2n$$

The translation of this constraint for the genetic representation of a fixed structure follows:

$$\forall j \quad \bigvee_{k=1}^{m} \Sigma[(k-1)n + j] + \sum_{\substack{i=1 \\ i \neq j}}^{n} \Sigma[r_{i,j}] \leq 1, \quad j = 1, 2, \ldots, n$$

where

$$r = n^2 + (m-1)n + (i-1)(n-1) + j - 1, \quad \text{for} \quad i < j$$
$$r = n^2 + (m-1)n + (i-1)(n-1) + j \quad \text{for} \quad i > j$$

4.5   Feasibility of Schema

The user-defined constraints for each individual fixed-structure organization result in a schema that forms the building blocks for the generation of future population of chromosomes or structures. The genes (interactions) that are ruled in or ruled out by the designer remain constant throughout the evolution process. The genetic difference among several chromosomes is due to the optional genes (x's in the bit string). Therefore, if there exist errors (violations of structural constraints) caused by the customary genes in the schema of an organization structure, they will be propagated through out the entire population of chromosomes; the evolution process will never yield any feasible organization structure. In order to avoid this wastage of time and computation effort, the following checks due to Zaidi and Levis [27] are performed on the chromosomes of the initial population of organisms prior to invoking the genetic process:

- The kernel chromosomes are checked for the constraint R2.
- The kernel chromosomes are checked for the constraint R3.
- The kernel chromosomes are checked for the constraint R4.

If at least one participating chromosome of the initial population fails any of these tests, the genetic process is immediately halted and the designer is warned of the infeasibility of the schema. The first check is based on the rationale that if an organizational structure with only the customary interactions among its DMUs lacks the acyclicity requirement, then acyclical structures, cannot be generated by adding more interactions to it. The same rationale applies to the rest of the checks performed on the initial population. Note that even after these checks are performed on the kernel chromosome, one cannot guarantee the feasibility of the schema in terms of the structural constraint R1. The check for the feasibility of schema for R1 is a very involved process and therefore is dropped in favor of the speed of the process. Similarly, even if the feasibility of individual schema is established, the feasibility of the entire organism cannot be established easily: the feasibility of user-defined constraints for each fixed structure only ensures that at least one feasible fixed-structure organization exists as the solution to the design problem, but it does not guarantee the existence of a combination of feasible fixed structures that when folded would yield a feasible variable-structure organization.

4.6   Computation of Solutions

In the present implementation of the genetic algorithm, an organism consists of several chromosomes each representing a constituent fixed organization. The requirements for one fixed organization are independent of the requirements of the others. Therefore, each chromosome in an organism is allowed to enhance its population independently of the others. The approach used to generate new populations of chromosomes, the genetic algorithm proposed by Zaidi and Levis [27], is applied to corresponding chromosomes of a population of organisms. Therefore, the approach runs parallel genetic algorithms for fixed structures corresponding to every input situation. During this stage there exists no interaction or exchange of information among these simultaneously running algorithms. However, when every algorithm reports production of at least one feasible solution, feasible chromosomes from these independent populations are selected by a selection criterion to be folded into a variable structure represented as an organism.

The organism is checked for the coordination constraint. In case the constraint is violated by an organism, the approach takes a notice of the error, and applies heuristics to correct it right away. This self-correction of an organism during its *lifetime* is termed the *learning cycle*. Finally, if the learning cycles fail to *train* a feasible solution, the information obtained (or learned) from the coordination inconsistency is used to tailor the genetic operators of the individual algorithms. At this stage, the independently running algorithms start interacting with each other by passing information on how to set different parameters of genetic operators. Each member (organism/ chromosome) of a population is evaluated against a fitness function. The evaluation results in an assignment of a fitness value of each and every member of the population.

Evaluation Function

The methodology may use several evaluation functions to evaluate individuals in genetically evolved populations. The algorithms for generating fixed structures corresponding to input situations may use their own evaluation functions reflecting the designer's requirements for the individual fixed structures. The current methodology employs the following evaluation function for all algorithms generating fixed-structure organizations:

$$\delta_f = \begin{cases} (4n + m)n + h_f & \text{if } \Sigma \text{ is feasible} \\ h_f & \text{otherwise} \end{cases}$$

where h_f is some user-defined measure reflecting the designer's bias toward (or against) a particular type of solution. The present implementation of the algorithms uses total number of 1s in a chromosome to be the value assigned to h_f. This reflects the designer's bias toward maximally connected organizations.

The fitness value assigned to an individual in a population of variable-structure organizations is calculated by the following evaluation mechanism:

$$\delta_v = f(\mathbf{x}, \mathbf{y}, \mathbf{z})$$

where $\mathbf{x}$ represents the parameter whose value depends upon the structural feasibility of individual fixed structures in the organism; $\mathbf{y}$ represents a parameter whose value depends upon the feasibility of coordination structure of the organism, determined by the coordination constraint; $\mathbf{z}$ represents a parameter whose value is determined by some user-defined criterion, e.g., number of interactional links.

The present implementation of the algorithm uses the following evaluation function:

$$\delta_v = \begin{cases} c(8n + 2m)n + \sum \delta_f & \text{if } \Pi \text{ is feasible} \\ \sum \delta_f & \text{otherwise} \end{cases}$$

where c is the number of participating chromosomes in an organism.

The evaluation function assigns fitness values to individuals in genetically evolved populations in such a manner that a fitness assigned to an individual clearly identifies the type of solution it represents. Table 1 outlines the distinct nonoverlapping ranges the algorithm uses to assign fitness values to three possible types of solutions in a population.

Genetic Operators

The fitness assigned to organism determines the "strong" and "weak" individuals in a population. The strongest elements are retained in the population and allowed to reproduce and generate following populations of organisms. Figure 17 and Figure 18 present illustrations of the two genetic operators, crossover and mutation, used in the approach. The two operators are

Table 1 Types of Solutions and Corresponding Ranges of Fitness Values

Type of solutions	Participating fixed structures	Range of fitness values	
		Fixed structure (each)	Variable structure
Variable structure			
Infeasible	Infeasible	$[0, 4n^2 + (m-3)n]$	$c[0, 4n^2 + (m-3)n]$
	Feasible	$[4n^2 + mn, 8n^2 + (2m-3_n]$	$c[4n^2 + mn, 8n^2 + (2m-3)n]$
Feasible	Feasible	$[4n^2 + mn, 8n^2 + (2m-3)n]$	$c[8n^2 + 2mn, 16n^2 + (2m+2n+3)n]$

n = number of DMUs, m = number of sensors, c = number of chromosomes in an organism.

Parent 1:	1	1	1	1	0	0	1	1	0	0	0	1
Parent 2:	1	0	1	0	0	0	0	0	0	0	0	0
Child 1:	1	0	1	0	0	0	1	0	0	0	0	0
Child 2:	1	1	1	1	0	0	0	1	0	0	0	1

(a)

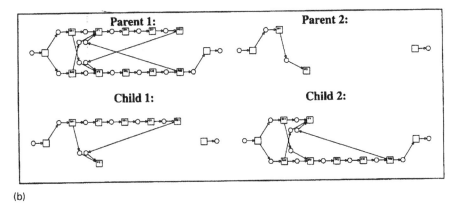

(b)

FIGURE 17
(a) Crossover. (b) Petri net representation of crossover.

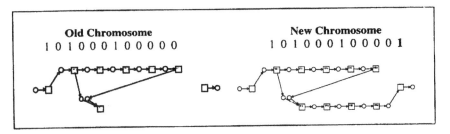

FIGURE 18
An example of bit mutation.

applied to chromosomes of organisms. The coordination structure of a *weak* organism provides useful information regarding the problematic interactions—links where the coordination constraint is violated. The algorithm uses several *learning cycles* to correct an individual by heuristically selecting a (some) link(s) causing the coordination inconsistency and, by probabilistically altering 1s to 0s, or vice versa, to remove the inconsistency. A specified number of such corrective attempts are allowed in each generation. This information—i.e., the presence or absence of link(s) causing coordination inconsistency—is also shared by the independent algorithms generating fixed structure to update their mutation rates or crossover points for the genetic operators used in the generation of subsequent generations; for example, during evaluation of the coordination constraint if a partition (associated with an optional link) is found with different elements in it. The mutation rate for that particular link in a fixed structure, which contributes to this infeasibility, is increased to eliminate this link in the next generation. In the present approach, we have investigated the effect of an increased mutation rate on the design procedure. The same information, however, can be used to determine the crossover point for the mating operation performed on the present generation.

5   APPLICATION—THE AIR SURFACE TRAFFIC PROBLEM [8]

This section illustrates the application of the methodology to the design of a variable-structure Airport Surface Traffic Control system (ASTC). The problem described in this paper has earlier been presented by Demaël and Levis in their paper on a methodology for generating variable-structure decision-making organizations [8]. The same design problem is taken for application of the GA-based approach and the corresponding results from both approaches are compared. The description of the problem is as follows.

ASTC is broadly defined as the portion of the Air Traffic Control system that is responsible for traffic on the runways and taxiways of an airport. The system encompasses people, procedures, and equipment. In major U.S. airports, the system consists of two control positions, Local Control and Ground Control, which are stationed in the tower cab using visual surveillance, voice radio, and ground surveillance radars wherever available. Local Control handles the traffic on the runways and in the airspace in the immediate vicinity of the airport, while Ground Control handles the traffic on the taxiways and, at some airports, issues advisories regarding airplane movements at the ramps. Local Control monitors landings and takeoffs by interacting with the portion of the Air Traffic Control system that is in charge of arrivals and departures in the flight corridors. Local Control can also communicate with Ground Control and with all planes on the runways and taxiways. Ground Control exchanges information with Local Control and with each plane on the ground.

The example presented in this paper describes the design of a variable ASTC system that encompasses one Local Controller (LC) and two Ground Controllers (GC). This example has been based on a simplified and a hypothetical design of an ASTC system for Logan Airport in Boston shown in Figure 19 [8].

The airport in Figure 19 has three terminals and two runways, A and B. Planes land and take off on runways, and move to and from the terminals on the taxiways. LC monitors the movements on the runways, while GC surveys the taxiways, the crossings of taxiways and runways, and the terminals. The guiding principle for the utilization of runways is that landings and takeoffs are done "against the wind": runway A is used if the wind blows from the North or from the South, and runway B if it blows from East or West, but both runways can be used under low wind conditions. However, due to noise abatement concerns in the communities around Boston Harbor, large planes land and take off from runway A exclusively, and runway B is used for general aviation. The safety standards require that there cannot be simultaneous use of both runways.

The assumptions for the design problems are as follows: One Ground Controller, called GC1, is responsible for the southern sector of the airport, while the other, called GC2, monitors the northern sector. Terminals 1 and 2 are monitored by GC1, and terminal 3 is monitored by GC2. Crossings 1, 2, and 3 in Figure 19 designate dangerous crossings between taxiways. Crossing 1 lies within the jurisdiction of GC2, and crossing 3 is under the jurisdiction of GC1. Crossing 2, however, stands on the boundary between the northern and southern sectors, and is monitored by both Ground Controllers. Crossing 4 is monitored by GC2, and crossing 5 is monitored by GC1. Both these plots indicate crossing between a taxiway and a runway. If a plane on a taxiway approaches crossings 4 or 5, a Ground Controller must interact with the Local Controller to get

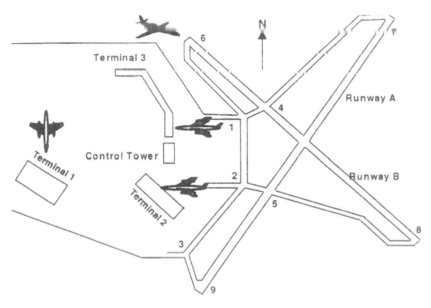

FIGURE 19
Example airport.

the status of the runway, and then authorize or deny the crossing. Finally, crossings 6, 7, 8, and 9 designate the ends of the runways, where the plane changes jurisdiction between Ground Control and Local Control. The following five sources of information can trigger variable patterns of interaction in the system.

5.1 Sensor Model

Sensor 1: Wind. The associated alphabet is $X1 = \{O, N, S, E, W\}$, where N (S, E, and W) indicates high wind coming from North (South, East, and West respectively). O models low wind conditions.

Sensor: Runway status. The associated alphabet is $X2 = \{LAA, LAB, TOA, TOB, CL\}$, where LAX ($X = A$, or B) indicates that a plane is landing on runway X, TOX ($X = A$, or B) indicates a plane taking off from runway X, and CL indicates no activity on both runways.

Sensor 3: Status at terminals 1 and 2. The alphabet is $X3 = \{DP1, NDP1\}$, where DP1 indicates departure from terminal 1 or 2, and NDP1 indicates no plane departing. Note that a departing plane must be directed to a runway. If both runways are operational, GC1 must ask the Local Controller where to direct the plane.

Sensor 4: Status at terminal 3. The alphabet is $X4 = \{DP3, NDP3\}$, where DP3 indicates departure from terminal 3, and NDP3 indicates no plane departing. As noted earlier, GC2 must ask the Local Controller to direct the plane when both runways are operational.

Sensor 5: Conflicts. The alphabet is $X5 = \{C, NC\}$, where C indicates that there is some conflict at the boundaries of the northern and southern sectors, and NC models the absence of any conflict.

The input space, $\mathbf{I} = X1 \times X2 \times X3 \times X4 \times X5$, contains 200 events, all of which are feasible events—$\mathbf{I}_f = \mathbf{I}$. These inputs model only the parameters that necessitate or influence coordination, and do not encompassing the additional parameters that are processed by the controllers. It is assumed that each DMU knows the direction of the wind, the output of Sensor 1. The output of Sensor 2, the status of the runway(s), is known to LC only. The output of Sensor 3 is monitored by GC1, but not by GC2. LC may also have access to this source of information. Similarly, Sensor 4 is in possession of GC2, and LC may also have access to its information. Finally, conflicts at the boundaries of the two sectors, output of Sensor 5, are only known to GCs. Note that the sensor model presented in this example is *deterministic* and *temporally consistent*. No degree of freedom is left for the design procedure to assign different input sensors to DMUs and no variability is introduced in the pattern of interaction between sensors and DMUs across different fixed structures. Similarly, an element output by a sensor, connected to several DMUs, is considered available to all the DMUs without any delay. In the matrix representation these input requirements can be represented as follows:

$$
\mathbf{E} = \begin{array}{c} \\ X1 \\ X2 \\ X3 \\ X4 \\ X5 \end{array} \begin{array}{ccc} LC & GC1 & GC2 \\ \begin{bmatrix} 1 & 1 & 1 \\ 1 & 0 & 0 \\ 1 & 1 & 0 \\ 1 & 0 & 1 \\ 0 & 1 & 1 \end{bmatrix} \end{array}
$$

Note that this sensor model will remain same across all fixed structures.

5.2   Design Requirements

As pointed out in [8], there are six input situations, which correspond to different patterns of interaction—fixed structures. The six input situations are listed as:

$E_{X1} = \{\mathbf{v} \mid \mathbf{v} = (v_1, v_2, v_3, v_4, v_5) \in X1 \times X2 \times X3 \times X4 \times X5, \text{ s.t. } v_1 = N \text{ or } W\}$

$E_{X2} = \{\mathbf{v} \mid \mathbf{v} = (v_1, v_2, v_3, v_4, v_5) \in X1 \times X2 \times X3 \times X4 \times X5, \text{ s.t. } v_1 = E \text{ or } S\}$

$E_{X3} = \{\mathbf{v} \mid \mathbf{v} = (v_1, v_2, v_3, v_4, v_5) \in X1 \times X2 \times X3 \times X4 \times X5, \text{ s.t. } v_1 = O, v_3 = DP1,$
$$\text{and } v_4 = DP3\}$$

$E_{X4} = \{\mathbf{v} \mid \mathbf{v} = (v_1, v_2, v_3, v_4, v_5) \in X1 \times X2 \times X3 \times X4 \times X5, \text{ s.t. } v_1 = O, v_3 = DP1,$
$$\text{and } v_4 = NDP3\}$$

$E_{X5} = \{\mathbf{v} \mid \mathbf{v} = (v_1, v_2, v_3, v_4, v_5) \in X1 \times X2 \times X3 \times X4 \times X5, \text{ s.t. } v_1 - O, v_3 = NDP1,$
$$\text{and } v_4 = DP3\}$$

$E_{X6} = \{\mathbf{v} \mid \mathbf{v} = (v_1, v_2, v_3, v_4, v_5) \in X1 \times X2 \times X3 \times X4 \times X5, \text{ s.t. } v_1 = O, v_3 = NDP1,$
$$\text{and } v_4 = NDP3\}$$

The corresponding user-defined constraints for six fixed-structure organizations are given as follows:

$$\Sigma_{x1}: \quad \mathbf{F} = \begin{bmatrix} \# & 1 & 0 \\ x & \# & x \\ x & x & \# \end{bmatrix} \quad \mathbf{G} = \begin{bmatrix} \# & 0 & 0 \\ 0 & \# & 0 \\ 0 & 0 & \# \end{bmatrix}$$

$$\mathbf{H} = \begin{bmatrix} \# & 0 & 0 \\ 0 & \# & 0 \\ 0 & 0 & \# \end{bmatrix} \quad \mathbf{C} = \begin{bmatrix} \# & 0 & 0 \\ 0 & \# & x \\ 0 & 0 & \# \end{bmatrix}$$

$$s = \begin{bmatrix} 1 & 1 & 1 \end{bmatrix}$$

$$\Sigma_{x2}: \quad \mathbf{F} = \begin{bmatrix} \# & 0 & 1 \\ x & \# & x \\ x & x & \# \end{bmatrix} \quad \mathbf{G} = \begin{bmatrix} \# & 0 & 0 \\ 0 & \# & 0 \\ 0 & 0 & \# \end{bmatrix}$$

$$\mathbf{H} = \begin{bmatrix} \# & 0 & 0 \\ 0 & \# & 0 \\ 0 & 0 & \# \end{bmatrix} \quad \mathbf{C} = \begin{bmatrix} \# & 1 & 1 \\ 0 & \# & x \\ 0 & 0 & \# \end{bmatrix}$$

$$s = \begin{bmatrix} 1 & 1 & 1 \end{bmatrix}$$

$$\Sigma_{x3}: \quad \mathbf{F} = \begin{bmatrix} \# & 1 & 1 \\ x & \# & x \\ x & x & \# \end{bmatrix} \quad \mathbf{G} = \begin{bmatrix} \# & 0 & 0 \\ 0 & \# & 0 \\ 0 & 0 & \# \end{bmatrix}$$

$$\mathbf{H} = \begin{bmatrix} \# & 0 & 0 \\ 0 & \# & 0 \\ 0 & 0 & \# \end{bmatrix} \quad \mathbf{C} = \begin{bmatrix} \# & 1 & 1 \\ 0 & \# & x \\ 0 & 0 & \# \end{bmatrix}$$

$$s = \begin{bmatrix} 1 & 1 & 1 \end{bmatrix}$$

$$\Sigma_{x4}: \quad \mathbf{F} = \begin{bmatrix} \# & 1 & 1 \\ x & \# & x \\ x & x & \# \end{bmatrix} \quad \mathbf{G} = \begin{bmatrix} \# & 0 & 0 \\ 0 & \# & 0 \\ 0 & 0 & \# \end{bmatrix}$$

$$\mathbf{H} = \begin{bmatrix} \# & 0 & 0 \\ 0 & \# & 0 \\ 0 & 0 & \# \end{bmatrix} \quad \mathbf{C} = \begin{bmatrix} \# & 0 & 1 \\ 0 & \# & x \\ 0 & 0 & \# \end{bmatrix}$$

$$s = \begin{bmatrix} 1 & 1 & 1 \end{bmatrix}$$

$$\Sigma_{x5}: \quad \mathbf{F} = \begin{bmatrix} \# & 1 & 1 \\ x & \# & x \\ x & x & \# \end{bmatrix} \quad \mathbf{G} = \begin{bmatrix} \# & 0 & 0 \\ 0 & \# & 0 \\ 0 & 0 & \# \end{bmatrix}$$

$$\mathbf{H} = \begin{bmatrix} \# & 0 & 0 \\ 0 & \# & 0 \\ 0 & 0 & \# \end{bmatrix} \quad \mathbf{C} = \begin{bmatrix} \# & 1 & 0 \\ 0 & \# & x \\ 0 & 0 & \# \end{bmatrix}$$

$$s = \begin{bmatrix} 1 & 1 & 1 \end{bmatrix}$$

$$F = \begin{bmatrix} \# & 1 & 1 \\ x & \# & x \\ x & x & \# \end{bmatrix} \quad G = \begin{bmatrix} \# & 0 & 0 \\ 0 & \# & 0 \\ 0 & 0 & \# \end{bmatrix}$$

$$\Sigma_{x6} : H = \begin{bmatrix} \# & 0 & 0 \\ 0 & \# & 0 \\ 0 & 0 & \# \end{bmatrix} \quad C = \begin{bmatrix} \# & 0 & 0 \\ 0 & \# & x \\ 0 & 0 & \# \end{bmatrix}$$

$$J = \begin{bmatrix} 1 & 1 & 1 \end{bmatrix}$$

These constraints can be summarized by the following description [8]. Every DMU has to produce a response to be sent to the planes under its jurisdiction; therefore, each DMU must have a fixed link from its RS stage to the effectors in all input situations. No constraints are imposed on sharing information between Ground Controllers or from a GC to LC. Some constraints are imposed on the exchange of information from LC to the Ground Controllers, because the LC must inform the Ground Controllers of the runway status. There is no need for fixed interactions because the utilization of the runways does not always create conflicts or dangers in both the northern and the southern sectors. If the wind is N or W (corresponding input situation is E_{X1}), the landing planes leave the runway at crossings 6 or 7, under the jurisdiction of GC2, and head for the terminals through the crossings 1 and 4, all monitored by GC2. The departing planes take off from crossing 8 or 9. The way these airplanes move on the taxiways to crossings 8 and 9 is mainly under the jurisdiction of GC1. Therefore, GC2 only needs to be informed by LC. Similarly if the wind is S or E (corresponding input situation is E_{X2}), GC1 needs to be informed by LC. If runways A and B are in use, both Ground Controllers need to be informed, because each GC monitors a crossing between a runway and a taxiway. It is also assumed that GCs cannot issue commands, to the LC because the movement on the runways has priority for safety purposes. The number of alternative courses of action that the LC can select shall never be restricted. Secondly, GC2 cannot issue a command to GC1, whereas GC1 may issue one to GC2. GC1 covers a larger area than GC2 and may need to restrict the courses of action of GC2 to resolve conflicts. finally, in the case of low wind conditions, the LC must instruct the Ground Controllers when a plane leaves a terminal. This variability is depicted by input situations E_{X3}, E_{X4}, E_{X5}, and E_{X6}.

5.3 Solutions

The design requirements for every fixed structure are encoded in the genetic representation described in Section 4. Six parallel genetic engines are initialized with the initial populations and allowed to run until every one of them has reported at least one feasible solution in the generated populations. Chromosomes with highest fitness in each populations are selected, with repetition, for folding into organisms—variable structures. The organisms so created are evaluated. The feasible solutions are reported to the designer, weak individuals are allowed to go through corrective cycles, and unresolved inconsistencies are reported to corresponding genetic engines, which, in turn, adjust their mutation rates on certain bit(s).

The first reported feasible solutions are shown in Figures 20 and 21. The Petri net representations of the two solutions are presented in Figures 22 and 23, respectively. The two solutions turn out to be the maximally and minimally (respectively) connected variable-structure organizations reported by Demaël and Levis [8].

The process is allowed to continue. In the next generation of variable structures the process finds an infeasible solution with all constituent feasible chromosomes. The algorithm tries to

Σ_{x1} :   111101111000000000000000100111
Σ_{x2} :   111011111000000000000000100111
Σ_{x3} :   111111111000000000000110100111
Σ_{x4} :   111111111000000000000010100111
Σ_{x5} :   111111111000000000000100100111
Σ_{x6} :   111111111000000000000000100111

FIGURE 20
The first reported feasible solution with fitness of 998.

Σ_{x1} :   111101111000000000000000100111
Σ_{x2} :   111011111000000000000000100111
Σ_{x3} :   111111111000000000000110100111
Σ_{x4} :   111111111000000000000010100111
Σ_{x5} :   111111111000000000000100100111
Σ_{x6} :   111111111000000000000000100111

FIGURE 21
The second reported feasible solution with fitness of 968.

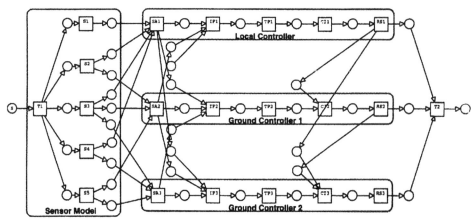

Labels on Links:
Link from SA1 to IF2: Ex_2
Link from SA1 to IF3: Ex_1
Link from RS1 to CI2: $Ex_1 \cup Ex_2 \cup Ex_4 \cup Ex_6$
Link from RS1 to CI3: $Ex_1 \cup Ex_2 \cup Ex_5 \cup Ex_6$

FIGURE 22
PN representation of first solution in Figure 20.

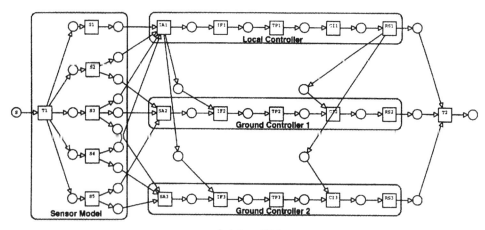

Labels on Links:
Link from SA1 to IF2: Ex_2
Link from SA1 to IF3: Ex_1
Link from RS1 to CI2: $Ex_1 \cup Ex_2 \cup Ex_4 \cup Ex_6$
Link from RS1 to CI3: $Ex_1 \cup Ex_2 \cup Ex_5 \cup Ex_6$

FIGURE 23
PN representation of second solution in Figure 21.

correct the coordination inconsistency by turning certain bits from 0 to 1 (the bias is toward the more connected organizations). After two cycles of self-correction, the algorithm succeeds in converting an infeasible organism into a feasible variable structure solution to the design problem. The solution is presented in Figures 24 and 25. The bits that were altered during the correction cycles are shown underlined in Figure 24.

4   CONCLUSION

We have presented results of an effort at generating variable structure organizations by genetic algorithm. The genetic approach offers an alternative to the previous approach of constructing variable organizations. The previous approach generates feasible fixed structures for all possible input situations, and then folds these structures by arbitrarily selecting them. The approach is computationally expensive since it generates all sets of feasible fixed structures first and then combinatorially evaluates these structures for coordination feasibility. The new genetic approach generates fixed structures in an incremental fashion, and checks them for coordination feasibility

$$
\begin{aligned}
\Sigma_{x1} &: \quad 111101111000000000000000100111 \\
\Sigma_{x2} &: \quad 111010011000000000000000000111 \\
\Sigma_{x3} &: \quad 111111\underline{1}11000000000000110000111 \\
\Sigma_{x4} &: \quad 1111111\underline{1}1000000000000010100111 \\
\Sigma_{x5} &: \quad 111111111000000000000100000111 \\
\Sigma_{x6} &: \quad 111111111000000000000000000111
\end{aligned}
$$

FIGURE 24
The self-corrected solution with fitness of 991.

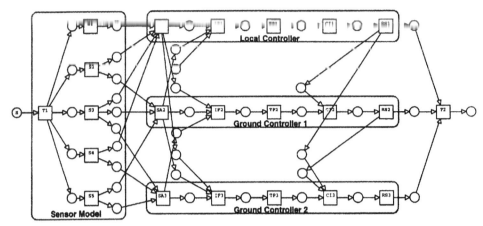

Labels on Links:
Link from SA1 to IF2: Ex_2
Link from SA1 to IF3: Ex_1
Link from SA2 to IF1: Ex_2
Link from SA2 to IF3: Ex_2
Link from RS1 to CI2: $Ex_1 \cup Ex_2 \cup Ex_4 \cup Ex_6$
Link from RS1 to CI3: $Ex_1 \cup Ex_2 \cup Ex_5 \cup Ex_6$
Link from RS2 to CI3: $Ex_1 \cup Ex_2 \cup Ex_3 \cup Ex_5 \cup Ex_6$

FIGURE 25
PN representation of solution in Figure 24.

right away. The information obtained during the evaluation of coordination constraint is used to direct the search for other feasible fixed structures. This information not only is useful in narrowing down the search for other feasible structures, but is also helpful in eliminating a potentially large number of feasible structures with infeasible coordination dynamics under variable structures. Another advantage of this approach is that additional structural, user, and performance criteria can be made an integral part of the design algorithm, by defining different evaluation mechanisms, to direct the search for the solution in a particular direction.

The results presented here are the outcome of the concept verification phase of the research. Now that it has been established that the genetic approach shows promise for solution of the design problem effort currently focuses on ways to improve the genetic operators used in the methodology and to explore the kind of domain-dependent information required by these operators, to yield better and earlier results. Work is also being done on a software tool for running experiments with different mixes of genetic operators and heuristics to gain an understanding of the nature of underlying solution space of the design problem.

Acknowledgment

This work was supported by the Office of Naval Research under contract No. N00014-93-1-0912.

REFERENCES

[1] S.K. Andreadakis and A.H. Levis, Synthesis of distributed command and control for the outer air battle, *Proc. 1988 Symposium on Command and Control Research*, pp. 352–364. Science Applications International Corporation, McLean, VA, 1988.

[2] K.L. Boettcher and A.H. Levis, Modeling the interacting decisionmaker with bounded rationality, *IEEE Trans. Systems, Man, and Cybernetics*, Vol. SMC-12, No. 3, 1982.

[3] B.P. Buckles and F.E. Petry, *Genetic Algorithms*, IEEE Computer Society Press, Los Alamitos, CA, 1992.

[4] A.B. Conru, A genetic approach to the cable harness routing problem, in *Proc. 1st IEEE Conf. Evolutionary Computation, Orlando, FL*, 1994.

[5] K.A. Dejong, *Analysis of the behavior of a class of genetic adaptive systems*, PhD Dissertation, Department of Computer Science, University of Michigan, Ann Arbor, 1975.

[6] J.J. Demaël and A.H. Levis, On the generation of a variable structure airport surface traffic control system, *Proc. 1990 IFAC World Congress*, Pergamon Press, Oxford, 1990.

[7] J.J. Demaël, On the generation of variable structure distributed architectures, *MIT Report LIDS-TH-1869*, 1989.

[8] J.J. Demaël and A.H. Levis, On generating variable structure architectures for decision-making systems, in *Information and Decision Technologies, 19*, pp. 233–255. Elsevier Science, Amsterdam, 1994.

[9] D.E. Goldberg, *Genetic Algorithms in Search, Optimization and Machine Learning*. Addison-Wesley, Reading, MA, 1989.

[10] J.H. Holland, *Adaptation in Natural and Artificial Systems*. University of Michigan Press, Ann Arbor, 1975.

[11] H. Iba, T. Kurita, H. deGaris, and T. Sato, System identification using structured genetic algorithms, in *Proc. 5th Int. Conf. Genetic Algorithms, Urbana-Champaign, IL*, 1993.

[12] K. Jensen, *Coloured Petri Nets*, 1. Springer-Verlag, Berlin, 1992.

[13] K. Kargupta and R.E. Smith, System identification with evolving polynomial networks, in *Proc. 4th Int. Conf. Genetic Algorithms, San Diego, CA*, 1991.

[14] K. Kristinnson and G.A. Dumont, System identification and control using genetic algorithms, *IEEE Trans. Systems, Man, and Cybernetics*, Vol. 22, No. 5, pp. 1033–1046, 1992.

[15] L. Davis, *Handbook of Genetic Algorithms*. Van Nostrand Reinhold, New York, 1991.

[16] A.H. Levis, A colored Petri net model of intelligent nodes, in J.C. Gentina and S.G. Tzafestas (eds.), *Robotics and Flexible Manufacturing Systems*. Elsevier Science, Amsterdam, 1992.

[17] A.H. Levis, N. Moray, and Hu Baosheng, Task allocation models and discrete event systems, *Automatica*, Vol. 29, 1993.

[18] Z. Lu and A.H. Levis, Coordination in distributed intelligence systems, *Proc. 1992 IEEE Int. Conf. Systems, Man, and Cybernetics, Chicago, IL*, pp. 668–673. IEEE Press, New York, 1992.

[19] M.D. Mesarovic, D. Macko, and Y. Takahara, *Theory of Hierarchical, Multilevel Systems*. Academic Press, New York, 1970.

[20] M. Minsky, *The Society of Mind*. Simon and Schuster, New York, 1986.

[21] J.M. Monguillet and A.H. Levis, Modeling and evaluation of command, control, and communications, in *Progress in Astronautics and Aeronautics*, Vol. 156. AIAA, Washington DC.

[22] S. Pierre and G. Legault, A genetic algorithm for designing distributed computer network topologies, *IEEE Trans. SMC, Part B: Cybernetics*, Vol. 28, No. X, pp. 249–258, 1998.

[23] P.A. Remy and A.H. Levis, On the generation of organizational architectures using Petri Nets, in G. Rozenberg (ed.) *Advances in Petri Nets 1988*, pp. 371–385. Springer-Verlag, Berlin, 1988.

[24] P.A. Remy, *On the generation of organizational architectures using Petri nets*, Report LIDS-TH-1630, Lab for Information and Decision Systems, MIT, Cambridge, MA, 1986.

[25] S. Uckun, S. Bagchi, and K. Kawamura, Managing genetic search in job shop scheduling, *IEEE Expert*, Vol. 8, No. 5, pp. 15–24, 1993.

[26] A.K. Zaidi and A.H. Levis, Algorithmic design of distributed intelligence system architectures, in M.M. Gupta and N.K. Sinha (eds.), *Intelligent Control Systems: Theory and Practice*. IEEE Press, New York, 1994.

[27] A.K. Zaidi and A.H. Levis, On generating distributed intelligence systems architectures using genetic algorithms, *IEEE Trans. Systems, Man, and Cybernetics*, Vol. 28, No. 3, pp. 453–459, 1998.

[28] D. Park and A. Kandel, Genetic-based new fuzzy reasoning models with application to fuzzy control, *IEEE Trans. Systems, Man, and Cybernetics*, Vol. 24, No. 1, pp. 39–47, 1994.

[29] D.A. Stabile and A.H. Levis, The design of information structures: Basic allocation strategies for organizations, *Large Scale Systems*, Vol. 6, pp. 123–132, 1984.

CHAPTER 6

Evolutionary Algorithms and Neural Networks

R.G.S. ASTHANA

Business Standard Ltd., 5 BSZ Marg, New Delhi 110 002, India

1   INTRODUCTION

Discovering relationships between sets of data has always been a very active research problem. Statistical methods were developed as valuable tools to find relationships of observed facts. These methods are based on assumptions such as that the data are normally distributed, that the equation relating the data is of a specific form (e.g. linear, quadratic or polynomial), and that the variables are independent. However, real-life problems seldom meet these criteria. Artificial neural networks (ANNs) are not limited by these assumptions and serve as strong predictive models. An ANN can uncover complex relationships but provides little insight into the underlying mechanisms that describe the relationship. Evolutionary algorithms are not only robust methods of exploring complex solution spaces, but also provide some insight into revealing the mechanisms relating data items.

While neural networks are metaphorically based on learning processes in individual organisms, evolutionary algorithms (EAs) are inspired by evolutionary change in populations of individuals. Relative to neural nets, evolutionary algorithms have only recently gained wide acceptance in academic and industrial circles. Evolutionary algorithms describe computer-based problem solving techniques that use computational models of some of the known mechanisms of evolution as key elements in their design and implementation. EAs maintain a population of structures that evolve according to rules of selection and through use of operators, which are referred to as "search" or "genetic operators," such as recombination and mutation. A measure of fitness in the environment is assigned to each individual in the population. Reproduction focuses attention on high-fitness individuals, thus exploiting the available fitness information. Recombination and mutation perturb those individuals, providing general heuristics for exploration.

The performance of ANN is critically dependent on factors such as the choice of primitives (neurons), network architectures and the learning algorithm used. The learning phase of an ANN involves the search for a suitable setting of weights, which are adjusted within a-priori specified network topology under guidance from training samples in a specified problem environment. Although one may obtain suitable settings for the parameters of the network, the capability of the resulting network to generalize on data not encountered during training, or the cost of the hardware realization and use of the network may be far from optimal. In addition, lack of sound design principles in the development of large-scale ANNs presents further difficulty for a variety of real-life problems.

This has led researchers to develop techniques for automating the design of neural architectures to solve specific problems under given design and performance constraints. The combination of ANNs and evolutionary techniques offers an attractive approach to solving complex problems where neither the detailed structure nor the size of the solution is known in advance. The evolutionary algorithm introduces changes in the topology of an ANN one step at a time and measures the performance of the network in terms of reduced errors and improved training times. The changes introduced in the network topology include aspects such as connectivity, number of layers in the network, and so on. Topology changes that result in improved performance are retained and others are discarded. Hence, an ANN can be forced to grow and perform a set of specified tasks better.

ANNs offer an attractive paradigm for the design and analysis of adaptive intelligent systems. Wide ranges of applications in artificial intelligence and cognitive modeling [2, 4, 5, 32, 42] using ANNs have been developed. These include 2- and 3-dimensional visual pattern recognition and classification, motion detection, speech recognition, language processing, signal detection, inductive and deductive inference, financial forecasting, adaptive control, planning, robotics, potential for massively parallel computation, robustness in the presence of noise, resilience to the failure of components, amenability to adaptation, and learning by the modification of computational structures. EAs [48], together with ANNs, offer an attractive and relatively efficient, randomized opportunistic approach to searching for near-optimal solutions in a variety of problem domains.

In this chapter, we give a brief review of the evolutionary algorithm followed by evolutionary design of neural networks. A few applications of EAs and combinations of EAs and neural networks are also described.

2 BRIEF REVIEW OF EVOLUTIONARY ALGORITHMS

The term EA covers topics such as genetic algorithms (GAs), evolutionary programming (EP), evolution strategies (ES), classifier systems (CS), and genetic programming (GP). EAs are iterative. Iteration is also referred to as a "generation." The basic EA begins with a population of randomly chosen individuals. In each generation, the individuals "compete' among themselves to solve a given problem. Individuals that perform better are more likely to "survive" to the next generation. Those surviving to the next generation may be subject to small, random modifications. If the algorithm is properly set up, the quality of the solutions contained in the population improves as the iteration progresses.

As in the case of neural nets, EAs vary widely in their degree of biological realism. There are wide ranges of implementation details, which can have a profound effect on the outcome. While the theory to explain the behavior of evolutionary algorithms exists, it is far from complete. EAs, therefore, are loosely modeled on processes that appear to be at work in biological evolution and working of the immune system. Evolution is determined by natural selection process, that is, each individual competes for resources in a specified environment. Individuals who are better than others are more likely to survive and propagate their genetic material.

The encoding for genetic information (the genome) is done in nature in a way that admits asexual reproduction—resulting in offspring that are genetically identical to the parent (e.g. in bacteria). The sexual reproduction process allows the exchange of pieces of genetic information between chromosomes, producing offspring that contain a combination of information from each parent. This operation is called recombination or crossover because of the way that biologists have observed strands of chromosome crossing over during the exchange.

In the recombination approach, the selection of who gets to mate is largely a function of the fitness of the individual. Luck (or random effect) often plays a major role in the selection. EAs use either a simple function of the fitness measure to select individuals for genetic operations such as crossover/asexual reproduction (a case in which the propagation of genetic material remains unaltered) or a model in which certain randomly selected individuals in a subgroup compete and the fittest is selected. This is called tournament selection.

Genotypes are binary strings of some fixed length (say n) that code for points in an n-dimensional Boolean search space [30] in a simple EA. A population of genotypes can be seen as elements of a high-dimensional search space or as an arrangement of genes represented as strings, where each gene takes on values from a suitably defined domain of values (also known as alleles). A simple crossover operator is defined as follows. Let $A = a_1, a_2, \ldots, a_n$ and $B = b_1, b_2, \ldots, b_n$ be genotypes from the population $P(t)$. Select at random a number x from $1, 2, \ldots, n - 1$. The two genotypes are formed from A and B by exchanging sets of alleles to the right of position of x, yielding $A_{\text{new}} = a_1, a_2, \ldots, a_x, b_{x+1}, b_2, \ldots, b_n$ and $B_{\text{new}} = a_1, a_2, \ldots, a_x, \ldots, b_{x+1}, b_2, \ldots, b_n$.

Crossover is performed with probability $pcross$ (a common value is 0.7) between parents (two selected individuals). Parents exchange parts of their genomes (i.e., encoding) to form two new individuals called offspring. In its simplest form, substrings are exchanged after randomly selected crossover point. The evolutionary process assisted by crossover operation moves toward "promising" regions of the search space.

The crossover operator is able to generate all possible values of the genotypes even if the population contains only one cope of a specific allele value. However, as the GA proceeds to generate new genotypes, it is always possible to lose the last copy of an allele value. With the second operator, called mutation, we prevent the population of genotypes from losing a specific value of an allele. This operator is an "insurance" against the loss of information inside a population of genotypes.

The mutation operator prevents premature convergence to local optima by randomly sampling new points in the search space. It is carried out by flipping bits at random, with some probability $pmut$.

Nature introduces diversity through mutation. In EAs, it is achieved by randomizing the genes in the population. A pseudo code for EAs is given below:

```
begin EA
    t := 0 {/initial time at the start of the EA/}
    Initialize population P(t)
    Evaluate population P(t) {/i.e., compute fitness of all initial individuals in population/}
    while not done do
        t := t + 1
        Select P(t) from P(t − 1) {/select sub-population for offspring production/}
    Crossover P(t)
    Mutate P(t)
    Evaluate P(t)
    end while
end EA
```

2.1 Genetic Algorithms (GA)

The most popular evolutionary algorithm is the genetic algorithm of J. Holland [28, 38]. GA is an iterative procedure and its starting condition is a large set of random strings called genes or the genome. The genes are linear arrays of numbers. Each number represents an aspect of the system to which the algorithm is being applied; for example, if we are dealing with neural network topology, then one of the numbers could represent the number of layers in a particular network.

When the algorithm is run, each of the networks represented by the population of genes is tested and graded according to its performance. The genes are then copied with a probability that is larger if their performance was greater. That is, the genes that produce a network with poor performance are less likely to get copied; those with good performance are more likely to get copied. The copying process therefore produces a population that has a large number of better-performing genes.

Having completed the copying process, the genes are then "bred" by crossing over some of the numbers in the arrays at random points. A small random change called a "mutation" is introduced to add some diversity. The whole process is then repeated.

Each genome or gene encodes a possible solution in a given problem space—referred to as the search space. This space comprises all possible solutions to the problem at hand. The symbol alphabet used is often binary but this has been extended in recent years to include character-based encodings, real-valued encodings, and tree representations.

The following steps are required to define a basic GA:

1. Create a population of random individuals (e.g., a mapping from the set of parameter values into the set of (0-1) such that each individual represents a possible solution to the problem at hand.

2. Compute each individual fitness, i.e., its ability to solve a given problem. This involves finding a mapping from bit strings into the reals, the so-called fitness function.

3. Select individual population members to be parents. One of the simplest selection procedure is the fitness-proportionate selection, where individuals are selected with a probability proportional to their relative fitness. This ensures that the expected number of times an individual is chosen is approximately proportional to its relative performance in the population. Thus, high-fitness individuals stand a better chance of "reproducing," while low-fitness ones are more likely to disappear.

4. Produce children by recombining patent material via crossover and mutation and add them to the population.

5. Evaluate the children's fitness.

6. Repeat step (3) to (5) until a solution with required fitness criteria is obtained.

Selection alone cannot introduce any new individuals into the population. Genetically inspired operators such as crossover and mutation are used to find new points in the search space. The most important genetic operator is the crossover operator. As in biological systems, the crossover process yields recombination of alleles via exchange of segments between pairs of genotypes. Genetic algorithms are stochastic iterative processes that are not guaranteed to converge. The termination condition may be specified either as some fixed, maximal number of generations, or on reaching a predefined acceptable fitness level.

So-called premature convergence is a problem often discovered in small population GAs. It arises from the fact that at the beginning there may be some extraordinary genotypes in a population of mediocre others. In the first couple of generations these genotypes take over a huge part of the population before the crossover operator is able to construct a more diverse set of good genotypes.

This leading cause of premature convergences can be avoided by fitness scaling. With this method, the few extraordinary genotypes are scaled down, while the lowly members of the population get scaled up.

The genetic algorithm is widely used in practical contexts [17, 18] such as financial forecasting and management science.

EXAMPLE [31, 50]
A simple example is given. The parameters are:

- *Population*:   4 individuals (Typical number is 50 to 1000)
- *Representation*: Binary-encoded strings (genomes) of length 8
- *Fitness value*:   Equals the number of ones in the bit string, with $pcross = 0.7$, and $pmut = 0.001$.

The initial (randomly generated) population might look like this:

Label	Genome	Fitness
A	00000110	2
B	11101110	6
C	00100000	1
D	00110100	3

- *Selection*: Choose 4 individuals or two sets of parents $\{B, D\}$ and $\{B, C\}$, with probabilities proportional to their fitness values. Selection was probabilistic so A was not selected.

- Crossover is effected between the selected parents with probability say, *pcross*, resulting in two offspring. If the crossover is not done, then the offspring will be exact copies of each parent. Let us assume that crossover takes place between parents B and D at the (randomly chosen) first bit position, forming offspring $E = 10110100$ and $F = 01101110$. No crossover is effected between parents B and C, forming offspring that are exact copies of B and C.

- *Mutation*: Each offspring is subjected to mutation with probability *pmut* per bit. Offspring E is mutated at the sixth position to form $E' = 10110000$, offspring B is mutated at the first bit position to form $B' = 01101110$, and offspring F and C are not mutated at all.

- *Next generation population*: The above operators of selection, crossover, and mutation create the next generation. The result is

Label	Genome	Fitness
E'	10110000	3
F	01101110	5
C	00100000	1
B'	01101110	5

Although in the new population the best individual with fitness 6 has been lost, the average fitness has been increased. Iterating this procedure, the genetic algorithm finds a perfect string, that is, with maximal fitness value of 8.

2.2 Single Gene Methods [41]

A single linear array is used in this method. As in the case of a GA, each number in the array represents a property of the network. For example, an ANN an array with four numbers is *a b c d* where *a* is a number representing the number of layers in the network, *b* represents the number of neurons, *c* represents the connectivity, and so on.

Mutation is introduced by picking one of the numbers at random. Two new values (at random) are taken, one being slightly above the original number and the other one slightly below, and two new genes are produced. These new genes are tested against the original gene and the best combination of numbers is kept. This process is repeated and so the numbers in the gene eventually converge to an optimum solution [5, 6].

This procedure might be thought of in terms of biology as a mutation producing a whole new species of animal, whereas a GA is a population of animals producing the fittest provided the range of the GA is not too large. A single gene and the GA approach can be combined in the same evolutionary algorithm in such a way that the single gene produces gross changes and the GA fine tunes the system.

2.2.1 Improving the Single Gene Approach. It was found that algorithm can converge faster if the network that produced the greatest changes in training times is prioritized. For example, if the quantum of change in the training times is higher then it is preferable to first change the number of neurons in a given layer. Attempts to change the bias of the network should be done later. Application of such strategies reduces search times for an optimal solution by one-third.

2.3 Evolutionary Programming (EP) [25, 26]

This is a stochastic optimization strategy similar to genetic algorithms. It places emphasis on the behavioral linkage between parents and their offspring, rather than seeking to emulate specific genetic operators as observed in nature. Evolutionary programming is similar to evolution strategies. Like both the ESs and GAs, EP is a useful method of optimization when other techniques such as gradient descent or direct analytical discovery are not possible. Combinatoric and real-valued function optimization, in which the optimization surface or fitness landscape is "rugged," possessing many locally optimal solutions, are well suited for evolutionary programming.

For EP, a fitness criterion can be characterized in terms of variables, for which an optimum solution exists in terms of these variables. For example, to find the shortest path in a Traveling Salesman problem, each solution would be a path. The length of the path (say, from location *a* to location *b*) can be expressed as a number, which in turn would serve as the fitness criteria for the solution. The fitness criteria for this problem could be characterized as a hypersurface proportional to the path lengths in a space of possible paths. The goal would be to find the globally shortest path in that space or, more practically, to find very short tours very quickly. The basic EP method involves three steps (repeated until a threshold for iteration is exceeded, or an adequate solution is obtained):

1. Choose an initial "population" of trial solutions at random. The number of solutions in a population is highly relevant to the speed of optimization, but no definite answers are available as to how many solutions are appropriate (other than > 1) and how many solutions are wasteful.

2. Each solution is replicated into a new population. Each of these offspring solutions is mutated.

3. Each offspring solution is assessed by computing its fitness. Typically, a stochastic tournament is held to determine N solutions to be retained for the population of solutions, although this is occasionally performed deterministically. The population size need not be held constant and more than one offspring can be generated from each parent.

Genetic programming and evolutionary programming are compared in Table 1 based on representation, extent of use of genetic operators, and optimization strategy.

Evolutionary strategy and evolutionary programming are compared in Table 2 based on selection and recombination strategies.

A pseudo-code for EP is given below:

```
begin EP
    t := 0                    {start with an initial time}
    Initialize population P(t) {initialize a usually random population of individuals}
```

Table 1 Differences between GA and EP

Item	Genetic algorithm (GA)	Evolutionary programming (EP)
Representation	No constraint (see note 1)	Follows from the problem (see note 2)
Genetic operators	No constraint in using crossover	Typically does not use any crossover
Mutation	Simple mutation used	Ranges from minor to extreme (see note 3)
Optimization strategy	Gradient descent or direct analytical discovery	Used where GA fails

1. The typical GA approach involves encoding the problem solutions as a string of representative tokens, the GENOME.
2. A neural network can be represented in the same manner as it is implemented, for example, because the mutation operation does not demand a linear encoding. In this case, for a fixed topology, real-valued weights could be coded directly. Mutation operates by perturbing a weight vector with a zero mean multivariate Gaussian perturbation. For variable topologies, the architecture is also perturbed, often using Poisson-distributed additions and deletions.
3. The mutation operation changes aspects of the solution according to a statistical distribution, which introduces minor variations in the behavior of the offspring. Further, the severity of mutations is often reduced as the global optimum is approached. The "meta-evolutionary" technique is commonly used in which the variance of the mutation distribution is subject to mutation by a fixed-variance mutation operator and evolves along with the solution.

Table 2 Main Differences between ES and EP

Item	Evolutionary programming (EP)	Evolution strategy (ES)
Selection	Uses stochastic selection via a tournament (see note 1)	Uses deterministic selection (see note 2)
Recombination	Not used as recombination does not occur between species (see note 3)	Used in many forms (see note 4)

1. Each trial solution in the population faces competition from a preselected number of opponents and receives a "win" if it is at least as good as its opponent in each encounter. Selection then eliminates those solutions with the least wins.
2. The worst solutions are purged from the population based directly on their function evaluation.
3. EP is an abstraction of evolution at the level of reproductive populations, also referred to as *species*.
4. ES is an abstraction of evolution at the level of individual behavior. When self-adaptive information is incorporated this is purely genetic information (as opposed to phenotypic).

Evaluate population $P(t)$ {compute fitness of all initial individuals in population}
                               {/test for termination criterion time, fitness, etc./}
while not done do
    $t := t + 1$
    Select $P(t)$ from $P(t-1)$ {/stochastically select the survivors from actual fitness/}
    Mutate $P(t)$
    Evaluate $P(t)$ {/evaluate its new fitness/}
end while
end EP

2.4 Evolution Strategy (ES) [45]

Until recently, ESs were only used by civil engineers to solve technical optimization problems as an alternative to standard solutions. Usually no closed form analytical objective function is available for technical optimization problems and, hence, no applicable optimization method exists but the engineer's intuition.

In a two-membered or $(1 + 1)$ ES, one parent generates one offspring per generation by applying normally distributed mutations, that is, smaller steps are more likely than big ones, until a child performs better than its ancestor and takes its place. Because of this simple structure, theoretical results for step-size control and convergence velocity can be derived. The ratio between successful and all mutations should come to 1/5—the so-called 1/5 success rule. This first algorithm using mutation only, has then been enhanced to an $(m + 1)$ strategy, which incorporated recombination due to several (i.e. m) parents being available. The mutation scheme and the exogenous step-size control were taken across unchanged from $(1 + 1)$.

Schwefel [57] later generalized these strategies to the multimembered ES, now denoted by $(m + 1)$ and $(m, 1)$, which imitates the following basic principles of organic evolution: a population leading to the possibility of recombination with random mating, mutation, and selection. These strategies are termed the Plus Strategy and the Comma strategy, respectively:

- In the Plus case, the parental generation is taken into account during selection.
- In the Comma case, only the offspring undergoes selection, as the parents die off.

Self-adaptation within ESs depends on the following agents:

- *Randomness*: Mutation cannot be modeled as a purely random process. This would mean that a child is completely independent of its parents.
- *Population size*: The population has to be sufficiently large. Both the current best as well as a set of good individuals should be permitted to reproduce.
- *Cooperation*: In order to exploit the effects of a population ($m > 1$), the individuals should recombine their knowledge with that of others (cooperate), because one cannot expect knowledge to accumulate only in the best individuals.
- *Deterioration*: In order to allow better internal models to evolve (step size), and to ensure progress in the future, one should accept deterioration from one generation to the next. A limited life span in nature is not a sign of failure but an important means of preventing a species from "freezing" genetically.

The main features of the ES are:

- It is adaptable to nearly all sorts of problems in optimization because they need very little information about the problem, especially no derivatives of the objective function.
- It is capable of solving high-dimensional, multimodel, nonlinear problems subject to linear and/or nonlinear constraints.
- The objective function can be the result of a simulation. It does not have to be given in a closed form. This also holds for the constraints, which may represent the outcome of, e.g., a finite elements method.
- It can be adapted to vector optimization problems [45]. They can also serve as a heuristic for NP-complete combinatorial problems like the Traveling Salesman problem, or problems with a noisy or changing response surface.

2.5   Classifier Systems

Cognitive models [10, 30] were initially referred to as "classifier systems" or CSs, and sometimes as CFS. A reinforcement component was added to the overall design of a CFS that emphasized its ability to learn. Thus, the name became "learning classifier systems" (LCSs). LCSs are also called "evolutionary reinforcement learning or ERL.

A classifier system is a set of decision rules, each endowed with a weight that determines the probability with which a rule applicable to the current environment situation is activated. The characteristic learning rule uses a credit assignment process by which the weights of the rules are updated as a function of the payoff they yield. The first learning task in a CS is to modify the strength of the classifiers as the CS accumulates experience. This credit-apportionment is tackled with a bucket brigade algorithm. The second learning task is to generate plausible new classifiers (a set of rules). The task is carried out by GA. Using classifiers as genotypes and their respective strength as fitness parameter, it generates new classifiers to be tested under the bucket brigade algorithm.

Much work is being done on intelligence through dynamic modeling of simple creatures (animat = animal + robot) that satisfy their needs in semirealistic simulated environments, thus requiring adaptiveness, generalization, and learning. One part of the research concerns evolution of wired-in adaptive behavior in populations of animals in response to physical characteristics in the environment (e.g., food availability). The other part concerns learning of adaptive behaviors by animals during their lifetime so as to maximize success at obtaining food expeditiously and avoiding dangers. Work is also done at the borderline between evolution and learning and this is often regarded as "artificial life" rather than evolutionary computation.

A CS obtains its information from an outside world by means of its detector and has a number of effectors that are used to select system action. The outside world is represented as an environmental object to be modified by application. An animat studied extensively by Wilson [65] is a good example to describe CS. An animat lives in a digital microcosm and is incarnated into the real world in the form of an autonomous robot vehicle with sensors/detectors (camera eyes, whiskers, etc.) and effectors (wheels, robot arms, etc.). A LCS algorithm acts as the "brain" of this vehicle, connecting the hardware parts with the software learning component.

The animat world is an artificially created digital world; for example, in Booker's Gofer system, a 2-dimensional grid that contains "food" and "poison" and the Gofer itself, which walks across this grid and tries to learn to distinguish between these two items, and survive well fed. Imagine a very simple animat: A simplified model of a frog, called "Kermit" living in little ponds—the environment—and having Eyes (i.e., sensorial input detectors) and Hands and legs (i.e. environment-manipulating effectors), which is a spicy-fly-detecting-and-eating device.

A single "if–then" rule can be referred to as a "classifier" and encoded into binary strings. Similarly, a set of classifiers (rules) is called a "classifier population" and is used to GA-generate new classifiers from the current population. A CFS starts from scratch, that is, without any knowledge, using a randomly generated classifier population, and we let the system learn its program by induction [40]. This reduces the input stream to recurrent input patterns that must be repeated over and over again to enable the animat to classify its current situation/context and react on events appropriately.

Kermit lives in its digital microwilderness where it moves randomly. Whenever a small flying object appears that has no stripes, Kermit should eat it because it is very likely a spicy fly, or other flying insect. If the insect has stripes (possibly a wasp, hornet, or bee), then Kermit should leave it. If Kermit encounters a large, looming object, it immediately uses its effectors to jump away as far as possible. So, part of these behavior patterns within a specified virtual environment, in this case "pond," are referred to as a "frame" in AI. This knowledge can be represented in a set of "if <condition> then <action>" rules as given in the second column of Table 4.

The set of rules for this virtual world is encoded for use within a CS. A possible encoding of the above rule set is CFS-C (Riolo) terminology (see Table 3). The encoded rules are given in the third column of Table 4. In CFS-C terminology rules are encoded as follows:

- NAND (/AND followed by NOT) operation is denoted by the '~' prefix character (see rule #5).
- Bits 1–4, i.e. pattern "0000" denotes small, and the pattern "00" in the first part of the second column (bits 5 and 6) denotes flying. The last two bits 7 and 8 of column #2 encode the direction of the object approaching, where "00" means left, "01" means right, etc.
- In rule #4 a "don't care" symbol "#" is used that matches "1" and "0". In other words, the position of the large, looming object is completely arbitrary: a simple fact that can save Kermit's life.

The following steps are required to convert the previous nonlearning CFS into a learning CS or LCS [40]:

Table 3   Knowledge Representation of Classifier System

Rule #	Knowledge represented as if <condition> then <action> rules	CFS-C (Riolo) terminology	
		IF	THEN
1	IF small, flying object to the left THEN send @	0000, 00	00 00 00
2	IF small, flying object to the right THEN send %	0000, 00	01 00 01
3	IF small, flying object centered THEN send $	0000, 00	10 00 10
4	IF large, looming object THEN send !	1111, 01	## 11 11
5	IF not large, looming object THEN send *	~1111, 01	## 10 00
6	IF * and @ THEN move head 15 degrees left	1000, 00	00 01 00
7	IF * and % THEN move head 15 degrees right	1000, 00	01 01 01
8	IF * and $ THEN move in direction head pointing	1000, 00	10 01 10
9	IF ! THEN move rapidly away from direction head pointing	1111, ##	## 01 11

Table 4   Nonlearning and Learning CFS

Algorithm	Nonlearning CFS	Learning CFS
Start	begin CFS	begin LCS
Initialize time	$t = 0$	$t = 0$
Initially empty message list	initMessageList ML (t);	initMessageList ML (t);
Randomly created population of classifiers	initClassifierPopulation $P(t)$;	initClassifierPopulation $P(t)$;
Test for cycle termination criterion (time, fitness, etc.) increase the time counter	while not done do $t = t + 1$;	while not done do $t = t + 1$;
1. Detectors check whether input messages are present	ML = readDetectors (t);	ML = readDetectors (t);
2. Compare ML to the classifiers and save matches	ML' = matchClassifiers ML,$P(t)$;	ML' = matchClassifiers ML,$P(t)$;
LCS: highest bidding classifier(s) collected in ML' wins the "race" and post the(ir) message(s)		ML' = selectMatchingClassifiers ML',$P(t)$;
LCS: tax bidding classifiers, reduce their strength		ML' = taxClassifiers ML',$P(t)$;
LCS: effectors check new message list for output msgs		ML: = sendEffectors ML' (t);
LCS: receive payoff from environment (reinforcement)		C: = receivePayoff (t);
LCS: distribute payoff/credit to classifiers		P' = distributeCredit C, $P(t)$;
LCS: Eventually (depending on t), a GA is applied to the classifier population		if criterion then P: = generateNewRules $P'(t)$; else P: = P'
CS: process new messages through output interface	ML = sendEffectors ML' (t);	
Iterate	end while	end while
end CFS		end LCS

Step 1: The major cycle has to be changed such that the activation of each classifier depends on some additional parameter that can be modified as a result of experience, i.e. reinforcement from the environment; and/or

Step 2: Change the contents of the classifier list, i.e., generate new classifiers/rules by removing, adding, or combining condition/action-parts of existing classifiers.

Table 4 gives (pseudo code both from non-learning and learning CFSs).

2.6   Genetic Programming (GP)

Genetic programming is an automatic programming technique for evolving computer programs that solve (or approximately solve) problems. Starting with thousands of randomly created computer programs, a population of programs is progressively evolved over many generations using for example, the Darwinian principle of survival of the fittest.

Linear GAs (the structure of an individual is a flat bitstring) are adept at developing rule-based systems. They cannot develop equations, GPs can generate symbolic expression and perform symbolic regressions to the limited extent of modifying structure of the expression but not its contents. In GP [43, 44, 64], the genome, can be represented by a LISP expression. Thus, the evolution is through computer programs, rather than bit strings as in the case of the usual genetic algorithm. Therefore, the objects that constitute the population are not fixed-length character strings that encode possible solutions to the problem but are programs that, when executed, become the candidate solutions to the problem. In GP these programs are called parse trees and not lines of code. Thus, for example, the simple program "$a + b * c$" would be represented as parse tree:

$$
\begin{array}{c}
+ \\
/ \quad \backslash \\
a \quad\quad * \\
/ \quad\quad \backslash \\
b \quad\quad c
\end{array}
$$

or as suitable data structures linked together to achieve this effect. GP methods can be implemented using either a LISP or a non-LISP programming environment.

The programs in the population are composed of elements from the function set and the terminal set, which are typically fixed sets of symbols selected to be appropriate to the solution of problems in the domain of interest.

In GP, the crossover operation is implemented by taking randomly selected subtrees in the individuals (selected according to fitness) and exchanging them. GP does not, usually, exercise any mutation as a genetic operator.

3   EVOLUTIONARY DESIGN OF NEURAL ARCHITECTURES

The key processes in this approach to the design of neural architectures [2, 3, 7–9, 11, 14, 29, 33, 39, 55, 62, 63] are depicted in Figure 1.

In a simple genetic algorithm. genotypes are binary strings of some fixed length (say n) that code for points in an n-dimensional Boolean search space. Each genotype may encode for typically one, but possibly a set of phenotypes or candidate solutions in the domain of interests, for example, a class of neural architectures. The encodings employ genes that taken on numeric values or complex symbol structures. The next step is to develop decoding processes to map these structures into phenotypes (in this case ANNs), which may also be equipped with learning algorithms that train it using environmental stimuli. For example, the weights of the network may also be derived by the encoding/decoding mechanism. This evaluation of a phenotype computes the fitness of the corresponding genotype.

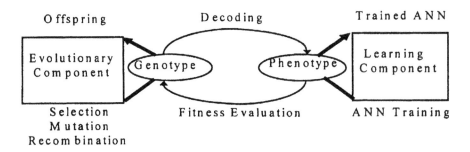

FIGURE 1
Evolutionary design of neural architectures.

The EA operates on the population of such genotypes, and selects genotypes that code for high-fitness phenotypes and reproduces them. Genetic operators, such as mutation, crossover, and inversion are used to introduce variety into the population. Thus, operating over several generations, a population gradually evolves toward genotypes that correspond to high-fitness phenotypes.

3.1   Genotype Representation

The evolutionary ANN design approach is to develop a scheme to represent or encode a variety of neural architectures as genotypes. This salient aspect determines the classes of neural architectures that could evolve and also constraints the choice and speed of the decoding process. For example, if it is necessary to discover neural networks with recurrent structures, the encoding scheme must be sufficiently flexible to describe recurrent neural architectures, and the decoding mechanism must make it into an appropriate recurrent network (phenotype).

The genotype representations may be broadly classified into two categories based on the decoding effort that is needed.

- *Direct encoding.* The transformation of the genotype into a phenotype is trivial. An example of such an encoding is a connection matrix (see Figure 2) that precisely and directly, specifies the architecture of the corresponding neural network.
- *Indirect encoding.* The complexity of the procedure required to decode and construct a phenotype varies from problem to problem. An example of such an encoding is one that uses rewrite rules to specify a set of construction rules that are recursively applied to yield the phenotype. Indirect encodings can be grouped into two broad categories:

  (1) Grammatical encodings, e.g., cellular grammars, graph grammars, genetic/biological grammars, geometric grammars etc.
  (2) Others, e.g., the genetic programming paradigm—LISP programs, development models, etc.

Other encoding schemes could be deterministic versus stochastic, hierarchical versus nonhierarchical, modular versus nonmodular, and so on.

3.2   Network Topology or Structure of the Phenotypes

Network topology, or the structure of the phenotype in an evolutionary design system, plays a crucial role in the success of a neural architecture in solving any problem. In the elementary (single layer) perceptron there are no hidden neurons; therefore, it cannot classify input patterns that are not linearly separable. In theory, for an m-class classification problem in which the union of the m distinct classes forms the entire input space, we need a total of m outputs to represent all of the classification decisions. A purely feed-forward neural network cannot discover or respond to temporal dependencies in its environment. A recurrent network is needed for this task. Neural network topologies may be classified into two broad types:

Feed-forward networks: those without feedback loops and all connections pointing in one (direction); and

Recurrent networks [6]: those with feedback connections or loops.

Each of the two basic types of topologies may be further classified as networks that are multilayered, strictly layered, randomly connected, locally connected, sparsely connected, fully connected, regular, irregular, modular, hierarchical, and so on

The choice of the target class of network structures dictates the choice of the genetic representation. This is very much analogous to the choice of the knowledge representation scheme for problem solving using state-space search in artificial intelligence. Thus, the search efficiency can be enhanced by restricting the search space based on a-priori knowledge about the properties of the solution set. Structures are selected based on cost and/or performance considerations with respect to a particular technology. For example, in a VLSI design, preference would be given to locally connected, fault-tolerant, highly modular neural network structures over globally connected nonmodular ones [42].

3.3 Variables of Evolution

Neural architectures are typically specified in terms of the topology (or connectivity pattern), functions computed by the neurons (e.g., threshold, sigmoid) and the connection weights, and/or the learning algorithm used [32]. A more complete description of a neural architecture requires the specification of coordination and control structures and learning structures [42, 46, 52]. Virtually any subset of these variables is a candidate to be operated on by evolutionary processes. For example, a system A might evolve the network connectivity as well as the weights (while maintaining everything else constant), whereas a system B might evolve the connectivity, relying on a perhaps more efficient local search for weights within each network. The time/performance trade-offs for the two systems, on the given problem, will be different, making the choice of variables subjected to evolution, which is an extremely critical factor.

In addition to the network connectivity and the weights, one might evolve a learning algorithm, control or regulatory functions, the functions computed by various neurons, distribution of different types of neurons, relative densities of connections, parameters (and/or processes) governing the decoding of a genotype into a phenotype, and so on.

3.3.1 Back-propagation or Backprop. "Backprop" is short for "back-propagation of error". Strictly speaking, back-propagation refers to the method for computing the error gradient for a feedforward network, a straightforward but elegant application of the chain rule of elementary calculus. By extension, backprop refers to a training method that uses back-propagation to compute the gradient. By further extension, a backprop network is a feedforward network trained by back-propagation.

One of the most widely used supervised training methods for neural nets is the generalized delta rule, the training algorithm that was popularized by Rumelhart et al. [54]. The generalized delta rule (including momentum) is called the "heavy ball method" in the numerical analysis literature. Standard backprop can be used for incremental training (in which the weights are updated after processing each case), but it does not converge to a stationary point on the error surface. To obtain convergence, the learning rate must be slowly reduced. This methodology is called "stochastic approximation."

Another supervised error-correcting learning algorithm realizes a gradient descent in error—the difference of the actual output of the system and a target output. The simple delta rule or the perceptron convergence procedure is used in networks with only one modifiable connection layer. It can be proven to find a solution for all input–output mappings that are realizable in the simpler architecture. The error surface in such networks has only one minimum, and the system moves on this error surface toward this minimum.

This is not true for back-propagation in a network with more than one modifiable connection layer. In a network with a hidden layer or hidden layers of nodes (i.e., nodes that are neither in the input nor in the output layer), the error surface has, in addition to the global minimum also a local minima, and the system can get stuck in such local error minima. In the simpler case—networks with only one modifiable connection layer—the system stays at the minimum.

The connectivity structure is feedforward between the input and the output layers, i.e., connections from the input layer nodes to the hidden layer nodes and from the hidden layer nodes to the output layer nodes. There are no connections backward, e g , from the hidden layer nodes to the input layer nodes. There is also no lateral connectivity within the layers. In addition, connectivity between the layers is total in that sense that each input layer node is connected to each hidden layer node and each hidden layer node is connected to each output layer node. Before learning, the weights of these connections are set to small random values. Back-propagation learning proceeds in the following way:

1. An input pattern is chosen from a set of input patterns. This input pattern determines the activations of the input nodes.
2. Setting of the activations of the input layer nodes is followed by the activation of the forward-propagation phase. The activation values of first the hidden units and then the output units are computed. This is done using a sigmoid activation function.

For batch processing, there is no reason to suffer through the slow convergence and the tedious tuning of learning rates and momenta of the standard backprop. Much of the ANN research literature is devoted to attempts to speed up backprop. However, conventional methods for nonlinear optimization are usually faster and more reliable than any of the "props." It is observed that the topology of the network plays an important role in selecting the learning algorithm as well as the convergence rate.

3.4 Application Domain: An Example [49]

The architecture of a network of n units is represented by a connectivity constraint matrix, C, of dimension $n \times (n + 1)$, with the first n columns specifying the constraints on the connections between the n units, and the final column denoting the constraint on the threshold bias of each unit. Each entry C_{ij} indicates the nature of the constraint on the connection from unit j to unit i, or the constraint on the threshold bias of unit i if $j = n + 1$. The value of C_{ij} can either be "0", denoting the absence, or "1", indicating the presence of a trainable connection between the corresponding units. The genotype is constructed by concatenating the rows of the matrix, to yield a bit-string of length $n \times (n + 1)$ as illustrated in Figure 2. The genetic algorithm maintains a population of such bit strings (each of length $n \times (n \mid 1)$). Each string codes for network architecture. A fitness-proportionate selection scheme chooses parents for reproduction—cross-over swaps rows between parents, while mutation randomly flips bits in the connectivity constraint matrix with some low, predetermined probability.

The architecture encoded by a genotype is first created only by providing connections corresponding to matrix entries of 1. All of the feedback connections are ignored even though they may be specified in the genotype. This system evolves thus on pure feedforward networks. The connections in the network are then set to small random values, and trained using the back-propagation learning rule for a fixed number of iterations. At the end of the learning phase, the total sum squared error E of the network is used as the fitness measure. A higher fitness attribute

Connectivity Constraint Matrix

From neurons	1	2	3	4	5	Bias			
To neurons 1	0	0	0	0	0	0	000000		
2	0	0	0	0	0	0		000000	
3	1	1	0	0	0	1			110001
4	1	1	0	0	0	1			110001
5	0	0	1	1	0	1			001101

Bit - String Genotype   000000000000110001110001001101

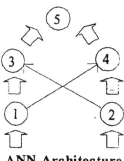

ANN Architecture

FIGURE 2
Evolutionary design of ANN.

for the corresponding genotype is assigned to low values of E as it corresponds to better learning of the task.

This system uses a constraint matrix to specify the network connectivity. The genotype is a simple concatenation of the rows of this matrix. This system uses a direct encoding method and decodes the genotype to construct the phenotype, which, in this case, is a trivial process. Further, feedback connections are ignored by the decoding process. Hence, only networks with feedforward topology are evolved by this system.

In addition, the only variable subjected to evolution is the connectivity (or the topology) of the network. The parameters (connection weights) are determined separately by the back-propagation procedure and are not subject to evolution.

The system was tested on three toy problems—XOR, the four-quadrant problem and the pattern-copying problem—which form its application domain.

3.5 Network Optimization Using Single Gene Technique

It was found that although a pseudo-random search through the gene was effective, a more structured approach of grading the strategies from the most effective to the least effective and applying them in that order produced better results. The effectiveness was estimated by testing how long the network took to train to a preset error target on a character recognition problem.

A survey of the work published in the past on the subject of network topology shows that there are several strategies for growing networks [47]. A fully connected two-layer standard network is used as a reference and growth strategies are described in Table 5.

The following strategies are selected out of those listed in Table 5 for use as other strategies that result in very simple schemes:

Table 5   Growth Strategies for ANNs

Growth strategies	Description	Figure
Reference standard network	Two layer fully connected	3
Change the number of neurons	Neurons in a layer are added or reduced without changing connectivity in that layer	4
Change the connections (network pruning)	Number of connections are increased or decreased	5
Asymmetry	Number of connections in the network may be reduced or increased	6
Sideways connections	In synchronous networks sideways connections can be introduced between neurons in the same layer	7
Skipping layers	Rather than connecting to the layer directly, below a connection may skip a layer. A three-layer network is, therefore, necessary	8
Feedback	Feedback may be added to the network and it may also skip layers	9
Bias units	Bias may be added to the network	10
Sideways growth	A network may add to the neurons in a particular layer by growing sideways	11

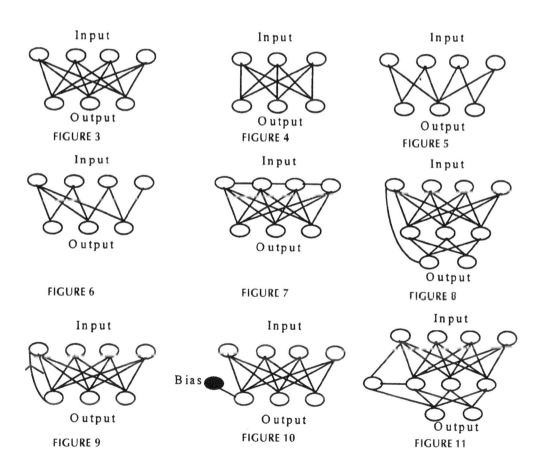

FIGURE 3

FIGURE 4

FIGURE 5

FIGURE 6

FIGURE 7

FIGURE 8

FIGURE 9

FIGURE 10

FIGURE 11

Changing the number of neurons

Changing the connectivity

Adding bias units

Sideways growth

EXAMPLE   CHARACTER RECOGNITION

- *Objective:* To identify the 26 letters of the alphabet.
- *General:* The network was tested on a character recognition problem using a 5×7 pixel grid (matrix). The output layer had a fixed number of 26 neurons, each representing one letter of the alphabet. The network was set up using the matrix handling commands in the MATLAB mathematics software package and trained using the back-propagation algorithm.
- *Figure of merit:* Number of cycles taken for the network to train.
- *The measure of performance:* The number of cycles a back-propagation algorithm takes to train the network to a sum squared error of 0.1 in a character recognition problem.
- *Observation:* As the network gets larger, the performance improves until the network starts to overfit. The network, therefore, has an optimum size for the problem, which we can find by growing it using evolutionary methods (in this case 16 neurons). This method thus represents a powerful means of optimization. Any further alterations to the network after this till result in a degradation of the training times.
- Experiments showed that the general approach worked on a variety of different neural network problems. However, the order in which the strategies were applied changed in the different applications. The pseudo-random nature of weight initialization in a back-propagation matrix means that consecutive runs may take slightly different training times to reach a given error goal. Therefore, the same problem was applied four times to the network to obtain an average answer. Table 6 and Figure 12 show the growth strategies adopted and the result of running the algorithm on a typical character recognition network.
- *Results:* The evolutionary algorithm changes the topology of the neural network one step at a time and measures the performance of the network in terms of reduced error and improved training times. Aspects of the network topology may be changed include connectivity, the number of layers in the network, addition of bias units, and sideways growth (found to be least effective). Alterations to the topology that result in better performance are kept, and the others are discarded. Hence, a network placed in an artificial "environment" can be forced to grow and perform its task better.

Table 6   Growth Strategy and Performance

Strategy	Number of cycles back-propagation takes to train network	Results
An increase in the number of neurons in the top layer of two layer network	Step 1 to 2	See Figure 12
	Step 2 to 3	
An increase in connectivity	Step 3 to 4	
Addition of bias	Step 5 to 6 and Step 6 to 7	Marginal reduction

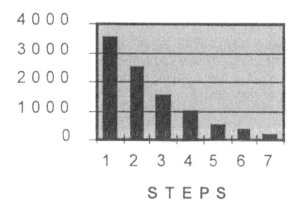

FIGURE 12
Number of cycles back-propagation takes to train network.

4 APPLICATIONS OF EVOLUTIONARY ALGORITHMS (EA)

In principle, EAs can analyze and solve any computable function, that is, do everything a normal digital computer can do. Special-purpose algorithms that have a certain amount of problem domain knowledge hard-coded into them, however, could outperform EAs. EAs are useful tools when there is no other known problem solving strategy and the problem domain is NP-complete. The following sections describe a few EA applications.

4.1 Biocomputing

Biocomputing, or bioinformatics, is the field of biology dedicated to the automatic analysis of experimental data. Several approaches to specific biocomputing problems have been described that involve the use of GA, GP and simulated annealing. There are three main domains in which GAs have been applied to bioinformatics, viz., protein folding, RNA folding, and sequence alignment. General information about software and databases can be found on the server of the European Bioinformatics Institute: http://www.ebi.ac.uk/ebi_home.html.

4.2 Evolvable Hardware (EHW or "E-HARD") [35–37, 56, 58, 60, 61]

This field is developing by using innovations from the evolutionary computation domain as well as from the hardware field. Recently, the term "evolware" has been used by some researchers to describe such evolving ware, with current implementations centering on hardware while raising the possibility of using other forms in the future, such as bioware. A more accurate title might have been "biologically inspired electronics" (bionics).

The concept of the FPGA (field programmable gate array) provides flexibility to the extent that the functioning of the circuit is determined not in the factory but in the field by the user with a "configuration bit string"—a piece of software that instructs the hardware how to configure itself or wire itself up. FPGAs based on static RAM can be written an infinite number of times. An approach toward designing a E-hard could be to configure bit strings as a genetic algorithm chromosome and then to find a pattern of bit strings that generates the "best" circuit in terms of some functional criterion. The best pattern is downloaded into an FPGA. In this approach most of the evolution occurs outside the actual piece of hardware.

Each chromosome would reconfigure the circuit for a GA with a population of P chromosomes, and G generations, the reconfigurable hardware would be rewritten a total of $P \times G$ times. That is, the evolution would occur principally inside the circuit. This inside–outside distinction [20] can be characterized as

Intrinsic E-hard: circuit gets configured for each chromosome for each generation.

Extrinsic E-hard: the evolution is simulated in software, and only the elite chromosome (i.e., the configuring bit string) gets written. Thus, the circuit is configured only once. This process is slower than the intrinsic approach. A hardware description language in the form of trees, which can be evolved GP-style, is also used [30].

Electronics is one of the world's largest industries, involving automobiles, aviation, housing, and oil. With Moore's law of doubling circuit speeds and densities every year or so, electronic circuits are getting so complex that designing them in the traditional "blueprinting" manner is reaching the breaking point. By using a "evolutionary engineering" approach, it is possible to evolve electronic circuits with a complexity beyond human design ability. In the words of de Garis [20]

eventually E-hard will grow into a trillion dollar industry. There is a limit to what is designable. Moore's law will continue right down to one bit per atom, single electron transistors, and the like. It will be totally impractical to design a trillion component electronic devices. It will have to self assemble in an embryological way, but the complexity will be so great that predicting the outcome will be impossible. Hence, the only way left is to test the result. Since the traditional link between structure and function (the basis of traditional electronic design) will be destroyed, the only way to make improvements will be by trial and error, i.e., by random mutation, building/executing the new circuit, and then testing it. If it performs well, it survives. Nature has used this evolutionary engineering technique for billions of years and it produced us.

4.3 Game Playing [26]

A simple game has just two moves, X and Y. The players receive a reward, analogous to Darwinian fitness, depending on which combination of moves occurs and which move they adopted. In complex models, there may be several players and several moves.

The players iterate such a game a number of times, and then move on to a new partner. At the end of all such moves, the players will have a cumulative payoff, their fitness. This fitness can then be used as a means of conducting something akin to roulette-wheel selection to generate a new population.

The real key in using a GA is to develop encodings to represent a player's strategies, one that is amenable to crossover and to mutation. Suppose at each iteration a player adopts X with some probability. A player can thus be represented as a real number or a bit string by interpreting the decimal value of the bit string as the inverse of the probability. If a player adopts a move X with probability $P(X)$ then the probability of move Y is given by $[1 - P(X)]$.

An alternative characterization is to model the players as finite state machines, or finite automata (FA). These can be thought of as a simple flow chart governing the behavior in the "next" play of the game depending upon previous plays. For example:

10 Play X
20 If opponent plays X go to 10
30 Play Y
40 If opponent plays X go to 10 clse go to 30

represents a strategy that does whatever its opponent did last, and begins by playing X, known as "tit-for-tat" (TFT). Such machines can readily be encoded as bit strings. Consider the encoding "101001" to represent TFT. The first three bits "101" are state 0. The first bit, "1", is interpreted as "play X". The second bit, "0", is interpreted as "if opponent plays X go to state 1". The third bit, "1", is interpreted as "if the opponent plays Y, go to state 1". State 1 has a similar interpretation. Crossing over such bit-strings always yields valid strategies.

EA-based commercial games are entering the market, viz., *Galapagos* and *Creatures* from Anark Software and Alife (see http://alife.santafe.edu/alife/www/), respectively.

4.4   Job Shop Scheduling Problem (JSSP) [19, 51]

The job shop scheduling problem is very difficult NP-complete, and branch and bound search techniques are used. GA is used to encode schedules. Research workers have used a variety of encoding schemes. A genome directly encodes the operation completion times instead of binary representation [66], and (ii) genomes represent implicit instructions [21] for building a schedule.

The open shop scheduling problem (OSSP) is similar to the JSSP. Fang et al [21] reported results showing reliable achievement (through use of GA) within less than 0.23% of optimal on moderately large OSSPs (so far, up to 20×20), including an improvement on the previously best known solution for a benchmark 10×10 OSSP. GA has been used successfully to solve the flow shop sequencing problem [53], a simple JSSP.

In contrast to job shop scheduling, some maintenance scheduling problems consider which activities to schedule within a planned maintenance period, rather than seeking to minimize the total time taken by the activities. The constraints on which parts may be taken out of service for maintenance at particular times may be very complex, particularly as they will, in general, interact. Expert systems have been widely used to solve such a problem.

4.5   Artificial Painter (AP)

The AP is a joint Danish–Italian research project between the Institute of Psychology, the National Research Council, Rome, Italy, and the Department of Computer Science, Århus University, Denmark. The AP software uses a GA on ANN. It evolves pictures to be used in artistic design. The evolution of pictures is based on the user's aesthetic evaluation on the number of pictures shown on the screen.

In this environment (a rectangular grid) a number of landmarks are placed, and the network senses the angle and distance of each of the landmarks. The output activity of each single output unit of the ANN is recorded by placing the network in each cell of the environment. Output activity can change due to changes in the angle and distance measures, which act as an input stimuli. To compose the final image each level of output activity is mapped in different colors and shown in a computerized picture in which each pixel is a cell in the environment.

In AP the genotype of each individual (ANN) is represented by a bit string codifying landmark coordinates, neural network weights, the output activation function type (sum, logistic, exponential, trigonometric, etc.), and color mapping (palette of color to map each level of the output to a specific color). Different landmark coordinates give different sensory input, while connection weights provide different activation flows in the ANN.

AP forms a population of individuals. The genotype of each individual is set randomly. Each individual builds a picture, which is shown to the user. According to the genotype, different images will appear. The user selects the most appealing picture. A new generation is formed by cloning each selected picture a fixed number of times (i.e., each picture will have fixed number of children/copies). Each clone is mutated in some randomly chosen parts of the genotype. Mutation alters parameters such as landmark coordinates, connection weights, output activation function type, and color mapping. The selection and cloning process continues until an acceptable picture is obtained.

4.6 Management Sciences

Application of EA in management science and closely related fields such as organizational ecology is a domain that has been covered by some EA researchers with considerable bias toward scheduling problems.

4.7 Nonlinear Filtering

GAs have already been successfully applied to a large class of nonlinear filtering problems found in radar/sonar/GPS signal processing. The new results also point out some natural connections between genetic-type algorithms, information theory, nonlinear filtering theory, and interacting and branching particle systems.

4.8 Timetabling [1, 15, 16]

The first application of GAs to timetabling was to schedule teachers in an Italian high school. At the Department of Artificial Intelligence, University of Edinburgh, UK timetabling of the M.Sc. examinations is now done using a GA [16]. In the examination timetabling case, the fitness function for a genome representing a timetable involves computing degrees of punishment for violating various preferences and avoiding clashes, such as instances of students having to take consecutive examinations, students having three or more examinations in one day, the degree to which heavily-subscribed examinations occur late in the timetable (which makes marking harder), overall length of timetable, and so on. The power of the GA approach is the ease with which it can handle arbitrary kinds of constraints and objectives. All such things can be handled as weighted components of the fitness function, making it easy to adapt the GA to the particular requirements of a very wide range of possible overall objectives.

4.9 Human Motion Modelling [12]

Human motion models are important in virtual reality applications. One approach is to use conceptual-level learning that imitates the way humans learn, i.e., through macro-instructions. The human motion modeling system receives input either as motion or as words from a training person. This information is transformed and stored as fuzzy-based knowledge. A tennis motion system was used in the experiments. A camera was developed that detected the human motion model using indicators on the body of a person playing. Several different tennis strokes such as forehand, backhand, and smash strokes were stored in the system. The strokes from other tennis players were then input to test the recognition robustness. On average, experiments showed correct recognition 84.2% of the time.

4.10   Paper Currency and Document Recognition [13, 27]

GA is adapted to find effective masks for paper currency recognition by using masking characteristic parts of an image. A perceptron neural network does the recognition itself. GA is used to find the optimal position of the masks both to obtain shortened training time and to improve the generalization. Recently, this problem has been dealt with by Glory Ltd., which has developed a neuro-board jointly with the University of Tokushima, Japan. They claim that the use of GA results in a machine ten times faster than conventional recognition machines.

4.11   Railway Bridge Fault Detection

Objective

- To develop methods for the inspection, evaluation, and fault detection of railway bridges.
- To instrument and remotely monitor the bridges.

Method. The passing of a train over the bridge is assumed to constitute a test. The measurements are used to evaluate the state of the bridge and to determine some key damage indices. Currently, the genetic algorithm is being used to determine the parameters of a model of the bridge by minimizing the differences between the model predictions and measurement.

5   FURTHER WORK

It has been observed that when a network becomes too large it starts to overfit and performance drops. Therefore, a different approach is required to tackle problems such as complex image recognition. Preliminary results show that one can use a hierarchical network consisting of several small networks each dedicated to one small task, and each feeding into another network in the layer above that collates the results. Research into the nervous systems of animals indicates that the biological neural structure is organized in this way, with functional areas of the brain having small areas of responsibility. The application of the evolutionary approach to the growth of hierarchical networks is an area with research potential.

Current ANNs use a neuron model of the perceptron. Although this shows good results under some circumstances, the functionality is strictly limited and it is a poor model of a biological neuron, which operates by sending a train of pulses the frequency of which is proportional to their stimulation. However, neurons in the nervous system have widely differing modes of operation and are therefore difficult to simulate. Evolutionary neural networks provide two methods, using (i) a neuron that is capable of producing any mathematical function of its input vector at its output, and (ii) a genetic algorithm to evolve the functionality of the cell itself.

To use evolutionary networks in practical applications, we need also to consider the wiring of the system. Only part of the biological neural network is used for processing. The majority is actually the "wiring" or control system that interfaces the neural network to the outside world. For the artificial neural network to become useful, we must also consider how to interface the network to a similar control system.

6   SUMMARY

Fuzzy logic, neural networks, genetic algorithms, and evolutionary strategies have been treated in parallel for a long time without recognition of the common aspects. Recently, hybrid systems have been developed to unify the advantages of these different strategies. Accepting the advantages of hybrid approaches, nowadays these systems are treated as integral parts of computational intelligence.

The process of evolution and natural selection has developed the biological brain from a simple bundle of cells into the nervous system of the higher species. The development of artificial evolutionary techniques has paved the way for the application of similar methods to ANNs, with excellent results in some specific application areas, but they have not lived up to the initial promise of a realistic simulation of the biological brain.

In this chapter, the current status of evolutionary approaches to the design of neural architectures has been presented. There is a need, however, to develop sound scientific principles to guide the development and application of evolutionary techniques in the design of artificial neural architectures given a variety of design and performance constraints for specific classes of problems.

REFERENCES

[1] Abramsson and Abela, '*A Parallel Genetic Algorithm for Solving the School Timetabling Problem*', Technical Report, Division of I.T., C.S.I.R.O, c/o Dept. of Communication and Electronic Engineering, Royal Melbourne Institute of Technology, PO POX 2476V, Melbourne 3001, Australia, April, 1991.

[2] *Advances in Fuzzy Logic, Neural Networks, and Genetic Algorithms*, IEEE/Nagoya-University World Wisepersons Workshop, Nagoya, Japan, August 9–10, 1994.

[3] E. Alba, J.F. Aldana, and J.M. Troya, Genetic algorithms as heuristics for optimizing ANN design, in R.F. Albrecht, C.R. Reeves, and N.C. Steele (eds.) *Proc. Int. Conf. Artificial Neural Nets and Genetic Algorithms*, pp. 683–690. Springer-Verlag, Berlin, 1993.

[4] Rudolf F. Albrecht, Colin R. Reeves, and Nigel C. Steele, (eds.) *Proc. Int. Conf. Artificial Neural Networks and Genetic Algorithms*. Springer-Verlag, Berlin, 1993.

[5] J.A. Anderson and E. Rosenfeld, *Neurocomputing*, Vols 1 and 2, MIT Press, Cambridge MA, 1991.

[6] Peter J. Angeline, G.M. Saunders, and J.B. Pollack, An evolutionary algorithm that constructs recurrent neural networks, *IEEE Trans. Neural Networks*, Vol. 5, pp. 54–64, 1994.

[7] F.Z. Brill, D.E. Brown, and W.N. Martin, Fast genetic selection of features for neural network classifiers, *IEEE Trans. Neural Networks*, Vol. 3, No. 2, pp. 324–328, Mar. 1992.

[8] Aviv Bergman, Variation and selection: An evolutionary model of learning in neural networks, *Neural Networks*, Vol. 1, No. 1, pp. 75, 1988.

[9] Pierre Bessiere, Genetic algorithms applied to formal neural networks, in P. Bourgine, (ed.) *ECAL91, 1st European Conference on Artificial Life, Paris*. MIT Press, Cambridge, MA, 1993.

[10] L.B. Booker, D.E. Goldberg, and J.H. Holland, Classifier systems and genetic algorithms, *Artificial Intelligence*, Vol. 40, Nos. 1–3, pp. 235–282, Sept., 1989.

[11] Stephan Bornholdt and Dirk Graudenz, General asymmetric neural networks and structure design by genetic algorithms, *Neural Networks*, Vol. 5, No. 2, pp. 327–334, 1992.

[12] Rodney A. Brooks, A robot that walks. Emergent behavior from a carefully evolved network, *Neural Computation*, Vol. 1, No. 2, pp. 253–262, 1989.

[13] Marcelo H. Carugo, Optimization of parameters of a neural network, applied to document recognition, using genetic algorithms, in *Nat. Lab. Technical note no. 049/91*, N.V. Philips, Eindhoven, The Netherlands, 1991.

[14] Thomas P. Caudell and Dolan P. Charles, Parametric connectivity: training of constrained networks using genetic algorithms, in *Proc. Third Int. Conf. Genetic Algorithms*, 1989, pp. 370–374.

[15] A. Colorni, M. Dorigo and V. Maniezzo, Genetic algorithms and highly constrained problems: The time-table case, in *Proc. First Int. Workshop Parallel Problem Solving from Nature, Dortmund, Germany*. (Lecture Notes in Computer Science No. 496). pp. 55–59, Springer-Verlag, Berlin, 1990.

[16] D. Corne, H.L. Fang, and C. Mellish, Solving the modular exam scheduling problem with genetic algorithm, *Proc. 6th Int. Conf. Industrial and Engineering Applications of Artificial Intelligence and Expert Systems, ISAI*, 1993.

[17] Lawrence Davis, *Genetic Algorithms and Simulated Annealing*. Morgan Kaufmann, Los Altos, CA, 1989.

[18] Lawrence Davis, *Handbook of Genetic Algorithms*. Van Nostrand Reinhold, New York, 1991.

[19] L. Davis, Job-shop scheduling with genetic algorithms, in *Proc. Int. Conf. Genetic Algorithm*, 1985, pp. 136–140.

[20] H. de Garis, Evolvable hardware: Genetic programming of a Darwin machine, in *Artificial Neural Nets and Genetic Algorithms, Proc. Int. Conf. Innsbruck, Austria*. Springer-Verlag, Berlin, 1993, pp. 441–449.

[21] H.-L. Fang, P. Ross, and D. Corne, A promising genetic algorithm approach to job-shop scheduling, resheduling and open-shop scheduling problems, in *Proc. Int. Conf. Genetic Algorithm*, 1993, pp. 375–382.

[22] L. Fogel, A. Owens, and M. Walsh, *Artificial Intellligence through Simulated Evolution*. Wiley, New York, 1966.

[23] D.B. Fogel, *Evolutionary Computation: Toward a New Philosophy of Machine Intelligence*. IEEE Press, Piscataway, NJ, 1995.

[24] D.B. Fogel, On the philosophical foundations of evolutionary algorithms and genetic algorithms, in D.B. Fogel and W. Atmar (eds.) *Proc. Second Annual Conf. Evolutionary Programming, La Jolla, CA*, 1993, pp. 23–29.

[25] L.J. Fogel, Evolutionary programming in perspective: The top-down view, in J.M. Zurada, R.J. Marks, and C.J. Robinson (eds.) *Computational Intelligence: Imitating Life*, pp. 135–146. Pisataway, NJ, IEEE Press, 1994.

[26] D.B. Fogel, Evolutionary programming: An introduction and some current directions, *Statistics and Computing*, Vol. 4, pp. 113–129, 1994.

[27] A. Frosini, M. Gori, and P. Priami, A neural network based model for paper currency recognition and verification, *IEEE Trans. Neural Networks*, Vol. 7, No. 6, pp. 1482–1490, Nov. 1996.

[28] D. Goldberg, *Genetic Algorithms in Search, Optimization and Machine Learning*. Addison-Wesley, Reading, MA, 1989.

[29] S. Grossberg, (ed.), *Neural Networks and Natural Intelligence*. MIT Press, Cambridge, MA, 1988.

[30] D. Goldberg, *Genetic Algorithms in Search, Optimization and Machine Learning*. Addison-Wesley, Reading, MA, 1989.

[31] D.E. Goldberg, *Genetic Algorithms*, Addison-Wesley, Reading, MA, 1989.

[32] S. Haykin, *Neural Networks*, Macmillan, New York, 1994.

[33] J. Hertz, A. Krogh, and R.G. Palmer, *Introduction to the Theory of Neural Computation*, Addison-Wesley, Reading, MA, 1991.

[34] H. Hemm, J. Mizoguchi, and K. Shimohara, Development and evolution of hardware behaviors, *Proc. Artificial Life IV*, MIT Press, Cambridge, MA, 1994.

[35] T. Higuchi, T. Niwa, T. Tanaka, H. Iba, H. de Garis, and T Furuya, Evolving hardware with genetic learning: A first step towards building a Darwin machine, *Proc. of 2nd. Int. Conf. Simulation of Adaptive Behavior*, MIT Press, Cambridge, MA, 1993.

[36] T. Higuchi, H. Iba, and B. Mandrake, Evolvable hardware, in *Massively Parallel Artificial Intelligence* (H. Kitano, ed.), MIT Press, Cambridge, MA, 1994.

[37] T. Higuchi, et al. (eds.), *Proc. First Int. Conf. Evolvable Systems: From Biology to Hardware (ICES96)*, (Lecture Notes in Computer Science). Springer-Verlag, Berlin, 1997.

[38] J. Holland, *Adaptation in Natural and Artificial Systems*, University of Michigan Press, Ann Arbor, 1975.

[39] J.H. Holland, *Adaptation in Natural and Artificial Systems*, MIT Press, Boston, MA, 1992.

[40] J.H. Holland, Escaping brittleness: The possibilities of general-purpose learning algorithms applied to parallel rule based system, in R.S. Michalski-J.G., J.G. Carbomel, and T.M. Mitchel (eds.) *Machine Learning: An Artificial Intelligence Approaches*, Vol. II, pp. 593–623, Morgan Kaufmann, Los Altos, CA, 1986.

[41] O. Holland and M. Snaith, The blind neural network maker: Can we use constrained embryologies to design Animat nervous systems, in *Proc. ICANN91, Espoo, Finland*, pp. 1261–1264, 1991.

[42] V. Honavar and L. Uhr, Symbolic artificial intelligence, artificial naural networks, and beyond in S. Goonatilake and S. Khebbal (eds.) *Hybrid Intelligent Systems*. Wiley, London, 1995.

[43] John R. Koza, *Genetic Programming: On the Programming of Computers by Means of Natural Selection*, MIT Press, Cambridge, MA, 1992.

[44] John R Koza, *Genetic Programming II: Automatic Discovery of Reusable Subprograms*, MIT Press, Cambridge, MA, 1994.

[45] F. Kursawe, *Evolution Strategies for Vector Optimization*, pp. 187–193. Taipei, National Chiao Tung University, 1992.

[46] P. Langley, *Elements of Machine Learning*. Morgan Kaufmann, Palo Alto, CA, 1995.

[47] P.H.W. Leong and M.A. Jabri, Connection topologies for digital neural networks, in *ACNN-91*, Sydney, Australia, 1991, pp. 34–37.

[48] Z. Michalewicz, *Genetic Algorithms + Data Structures = Evolutionary Programs*. Springer-Verlag, New York, 1992.

[49] G. Miller et al., Designing neural networks using genetic algorithm, in *Proc. 3rd Int. Conf. Genetic Algorithm*, 1989, pp. 379–384.

[50] M. Mitchell, *An Introduction to Genetic Algorithms*, MIT Press, Cambridge, MA, 1996.

[51] R. Nakano, Conventional genetic algorithms for job-shop problems, in *Proc. 4th Int. Conf. Genetic Algorithm, 1991*, pp. 474–479.

[52] N. Nilsson, *Learning Machines*. McGraw-Hill, New York, 1965.

[53] C.R. Reeves, *A Genetic Algorithm for Flowshop Sequencing*, Coventry Polytechnic Working Paper, Coventry, UK, 1993.

[54] D.E. Rumelhart, G.E. Hinton, and R.J. Williams, Learning internal representation by error propagation, in D.E. Rumelhart and J.L. McClelland (eds.) *Parallel Distributed Processing, Vol. 1: Foundations*, pp. 318–362, MIT Press, Cambridge, MA, 1986.

[55] M.A. Rudnick, *Bibliography: The Intersection of Genetic Search and Artificial Neural Networks*, Technical Report CSE-90-001, Department of Computer Science and Engineering, Oregon Graduate Institute, 1990.

[56] E. Sanchez and M. Tomassini (eds.), *Towards Evolvable Hardware, (Lecture Notes in Computer Science No. 1062)*, Springer-Verlag, Berlin, 1996.

[57] H.P. Schwefel, Collective phenomena in evolutionary systems, in *31st Annual Meeting Int. Soc. General Systems Research, Budapest*, 1987, pp. 1025–1033.

[58] M. Sipper, et al., A phylogenetic, ontogenetic, and epigenetic view of bio-inspired hardware systems, *IEEE Trans. Evolutionary Computation*, Vol. 1, No. 1, pp. 83–97, 1997.

[59] Stephen Bornholdt and Dirk Graudenz, General asymmetric neural networks and structure design by genetic algorithms, *Neural Networks*, Vol. 5, No. 2, pp. 327–334, 1992. (DESSY 91-046, Deutsches Electronen-Synchrotron, Hamburg, Germany, May 1991.)

[60] S. Nolfi, O. Miglino, and D. Parisi, Phenotypic plasticity in evolving neural networks, in P. Gaussier and J.-D. Nicoud (eds.) *Perception Action Conference*, IEEE Computer Society Press, pp. 146–157, 1994.

[61] A. Thompson, Evolving electronic robot controllers that exploit hardware resources, in *Proc. 3rd European Conf. Artificial Life*. Springer-Verlag, Berlin, 1995.

[62] Vaario Jari and Setsuo Ohsuga, Adaptive neural architectures through growth control, in *Intelligent Engineering Systems through Artificial Neural Networks*, Conference Proceedings, pp. 11–16, 1991.

[63] Mark Watson, *Common Lisp Modules—Artificial Intelligence in the Era of Neural Networks and Chaos Theory*, Springer-Verlag, Berlin, 1991.

[64] A. Walter, Tackett genetic programming for feature discovery and image discrimination, in Stephanie Forrest (ed.) *Proc. Fifth Int. Conf. Genetic Algorithms*. Morgan Kauffman, Palo Alta, CA, 1993.

[65] S.W. Wilson and D.E., Goldberg, A critical review of classifier systems, *Proc. 3rd Int. Conf. Genetic Algorithm*, 1989, pp. 244–255.

[66] T. Yamada and R. Nakano, A genetic algorithm applicable to large-scale job-shop problems, in R. Männer and B. Manderick (eds.), *Parallel Problem Solving from Nature (PSN92)*, pp. 281–290, North-Holland, Amsterdam, 1992.

CHAPTER 7

Neural Networks and Fuzzy Systems

PETR MUSÍLEK and MADAN M. GUPTA

Intelligent Systems Research Laboratory, College of Engineering, University of Saskatchewan, Saskatoon, Saskatchewan, Canada S7N 5A9

1 INTRODUCTION

There still lies a challenge in the understanding of the capabilities of biological systems dealing with complex problems of the real world. Distinguishing between different objects, or the skill of writing, are just two examples of the amazing abilities of information processing systems embodied in human cognitive faculty. The information processing abilities of biological neural systems, such as classifiers or controllers used as examples above, are quite successful in dealing with complex, imprecise, or even ambiguous data. Along with this robustness there is an ability to improve corresponding faculties and to learn new ones, that is to increase the accuracy of recognition or to reduce the time necessary for writing a letter.

Many advances have been made in mimicking some of these human cognitive capabilities, mostly inspired by certain substantial aspects of their biological examples. The corresponding approaches include the theories of neural networks, fuzzy systems, and genetic algorithms, to name the most significant ones. Recently a new field of *soft computing* has emerged that combines these different approaches in a synergetic way. The resulting compound systems combine favorable properties of the primary constituents to achieve a new quality of behavior characterized in particular by great adaptability and tolerance for vagueness. Let us cite the definition of soft computing given by Professor Lotfi A. Zadeh, the father of fuzzy logic [18]:

> Soft computing differs from conventional (hard) computing in that, unlike hard computing, it is tolerant of imprecision, uncertainty and partial truth. In effect, the role model for soft computing is the human mind. The guiding principle of soft computing is: Exploit the tolerance for imprecision, uncertainty and partial truth to achieve tractability, robustness and low solution cost.

Here, we focus our attention on systems combining two important constituents of soft computing: neural network and fuzzy systems. *Fuzzy neural systems* are distributed parallel information processing schemes that employ neuronlike processing units and fuzzy operations for dealing with fuzzy signals. Such definition is very general as it covers not only fuzzy neural networks, but also other approaches combining neural networks and fuzzy systems. However, the primary constituents can have a different function in the resulting system [14].

In this chapter, we give a concise overview of the two constituent fields of fuzzy neural networks: neural networks and fuzzy systems. The main contents of this chapter are given in the following sections.

In Section 2 we give an introduction to the theory of neural networks. We start with a formal definition of a neural network followed by a detailed treatment of single-neuron structures. This is because we consider a sound model of the single neuron crucial for further development of more complicated network structures. In addition, we have found that it is just the model of single neuron that induces most of confusion encountered in the field of fuzzy neural networks.

Section 3 introduces two important concepts of the theory of fuzzy systems: fuzzy sets and fuzzy numbers. Each of these two mathematical structures offers a different approach for coping with fuzzy uncertainty. Also, different mathematical tools are used to manipulate them. The partial goal of this section is to bring forward the variety of resources offered to fuzzy neural networks by the theory of fuzzy systems.

Finally, Section 4 summarizes the main contents of the chapter, and gives some concluding remarks.

2   NEURAL NETWORKS

A *neural network* (NN) is a parallel distributed information processing structure [4] consisting of a number of processing units called *neurons*. These processing units are inspired by the structure and operation of the biological neurons which are the basic elements of the neural systems of living organisms. In this section, we give a simplified overview of the biological neurons followed by some implications crucial for their modeling. Next, we introduce a generalized mathematical model of the neuron which will be elaborated on later when developing fuzzy neurons [13]. Finally, we show two important instances of the generalized model and examples of their use in simple classification problems.

2.1   Biological Neurons: A Brief Introduction

A nerve cell with freely branched projections forms a *neuron*, which is the primary element involved in information processing in the central nervous system. There are many different types of neurons, but the basic *structure* is consistently the same as shown in Figure 1. There are four main parts of a neuron: soma, axon, synapses, and dendrites.

1. *Soma*, the main part of the neuron, provides weighted aggregation and nonlinear operation to the received signals, and gives an output signal through an axon.
2. The *axon* serves as an output branch of the nerve cell. There is only one axon in a neuron; however, it is branched into colateral fibers carrying signals to other neurons.
3. *Synapses* are the junction points of the axons (outputs radiating form different neurons) and dendrites (input terminals of the neuron). The synapses act as a storage place of the past experience (memory).
4. The *dendrites* carry the synaptic information toward the main body (soma) of the neuron. The number of dendrites in a typical neuron ranges from a very few, say 10, to a very large number, up to 10000.

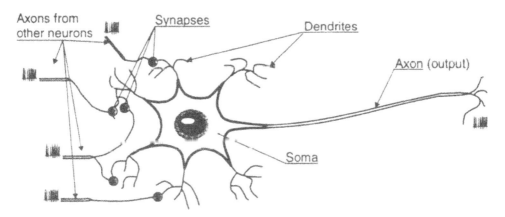

FIGURE 1
A biological neuron.

Important *functional* properties of biological neurons determine the way of processing signals and communication among neural populations. In general, neuronal functions can be classified into two groups: synaptic operations and somatic operations [2].

1. *Synaptic operations.* Synaptic operations provide processing of the incoming neural signals to a neuron in the synapses and dendrites. They can be classified into two groups: synaptic and dendritic processing.

   (a) *Synaptic processing.* Synapses continuously learn and adapt by changing their ability to transmit signals incoming from other neurons, that is by changing their weights. Based on the encountered local information, learning is provided by various mechanisms of neural plasticity [11]. New signals are then processed with respect to the stored weights—the attributes of the past experience. More precisely, depending on the state of the synapses, the input signals can be either amplified or attenuated, and they may cause either excitatory or inhibitory contributions to the inner potential of the neuron.

   (b) *Dendritic processing.* Dendrites allow synergistic interactions of the input signals [10]. While synapses can provide gradation of single input signals, dendrites can carry out nonlinear operations among the inputs (e.g., their multiplication or power). In addition, it is believed that dendrites also play a very active role in the processes of learning and adaptation [9].

2. *Somatic operations.* Two main operations take place in the soma: aggregation of the input signals processed by synapses, and generation of action potentials (i.e., determining the output signal of the neuron).

   (a) *Aggregation.* Synaptic aggregation is a sort of averaging process to the synaptic signals fed into the soma. It consists of gathering contributions of input signals reaching a neuron in close spatial or temporal relation.

   (b) *Action potential.* Communication among neurons is performed through certain pulse code modulated signals. The pulses, called action potentials, are generated in the soma and propagated through the axon. An action potential is characterized by the following significant attributes (see Figure 2):

   Threshold. An action potential is fired only if the aggregated potential of the neuron exceeds certain threshold value, about −50 mV.

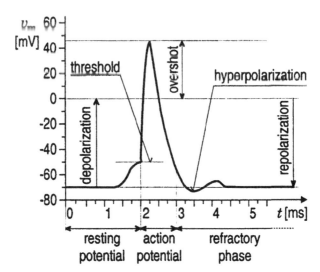

FIGURE 2
Action potential of a neuron.

> *Pulse coding.* Aggregated somatic information is converted from the amplitude signal into a form of pulse code modulated signal that is then transmitted to other neurons. Recent theories assume existence of several different pulse codes in various parts of the nervous system [9].
>
> *Saturation.* There is an upper limit of the frequency of the spikes. It is caused by the finite width of the spikes and by the refractory period during which a second spike cannot be initiated [12].

The description of the biological neuron given above is only in a simplified form. However, other simplifications frequently apply when employing these neural models for artificial information processing systems. Two typical simplified models of neuron will be described later in this section.

2.2 Neuronal Functions: Some Implications

It would be useful to complement the brief description of the biological neuron given in the previous subsection by some implications interpreting the meaning of the single neuronal functions.

Neuronal operation can be characterized by two main modes: (i) the learning and adaptation mode, and (ii) the information processing mode. Although neither of them can be omitted, and information processing is the main function of the neuron, the learning mode is perhaps the more characteristic one, giving the neuron ability to learn new knowledge and adapt to new conditions.

Learning and adaptation take place mainly in the synapses of the neuron. Their properties change in accordance with situations (i.e., signals, states, configurations, and spatiotemporal correlations) met during the lifetime of the neuron. This experience is stored by changing the processing properties of the neuron, in particular the weights associated with the synapses.

Operation of the neuron in the *processing mode* is associated with all parts of the neuron. Signals coming from the other neurons are first confronted with the past experience stored in the dendrites and synapses. Then they are fed into the soma to determine the output behavior of the neuron. In other words, the synaptic part of the neuron may be regarded as a memory unit continuously storing experience and passing all the stored experience to the signals under processing. Soma, on the other hand, may be considered as a decision making unit that determines the output signal of the neuron based on the stored experience and actual inputs feeding into the neuron from other neurons or from the environment.

Neuronal information processing uses two important processes to determine the actual output behavior of the neuron. The first is the evaluation of similarity between the input signals and the experience stored in synapses. It is followed by a nonlinear mapping operation providing the neural output based on the actual similarity. The process of similarity evaluation (or matching) is realized by an element-by-element comparison of the fresh neural input with the stored experience (i.e., synaptic processing) and the collection of the partial results (i.e., somatic aggregation). It provides a global measure of mutual relationship, or a measure of *confluence*, between the fresh neural inputs and stored information. The succession of the operations provided in the course of information processing by a neuron can be depicted by the simplified block diagram given in Figure 3.

As depicted in this diagram, a neuron can be regarded as a multi-input–single-output (MISO) processing unit. From the structural point of view, we can identify the two main parts of the neuron: the synapses and soma. Comparison of the stored past experience with the fresh neural inputs is executed in the synaptic part (including the dendritic processing as well). The results of the element-wise synaptic operations are then aggregated in the soma, determining an internal potential of the neuron. Finally, the neural output is generated through a nonlinear output operation in the soma.

Although this greatly simplified general description is perhaps obvious, some of the principles are omitted when describing the so-called neural and, more frequently, fuzzy neural models. In the following subsection we define a generalized model of neuron based on the principles outlined above. The generalized model will be used later to review some established fuzzy neural models, to propose several new models, and to show the weaknesses of some models found in the literature.

2.3 A Generalized Model of Neuron

We can formalize the operations provided by a biological neuron to obtain its generalized mathematical model. The neuron can be considered to operate as a *mathematical processor* performing certain mathematical operations on its inputs in order to determine an output. We can identify two parts of the mathematical processor, and its functions can be divided likewise into two distinct groups of operations: *synaptic* and *somatic* operations. The synaptic operations consist of the controlled synaptic transmission, which is continuously modified through learning and adaptation. These processes affect the parameters of the synaptic operation and they are usually derived from the overall activity of the corresponding neural network consisting of a

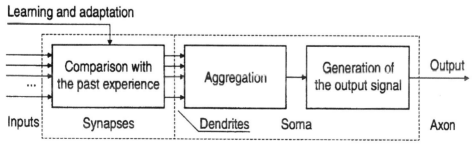

FIGURE 3
A general view of neuronal operation.

large number of mutually interconnected neurons. The somatic operations comprise aggregation and generation of the output of the neuron.

Synaptic Operations. The synaptic transmission provides combination of the fresh neural inputs and the past experience by applying the *synaptic operation* between the vector of fresh neural inputs $\mathbf{x} = [x_1, x_2, \ldots, x_n]^T \in \mathbb{R}^n$ and the vector of synaptic weights $\mathbf{w} = [w_1, w_2, \ldots, w_n]^T \in \mathbb{R}^n$. The vector of synaptic weights $\mathbf{w} \in \mathbb{R}^n$ thus serves in weighting the incoming information with respect to the learned knowledge (past experience) and the single synaptic coefficients w_i, $i = 1, 2, \ldots, n$, can be viewed as representations of the knowledge (in addition with the ability to adapt to new events). Thus, the synaptic operation assigns a relative value z_i to each component x_i of the incoming neural input with respect to the past experience stored in the synaptic coefficient w_i. The weighted synaptic output can be expressed as

$$z_i = w_i \odot x_i, \qquad z_i \in \mathbb{R}, \ i = 1, 2, \ldots, n \tag{1}$$

or in the vector form

$$\mathbf{z} = \mathbf{w}^T \odot \mathbf{x}, \ \mathbf{z} \in \mathbb{R}^n \tag{2}$$

where $\odot$ denotes generalized synaptic operators for scalar (1) or vector (2) arguments, and T denotes the transpose.

Somatic Operations. The soma of a biological neuron provides the operations of aggregation and generation of the neural output.

The somatic operation of *aggregation* ensures the combination of the weighted inputs z_i, $i = 1, 2, \ldots, n$. It maps the vector $\mathbf{z} \in \mathbb{R}^n$ on a scalar value $u \in \mathbb{R}$ using an aggregation operation

$$u = \bigoplus_{i=1}^{n} z_i \tag{3}$$

or considering equation (1)

$$u = \bigoplus_{i=1}^{n} w_i \odot x_i \tag{4}$$

where $\oplus$ is the generalized operator of aggregation.

The synaptic and aggregation operations can be unified to obtain a simple mathematical expression that describes the *confluence* between the neural input vector $\mathbf{x} \in \mathbb{R}^n$ and the vector of synaptic weights $\mathbf{w} \in \mathbb{R}^n$, and yields a scalar value $u \in \mathbb{R}$,

$$u = \mathbf{w}^T \copyright \mathbf{x} \in \mathbb{R} \tag{5}$$

where $\copyright$ is for the generalized operator of confluence implementing the function of weighted aggregation.

The other somatic operations are thresholding, and generation of the output signal form the weighted and aggregated signal $u \in \mathbb{R}$. They can generally be described by the relation

$$y = \phi[u, w_0] \tag{6}$$

where ϕ is a nonlinear output function, and w_0 is a threshold (bias) value. It can easily be seen that the output signal of the neuron y is function of its internal state u. Therefore, by considering equation (5) and its interpretation, the output signal is dependent on the similarity between the vector of the neural input signals $\mathbf{x} \in \mathbb{R}^n$ and the vector of synaptic weights $\mathbf{w} \in \mathbb{R}^n$. If the measure of confluence between the two vectors is smaller than the threshold value w_0, the output signal corresponds to the passive state of the neuron. If the value of the relative measure u overreaches the threshold w_0, the output signal follows the output function ϕ.

If we introduce a new auxiliary quantity $v = u + w_0$, equation (6) can be rewritten as

$$y = \phi[v] \tag{7}$$

General properties imposed on the function $\phi[\cdot]$ (i.e., requirements of continuity, monotonicity, etc.) depend on the particular measure of similarity used in the neural model.

Finally, we can include the threshold term w_0 into the weight vector by introducing an augmented weight vector $\mathbf{w}_a = [w_0, w_1, \ldots, w_n]^T \in \mathbb{R}^{n+1}$, and by setting $x_0 = 1$ as a component of an augmented input vector $\mathbf{x}_a = [x_0, x_1, \ldots, x_n]^T \in \mathbb{R}^{n+1}$. Thresholding is thus realized in the process of aggregation itself. Consequently, the confluence operation can be written as

$$v = \mathbf{w}_a^T \, \copyright \, \mathbf{x}_a \tag{8}$$

and the output signal v is defined directly by equation (7), that is,

$$y = \phi[v]$$

Let us sum up the generalized model of a neuron, as shown in Figure 4, using the following definition.

Definition 1. *The generalized model of A neuron* is an information processing unit N $(\mathbf{x}_a, \mathbf{w}_a, y, \odot, \oplus, \phi)$ with the following specifications:

(a) The augmented input vector $\mathbf{x}_a \in \mathbb{R}^{n+1}$ represents $n + 1$ inputs $x_0, \ldots, x_n$, $n \geq 1$, where the threshold term $x_0 = 1$.

(b) The augmented weight vector $\mathbf{w}_a \in \mathbb{R}^{n+1}$ contains $n + 1$ weights $w_0, \ldots, w_n$, $n \geq 1$, each of them w_i associated with a component x_i of the input vector; w_0 is the threshold term.

(c) $y \in \mathbb{R}$ is the scalar neural output.

(d) $\odot$, $\oplus$ and ϕ are respectively the generalized synaptic operator, operator of aggregation and output function. The synaptic operation $\odot$ and the process of aggregation $\oplus$ can be compounded into the confluence operation $\copyright$ defined in equation (8).

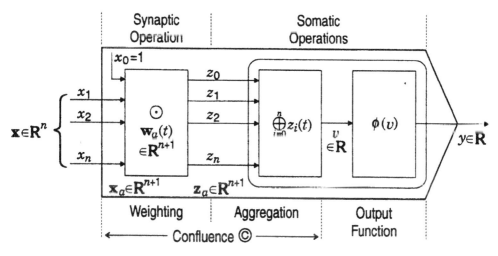

FIGURE 4
Generalized model of neuron.

2.4   Specific Neural Models

As was outlined in the previous subsections, the synaptic operation can be regarded as an element-by-element comparison of the augmented vector of input signals x_a describing the fresh neural input with the vector of synaptic weights w_a containing the past experience. The confluence operation then provides a measure of similarity between these two vectors by aggregating the partial contributions z_i obtained by the synaptic operation.

In this subsection, we describe two groups of neuronal models based on two different methods for evaluating the mutual relation of the vectors w_a and x_a. Consequently, they also use different mathematical functions to generate the neural output. Examples of their applications to simple classification tasks are given for illustrative purpose.

2.4.1   Product-based Neural Model.
In this type of neuron, the confluence operation is based on the inner product between the weight vector and the fresh neural inputs.

The synaptic operation $\odot$ is realized by *product*

$$z_i = w_i \odot x_i = w_i \cdot x_i, \qquad i = 0, 1, \ldots, n \qquad (9)$$

while the somatic operation of aggregation is executed by *summation* of the weighted inputs z_i,

$$v = \bigoplus_{i=0}^{n} z_i = \sum_{i=0}^{n} z_i \qquad (10)$$

By combining equations (9) and (10), the internal state v is defined as a weighted aggregation of the neural inputs that corresponds to the scalar product of the vectors x_a and w_a:

$$v = \sum_{i=0}^{n} w_i \cdot x_i = w_a^T x_a = |w_a| |x_a| \cos \psi \qquad (11)$$

where $|\cdot|$ is for the length of a vector, and ψ is the angle between the two vectors.

The inner product of the vectors w_a and x_a can also be viewed as a projection of the augmented vector of fresh neural inputs x_a onto the vector of synaptic weights w_a representing the learned knowledge. A geometric representation of the projection is shown in Figure 5.

Let us examine the process of confluence operation (equation 11) with the following three cases of phase ψ between the vectors w_a and x_a:

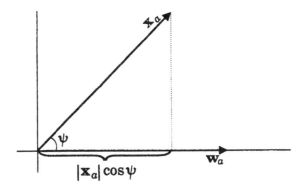

FIGURE 5
Inner product of the two vectors w_a and x_a: $v = w_a^T x_a = |w_a| |x_a| \cos \psi$.

(i) $|\psi| < 90°$: The phase ψ in the first or fourth quadrant $-90° < \psi < 90°$ implies a positive correlation between the learned experience stored in $\mathbf{w}_a$ and the fresh neural inputs $\mathbf{x}_a$. The positive correlation has its maximum value for $\psi = 0°$.

(ii) $\psi = \pm 90°$: Either of these values of phase ψ implies that the two vectors $\mathbf{w}_a$ and $\mathbf{x}_a$ are orthogonal to each other, providing a zero correlation between the learned experience and fresh neural inputs.

(iii) $|\psi| > 90°$: If the phase is in the second or third quadrant, the correlation between the learned experience and the fresh neural inputs is negative. It has its maximum negative value at $\psi = \pm 180°$.

Nondecreasing functions are used to generate the neural output in the product-based models to ensure proportionality of the neural output signal to the measure of similarity between the input vector $\mathbf{x}_a \in \mathbb{R}^{n+1}$ and the weight vector of the neuron, $\mathbf{w}_a \in \mathbb{R}^{n+1}$.

Many different types of functions can be used to realize this kind of function. Typically, a sigmoidal (S-shaped) function is used to perform the neural output function. For unipolar output signals (which are closest to biological neurons), the sigmoidal function

$$y = \frac{1}{1 + \exp(-gv)} \tag{12}$$

with the slope

$$\frac{dy}{dv} = \frac{g \exp(-gv)}{[1 + \exp(-gv)]^2} \tag{13}$$

is the most frequently used output function for the product-based neural models. It is an increasing sigmoidal function with positive gain coefficient $g > 0$ that determines the slope of the S-curve. Graphs of the unipolar sigmoidal function and its slopes for different values of the gain g are shown in Figure 6. Other examples of the output functions for use in the product based neural models are shown in Figure 19 in Appendix A.

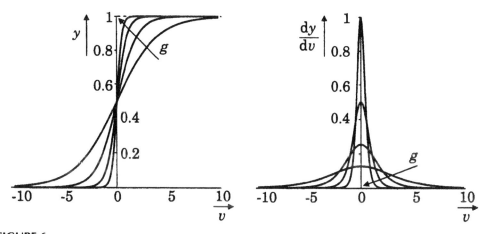

FIGURE 6
Unipolar sigmoidal function and its slope for different values of the gain $g = \{0.5, 1, 2, 4\}$.

EXAMPLE 2.4.1

To illustrate the function of the neural model described above, we will consider the following simple classification problem. Six patterns, described by the feature vectors $x^{(i)}$, should be classified according to their membership in classes 1 and 2 as follows:

Patterns	Class
$x^{(1)} = [1.0, \ 1.0]^T, \ x^{(2)} = [0.9, \ 0.9]^T, \ x^{(3)} = [0.6, \ 0.7]^T$	1
$x^{(4)} = [0.4, \ 0.5]^T, \ x^{(5)} = [0.4, \ 0.2]^T, \ x^{(6)} = [0.0, \ 0.0]^T$	2

The pattern space can be arbitrarily divided as shown in Figure 7, and the division can be performed by a simple product-based neural classifier shown in Figure 8.

The line separates the pattern space into two half-planes corresponding, respectively, to the positive and negative correlation between the weights and the neural inputs. A critical thresholding condition occurs when the correlation v equals zero,

$$v = w_0 + w_1 x_1 + w_2 x_2 = 0 \tag{14}$$

that is, the separating line is described by the linear relation

$$x_2 = -\frac{w_0}{w_2} - \frac{w_1}{w_2} x_1 \tag{15}$$

The three components of the augmented weight vector $w_a = [w_0, \ w_1, \ w_2]^T$ determine the slope of the separating line and its interception of the vertical axis, as shown in Figure 7. Weight vector of the neuron is set to $w_a = [-1, \ 1, \ 1]^T$ corresponding to the chosen separating line. It determines the slope $k = -w_1/w_2 = -1$, and the intercept $-w_0/w_2 = 1$.

Based on the value of the correlation v, the output function ϕ generates the output of the neuron. Depending on the particular problem, various output functions can be used.

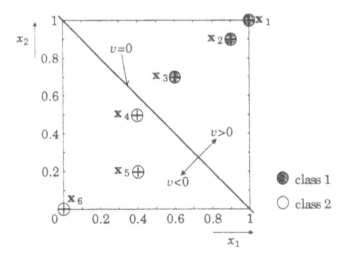

FIGURE 7
The patterns and separating line for Example 2.4.1.

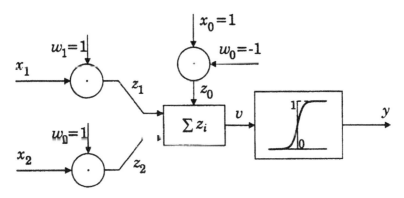

FIGURE 8
The product-based neural classifier.

First, let us consider the unipolar hard-limiting output function. The neural output is, in this case, found by calculation:

$$y = \begin{cases} 1 & \text{if } v > 0 \\ 0 & \text{if } v \leq 0 \end{cases}$$

and interpreted as follows:

$$\text{If } y(\mathbf{x}^{(i)}) = \begin{cases} 1 & \text{then pattern } \mathbf{x}^{(i)} \text{ belongs to class 1} \\ 0 & \text{then pattern } \mathbf{x}^{(i)} \text{ belongs to class 2} \end{cases}$$

The results of classification by the product based neuron with the hard-limiting output function are summarized in Table 1.

Another output function that can be used to solve our classification problem is the unipolar sigmoidal function:

$$y = \frac{1}{1 + \exp(-gv)}, \qquad g = 5$$

This type of output function offers finer discrimination of membership of the patterns in the classes [19], as it attains values in the continuous interval [0, 1] instead of in the binary set {0, 1}. The results of classification by the product-based neuron with the sigmoidal output function are summarized in Table 2.

Table 1 The results of classification by the product-based neuron with the hard-limiting output function

Pattern	x_1	x_2	v	y
$\mathbf{x}^{(1)}$	1.0	1.0	1.0	1
$\mathbf{x}^{(2)}$	0.9	0.9	0.8	1
$\mathbf{x}^{(3)}$	0.6	0.7	0.3	1
$\mathbf{x}^{(4)}$	0.4	0.5	−0.1	0
$\mathbf{x}^{(5)}$	0.4	0.2	−0.4	0
$\mathbf{x}^{(6)}$	0.0	0.0	−1.0	0

Table 2   The results of classification by the product-
based neuron with the sigmoidal output function

Pattern	x_1	x_2	v	y
$\mathbf{x}^{(1)}$	1.0	1.0	1.0	1.00
$\mathbf{x}^{(2)}$	0.9	0.9	0.8	0.98
$\mathbf{x}^{(3)}$	0.6	0.7	0.3	0.82
$\mathbf{x}^{(4)}$	0.4	0.5	−0.1	0.38
$\mathbf{x}^{(5)}$	0.4	0.2	−0.4	0.11
$\mathbf{x}^{(6)}$	0.0	0.0	−1.0	0.00

2.4.2 Distance-based Neural Model.

In this type of neuron, the confluence operation is based on the distance between the weight vector and the vector of fresh neural inputs.

Synaptic distance operation and somatic operation of aggregation compose another similarity measure, which is based on various metrics. The distance measure between two vectors[1] $\mathbf{w}$ and $\mathbf{x}$ can be generally described as

$$\ell^d(\mathbf{w},\ \mathbf{x}) = \sqrt[d]{\sum_{i=1}^{n} |w_i - x_i|^d} \tag{16}$$

where $\ell^d(\mathbf{w},\ \mathbf{x})$ is the distance measure with rank d. Although the general formulation allows definition of a metric with an arbitrary rank d, only ℓ^1 (i.e., Hamming distance) and ℓ^2 (i.e., Euclidean distance) are commonly used.

For example, the confluence operation corresponding to the Euclidean distance of two vectors $\mathbf{w}$ and $\mathbf{x}$ is defined as

$$u = \ell^2(\mathbf{w},\ \mathbf{x}) = \|\mathbf{w} - \mathbf{x}\| = \sqrt[2]{\sum_{i=1}^{n}(w_i - x_i)^2} \tag{17}$$

It can easily be seen that the properties of the (Euclidean) distance-based confluence operation differ greatly from that of the inner product-based one. While the inner product-based confluence operation has a maximum value for two parallel vectors, the distance based measure equals to zero for two identical vectors. In addition, the distance-based similarity measure compares positions of the vectors' end points rather than their directions (see Figure 9).

Radial kernels are used to generate the neural output in the models with distance-based confluence operations. A kernel is called radial if it is only a function of the norm of its argument [15]. A Gaussian function defined as

$$y = \exp\left(-\frac{u^2}{4\sigma^2}\right) \tag{18}$$

with the slope

$$\frac{dy}{du} = -\frac{u}{2\sigma^2}\exp\left(-\frac{u^2}{4\sigma^2}\right) \tag{19}$$

is frequently used to perform the mapping.

[1] Note that, unlike in the product-based model, unaugmented (without threshold) vectors $\mathbf{w}$ and $\mathbf{x}$ are considered instead of the augmented vectors $\mathbf{w}_a$ and $\mathbf{x}_a$.

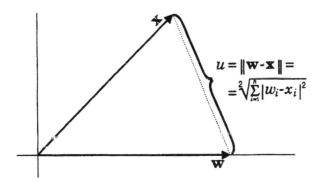

$$u = \| \mathbf{w}\text{-}\mathbf{x} \| = \sqrt[2]{\sum_{i=1}^{n} |w_i\text{-}x_i|^2}$$

FIGURE 9
Euclidean distance of two vectors **w** and **x**.

The parameter σ determines the width of the Gaussian curve. Graphs of the function and its slopes for different values of the parameter σ are shown in Figure 10. Other examples of the output functions for use in the distance-based neural models are shown in Figure 20 in Appendix A.

EXAMPLE 2.4.2
To illustrate the function of the distance-based neural model, we will consider the following simple classification problem. Six patterns, described by the feature vectors $\mathbf{x}^{(i)}$, should be classified according to their membership in classes 1 and 2 as follows:

Patterns	Class
$\mathbf{x}^{(1)} = [1.0,\ 1.0]^T,\ \ \mathbf{x}^{(2)} = [1.0,\ 0.5]^T,\ \ \mathbf{x}^{(3)} = [0.5,\ 1.5]^T$	1
$\mathbf{x}^{(4)} = [0.5,\ 0.4]^T,\ \ \mathbf{x}^{(5)} = [2.0,\ 1.0]^T,\ \ \mathbf{x}^{(6)} = [2.0,\ 2.0]^T$	2

The pattern space can be arbitrarily divided by a circle as shown in Figure 11a. Such division can be performed by a simple distance-based neural classifier shown in Figure 12.

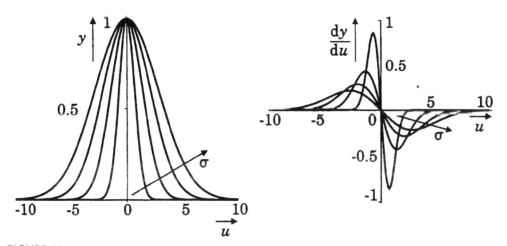

FIGURE 10
Gaussian output function and its slope for different values of the parameter $\sigma = \{0.5,\ 1,\ 1.5,\ 2\}$.

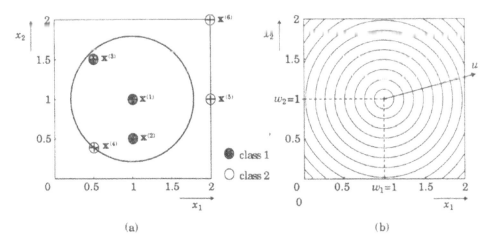

(a)   (b)

FIGURE 11
Example 2.4.2: (a) the patterns and the separating circle; (b) contour plot of the gradient surface of the Euclidean distance measure.

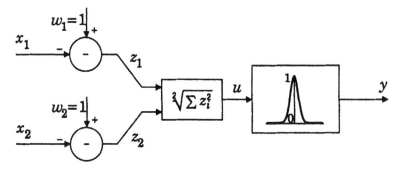

FIGURE 12
The distance-based neural classifier.

The weight vector of the neuron $\mathbf{w} = [w_1,\ w_2]^T$ determines the center of the circle corresponding to a prototype configuration of the neural input $\mathbf{x} = [x_1,\ x_2]^T$. If the input $\mathbf{x}$ is identical to the prototype configuration, the distance measure equals to zero, $u = 0$. The weight vector of the neuron is set to $\mathbf{w} = [1,\ 1]^T$ corresponding to the chosen prototype. The shape of the pattern space off the center depends on the particular distance measure used. In the case of Euclidean distance,

$$u = \|\mathbf{w} - \mathbf{x}\| = \sqrt[2]{\sum_{i=1}^{2}(w_i - x_i)^2}$$

a gradient surface is formed with the shape depicted by the contour plot in Figure 11b.

Based on the value of the distance u, the output function ϕ generates the output of the neuron. Depending on the particular problem, various output functions can be used. First, let us consider the unipolar hard-limiting output function. The neural output is found by calculation:

$$y = \begin{cases} 1 & \text{if } u < \sigma \\ 0 & \text{if } u \geq \sigma \end{cases}$$

Table 3 The results of classification by the distance-based neuron with the hard-limiting output function

Pattern	x_1	x_2	u	y
$x^{(1)}$	1.0	1.0	0.00	1
$x^{(2)}$	1.0	0.5	0.50	1
$x^{(3)}$	0.5	1.5	0.71	1
$x^{(4)}$	0.5	0.4	0.78	0
$x^{(5)}$	2.0	1.0	1.00	0
$x^{(6)}$	2.0	2.0	1.41	0

Table 4 The results of classification by the distance-based neuron with the Gaussian output function

Pattern	x_1	x_2	u	y
$x^{(1)}$	1.0	1.0	0.00	1.00
$x^{(2)}$	1.0	0.5	0.50	0.77
$x^{(3)}$	0.5	1.5	0.71	0.61
$x^{(4)}$	0.5	0.4	0.78	0.45
$x^{(5)}$	2.0	1.0	1.00	0.36
$x^{(6)}$	2.0	2.0	1.41	0.14

where $\sigma = 0.78$ is a bias value corresponding to the radius of the dividing circle. The output is then interpreted as follows:

$$\text{If } y(x^{(i)}) = \begin{cases} 1 & \text{then pattern } x^{(i)} \text{ belongs to class 1} \\ 0 & \text{then pattern } x^{(i)} \text{ belongs; to class 2} \end{cases}$$

The results of classification by the distance-based neuron with the hard-limiting output function are summarized in Table 3.

Another output function which can be used to solve our classification problem is the Gaussian function

$$y = \exp\left(-\frac{u^2}{4\sigma^2}\right), \qquad \sigma = 0.5,$$

where parameter σ determines the selectivity of the function, which is also coupled with the radius of the dividing circle. The results of classification by the distance-based neuron with the Gaussian output function are summarized in Table 4.

Analogously to the product-based neuron with the sigmoidal output function, the Gaussian output function offers finer discrimination of membership of the patterns in the classes as it attains values in the continuous interval [0, 1] instead of in the binary set {0, 1}.

3 FUZZY SYSTEMS

In this section, we give a sample of those attributes of fuzzy systems that are important for the development and understanding of fuzzy neural networks. Indeed, the area of fuzzy systems is much larger, beyond the scope of this concise introduction. An extensive overview of fuzzy systems can be found in [6, 7, 8].

The following two subsections contain a fundamental description of fuzzy sets and fuzzy numbers, including their basic properties. The corresponding fuzzy logic and fuzzy arithmetic operations are also briefly treated. These tools for manipulating the mathematical structures are described in more detail in Chapter 8 of this volume [13].

3.1   Fuzzy Sets

The theory of fuzzy systems is based on the notion of *fuzzy set* introduced by Zadeh in [16]. It is a set with graded membership over the interval [0, 1]. A fuzzy set A, which is a fuzzy subset of an universe of discourse X, is denoted by

$$A = \int_A \mu_A(x)/x \tag{20a}$$

or, in the case of a discrete universe X,

$$A = \sum_{i=1}^n \mu_A(x_i)/x_i \tag{20b}$$

$$= \mu_A(x_1)/x_1 + \mu_A(x_2)/x_2 + \cdots + \mu_A(x_m)/x_m \tag{20c}$$

where $\mu_A(x)$ is a membership function describing the degree of membership of points in X in the fuzzy subset A. An example fuzzy set is shown in Figure 13. It also contains a description of some important parameters of fuzzy sets defined later in this section.

3.1.1   Properties of Fuzzy Sets.   The *height* of a fuzzy set A is defined as

$$\text{hgt}(A) = \sup_{x \in X} \mu_A(x) \tag{21}$$

where sup is for supremum of a set. The height of the so called *normal* fuzzy set is equal to 1, while fuzzy sets with $\text{hgt}(A) < 1$ are called *subnormal*.

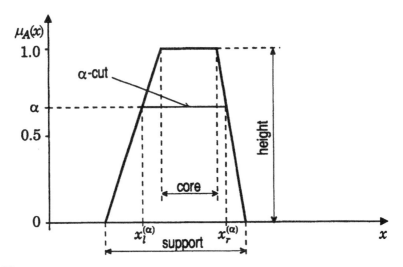

FIGURE 13
A fuzzy set A and its basic parameters.

The *support* of a fuzzy set A is a crisp subset of X with nonzero membership, i.e.,

$$\text{supp}(A) = \{x \in X | \mu_A(x) > 0\} \tag{22}$$

and the *core* (or kernel) of the fuzzy set is a crisp subset of X with membership equal to 1, that is,

$$\text{core}(A) = \{x \in X | \mu_A(x) = 1\} \tag{23}$$

The α-cut of a fuzzy set expresses interval of confidence for the level of presumption α [7] Again, it is defined using a crisp subset of the universe X,

$$A_\alpha = \{x \in X | \mu_A(x) \geq \alpha\} \tag{24}$$

An important attribute of a fuzzy set is its *convexity.* A convex fuzzy set is characterized by the relation

$$\forall x_1, x_2, x_3 \in X, \ x_1 \leq x_2 \leq x_3; \quad \mu_A(x_2) \geq \min(\mu_A(x_1), \ \mu_A(x_3)) \tag{25}$$

Hence, the fuzzy set shown in Figure 13 is convex.

The last structure described in this subsection is fuzzy partition. An n-tuple of fuzzy subsets $(A_1, A_2, \ldots, A_n)$ of X is called a *fuzzy partition* if

$$\forall x \in X: \ \sum_{i=1}^{n} \mu_{A_i}(x) = 1 \tag{26}$$

provided that $A_i \neq \emptyset$ and $A_i \neq X$.

3.1.2 *Operations on Fuzzy Sets: Fuzzy Logic.*

The possible operations over fuzzy sets are the generalizations of the corresponding classical set operations. For each of these generalized operations there is an extensive group of possible instances. In the following we define the necessary basic concepts and show the standard cases of the operations.

- *Fuzzy complement* $\mathbf{C}(A)$ of the fuzzy set A is generally defined by a function

$$\mathbf{C}: \quad [0, \ 1] \to [0, \ 1] \tag{27}$$

which assigns a value $\mathbf{C}(A(x))$ to each point x of the fuzzy set A. The basic properties of the operation of fuzzy complement $\mathbf{C}$ are

Boundary conditions: $\mathbf{C}(0) = 1 \wedge \mathbf{C}(1) = 0$
Monotonicity: $\forall a, b \in [0, \ 1]: a \leq b \Rightarrow \mathbf{C}(a) \geq \mathbf{C}(b)$
Involutivity: $\forall a \in [0, \ 1]: \mathbf{C}(\mathbf{C}(a)) = a$

Another frequently considered requirement is the continuity of the operation $\mathbf{C}$ on the interval $[0, 1]$.

The standard fuzzy complement is described by the relation

$$\mathbf{C}(a) = 1 - a \tag{28}$$

illustrated in Figure 14.

- *Fuzzy intersection* (T-norm operation) of fuzzy sets A and B is generally described by the relation

$$(A \cap B)(x) = \mathbf{T}[A(x), \ B(x)] \tag{29}$$

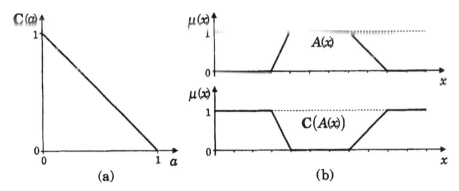

(a)   (b)

FIGURE 14
The standard fuzzy complement: (a) graph of the fuzzy complement; (b) the fuzzy complement of a fuzzy set $A(x)$.

where **T** is the operator for fuzzy intersection. The basic properties of the operation are

Commutativity:	$\mathbf{T}(a, b) = \mathbf{T}(b, a)$
Associativity:	$\mathbf{T}(a, \mathbf{T}(b, c)) = \mathbf{T}(\mathbf{T}(a, b), c)$
Monotonicity:	$b \le c \Rightarrow \mathbf{T}(a, b) \le \mathbf{T}(a, c)$
Idempotency:	$\mathbf{T}(a, a) = a$
Boundary condition:	$\mathbf{T}(a, 1) = a$

The standard fuzzy intersection is defined by the relation

$$\mathbf{T}(a, b) = \min(a, b) \tag{30}$$

illustrated in Figure 15.

- *Fuzzy union* (T-conorm operation) of fuzzy sets A and B is generally described by the relation

$$(A \cup B)(x) = \mathbf{S}[A(x), B(x)] \tag{31}$$

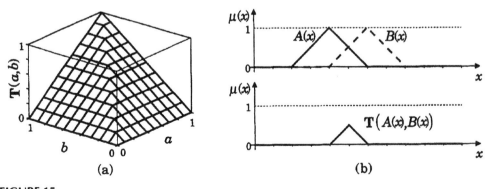

(a)   (b)

FIGURE 15
The standard fuzzy intersection: (a) graph of the fuzzy intersection; (b) the fuzzy intersection of fuzzy sets $A(x)$ and $B(x)$.

where **S** is the operator for fuzzy union. The basic properties of the operation are

Commutativity: $S(a, b) = S(b, a)$
Associativity: $S(a, S(b, c)) = S(S(a, b), c)$
Monotonicity: $b \leq c \Rightarrow S(a, b) \leq S(a, c)$
Idempotency: $S(a, a) = a$
Boundary condition: $S(a, 0) = a$

The standard fuzzy union is defined by formula

$$S(a, b) = \max(a, b) \tag{32}$$

illustrated in Figure 16.

3.2 Fuzzy Numbers

Fuzzy numbers are polarization sets with some special properties. A fuzzy number A is a fuzzy subset of the set of real numbers $\mathbb{R}$ with membership function $\mu_A: \mathbb{R} \to [0, 1]$ with the following attributes

Convexity: $\forall x_1, x_2, x_3 \in A,\ x_1 \leq x_2 \leq x_3:\quad \mu_A(x_2) \geq \min(\mu_A(x_1), \mu_A(x_3))$
Delimitation: $\exists x_1, x_2 \in \mathbb{R},\ x_1 < x_2,\ \forall x \in \mathbb{R}:\quad x \notin (x_1, x_2) \Rightarrow \mu_A(x) = 0$
Normality: $\sup_{x \in \mathbb{R}} \mu_A(x) = 1$

We use symbol $\mathbb{F}$ to denote the set of all fuzzy subsets of $\mathbb{R}$.

3.2.1 Properties of Fuzzy Numbers.
The shape of the membership function describing a fuzzy number can, in general, be arbitrary. However, in practice there are several types of fuzzy numbers that can be described by a suitable set of parameters. *Triangular fuzzy numbers* have a symmetric or asymmetric triangular shape, and are described by three parameters: the modal value a_m, and two side values a_l and a_r corresponding, respectively, to the lower and upper boundaries of the α-cut A_α for the level $\alpha = 0$. As triangular fuzzy numbers are easy to represent and simple to operate with, we consider all fuzzy numbers to be of triangular shape, unless stated otherwise. Other typical examples are *trapezoidal* and *bell-shaped* fuzzy numbers. For a brief overview of fuzzy numbers see [5, 7].

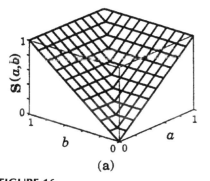
(a)

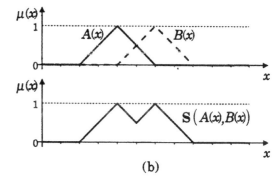
(b)

FIGURE 16
The standard fuzzy union: (a) graph of the fuzzy union; (b) the fuzzy union of fuzzy sets $A(x)$ and $B(x)$.

Fuzzy numbers are associated with some fuzzy uncertainty, that is vagueness or *fuzziness*. For the evaluation of the uncertainty of fuzzy values in some types of fuzzy neural networks, we have chosen a quadratic energy index

$$k_2(A) = \int_{a_l}^{a_r} \mu_A^2(x)\, dx \tag{33}$$

where a_l and a_r are, respectively, the lower and upper boundary of the α-cut $A_\alpha = [a_l^{(\alpha)}, \ a_r^{(\alpha)}]$ for the level $\alpha = 0$.

The simple energy index $k_1(A) = \int \mu_A(x)\, dx$ would give the same value of fuzziness for both the fuzzy set A, and its nearest crisp interval $\underline{A}$, as shown in Figure 17. The quadratic energy index (33) separates these two sets, $k_2(A) \neq k_2(\underline{A})$ [6].

3.2.2 Operations on Fuzzy Numbers: Fuzzy Arithmetic.
A general framework for extending nonfuzzy mathematical operations to deal with fuzzy operands is provided by the *extension principle* introduced by Zadeh [17]. It asserts that

$$f(A) = f(\mu_1/x_1 + \cdots + \mu_n x_n) \equiv \mu_1/f(x_1) + \cdots + \mu_n/f(x_n)$$

or, for the continuous support of A,

$$f(A) = f\left(\int_X \mu_A(x)/x \right) \equiv \int_Z \mu_A(x)/f(x)$$

where $f(x)$ is a point in Z and $\mu_A(x)$ is corresponding grade of membership in $f(A)$, which is a fuzzy subset of Z.

Using the extension principle, the basic operations over fuzzy quantities A and B can be expressed as a convolution in terms of the corresponding membership functions

$$\mu_{A*B}(z) = \sup_{z=x*y} \min(\mu_A(x), \mu_B(y)) \tag{34}$$

where $*$ is for any basic arithmetic operation, i.e., $* = \{+, \ -, \ \cdot, \ \backslash\}$. The basic fuzzy arithmetic operations are illustrated in Figure 18.

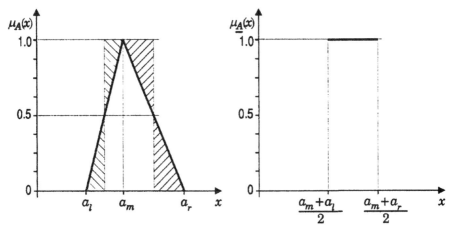

FIGURE 17
A fuzzy number A and its nearest crisp interval $\underline{A}$.

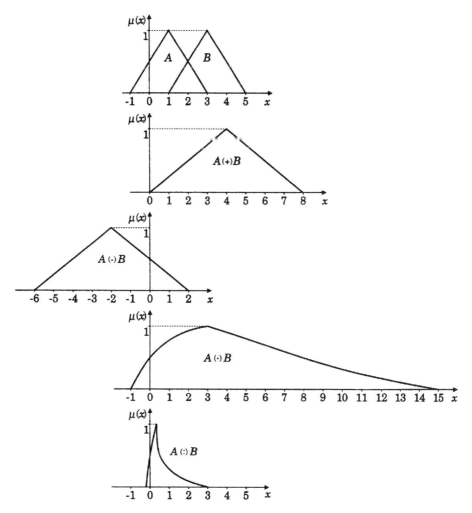

FIGURE 18
The basic fuzzy arithmetic operations.

4 CONCLUDING REMARKS

This chapter is the first one in a series treating theory of fuzzy neural networks. It describes the most important aspects of the basic constituent tools: neural networks and fuzzy systems.

In describing the basics of neural networks, we have focused on the most important aspects of neural information processing: the mechanisms of comparison of the new and learned knowledge, and corresponding processes of generation of the neural output signals. As we consider a sound model of the single neuron to be essential for the development of any more complicated network structures, we have devoted a considerable part of this chapter to the development and description of various models of neurons.

The overview of fuzzy systems aims to stress the distinctions of fuzzy sets and fuzzy numbers. Although these mathematical structures have common basis and many similar properties, they can be used to handle different aspects of fuzzy uncertainty. We have confined the overview to the basic definition and to description of some important properties of these structures. Mathematical tools for handling fuzzy sets and fuzzy numbers are also briefly described, and they will be treated in detail in the forthcoming part of the series regarding simple fuzzy neural models.

The knowledge presented in this chapter is the first step towards building a solid basis for fuzzy neural networks. In the next part, included in this volume [13], we introduce various models of fuzzy neurons and examine their capabilities. The future work will include the study of learning mechanisms of single fuzzy neurons, and the development of sophisticated fuzzy neural network structures.

APPENDIX A: OUTPUT FUNCTIONS

In this appendix we show various output functions that can be used in the (crisp) neural models described in this chapter. More detailed treatment of these and other functions can be found in [1, 3].

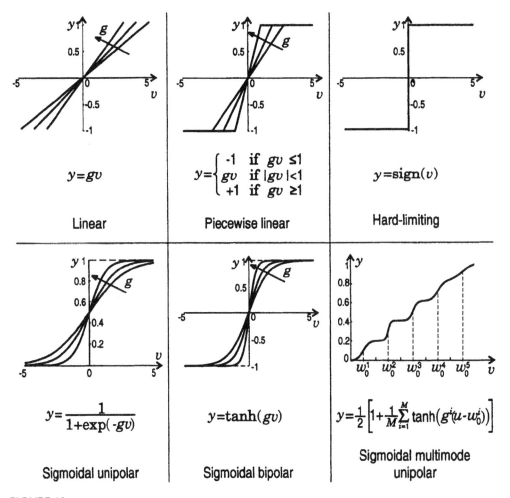

FIGURE 19
Variants of possible output functions for the product-based neural models.

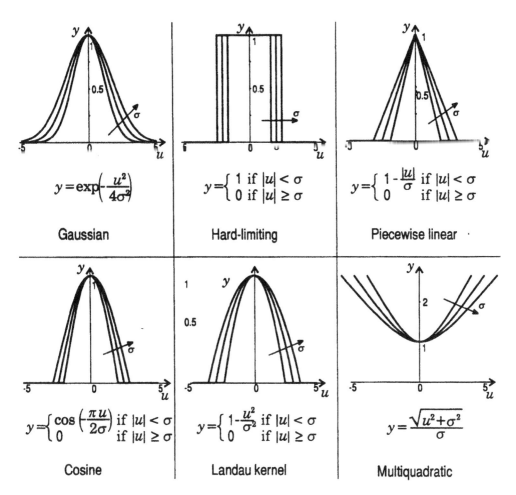

FIGURE 20

Variants of possible output functions for the distance-based neural models.

REFERENCES

[1] W. Duch and N. Jankowski, New neural transfer functions, *Applied Mathematics and Computer Science*, Vol. 7, No. 3, pp. 639–658, 1997.

[2] M.M. Gupta, Fuzzy logic and neural networks, in *Proc. 10th Int. Conf. Multiple Criteria Decision Making (TAIPEI'92)*, Japan, 1998, Vol. 3, pp. 281–294.

[3] K. Hlaváčková, *Some Estimations of the Approximation Error of Continuous Functions by RBF and KBF Networks*, TR-602, ICS, Academy of Sciences of the Czech Republic, Prague, 1994.

[4] R. Hecht-Nielsen, *Neurocomputing*. Addison-Wesley, Reading, MA, 1991.

[5] J.R. Jang and C. Sun, Neuro-fuzzy modeling and control. *Proc. IEEE*, Vol. 83, No. 3, pp. 378–405, 1995.

[6] A. Kaufmann and M.M. Gupta, *Fuzzy Mathematical Models in Engineering and Management Science*. North-Holland, New York, 1988.

[7] A. Kaufmann and M.M. Gupta, *Introduction to Fuzzy Arithmetic*. Van Nostrand Reinhold, New York, 1991.

[8] G.J. Klir and B. Yuan, *Fuzzy Sets and Fuzzy Logic*. Prentice-Hall, Englewood Cliffs, NJ, 1995.

[9] C. Koch, Computation and the single neuron, *Nature*, Vol. 385, pp. 207–211, 1997.

[10] C. Koch and T. Poggio, Multiplying with synapses and neurons, in T. McKenna, J. Davis, and S.F. Zornetzer (eds.) *Single Neuron Computation*, pp. 315–345, Academic Press, Boston, 1992.

[11] B. Kolb. *Brain Plasticity and Behavior.* Lawrence Erlbaum Associates, Mahwah, NJ, 1995.

[12] S.W. Kuffler, J.G. Nicholls, and A.R. Martin, *From Neuron to Brain: A Cellular Approach to the Function of the Nervous System.* Sinauer Associates, Sunderland, MA, 1984.

[13] P. Musílek and M.M. Gupta. Fuzzy Neural Networks, in N.K. Sinha and M.M. Gupta (eds.), this volume, Chapter 8.

[14] D. Nauck, Beyond neuro-fuzzy: Perspectives and directions, in *Proc. 3d European Congress on Intelligent Techniques and Soft Computing (EU-FIT'95) Aachen,* 1995, pp. 1159–1164.

[15] M. Verleysen, P. Thissen, J.-L. Voz, and J. Madrenas, An analog processor architecture for a neural network classifier, *IEEE Micro,* Vol. 14, pp. 16–28, 1994.

[16] L.A. Zadeh. Fuzzy sets, *Information and Control,* Vol. 8, pp. 338–353, 1965.

[17] L.A. Zadeh, The concept of a linguistic variable and its application to approximate reasoning. *Information Sciences,* Vol. 8, pp. 199–251, 1975.

[18] L.A. Zaadeh, What is soft computing? *http://www.cs.berkeley.edu/projects/Bisc/bisc.memo.html,* 1994.

[19] J.M. Zurada, *Introduction to Artificial Neural Systems,* West Publishing Company, St. Paul, MN, 1992.

CHAPTER 8

Fuzzy Neural Networks

PETR MUSÍLEK and MADAN M. GUPTA

Intelligent Systems Research Laboratory, College of Engineering, University of Saskatchewan, Saskatoon, Saskatchewan, Canada S7N 5A9

1 INTRODUCTION

Fuzzy neural networks and fuzzy neurons were first introduced in the early 1970s [16, 17]. They were understood as a fuzzy generalization of the McCulloch–Pitts model of the neuron [20]. The development of the field in the following years can be called "quiet" because almost no research projects were conducted, or made public. There was very little activity in the field during the 1980s [11, 25], but extensive research, resulting in some novel designs and applications, has been observed during the 1990s. The boom started at the beginning of the 1990s when several promising papers [2, 6, 24] appeared. From this point, many researchers have begun their activities in the field of fuzzy neural networks and produced substantial amounts of theoretical and applicative results.

Nevertheless, as in almost any new and developing field, that of fuzzy neural networks encounters controversies and obscurities. These mostly stem from the popularity of the concepts and their overuse. The term "fuzzy neural network" is frequently used without rationale or without sufficient specification. This can lead to unclear terminology and confusion. Some of these problems are addressed in this chapter and possible approaches to the "defuzzification" of fuzzy neural networks are presented. The particular intents of this chapter are:

- to point out to some controversies and misunderstandings encountered in this field;
- to set its boundaries and make corresponding terminology more accurate; and
- to develop general models of the basic units of fuzzy neural networks—the fuzzy neurons.

The main contents of this chapter are given in the following sections.

At the beginning of Section 2, we give a formal definition of fuzzy neural networks that clearly specifies the bounds of this field. It is followed by a detailed analysis of its implications. The most important one results in introduction of two distinctive classes of fuzzy neural networks treated separately in the following two sections.

Section 3 is devoted to the fuzzy neural networks based on principles and operations of fuzzy arithmetic, while Section 4 describes the fuzzy neural networks subsuming fuzzy logic. Each of

161

these sections begins with development of a corresponding generalized neural model followed by the definition of several types of specific models. In both sections, we also introduce several novel techniques for fuzzy arithmetic and fuzzy logic computations. The single neural structures are of prime interest because of their constructive role in building various models of fuzzy neural networks. To support our understanding, we give several examples of their use in simple classification problems.

Finally, Section 5 summarizes the contents of the chapter, and gives some concluding remarks. Appendices A and B give, respectively, concise overviews of basic fuzzy arithmetic and fuzzy logic operations necessary for the development of fuzzy neural models.

2   FUZZY NEURAL NETWORKS (FNNs)

In this section, we provide a basis for the theory of fuzzy neural networks (FNNs). First, we elaborate a general definition of fuzzy neural networks. The proposed paradigm is broad enough to accommodate many different models of fuzzy neural networks, but at the same time, it clearly specifies the bounds of this field.

Definition 1. A *fuzzy neural network* is a structure FNN (U, **W**, **X**, **Y**, L) with the following specifications:

(a) U is a nonempty set of fuzzy neurons and auxiliary units.

(b) The structure and parameters of the fuzzy neural network are described by the weight matrix **W** given by cartesian product $U \times U \to D_W$ (D_W is the domain of weights).

(c) The vector of fuzzy inputs **X** $\in D_X$ describes the input for the fuzzy neural network (D_X is the domain of the input vector).

(d) The vector of fuzzy outputs **Y** $\in D_Y$ describes the output of the fuzzy neural network (D_Y is the domain of the output vector).

(e) The learning algorithm L describes the mechanism for learning and adaptation to the new information (usually by changing the weight matrix **W**).

By realizing the confines given in the definition, one may see that the term "fuzzy neural network" is frequently used confusingly, without a rationale. In the following paragraphs, we describe two of the most common problems associated with fuzzy neural networks that are encountered frequently in recent literature.

First, the name "fuzzy neural network" implies a likeness between fuzzy neurons and biological neurons—the natural elements for information processing. This clear assumption is frequently left out of consideration, especially in the case of fuzzy logic-based FNNs. Namely, some of the so-called fuzzy neural networks are based on processing units realizing only elementary fuzzy logic operations [18, 23], and others do not retain some of the fundamental structural properties of neurons [9, 15]. From the theoretical and/or applications points of view, most of the papers present interesting new ideas. Nevertheless, the use of the tag "neural" is not appropriate and may cause confusion. We feel that the name "neuron" and its derivatives should be reserved for the information processing units resembling the structure and operation of their biological counterparts. We propose to use the name "fuzzy network" for schemes having a network structure based on fuzzy logic or fuzzy arithmetic operations, but not using the real neuron-like processing units.

The second implication, obvious from the name "fuzzy neural network" itself, is that FNNs are neural networks that are fuzzy, that is, they are able to process fuzzy information. A straightforward way of allowing such a processing mode consists of the use of fuzzy arithmetic operations to handle fuzzy quantities. However, most fuzzy neural networks introduced so far have used fuzzy logic operations to handle fuzzy sets. This is too correct, but it should be considered as a secondary approach to fuzzification of neural networks. The prevalence of the term "fuzzy neural network" can be compared to the use of the term "fuzzy logic" for all techniques based on the theory of fuzzy sets, sometimes called "fuzzy logic in the wide sense" [27]. It is acceptable when referring to fuzzy neural networks in general. However, we propose a refined classification that respects the existence of the two families of FNNs and prevents potential misunderstandings.

The classification consists of the separate treatment of the fuzzy neural networks operating with fuzzy sets describing linguistic terms, and the fuzzy neural networks operating with fuzzy sets in the form of fuzzy numbers. Each of these groups is suitable for different tasks, and requires the use of different mathematical tools. With respect to the mathematical aspect, we define the two groups of fuzzy neural networks as follows:

Fuzzy arithmetic neural networks (FANNs) operating on fuzzy numbers using fuzzy arithmetic; and

Fuzzy logic neural networks (FLNNs) operating on fuzzy sets of linguistic terms using fuzzy logic.

In the rest of this chapter, we describe the principles of operation of these two groups of FNNs. As was stated in the introduction, we are interested first in the basic building blocks of fuzzy neural networks—the fuzzy neurons.

3 FUZZY ARITHMETIC NEURAL NETWORKS (FANNs)

The basic building blocks of FANNs are *fuzzy arithmetic neurons* (FANs). They use fuzzy arithmetic operations to process an input vector of fuzzy quantities[1], $\mathbf{x} \in \mathbb{F}^n$, and yield a scalar fuzzy output $y \in \mathbb{F}^1$. Thus, the inputs and the output of a FAN are fuzzy numbers representing uncertain (vague) numerical values.

The FANs provide a natural extension of the original concept of the crisp neural models described in [22]. They allow us to introduce fuzzy uncertainty into the modeling without affecting the variety of functions to be used to perform single synaptic and somatic operations. In addition, the FANs preserve the absolute values of the quantities being processed (fuzzy logic neurons, discussed in Section 4, enable only operation with relative grades of membership).

Generally, the FANs can perform operations similar to the crisp neural models. In addition, they have the ability to cope with omnipresent vagueness and ambiguity. On the other hand, fuzzy arithmetic operations are generally harder to implement and the implementation usually brings some computational difficulties.

3.1 Generalized Fuzzy Arithmetic Neural Model

The generalized model of FAN can be derived from the generalized model of the crisp neuron by assuming that the input vector $\mathbf{x}_a \in \mathbb{F}^{n+1}$, the weight vector $\mathbf{w}_a \in \mathbb{F}^{n+1}$, and the output signal

---

[1] For a definition of fuzzy quantities see Appendix A.

$y \in \mathbb{F}$ are fuzzy quantities. Consequently, the operations $\odot$, $\oplus$, and ϕ are, respectively, the fuzzy synaptic operation, fuzzy aggregation operation, and fuzzy output function. This can be specified formally in the following definition.

Definition 2. *Generalized model of fuzzy arithmetic neuron* is an information processing unit FAN $(\mathbf{x}_a, \mathbf{w}_a, y, \odot, \oplus, \phi)$ with the following specifications:

    (a) The vector of fuzzy inputs $\mathbf{x}_a \in \mathbb{F}^{n+1}$ represents $n+1$ inputs $x_0, \ldots, x_n$, $n \geq 1$, where the threshold term $x_0 = 1$.

    (b) The vector of fuzzy weights $\mathbf{w}_a \in \mathbb{F}^{n+1}$ contains $n+1$ weights $w_0, \ldots, w_n$, $n \geq 1$, each w_i associated with a component x_i of the input vector; w_0 is the threshold term.

    (c) $y \in \mathbb{F}$ is the scalar fuzzy neural output.

    (d) $\odot$, $\oplus$, and ϕ are, respectively, the fuzzy arithmetic-based synaptic operator, operator for aggregation, and output function.

A brief overview of fuzzy arithmetic operations is given in Appendix A.

3.2 Specific Fuzzy Arithmetic Neural Models

In the following subsections, we develop two important instances of FANs using specific cases of the fuzzy arithmetic operators named in the general definition of FAN. They generally conform with the two crisp neural models described in [22]. In the fuzzy models, the corresponding synaptic and somatic operations are fuzzified for processing of fuzzy quantities.

3.2.1 *Product-based Fuzzy Arithmetic Neurons.*
Analogously to the crisp neural models, the synaptic operation is provided by the operation of multiplication. In the product-based FAN, fuzzy multiplication is used. It is a mapping $\mathbb{F} \times \mathbb{F} \rightarrow \mathbb{F}$, presuming the inputs and weights to be fuzzy quantities in accordance with the definition of the generalized model of a FAN. We can describe this type of fuzzy synaptic operation by the relation

$$z_i = w_i \odot x_i = w_i(\cdot)x_i, \qquad i = 0, 1, \ldots, n \tag{1}$$

where $(\cdot)$ is the operator for fuzzy multiplication. In standard fuzzy arithmetic, it is defined as in equation (25) in Appendix A. However, such a way of multiplying fuzzy numbers has one problematic feature: the fuzziness of the product is biased by the absolute value of the factors. Consequently, the standard product-based FANs are monotonic [3], and the correspond FANNs do not have the ability of universal approximation[2], as one would expect analogously to multilayer neural networks with crisp values [10].

    To overcome this difficulty, we have proposed a modified approach to multiplication of fuzzy numbers, based on the assumption that neural inputs and weights can be treated as interactive quantities. It performs multiplication of the model values of the factors, and adopts the fuzziness of the fuzziest of the fuzzy numbers, as follows:

$$z_i = w_i[\cdot]x_i \begin{cases} z_m = w_m x_m \\ z_1^{(0)} = z_m - \max(l_x, l_w) \\ z_2^{(0)} = z_m + \max(r_x, r_w) \end{cases} \tag{2}$$

---

[2] The approximation properties of an information processing scheme express its capacity to approximate the given function f on a compact domain to an arbitrary degree of accuracy ε.

where $[\cdot]$ is the operator for modified fuzzy multiplication, and $l_{(\cdot)}$ and $r_{(\cdot)}$, respectively, represent the left and right parts of the support of the corresponding fuzzy number. Such modified operation of fuzzy multiplication keeps the same modal value of the product as does the extension principle based fuzzy multiplication. In addition, unlike in the other case, the fuzziness of the product depends only on the fuzziness of the factors. The convenience of this approach in fuzzy neural networks is shown below in Example 3.2.1.

Fuzzy arithmetic-based *aggregation* can be realized by fuzzy summation, which is a mapping $\mathbb{F}^{n+1} \rightarrow \mathbb{F}$, generally described as

$$v = \overset{n}{\underset{i=0}{(+)}} z_i = \overset{n}{\underset{i=0}{(+)}} [w_i(\cdot)x_i] \tag{3}$$

where $(+)$ is the operator of fuzzy summation. The extension principle-based fuzzy summation is defined by equation (24) in Appendix A. This type of fuzzy computation involves a serious problem. When adding a substantial number of fuzzy quantities, the fuzziness of the sum can grow to such values that the result lacks a clear interpretation.

We have proposed a modified approach to summation of fuzzy numbers that corresponds to addition of interactive quantities [4]. It performs summation of the modal values of the fuzzy numbers, and adopts the fuzziness of the fuzziest of summed numbers, as follows:

$$v = \overset{n}{\underset{i=0}{[+]}} z_i \begin{cases} v_m = \displaystyle\sum_{i=0}^{n} z_{im} \\ v_1^{(0)} = v_m - \displaystyle\max_{i=0}^{n} l_{z_i} \\ v_2^{(0)} = v_m + \displaystyle\max_{i=0}^{n} r_{z_i} \end{cases} \tag{4}$$

where $[+]$ is the operator for modified fuzzy summation. The advantages of this technique are similar to those of the modified fuzzy multiplication described above.

The fuzzy arithmetic *output function* could be, analogously to the crisp neural models, realized by a fuzzy sigmoidal function obtained by the extension principle (equation 23). The general formula for fuzzy exponentiation (equation 26) can, for the special case e^v, $v \in \mathbb{F}$, be simplified to the form [19]:

$$\mu_{e^v}(x) = \mu_v(\ln x), \qquad x > 0 \tag{5}$$

The exponential functions evaluated using equation (5) would be then used to compute a sigmoidal function, for example, the unipolar logistic function. However, as sigmoidal functions are generally based on exponentiation, the use of extension principle-based output functions produces problems connected with zero and negative exponents. To cope with these problems, some researchers have assigned specific shapes of membership functions to the fuzzy sets [8], or used simplified formulas to compute the output fuzzy quantity of the fuzzy neuron [5].

We have proposed the use of a set of equations to determine the fuzzy neural output $y \in \mathbb{F}$ in a triangular shape. It is generally based on the simplification of the calculations using the characteristic values of fuzzy numbers. In the case of triangular fuzzy numbers, the fuzzy sigmoidal function can be computed using the following three equations:

$$y = \begin{cases} y_m = \dfrac{1}{1 + \exp(-gv_m)} \\ y_1^{(0)} = \dfrac{1}{1 + \exp(-gv_1^{(0)})} \\ y_2^{(0)} = \dfrac{1}{1 + \exp(-gv_2^{(0)})} \end{cases} \tag{6}$$

where $\{v_1^{(0)}, v_m, v_2^{(0)}\}$ and $\{y_1^{(0)}, y_m, y_2^{(0)}\}$, respectively, describe the triangular fuzzy numbers v and y. This approach ensures the validity of the used output function over the whole domain of real fuzzy numbers Γ. In addition, the output fuzzy quantity retains the triangular form, which is easy to store and manipulate, and its fuzziness is connected with both the ambiguity of the aggregated internal state of the neuron v and its modal value expressing the similarity of the fresh neural inputs and the learned experience. The situation is shown in Figure 1 (fuzziness of the input fuzzy number is $k_2(v) = 1.3$, parameter $g = 1$).

Such dependence conforms well to the nature of human information processing. Consider that observations, corresponding to the fresh neural inputs, are obtained with some degree of uncertainty. If these observations do not show any correlation to the expectations, corresponding to the learned experience stored in the synaptic weights, the uncertainty of the associated conclusion remains relatively high. If, on the other hand, the observations are positively or negatively correlated to the expectations, the uncertainty of the conclusion is reduced despite the original fuzziness of the observations.

EXAMPLE 3.2.1
To illustrate the function of the product-based FAN, we will consider the following simple classification problem. Six patterns, described by the feature vectors $x^{(i)}$ of triangular fuzzy numbers, should be classified according to their membership in classes 1 and 2 as follows

	Patterns	Class
$x^{(1)} = [\{0.9,\ 1.0,\ 1.1\},\ \{0.9,\ 1.0,\ 1.1\}]^T$		1
$x^{(2)} = [\{0.8,\ 0.9,\ 1.0\},\ \{0.8,\ 0.9,\ 1.0\}]^T$		1
$x^{(3)} = [\{0.5,\ 0.6,\ 0.7\},\ \{0.6,\ 0.7,\ 0.8\}]^T$		1
$x^{(4)} = [\{0.3,\ 0.4,\ 0.5\},\ \{0.4,\ 0.5,\ 0.6\}]^T$		2
$x^{(5)} = [\{0.3,\ 0.4,\ 0.5\},\ \{0.1,\ 0.2,\ 0.3\}]^T$		2
$x^{(6)} = [\{-0.1,\ 0.0,\ 0.1\},\ \{-0.1,\ 0.0,\ 0.1\}]^T$		2

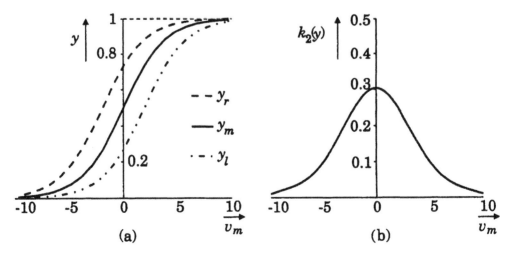

FIGURE 1
Modified fuzzy sigmoidal function. (a) Graph of the three characteristic values of the output triangular fuzzy number $y = \{y_1^{(0)}, y_m, y_2^{(0)}\}$. (b) Graph of the fuzzy uncertainty determined by the energy index k_2.

This problem can be solved by a simple product-based FAN classifier as shown in Figure 2. Analogously to the crisp product-based neuron, the weights separate the pattern space into two half-planes corresponding to the positive and negative correlation between the neural weights and inputs. In the case of a product-based FAN, the separating line represents only the modal values $v_m = 0$ of the corresponding fuzzy numbers $v \in \mathbb{F}$. The slope and intercept of the line are thus determined by the modal values of the weight vector. Although the fuzzy numbers lying on the line have zero modal value, the fuzziness of the fuzzy numbers depends on the fuzziness of the corresponding inputs and weights. In this example, the components of the weight vector are set to triangular fuzzy numbers

$$\mathbf{w}_a = [w_0, \ w_1, \ w_2]^T = [\{-1.1, \ -1.0, \ -0.9\}, \ \{0.9, \ 1.0, \ 1.1\}, \ \{0.9, \ 1.0, \ 1.1\}]^T$$

In the preceding section, we described two different product-based FAN models based on the standard and the modified fuzzy arithmetic computations. Therefore, in this example, we show results obtained using both the models. The standard product-based FAN uses the standard fuzzy arithmetic operations based on the extension principle, i.e., fuzzy summation and fuzzy multiplication defined, respectively, in equations (24) and (25) in Appendix A. The modified product-based FAN uses the modified fuzzy arithmetic operations defined by equations (2) and (4). Both the product-based FANs use the modified fuzzy sigmoidal function described by equation (6) with parameter $g = 5$. Results of classification for six different patterns are given in Tables 1 and 2.

In both cases the classification results represent the membership of the patterns in a given class by graded values. If we compare the numeric values of the example patterns and the corresponding results to those obtained for the crisp product-based neuron in [22], we see that the corresponding modal values are identical. However, the FANs provide additional information on fuzzy uncertainty connected with the results.

From the results given in the tables, it is obvious that the modified product-based FAN is able to perform the classification task in a better way than the standard product-based FAN based on the extension principle. Although the modal values of output fuzzy quantities are identical, their fuzziness differ:

- The fuzziness of the results of the standard FAN is coupled with the modal value of the neural inputs. It is, in general, considerably larger than the fuzziness of inputs and weights of this FAN.

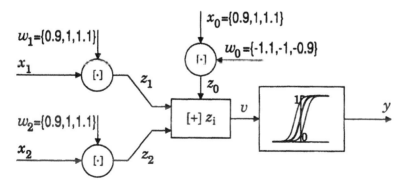

FIGURE 2
The product-based FAN classifier.

Table 1 The Results of Classification by the Standard Product-based FAN (modal values of fuzzy numbers are shown in bold; fuzziness of the input fuzzy numbers, weights, and threshold is uniform ($k - 0.13$)

	$x_{11}^{(0)}$	x_{1m}	$x_{12}^{(0)}$	$x_{21}^{(0)}$	x_{2m}	$x_{22}^{(0)}$	$y_1^{(0)}$	y_m	$y_2^{(0)}$	$k_2(y)$
	Input pattern						Standard product-based FAN			
1	0.9	**1.0**	1.1	0.9	**1.0**	1.1	0.96	**1.00**	1.00	0.03
2	0.8	**0.9**	1.0	0.8	**0.9**	1.0	0.90	**0.98**	1.00	0.07
3	0.5	**0.6**	0.7	0.6	**0.7**	0.8	0.60	**0.82**	1.00	0.27
4	0.3	**0.4**	0.5	0.4	**0.5**	0.6	0.20	**0.38**	1.00	0.53
5	0.3	**0.4**	0.5	0.1	**0.2**	0.3	0.02	**0.11**	1.00	0.65
6	−0.1	**0.0**	0.1	−0.1	**0.0**	0.1	0.00	**0.00**	0.84	0.56

Table 2 The Results of Classification by the Modified Product-based FAN (modal values of fuzzy numbers are shown in bold; fuzziness of the input fuzzy numbers, weights, and threshold is uniform ($k=0.13$)

	$x_{11}^{(0)}$	x_{1m}	$x_{12}^{(0)}$	$x_{21}^{(0)}$	x_{2m}	$x_{22}^{(0)}$	$y_1^{(0)}$	y_m	$y_2^{(0)}$	$k_2(y)$
	Input pattern						Modified product-based FAN			
1	0.9	**1.0**	1.1	0.9	**1.0**	1.1	0.99	**1.00**	1.00	0.00
2	0.8	**0.9**	1.0	0.8	**0.9**	1.0	0.97	**0.98**	0.99	0.01
3	0.5	**0.6**	0.7	0.6	**0.7**	0.8	0.73	**0.82**	0.88	0.10
4	0.3	**0.4**	0.5	0.4	**0.5**	0.6	0.27	**0.38**	0.50	0.15
5	0.3	**0.4**	0.5	0.1	**0.2**	0.3	0.08	**0.11**	0.18	0.07
6	−0.1	**0.0**	0.1	−0.1	**0.0**	0.1	0.00	**0.00**	0.01	0.00

- The fuzziness of the results of the modified FAN is inversely coupled exclusively with the absolute value of correlation between the presented patterns and the weight vector. It is, in general, comparable to the fuzziness of inputs and weights of this FAN.

Based on these observations, we conclude that the modified product-based FAN provides more consistent model for the processing of fuzzy uncertain information than the standard product-based FAN. The fuzziness of the output quantities of the modified product-based FAN corresponds inversely to the absolute value of correlation between the fresh neural inputs and the learned knowledge. The graphical representation of the results is given in Figure 3.

3.2.2 Distance-based Fuzzy Arithmetic Neurons.
The distance-based fuzzy arithmetic neurons provide an alternative way of evaluating confluence of vectors of fuzzy numbers. The most obvious measure can be described by the distance relation

$$z_i = x_i \odot w_i = |x_i(-)w_i| \tag{7}$$

which provides the partial (element-by-element) distance z_i between the corresponding components of the input and weight vectors. The aggregation of these partial results then provides an alternative fuzzy confluence operation ©. Similarly to the crisp distance-based models, we can use the general distance relation,

$$u = \mathbf{x} \text{ © } \mathbf{w} = \ell(\mathbf{x}, \ \mathbf{w}) = \sqrt[r]{(+) \sum_{i=1}^{n} |x_i(-)w_i|^r} \tag{8}$$

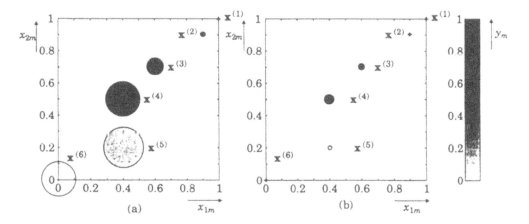

FIGURE 3
Application of the product-based FANs for pattern classification. (a) The results obtained by the standard product based FAN. (b) The results obtained by the modified product-based FAN (brightness of the ith circle represents the modal value of the corresponding output fuzzy number $y^{(i)}$ on the scale shown on the right; its diameter represents the fuzziness $k_2^{(i)}$).

where n is the dimensionality of the input space, and r is the order of the distance measure. In the crisp distance-based models, Euclidean distance ($r = 2$) is most commonly used. However, in the case of fuzzy arithmetic neurons, the use of such distance measures may be potentially complicated because of the difficulties connected with computing the roots with the order $r \geq 2$. In addition, the fuzzy arithmetic operation of aggregation (+) obtained by the extension principle (equation 24) would bring similar difficulties as in the case of the standard product-based FAN described in the preceding section.

Therefore, we have proposed a modified fuzzy confluence operation that provides a simplified computation of the distance between the two vectors of fuzzy numbers $\mathbf{w}$, $\mathbf{x} \in \mathbb{F}^n$. It can be generally described by the relation

$$u = \mathbf{w} \, \textcircled{c} \, \mathbf{x} = \frac{\overset{n}{[+]} |w_i[-]x_i|}{n} \tag{9}$$

where $[-]$ is the modified operator for fuzzy subtraction defined as the modified addition of two fuzzy numbers w_i and x_i^- (the image of x_i)

$$w_i[-]x_i = w_i[+]x_i^- \tag{10}$$

The image of a fuzzy number [13] is defined as follows: If $x_i = \{x_{i1}^{(0)}, x_{im}, x_{i2}^{(0)}\}$, then $x_i^- = \{-x_{i2}^{(0)}, -x_{im}, -x_{i1}^{(0)}\}$. The same method is used when determining the absolute value of a fuzzy number in equation (9).

The distance measure (9) corresponds to the arithmetic mean of the distances between the components of the input and weight vectors. It can be used instead of the quadratic mean (8), which can produce potential problems connected with computing the roots of negative arguments[3].

The fuzzy arithmetic *output function* for this type of FAN can be taken as a fuzzy variant of the Gaussian function. The function is generally based on exponentiation, which can lead to potential formal complications as mentioned in the previous section. Therefore, we have

---

[3] Any fuzzy number, though positive in terms of its modal value, can partially reach the negative values through its lower part.

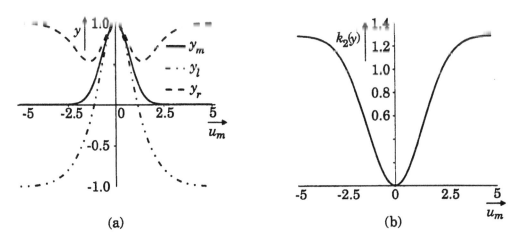

FIGURE 4
Modified fuzzy Gaussian function. (a) Graph of the three characteristic values of the output triangular fuzzy number $y = \{y_1^{(0)}, y_m, y_2^{(0)}\}$. (b) Graph of the fuzzy uncertainty determined by the energy index k_2.

proposed the use of a modified fuzzy Gaussian function defined by the following set of equations:

$$y = \begin{cases} y_m = \exp\left(-\dfrac{u_m^2}{4\sigma^2}\right) \\[2ex] y_1^{(0)} = y_m - l_y; \ l_y = 1 - \exp\left(-\dfrac{u_m^2}{4l_u^2}\right) \\[2ex] y_2^{(0)} = y_m + r_y; \ r_y = 1 - \exp\left(-\dfrac{u_m^2}{4r_u^2}\right) \end{cases} \qquad (11)$$

where u_m is the modal value of the fuzzy number u, $\{y_m, y_1^{(0)}, y_2^{(0)}\}$ describe the triangular fuzzy number y, and $l_{(\cdot)}$ and $r_{(\cdot)}$, respectively, represent the left and right part of the support of the corresponding triangular fuzzy number. This approach ensures the validity of the used output function over the whole domain of fuzzy numbers $\mathbb{F}$. Additionally, the output fuzzy quantity retains the triangular form, and its fuzziness is connected with both the ambiguity of the aggregated internal state of the neuron u and its modal value expressing the similarity of the fresh neural inputs and the stored weights. The situation is shown in Figure 4 (fuzziness of the input fuzzy number is $k_2(u) = 1.3$, parameter $\sigma = 1$).

Finally, let us note some other important operations belonging to the group of distance-based fuzzy arithmetic operations. These are *Hausdorff distance* [1] applicable to arbitrary sets, and the *dissemblance index* [13] referring particularly to fuzzy numbers. In contrast to the measures based on the norms (7) and (9), these operations evaluate distance between two fuzzy sets by a crisp real number. Consequently, we obtain the output of such a fuzzy neuron in terms of a crisp real value. This may be used to construct hybrid (fuzzy/crisp or fuzzy arithmetic/logic) fuzzy neural networks[4].

---

[4] The term "hybrid fuzzy neural network" is used in [3] to denote a fuzzy neural network with various fuzzy arithmetic functions. We consider such use of the tag "hybrid" not to be adequate as the signals are uniform over the whole fuzzy neural network.

EXAMPLE 3.2.2

To illustrate the function of the distance-based fuzzy arithmetic neuron, we will consider the following classification problem. Six patterns, described by the feature vectors $\mathbf{x}^{(i)}$ of triangular fuzzy numbers, should be classified according to their membership in classes 1 and 2 as follows

Patterns	Class
$\mathbf{x}^{(1)} = [\{0.9, \ 1.0, \ 1.1\}, \ \{0.9, \ 1.0, \ 1.1\}]^T$	1
$\mathbf{x}^{(2)} = [\{0.9, \ 1.0, \ 1.1\}, \ \{0.4, \ 0.5, \ 0.6\}]^T$	1
$\mathbf{x}^{(3)} = [\{0.4, \ 0.5, \ 0.6\}, \ \{0.4, \ 0.5, \ 0.6\}]^T$	1
$\mathbf{x}^{(4)} = [\{0.4, \ 0.5, \ 0.6\}, \ \{0.4, \ 0.5, \ 0.6\}]^T$	2
$\mathbf{x}^{(5)} = [\{1.9, \ 2.0, \ 2.1\}, \ \{0.9, \ 1.0, \ 1.1\}]^T$	2
$\mathbf{x}^{(6)} = [\{1.9, \ 2.0, \ 2.1\}, \ \{1.9, \ 2.0, \ 2.1\}]^T$	2

This problem can be solved by a simple distance-based FAN classifier shown in Figure 5.

Analogously to the crisp distance-based neuron, the weights describe a prototype configuration of the features x_1, x_2 representing a given class. In the case of a distance-based FAN, the modal values u_m describe the modal part of the fuzzy gradient surface defined by the distance measure u. The fuzziness of the gradient surface depends on the fuzziness of the corresponding inputs and weights. Here, the weight vector is set to $\mathbf{w} = [\{0.9, \ 1.0, \ 1.1\}, \ \{0.9, \ 1.0, \ 1.1\}]^T$.

The modified distance-based FAN used in this example is based on the modified fuzzy distance measure (9) and the modified fuzzy Gaussian function described by equation (11). Results of classification for six different patterns are given in Table 3.

The classification results represent the membership of the patterns in a given class by graded values. If we compare the numeric values of the example patterns and the corresponding results to those obtained for the crisp distance-based neuron in [22], we see that the corresponding modal values are similar (the difference for patterns $\mathbf{x}^{(2)} - \mathbf{x}^{(6)}$ stems from the different distance measure used in either case). However, the FANs provide additional information on fuzzy uncertainty connected with the results. Implications on fuzziness of the neural outputs stated in Example 3.2.1 are valid for the distance-based FAN as well. That is, the fuzziness of the output quantities of the modified distance-based FAN corresponds inversely to the distance between the

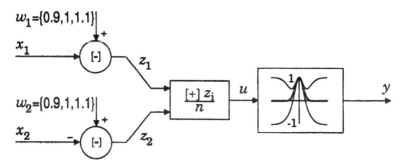

FIGURE 5
The distance-based FAN classifier.

Table 3   The Results of Classification by the Distance-based FAN (modal values of fuzzy numbers are shown in bold; fuzziness of the input fuzzy numbers and weights is uniform $\lambda_j = 0.13$)

	Input patterns					Modified distances-based FAN			
	$x_{11}^{(0)}$	x_{1m}	$x_{12}^{(0)}$	$x_{21}^{(0)}$	x_{2m}	$x_{22}^{(0)}$	$y_1^{(0)}$	y_m	$y_2^{(0)}$	$k_2(y)$
1	0.9	**1.0**	1.1	0.9	**1.0**	1.1	1.00	**1.00**	1.00	0.00
2	0.9	**1.0**	1.1	0.4	**0.5**	0.6	0.46	**0.78**	1.10	0.43
3	0.4	**0.5**	0.6	0.4	**0.5**	0.6	−0.42	**0.37**	1.15	1.05
4	0.4	**0.5**	0.6	0.3	**0.4**	0.5	−0.55	**0.30**	1.14	1.13
5	1.9	**2.0**	2.1	0.9	**1.0**	1.1	−0.42	**0.37**	1.15	1.05
6	1.9	**2.0**	2.1	1.9	**2.0**	2.1	−0.98	**0.01**	1.02	1.33

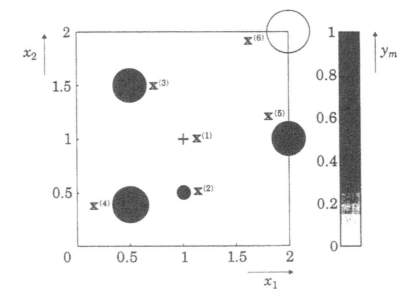

FIGURE 6

Application of the modified distance-based FAN for pattern classification (brightness of the ith circle represents the modal value of the corresponding output polarization number $y^{(i)}$ on the scale shown on the right; its diameter represents the fuzziness $k_2^{(i)}$).

fresh neural inputs and the learned knowledge. The graphical representation of the results is given in Figure 6.

4   FUZZY LOGIC NEURAL NETWORKS (FLNNs)

The basic building blocks of fuzzy logic-based fuzzy neural networks are neurons with fuzzy logic, termed *fuzzy logic neurons* (FLNs). They use fuzzy logic operations to process the fuzzy inputs **x** from the unit hypercube $[0, 1]^n$ to obtain an output $y \in [0, 1]^1$. The inputs and the output of such a fuzzy logic neuron express the degree of membership of certain quantities to the given polarization sets (e.g. concepts, or linguistic hedges) rather than the fuzzy (uncertain) value as in the case of the FANs.

The FLNs are presently the most frequently used types of fuzzy neural models [7, 9, 15]. Fuzzy logic operations, such as T-norms and T-conorms, are easy to implement and they generally do not bring any computational difficulties. The learning algorithms for these processing units are also easier and satisfying. The corresponding fuzzy neural networks are largely characterized by the local representation of well-defined fuzzy concepts. These local-representation schemas are closer to the rule-based fuzzy systems than to the original concept of neural networks.

4.1 Generalized Fuzzy Logic Neural Model

The generalized model of FLN can be derived from the generalized model of the crisp neuron by assuming the input vector $\mathbf{x} \in [0, 1]^n$, the weight vector $\mathbf{w} \in [0, 1]^n$, and the output signal $y \in [0, 1]$ are expressed in terms of their membership functions. Consequently, the operations $\odot$, $\oplus$, and ϕ are, respectively, the fuzzy logic synaptic operation, fuzzy logic aggregation operation, and fuzzy logic output function. This can be formally specified in the following definition.

Definition 3. The *generalized model of fuzzy logic neuron* is an information processing unit FLN $(\mathbf{x}, \mathbf{w}, y, \odot, \oplus, \phi)$ with the following specifications:

(a) The input vector $\mathbf{x} \in [0, 1]^n$ represents n fuzzy inputs $x_1, \ldots, x_n$, $n \geq 1$.

(b) The weight vector $\mathbf{w} \in [0, 1]^n$ contains n fuzzy weights $w_1, \ldots, w_n$, $n \geq 1$, each w_i associated with a component x_i of the input vector.

(c) $y \in [0, 1]$ is the scalar fuzzy neural output.

(d) $\odot$, $\oplus$, and ϕ are, respectively, the fuzzy logic-based synaptic operator, operator for aggregation, and output function.

A brief overview of fuzzy logic operations is given in Appendix B. The application of these operations is not arbitrary, but should comply with the information processing scheme of the biological neurons described in [22]. From this perspective, constructions such as MAX or MIN fuzzy neurons [15, 18], OR/AND neurons [9], and the like, should be understood as the misuse of the terms fuzzy neuron and fuzzy neural network (perhaps fuzzy networks would be a more fitting name). In addition, some such devices [15] do not observe the requirement of the sole output signal resulting from the principle of likeness to the biological neurons.

4.2 Specific Fuzzy Logic Neural Models

In the following subsections, we develop two important classes of FLNs conforming to two crisp neural models described in [22].

4.2.1 Product-based Fuzzy Logic Neurons. Product-based fuzzy logic neurons use the confluence operation realized by **T** and **S** fuzzy logic operations.

Variants of **T** operations (T-norms) are used to realize the fuzzy logic synaptic operator. $\odot$ most frequently. The fuzzy logic synaptic operation based on the standard **T** operation is described by the relation

$$z_i = w_i \odot x_i = \min(w_i, x_i) \tag{12}$$

Other possible **T** operations are the algebraic product described by equation (32), and the bounded difference represented by equation (33).

The fuzzy logic-based aggregation can be realized by **S** operations (T-conorms). Using the standard **S** operation (35), it can be defined as

$$u = \bigoplus_{i=1}^{n} z_i = \max_{i=1}^{n} z_i \qquad (13)$$

Other possible T-conorms are the algebraic sum described by equation (36), and the bounded sum represented by equation (37). Besides T-conorms, there are many other aggregation operations such as the harmonic and arithmetic means [14].

In the FLNs, the output function performs the mapping

$$u \rightarrow y \qquad (14)$$

where $u \in [0, 1]$ is the internal state of the neuron, and $y \in [0, 1]$ is the neural output. The output functions for the product-based fuzzy logic neurons are monotonically increasing, correspondingly to the sigmoidal output functions used in the product-based neural models. The simplest output function is the equality relation $y = u$. Its generalization

$$y = u^{\gamma} \qquad (15)$$

enables us to introduce a nonlinear output function, which is in many instances desirable and is biologically more plausible. The operation realized depends on the value of the parameter γ. For $\gamma < 1$ the operation is *dilatation*, while for $\gamma > 1$ the operation is *contraction*. The operation converts to the linear case of the equality for $\gamma = 1$. Graphs of the functions for the typical values of γ are shown in Figure 10a.

EXAMPLE 4.2.1
To illustrate the function of the product-based FLN, we will consider the following classification problem. Six patterns, described by the feature vectors $x^{(i)}$, should be classified according to their membership in classes 1 and 2 as follows:

Patterns	Class
$x^{(1)} = [1.0, \ 1.0]^T, \ x^{(2)} = [0.9, \ 0.9]^T, \ x^{(3)} = [0.6, \ 0.7]^T$	1
$x^{(4)} = [0.4, \ 0.5]^T, \ x^{(5)} = [0.4, \ 0.2]^T, \ x^{(6)} = [0.0, \ 0.0]^T$	2

The product based FLNs can be used for classification of patterns described by features expressed in terms of their membership to given fuzzy sets. Therefore, the crisp input patterns have to be fuzzified before further processing by the classifier. The patterns can be fuzzified using the following fuzzy partition:

$$\mu_{X_{i1}}(x_i) = \max\left[\min\left(1, \frac{b_1^u - x_i}{b_1^u - c_1}\right), \ 0\right] \qquad (16a)$$

$$\mu_{X_{i2}}(x_i) = \max\left[\min\left(\frac{b_2^l - x}{c_2 - b_2^l}, \ 1\right), \ 0\right] \qquad (16b)$$

The graph of the fuzzy partition is shown in Figure 7. We use the notation $\bar{x}$ to denote the fuzzified input vector, i.e.,

$$\bar{x} = [\bar{x}_1, \bar{x}_2, \bar{x}_3, \bar{x}_4]^T = [\mu_{X_{11}}(x_1), \mu_{X_{12}}(x_1), \ \mu_{X_{21}}(x_2), \ \mu_{X_{22}}(x_2)]^T$$

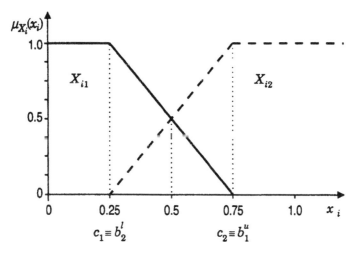

FIGURE 7
The fuzzy partition used in Examples 4.2.1 and 4.2.2.

The product-based FLN uses the standard fuzzy logic operations described in equations (12)–(15). The diagram of the simple FLN classifier is shown in Figure 8. The weight vector is set to $\mathbf{w} = [0,\ 1,\ 0,\ 1]^T$. The classification results for six different patterns are shown in Table 4.

From the table, it is obvious that the classification results are similar to the results obtained by the crisp product-based neuron in [22]. However, the FLN classifier can be used to solve problems described in linguistic terms, that is, in terms of linguistic variables and hedges. Also, the results are expressed in terms of membership of a given class determined by the weight vector and the parameters of fuzzification.

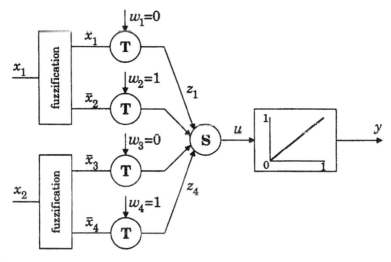

FIGURE 8
The product-based FLN classifier.

Table 4   The Results of Classification by the Product-based FLN

	Input pattern						Output
	x_1	x_2	$\bar{x}_1$	$\bar{x}_2$	$\bar{x}_3$	$\bar{x}_4$	y
1	1.0	1.0	0.0	1.0	0.0	1.0	1.0
2	0.9	0.9	0.0	1.0	0.0	1.0	1.0
3	0.6	0.7	0.3	0.7	0.1	0.9	0.9
4	0.4	0.5	0.7	0.3	0.5	0.5	0.5
5	0.4	0.2	0.7	0.3	1.0	0.0	0.3
6	0.0	0.0	1.0	0.0	1.0	0.0	0.0

4.2.2   Distance-based Fuzzy Logic Neurons. T-operations are the only possible fuzzy logic-based measures of similarity between the input and the weight vectors of membership functions[5]. However, analogously to the processing pattern found in the distance-based crisp neural models, we have introduced a distance-based information processing scheme for the FLNs. Fuzzy logic neurons of this group use the distance between the components of the input and weight vectors of membership values to evaluate their dissimilarity.

We have proposed several operations to realize this type of synaptic processing. By introducing the so-called fuzzy dissimilarity measure **D**, we have obtained a fuzzy logic-based method for the evaluation of the distance of two points with respect to a fuzzy set. When using algebraic variants of the basic fuzzy logic operations (equations 32 and 36), we can determine the result of the fuzzy logic synaptic operation as

$$z_i = w_i \odot x_i = \mathbf{D}(w_i, \ x_i) = w_i + x_i - 3w_ix_i + w_ix_i^2 + w_i^2x_i - w_i^2x_i^2 \tag{17}$$

where **D** is the operator for fuzzy dissimilarity. Equation (17) describes a quadratic surface in the unit cube as shown in Figure 9. For details on the fuzzy dissimilarity operation and the corresponding fuzzy logic neuron see [21].

The fuzzy logic-based somatic operation of aggregation can be realized by the various T-conorms. Using the standard T-conorm (equation 35), the operation can be defined as

$$u = \bigoplus_{i=1}^{n} z_i = \max_{i=1}^{n} z_i \tag{18}$$

Other possible aggregative operations are the algebraic sum, the bounded sum and the harmonic and arithmetic means [14].

In the case of distance-based FLNs, the output mapping (14) is provided by a decreasing function corresponding to the positive part of the bell-shaped output function of the crisp distance-based neurons. The neural output can be obtained, for example, as the complement (28), of the internal state of the neuron. The fuzzy complement **C** can be generalized as follows:

$$y = \mathbf{C}(u) = (1 - u)^\gamma \tag{19}$$

where the parameter γ has similar effect as in equation (15). Graphs of the functions for the typical values of γ are shown in Figure 10b. The Sugeno class of fuzzy complements (29) can be employed as another group of suitable fuzzy output functions for distance-based FLNs.

---

[5] S-operations are sometimes also used to perform the synaptic operations; however, this does not comply with the general framework derived from the basic principles of biological neurons.

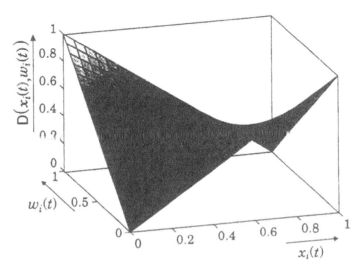

FIGURE 9
Graph of the dissimilarity operation defined by equation (17).

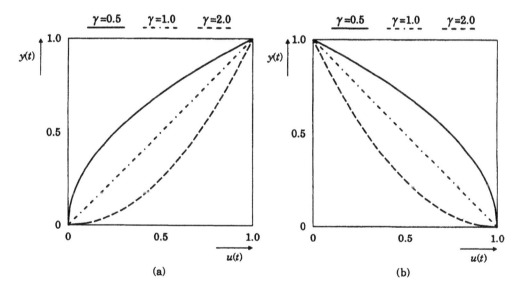

FIGURE 10
Fuzzy logic output functions (a) the increasing function $y = u^{\gamma}$, and (b) the decreasing function $y = (1 - u)^{\gamma}$ for various values of the parameter γ: dilatation ($\gamma < 1$), equality ($\gamma = 1$), contraction ($\gamma > 1$).

EXAMPLE 4.2.2
In order to illustrate the function of the distance-based FLN, we will consider the following classification problem. Six patterns, described by the feature vectors $\mathbf{x}^{(i)}$, should be classified according to their membership in classes 1 and 2 as follows:

Patterns	Class
$x^{(1)} = [1.0,\ 1.0]^T,\ ;\ x^{(2)} = [0.9,\ 0.9]^T,\ x^{(3)} = [0.6,\ 0.7]^T$	1
$x^{(4)} = [0.4,\ 0.5]^T,\ x^{(5)} = [0.4,\ 0.2]^T,\ x^{(6)} = [0.0,\ 0.0]^T$	2

The distance-based FLNs can be used for classification of patterns described by features expressed in terms of their membership to given fuzzy sets. Therefore, before further processing, the crisp input patterns have to be fuzzified, for example, by the fuzzy partition described by equations (16a) and (16b), shown in Figure 7.

The distance-based FLN uses the fuzzy logic operations described in equations (17)–(19). The diagram of the simple FLN classifier is shown in Figure 11. The weight vector is set to $w = [0,\ 1,\ 0,\ 1]^T$. The classification results for six different patterns are shown in Table 5.

From the table, it is obvious that the classification results are similar to the results obtained by the product-based FLN: the results are expressed in terms of membership of a given class determined by the weight vector and the parameters of fuzzification.

Table 5   The Results of Classification by the Distance-based FLN

			Input pattern				Output
	x_1	x_2	$\bar{x}_{11}$	$\bar{x}_{12}$	$\bar{x}_{21}$	$\bar{x}_{22}$	y
1	1.0	1.0	0.0	1.0	0.0	1.0	1.0
2	0.9	0.9	0.0	1.0	0.0	1.0	1.0
3	0.6	0.7	0.3	0.7	0.1	0.9	0.7
4	0.4	0.5	0.7	0.3	0.5	0.5	0.3
5	0.4	0.2	0.7	0.3	1.0	0.0	0.0
6	0.0	0.0	1.0	0.0	1.0	0.0	0.0

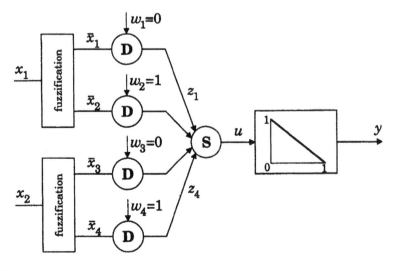

FIGURE 11
The distance-based FLN classifier.

5   CONCLUDING REMARKS

In this chapter, we have presented a new refined classification of fuzzy neural networks. This classification conforms to the nature of the processed information and to the corresponding mathematical fields: fuzzy arithmetic and fuzzy logic. As we consider a sound model of the single neuron to be essential for the development of any more complicated network structures, we have devoted a considerable part of this chapter to the development and description of various models of fuzzy neurons. We have also introduced several novel techniques for fuzzy arithmetic and fuzzy logic computations in the fuzzy neural networks.

Two distinctive aspects have been found among these models. First, they can be classified, with respect to the mathematical tools used, into three groups: crisp neurons, fuzzy arithmetic neurons, and fuzzy logic neurons. Second, there are two families of the confluence operations in each of the three groups: product-based and distance-based ones. All the cases have been treated in detail and supplemented by illustrative examples of their use for simple classification problems.

The knowledge presented in this chapter is the outcome of our recent endeavors to build a solid basis for fuzzy neural networks. This field is not settled yet, and it contains many controversies and confusions. We regard the definition of fuzzy neurons and examination of their capabilities as the first step in building the theory of fuzzy neural nets. Future work will include the study of learning mechanisms of the single fuzzy neurons, and the development of sophisticated fuzzy neural network structures.

APPENDIX A.   FUZZY ARITHMETIC OPERATIONS

In this appendix, we define *fuzzy quantities*[6] and the basic *arithmetic* operations [13] over them.

Definition A.1:   *Fuzzy quantity.* A fuzzy quantity is a fuzzy subset A of the set $\mathbb{R}$ of real numbers. Its membership function $\mu_A : \mathbb{R} \to [0, 1]$ conforms to following conditions:

$$\forall x_1, x_2, x_3 \in A, \ x_1 \leq x_2 \leq x_3: \quad \mu_A(x_2) \geq (\mu_A(x_1), \mu_A(x_3)) \tag{20a}$$

$$\exists x_1^A, x_2^A \in \mathbb{R}, \ x_1^A < x_2^A, \ \forall x \in \mathbb{R}: \quad x \notin (x_1^A, x_2^A) \Rightarrow \mu_A(x) = 0 \tag{20b}$$

$$\sup_{x \in \mathbb{R}} \mu_A(x) = 1 \tag{20c}$$

that is, a fuzzy quantity is a fuzzy subset A of $\mathbb{R}$, which is convex (20b), delimited (20c), and normal (20c). We use the symbol $\mathbb{F}$ to denote the set of all fuzzy quantities fulfilling these assumptions.

Fuzzy quantities are associated with some *fuzziness* that can be evaluated by various measures [12]. An important measure of fuzziness is the quadratic energy index k_2:

$$k_2(A) = \int_{a_1^{(0)}}^{a_2^{(0)}} \mu_A^2(x) \, dx \tag{21}$$

where $a_1^{(0)}$ and $a_2^{(0)}$ are, respectively, lower and upper boundaries of the α-level $A_\alpha = [a_1^{(0)}, a_2^{(0)}]$ for $\alpha = 0$.

The *extension principle* introduced by Zadeh provides a general framework for extending nonfuzzy mathematical operations in order to deal with fuzzy quantities. It asserts that

$$f(A) = f(\mu_1/x_1 + \cdots + \mu_n/x_n) \equiv \mu_1/f(x_1) + \cdots + \mu_n/f(x_n)$$

[6] Other terms such as *fuzzy variable* or *fuzzy number* can also be used

or, for the continuous support of A,

$$f(A) = f\left(\int_X \mu_A(x)/x\right) = \int_Z \mu_A(x)/f(x)$$

where $f(x)$ is a point in Z and $\mu_A(x)$ is corresponding grade of membership in $f(A)$, which is a fuzzy subset of Z [26].

Using the extension principle, the basic operations over two fuzzy quantities A and B can be expressed as a convolution

$$(A * B)(z) = \sup_{z=x*y} \min(A(x), B(y)) \tag{22}$$

or, in terms of membership functions,

$$\mu_{A*B}(z) = \sup_{z=x*y} \min(\mu_A(x), \mu_B(y)) \tag{23}$$

where $*$ is for any basic arithmetic operation, i.e., $* = \{+, -, \cdot, /\}$.

In the following, we define the fuzzy arithmetic operations needed for computations in the fuzzy arithmetic neurons, that is, the operations of fuzzy addition, fuzzy multiplication, and fuzzy exponentiation.

Definition A.2: *Fuzzy addition.* Let A and B be two fuzzy quantities from $\mathbb{F}$ with the corresponding membership functions μ_A and μ_B. Then the fuzzy quantity $C = A(+)B$ with membership function

$$\mu_C(z) = \sup_{z=x+y} \min(\mu_A(x), \mu_B(y)) \tag{24}$$

is called *fuzzy sum of A and B.*

Theorem A.1. if A and B are the fuzzy quantities in $\mathbb{F}$, then $C = A(+)B$ is also a fuzzy quantity in $\mathbb{F}$ (i.e., it is a fuzzy subset in $\mathbb{R}$ that is convex, delimited, and normal).

The algebraic properties of addition of fuzzy quantities can be summed up as follows. For all A, B, and C fuzzy quantities in $\mathbb{F}$, the following properties hold:

$$\begin{aligned}
\text{Commutativity:} \quad & A(+)B = B(+)A \\
\text{Associativit:} \quad & (A(+)B)(+)C = A(+)(B(+)C) \\
\text{Neutrality:} \quad & A(+)0 = 0(+)A = A
\end{aligned}$$

Thus, the set of fuzzy quantities in $\mathbb{F}$ with the operation of addition is *commutative additive monoid.* However, the image of a fuzzy quantity is not generally symmetric:

$$A(+)A^- = A^-(+)A \neq 0$$

Hence the operation of addition of fuzzy quantities in $\mathbb{F}$ does not have group structure.

Definition A.3: *Fuzzy multiplication.* Let A and B be two fuzzy quantities from $\mathbb{F}$ with corresponding membership functions μ_A and μ_B. Then the fuzzy quantity $C = A(\cdot)B$ with membership function

$$\mu_C(z) = \sup_{z=x\cdot y} \min(\mu_A(x), \mu_B(y)) \tag{25}$$

is called *fuzzy product of A and B.*

Theorem A.2. If A and B are fuzzy quantities in $\mathbb{F}$, then $C = A(\cdot)B$ is also a fuzzy quantity in $\mathbb{F}$ (i.e., it is a fuzzy subset in $\mathbb{R}$ that is convex, delimited, and normal).

The algebraic properties of multiplication of fuzzy quantities can be summed up as follows. For all A, B, and C fuzzy quantities in $\mathbb{F}$, the following properties hold:

$$
\begin{array}{ll}
\text{Commutativity:} & A(\cdot)B = B(\cdot)A \\
\text{Associativity:} & (A(\cdot)B)(\cdot)C = A(\cdot)(B(\cdot)C) \\
\text{Neutrality:} & A(\cdot)1 = 1(\cdot)A = A
\end{array}
$$

Thus, the set of fuzzy quantities in $\mathbb{F}$ with the operation of multiplication is *commutative multiplicative monoid*. However, the inverse element of a fuzzy quantity is not generally symmetric:

$$
A(\cdot)A^{-1} = A^{-1}(\cdot)A \neq 1
$$

Hence the operation of multiplication of fuzzy quantities in $\mathbb{F}$ does not have group structure.

Definition A.4: *Fuzzy exponentiation.* Let A and B be two fuzzy quantities from $\mathbb{F}$ with corresponding membership functions μ_A and μ_B. Then the fuzzy quantity $C = A^B$ with membership function

$$
\mu_C(z) = \sup_{z=x^y} \min(\mu_A(x), \mu_B(y)) \tag{26}
$$

is called the Bth fuzzy power of A.

APPENDIX B. FUZZY LOGIC OPERATIONS

In this appendix, we define *fuzzy sets* and the basic *logic* operations [14] over them.

Definition B.1: *Fuzzy set.* A fuzzy set A in an universe of discourse X is characterized by a membership function $\mu_A \in [0, 1]$ that associates with each point $x \in X$ a real-valued grade of membership of the point x in the universe X.

The possible logic operations over fuzzy sets are the generalizations of corresponding classical set operations (i.e., complement, intersection, and union). For each of these generalized operations there is an extensive group of possible instances. In the following we define the necessary basic concepts, provide important properties of these operations, and show some frequently used cases.

Definition B.2: *Fuzzy complement.* Let A be a fuzzy set on the universe X with the corresponding membership functions μ_A. The fuzzy set

$$
\mathbf{C}(A(x)) \tag{27}
$$

is called *fuzzy complement* of the fuzzy set A.

Important properties of the operation of fuzzy complement $\mathbf{C}$ are

$$
\begin{array}{ll}
\text{Boundary conditions:} & \mathbf{C}(0) = 1 \wedge \mathbf{C}(1) = 0 \\
\text{Monotonicity:} & \forall a, b \in [0, 1]: \quad a \leq b \Rightarrow \mathbf{C}(a) \geq \mathbf{C}(b) \\
\text{Involutivity:} & \forall a \in [0, 1]: \quad \mathbf{C}(\mathbf{C}(a)) = a
\end{array}
$$

Another frequently considered requirement is the continuity of the operation $\mathbf{C}$ on the interval $[0, 1]$.

The *standard fuzzy complement* is obtained by application of the relation

$$\mathbf{C}(a) = 1 - a \tag{28}$$

The more general operation, offering a broad class of fuzzy complements, is defined by the *Sugeno class* of fuzzy complements

$$\mathbf{C}(a) = \frac{1 - a}{1 + \lambda a}, \qquad \lambda \in (-1, \infty) \tag{29}$$

which is reduced to the standard fuzzy complement (28) for $\lambda = 0$.

Definition B.3:   T-*norm operation.* Let A and B be two fuzzy sets on the universe X with the corresponding membership functions μ_A and μ_B. The fuzzy set

$$(A \cap B)(x) = \mathbf{T}[A(x), \; B(x)] \tag{30}$$

is the result of T-*norm operation* $\mathbf{T}$ (or fuzzy intersection).

The algebraic properties of T-norm operation can be summed up as follows. For all $a, b, c \in [0, 1]$, the following properties hold:

Commutativity:	$\mathbf{T}(a, b) = \mathbf{T}(b, a)$
Associativity:	$\mathbf{T}(a, \mathbf{T}(b, c)) = \mathbf{T}(\mathbf{T}(a, b), c)$
Monotonicity:	$b \le c \Rightarrow \mathbf{T}(a, b) \le \mathbf{T}(a, c)$
Idempotency:	$\mathbf{R}(a, a) = a$
Boundary condition:	$\mathbf{T}(a, 1) = a$

Some other conditions such as continuity, subidempotency, and strict monotonicity are often considered.

The *standard fuzzy intersection* is defined by the relation

$$\mathbf{T}(a, b) = \min(a, b) \tag{31}$$

The other T-norm frequently used as the fuzzy intersection is the *algebraic product*

$$\mathbf{T}(a, b) = ab \tag{32}$$

The last example of the usual T-norms is the *bounded difference*

$$\mathbf{T}(a, b) = \max(0, a + b - 1) \tag{33}$$

Definition B.4:   T-*conorm operation.* Let A and B be two fuzzy sets on the universe X with the corresponding membership functions μ_A and μ_B. The fuzzy set

$$(A \cup B)(x) = \mathbf{S}[A(x), B(x)] \tag{34}$$

is the result of the T-*conorm operation* $\mathbf{S}$ (or fuzzy union).

The algebraic properties of T-conorm operation can be summed up as follows. For all $a, b, c \in [0, 1]$, the following properties hold:

Commutativity:	$S(a, b) = S(b, a)$
Associativity:	$S(a, S(b, c)) = S(S(a, b), c)$
Monotonicity:	$b \leq c \Rightarrow S(a, b) \leq S(a, c)$
Idempotency:	$S(a, a) = a$
Boundary condition:	$S(a, 0) = a$

Some other conditions such as continuity, superidempotency, and strict monotonicity are often considered as well.

The *standard fuzzy union* is defined by the formula

$$S(a, b) = \max(a, b) \tag{35}$$

The other T-conorm frequently used as the fuzzy union is the *algebraic sum*

$$S(a, b) = a + b - ab \tag{36}$$

The last example of the usual T-conorms is the *bounded sum*

$$S(a, b) = \min(1, a + b) \tag{37}$$

REFERENCES

[1] M. Barnsley, *Fractals Everywhere*. Academic Press, Orlando, FL, 1988.

[2] J.J. Buckley and Y. Hayashi, Fuzzy neural nets and applications, *Fuzzy Systems and AI*, Vol. 3, pp. 11–41, 1992.

[3] J.J. Buckley and Y. Hayashi, Can fuzzy neural nets approximate continuous fuzzy functions? *Fuzzy Sets and Systems*, Vol. 61, pp. 43–51, 1994.

[4] D. Dubois and H. Prade, Additions of interactive fuzzy numbers, *IEEE Trans. Automatic Control*, Vol. 26, pp. 926–936, 1981.

[5] T. Feuring and W.M. Lippe, Fuzzy neural networks are universal approximators, in *6th IFSA World Congress, Sao Paulo*, 1995, pp. 659–662.

[6] M.M. Gupta and G. Knopf, Fuzzy neural network approach to control systems, in *Proc. 1st Int. Symp. Uncertainty Modeling and Analysis, Maryland*, 1990, pp. 483–488.

[7] M.M. Gupta, Fuzzy logic and neural networks, in *Proc. 10th Int. Conf. Multiple Criteria Decision Making (TAIPEI'92)*, Taipei, 1992, Vol. 3, pp. 281–294.

[8] Y. Hayashi, J.J. Buckley, and E. Czogala, Fuzzy neural network with fuzzy signals and weights, in *Proc. IJCNN, Baltimore*, 1992, Vol. 2, pp. 696–701.

[9] K. Hirota and W. Pedrycz, OR/AND neuron in modeling fuzzy set connectives, *IEEE Trans. Fuzzy Systems*, Vol. 2, pp. 151–161, 1994.

[10] K. Hornik, Approximation capabilities of multilayer feedforward networks. *Neural Networks*, Vol. 4, pp. 251–257, 1991.

[11] D.J. Hunt and J.M. Keller, Incorporating fuzzy membership functions into the perceptron algorithm, *IEEE Trans. Pattern Analysis and Machine Intelligence*, Vol. 7, No. 6, pp. 693–699, 1985.

[12] A. Kaufman and M.M. Gupta, *Fuzzy Mathematical Models in Engineering and Management Science*. North-Holland, New York, 1988.

[13] A. Kaufman and M.M. Gupta, *Introduction to Fuzzy Arithmetic*. Van Nostrand Reinhold, New York, 1991.

[14] G.J. Klir and B. Yuan, *Fuzzy Sets and Fuzzy Logic*. Prentice-Hall, Englewood Cliffs, NJ, 1995.

[15] H.K. Kwan and Y. Cai, A fuzzy neural network and its application to pattern recognition, *IEEE Trans. Fuzzy Systems*, Vol. 2, No. 3, pp. 185–193, 1994.

[16] S.C. Lee and E.T. Lee, Fuzzy neurons and automata, in *Proc. 4th Princeton Conf. Information Science Systems*, 1970, pp. 381–385.

[17] S.C. Lee and E.T. Lee, Fuzzy neural networks, *Mathematical Biosciences*, Vol. 23, pp. 151–177, 1975.

[18] C.T. Lin and Y.C. Lu, A neural fuzzy system with linguistic teaching signals *IEEE Trans. Fuzzy Systems*, Vol. 3, no. 2, pp. 169–189, 1995.

[19] M. Mareš, *Computation over Fuzzy Quantities*, CRC Press, Boca Raton, FL, 1994.

[20] W.S. McCulloch and W. Pitts, A logical calculus of the ideas immanent in nervous activity, *Bull. Mathematical Biophysics*, Vol. 5, pp. 115–133, 1943.

[21] P. Musílek and M.M. Gupta, Dissimilarity based fuzzy logic neuron, in *Proc. Int. Conf. Soft Computing and Information/Intelligent Systems (IIZUKA'98)*, Iizuka, Fukuoka, Japan, 1998, pp. 763–766.

[22] P. Musílek and M.M. Gupta, Neural networks and fuzzy systems, in N.K. Sinha and M.M. Gupta (eds.) *Soft Computing and Intelligent Systems* (this volume, Chapter 7).

[23] W. Pedrycz and A.F. Rocha, Fuzzy-set based models of neurons and knowledge-based networks, *IEEE Trans. Fuzzy Systems*, Vol. 1, No. 1, pp. 254–266, 1993.

[24] H. Takagi, Fusion technology of fuzzy theory and neural networks, in *Proc. Int. Conf. Fuzzy Logic and Neural Networks (IIZUKA'90)*, Iizuka, Fukuoka, Japan, 1990, pp. 13–26.

[25] T. Yamakawa, A fuzzy neuron and its application to pattern recognition, in *Proc. 3rd IFSA Congress, Seattle*, 1989, pp. 30–38.

[26] L.A. Zadeh, The concept of a linguistic variable and its application to approximate reasoning, *Information Sciences*, Vol. 8, pp. 199–251, 1975.

[27] L.A. Zadeh, Why the success of fuzzy logic is not paradoxical, *IEEE Expert*, Vol. 9, No. 4, pp. 43–46, 1994.

CHAPTER 9

A Cursory Look at Parallel Architectures and Biologically Inspired Computing

S.K. BASU,
Computer Centre, Banaras Hindu University, India

1 INTRODUCTION

The speed of serial computers has increased enormously over the years, about a 10-fold increment in speed over seven years. The speed of circuits is approaching the limiting point. Hence serial computers using faster circuit technology are not able to cope with the massive computational demands of many problems such as the simulation of biological systems, weather forecasting, quantum chromodynamics, simulation of subatomic particle dynamics, computational fluid mechanics, and so on, beyond a certain problem size. Many of these problems require 1000 MFLOPS or more of computing power. Sequential machines offer far less computing power. However, by performing some or all of a desired computation in parallel using multiple processors or processing elements, faster execution time can be achieved. The important issues to be addressed by a computer architect are:

- How the processing elements should be interconnected
- How the problem should be partitioned into subtasks and mapped on the processors
- How data routing and synchronization among subtasks executing on different processors or processing elements should be done
- How much time is wasted in interprocessor communication
- What model of computation should be used

Parallelism can be exploited through the technique of pipelining or through multiprocessing, or through a suitable combination of the two. The main problem with pipeline design is decomposing the whole process into a number of functionally distinct stages each requiring more or less the same time. Otherwise, throughput of the pipeline will be decided by the slowest-running stage and all the other stages will be constrained to work at this speed by the introduction of suitable interstage buffers that will effectively slow down the speed of faster stages. This simple idea has been exploited not only in the design of functional units in advanced microprocessors but also in architectures for parallel processing. The major problems with pipeline designs are finding suitable functional decomposition of the original job into a number of stages, synchronization among these stages, and constant supply of inputs to the pipelines to offset the setup overhead of pipelining.

Multiprocessing means recruiting many processors or processing elements (tiny processors) with more or less same functional capabilities to decrease the processing time of a job or computational task. These processors may work together to complete the task in perfect synchrony or in an asynchronous mode. If the processors are powerful enough, only a few of them are used in a system because of cost and they generally work in asynchronous mode. These processors have their own local memories and they may or may not be sharing memory for interprocessor communication. For multiprocessors having no globally shared memory, inter-processor communication takes place through message passing. Conventional multiprocessors belong to this category of multiprocessing. For multiprocessors having shared global memory, interprocessor communication takes place through shared memory. Synchronization of processes running on different processors is effected by writing and reading into the shared memory. For synchronization of two processes running on different processors, one process writes into the global memory and the other process reads from it. For processes running on the same processor, synchronization is effected similarly, but writing and reading take place in the local memory.

The architectural innovations in the parallel processing domain include the well-known pipelined vector processor, SIMD architectures, systolic architectures, data flow architecture, reduction or demand driven architectures, wavefront array architectures, and MIMD architectures. Parallel VLSI architecture includes both application-specific and general, multipurpose systems. Examples of application-specific architectures include systolic arrays and examples of general-purpose multiprocessors include tree machines, hypercube, and various data flow, reduction and recursive machines.

An artificial neural network comprises many nonlinear computational elements (nodes) that are massively linked by weighted connections. A node receives its inputs, performs the weighted summation, applies an activation function to the weighted sum and outputs its result to other nodes. Considering that $1\,mm^2$ of human cortex contains about $100\,000$ neurons, each with several thousand connections, it is not too surprising that most neural models so far have been either constructed for analytical treatment or their behaviour has been studied only for small to medium-sized networks far below their natural scale with regard to the number of neurons and neural connections involved.

Simulation of large neural networks on a sequential computer frequently requires days and even weeks of computation and this long computational time had been a critical obstacle to progress in neural network researches. The computational power of even the fastest serial computer is still inferior to the biological computation taking place in the brain. The mass of processing elements and the interconnections that comprise an artificial neural network (ANN) make ANNs inherently computation-intensive. ANN algorithms are known to scale very poorly. Even serial supercomputers are bound to be overwhelmed by the computational demands of ANNs. ANNs have, in addition to their endemic computational intensity, a variety of inherent parallel aspects. Massively parallel computers have the potential to exploit the parallel nature of neural nets and to provide the computational power of such simulations.

Parallel architectures are mostly used for conventional computing. In this chapter an attempt has been made to examine the various generic parallel architectures for biologically inspired computation. In Section 2, readers are taken on a tour of the parallel architectures. In Section 3, these architectures are examined in the light of conventional numeric processing. In Section 4, the requirements of biologically inspired processing such as those in the fields of artificial intelligence, genetic algorithm and artificial neural computing are assessed. Section 5 addresses the issue of biologically inspired computing (mainly artificial neural computing) on the parallel architectures discussed in Section 2. Section 6 concludes the article.

2 ARCHITECTURE OF PARALLEL COMPUTERS

The success of an architect's design depends on how far the design meets the requirements of the end users efficiently and economically. These requirements are varied and often mutually conflicting. That is why no formal set of parameters have been identified unanimously for the analysis of architectures. No standardized benchmarks have been evolved. Practically, no systematic evaluations of different proposed computer interconnection network structures have been made. Nor have these criteria and their importance and value been investigated more than casually.

There has been rapid development in parallel architectures, especially during the 1980s and 1990s. Because of the diversity of parallel computer architectures, the situation has become bewildering for nonspecialists. It is difficult to define the term parallel architecture precisely in the absence of a suitable taxonomy. Nonetheless, some notion has evolved as to what should be accepted as parallel architecture:

- Architectures incorporating only low level parallel mechanisms are not regarded as parallel machines.
- Architectures under SIMD (single instruction and multiple data) and MIMD (multiple instructions and multiple data) categories in Flynn's taxonomy [1, 49] are regarded as parallel machines.
- Pipelined vector processors and other architectures that intuitively seem to merit inclusion as parallel architectures but that are difficult to accommodate gracefully within Flynn's taxonomy are also regarded as parallel machines.

Architectural innovations in the parallel processing domain include the well-known pipelined vector processors (e.g., Cray-X-MP/4 and ETA-10), SIMD architectures (e.g., ILLIAC-IV, Burroughs scientific processor, ICL's DAP, Loral's massively parallel processor, connection machines, GF11), and associative memory architecture, a distinct type of SIMD architecture (e.g., Bell Labs' parallel element processing ensemble, Loral's associative processor), systolic architectures (e.g., CMU's WARP and Saxby's Matrix-1), data flow (e.g., Manchester data flow computer, MIT tagged token data flow architecture, Toulouse LAU system), reduction or demand-driven architectures (e.g., Newcastle reduction machine, North Carolina cellular tree machine, Utah applicative multiprocessing system), wavefront array architectures (e.g., wavefront arrays constructed at Johns Hopkins University, Standard Telecommunications Company and the Royal Signals and Radar Establishment), and MIMD architectures (both distributed memory and shared memory architectures). Distributed memory architectures connect processing nodes (consisting of an autonomous processor and its local memory) through a processor-to-processor interconnection network. These distributed memory architectures are results of research of the 1980s and 1990s and is motivated by the effort to provide a multiprocessor architecture that scales well and satisfies the performance requirements of large scientific applications characterized by local data references. Various interconnection network topologies have been proposed to support architectural expandability and provide efficient performance for parallel programs with differing interprocessor communication patterns. Some of the important topologies reported in the literature are ring, mesh, tree, hypercube, cube-connected cycles and reconfigurable topology (e.g., Snyder's CHiP, Siegel's SIMD/MIMD System or PASM). Shared memory architectures accomplish interprocessor communication by providing a global shared memory that each processor in the system can access. Commercial systems under shared memory architectures include Flexible Corporation's Flex/32 and Encore Computer's Multimax. There are some alternatives for connecting multiple processors to shared memory such as time-shared busses (e.g., CMU's Cm*), crossbar interconnection (such as Alliant FX/8), and multistage interconnection networks (e.g., BBN Butterfly).

Parallel architecture includes both special-purpose and general-purpose systems. Special-purpose processors are usually designed to function as peripheral devices attached to a conventional host computer. General-purpose processors are designed to function as independent computers. Multiprocessors, both special-purpose and general-purpose, are designed so that a number of usually identical chips can be interconnected to form a larger computer system. These processors are organized into a regular structure such as a linear array, tree, and cooperate in the concurrent execution of a program. These regular structures give rise to integrated circuits having regular interconnections, local communications and many repetitions of simple cells. Examples of special-purpose multiprocessors include systolic arrays and examples of general-purpose multiprocessors include tree machines, hypercube, and various data flow, reduction and recursive machines. These special-purpose and general-purpose processors considerably broaden our view of computer architecture from that traditionally associated with the Von Neumann computer. In addition, all these special-purpose and general-purpose processors may be considered potential building blocks for even larger multiprocessor computer systems including mixtures of special-purpose and general-purpose processors. We categorize the parallel architectures into a number of generic groups as shown in Figure 1.

2.1   Vector Processor [1, 33, 35]

In many scientific and engineering applications, most of the time is spent in carrying out typical operations on large sets of data. Examples of these are the calculation of the dot product of two vectors, the addition or subtraction of matrices, the multiplication of two matrices, the convolution of two vectors, and so on. These operations may occur within loops to be carried out for a number of vector/matrix pairs. One thing that is common among these types of computation is repetitive multiplication on different sets of data and accumulation of sums of these products. Let us analyze what goes on in finding the dot product of two vectors using

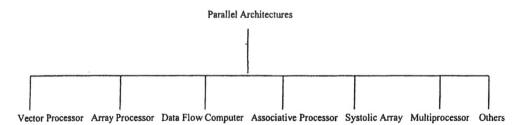

FIGURE 1
Classification of parallel architectures.

conventional sequential processor. The pseudocode for dot product calculation of two vectors $A(i)$ and $B(i)$ on a sequential machine may be written as

```
      C = 0
      DO 10 I = 1, n, 1
10    C = C + A(i)*B(i)
```

Execution of this loop proceeds as follows: C is initialized to zero. $A(1)$ and $B(1)$ are fetched from memory and multiplied. The product is added to C and stored in memory. Then $A(2)$ and $B(2)$ are fetched from memory and then multiplied and added to C and the result is stored in memory. Execution of the entire computation will require $2n$ nonoverlapping fetchings of the operands ($A(i)$ and $B(i)$) from memory. C is fetched from memory at the beginning of each iteration and stored in memory at the end of each iteration of the loop. This will also involve $2n$ references to memory if the compiler does not earmark any ALU register for C. So we find that there are $4n$ accesses to memory (in the worst case) and n multiplications and n additions. Memory accesses require more time than ALU operations because of memory latency. The computation can be made faster if we can reduce the memory access overhead. The best thing would be to have faster ALU operations and a matching effective memory bandwidth. ALU operations can be made faster by using pipelining in each functional unit of the ALU and having multiple such pipelined functional units in the ALU. But this will aggravate the existing memory bottleneck. To cope with faster ALU operations because of ALU pipelining, a commensurate increase in effective bandwidth of memory has to be made. Vector computers attempt to do this. A computer that can operate on vector operands in addition to scalar operands is called a vector computer. The vector computer has emerged as the most important high-performance architecture for numerical problems.

Most vector computers have pipelined structures and many of them provide for multiple pipelines. Such processors support streaming mode of data flow through the pipelines and support both temporal and spatial parallelism by allowing multiple pipelines to execute concurrently on independent streams of data. As the code for any real problem cannot be entirely executed in parallel, because of the presence of data dependency, similarly, not all of the code for a numerical application can be entirely vectorized or executed in vector mode. Practical applications involve code that can be partly vectorized. A standalone vector processor should therefore have the capability for both scalar and vector processing. A system with only vector processing capability cannot be used as a standalone system and has to be attached to a scalar processing system for real-life applications.

The way in which the hunger of the functional units for data is satisfied leads to a dichotomy of vector computer architecture. A pipelined vector computer can be classified either as memory–memory or register–register architecture. In the memory–memory architecture, vector components are streamed directly from the memory to the pipelined functional units and the generated results also go back to the memory. In register–register architecture, high-speed internal registers are used to supply the vector components to the pipelined functional units and the results from the functional units are also stored in the registers. CRAY-1 is an example of register–register architecture and CDC CYBER-205 is an example of memory–memory architecture. Figure 2 depicts block diagrams of vector processor architectures.

An intermediate approach to vector computing is to provide an optional, integrated vector capability with a general-purpose scalar system. This approach was used in the IBM 3090 system, which was basically an extension of the IBM System/370 with vector capability. System/370 vector architecture includes vector registers. Its instructions can designate three operands: two source operands and one result, where one of the source operands can be from

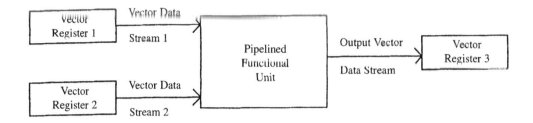

Register-Register Architecture

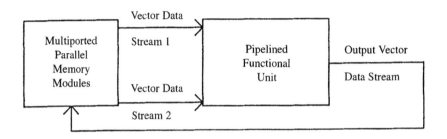

Memory-Memory Architecture

FIGURE 2
Vector processor architectures.

storage. Both the Cray and Cyber machines have been the dominating supercomputers in the market since the middle 1970s. Later, a number of machines appeared on the market from Japanese companies in addition to recent systems marketed by U.S. companies like Cray Corporation, CDC, etc.. The prominent machines from Japan include the Hitachi 820/80, a uniprocessor with 18 functional pipelines and a 4 ns clock period, in 1987; NEC SX-X/44, four processors with four sets of pipelines per processor and a clock period of 2.9 nanoseconds, in 1991; and the Fujitsu VP2600/10, a uniprocessor with five vector pipes and dual scalar processor with a clock period of 3.2 ns, in 1991. Some of the important machines from the United States are CDC's ETA 10E, a uniprocessor with a 10.5 ns clock period, in 1985 as a successor to Cyber 205; Cray X-MP 416, four processors with a 8.5 ns clock period, introduced in 1982; the Cray 2S/4-256, a four processor with a 4.1 ns clock period, introduced in 1985; Cray Y-MP 832, eight processors with a 6 ns clock period (enhanced from X-MP), introduced in 1988; and the Cray Y-MP C-90, 16 processors with two vector pipes per processor and a 4.2 ns cycle time, introduced in 1991.

2.2   Array Processor [4, 96]

An array processor may be used either as an attached processor interfacing with a compatible host machine or as a standalone processor equipped with a global control processor. Figure 3 depicts the architecture of an array processor. The desirable features of an array processor system are high speed, flexibility, reliability, and cost-effectiveness. The most important issue in the design of array processor is making a reasonable trade-off between the number and the size of the processors. This boils down to several questions: How many processors are needed? How big

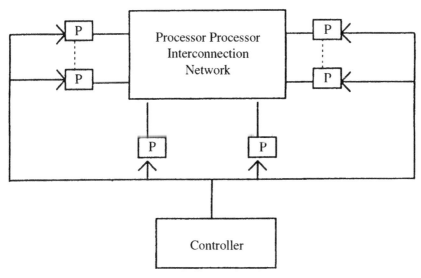

FIGURE 3
Array processor.

does each processor have to be? How simply can or should the individual processing element be made?

A processor array consists of a number of processing elements (PEs) linked by a network with regular topology. Each processing element has its own memory to store local data. As in a conventional machine, it is important that an array processor implementation supports a balance of processing and input/output. In some applications, such as the simple image processing of high-resolution satellite or radar data, the input/output bandwidth may actually dominate the performance of the machine. The success of an implementation depends on how well it fits all the aspects of the application, not just the processing. For the communication network, the important decision is the choice of the physical wiring pattern or topology of the network. A number of processor arrays such as linear array, mesh, hypercube, tree, etc. are quite popular. The choice of array structure depends on the communication requirements of the algorithms for the given application. Dynamic interconnection or reconfigurable array structures allow an array to support a large class of algorithms efficiently. Such structures usually involve significant hardware overhead. The host computer or the array control unit provides system monitoring, batch data storage, management and formatting. It determines the schedule program that controls the interface unit and interconnection network and generates global control codes and object codes for the PEs. The host determines and schedules the parallel processing tasks and matches them with the available array processor modules. It generates control codes to coordinate all system units. The array control unit follows the schedule commands, performs data rearrangement and handles direct data transfer traffic. The interface unit is connected to the host via the host bus or through DMA. It downloads, uploads, buffers array data, handles interrupts, and formats data. Since an array processor is used as an attached processor, the design of this unit is important. The interface unit is monitored by the host or the array control unit according to the schedule program. In the control area there is the question of how much autonomy should be given to the individual processing elements and how to manage the interaction between the processor array and the host. There is also a set of system issues that occur in the design of any computer such as clocking disciplines, fault tolerance, scalability, input/output, etc.

Array processors work in the SIMD mode, that is, a single instruction stream is broadcast to all the PEs. Each PE has the option of executing the instruction on the data available in its local memory or ignoring it, depending on its own internal state. Although every processing element does not necessarily execute the same sequence of instructions, each processing element is presented with the same sequence. Processing elements not executing must "wait out" while the active processing elements execute. The operation of an array processor is synchronized to a single central clock. The primary reason for this is simplicity of design. One problem with synchronous clocking is that, as machines grow physically larger it becomes increasingly difficult to synchronize the array. The skewing in signal while propagating from one part of the machine to another part becomes significant. There is also a time penalty for synchronization because all components must operate at the speed of the slowest.

Many successful array processors have been designed and used. Notable among them are the DAP, MPP, PEPE (parallel element processing ensemble), ILLIAC IV, GAPP (geometric arithmetic parallel processor), Connection Machine, GAM and CLIP4 (cellular logic image processor), adaptive array processor, GF11, CLIP7, etc..

2.2.1 Interconnection Networks for Array Processing.
In this subsection, we undertake a short tour of the important interconnection networks.

Ring [26]. Ring networks have mostly been used in local area networks. A ring network is a closed chain of processing elements. Each node in the ring has a unique predecessor and successor nodes. The degree of each node is 2, so that it is a regular network. A ring network with N nodes has a diameter $N/2$ (i.e., $O(N)$) and it can tolerate one fault, i.e., communication among the processing elements can be maintained in the event of failure of only one of the processing elements. The symmetrical nature of a ring makes it possible to have a simple routing algorithm. The large diameter of ring is the major disadvantage of its being used in massively parallel processing.

Binary tree [7]. In a binary tree machine, each PE has three ports connected to three other PEs designated as parent PE, left-child PE and right-child PE, respectively, excepting the root PE, which does not have a connection to a parent, and the other leaf PEs, which do not have connections to child PEs. Since the connection is regular and the maximum degree of any node is 3, the structure is suitable for VLSI implementation. The number of nodes (PEs) is $2N - 1$, the number of links is $2N - 2$, and the diameter is $2 \log N$. The line connectivity in the tree structure is 1 and hence it has no inherent fault-tolerance capability.

Hypertree [2]. This combines the easy expansibility of tree structures with the compactness of the hypercube. The addition of hypercube links to the binary tree structure provides direct paths between nodes that have frequent data exchange in algorithms such as sorting and fast Fourier transforms. The basic skeleton of a hypertree is a binary tree structure. Additional hypercube links are added to connect nodes at the same level of the tree. In particular, they are chosen to be a set of hypercube connections connecting nodes that differ by only one bit in their addresses.

Fat tree [5]. Unlike a computer scientist's traditional notion of a tree, fat trees are more like real trees in that they get thicker farther from the leaves. The processors of a fat tree are located at the leaves of a complete binary tree, and the internal nodes are switches. Going up the fat tree, the number of wires connecting a node with its parent increases, and hence the communication bandwidth increases. The rate of growth influences the size and cost of the hardware as well. Boolean hypercube networks suffer from wiring and packaging problems and require a nearly physical volume of nearly $N^{3/2}$ to interconnect N processors. There are many applications that do not require the full communication potential of a hypercube-based network. For example, a parallel finite-element algorithm would waste much of the communication bandwidth provided by a hypercube-based routing network.

Fat trees are a family of general-purpose interconnection strategies that effectively uitilize any given amount of hardware resource devoted to communication. Each edge of the underlying tree corresponds to two channels of the fat tree: one from parent to child, the other from child to parent. Each channel consists of a bundle of wires, and the number of wires in a channel is called its capacity. The capacities of channels in the routing network are determined by how much hardware one can afford. The channel leaving the root of the tree corresponds to an interface with the external world. Each (internal) node of the fat tree contains circuitry that switches messages between incoming channels and outgoing channels. A fat tree node has three input ports and three output ports connected in the natural way to the wires in the channels.

Mesh of tree [36]. A $N \times N$ mesh of tree (where N is some positive integer power of 2) is formed by taking a two-dimensional lattice of $N \times N$ PEs, where PEs along both the orthogonal axes are joined by tree connections. Each PE in the lattice becomes the leaf of one row tree and one column tree. PEs in the lattice are referred by their row and column numbers. Thus PE(i, j) refers to the PE in the jth column of the ith row of the lattice and this PE is the jth leaf of the ith row tree and also the ith leaf of the jth column tree. A $N \times N$ mesh of tree has $3N^2 - 2N$ PEs and $4N^2 - 4N$ bidirectional links, and its diameter is $4 \log N$.

Pyramid [8]. A pyramid network of size p is a complete 4-ary rooted tree of height $\log_4 p$ augmented with additional interprocessor links so that the processors in every tree level form a two-dimensional grid network. A pyramid of size p has at its base a two-dimensional grid network containing $p = k^2$ processors where k is an integer power of 4. The total number of processors in a pyramid of size p is $(4/3)p - 1/3$. Every interior processor is connected to nine other processors: one parent, four mesh neighbours, and four children. A pyramid with $N \times N$ PEs at its base will have a total of $(4/3)N^2 - 1/3$ PEs and $4N(N - 1)$ links, of which there are $(4/3)(N^2 - 1)$ tree links and $(2/3)(4N - 2)(N - 2)$ grid links. The diameter of a pyramid machine is $2 \log_2 N$. A pyramid is a very good architecture for low-level image processing applications.

Linear array. The simplest interconnection network for parallel processing is a linear array. Here we have N processors numbered $P(1), P(2), \ldots, P(N)$, each processor $P(i)$ being linked by a communication path to processors $P(i - 1)$ and $P(i + 1)$, where $1 < i < N$, with no other links available, and processors $P(1)$ and $P(N)$ each has only one nearest neighbour. Processor $P(1)$ is connected with $P(2)$ and processor $P(N)$ is connected with $P(N - 1)$. Obviously, the number of links is $O(N)$ and the diameter is also $O(N)$. In general, the inputs and outputs are restricted to the end processors $P(1)$ and $P(N)$ because doing I/O through all the N processors in parallel is not technologically feasible for large values of N as I/O pads occupy large areas on VLSI chips. Snapping of links between two neighbouring PEs on the linear array leads to two linear arrays of smaller sizes and hence it has line connectivity 1.

Mesh array. This is a two-dimensional extension of a linear array. Here N^2 processors are distributed over N linear arrays each containing N processors. These linear arrays are placed side by side in the north-to-south direction and are connected by north and south links through the PEs on the corresponding positions. If the numbering of the PEs of the linear arrays is 1 through N in the left-to-right direction and the linear arrays are numbered successively 1 through N from north to south, then the kth ($1 \leq k \leq N$) PE on linear array number i ($1 < i < N$) would be connected to kth PE on linear array number ($i - 1$) and to the kth PE on linear array number ($i + 1$). PEs on the first linear array do not have north links; similarly, PEs on the Nth linear array do not have south links. So each PE excepting the boundary PEs in the mesh has four connections, two to its two neighbours on the same linear array and two to the corresponding PEs on the previous and the next linear arrays. Boundary PEs have either two or three connections. PEs on the first and Nth linear arrays have two connections each and the other boundary PEs have three connections. The number of links for a $N \times N$ mesh array is $2N^2 - 2N$ which is $O(N^2)$, the diameter is $O(N)$, and line connectivity is 2. Mesh array forms an important model for study of parallel algorithms.

ILLIAC IV [1, 8]. ILLIAC IV connection is an augmented two-dimensional mesh. Each PE in a mesh is connected to its four nearest neighbours in the mesh. The augmentation is done as follows:

   (i)   PEs in the same columns are joined in the form of rings.
   (ii) PEs of all rows are joined to form a single big ring in the row-major way.

Torus [1, 8]. This is also an augmented two-dimensional mesh network where each row of PEs forms a ring and each column of PEs also forms a ring. Total number of PEs is N^2, total number of links is $2N^2$, and diameter is N. Torus differs from ILLIAC IV in having separate row rings instead of single row ring comprising all the PEs.

Hypercube [11, 28]. A hypercube is a k-dimensional cube where each node has k-bit address and is connected to k other nodes. Two nodes in the hypercube are directly connected if their node addresses differ exactly in one bit position. Since each node is representable by k bits, it has k directly connected neighbors. There is an elegant recursive definition of hypercube. An isolated node is a 0-cube. Two 0-cubes connected by a line form a 1-cube. In general, a k-cube is defined as the structure resulting from two ($k - 1$)-cubes after the corresponding nodes of these two ($k - 1$)-cubes are connected by links.

    The total number of PEs in a k-dimensional hypercube is 2^k and the total number of links and the diameter are $0.5 \times 2^k k$ and k, respectively. There are k alternative paths between any two PEs, which is a good situation from the point of view of fault-tolerance. However, the structure is not modularly expandable and expansion involves changing the number of ports per node. Since several common interconnection topologies such as ring, tree, and mesh can be embedded in a hypercube, the architecture is suitable for both scientific and general-purpose parallel computation. The novelty of this architecture has resulted in several experimental and commercial products such as the Cosmic Cube, Intel iPSC, Ametek System/14, NCUBE/10, Caltech/JPL Mark III, and the Connection Machine.

Cube-connected cycles [12]. The degree of nodes in hypercube is dependent on the size of hypercube. Degree of each node in a hypercube of size N is log N. This is not a desirable feature from the point of VLSI design. The cube-connected cycle (CCC) is a feasible substitute for the hypercube network and has desirable VLSI implementable features. The operation of cube-connected cycles is based on the combination of pipelining and parallelism. Formally, a cube-connected cycle is formed by taking a hypercube of N nodes (N is an integer power of 2) and replacing each vertex of the hypercube by a cycle of log N vertices, each with three ports. The log N edges connected to each vertex of the hypercube are now separately connected to log N vertices in the chain, one per vertex. The total number of nodes in cube-connected cycles is N log N and the number of links is 1.5 N log N. The number of disjoint paths between any two nodes in cube-connected cycles is three and the diameter is $(1 + 0.5 \log N)$ log N.

In CCC, the number of connections per processor is reduced to three and the processing time is not significantly increased with respect to that achievable on the hypercube network. The overall structure complies with the basic requirements of VLSI technology.

2.3 Data Flow Computer [27, 40–45, 51–60, 92]

A data flow model of computation has been proposed as an alternative to the conventional Von Neumann principle of execution. In the conventional Von Neumann model, an instruction is executed only when the control reaches the instruction, although there might be no reason not to execute the instruction earlier. Let us consider the following code segment:

$$A = B + C \quad (1)$$
$$R = A * S \quad (2)$$
$$Q = D - E \quad (3)$$
$$SS = C + E \quad (4)$$

In the conventional Von Neumann model, the instructions are executed in the sequence 1, 2, 3, 4. It is understood that instruction (2) has to wait until instruction (1) is completed because instruction (1) generates one of the operands of instruction (2). But there is no reason to delay the execution of instructions (3) and (4) and they could be executed at the same time as or even earlier than the execution of instruction (1).

Instead of relying on a program counter for the sequencing of instruction execution and on the notion of updatable global memory for the supply of instructions and operands, the data flow computation paradigm allows an instruction to execute as soon as its operands are available. The instruction is said to fire as soon as its operands are available. That is why it is also referred as data-driven computation. Data flow computation is asynchronous and can exploit fine-grain (at the operation level) parallelism. The data flow model deals only with values and not with addresses, and is free from side-effects. An operator produces a value that is used by other operators. Enabled instructions consume input values and produce output values that are sent to the other instructions consuming these values as operands.

A data flow computation is represented by a data flow graph (DFG) whose nodes represent functions, and arcs represent data dependencies between functions. In the graph, the values are represented as tokens on the arcs. Data flow processors are stored-program computers in which the stored program is a representation of data flow graphs. Like other forms of parallel computers, data flow computers are best programmed in special languages. The important properties of data flow languages are freedom from side-effects, locality of effect, equivalence of instruction scheduling constraints with data dependencies, and single assignment.

The DFG may be regarded as a representation of the machine-language program of a data flow computer. A data flow graph consists of a number of nodes called actors or operators connected by directed arcs or links. The arcs contain tokens or data values. For each actor, there may be one or more input arcs and one or more output arcs. Whenever there is token on each of the input arcs of an actor and there are no tokens on the output arcs, the actor is said to fire, that is, it consumes or removes the tokens from the input arcs and produces tokens on the output arcs. Figure 4 shows the DFG for solution of a quadratic equation where circles represent actors. Circles with 'L' inscribed represent link actors. Circles with no input arc represent constant actors producing constant values when the output arcs do not contain any token. The requirement of the

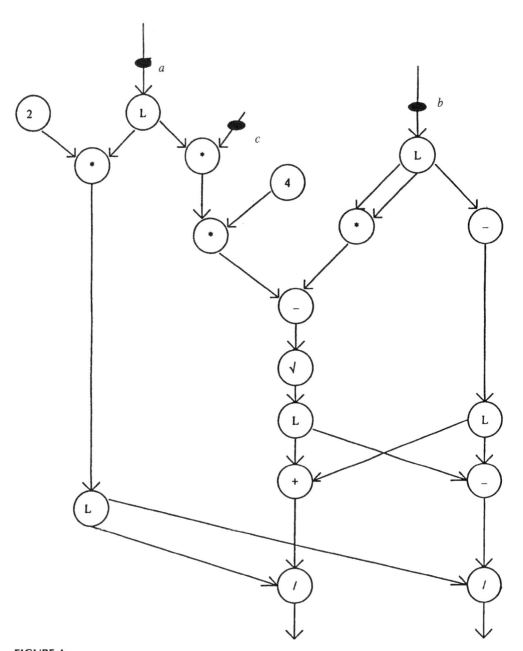

FIGURE 4
DFG for solution of a quadratic equation.

absence of tokens on the output arcs is relaxed in some variants of data flow computers called dynamic data flow machines. There is no explicit synchronization in data flow computation. Synchronization is achieved through the requirement of the presence of tokens on each of the input arcs. The firing of an actor produces result tokens on its output arcs and these serve as input tokens for those actors to which these arcs are the input. The relaxation of the firing rule in the case of dynamic data flow machines is tackled through coloring of tokens to indicate for which instance of computation, these result tokens will serve as input operands.

The dynamic model, also known as the tagged token model, was developed as an alternative to the static model. In the dynamic model several tokens may be present simultaneously on an arc corresponding to different instantiations of that part of the DFG. The tokens on an arc are distinguished from one another by distinct tags that form part of the token. In the dynamic model, provisions should be made for tokens on distinct arcs to an actor to be matched as belonging to the same instantiation. When matching tagged tokens on all the input arcs are detected, the actor consumes them and fires. The development of dynamic data flow machines was made independently by many groups; notable among them are Arvind and his colleagues at MIT [43, 45] and Gurd and his colleagues [27, 40] at Manchester University.

A data flow graph can be evaluated in two ways: demand-driven and data-driven. In the demand-driven mode, activation of an operation is delayed until its result is known to be useful for some other operation and needed for the final results. This mode of operation may be termed *lazy evaluation*. This mode is usually implemented by propagating demands backward through the data flow graph and then activating useful computations. The overhead in this mode of execution is high since the data flow graph must be traversed twice, first to propagate the demands for inputs and then to carry out the operations. The actual evaluation of the data flow graph does not begin until demands have propagated all the way through the data flow graph. Data-driven computation activates an operation as soon as all of its inputs are available. This scheme may loosely be called *eager evaluation*. The main drawback of data-driven computation is useless computation—computations that do not contribute to the final result. In the worst case, useless computations that are infinite may tie up machine resources and prevent program termination.

The best of the two schemes can be achieved if the data flow graph can be compiled so that parallelism is maximized and useless computation is minimized. It has been shown that many programs show greater parallelism under data-driven evaluation than under demand-driven evaluation. A typical example is the producer–consumer problem. If the producer is allowed to compute values only in response to requests from the consumer, pipelined operation of the producer and the consumer is often not possible. The data-driven execution scheme does not have this problem, but there is also no control over the activation of useless computations.

2.4 Associative Processor [1, 79]

Associative processing is mainly based on searching associative memory. An associative memory is one in which any stored item can be accessed directly by using partial contents of the item in question. Associative memories are also commonly known as content-addressable memories (CAMs). The subfield chosen to address the memory is called the key. In contrast, for accessing RAM, the physical address of the memory cell is used. RAM cells are accessed sequentially using addresses, whereas cells of a CAM are accessed in parallel using content.

In conventional Von Neumann machines, the central processor communicates with the memory by giving to the memory the address of the cell. After a certain delay, the memory delivers the contents of this cell. One of the obstacles preventing the speed acceleration in these types of machines is that the processing capability is separated from the storage cells, that is, processing requires information transfers between the processing units and storage cells. These transfers are carried out by slow busses. In associative processing, some of the processing abilities are put into the memory cells to remove this disadvantage. An associative memory has the facility of storing information, comparing it with other information and discovering agreement or disagreement. It can quickly answer questions, such as "Does there exist a cell in associative memory containing an item x?" or "What is the maximum value of the components of a given vector?." Associative memory contains processing logic that can determine in parallel whether a given cell does or does not contain data having given properties or it can search in parallel over its words and serially over its bits; that is, processing is done word-parallel and bit-serial.

An associative memory (AM) has n words each with m bits. Each word W_i is connected to a tagbit T_i. A response register T is formed by the bits T_i, $i = 1, 2, \ldots, n$ and is connected by a data-gathering device with the central control unit (CCU). From the CCU, instructions go in parallel to each word W_i. The CCU contains a comparand register $C = C_1 C_2 \cdots C_m$ and a mask register $M = M_1 M_2 \cdots M_m$. C contains the word that is to be compared in parallel with all or with selected words in the associative memory. Bits that are to be compared in these words are determined by the content of the mask register M. If the jth bit of M is 1 and others are 0, then the jth bit of each word, i.e., the jth bit slice, will be compared with C_j. T_i will be set 1 if jth bit of word i tallies with C_j and for others corresponding bit of T will be made 0. The pattern is stored in the register C where, on the basis of some condition, it is compared serially bit by bit, but in parallel with all or with selected words of the associative memory. The result of this operation is a subset of the original array containing all of the elements that satisfy the given retrieval condition. Such a condition can be an exact match, less than, greater than, nearest less than, nearest greater than, etc.. Among these operations there also belong searching for minima and maxima, and searching for all of the elements lying or not lying in a given interval. Figure 5 shows the block diagram of an associative processor.

The main advantage of such an organization of computation is the acceleration of speed. On a conventional computer, the execution of n identical operations over m-bit words lasts n times as long as the execution of one operation. Computation on an associative processor does not depend on n because it can be executed in parallel: it depends on m, where usually $n \gg m$. For example, searching for the maximum from n elements, where each element has m bits, takes n steps on conventional computers whereas on an associative memory it requires just m steps.

2.5   Systolic Array [4, 6, 9]

Systolic processors are a new class of pipelined array architectures. According to [9], a systolic system is a network of processors that rhythmically compute and pass data through the system. A

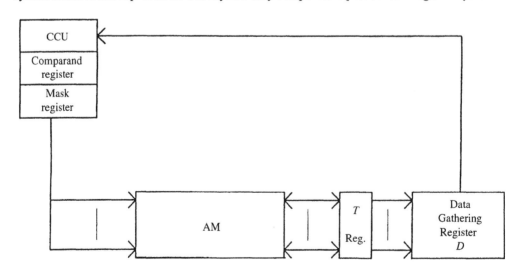

FIGURE 5
Associative processor.

systolic array has the characteristic features of modularity, regularity, local interconnection, high degree of pipelining, and highly synchronized multiprocessing. Since a large number of cells drawn from a small set of cell types with bounded degrees are connected with neighboring cells in a regular fashion, systolic arrays are easily realized in contemporary VLSI technology. Computational tasks can be divided into compute-bound computations and I/O-bound computations. Speeding up I/O-bound computations requires an increase in memory bandwidth, which is difficult in current technologies. Speeding up a compute-bound computation, however, may often be accomplished by using systolic arrays. In systolic arrays, once data is brought out from the memory, it can be used effectively at each cell of the array it passes while being pumped from cell to cell along the array, thus avoiding the classic memory access bottleneck problem commonly incurred in Von Neumann machines. Figure 6 shows a systolic array for matrix multiplication of two 3×3 matrices A and B where $C = AB$. Systolic arrays are descendants of arraylike architectures such as iterative arrays, cellular automata, and processor arrays. These architectures capitalize on regular and modular structures that match the computational requirements of many algorithms.

A number of definitions of systolic arrays are available in the literature. We cite the definition given in [4].

A systolic array is a computing network possessing the following features:

(i) *Synchrony*: The data are rhythmically (timed by a global clock) passed through the network.

(ii) *Modularity and regularity*: The array consists of modular processing units with homogeneous interconnections. Moreover, the computing network may be extended indefinitely.

(iii) *Spatial and temporal locality*: The array manifests a locally-communicative interconnection structure, i.e., spatial locality. There is at least one unit time delay allotted so that signal transactions from one node to the next can be completed, i.e., temporal locality.

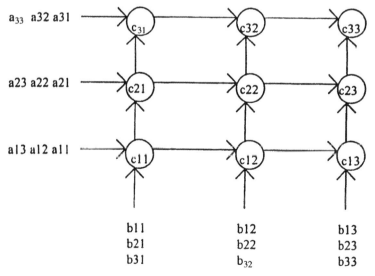

FIGURE 6
Systolic array for matrix multiplication.

(iv) *Pipelinability*: The array exhibits a linear rate pipelinability, i.e., it should achieve an $O(N)$ speedup in terms of processing rate where N is the number of processing elements in the network.

Systolic algorithms schedule computations in such a way that a data item is not only used when it is input but is also reused as it moves through the pipelines in the array. This results in balancing the processing and input/output bandwidths, especially in compute-bound problems that have more computations to be performed than they have inputs and outputs.

2.6 Multiprocessor [1, 35, 47]

Most of the parallel processing systems work in SIMD mode. These systems have good performance for certain classes of problem but they lack generality; programming these machines for wide classes of problems is sometimes difficult and does not have the desired level of performance. On the other hand, multiprocessors are general-purpose in nature and can be used for wide classes of problems. However, unlike SIMD machines, these work mainly in the asynchronous mode. So programmers of these machines must explicitly take care of synchronization and mutual exclusion problems in the code. Multiprocessing [1] is the cooperative and integrative use of programming, architectural, and technological means to establish multiple processor-based computer systems capable of executing two or more processes in parallel. A multiprocessor is an integrated computer system with the following characteristics: (i) It involves two or more processors all of roughly the same computational power and each capable of executing processes autonomously; (ii) The processes share a (logically) single, system-wide, memory space; (iii) The processors interact through message passing; and (iv) The hardware system as a whole is managed by a single operating system.

The design of any multiprocessor architecture involves the resolution of a common set of fundamental problems, some of which are new to the multiprocessing context, whereas others are inherited from the uniprocessor domain but in an exaggerated form. The major issues to be addressed in the design of multiprocessor systems are: (i) the "grains" of parallelism to be supported by the multiprocessor; (ii) synchronization mechanisms for access to shared memory and interprocessor communication; (iii) memory latency and its resolution; (iv) interconnection network problem; (v) processor scheduling strategies; (vi) concurrent programming languages and techniques.

Multiprocessors are generally classified into tightly coupled multiprocessor and loosely coupled multiprocessor. Figure 7 shows the architectures of multiprocessor systems. In the case of tightly coupled multiprocessors, processors communicate through a shared main memory. Hence, the rate at which data can be communicated from one processor to the other is on the order of the bandwidth of the memory. A small local memory or high-speed buffer (cache) may exist in each processor. A complete connectivity exists between the processors and memory. One of the limiting factors to the expansion of a tightly coupled system is the performance degradation due to memory contentions that occur when two or more processors attempt to access the same memory unit concurrently.

Loosely coupled multiprocessor systems do not generally encounter the degree of memory conflict experienced by tightly coupled systems. In such systems, each processor has a set of I/O devices and a large local memory where it accesses most of the instructions and data. We refer to the processor, its local memory and its I/O interfaces as a computer module. Processes that execute on different computer modules communicate by exchanging messages through the message transfer network. The degree of coupling in such a system is very loose. Loosely coupled systems are usually efficient when the interactions between tasks are minimal. Tightly

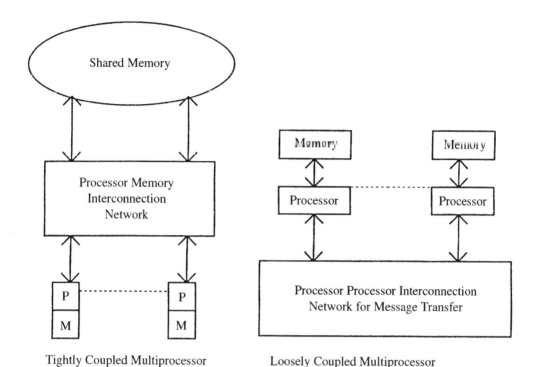

FIGURE 7
Architecture of multiprocessors.

coupled systems can tolerate a higher degree of interaction between tasks without significant deterioration in performance.

A message transfer network (or system) can take the forms of single shared bus or a shared memory system. The latter case can be implemented with a set of memory modules and a processor–memory interconnection network or a multiported main memory. Processes can communicate with other processes allocated to the same processor, or with processes allocated to other processors. Communication between tasks allocated to the same processor takes place through the local memory only. Communication between tasks allocated to different processors is through a communication port residing in the communication memory. One communication port is associated with each processor as its input port.

Multiprocessors are nowadays more aptly classified as UMA (for uniform memory access) and NUMA (nonuniform memory access). As the name implies, in UMA any processor can access any memory location in the same time. In NUMA, memory locations do not all require the same time. In NUMA, accessing local memory locations requires much less time than accessing locations from remote memory. C.mmp is a UMA type multiprocessor and Cm* is a NUMA-type multiprocessor.

3 CONVENTIONAL PROCESSING AND PARALLEL ARCHITECTURES

The two most important metrics used for evaluation of parallel machines are the speedup and efficiency of the processors. Speedup is defined as the ratio of the time taken for the solution of a problem on a serial computer using the best sequential algorithm to the time taken for the solution of the same problem on a parallel machine. Efficiency is the ratio of the speedup and the number of processors in the parallel machine. Efficiency indicates the contribution of individual processor toward the speedup achieved on the machine. Instead of trying to find a single figure of merit like speedup or efficiency for evaluation of parallel architectures, it is more meaningful to examine these architectures from the standpoints of a number of desirable characteristics.

- Present-day technology favors VLSI implementation of large circuits and VLSI technology demands small chip area for higher yields. Hence, as many nodes should be packed as possible into small area. Technological constraints also demand bounded-degree networks.
- For proper working of the chip, the maximum edge length in the VLSI layout of the network should be minimum.
- Regularity in the network facilitates efficient VLSI layout, easy routing of the data among the PEs of the network, as well as simple control.
- From the operational point of view, fault tolerance is an important aspect and the network should have as many alternative paths as possible between nodes of the network to have higher fault-tolerance capability.
- The network should have balanced I/O and computational bandwidths.
- It should be easy to map common algorithms on these architectures, and the mapped algorithms should be efficient on these architectures. Inefficiency of these mapped algorithms depends on the mismatch between the communication graph of the algorithm and the interconnection graph of the architecture.
- Another important consideration is whether the architecture is tailored to specific application or is for multipurpose applications.
- The diameter of a network is assumed to be an index for representing the efficiency of parallel computation on the network. But a lower network diameter, or even a lower average internode distance, does not always indicate a superior stochastic performance.

3.1   Vector Processor

A vector processor used for an application dominated by code for scalar processing performs very poorly. For a vector processor to be effective, the ratio of the vector code to the scalar code should be high. A vector processor should have the speeds of vector processing unit and scalar processing unit matching, otherwise one of them may be the bottleneck. The performance of a vector computer is dependent on the following factors: (i) the relative speeds of the vector and scalar processing units; (ii) the rate of supply of vector components to the functional units; and (iii) the ratio of vector code to the scalar code in the application.

In vector instructions the same operation is performed on a large number of elements. It is natural to implement vector computers as pipelined processors. In most of the vector computers implemented, the major source of strength is concurrent execution in multiple pipelines and dynamic chaining of these pipelines for higher throughput. A major advantage of a vector architecture is that a single instruction fetch can initiate a very long vector operation. The major problem faced by a computer architect is how to sustain a continuous flow of vector components (data) from the memory to the arithmetic units and subsequent use or storage of the generated intermediate results, which may be components of a generated vector.

The answers to this challenge are:

- Build necessary bandwidth in the main memory by using necessary number of independent memory modules to support concurrent access matching the demand of the functional unit(s).

- Use large numbers of high-speed vector registers to provide the necessary bandwidth. Vector registers are ordered collections of scalar registers and provide intermediate storage space for the components of a vector of moderately large size.

3.2 Array Processing

In choosing a topology, the goals can be divided roughly into two categories: cost and performance. On the performance side, we look for an optimal combination of the following parameter values:

- *Small diameter:* If the diameter is small, the processors are likely to be able to communicate more quickly.
- *Extendability:* It should be possible to build an arbitrarily large version of the network.
- *Short wires:* If the network can be efficiently embedded in two- or three-dimensional space such that all the wires are relatively short, information can propagate quickly among the PEs.
- *Redundant paths:* If there are multiple paths between each pair of processors, a partially defective network may continue to function.

On the cost side we look for the following:

- *Minimum number of wires:* Each physical connection costs money. Thus, if the number of wires is small, the cost is likely to be small also.
- *Efficient layout*: If the topology can be tightly and neatly packed into a small space, the packaging job becomes easier.
- *Fixed degree:* If each PE is connected to a fixed number of other PEs, then one PE design can serve for all sizes of networks.

It is a nontrivial task to find an optimal combination of these parameters. The list of desirable features contain contradictions: for example, minimum number of wires and redundant paths, or small diameter and fixed degree. Any decision will be a compromise.

3.3 Data Flow Computer

The data flow model apparently requires more instructions than the Von Neumann model. This code inefficiency arises because of distributed control and absence of explicit storage. In terms of the raw speed on small programs, the Von Neumann model requires less time. This performance advantage comes because of instruction pipelining and local storage. Although a data flow processor is slower in raw speed, it may be faster because it contains many overlapped processing units operating in parallel. In a crude approximation, the data flow machine can be thought of as a long pipeline. To keep the pipeline saturated, the degree of parallelism must be larger than the number of stages in the pipeline. Under low parallelism, the pipeline is not saturated for a long period of time and so serious degradation of performance occurs. The data flow machines have long pipelines that include functional units, a communication network, and instruction memory, so they are expected to perform poorly under low parallelism. Data flow machines require a parallelism of several hundred independent instructions to saturate the pipeline. Most of the programs with a high degree of parallelism are intensive numerical computations that operate on large arrays of data. Unfortunately, data flow machines do not handle arrays of data efficiently.

The most important argument put forward by the proponents of data flow architectures is the ability to tolerate long and unpredictable latencies by providing cheap, fine-grained dynamic scheduling and synchronization. Unfortunately, this argument ignores the storage hierarchy and the pitfalls of naive scheduling. Reality has proved less favorable to this approach than the arguments of the data flow community would suggest. Moreover, data flow notions are appealing at the scalar level, but array, recurrence, and other high-level operations become difficult to manage [41]. The handling of data structures is an area of active investigation. The crucial questions about data flow approach are concerned with handling of data structures, load balancing, and control of parallelism.

3.4 Associative Processor

Associative memory provides a naturally parallel and scalable form of data retrieval both for structured data such as sets, arrays, tables, trees and graphs, and for unstructured data such as raw data and digitized signals [79]. Associative memory is frequently needed in many important applications, such as the storage and retrieval of rapidly changing databases, radar signal tracking, image processing, computer vision and artificial intelligence. The major disadvantage of associative memory is its high cost, thus preventing the large-scale use of associative memory.

3.5 Systolic Array

Algorithms suitable for implementation in systolic arrays can be found in many applications, such as digital signal and image processing, linear algebra, pattern recognition, linear and dynamic programming and graph problems [6]. In fact, most of these algorithms are computationally intensive and require systolic architectures for their implementations when used in real-time environments. One should remember that although systolic array has similarity to data flow computation, these two paradigms of computation are distinct. While operations can occur as data are pumped through each processor, the overall computation is not a data flow computation, since the operations are executed according to a schedule determined by the systolic array design. Typically, a systolic array can be thought of as an algorithmically specialized system in the sense that its design reflects the requirements of a specific algorithm. Systolic arrays have regular and modular structures matching the computational needs of many algorithms. These arrays can be seen as hardware implementations of the respective algorithms.

3.6 Multiprocessor

The goals of multiprocessor systems are: (i) to reduce the execution time of a single program (job) by decomposing it into processes, assigning processes to distinct processors and executing processes concurrently whenever possible; (ii) to increase the overall throughput of a system's work load by allowing several jobs to be processed simultaneously by the system; and (iii) to establish, through redundancy, a level of fault tolerance for the system such that the failure of a processor will still allow the system to function correctly, though perhaps at reduced performance.

A multiprocessor has an overhead cost that is not present in uniprocessor. This cost includes the cost of scheduling, delay due to contention of shared resources such as shared memory, shared communication path, synchronization, etc. Although the time required for computational portion of a programme decreases as the number of processors working on that programme increases, the overhead costs tend to increase sometimes superlinearly in the number of processors. To increasingly exploit the parallelism in a problem, the number of processors employed is to be increased, but this will lead to increased overhead. Because of this dilemma, multiprocessor systems cannot be made faster by simply adding processors. In fact, there is an upper limit to the number of processors that can be cost-effectively used in a multiprocessor system. This upper limit depends to a great extent on the architecture of the machine, on the underlying technology, and on the characteristics of each specific application. To keep the overhead cost low compared to useful computation, multiprocessors are best suited for large problems that cannot easily be handled on a single processor. Multiprocessors are less attractive for dealing with problems that are solvable in reasonable time on a uniprocessor.

4 REQUIREMENTS OF BIOLOGICALLY INSPIRED PROCESSING

4.1 Computing in Artificial Intelligence

The processing required for artificial intelligence (AI) applications is drastically different from that required for conventional number-crunching. Acquisition, representation, and intelligent use of information and knowledge are fundamental to computing in AI. The information is sometimes incomplete and contradictory. The processing is symbolic rather than numeric and involves nondeterminism. The knowledge is voluminous and requires suitable representation. The processing requires extensive search.

Parallel architectures for implementing AI system include multiprocessors that support interactive MIMD operations through shared memory; multicomputers for supporting multiple SISDs (single instruction–single data) via message-passing among distributed processors with local memories; and massively parallel architectures consisting of processing–memory nodes cooperating in SIMD (single instruction–multiple data) or multiple SIMD or MIMD (multiple instruction–multiple data) fashion. At present most of the AI architectures are software-oriented. Four major classes of AI machines have been identified by Hwang et al [76]: language-based machines designed to execute languages like Lisp, Prolog, etc.; knowledge-based machines for efficiently supporting a particular knowledge representation system such as semantic nets, rules frames or objects; connectionist machines where knowledge is not represented by symbols but by direct encoding into the pattern of interconnections between processing elements; and intelligent interface machines where the man–machine interface is highly specialized and made as humanlike as possible.

4.2 Genetic Algorithm [21, 22, 95]

John Holland first introduced the concept of genetic algorithms [22]. The idea is to evolve a population of candidate solutions to a given problem using operators inspired by natural genetic variation and natural selection. The genetic algorithm is a method for moving from one population of chromosomes (encoded solution) to a new population by using a kind of natural selection together with the genetics-inspired operators of crossover, mutation, and inversion. The genetic algorithm should provide for chromosomal representation of solutions to the problem, creation of an initial population of solutions, an evaluation function for rating solutions in terms of their fitness, genetic operators that alter the composition of offsprings during reproduction, and parameter values for population size, probabilities of genetic operators, etc. These algorithms are suitable for problems having large search spaces that are multimodal or not well understood, or if the fitness function is noisy, and if the task does not require a global optimum to be found—i.e., finding a sufficiently good solution is enough. In these situations, a genetic algorithm will have a good chance of being competitive with or surpassing other weak methods, that is, methods that do not use domain-specific knowledge in their search procedure. The genetic algorithm is computation-intensive and is amenable for parallel implementation. Depending on the architectural features of a parallel machine, different aspects of genetic algorithms such as generation of initial population, evaluation of fitness of the chromosomes, etc. can be executed in parallel.

4.3   Artificial Neural Computing

Understanding the mechanism of information processing by the human brain is a challenging problem to scientists. Since there is no direct way of understanding the functions of a human brain, researchers have proposed various ideas and models to explain different aspects of the information-processing capability of brain. Modern high-speed computers operate with processing units that function at speeds of the order of tens or hundreds of nanoseconds, while the human brain consists of processing units that operate on the order of milliseconds [19]. Yet the brain is unquestionably able to perform certain processing feats in a few hundred milliseconds that have been proved to be impossible in hundreds of minutes of computer time. On the other hand, human beings fail miserably in performing number-crunching operations compared to conventional computers. This suggests that there is a basic difference in the functioning of the human brain and a digital computer.

The large number of neurons (about 10^{11}) in the human brain are organized in a complex, unknown interconnection structure. The individual neurons (the processing elements) in the brain may be connected to several thousand other neurons. Figure 8 shows a schematic diagram of a neuron. It is not understood how this massive collection of interconnected neurons allows us to store, represent, retrieve and manipulate different types of data. In artificial neural computing (ANC), a simple model of the neuron is assumed. The neuron sums its N weighted inputs and

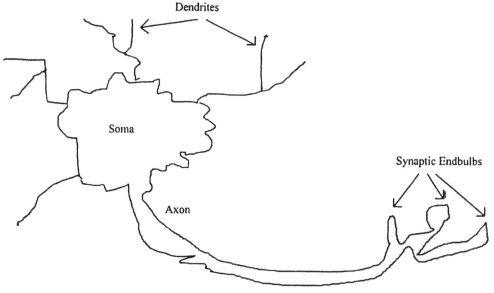

FIGURE 8
Schematic of a neuron.

outputs the result through a nonlinearity. This biologically influenced model (which is not biologically accurate) is used as a computational paradigm for solving difficult optimization problems. The major issues in ANC are deciding the interconnection of the simple neurons, and deciding the various rules for adjustment of weights.

Computer simulations can provide a means to study the complex functional relationships between neurons that comprise neural networks. Neural networks are complex interconnections of neurons. Most neural networks model the macroscopic functionality of systems of simplified neuronal units. Because of the advent of high-performance computers such as parallel and distributed processors, vector processors, etc., simulation of neural networks with considerable complexity has been possible. While modeling a complex system like a neural network, the modeler has to select the parameter space of the model that needs to be explored to tune and characterize the behavior of complex network models. As the model is expanded to make it biologically realistic, the size of the parameter space increases, requiring more and more computational power from the machines. This ever-increasing computational demand is difficult to meet by sticking to the sequential Von Neumann machines. Systems such as array processors, vector processors, etc. known to belong to the parallel processing category can be used effectively to meet the demand of increasing computational power.

The two important considerations for large-scale neural network modeling are:

1. Although there has been tremendous progress in our understanding of the physiological and anatomical basis of neural networks, no neural structure has yet been described in all its structural details.
2. Although parallel processors provide a large amount of computing power and storage, in simulating a large neural network, with all that is known about it biologically, the power of the machine becomes the limiting factor.

So the modeler has to introduce certain approximations into his model. These approximations are generally made at two levels of the model: at the neuronal level and at the network level.

There are three important components in neural computation: network structure, learning algorithms, and knowledge representation. Each neuron receives inputs from other cells, integrates the inputs and generates an output that it then sends to other neurons and in some cases to the effector organs such as muscles, glands, etc. A simple neuron can receive hundreds or thousands of inputs and may send its output to a similar number of other neurons. In the network, many cells are active at the same time. A description of the system involves the activities of all the cells in the system at that time. In neural networks, many computing elements are connected to many other elements. The overall behavior of the system is determined by the structure and strengths of the connections. The strength of the connections are modified in the learning phase. A number of learning algorithms have been proposed to set connection strengths. There have been several proposals about the connections of the computing elements in neural networks. Important among them are autoassociative networks, where a single layer of neurons connects to itself. Another structure is a two-layer system, where there is one input layer and one output layer. These networks are easy to analyze compared to general multilayer networks. In a multilayer network, the neurons are distributed over a number of layers: the input, the output, and one or more hidden layers. Its layers are completely connected but lack internal node connections. It uses supervised learning, implemented in two phases. In the forward pass, the network node output is computed and in the backward pass weights are adjusted to minimize the error between the observed and desired outputs. Multilayer neural networks are more powerful but are difficult to analyse. The issue of representation is not clearly settled. It is mostly hand-crafted to make the systems work.

5   PARALLEL ARCHITECTURES AND ARTIFICIAL NEURAL COMPUTING

There are various models for neural computing in the literature [65 70, 73, 88, 93]. Among them, the multilayer network with back-propagation learning algorithm [19, 48] is the most popular. We will mainly concentrate on this model of neurocomputing for our discussion in this section. The parallelisms exploitable in ANC [97] are:

- Training-session parallelism, i.e., simultaneous execution of different sessions.
- Training-example parallelism, i.e., simultaneous learning on different training examples; for example, the forward and backward passes of different training patterns can be processed in parallel.
- Layer parallelism, i.e., concurrent execution of layers within a network.
- Node parallelism, i.e., parallel execution of nodes for a single input.
- Weight parallelism, i.e., simultaneous weighted summation within a node.

Among these parallelisms the weight parallelism is the finest-grained and the training-session parallelism is the coarsest. Depending on the features of the parallel machine, one or more of the above parallelisms may be exploited to expedite ANC.

Owing to the specific nature of neural processing, standard efficiency measures do not guarantee good neuroperformance [23]. To reflect the needs of ANC, two measures are commonly used: CPS (connections per second), which measures how fast a network performs the recall phase, i.e., mapping from input to output, and CUPS (connection updates per second), which measures how fast a network learns. DARPA defined two measures for estimating the performance of ANC: IPS (interconnection per second) defined as the number of multiply-and-add operations that can be performed in a second on a back-propagation network, and WUPS (weight update per second), defined as the time required to read in the input pattern, propagate activation forward through the net, read in the correct output pattern, propagate the error signal backward through the net, compute weight changes, and change the weights. Among the benchmarks for ANC, the most popular is NETtalk, a back-propagation network that translates a text into phonemes.

5.1   Vector Computer and ANC

Let us consider a multilayer ANN. The output of neuron j in level l may be written

$$y_{lj} = g_l\left(\sum_i x_{li}w_{lij} - L_{lj}\right)$$

where g_l is the output function at the level l, x_{li} are the inputs, w_{lij} are the synaptic weights and L_{lj} is the threshold. This computation can be decomposed into pipeline stages as an accumulation of the product terms xws, subtraction of threshold from the accumulated product, and then application of output function. These computations are to be done for all the neurons of the layer and for all the layers of the network. Since the output of the neurons of layer l is fed as input to the neurons of layer $l + 1$, there is scope for exploitation of temporal parallelism between the computation of different layers. Spatial parallelism can be exploited within the computations in a layer. Most vector computers exploit temporal parallelism through extensive use of pipelining, so we restrict ourselves to temporal parallelism only. The product accumulation is facilitated in many vector computers through the use of compound vector instructions. For example, the IBM 3090 vector facility includes compound instructions such as multiply-and-add, multiply-and-subtract, and multiply-and-accumulate. Theoretically, the computations in the different layers could have been put into a macropipeline had there been a regular pattern of data dependency between the computations carried out by the neurons in different layers. Since the synaptic connections are not uniform, exploitation of macropipelining is less probable for ANC.

5.2   Array Processor and ANC

While using an array processor for any computation, the most important issue is the connection patterns among the processing elements. The connection patterns used in different array processors as discussed in Section 2.2 are regular and the fan in/out of each processor is low because of technological constraints. This regularity of connection leads to easy implementation in VLSI and also makes the design of algorithms for conventional processing easier. Since different problems have different connectivity requirements, no fixed connectivity pattern can suffice for the majority of problems. In the case of ANC, the operations are very simple: each neuron calculates a sum of the product of input values and their corresponding weights and applies a threshold function to this product sum, and so very simple PEs suffice for this purpose. In the case of neurons, the number of connections is very high and the connectivity does not have regularity such as we find in array processors. To perform ANC on an array processor, the first step is to find the array architecture that is closest to the ANC under consideration. Since the number neurons is very large compared to the number of PEs available in an array processor, the computational load of a group of neurons is to be assigned to a PE. This grouping of neurons and subsequent assignment to a PE can be done by a technique very close to the node-collapsing technique used in graph algorithms. To select the suitable array connection, one has to find a metric of closeness between the array and the reduced ANN. In the process one has to keep in mind that the supernodes (corresponding to conglomeration of neurons) are more or less of the same size, otherwise this will lead to imbalanced computational loads on the PEs, in turn leading to performance degradation. Since the computational load of each neuron is more or less the same, the computational load of a PE is basically proportional to the number of neurons in the supernode that has been assigned to the PE.

In the nervous system, there is no standard connectivity pattern that spans all neurons in all structures. Different brain regions have different characteristic patterns of cell-to-cell connectivity. Within regions, connections range from highly irregular to highly regular.

There is another important aspect of ANC implementation on array processor: the communication overhead. As with conventional computing using multiple PEs, communication plays an important role in deciding the performance of ANC on array processors. If the node groupings and assignment of these groups to the PEs of the array processor are such that for the ANC to progress a lot of inter-PE communication has to take place in the array processor, this will have an adverse effect on the performance.

In Zhang et al. [87], show how to map back propagation algorithm onto a 2-D mesh communication network and how to improve the mapping using a hypercube network. In [89, 107] ANC is expressed in terms of matrix and vector computations on a mesh without wraparound connections. Using graph theory-based mapping, the authors have shown how to implement a neural network of n neurons and e synaptic connections on a mesh. When the mesh size $N > n + e$, the data routing for a single iteration of the recall phase requires $24(N - 1)$ elemental shift operations, whereas the learning iteration takes $60(N - 1)$ shifts. How the different topologies of array processors (Section 2.2.1) can be exploited beneficially for parallel implementation of ANC and what their relative performances are remain interesting exercises to undertake.

5.3 Data Flow Computer and ANC

Data flow computers exploit fine-grain parallelism in an asynchronous manner. The parallel processing performed by many nodes in each layer of ANN is perhaps the most obvious form of parallelism that can be exploited on data flow multiprocessors. Multilayer ANC corresponds in a straightforward manner to a data flow graph with the exception that each node in ANN has multiple input arcs and multiple output arcs, while the data flow graph (DFG) nodes (referred as actors) have one or two inputs and one output, excepting that of the link actor. ANN can be converted into DFG for execution on data flow machines by the following steps:

1. Each arc connects node (i) of the kth layer to a node (j) of the $(k + 1)$th layer by a multiplier actor with two inputs, w_{ij} (synaptic strength) and O_i (output of node i of kth layer).
2. The outputs of these multiplier actors are fed as input to a binary tree of addition actors. If there are n nodes in the kth layer feeding a node in the $(k + 1)$th layer, the fan-in tree of addition actors will have $n/2$ leaf actors and a maximum height of $\lceil \log n - 1 \rceil$. The root of this fan-in tree replaces the original node of the ANN functionally.
3. The fan-out problem can be tackled in a similar manner. If the output of the node feeds n nodes on the next layer, a fan-out tree of height $\lceil \log n - 1 \rceil$ of link actors may be used to set up connections with the next layer. Of course, these transformations introduce more delay in the computation and are likely to offset the supposed advantages of data flow computers for fine-grain parallelism.

5.4 Associative Processor and ANC

An associative processor provides an ideal architecture for the solution of problems having a large amount of potential parallelism and involves a few primitive operations such as searching, summing, and selection. This architecture has not yet proved very popular for biologically inspired computations like GA and ANC because applications in these areas require large associative memory (AM), which is not possible because of the cost. But with the current advances in integration technology, researchers are using larger and larger associative memories for ANC and GA applications in addition to the traditional applications of associative memory.

Sometimes a network is used to represent the knowledge base. An important example of this representation is the semantic network. In the network, the nodes represent concepts and the links represent the association of the concepts. In processing a network-structured knowledge base, three fundamental operations generally used are association, set intersection, and marker propagation. Processing with markers is suitable for implementation in systems with associative memories because in such systems execution times are independent of the data stored. In the associative memory, the problem data is stored word-wise. The data contents are compared in parallel at every bit with the data in the comparand register. A tag bit is associated with each word of the AM. This bit is set when the word exactly matches the data in the comparand register. When a part of the word is required to be matched, the mask register is set appropriately. For processing network-based data, each word of the AM is assumed to have a field for node identification, a field for the marker bits, and a group identifier for parallel marker propagation. Sequential marker propagation requires time proportional to the number of links on which markers are propagated, while parallel marker propagation can be done in constant times regardless of the number of links. Information about the connections among the nodes is kept in the RAM of the controller of the AM. In Higuchi et al. [78], demonstrate how associative processing can be effectively used for memory-based speech-to-speech translation.

In Lawton et al. [81], demonstrate how a content-addressable processor can be used as an effective means of decomposing a computed flow field into its rotational and translational components to recover the parameters of sensor motion. In [82], Tavangarian introduced the concept of flag-oriented associative architecture. In this architecture, word-oriented data is transformed into flag-oriented data. The flag transformation allows parallel processing of associative or content-addressable data in a uniprocessor architecture. The flag-oriented architecture can be applied to ANC such as feed forward ANN and optimization ANN. Two operational phases of ANN are the learning phase and the association (search) phase. In the learning phase, the weights connecting the neurons are adjusted when iterative input patterns are applied to the ANN and modifications are made to the weights to produce a dedicated output. In the association phase, output patterns are generated from input patterns and the information stored during the learning phase. In the association phase, the weights have values as fixed in the learning phase through adjustments. Since one learning phase is generally followed by a number of association processes, accelerating the association process greatly improves ANC performance. Flag-oriented architecture can be used for acceleration of the association phase by combining output/input association with parallel processing.

5.5 Systolic Array and ANC

In this subsection, we discuss how a systolic array is used for artificial neural computing. We consider a multilayer feedforward artificial neural network. Implementation of this network on a parallel computer is nontrivial if efficiency is considered. The network communication pattern leads to nonscalable mapping of the network onto any target multiprocessor. If there is a change in the number of neurons in any of the layers, this may require major changes in the way load is distributed among the processors and the data is moved around.

As pointed out in Section 2.5, systolic arrays are more effective for computationally intensive problems. The evaluation of the activation values by the neurons is the most intensive part of the computation. In Petkov [80] shows how a systolic algorithm for matrix–vector multiplication can be used to realize a feedforward neural network model. At each layer (i) the matrix of the synaptic weights between the current layer (i) and its previous layer ($i - 1$) is multiplied by the output vector of the previous layer ($i - 1$) which is the input vector for the current layer (i). In Chung et al. [50], show how a two-dimensional systolic array for a back-propagation neural network can be implemented. This design is also based on the classical systolic algorithm of matrix–vector multiplication. The array executes forward and backward passes in parallel and exploits the pipelined parallelism of multiple patterns in each pass. In Margaritis et al. [101], describe a systolic architecture implementing an artificial neural network algorithm for the solution of the problem of detecting a subset of elements of a set having a given property. The algorithm has been implemented as a series of matrix–vector multiplications on a systolic architecture of two pipelined arrays. This design has two shortcomings: (i) the need for a feedback mechanism, which is undesirable from the VLSI implementation point of view; (ii) suboptimal time-complexity originating from the need for an initial fill-in stage for the systolic arrays.

5.6 Multiprocessor and ANC

Multiprocessors have been designed primarily for exploitation of coarse-grain parallelisms because the interprocessor communication is costly in such systems. In multiprocessors, subtasks are assigned to the individual processors, which are powerful and limited in number, and the processors perform the computations of the assigned subtasks and occasionally

Table 1   The Most Obvious Parallelism of ANC Exploitable in Generic Parallel Architectures

Generic parallel architectures	Weight parallelism	Node parallelism	Layer parallelism	Training-example parallelism	Training-session parallelism
Vector computer		Yes	Yes		
Array processor	Yes	Yes	Yes		
Data flow computer	Yes	Yes			
Associative processor			Yes	Yes	
Systolic array	Yes	Yes	Yes		
Multiprocessor				Yes	Yes

communicate with the peer processors. Since the communication (either through shared memory or by message-passing) is costly, the higher the ratio of computation time to the communication time, the higher is the performance. If the subtasks of the computation are organized in such a way that the communication is minimum, the performance of the system will be the highest. The most obvious parallelism that can be exploited on a multiprocessor is training-session parallelism. This means that we start different training sessions on different processors. This is not very interesting. More interesting would be the training-example parallelism. Since the number of training examples is usually very large, the parallelism of the training set can be exploited by mapping different training examples to different processors and letting each processor calculate outputs for its training example. When all the processors have finished, the weight changes can be summed to give the final synaptic weights of the network. If the network consists of N nodes and e edges and for computation of each training example the weights are retrieved k times, each processor will require ket_m time where t_m is the time to access one weight-value from the memory. Let the maximum time required by any processor for the computation of the training example be t_{mc}. If there are p processors in the system, p training examples can be simultaneously worked on and ep weight changes are to be made for synapses, and this will require ept_m time. Assuming that no time is lost due to memory contention, the total time required will be $ket_m + ept_m + t_{mc} = (k+p)et_m + t_{mc}$. The other forms of parallelism, such as layer parallelism and node parallelism, are not suitable for exploitation on multiprocessors. However, if each processor has multiple ALUs, weight parallelism can be exploited to some extent.

Table 1 shows the obvious parallelism of ANC that can be exploited on different generic parallel architectures.

6   CONCLUSIONS

An attempt has been made to assess the utility of various generic parallel systems for artificial neural computing. The existing parallel architectures have been divided into six groups: vector processor, array processor, data flow computer, associative processor, systolic array and multiprocessors. These systems are examined in the light of conventional numeric computing in Section 3. After characterizing the requirements of the three most important biologically inspired computing paradigms, namely, those of AI, genetic algorithms and ANC in Section 4, an attempt was made in Section 5 to assess the suitability of these systems for ANC. The two most general approaches for ANC as reported in the literature are (i) to use all the processors to simulate one copy of the network, (ii) to use each processor to simulate a complete copy of the network. Most people have used fully connected networks for this purpose. How to implement an arbitrarily connected neural network efficiently on the different parallel machine architectures remains an important direction to explore. The field of ANC abounds in a number of models, the number of neurons in any practical system of ANC is high, and the interneuron connectivities are complex. It is not clear which of the parallel systems will ultimately be accepted as the most suitable system for parallel computing of practical artificial neural ncts. The SIMD array processors seems to be the best choice for parallel execution of ANC. For application-specific ANN, systolic array is the other generic parallel architecture of choice.

REFERENCES

[1] Kwai Hwang and F.A. Briggs, *Computer Architecture and Parallel Processing*. McGraw-Hill, New York, 1984.

[2] J.R. Goodman and C.H. Sequin, Hypertree: A multiprocessor interconnection topology, *IEEE Trans. Computers*, Vol. C-30, No. 12, pp. 923–933, Dec. 1981.

[3] A.V. Aho, J.E. Hopcroft, and J.D. Ullman, *The Design and Analysis of Computer Algorithms*. Addison-Wesley, Reading, MA, 1974.

[4] S.Y. Kung, On supercomputing with systolic/wavefront array processors, *Proc. IEEE*, Vol. C-72, No. 7, pp. 867–884, July 1984.

[5] C.E. Leisserson, Fat-trees: Universal networks for hardware efficient supercomputing, *IEEE Trans. Computers*, Vol. C-34, No. 10, pp. 892–901, Oct. 1985.

[6] J.A.B. Fortes and B.W. Wah, Systolic arrays—From concepts to implementation, *IEEE Computer*, pp. 12–17, July 1987.

[7] E. Horowitz and A. Zorat, The binary tree as an interconnection network: Applications to multiprocessor systems and VLSI, *IEEE Trans. Computers*, Vol. C-30, No. 4, pp. 247–253, Apr. 1981.

[8] M.J. Quinn, *Designing Efficient Algorithms for Parallel Computers*. McGraw-Hill, New York, 1987.

[9] H.T. Kung and C.E. Leiserson, Systolic arrays (for VLSI), *Proc. Sparse Matrix Symposium*, 1978, pp. 256–282, SIAM.

[10] S.P. Levitan, Measuring communication structures in paralel architectures and algorithms, in L.H. Jemieson, et al. (eds.), *The Characteristics of Parallel Algorithms*, pp. 101–137. MIT Press, Cambridge, MA 1987.

[11] M.C. Pease, The indirect binary *N*-cube microprocessor array, *IEEE Trans. Computers*, Vol. C-26, No. 5, pp. 458–473, May, 1977.

[12] F.P. Preparata and J.E. Vuillemin, The cube-connected cycles: A versatile network for parallel computation, *Communications of the ACM*, pp. 300–309, May, 1981.

[13] L. Synder, Introduction to the configurable highly parallel computer, *IEEE Computer*, pp. 47–56, Jan. 1982.

[14] B.J. Lint, Communication issues in parallel algorithms and computers, Ph.D. Thesis, University of Texas at Austin, 1979.

[15] L.S. Haynes, et al., A survey of highly parallel computing, *IEEE Computer*, pp. 9–24, Jan. 1982.

[16] T.Y. Feng, A survey of interconnection networks, *IEEE Computer*, pp. 12–27, Dec. 1981.

[17] R. Duncan, A survey of parallel computer architectures, *IEEE Computer*, pp. 5–16, Feb. 1990.

[18] Leonard Uhr, *Algorithm-Structured Computer Arrays and Networks*. Academic Press, Orlando, 1984.

[19] Bruce D. Shriver, Artificial neural systems, *IEEE Computer*, pp. 8–9, Mar. 1988.

[20] L.D. Wittie, Communication structures for large networks of microcomputers, *IEEE Trans. Computers*, Vol. C-30, No. 4, pp. 264–273, Apr. 1981.

[21] Lawrence Davis, *Genetic Algorithms and Simulated Annealing*. Morgan Kaufmann, San Mateo, 1987.

[22] John H. Holland, *Adaptation in Natural and Artificial Systems*, University of Michigan Press, Chicago, 1975.

[23] Nikola B. Serbedzija, Simulating artificial neural networks on parallel architectures, *IEEE Computer*, pp. 56–63, Mar. 1996.

[24] J.C. Wyllie, *The complexity of parallel computations*, Ph.D. Thesis, Cornell University.

[25] W.D. Hillis and G.L. Steele, Jr., Data parallel algorithms, *CACM*, Vol. 29, No. 12, pp. 1170–1183, Dec. 1986.

[26] J.M. Crichlow, *An Introduction to Distributed and Parallel Computing*. Prentice-Hall, Englewood Cliffs, NJ, 1988.

[27] J.R. Gurd, et al., The Manchester prototype data flow computer, *CACM*, Vol. 28, No. 1, pp. 34–52, Jan. 1985.

[28] K. Padmanabhan, Cube structures for multiprocessors, *CACM*, Vol. 33, No. 1, pp. 43–52, Jan. 1990.

[29] Joseph Ja Ja, *Introduction to Parallel Algorithms*. Addison-Wesley, Reading, MA, 1992.

[30] K.M. Chandy and J. Mishra, *Parallel Program Design: A Foundation*. Addison-Wesley, Reading, MA, 1988.

[31] S.G. Akl, *The Design and Analysis of Parallel Algorithms*. Prentice-Hall, Englewood Cliffs, NJ, 1989.

[32] G. Brassard and P. Bratley, *Fundamentals of Algorithmics*. Prentice-Hall, Englewood Cliffs, NJ, 1996.

[33] P.M. Kogge, *The Architecture of Pipelined Computers*. McGraw-Hill, New York, 1984.

[34] M.J. Quinn, *Parallel Computing: Theory and Practice*. McGraw-Hill, New York, 1994.

[35] Kai Hwang, *Advanced Computer Architecture: Parallelism, Scalability, Programmability*. McGraw-Hill, New York, 1993.

[36] F.T. Leighton, *Introduction to Parallel Algorithms and Architectures: Arrays, Trees, Hypercubes*. Morgan Kaufmann, San Mateo, 1992.

[37] S. Lakshmivarahan and S.K. Dhall, *Analysis and Design of Parallel Algorithms: Arithmetic and Matrix Problems*. McGraw-Hill, New York, 1990.

[38] A. Gibbons and W. Rytter, *Efficient Parallel Algorithms*. Cambridge University Press, New York, 1988.

[39] John P. Fishburn, *Analysis of speedup in distributed algorithms*, Ph.D. Thesis, Department of Computer Science, University of Wisconsin-Madison, 1981.

[40] I. Watson and J. Gurd, A practical data flow computer, *IEEE Computer*, pp. 51–57, 1982.

[41] D.D. Gajski, et al., A second opinion on data flow machines and languages, *IEEE Computer*, pp. 58–67, Feb. 1982.

[42] K.P. Gostelow and R.E. Thomas, Performance of a simulated data flow computer, *IEEE Trans. Computers*, Vol. C-29, No. 10, pp. 905–919, Oct. 1980.

[43] Arvind and V. Kathail, A multiple processor data flow machine that supports generalized procedures, *Computation Structures Group Memo 205-1*, MIT, 1981.

[44] R.A. Iannucci, Implementation strategies for a tagged-token data flow machine, *Computation Structures Group Memo 218*, MIT, 1982.

[45] Arvind and R.A. Iannucci, A critique of multiprocessing Von Neumann Style, *Computation Structures Group Memo 226*, MIT, 1983.

[46] J.J. Hack, On the promise of general-purpose parallel computing, *Parallel Computing*, Vol. 10, pp. 261–275, 1989.

[47] Anita K. Jones and Peter Schwarz, Experience using multiprocessor systems—A status report, *Computing Surveys*, Vol. 12, No. 2, pp. 121–165, June 1980.

[48] A.K. Jain, Artificial neural networks: A tutorial, *IEEE Computer*, pp. 31–44, Mar. 1996.

[49] John P. Hayes, *Computer Architecture and Organization*. McGraw-Hill, New York, 1988.

[50] Jai-Hoon Chung, Ilyunsoo Yoon, and Seung Ryaul Maeng, A systolic array exploiting the inherent parallelisms of artificial neural networks, *Microprocessing and Microprogramming*, Vol. 33, pp. 145–159, 1991/92.

[51] J.B. Dennis, The varieties of data flow computers, *Proc. First Int. Conf. Distributed Computing Systems*, Oct. 1979, pp. 430–439.

[52] Kei Hiraki, Toshio Shimada, and Kenji Nishida, A hardware design of the SIGMA-1, a data flow computer for scientific computations, *Proc. 1984 Inter. Conf. Parallel Processing*, 1984, pp. 524–531.

[53] G.M. Papadopoulos, *Implementation of a General-Purpose Data flow Multiprocessor*. Pitman Publishing, London, 1991.

[54] J.R. Gurd, C.C. Kirkham, and I. Watson, The Manchester prototype data flow computer, *CACM*, Vol. 28, No. 1, pp. 34–52, Jan. 1985.

[55] A.H. Veen, Data flow machine architecture, *ACM Computing Surveys*, Vol. 18, No. 4, pp. 365–396, Dec. 1986.

[56] Arvind and R.S. Nikhil, Executing a program on the MIT tagged-taken data flow architecture, *IEEE Trans. Computers*, Vol. 39, No. 3, pp. 300–317, Mar. 1990.

[57] V.P. Srini, An architectural comparison of data flow systems, *IEEE Computer*, pp. 68–88, Mar. 1986.

[58] J.B. Dennis, Data flow supercomputers, *IEEE Computer*, pp. 48–56, Nov. 1980.

[59] J.R. McGraw, Data flow computing—Software development, *IEEE Trans. Computers*, Vol. C-29, No. 12, pp. 1095–1103, Dec. 1980.

[60] J.B. Dennis, G.-R. Gao, and K.W. Todd, A data flow supercomputer, *Computation Structures Group Memo 213*, MIT, 1982.

[61] D.P. Bertsekas and J.N. Tsitsiklis, *Parallel and Distributed Computation*. Prentice-Hall, Englewood Cliffs, NJ, 1989.

[62] G. Fox, M. Johnson, G. Lyzenga, S. Otoo, J. Salmon, and D. Walker, *Solving Problems on Concurrent Processors*, Vol. 1. Prentice-Hall, Englewood Cliffs, NJ, 1988.

[63] V.C. Barbosa, *Massively Parallel Models of Computation*. Ellis Herwood, New York, 1993.

[64] M.V. Mascagni,, Numerical methods for neuronal modeling, in Christof Koch and Idan Segev (eds.) *Methods in Neuronal Modeling*, pp. 439–484, MIT Press, Cambridge, MA, 1990.

[65] M.E. Nelson, W. Furmanski, and J.M. Bower, Simulating neurons and networks on parallel computers, in Christof Koch and Idan Segev (eds.) *Methods in Neuronal Modeling*, pp. 397–437. MIT Press, Cambridge, MA, 1990.

[66] M.A. Wilson and J.M. Bower, The simulation of large-scale neural networks, in Christof Koch and Idan Segev (eds.) *Methods in Neuronal Modeling*, pp. 291–333. MIT Press, Cambridge, MA, 1990.

[67] K. Fukushima, A neural network for visual pattern recognition, *IEEE Computer*, pp. 65–74, Mar. 1988.

[68] H.P. Graf, L.D. Jackel, and W.E. Hubbard, VLSI implementation of a neural network model, *IEEE Computer*, pp. 41–49, Mar. 1988.

[69] R. Linsker, Self-organization in a perceptual network, *IEEE Computer*, pp. 105–117, Mar. 1988.

[70] S.K. Basu and B.P. Sinha, A model for neuro-computing, *Proc. IEEE TENCON'90*, 1990, Vol. 1, pp. 55–58.

[71] S. Kirkpatrick, C.D. Gelatt, Jr., and M.P. Vecchi, Optimization by simulated annealing, *Science*, Vol. 220, No. 4598, pp. 671–680, May 1983.

[72] G.A. Carpenter and S. Grossberg, The ART adeptive pattern recognition by a self-organizing neural network, *IEEE Computer*, pp. 77–88, Mar. 1988.

[73] J.J. Hopfield and D.W. Tank, Computing with neural circuits: A model, *Science*, Vol. 233, pp. 625–633, Aug. 1986.

[74] D.W. Tank and J.J. Hopfield, Neural computation by concentrating information in time, *Proc. Natl. Acad., Sci., USA*, Vol. 84 (Biophysics), pp. 1896–1900, Apr. 1987.

[75] D.W. Tank and J.J. Hopfield, Simple 'neural' optimization networks: An A/D converter, signal decision circuit, and a linear programming circuit, *IEEE Trans. Circuits and Systems*, Vol. CAS-33, No. 5, pp. 533–541, May 1986.

[76] K. Hwang, J. Ghosh, and R. Chowkwanyun, Computer architectures for artificial intellience processing, *IEEE Computer*, pp. 100–109, Jan. 1987.

[77] K. Twardowski, An associative architecture for genetic algorithm-based machine learing, *IEEE Computer*, pp. 27–38, Nov. 1994.

[78] T. Higuchi, K. Handa, N. Takahashi, T. Furuya, H. Iida, E. Sumita, K. Oi, and H. Kitano, The IXM2 parallel associative processor for AI, *IEEE Computer*, pp. 53–62, Nov. 1994.

[79] A. Krikelis and C.C. Weems, Associative processing and processors, *IEEE Computer*, pp. 12–17, Nov. 1994.

[80] N. Petkov, Systolic simulation of multilayer feed-forward neural networks, In R. Eckmiller, G. Hartmann and G. Hanske (eds.) *Parallel Processing in Neural Systems and Computers*, pp. 303–306, Elsevier Science, New York, 1990.

[81] D.T. Lawton, J. Rieger, and M. Steenstrup, Computational techniques in motion processing in M.A. Arbib and A.R. Hanson (eds.) *Vision, Brain and Cooperative Computation*, pp. 419–488, MIT Press, Cambridge, MA, 1987.

[82] D. Tavangarian, Flag-oriented parallel associative architectures, *IEEE Computer*, pp. 41–52, Nov. 1994.

[83] Michael Witbrock and Macro Zagha, An implementation of backpropagation learning on GF11, a large SIMD parallel computer, *Parallel Computing*, Vol. 14, pp. 329–346, 1990.

[84] F.J. Smieja and H. Muhlenbein, The geometry of multi-layer perceptron solutions, *Parallel Computing*, Vol. 14, pp. 261–275, 1990.

[85] Alexander Singer, Implementations of artificial neural networks on the connection machine, *Parallel Computing*, Vol. 14, pp. 305–315, 1990.

[86] G.M. Megson and I.M. Bland, Generic systolic array for genetic algorithms, *IEEE Proc. Computers and Digital Technology*, Vol. 144, No. 2, pp. 107–119, Mar. 1997.

[87] Xiru Zhang, Michael McKenna, Jil Mesirov, and David Waltz, The backpropagation algorithm on grid and hypercube architectures, *Parallel Computing*, Vol. 14, pp. 317–327, 1990.

[88] K. Obermayer, H. Ritter, and K. Schulten, Large-scale simulations of self-organizing neural networks on parallel computers. Application to biological modelling, *Parallel Computing*, Vol. 14, pp. 381–404, 1990.

[89] V.K. Prasanna Kumar and K.W. Przytula, Algorithmic mapping of neural network models onto parallel SIMD machines, *Proc. Int. Conf. Application Specific Array Processors*, pp. 259–271. IEEE Computer Society Press, New York, 1990.

[90] U. Ramachcher and W. Raab, Fine grain system architectures for systolic emulation of neural algorithms, *Proc. Int. Conf. Application Specific Array Processors*, pp. 554–566. IEEE Computer Society Press, New York, 1990.

[91] A. Hiraiwa, M. Fujita, S. Kurosu, S. Ariasawa, and M. Inoue, Implementation of ANN on RISC processor array, *Proc. Int. Conf. Application Specific Array Processors*, pp. 677–688. IEEE Computer Society Press, New York, 1990.

[92] G.R. Gao, Exploiting fine-grain parallelism on data flow architectures, *Parallel Computing*, Vol. 13, pp. 309–320, 1990.

[93] B. Muller and J. Reinhardt, *Neural Networks: An Introduction*. Springer-Verlag, Berlin, 1990.

[94] H. Muhlenbein, Limitations of multi-layer perception networks—Steps towards genetic neural networks, *Parallel Computing*, Vol. 14, pp. 249–260, 1990.

[95] Melanie Mitchell, *An Introduction to Genetic Algorithms*. MIT Press, Cambridge, MA, 1996.

[96] S.Y. Kung, *VLSI Array Processors*, Prentice-Hall, Englewood Cliffs, NJ, 1988.

[97] T. Nordstrom and B. Svensson, Using and designing massively parallel computers for artificial neural networks, *J. Parallel and Distributed Computing*, Vol. 14, No. 3, pp. 260–285, 1992.

[98] I. De Falco, R. Del Balio, E. Tarantino, and R. Vaccaro, Simulation of genetic algorithms on MIMD multicomputers, *Parallel Processing Letters*, Vol. 2, No. 4, pp. 381–389, Dec. 1992.

[99] D. Whitley, T. Starkweather, and C. Boogart, Genetic algorithms and neural networks: optimizing connections and connectivity, *Parallel Computing*, Vol. 14, pp. 347–361, 1990.

[100] H. Muhlenbein, M. Schomisch, and J. Born, The parallel genetic algorithm as function optimizer, *Parallel Computing*, Vol. 17, pp. 619–632, 1991.

[101] K.G. Margaritis and D.J. Evans, Systolic implementation of neural networks for searching sets of properties, *Parallel Computing*, Vol. 18, pp. 325–334, 1992.

[102] Tzung-Pei Hong and Shiam-Shyong Tseng, Parallel perceptron learning on a single-channel broadcast communication model, *Parallel Computing*, Vol. 18, pp. 133–148, 1992.

[103] Chwan-Hwa Wu, Russel E. Hodges, and Chia-Jiu Wang, Parallelizing the self-organizing feature map on multiprocessor systems, *Parallel Computing*, Vol. 17, pp. 821–832, 1991.

[104] Tom Tollenaere and Guy A. Orban, Simulating modular neural networks on message-passing multiprocessors, *Parallel Computing*, Vol. 17, pp. 361–379, 1991.

[105] Nigel Dodd, Graph matching by stochastic optimization applied to the implementation of multilayer perceptrons on transputer networks, *Parallel Computing*, Vol. 10, pp. 135–142, 1989.

[106] A. De Gloria, P. Faraboschi, and S. Ridella, A dedicated massively parallel architecture for the Boltzman machine, *Parallel Computing*, Vol. 18, pp. 57–73, 1992.

[107] W-M. Lin, V.K. Prasanna, and K.W. Przytula, Algorithmic mapping of neural network models onto parallel SIMD machines, *IEEE Trans. Computers*, Vol. 40, No. 12, pp. 1390–1401, Dec. 1991.

[108] Mark James and Doan Hoang, Design of low-cost real-time simulation systems for large neural networks, *J. Parallel and Distributed Computing*, Vol. 14, pp. 221–235, 1992.

[109] S.Y. Kung and J.N. Hwang, Parallel architectures for artificial neural nets, *Proc. IEEE Int. Conf. Neural Networks*, San Diego, 1988, Vol. II, pp. 165–172.

CHAPTER 10

Developments in Learning Control Systems

JIAN XIN XU, TONG HENG LEE, CHANG CHIEH HANG, and YANGQUAN CHEN
Department of Electrical Engineering, National University of Singapore,
10 Kent Ridge Crescent, Singapore 119260

1 INTRODUCTION

Learning is the underlying property of all intelligent systems ranging from machines to human beings. Similarly, learning is the indispensable function of any intelligent control systems. In a learning control system, learning is a process during which the system extracts the relevant control information from the previous control actions, and generates the necessary control signals for the new action. Generally speaking, learning in a control system can be conducted in two ways: pattern-based learning and repetition-based learning. Neural learning is pattern-based learning. A neural network learns from a variety of distinct control input–output patterns that are obtained a priori and reflect the inherent relation of the process. On the other hand, repetition-based learning acquires the necessary control directly from previous control profiles whenever the control task is repeated.

This chapter focuses on developments in learning control systems in general, and recent advances in iterative learning control (ILC) and direct learning control (DLC) systems in particular. The objective of this chapter is to present a number of new developments by the authors with two types of learning control methods: iterative learning control and direct learning control. Iterative learning control is one of the repetition-based learning schemes, whereas DLC is one of the pattern-based learning schemes. Iterative learning control differs from most existing control methods in the sense that it exploits every possibility to incorporate past control information, such as tracking errors and control input signals, into the construction of the present control action. There are two phases in iterative learning control: first, the long-term memory components are used to store past control information; second, the stored control information is fused in a certain manner so as to ensure that the system meets control specifications such as convergence, robustness, etc. It is worth noting that these control specifications may not be easily satisfied by other control methods as they require more *prior* knowledge of the process in the controller design stage. ILC requires much less information of the system variations to yield the desired dynamic behaviors. Due to its simplicity and effectiveness, ILC has received consider-able attention and application in many areas since the mid 1980s. Most contributions have focused on developing new ILC algorithms with property analysis.

Research in ILC has progressed by leaps and bounds since 1992. On the one hand, substantial work has been conducted and reported in the core area of developing and analyzing new ILC algorithms. On the other hand, researchers have realized that integration of ILC with other control techniques may give rise to better controllers that exhibit desired performance that is impossible by any individual approach. Integration of adaptive, robust or other learning techniques into ILC for various control problems has frequently been reported to remove usual requirements on conventional ILC algorithms. Research into ILC has even seen "inva-sions" into areas that were traditionally noncontrol areas. For instance, iterative learning schemes have been used to improve system identification or curve fitting.

Generally speaking, two kinds of nonrepeatable problems are encountered in learning control: nonrepeatability of a motion task and nonrepeatability of a process. The *nonrepeatable motion task* can be shown by the following example: An XY table draws two circles with the same period but different radii. *Nonrepeatability of a process* can be due to the nature of system, such as welding different parts in a manufacturing line. Without loss of generality, we refer to these two kinds of problems as nonrepeatable control problems that result in extra difficulty when a learning control scheme is to be applied.

From the practical point of view, nonrepeatable learning control is more important and indispensable. To deal with nonrepeatable learning control problems, we need to explore the inherent relations of different motion trajectory patterns. The resulting learning control scheme might be both plant-dependent and trajectory-dependent. On the other hand, since the learning control task is essentially to drive the system tracking the given trajectories, the inherent spatial and speed relationships among distinct motion trajectories actually provide useful information. Moreover, in spite of the variations in the trajectory patterns, the underlying dynamic properties of the controlled system remain the same. Therefore, it is possible for us to deal with nonrepeatable learning control problems.

On the other hand, a control system may have much prior control knowledge obtained through all the past control actions, although they may correspond to different tasks. These control profiles are obviously correlated and contain a lot of important information about the system itself. In order to utilize this prior control knowledge effectively and explore the possibility of solving nonrepeatable learning control problems, *direct learning control* (DLC) schemes were proposed [1, 2].

Direct learning control is defined as the direct generation of the desired control profile from existing control inputs without any repeated learning. The ultimate goal of DLC is to utilize fully all the prestored control profiles and to eliminate the time-consuming iteration process thoroughly, even though these control profiles may correspond to different motion patterns and be obtained using different control methods. In this way, DLC provides a new kind of feedforward compensation that differs from other kinds of feedforward compensation methods. A feedforward compensator has hitherto been constructed in terms of the prior knowledge with regard to the plant structure or parameters. Its effectiveness therefore depends on whether a good estimation or guess is available for these system uncertainties. In contrast with the conventional schemes, the DLC scheme provides an alternative method: generating a feedforward signal by directly using the information of past control actions instead of the plant parameter estimation. Another advantage of DLC is that it can be used where repetitive operation may not be permitted.

It is interesting to note that direct learning control and iterative learning control function in a somewhat complementary manner. The main features of the existing iterative learning control methods are: (1) little a priori knowledge about the system is required; (2) it is only effective for a single motion trajectory; (3) a repeated learning process is needed. The features of the direct learning methods are: (1) prior control information is required to be accurate and sufficient; (2) it is able to learn from different motion trajectories; (3) there is no need for repetitive learning because the desired control input can be calculated directly. Therefore, DLC can be regarded as an alternative for the existing learning control schemes under certain conditions.

The organization of this chapter is as follows. In Section 2, developments in iterative learning control are presented. A current cycle P-type learning scheme is developed and analyzed in Section 2.2 for nonlinear servocontrol systems [3]. It shows that the existing feedback controller is very helpful in improving the control performance. In Section 2.2, a high-order PID-type learning scheme is developed for nonlinear uncertain systems with state delays [4]. A dual-PID scheme in both time axis and iteration number axis is suggested that shows the potential link with the well-established PID tuning methods [5, 6, 7]. Section 3 introduces a new learning control method—direct learning control—that differs from all other iterative learning control methods in that it is a pattern-based learning method [2]. Three typical applications of learning control methods are described in Section 4. The first is the application of ILC methods to the temperature control of a batch chemical reactor [8]. The second application is the direct learning control of a robotic manipulator. In the last application, we show that ILC is a useful tool for solving noncontrol problems. An example is learning-based aerodynamic curve identification [9]. Finally, some concluding remarks are presented in Section 5.

The following norms are used in this chapter:

$$\|f\| = \max_{1 \le i \le n} |f_i|, \qquad \|G\| = \max_{1 \le i \le m} \left(\sum_{j=1}^{n} |g_{i,j}| \right), \qquad \|h(t)\|_\lambda = \sup_{t \in [0,T]} e^{-\lambda t} \|h(t)\|$$

where $f = [f_1, \ldots, f_n]^T$ is a vector, $G = \lfloor g_{i,j} \rfloor_{m \times n}$ is a matrix and $h(t)(t \in [0, T])$ is a real function. The partial derivatives of a function $g(x, t)$ are denoted by g_x and g_t, i.e.,

$$g_x = \frac{\partial g}{\partial x}, \qquad g_t = \frac{\partial g}{\partial t}$$

2   ITERATIVE LEARNING CONTROL

2.1   P-type Iterative Learning Control

In this subsection, two learning control enhancement schemes applicable to nonlinear dynamical systems of the type commonly encountered in many practical servomechanisms are developed. The key difference between the two schemes lie in the fact that the first scheme utilizes previous-cycle errors in the learning strategy while the second utilizes present-cycle errors. The uniqueness of these learning controllers is that, in contrast to existing learning methods, they make full use of available a priori information on nominal models of the system and, as a result, overcome the problem of large swings in the control effort during the learning process, which is a major problem with conventional learning controllers. The properties of the schemes are discussed, and it is shown that the strategies developed assure iterative improvement in repetitive operation and asymptotic tracking of the reference signal.

A Framework for Incorporating Learning Control Enhancements. Consider the nonlinear dynamical system described by

$$m(q, \dot{q})\ddot{q} + v(q, \dot{q}) = u \qquad (1)$$

where q represents an appropriate output of the system (such as an angular position signal), and u represents an applied input to the system. It is assumed here that $m(., .)$ and $v(., .)$ are nonlinear continuous functions with $m(., .) > 0$.

Many practical servomechanisms are described by this particular structure of differential equations. For such systems, the function $m(q, \dot{q})$ typically models an equivalent mass function (thus the condition $m(q, \dot{q}) > 0$ is satisfied) while the function $v(q, \dot{q})$ represents the viscous damping and gravity effects. As examples, servomechanisms with asymmetrical loading [10] have dynamics of the form given by the above dynamic equation. Likewise, position control systems that utilize limited rotation pancake motors (which offer the advantages of small form factor, high torque, and brushless operation without requiring high-speed switching inverters and electronic commutation) as actuators also result in dynamics of the type described above.

It is very often the case that the nonlinear functions $m(q, \dot{q})$ and $v(q, \dot{q})$ are not known accurately. Nevertheless, some a priori information will exist in the form of nominal functions $\bar{m}(q, \dot{q}) > 0$ and $\bar{v}(q, \dot{q})$ in practical applications, and these are typically used to construct the basic control system for the servomechanism. For this basic part of the control system, a commonly used control law for nonlinear servomechanisms is the computed torque strategy [10] given by

$$u_c = \bar{m}[\ddot{q}_{\text{ref}} + k_1(\dot{q}_{\text{ref}} - \dot{q}) + k_2(q_{\text{ref}} - q)] + \bar{v} \qquad (2)$$

with $k_1 > 0$ and $k_2 > 0$, where q_{ref} is some given desired trajectory. Note that in many engineering applications, a priori information for the nominal functions $\bar{m}$ and $\bar{v}$ is usually available from technical data sheets used in combination with physical modeling considerations [10]. For more complex systems, these nominal functions $\bar{m}$ and $\bar{v}$ may be practically modeled and emulated via simple identification experiments utilizing model representations based on the use of suitable linear parameterizations and sensitivity functions.

As the nominal functions would not, in general, represent the actual servomechanism exactly, the functions $m(q, \dot{q})$ and $v(q, \dot{q})$ can be rewritten as

$$m(q, \dot{q}) = \bar{m}(q, \dot{q}) + \tilde{m}(q, \dot{q})$$
$$v(q, \dot{q}) = \bar{v}(q, \dot{q}) + \tilde{v}(q, \dot{q})$$

where $\tilde{m}(q, \dot{q})$ and $\tilde{v}(q, \dot{q})$ represent the modeling errors. In applications where these modeling errors are significant, the basic control system based on the nominal functions would require additional enhancements to achieve effective control and it is useful to consider an overall control law with two components in the form

$$u = u_c + u_l \qquad (3)$$

where u_c is the previously mentioned basic (computed torque) control component based on the nominal system, and u_l is a suitably designed enhancement component.

Considerations for Development of Learning Control Enhancements. As a result of the presence of the modelling errors $\tilde{m}(., .)$ and $\tilde{v}(., .)$, from (1), (2) and (3) the closed loop dynamics will thus be

$$\ddot{\tilde{q}} = -k_1\dot{\tilde{q}} - k_2\tilde{q} + \bar{m}^{-1}[\tilde{m}\ddot{q} + \tilde{v}] - \bar{m}^{-1}u_l$$
$$= -k_1\dot{\tilde{q}} - k_2\tilde{q} + f - \bar{m}^{-1}u_l \qquad (4)$$

where $\tilde{q} = q_{\mathrm{ref}} - q$ and $f = \bar{m}^{-1}[\tilde{m}\ddot{q} + \bar{v}]$. With the available a priori knowledge of the system already used in the basic (computed torque) law u_c, the next issue to resolve is the structure of the learning law component u_l.

Some common conditions for the successful incorporation of learning control methodology are:

- Each operation of the system ends in a fixed duration $T > 0$.
- A reference signal is given to the system a priori over that time duration $t \in [0, T]$.
- The system is reinitialized at the beginning of each trial; namely the initial states of the system at $t = 0$ are set at the reference states.
- The learning control effort at the present trial $u_{l,k+1}$ is composed of the error e_k and learning control effort $u_{l,k}$ of the previous trial through some law F:

$$u_{l,k+1}(t) = F(u_{l,k}(t), e_k(t))$$

- Invariance of the system dynamics is maintained throughout the trials.

As an example, a PID-type learning law [11] is given as

$$u_{l,k+1} = u_{l,k} + \left[\Gamma + \Phi\frac{d}{dt} + \Psi\int dt\right]e_k \tag{5}$$

$$e_k(t) = y_{\mathrm{ref}}(t) - y_k(t)$$

where $e_k(t)$ is the error between the reference trajectory $y_{\mathrm{ref}}(t)$ and the actual trajectory $y_k(t)$ of the previous trial. The variables $u_{l,k+1}$ and $u_{l,k}$ are the control efforts of the present and previous trial respectively. The constants Φ, Γ and Ψ are the learning gains.

It is pertinent to note that the method of learning control was developed primarily as an approach to controlling nonlinear dynamical systems without bothering to obtain any a priori knowledge of the system. In this purpose, it has achieved some measure of success, though the engineering trade-offs are that lengthy learning trials are required, and early trials typically result in fairly large swings in the control signal [12, 13]. The learning control laws developed and considered here extend some of the ideas previously pioneered in [14]. However, the work here adopts a philosophy that is different on two significant counts, namely:

P1. The chosen design approach should not attempt to dispense with a priori knowledge. All available a priori knowledge should be obtained carefully, and used in a basic control component.

P2: By design, learning control is to be incorporated as an enhancement component.

As mentioned earlier, in many nonlinear servomechanisms used in engineering applications, it is usually the case that some a priori knowledge about the system is available, e.g., from data sheets and from simple identification experiments. This is the basis for the principle **P1**, which prescribes that the design philosophy chosen should attempt to obtain all available a priori knowledge and utilize this in a basic control component. As we shall see later, this also has practical advantages in that it yields reductions in maximal swings of the control effort during the learning process. Principle **P2** then prescribes the use of learning control as an enhancement component to improve on the performance of the system.

Thus, as discussed previously, the enhancement structure (3) will be used. For the learning update, elements of the learning rule (5) will be incorporated in a suitably modified form. As we will see in a later subsection, the modified learning control enhancements that we use are designed with the intention that they should attain uniformly stable operation and assure convergence of the learning process. In the development here, two learning control laws will be investigated. To facilitate the discussion that follows, some terminology is first stated. The error e_k is defined as $e_k = \dot{q}_{ref} - \dot{q}_k$. Hence, e_k is the angular velocity error of the servomechanisms. The kth cycle refers to the previous trial while the $(k+1)$th cycle refers to the current (present) trial. Also, to avoid cumbersome notation, and where there is no risk of ambiguity, $\bar{m}(q_k, \dot{q}_k)$ will often be written as $\bar{m}_k$.

The proposed learning control laws are:

- Scheme 1: *Learning Law Using Error of Previous Cycle*:

$$u_{l,k+1} = \bar{m}_{k+1}[\bar{m}_k^{-1} u_{l,k} + \Gamma e_k] \tag{6}$$

- Scheme 2: *Learning Law Using Error of Present Cycle*

$$u_{l,k+1} = \bar{m}_{k+1}[\bar{m}_k^{-1} u_{l,k} + \Gamma e_{k+1}] \tag{7}$$

The key difference between these two schemes is that the error of the previous cycle (e_k) is used in Scheme 1 while the error of the present cycle (e_{k+1}) is used in Scheme 2. Learning laws utilizing previous-cycle errors are commonly encountered in earlier work [12, 13, 15]; the development of a learning law utilizing present-cycle errors is deliberately pursued here to investigate its comparative potential.

The improvements obtained by incorporating the learning elements described above are summarized in the following two propositions:

Proposition 1. For the nonlinear servomechanism described by (1), consider the control law (12) which is based on the nominal functions of the system, and the learning law (6) that makes use of the error in the *previous* cycle. If the computed torque and the learning gains satisfy the inequalities

$$k_1 > 0$$
$$k_2 > 0 \text{ AND } k_2 > -\alpha_3$$
$$\Gamma > 0 \text{ AND } \Gamma < 2\alpha_2 + 2k_1$$

where α_2 and α_3 are constants defined in [3], then this design of the learning control enhancement scheme based on the error of the previous trial ensures that the sum-of-squares of error of each trial is uniformly nonincreasing in the iterative learning procedure, and furthermore,

$$\lim_{k \to \infty} e_k(t) = 0$$

Remark 1a It is insightful to note in detail the implications of Proposition 1. The results stated imply that the learning enhancement control scheme consisting of (2), (3) and (6) together ensure the following features:

- **F1** (*Feature of Iterative Improvement through Learning*): This is seen from the fact that

$$\int_0^T e_{k+1}^2 \, d\tau \le \int_0^T e_k^2 \, d\tau$$

i.e., the sum-of-squares of tracking errors is a monotone nonincreasing function, so that practically, the learning yields iterative improvement.

- **F2** (*Feature of Asymptotic Tracking*): This is implied by the result in the proposition where

$$\lim_{k\to\infty} e_k(t) = 0$$

This feature thus assures that the learning process yields asymptotic convergence of the tracking error to zero.

For Scheme 2, similarly we have the following proposition:

Proposition 2. For the nonlinear servomechanism described by (1), consider the control law (2), which is based on the nominal functions of the system, and the learning law that makes use of error in the *present cycle* (7). If the computed torque gain and the learning gain satisfy the inequalities

$$k_1 > 0$$
$$k_2 > 0 \text{ AND } k_2 > -\alpha_3$$
$$\Gamma > 0 \text{ AND } \Gamma < -2\alpha_2 - 2k_1$$

then this design of the learning control enhancement scheme based on the error of the *present trial* ensures that the sum-of-squares of error of each trial is uniformly nonincreasing in the iterative learning procedure, and furthermore,

$$\lim_{k\to\infty} e_k(t) = 0$$

Remark 1b. It is straightforward to note that the features **F1** and **F2** discussed in Remark 1a are also attained here. The main difference is that this proposed scheme utilizes *present-cycle* errors in the learning law, and the relative performance of the two schemes remains to be investigated.

Remark 1c. For detailed derivations and analyses of Propositions 1 and 2, see [3].

2.2 D-type Iterative Learning Control

In this subsection, for a better learning transient along the iteration number direction, a PID-type iterative learning control algorithm is proposed for a class of delayed uncertain nonlinear systems that perform a given task repeatedly. The convergence conditions for the proposed high-order learning control have been established. The tracking error bound is shown to be a class-K function of the bounds of reinitialization errors, uncertainties, and disturbances of the systems. It is also indicated that the time delays in the system states do not play a significant role in the ILC convergence property.

High-order D-type ILC. Most existing ILC schemes are based on the first-order updating laws, i.e., only the information of one previous ILC iteration is employed. In [16], the idea of the high-order ILC algorithm is introduced, which utilizes the information of several previous learning iterations. In fact, high-order ILC schemes can be used to improve the transient learning behavior along the learning iteration number direction. Consider the ILC updating law proposed by [12],

$$u_{i+1}(t) = u_i(t) + \Gamma\dot{e}_i(t)$$

along the ILC iteration number i direction. Clearly, it is only an *integral controller* w.r.t. i. By using the difference $\dot{e}_i(t) - \dot{e}_{i-1}(t)$ as the derivative approximation along the i-direction, the PID controller in the i-direction will result in the following form of the ILC updating law:

$$u_{i+1}(t) = u_i(t) + \Gamma\dot{e}_i(t) + \Gamma_1\dot{e}_{i-1}(t) + \Gamma_2\dot{e}_{i-2}(t)$$

which is actually a third-order iterative learning controller. As is well known that PID controllers generally give better performance than integral controllers alone, one can expect that the high-order ILC is capable of giving better ILC performance than traditional first-order ILC. Therefore, it is beneficial to investigate high-order ILC schemes for the tracking control of nonlinear uncertain systems.

Consider a time-varying delayed uncertain nonlinear system that performs a given task repeatedly as follows:

$$\begin{cases} \dot{x}_i(t) = f(x_i(t), x_i(t - t_{d1}), t) + B(x_i(t), x_i(t - t_{d2}), t)u_i(t) + w(x_i(t), t) \\ y_i(t) = g(x_i(t), t) + v_i(t) \end{cases} \tag{8}$$

where $x_i(t) \in R^n$, $u_i(t) \in R^m$, and $y_i(t) \in R^r$ are the state control input and output of the system, respectively; $w(.,.)$, $v_i(.)$ are bounded uncertainties or disturbances to the system; $t \in [0, T]$ is the time and T is given; $t_{d_j} \le T(j = 1, 2)$ are unknown time delays. It is assumed that when $t < 0$, $x_i(t) = 0$. The functions $f: R^n \times R^n \times [0, T] \to R^n$ and $B: R^n \times R^n \times [0, T] \to R^{n \times m}$ are piecewise continuous in t, and $g: R^n \times [0, T] \to R^r$ is a C^2 function in $[0, T]$, i.e., the partial derivatives $g_x(.,.)$ and $g_t(.,.)$ are also differentiable in x and t.

Given a desired output trajectory $y_d(t)$, the control objective is to find a control input $u_i(t)$ such that when $i \to \infty$, the system output $y_i(t)$ will track the desired output trajectory $y_d(t)$ as closely as possible. The control input $u_{i+1}(t)$ is obtained by

$$u_{i+1}(t) = U(I_i)$$

where U is an updating law and I_i represents the information of the previous iterations, which is available at the current $((i + 1)$th$)$ iteration and is given by

$$I_i = \{u_j(t), y_j(t), y_d(t) | (i - N + 1) \le j \le i\}$$

where the integer N $(N \ge 1)$ is the order of ILC algorithm.

Now, the following high-order ILC updating law for the system (8) is proposed that uses the P, I, and D information of tracking errors:

$$u_{i+1}(t) = \sum_{k=1}^{N}(1 - \gamma)P_k u_l(t) + \gamma u_0(t)$$

$$+ \sum\left\{Q_k(y_l(t), t)e_l(t) + R_k(y_l(t), t)\dot{e}_l(t) + S_k(y_l(t), t)\int_0^t e_l(\tau)\,d\tau\right\} \tag{9}$$

where $l = i - k + 1$, $e_l(t) = y_d(t) - y_l(t)$, integer $N \ge 1$ is the order of the ILC algorithm; Q_k, R_k, and S_k are learning gain matrices; and γ $(0 \le \gamma \le 1)$ is a weighting parameter to restrain the large fluctuation of the control input at the beginning of the ILC iterations. The learning operators Q_k, R_k, and S_k are chosen to be bounded and their upper bounds, denoted by b_Q, b_R, and b_S, respectively, are defined, for example, by

$$b_Q - \max_{1 \le k \le N} \sup_{t \in [0,T]} \sup_{\forall y \in R^r} \|Q_k(y, t)\|$$

The weighting parameter γ can be selected to be a monotonic decreasing function w.r.t. the ILC iteration times i. As usual, it is assumed that $e_i(t) = 0$ and $u_i(t) = 0$ for $I < 0$.

Properties of Convergence and Robustness. Assume that the system (8) satisfies the following three assumptions:

A1 The system (8) is causal. Furthermore, for a given bounded desired output, $y_d(t)$, there exists a unique bounded input, $u_d(t)$, $t \in [0, T]$ such that when $u(t) = u_d(t)$, the system has a unique bounded state, $x_d(t)$, and $y_d(t) = g(x_d(t), t)$, $t \in [0, T]$.

A2 The functions f, B, w, g, and the partial derivatives g_x, g_t are uniformly globally Lipschitzian in x on $[0, T]$, i.e., there exist constants k_h, k_{f_j}, k_{B_j} $(j = 1, 2)$ such that

$$\|h(x_1(t), t) - h(x_2(t), t)\| \le k_h \|x_1(t) - x_2(t)\|$$

$$> \| f(x_1(t), x_1(t - t_{d1}), t) - f(x_2(t), x_2(t - t_{d1}), t)\|$$
$$\le k_{f_1} \|x_1(t) - x_2(t)\| + k_{f_2} \|x_1(t - t_{d1}) - x_2(t - t_{d1})\|$$

$$\|B(x_1(t), x_1(t - t_{d2}), t) - B(x_2(t), x_2(t - t_{d2}), t)\|$$
$$\le k_{B_1} \|x_1(t) - x_2(t)\| + k_{B_2} \|x_1(t - t_{d2}) - x_2(t - t_{d2})\|$$

where $h \in \{g, g_x, g_t, w\}$.

A3 The functions g_x, v_i, $\dot{v}_i$, and B are uniformly bounded. In the sequel, b_{g_x}, b_v, $b_{\dot{v}}$, and b_B are used to denote the upper bounds for g_x, v_i, $\dot{v}_i$, and B, respectively. For example,

$$b_B = \sup_{\forall (x_1, x_2) \in R^n \times R^n} \sup_{t \in [0,T]} \|B(x_1, x_2, t)\|$$

The stability of the above high-order ILC is shown in the following theorem [4].

Theorem 2.1. Consider the repetitive system (8) satisfying assumptions **A1**–**A3** and assume that the initial state bias $x_d(0) - x_i(0)$ is bounded. If

$$\sum_{k=1}^{N} P_k(t) = I_m \tag{10}$$

and there exist positive numbers ρ_k satisfying

$$\|(1 - \gamma)P_k(t) - R_k g_x B\| \le \rho_k, \quad \forall (x, t) \in R^n \times [0, T]$$
$$\sum_{k=1}^{N} \rho_k = \rho < 1 \tag{11}$$

then when $i \to \infty$, the bounds of the tracking errors $\|u_d(t) - u_i(t)\|$, $\|x_d(t) - x_i(t)\|$ and $\|y_d(t) - y_i(t)\|$ converge asymptotically to a residual ball centered at the origin. Furthermore, the tracking error bounds are class-K function of the bounds of reinitialization errors, uncertainties, and disturbances of the systems.

Remark 2.1. Under the conditions (10) and (11), one knows that the ILC stability is not affected by the uncertainties, disturbances, and the initial state bias, nor by the selection of γ. However, the bounds of the ILC final tracking errors are directly affected by those factors. As a high-order version ILC updating law of [17], it utilizes the past experiences comprehensively and has more flexibility in choosing learning operators and parameters. Hence, the better ILC performance can be expected. If the system dynamics are totally unknown, like the selection of learning parameters in traditional ILC algorithms [12, 17], the order N selection is also a trial-and-error process and needs "iterative learning." In practice, N should normally be chosen to be less than or equal to 3.

Remark 2.2. Similarly to Scheme 2 (equation 7), a current iteration tracking error information (CITE) may be included in the ILC updating law to improve the robustness as shown in [3, 18]. This is, in essence, a feedback–feedforward configuration similar to those discussed in [19, 20, 21].

Remark 2.3. The proportional and integral (PI) components in the ILC updating law do not affect the ILC stability [22], but PI components will be directly related to the robustness performance of ILC w.r.t. bounded initial positioning errors, uncertainties, and disturbances while the derivative component governs the ILC convergence property [23]. Conceptually, the PI learning operators can be used as design factors to make better the ILC performance when there exist bounded initial errors and uncertainties. High-order ILC updating law can be regarded as the PID controller in the i-direction where the high-order information is used to approximate the D information in the i-direction. Hence, the dual PIDs, both in the time t-direction and in the i-direction, can make the ILC application easier by taking the advantage of the long history of PID usage in conventional control engineering.

Remark 2.4. The ILC schemes presented above have their discrete-time counterparts. Detailed discussions on discrete-time ILC schemes can be found in [24, 25, 26].

3   DIRECT LEARNING CONTROL

In this section, a direct learning control (DLC) scheme for a class of high-order nonlinear systems with different magnitude scales is introduced. It has been shown that if the preobtained control profiles are chosen properly, the desired control input can be obtained directly and precisely by using DLC without the repeated learning process. Singularity problems have been discussed and a revised algorithm is proposed to deal with these problems.

DLC problems can be classified into the following three subcategories:

1. Direct learning of trajectories with the same time period but different magnitude scales, which can further be classified into the following two categories,
   (i) DLC learning of trajectories with single-magnitude scale relations.
   (ii) DLC learning of trajectories with multiple-magnitude scale relations.
2. Direct learning of trajectories with the same spatial path but different time scales. It can also be classified into two subcategories:
   (i) DLC learning of trajectories with linear time scale relations.
   (ii) DLC learning of trajectories with nonlinear time scale mapping relations.
3. Direct learning of trajectories with variations in both time and magnitude scales.

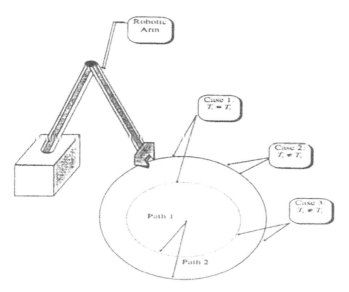

FIGURE 1
Classifications of DLC schemes.

A typical example of nonuniform task specifications can be illustrated as follows: A robotic manipulator draws circles in Cartesian space with the same radius but different periods, or, draws circles with the same period but different radii as shown in Figure 1.

In this section, we will explore the DLC schemes that deal with trajectories of single-magnitude scale relations, which belong to the first category of DLC problems. Other types of DLC schemes, such as multiple-magnitude-scale DLC schemes for high-order systems or time-scale DLC schemes for high-order systems or dual-scale DLC schemes have also been developed [27, 28, 29].

In the following we propose a general DLC scheme for high-order systems. The new scheme incorporates [1] as a subset.

3.1   Problem Formulation

Consider a nonlinear dynamic system described by the following equations:

$$M(\mathbf{x}(t), t)\mathbf{x}^{(p)}(t) = \sum_{j=1}^{q_0} \beta_{0,j}(\mathbf{x}(t), t)A_j(t)\xi_{0,j-r_0}(\mathbf{x}(t)) + B(t)\mathbf{u}(t)$$

$$\mathbf{y}(t) = C\mathbf{x}(t)$$

(12)

where

$$M(\mathbf{x})(t), t) = \left[\sum_{j=1}^{q_1} \beta_{1,j}(\mathbf{x}(t), t)G_{1,j}(t)\xi_{1,j-r_1}(\mathbf{x}(t)), \ldots, \sum_{j=1}^{q_m} \beta_{m,j}(\mathbf{x}(t), t)G_{m,j}(t)\xi_{m,j-r_m}(\mathbf{x}(t)) \right] \quad (13)$$

is a matrix of unknown nonlinear functions and $\mathbf{u}(t) \in R^m$ is the input vector, $\mathbf{y}(t) \in R^m$ is the output vector, and $\mathbf{x}(t) \in R^m$ is a measurable system state vector. $A_j(t)$, $B(t)$, and $G_{i,j}(t) \in R^{m \times m}$ are unknown time-varying matrices that are functions of time t only. $C \in R^{m \times m}$ is an unknown constant matrix. $\xi_{0,j-r_0}(\mathbf{x}(t))$ and $\xi_{i,j-r_i}(\mathbf{x}(t) \in R^m$ are partially known homogeneous function vectors that will be explained later in assumption **A2.1**. $\beta_{i,j}(\mathbf{x}(t), t)$ are known scalar nonhomogeneous functions of $x(t)$ and t. The numbers m, r_i, p, q are appropriate finite positive integers.

The following definition describes the inherent relations among trajectories with distinct magnitude scales. This definition is crucial in the derivation of this single-magnitude scale DLC scheme.

Definition. A trajectory $y_i(t)$ is said to be *proportional in magnitude scale* to another trajectory $y_d(t)$ if and only if both trajectories have the same time period and there exists a unique constant k_i such that $y_i(t) = k_i y_d(t)$ holds for any time instant $t \in [0, T]$ where T is the operation period.

This nonlinear system is assumed to satisfy the following conditions:

A2.1 All the elements of the vector $\xi_{i,j-r_i}(x(t))$ are homogeneous functions of order $j - r_i$. Consequently, $\xi_{i,j-r_i}(x(t))$ constitutes a power of $j - r_i$ for $x(t)$ such that $\forall k \neq 0$, $\xi_{i,j-r_i}(kx(t)) = k^{j-r_i}\xi_{i,j-r_i}(x(t))$.

A2.2 $\forall t \in [0, T]$, $\forall x(t) \in D \subset R^m$, the matrices $M(x(t), t)$, $B(t)$, C are nonsingular and D is a compact set in which the control solution uniquely exists with respect to the given trajectory.

A2.3 There are sufficient number of prestored trajectories $y \in [0, T]$. The corresponding desired control input signals $u_i(t)$ have been achieved a priori through learning or other control methods. All the prestored trajectories and the desired trajectory y_d are inherently related with each other through a distinct set of known constants k_i such that $y_i(t) = k_i y_d(t)$ where $\forall t \in [0, T]$, k_i. In other words, trajectories $y_i(t)$ and $y_d(t)$ are said to be *proportional in magnitude* with a scale k_i.

Remark 3.1. A direct inference of the Definition is that if the previous trajectory $y_i(t)$ is proportional in magnitude to $y_d(t)$ then the following equation exists:

$$x_i(t) = C^{-1}y_i(t) = C^{-1}k_i y_d(t) = k_i C^{-1}y_d(t) = k_i x_d(t)$$

Therefore assumption **A2.3** actually implies that the systems states of all the prestored trajectories and the desired trajectory are related with each other through the above-mentioned set of known constants k_i.

Remark 3.2. $\xi_{j-r_i}(x(t))$ can take different forms; for example, the following two functions

$$\xi_4(x(t)) = \begin{bmatrix} x_1^{(1)}(t)x_2^{(2)}(t)x_3^{(1)}(t) \\ x_1^{(3)}(t)x_2^{(1)}(t) \\ x_2^{(4)}(t) \\ x_2^{(2)}(t)x_3^{(2)}(t) \\ x_1^{(1)}(t)x_3^{(3)}(t) \end{bmatrix}, \quad \xi_3(x(t)) = \begin{bmatrix} x_1^{(2)}(t)x_2^{(1)}(t) \\ x_2^{(1)}(t)x_3^{(2)}(t) \end{bmatrix}$$

have "homogeneous order" of 4 and 3, respectively.

The control objective is to generate the desired control signal profile $u_d(t)$ over $t \in [0, T]$, for a new trajectory directly from the prestored control inputs u_i that is related to other prestored trajectories through the relations $y_d(t) = k_i^{-1}y_i(t_i)$, $k_i \neq 1$.

For simplicity of expressions, we write $x_i(t)$ as x_i in the subsequent derivation.

3.2   Direct Generation of the Desired Control Profiles

The following theorem relates the high-order DLC scheme for trajectories with different magnitude scales.

Theorem 3.1. For the plant given by (12), the desired control input $\mathbf{u}_d(t)$ with respect to a new trajectory $\mathbf{x}_{l,d}(t)$, $t \in [0, T]$ can be directly obtained using past control inputs according to the following relations

$$\mathbf{u}_d(t) = \vec{\mathbf{u}}K^{-1}\begin{bmatrix} \gamma_1(\mathbf{x}_d, t) \\ \vdots \\ \gamma_{q_s}(\mathbf{x}_d, t) \end{bmatrix}$$

where $\vec{\mathbf{u}} = [\mathbf{u}_1 \ \cdots \ \mathbf{u}_p]$ and $\mathbf{u}_i(t)$ is the ith known control input profile; ρ is an appropriate positive integer; $\gamma_i(\mathbf{x}_d, t)$ are known nonlinear function vectors; and K is a known matrix to be given in the following context.

Proof: Premultiplying each side of equation (12) with C, we have

$$CM(\mathbf{x}(t), t)\dot{\mathbf{x}}^{(p)}(t) = \sum_{j=1}^{q_0} \beta_{0,j}(\mathbf{x}(t), t)CA_j(t)\xi_{0,j-r_0}(\mathbf{x}(t)) + CB(t)\mathbf{u}(t) \qquad (14)$$

Since $CB(t)$ is invertible as stated in assumption **A2.2**, multiplying equation (14) by the inverse of $CB(t)$ and rearranging, it becomes

$$\mathbf{u}(t) = (CB)^{-1}CM(\mathbf{x}(t), t)\mathbf{x}^{(p)}(t) - (CB)^{-1}\sum_{j=1}^{q_0} \beta_{0,j}(\mathbf{x}(t), t)CA_j(t)\xi_{0,j-r_0}(\mathbf{x}(t)) \qquad (15)$$

The desired control input signal with respect to the new trajectory $\mathbf{y}_d(t)$, $t \in [0, T]$ can thus be expressed as

$$\mathbf{u}_d(t) = (CB)^{-1}CM(\mathbf{x}_d(t), t)\mathbf{x}_d^{(p)}(t) - (CB)^{-1}\sum_{j=1}^{q_0} \beta_{0,j}(\mathbf{x}_d(t), t)CA_j(t)\xi_{0,j-r_0}(\mathbf{x}_d(t))$$

Note that $\mathbf{u}_d(t)$ are not directly available in terms of the above formula due to the existence of system uncertainties in C, $A_j(t)$, $B(t)$, $M(\mathbf{x}_d(t), t)$ and $\xi_{j-r}(\mathbf{x}_d(t))$.
   Substituting (13) into (15) yields

$$\mathbf{u}(t) = (CB)^{-1}(t)\left[\sum_{j=1}^{q_1} \beta_{1,j}(\mathbf{x}(t), t)CG_{1,j}(t)\xi_{1,j-r_1}(\mathbf{x}(t)), \dots, \right.$$

$$\left. \sum_{j=1}^{q_m} \beta_{m,j}(\mathbf{x}(t), t)CG_{m,j}(t)\xi_{m,j-r_{1m}}(\mathbf{x}(t)) \right]\mathbf{x}^{(p)}(t)$$

$$- (CB)^{-1}\sum_{j=1}^{q_0} \beta_{0,j}(\mathbf{x}(t), t)CA_j(t)\xi_{0,j-r_0}(\mathbf{x}(t)) \qquad (16)$$

By defining the matrices

$$E_{0,j}(t) = (CB)^{-1}CA_j(t)$$
$$E_{1,j}(t) = (CB)^{-1}CG_{1,j}(t)$$

$$\vdots$$

$$E_{m,j}(t) = (CB)^{-1}CG_{m,j}(t)$$

equation (16) can be rewritten as

$$\mathbf{u}(t) = \sum_{l=1}^{m}\sum_{j=1}^{q_l}\beta_{l,j}(\mathbf{x}(t), t)\mathbf{x}_l^{(p)}(t)F_{l,j}(t)\xi_{l,j-r_l}(\mathbf{x}(t)) - \sum_{j=1}^{q_0}\beta_{0,j}(\mathbf{x}(t), t)E_{0,j}(t)\xi_{0,j-r_0}(\mathbf{x}(t))$$

On the other hand, for the output trajectories $y_i(t)$, $t \in [0, T]$, their control profiles have been obtained a priori, that is

$$\mathbf{u}(t) = \sum_{l=1}^{m}\sum_{j=1}^{q_l}\beta_{l,j}(\mathbf{x}_i(t), t)\mathbf{x}_{l,i}^{(p)}(t)E_{l,j}(t)\xi_{l,j-r_l}(\mathbf{x}(t)) - \sum_{j=1}^{q_0}\beta_{0,j}(\mathbf{x}_i(t), t)E_{0,j}(t)\xi_{0,j-r_0}(\mathbf{x}_i(t)) \qquad (17)$$

are known prestored input vectors.

According to Definition 2.1 the states of prestored trajectories $\mathbf{x}_i(t)$ and the desired trajectory $\mathbf{x}_d(t)$ are *proportional in magnitude*. By substituting $\mathbf{x}_i(t)$ with $k_i\mathbf{x}_d(t)$ in (17), we obtain

$$\mathbf{u}_i(t) = \sum_{l=1}^{m}\sum_{j=1}^{q_l}k_i^{j+1-r_l}\beta_{l,j}(k_i\mathbf{x}_d(t), t)\mathbf{x}_{l,d}^{(p)}(t)E_{l,j}(t)\xi_{l,j-r_l}(\mathbf{x}_d(t))$$

$$- \sum_{j=1}^{q_0}k_i^{j-r_0}\beta_{0,j}(k_i\mathbf{x}_d(t), t)E_{0,j}(t)\xi_{0,j-r_0}(\mathbf{x}_d(t)) \qquad (18)$$

Note that $E_{i,j}(t)$ are functions of t only, and it remains the same for identical time periods. By inspecting (18), we can see that the left-hand side of $\mathbf{u}_i(t)$ is known for each $t \in [0, T]$, whereas in the right-hand side the unknown terms $\mathbf{x}_{l,d}^{(p)}E_{l,j}(t)\xi_{l,j-r_l}(\mathbf{x}_d(t))$, $l = 1, \ldots, m$ are common for all trajectories. Therefore, those unknown but common factors can be calculated in a point-wise manner for each $t \in [0, T]$, provided that the number of prestored trajectories available is at least the same as the number of unknown elements in equation (18).

Now let us rearrange the items in equation (18). First collect all the vectors with the same power of the scaling factor of k_i^j from the $\rho = \sum_{i=0}^{m} q_i$ column vectors in equation (18). Note that each column vector is expressed as a product of a known scalar function and an unknown column vector. Assume that for all the known scalar functions $\beta_{l,j}$, $l = 1, \ldots, m$ there are only ρ_j distinct functions corresponding to the jth power of the scaling factor k_i^j. Note that $\rho_j \le m+1$. They constitute a known column vector denoted as

$$\gamma_j(k_i\mathbf{x}_d, t) = [\gamma_{j,1}(k_i\mathbf{x}_d, t), \cdots, \gamma_{j,\rho_j}(k_i\mathbf{x}_d, t)]^T$$

Their corresponding vectors $\mathbf{x}_{l,d}^{(p)}E_{l,j}(t)\xi_{l,j-r_l}(\mathbf{x}_d(t))$ and $E_{0,j}(t)\xi_{l,j-r_0}(\mathbf{x}_d(t))$ can therefore be arranged as a matrix

$$D_j(\mathbf{x}_d(t)) = [\mathbf{d}_{j,1}(\mathbf{x}_d, t), \ldots, \mathbf{d}_{j,\rho_j}(\mathbf{x}_d, t)]$$

Note that $D_j(\mathbf{x}_d(t)) \in R^{m \times \rho_j}$.

After defining

$$r_s = \max\{r_0 - 1, \quad r_1 - 1, \quad \ldots, \quad r_m - 1\}$$

$$q_s = \max\{q_0 - r_0 + 1, \quad q_1 - r_1 + 1, \quad \ldots, \quad q_m - r_m + 1\} + r_s$$

$$\rho = \sum_{j=1}^{q_s}\rho_j$$

$\mathbf{u}_i$ in equation (18) can be reformulated into the following compact form:

$$\mathbf{u}_i = \sum_{j=1}^{q_s}k_i^{j-r_s}D_j(\mathbf{x}_d, t)\gamma_j(k_i\mathbf{x}_d, t) \qquad (19)$$

Note that in assumption **A2.3** it has been assumed that there are a sufficient number of prestored trajectories available in the system. We are now ready to rewrite equation (18) for ρ distinct trajectories in matrix form:

$$\vec{u} = \vec{D}K,$$

where

$$\vec{u} = [\mathbf{u}_1 \ \cdots \ \mathbf{u}_\rho] \tag{20}$$

$$\vec{D} = [\mathbf{D}_1(\mathbf{x}_d(t)) \ \cdots \ \mathbf{D}_{q_s}(\mathbf{x}_d(t))]$$

$$K = \begin{bmatrix} k_1^{1-r_s}\gamma_1(\mathbf{x}_1, t) & \cdots & k_\rho^{1-r_s}\gamma_1(\mathbf{x}_\rho, t) \\ \vdots & & \vdots \\ k_1^{q_s-r_s}\gamma_{q_s}(\mathbf{x}_1, t) & \cdots & k_\rho^{q_s-r_s}\gamma_{q_s}(\mathbf{x}_\rho, t) \end{bmatrix} \tag{21}$$

and $\vec{u} \in R^{m \times \rho}$, $K \in R^{\rho \times \rho}$, $\vec{D} \in R^{m \times \rho}$. It can be observed that $\vec{D}$ is invariant for all ρ trajectories at each time instant. Therefore, if the known matrix $K \in R^{\rho \times \rho}$ is of full rank for all $t \in [0, T]$, the matrix $\vec{D}$ can be solved directly by $\vec{D} = \vec{u}K^{-1}$.

As a consequence, the desired control input can be achieved directly as below:

$$\mathbf{u}_d(t) = \sum_{j=1}^{q_s} D_j(\mathbf{x}_d, t)\gamma_j(k_i\mathbf{x}_d, t)$$

$$= \vec{u}K^{-1}\begin{bmatrix} \gamma_1(\mathbf{x}_d, t) \\ \vdots \\ \gamma_{q_s}(\mathbf{x}_d, t) \end{bmatrix} \tag{22}$$

It is clear that at least ρ distinct trajectories are needed to obtain the matrix $\vec{D}$. ∎

Remark 3.3. If the nonhomogeneous functions $\beta_{i,j}$ in equation (12) do not exist, i.e, they are all ones, then the system states $\mathbf{x}(t)$ do not have to be measurable.

Remark 3.4. The initial position of the system is assumed to be aligned with the desired trajectory. This condition can be guaranteed in many real systems and is also required by most ILC algorithms.

Remark 3.5. From the formation of the DLC algorithm, we can also observe that it is actually not necessary to know the exact numbers $\{q_i, r_i\}$ of the homogeneous functions $\xi_{l,j}$. The only prior information used in DLC design is the highest and lowest orders of $\xi_{l,j}$. For example, if a real plant only has a nonlinear term x^2, whereas the plant model may include an extra term x, we can still apply the DLC scheme without affecting the results, provided that a sufficient number of prestored trajectories are available. Therefore, the DLC algorithm can allow, to some extent, the system model to be redundant or overstructured.

Remark 3.6. For a time-varying output matrix $C(t)$, the above procedure can still be applied to generate the desired signals directly.

Remark 3.7. If the previous information is not accurate, DLC can still function as an effective feedforward compensator to provide useful information. We will demonstrate this point in the subsequent section when applying DLC to a robotic manipulator control problem.

3.3 Modified DLC Scheme in the Presence of Singularity

To implement the direct learning control scheme, the singularity problem has to be addressed. Consider the matrix K of (21): it is considered "singular" if $\det(K) = 0$ at certain time instant. In some cases, det(K) is nonzero but the condition number of K is too large to achieve accurate results.

There are two possible circumstances resulting in the singularity of K, and each needs a different approach to deal with.

Case 1. A nonhomogeneous function $\gamma_{j,l}(\mathbf{x}_i, t)$ is zero for all trajectories at a certain time instant. For example, suppose the lth element of $\gamma_j(\mathbf{x}_i, t)$ takes the form $\gamma_{j,l}(\mathbf{x}_i, t) = \sin(\mathbf{x}_i)$. Then the row that corresponds to l will be zero when $\mathbf{x}_d = 0$.

However, it can be noted that a zero $\gamma_{j,l}(\mathbf{x}_i, t)$ implies that the corresponding vector $\mathbf{d}_{j,l}(\mathbf{x}_d(t), t))$ in $D_{j,l}(\mathbf{x}_d, t)$ is irrelevant to the control input $\mathbf{u}_j(t)$ and consequently irrelevant to $\mathbf{u}_d(t)$. We can simply delete the row of zeros from the original K matrix such that the reduced matrix $K_o \in R^{(\rho-1)\times\rho}$. The corresponding column vector $\mathbf{d}_{j,l}$ should also be removed from the $\vec{\mathbf{D}}$ matrix to generate a reduced $\vec{\mathbf{D}}_o$. That is, $\vec{\mathbf{u}} = \vec{\mathbf{D}}_o K_o$ where $\vec{\mathbf{D}}_o \in R^{m\times(\rho-1)}$ and $K_o \in R^{(\rho-1)\times\rho}$.
The reduced matrix $\vec{\mathbf{D}}_o$ can be solved by

$$\vec{\mathbf{D}}_o = \vec{\mathbf{u}} K_o^T (K_o K_o^T)^{-1}$$

In terms of equation (22), $\mathbf{u}_d(t_s)$ can still be obtained except that one column of $\vec{\mathbf{D}}$ is removed. This procedure can also be applied analogously to cases where multiple rows in $\vec{\mathbf{D}}$ are zeros.

Case 2. If det(K) $= 0$, whereas no row in K is zero, we can use an extra trajectory and the matrix K becomes augmented, K_e,

$$K_e = \begin{bmatrix} k_1^{1-r_s}\gamma_1(\mathbf{x}_1(t), t) & \cdots & k_\rho^{1-r_s}\gamma_1(\mathbf{x}_\rho(t), t)) & k_{\rho+1}^{1-r_s}\gamma_1(\mathbf{x}_{\rho+1}(t), t) \\ \vdots & & \vdots & \vdots \\ k_1^{q_s-r_s}\gamma_{q_s}(\mathbf{x}_1(t), t) & \cdots & k_\rho^{q_s-r_s}\gamma_{q_s}(\mathbf{x}_\rho(t), t) & k_{\rho+1}^{q_s-r_s}\gamma_{q_s}(\mathbf{x}_{\rho+1}(t), t) \end{bmatrix}$$

Since we have assumed that there are sufficient number of different trajectories, it is always possible to choose such an extra trajectory that the expanded matrix $K_e \times K_e^T$ is of full rank. Therefore, the matrix $\vec{\mathbf{D}}$ can be solved using

$$\vec{\mathbf{D}}_o = \vec{\mathbf{u}}_e K_e^T (K_e K_e^T)^{-1}$$
$$\vec{\mathbf{u}}_e = [\mathbf{u}_1 \quad \cdots \quad \mathbf{u}_\rho \; \mathbf{u}_{\rho+1}],$$

The desired $\mathbf{u}_d$ can be calculated using equation (22).

4   LEARNING CONTROL APPLICATIONS

4.1   Temperature Profile Tracking in Batch Chemical Reactor

This subsection presents an application of the ILC methodology to the temperature profile control of a batch chemical reactor. The P-type and D-type ILC schemes are applied and compared. The *feedback-assisted* (FA) ILC and the ILC with *current-iteration tracking error* (CITE) are discussed together with the *high-order* ILC schemes. The effectiveness of the proposed schemes is demonstrated by simulation studies using a simplified polymerization reactor model.

Background. Most large-scale chemical engineering processes have traditionally been operated in a continuous manner. However, batch processes, particularly batch chemical reactors, have drawn increasing attention from industry.

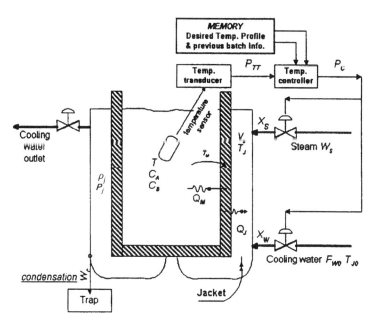

FIGURE 2
A batch chemical reactor.

A typical batch reactor is shown in Figure 2. Reactant is charged into the vessel. Steam is fed into the jacket to bring the reaction mass up to a specified temperature. Cooling water is then added to the jacket to remove the exothermic heat of reaction such that the reactor temperature can follow the *prescribed temperature profile*.

It is well known that it is difficult for a conventional control to track a given trajectory (pattern) in a finite (batch duration) interval. An *iterative learning control*, on the other hand, is able to utilize the system's repetition to compensate or reject uncertainties and disturbances and hence able to track the prescribed trajectory in a finite interval. In particular, the control efforts of the current batch incorporate the control efforts and tracking errors of the previous batch.

4.1.1 A Batch Reactor Model. A simplified batch polymerization reaction model [30] is used for the simulation study in which the jacket effect is neglected. A more complete batch reactor model can be found in [31]. An equivalent thermal flow Q comes from manipulating the valves for steam or cooling water flow control. The valves are under split range control so that the steam valve and cooling water valve cannot be opened simultaneously. Hence, Q is regarded as a total control. The reaction equations are given as follows:

$$\begin{cases} \dfrac{dc}{dt} = -a_1 k_d c + Q' \\[2mm] \dfrac{dx_M}{dt} = -a_2 k_p \sqrt{\dfrac{2\eta k_d}{k_1}} \sqrt{c} x_M \\[2mm] \dfrac{dp}{dt} = a_3 \eta k_d c \\[2mm] \dfrac{dT}{dt} = H_r \dfrac{dx_M}{dt} + Q \end{cases} \qquad (23)$$

where c, x_M and p are the concentrations of the initiator, monomer and polymer respectively; T is the temperature inside the reactor (K). Q' is assumed to be 0, which means that no additional initiator is added during the reaction, i.e., all reactants have been filled in the reactor at the beginning. The reaction rate constants k_i, $i \in \{d, p, t\}$ are functions of T where the subscripts d, p, t represent the phases of beginning, growing and stopping, and

$$k_i = k_{i0} \exp\left(-\frac{E_i}{RT}\right), \qquad i = d, p, t \tag{24}$$

The relevant constants in (23) and (24) are given in [30]. The initial states are $c(0) = 200$, $x_M(0) = 500$, $p(0) = 0$ and $T(0) = 300$ K.

A well-planned temperature profile $T_d(t)$ is given as

$$T_d(t) = \begin{cases} \dfrac{T_e}{t_m} t & \text{if } 0 \le t \le t_m \\ T_e & \text{if } t_m \le t \le t_e \end{cases} \tag{25}$$

with settings $t_e = 2$ h; $t_m = 1$ h and $T_e = 435$ K.

For comparative purposes, a simple P-type feedback controller

$$Q(t) = K_p e(t), \qquad e(t) = T_d(t) - T(t) \tag{26}$$

is first applied and the responses are shown in Figure 3. Clearly, a conventional controller is not able to track the temperature profile in a finite time interval.

Iterative Learning Control Schemes.   The basic idea of ILC is to update the control signal during tracking period $[0, T]$ in a pointwise manner. In the following, we briefly introduce four ILC schemes used for the temperature control of the batch polymerization reaction.

(1) D-type ILC. The D-type ILC input signals are updated by using the derivative of the tracking error in the previous iteration. In this case, the ILC updating law is given by

$$Q_{i+1} = Q_i + K_d \dot{e}_i(t), \qquad \dot{e}_i(t) = \dot{T}_d - \dot{T}_i \tag{27}$$

where K_d is the learning gain, which is to be properly chosen such that $e_i \to 0$ as $i \to \infty$. As a simplified case of Theorem 2.1, the convergence condition can be given by

$$\|1 - CBK_d\| < 1 \tag{28}$$

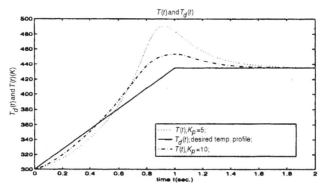

FIGURE 3
Responses for a simple P-controller.

where B and C are the input distribution matrix and output matrix, respectively. In (23), the system input is Q and the output is T. Hence, $CB = 1$. K_d should be selected to satisfy the condition $|1 - K_d| < 1$.

(2) High-order ILC. It is quite intuitive that if more of the previous control efforts and tracking errors are used, a better ILC performance can be expected. This has been well discussed in Section 1.2. In general, an Nth-order D-type ILC updating law is

$$Q_{i+1} = Q_i + \sum_{j=1}^{N} K_{d_j} \dot{e}_{i-j+1}(t) \tag{29}$$

where the learning gains should satisfy the condition that the roots of (30) are inside the unit circle,

$$(1 - CBK_{d_1})z^{-1} - \sum_{j=2}^{N} CBK_{d_j}z^{-j} = 0 \tag{30}$$

where z is one step shifting operator. According to Theorem 2.1, a sufficient condition is given by

$$|1 - CBK_{d_1}| + \sum_{j=2}^{N} |CBK_{d_j}| = 0 \tag{31}$$

(3) P-type Iterative Learning Feedback Control. From [11], it is clear that a better ILC performance can be achieved by introducing a feedback loop. The control system is actually an ILC controller in the iteration number direction and simultaneously a feedback controller in the time direction. In practice, P-type ILC scheme is preferred because the D-type ILC (27) is sensitive to the measurement noise. The P-type scheme can be written as

$$\begin{cases} Q_i(t) = Q_i^{ff}(t) + Q_i^{fb}(t) \\ Q_i^{fb}(t) = K_p e_i(t) \\ Q_i^{ff}(t) = Q_{i-1}(t) + K_{pl}e_{i-1}(t) \\ \quad = Q_i^{ff}(t) = (K_p + K_{pl})e_{i-1}(t) \end{cases} \tag{32}$$

A convergence condition can be found in [26] for discrete-time nonlinear systems where the role of feedback is regarded as an assistance to the ILC.

(4) P-type ILC with CITE. Consider the PI-controller in the ILC iteration direction as follows:

$$Q_i(t) = k_I' \sum_{j=0}^{i} e_j(t) + k_P' e_i(t) \tag{33}$$

Writing (33) in an iterative form, we have

$$Q_i(t) = Q_{i-1}(t) + k_I' e_i(t) + k_P'(e_i(t) - e_{i-1}(t))$$
$$= Q_{i-1}(t) + K_P e_i(t) + K_{pl} e_{i-1}(t) \tag{34}$$

where $K_p = k_I' + k_P'$, $K_{pl} = -k_P'$. Updating law (34) is called the *ILC with current-iteration tracking error* (CITE). A convergence condition was given in [32] where k_P' was assumed to be 0. It was shown in [32] that the convergence as well as the robustness of the ILC with CITE scheme (34) is independent of the choice of K_p, the CITE gain. This actually invokes a high-gain ILC as indicated in [33].

High-order schemes can be synthesized with P-type ILC and CITE:

$$Q_i(t) = p'Q_{i-1}(t) + (1 - p')Q_{i-2}(t) + K_p e_i(t) + K_{pl} e_{i-1}(t) \qquad (35)$$

where p' is a positive fraction $p' \in [0, 1]$. An improved ILC convergence property can be expected as discussed in the above.

Simulation Studies. Simulations were carried out with a fixed step $h = 0.1$ h. We now concentrate on the P-PI scheme (33), which used the P component of the tracking error in the time t-direction and PI components of the tracking error in the ILC iteration number i-direction. We will investigate the effects of different choices of learning gains K_p and K_{pl} on the convergence performance of the ILC scheme (34).

Case 1. $K_{pl} = 0$. In this case, only CITE is used, i.e.,

$$Q_i(t) = Q_{i-1}(t) + K_p e_i(t) \qquad (36)$$

This can be regarded as a P-I scheme as discussed in the above. It is interesting to note that from the analysis of [32], the convergence and robustness of the ILC scheme (36) are independent of the choice of K_p. However, larger K_p will give better ILC performance as also indicated in [18]. This is clearly illustrated by Figure 4.

Case 2. $K_{pl} \neq 0$. This is P-PI type ILC. Along the i-direction, the PI gains $k'_p = -K_{pl}$, $k'_I = K_p + K_{pl}$. It is intuitive from conventional PID controller tuning that increasing k_I will reduce the convergence bound of the tracking error. This is similar to the effect of an integral (I) controller in the time-domain. This effect is illustrated in Figure 5.

We now observe the effect of K_{pl} under a fixed K_p. Qualitatively speaking, to guarantee the ILC convergence (stability in the i-direction), k'_p, (i.e., K_{pl}) cannot be arbitrarily chosen. We considered five subcases for $K_{pl} = 2$, 0.5, 0, -2 and -4 respectively. The results are presented in Figure 5. From the comparison in Figure 5, the tuning of K_{pl} and K_p is possible based on the existing PID tuning method, which deserves future research.

Case 3. *High-order in Control.* As described in (35), the high order can be in control terms. This, in fact, adds an input signal filter, which in this case, is a first-order filter. Different choices

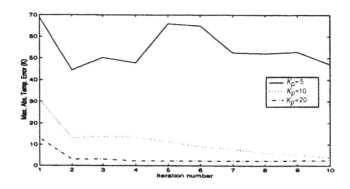

FIGURE 4
Convergence comparisons for P-I type (ILC+CITE) schemes.

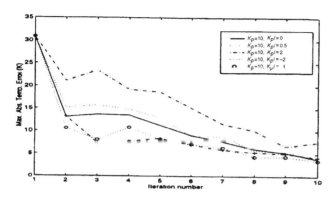

FIGURE 5
Convergence comparisons for P-PI type (ILC+CITE) schemes.

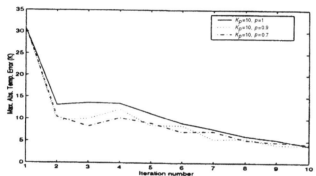

FIGURE 6
Convergence comparisons for P-type scheme (35).

of p' may result in different ILC convergence transients. Figure 6 shows the results for $p' = 1$, 0.9, and 0.7 respectively. It is interesting to observe that the ILC convergence performance improves as p' decreases slightly from 1.

Case 4. $K_{pl} = 4$; $K_p - 5$, 10, 15. Similar to Case 1, we will show that under a fixed K_{pl}, the ILC convergence improves when K_p increases. This is well illustrated by Figure 7.

The converged results are almost the same. A set of plots for the system states in the 10th ILC is given in Figure 8. The monomer condensation finally decreases to 0 while the polymer condensation keeps increasing, according to the predesigned temperature profile $T_d(t)$.

4.2 Direct Learning Control of Robotic Manipulators

Robotic Model. The plant to be controlled is a two-link robotic manipulator. Its dynamic equation can be represented by

$$\begin{bmatrix} h_{11} & h_{12} \\ h_{21} & h_{22} \end{bmatrix} \begin{bmatrix} \ddot{\theta}_1 \\ \ddot{\theta}_2 \end{bmatrix} + \begin{bmatrix} -h\dot{\theta}_2 & -h\dot{\theta}_1 - h\dot{\theta}_2 \\ h\dot{\theta}_1 & 0 \end{bmatrix} \begin{bmatrix} \dot{\theta}_1 \\ \dot{\theta}_2 \end{bmatrix} + \begin{bmatrix} g_1 \\ g_2 \end{bmatrix} = \begin{bmatrix} u_1 \\ u_2 \end{bmatrix}$$

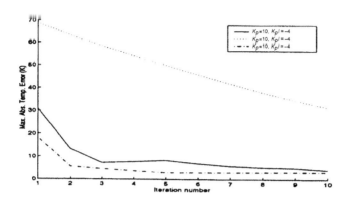

FIGURE 7
Convergence comparisons for P-PI type (ILC+CITE) schemes.

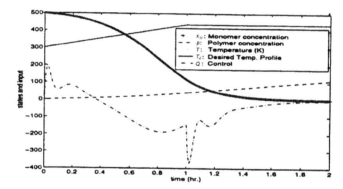

FIGURE 8
Converged system states and input (at the 10th ILC iteration).

with $\theta = [\theta_1 \theta_2]^T$ being the two joint angles, $\mathbf{u} = [u_1 u_2]^T$ being the joint inputs and

$$h_{11} = m_1 l_{c_1}^2 + I_1 + m_2[l_1^2 + l_{c_2}^2 + 2l_1 l_{c_2} \cos \theta_2] + I_2$$

$$h_{22} = m2l_{c_2}^2 + I_2$$

$$h_{12} = h_{21} = m_2 l_1 l_{c_2} \cos \theta_2 + m_2 l_{c_2}^2 + I_2$$

$$h = m_2 l_1 l_{c_2} \sin \theta_2$$

$$g_1 = m_1 l_{c_1} g \cos \theta_1 + m_2 g[l_{c_2} \cos(\theta_1 + \theta_2) + l_1 \cos \theta_1]$$

$$g_2 = m_2 l_{c_2} g \cos(\theta_1 + \theta_2)$$

where the pairs $\{m_1, m_2\}$, $\{I_1, I_2\}$, $\{l_1, l_2\}$ and $\{l_{c1}, l_{c2}\}$ are the masses, moments of inertia, lengths, and center of gravity coordinates of the two robotic arms, respectively. For complicity, the payload is also included in m_2. The prestored tracking trajectories are specified as

$$\theta_{1,i}(t) = k_i \left\{ \theta_{01} + (\theta_{01} - \theta_{f1}) \left[15 \left(\frac{t}{T} \right)^4 - 6 \left(\frac{t}{T} \right)^5 - 10 \left(\frac{t}{T} \right)^3 \right] \right\}$$

$$\theta_{2,i}(t) = k_i \left\{ \theta_{02} + (\theta_{02} - \theta_{f2}) \left[15 \left(\frac{t}{T} \right)^4 - 6 \left(\frac{t}{T} \right)^5 - 10 \left(\frac{t}{T} \right)^3 \right] \right\}$$

where θ_0 and θ_f denote the initial and final angular positions, respectively. The desired trajectories for the two links are

$$\theta_{1,d}(t) = \left\{ \theta_{01} + (\theta_{01} - \theta_{f1}) \left[15\left(\frac{t}{T}\right)^4 - 6\left(\frac{t}{T}\right)^5 - 10\left(\frac{t}{T}\right)^3 \right] \right\}$$

$$\theta_{2,d}(t) = \left\{ \theta_{02} + (\theta_{02} - \theta_{f2}) \left[15\left(\frac{t}{T}\right)^4 - 6\left(\frac{t}{T}\right)^5 - 10\left(\frac{t}{T}\right)^3 \right] \right\}$$

The parameters were chosen as follows: $m_1 = 1$ kg, $m_2 = 2$ kg, $l_1 = 1$ meter, $l_2 = 1$ meter, $l_{c1} = 0.5$ meter, $l_{c2} = 0.6$ meter, $I_1 = 0.12$ kg $\cdot$ meter^2, $I_2 = 0.25$ kg $\cdot$ meter^2, $\theta_{01} = 120°$, $\theta_{f1} = 140°$, $\theta_{02} = 30°$, $\theta_{f2} = 50°$, and $T = 1$ s to be the operation period. All the prestored trajectories are *proportional in magnitude* with respect to θ_d through scales $k_1 = -0.75$, $k_2 = -1.5$, $k_3 = 2$, $k_4 = 1.5$, and $k_5 = 0.75$.

Inverse Model Suitable for DLC Scheme.   To facilitate DLC design, an inverse model such as (19) describing the constitution of the control input $\mathbf{u}$, is needed. First define the following:

$$h_{11} = c_1 + c_2 \cos\theta_2$$
$$h_{22} = c_3$$
$$h_{12} = h_{21} = c_3 + c_4 \cos\theta_2$$
$$h = c_4 \sin\theta_2$$
$$g_1 = c_5 \cos\theta_1 + c_6 \cos(\theta_1 + \theta_2)$$
$$g_2 = c_6 \cos(\theta_1 + \theta_2)$$

where $\{c_1, c_2, c_3, c_3, c_4, c_5, c_6\}$ are unknown constants. Then we have

$$
\begin{bmatrix} u_1 \\ u_2 \end{bmatrix} = \begin{bmatrix} c_1 + c_2 \cos\theta_2 & c_3 + c_4 \cos\theta_2 \\ c_3 + c_4 \cos\theta_2 & c_3 \end{bmatrix} \begin{bmatrix} \ddot\theta_1 \\ \ddot\theta_2 \end{bmatrix}
$$
$$
+ c_4 \sin\theta_2 \begin{bmatrix} -\dot\theta_2 & -\dot\theta_1 - \dot\theta_2 \\ \dot\theta_1 & 0 \end{bmatrix} \begin{bmatrix} \dot\theta_1 \\ \dot\theta_2 \end{bmatrix}
$$
$$
+ \begin{bmatrix} c_5 \cos\theta_1 + c_6 \cos(\theta_1 + \theta_2) \\ c_6 \cos(\theta_1 + \theta_2) \end{bmatrix} \tag{37}
$$

The state variables and output vector were chosen as

$$y = [y_1 \ y_2]^T = [x_1 \ x_2]^T = [\theta_1 \ \theta_2]^T$$

Then, we can rewrite (37) as

$$
\begin{bmatrix} u_1 \\ u_2 \end{bmatrix} = \begin{bmatrix} c_1 + c_2 \cos x_2 & c_3 + c_4 \cos x_2 \\ c_3 + c_4 \cos x_2 & c_3 \end{bmatrix} \begin{bmatrix} \ddot x_1 \\ \ddot x_2 \end{bmatrix}
$$
$$
+ c_4 \sin x_2 \begin{bmatrix} -\dot x_2 & -\dot x_1 - \dot x_2 \\ \dot x_1 & 0 \end{bmatrix} \begin{bmatrix} \dot x_1 \\ \dot x_2 \end{bmatrix}
$$
$$
+ \begin{bmatrix} c_5 \cos x_1 + c_6 \cos(x_1 + x_2) \\ c_6 \cos(x_1 + x_2) \end{bmatrix} \tag{38}
$$

or

$$u_1 = (c_1 + c_2 \cos x_2)\ddot{x}_1 + (c_3 + c_4 \cos x_2)\ddot{x}_2 - c_4 \sin x_2(2\dot{x}_1\dot{x}_2 + \dot{x}_2^2) + c_5 \cos x_1 + c_6 \cos(x_1 + x_2)$$
$$u_2 = (c_3 + c_4 \cos x_2)\ddot{x} + c_3\ddot{x}_2 + c_4\dot{x}_1^2 \sin x_2 + c_6 \cos(x_1 + x_2)$$

$$(39)$$

Because the ith trajectories are related to the desired trajectory with constant k_i, i.e.,

$$[x_{1,i}x_{2,i}]^T = k_i[x_{1,d}x_{2,d}]$$

the dynamic equation for the ith trajectory can be written as

$$u_{1,i} = k_i(c_1\ddot{x}_{1,d} + c_3\ddot{x}_{2,d}) + k_i(c_2\ddot{x}_{1,d} + c_4\ddot{x}_{2,d})\cos x_{2,i} - k_i^2 c_4(2\dot{x}_{1,d}\dot{x}_{2,d} + \dot{x}_{2,d}^2)\sin x_{2,i}$$
$$\qquad + c_5 \cos x_{1,i} + c_6 \cos(x_{1,i} + x_{2,i})$$

$$(40)$$

$$u_{2,i} = k_i(c_3\ddot{x}_{1,d} + c_3\ddot{x}_{2,d}) + k_i c_4\ddot{x}_{1,d} \cos x_{2,i} + k_i^2 c_4\dot{x}_{2,d}^2 \sin x_{2,i} + c_6 \cos(x_{1,i} + x_{2,i})$$

It can be written as a summation of vectors according to the power of k_i:

$$\mathbf{u}_i(t) = k_i^0 \begin{bmatrix} c_5 & c_6 \\ 0 & c_6 \end{bmatrix} \begin{bmatrix} \cos x_{1,i} \\ \cos(x_{1,i} + x_{2,i}) \end{bmatrix}$$
$$\qquad + k_i^1 \begin{bmatrix} c_1\ddot{x}_{1,d} + c_3\ddot{x}_{2,d} & c_2\ddot{x}_{1,d} + c_4\ddot{x}_{2,d} \\ c_3\ddot{x}_{1,d} + c_3\ddot{x}_{2,d} & c_4\ddot{x}_{1,d} \end{bmatrix} \begin{bmatrix} 1 \\ \cos x_{2,i} \end{bmatrix}$$
$$\qquad + k_i^2 \begin{bmatrix} -c_4(2\dot{x}_{1,d}\dot{x}_{2,d} + \dot{x}_{3,d}^2) \\ c_4\dot{x}_{2,d}^2 \end{bmatrix} \sin x_{2,i}$$

$$(41)$$

Comparing with (19), it can be seen that the following relations hold:

$$q_s = 3, \qquad r_s = 1, \qquad p_1 = p_2 = 2, \qquad p_3 = 1,$$

$$D_1(x_d)0 = \begin{bmatrix} c_5 & c_6 \\ 0 & c_6 \end{bmatrix}$$

$$\gamma_1 = \begin{bmatrix} \cos x_{1,i} \\ \cos(x_{1,i} + x_{2,i}) \end{bmatrix}$$

$$D_2(\mathbf{x}_d) = \begin{bmatrix} c_1\ddot{x}_{1,d} + c_3\ddot{x}_{2,d} & c_2\ddot{x}_{1,d} + c_4\ddot{x}_{2,d} \\ c_3\ddot{x}_{1,d} + c_3\ddot{x}_{2,d} & c_4\ddot{x}_{1,d} \end{bmatrix}$$

$$\gamma_2 = \begin{bmatrix} 1 \\ \cos x_{2,i} \end{bmatrix}$$

$$D_3(\mathbf{x}_d) = \begin{bmatrix} -c_4(2\dot{x}_{1,d}\dot{x}_{2,d} + \dot{x}_{3,d}^2) \\ c_4\dot{x}_{2,d}^2 \end{bmatrix}$$

$$\gamma_3 = \sin x_{2,i}$$

It can easily be checked that $\rho = \rho_1 + \rho_2 + \rho_3 = 5$. Therefore, the control information of at least five distinct previous trajectories is needed. By following similar steps, the DLC control input for this two-link model can be expressed as

$$\mathbf{u}_d(t) = \vec{\mathbf{u}} K^{-1} \begin{bmatrix} \cos x_{1,d} \\ \cos(x_{1,d} + x_{2,d}) \\ 1 \\ \cos x_{2,d} \\ \sin x_{2,d} \end{bmatrix} \tag{42}$$

where

$$\vec{\mathbf{u}} = \begin{bmatrix} u_{1,1} & u_{1,2} & u_{1,3} & u_{1,4} & u_{1,5} \\ u_{2,1} & u_{2,2} & u_{2,3} & u_{2,4} & u_{2,5} \end{bmatrix}$$

$$K = \begin{bmatrix} \cos x_{1,1} & \cos(x_{1,1} + x_{2,1}) & k_1 & k_1 \cos x_{2,1} & k_1^2 \sin x_{2,1} \\ \cos x_{1,2} & \cos(x_{1,2} + x_{2,2}) & k_2 & k_2 \cos x_{2,2} & k_2^2 \sin x_{2,2} \\ \cos x_{1,3} & \cos(x_{1,3} + x_{2,3}) & k_3 & k_3 \cos x_{2,3} & k_3^2 \sin x_{2,3} \\ \cos x_{1,4} & \cos(x_{1,4} + x_{2,4}) & k_4 & k_4 \cos x_{2,4} & k_4^2 \sin x_{2,4} \\ \cos x_{1,5} & \cos(x_{1,5} + x_{2,5}) & k_5 & k_5 \cos x_{2,5} & k_5^2 \sin x_{2,5} \end{bmatrix}$$

Simulation Results and Discussions. Three sets of simulations are conducted to investigate the effectiveness of DLC from different aspects.

Case 2.1: DLC with perfect past control information. Assume that perfect tracking control profiles have been obtained in advance with respect to the five distinct trajectories. The simulation results are shown in Figures 9 and 10.

Figure 9 shows the output trajectory and the tracking errors of the two robotic arms with sampling interval $\delta t = 2.5$ ms. It can be seen that the robotic links can track the desired trajectory but with certain deviations. This can be readily explained: DLC is, in fact, an open-

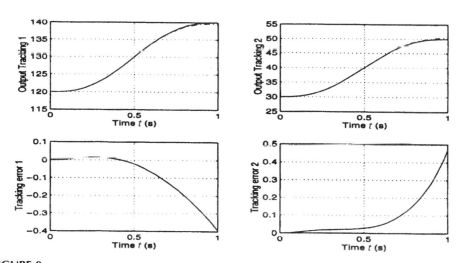

FIGURE 9
Direct learning using accurate previous control profiles ($\delta t = 2.5$ ms): (1) dash-dot line, DLC learned trajectory; (2) solid line, ideal trajectory.

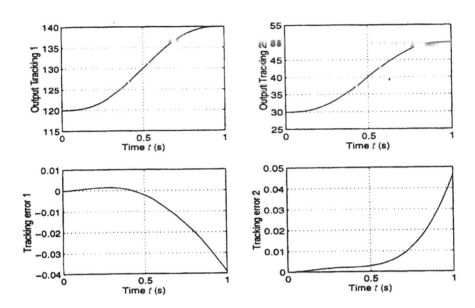

FIGURE 10
Direct learning using accurate previous control profiles ($\delta t = 0.25$ ms): (1) dash-dot line, DLC learned trajectory; (2) solid line, ideal trajectory.

loop controller; hence, it does not have the ability to correct motion when errors occur. The errors here were caused mainly by the limited sampling rate. From the derivation of the DLC scheme, we know that the control inputs are exact only at each sampling point. Therefore, we can expect that the tracking errors can be reduced by shortening the sampling interval. This is shown in Figure 10, where we choose $\delta t = 0.25$ ms. It can be observed that the tracking error of DLC was reduced by approximately ten times by shortening the sampling interval to one-tenth of the previous interval.

Case 2.2: DLC with feedback. In practice, DLC can be combined with other kinds of control methods to improve the system performance. Figure 11 is the simulation result obtained by combining DLC with a PD controller, i.e.,

$$\mathbf{u} = \mathbf{u}_{DLC} + \mathbf{u}_{PD}$$

$$\mathbf{u}_{PD} = K_P(\theta_d - \theta) + K_d \frac{d}{dt}(\theta_d - \theta)$$

where $K_p = 100$ and $K_d = 20$ were chosen.

It can be seen that the tracking errors were greatly reduced despite the sampling interval of 2.5 ms. The tracking accuracy was almost the same as in the previous case where the sampling interval was 0.25 ms. As a comparison, we also provide simulation results using only a PD controller as shown in Figure 12 with the same K_p and K_d. It is obvious that the PD controller, alone, cannot work properly for such a highly nonlinear and uncertain dynamics. This clearly shows that DLC can work as a suitable feedforward compensator for different trajectories and be obtained only from past control inputs.

Case 2.3: DLC with imperfect past control information. Note that the prestored control profiles are obtained through past control experiences using any control methods such as ILC, PID, VSC, adaptive control, or any combination of them. From the practical point of view, those

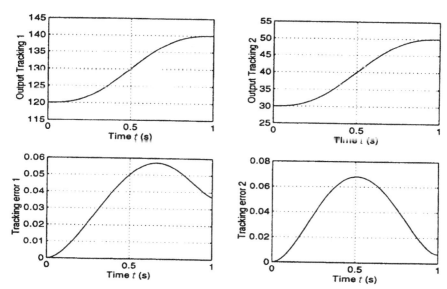

FIGURE 11

Direct learning using accurate previous control profiles and combined with PD ($\delta t = 2.5$ ms): (1) dash-dot line, DLC learned trajectory; (2) solid line, ideal trajectory.

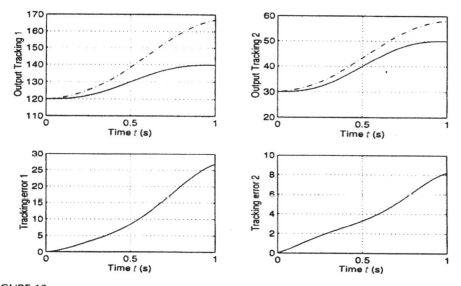

FIGURE 12

PD control alone ($\delta t = 2.5$ ms) . (1)$dash - dotline, PD control trajectory$; (2)$solidline, ideal trajectory$.

signals may not be as *accurate* as desired. Nevertheless, the DLC scheme can still work as a feedforward compensator. It tries to extract the useful information from past tracking control experiences for the new control attempt. To see whether the proposed DLC method can work when the prestored control information is imperfect, we used two sets of prestored control profiles, which resulted in different tracking errors as listed in Tables 1 and 2. The simulation results are shown in Figures 13 and 14.

From the simulation results, we can see that DLC worked well as a feedforward compensator even if the previous control was not precise. If the previous information was relatively accurate

Table 1.1   First set of Control Profile

	Prestored Trajectory No.				
	1st	2nd	3rd	4th	5th
Max error of 1st link (degree)	0.50	1.3	0.38	0.95	0.80
Max error of 2nd link (degree)	0.25	0.40	0.32	0.20	0.42

Table 1.2   Second set of Control Profile

	Prestored Trajectory No.				
	1st	2nd	3rd	4th	5th
Max error of 1st link (degree)	1.7	5.6	1.7	3.5	3
Max error of 2nd link (degree)	0.9	1.8	1.6	0.5	1.4

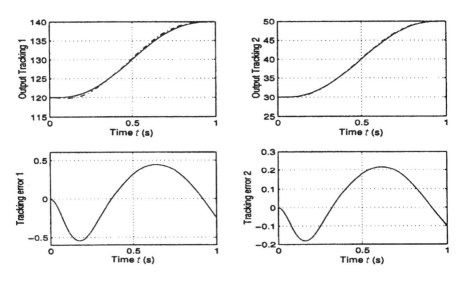

FIGURE 13
Direct learning using first set previous control profiles and combined with PD ($\delta t = 2.5$ ms): (1) dash-dot line, DLC learned trajectory; (2) solid line, ideal trajectory.

(the first set), it provided satisfactory performance with regard to the new trajectory (Figure 13). When using information which involved larger tracking errors (the second set), DLC could still maintain the feedforward compensation (Figure 14). Comparing Figures 14 and 12, we can observe that the maximum tracking errors of PD control with DLC based feedforward compensation were reduced to less than one-tenth of that of PD control alone.

Remark 1.4.1. It is interesting to note that DLC also provides the possibility of improving the iterative learning control performance. When a new trajectory is assigned to ILC, we can use DLC to generate the initial control profile, which is much more accurate than the 0th trial result of an ILC with either open-loop or PD control alone. Comparing Figure 12 with Figure 13 or

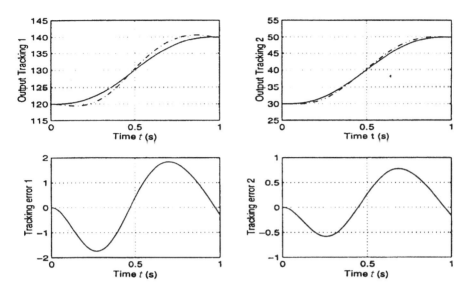

FIGURE 14
Direct learning using second set previous control profiles ($\delta t = 2.5$ ms): (1) dash-dot line, DLC learned trajectory; (2) solid line, ideal trajectory.

Figure 14, it is obvious that a better convergence of ILC can be achieved by incorporating DLC-based feedforward compensation as the initial learning control signals.

4.3   Aerodynamic Curve Identification by Iterative Learning

This subsection focuses on extracting a single aerodynamic drag coefficient curve of aeronautical bomb from three-dimensional theodolite film data, i.e., from the measured spatial positions of the aeronautical bomb. In increasing the bombing accuracy of aircraft, the aeronautical bomb's drag coefficient curve plays a crucial role. The mechanism of the interference air flow field between the aircraft and the aeronautical bomb when bombing is not yet clear. Therefore, the drag coefficient curve obtained from wind tunnel measurements or from theoretical numerical prediction under the free airflow condition cannot be applied directly. The curve deduced from flight testing data is obviously advantageous in practical applications. Many efforts have been made to extract aerodynamic properties of real or full-scale flying vehicles from flight testing data [34, 35]. Most of the literature, however, only emphasizes the aerodynamic *coefficient* extraction by parameter identification, which is clearly a special case of *curve* extraction. In practice, to utilize the flight testing data, aerodynamic *curve* extraction or identification is preferred. The *optimal dynamic fitting* method [36, 37] has been used to directly extract the aerodynamic coefficient *curve*. However, this method suffers from computational complexity and the need for a good estimate of the initial curve.

A new approach, iterative learning identification [9, 37] has been introduced and applied. By properly setting the learning gain, the learning convergence can be guaranteed. The convergence is shown to be quite robust with respect to the initial control estimate. To improve the learning convergence, several schemes for the learning gain determination have been examined. Results from actual flight testing data for three bombing flight paths have been presented to validate the effectiveness of the proposed iterative learning scheme. The extracted results are convincing and comprehensively reflect the effects of interference air flow field and the angular motion around the center of mass. Conventionally, generation of the bombing table is based on a single ballistic coefficient, a drag law, and some fitting factors. More accurate firing tables can then be produced when the extracted C_{df} of this application is utilized directly.

Problem Formulation.   Suppose that at time t the aeronautical bomb's position in the earth coordinate system (ECS) is $[x(t), y(t), z(t)]^T$, and its velocity $\vec{u}$ w.r.t ECS is $[u_x(t), u_y(t), u_z(t)]^T$. We have

$$\begin{cases} \dot{u}_x(t) = -\rho s V(t)(u_x(t) - w_x(t))C_{df}(t)/2m \\ \dot{u}_y(t) = -\rho s V(t)u_y(t)C_{df}(t)/2m - g \\ \dot{u}_z(t) = -\rho s V(t)(u_z(t) - w_z(t))C_{df}(t)/2m \\ \dot{x}(t) = u_x(t); \ \dot{y}(t) = u_y(t); \ \dot{z}(t) = u_z(t) \end{cases} \tag{43}$$

where $X(t) = [x(t), y(t), z(t), u_x(t), u_y(t), u_z(t)]^T$ is the state vector of system (43); g is the gravitational acceleration; $w_x(t), w_z(t)$ are the wind components in ECS; $V(t)$ is the aeronautical bomb's relative velocity w.r.t wind and

$$V(t) = \sqrt{(u_x(t) - w_x(t))^2 + u_y^2(t) + (u_z(t) - w_z(t))^2} \tag{44}$$

In (43), ρ is the air density; $s = 2\pi d^2/4$ is the reference area of the aeronautical bomb, and d is the aeronautical bomb's reference diameter; m is the mass of the bomb. $C_{df}(t)$ is the aerodynamic drag coefficient curve w.r.t. the trajectory model (43), which is regarded as a "control" function to be determined optimally.

Denote by $\{x_m(t), y_m(t), z_m(t)|t = t_0, t_0 + h, \dots, t_0 + Nh\}$ the measured positional trajectories of aeronautical bomb from theodolite films, where N is the number of points and h is the time step. By a proper use of the spline fitting method, the velocity data $u_m(t) = \sqrt{u_{x_m}^2(t) + u_{y_m}^2(t) + u_{z_m}^2(t)}$ can be obtained and hence $X(t_0)$ is known. The initial state $X(t_0)$ can also be obtained from test planning and other recording devices. Taking $u_m(t)$ as the desired trajectory to be followed, the control objective is to minimize the tracking error $e(t) = u_m(t) - u(t)$, i.e.,

$$\min_{C_{df}} J[C_{df}] = \min_{C_{df}} e_b = \min_{C_{df}} \sup_{t \in [t_0, t_0 + Nh]} |e(t)| \tag{45}$$

where

$$u(t) = \sqrt{u_x^2(t) + u_y^2(t) + u_z^2(t)} \tag{46}$$

which can be regarded as the "output" equation for system (43). Clearly, (43), (46), and (45) formulate an optimal tracking control problem (OTCP). It should be pointed out that this OTCP is a singular optimal control problem (SOCP) and the performance index is a *minimax* one, which is difficult to solve.

Curve Extraction by Iterative Learning.   The differences between iterative learning control and iterative learning-based curve extraction are as follows:

- *Iterative learning control*: Given a desired output trajectory, to solve a desired control function iteratively along with the system repetitive operations.

- *Iterative learning-based curve extraction*: To extract an unknown nonlinear function, which is regarded as a *virtual* control function, iteratively from input/output data; this is taken as the desired output trajectory.

The key issue in implementing an iterative learning extraction method is how the *system* is operated repeatedly. In fact, a system repetition here is simply the numerical integration of the trajectory model (43) from t_0 to $t_0 + Nh$ with a known initial condition $X(t_0)$ under the current control $C_{df}(t)$. Therefore, the iterative learning extracting procedures can be summarized as follows:

- *Step 1*. Set $k = 0$ and give an arbitrary $(C_{df}(t))_0$. Specify a maximum error ε^* allowed and a maximum number of iterations N_i for the extraction.
- *Step 2*. Integrate the ballistic model (43) with $(C_{df}(t))_k$ from t_0 to $t_0 + Nh$ with initial condition $X(t_0)$; then obtain the tracking error $e_k(t)$ according to (46).
- *Step 3*. Learning updating:

$$(C_{df}(t))_{k+1} = (C_{df}(t))_k = K(t)\dot{e}_k(t) \tag{47}$$

  where $K(t)$ is a learning gain, which will be discussed in the following.
- *Step 4*. If either $e_b < \varepsilon^*$ or $k \geq N_i$ then go to step 6; else go to Step 5.
- *Step 5*. $k = k + 1$ and store $(C_{df}(t))_k$ and $\dot{e}_i(t)$ for use in the next repetition. Go to Step 2.
- *Step 6*. Stop.

Selection of Learning Gain.   The selection of the learning gain is mainly based on a learning convergence condition that is a simplified version of Theorem 2.1.

In (11), $\bar{\rho}$ is the rate of convergence. The smaller $\bar{\rho}$, the faster the convergence. A constant learning gain may be used provided at all time instants $\bar{\rho}$ is smaller than 1. To have the fastest convergence, one may set $\bar{\rho} = 0$ to get the best $K(t)$. According to Theorem 2.1, from (43) and (46), one obtains

$$\bar{g}_{\bar{x}} = \left[\frac{u_x}{u}, \frac{u_y}{u}, \frac{u_z}{u}, 0, 0, 0\right], \qquad B(\bar{x}(t), t) = -\frac{\rho V s}{2m}[u_x - w_x, \ u, u_z - w_z, \ 0, \ 0, \ 0]$$

Then, applying (11) yields

$$K(t) = -\left(\frac{\rho V s}{2mu}[u^2 - u_x w_x - u_z w_z]\right)^{-1} \tag{48}$$

a time-varying learning gain for convenient application in learning updating. Note that $u_x \gg w_x$, $u_z \gg w_z$, and $V \approx u$. Thus, based on (48), the first choice for $K(t)$ is

$$K^{(1)}(t) = -\frac{2m}{\rho_0 s u_m^2(t)} \tag{49}$$

where ρ_0 is the standard air density at sea level and the superscript [1] denotes the first design of the learning gain. $K^{(1)}(t)$ is simple to use as it varies only w.r.t. time t. In fact, one may consider that $K(t)$ is not only a function of time t but also a function of the iteration number k. This is essential because, in (48), ρ and V vary from iteration to iteration. We thus get the second formula for learning gain as follows:

$$K^{(2)}(t) = -\frac{2m}{(\rho)_k s (u^2(t))_k} \tag{50}$$

Intuitively, one may wish to replace $u^2(t)$ with the "desired" $u_m^2(t)$, which gives the third learning gain formula:

$$K^{(3)}(t) = -\frac{2m}{(\rho)_k s (u_m^2(t))_k} \tag{51}$$

In what follows, the extracted results associated with the above three varying learning gains are given and discussed.

Extracted Results from Flight Tests. The main purpose of the flight tests is to *measure* the aerodynamic drag coefficient curve of the aeronautical bomb. Several tests were carried out under different bombing conditions. Here we present the curve-extraction results from three-dimensional theodolite film data sets of three bombing flight paths supplied by a Proving Ground. Figure 15 illustrates the measured trajectories. From Figure 15, the numerically computed velocities are used to extract the C_{df} curve. According to the standardization processing result from the Proving Ground, for flights #7–9, respectively, the elevation angles (degrees) when bombing were 0.15, 0.11, and −0.04; the heights (meters) when bombing were 4101, 4103, and 4106; and the velocities (meters/s) when bombing were 127, 129, and 125. The ballistic coefficients c obtained were 0.60553, 0.61213, and 0.60274, and the obtained shape coefficients i_{cp1} were 0.757, 0.765, and 0.753. In the above, c is obtained as a fitting factor to fit the range measurements under practical bombing conditions,

$$c = \frac{id^2}{m} \times 10^3, \qquad i = \frac{c_x}{\bar{c}_{x0}} \tag{52}$$

where i is the aeronautical bomb's shape coefficient, c_x is the drag coefficient and $\bar{c}_{x0}$ is the so-called drag law. i_{cp1} is also a fitting result provided by the Proving Ground based on a fitted c.

Using the method and relevant data reduction program of this work, three c curves corresponding to flight paths #7–9 were obtained. The results are shown in Figure 16, where the drag law $\bar{c}_{x0}(M)$ (local) is also plotted for comparison. For each flight path, the final converged results are the same using different choices of learning gain.

Validation of the extracted results is quite difficult because the effect of airflow interference–interaction between aircraft and aeronautical bomb is not yet clear. From Figure 16, the shape coefficient curve $i(M)$ of each flight path can be determined by

$$i(M) = \frac{C_{df}(M)}{\bar{c}_{x0}(M)} \tag{53}$$

Taking the mean value of this $i(M)$, one can obtain the average shape coefficient i_{cp2}. It is important to note that i_{cp2} obtained in this application is with the *comparability* w.r.t. i_{cp1} given above. See Table 3 for the shape coefficient comparison and the induced range error comparison according to an evaluation formula of the Proving Ground. From Figure 16 and Table 3, it can be validated that the $C_{df}(M)$ curve extracted in this study is correct. The form of $C_{df}(M)$ fits the qualitative theoretical conjecture. In these sets of flight test data, the maximal Mach number (M) was about 0.65. Theoretically $C_{df}(M)$ should be constant when $M \leq 0.65$ (lower subsonic region). It is interesting to note that the form of $C_{df}(M)$ is an approximately exponential decay in the early stage of the Mach range and then smoothly approaches constant value. The latter

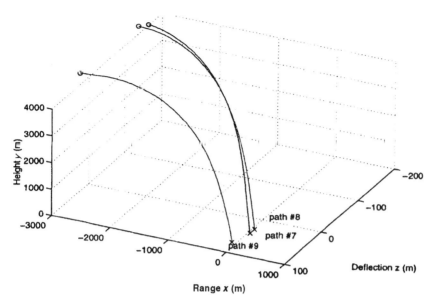

FIGURE 15
The measured three flight paths #7, # 8 and #9.

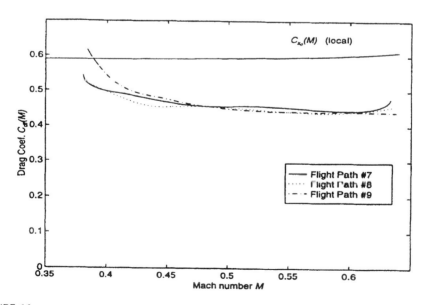

FIGURE 16
The extracted $C_{df}(M)$ by iterative learning.

Table 3   Comparison of Shape Coefficients

Flight Path Number	i_{cp2}	Shape Coefficient Error: $\dfrac{i_{cp1} - i_{cp2}}{i_{cp1}}$	Range Error $\Delta A / A$
7	0.787	−3.991%	−0.598%
8	0.782	−2.253%	−0.338%
9	0.819	−8.715%	−1.307%
Average value	0.796	−4.986%	−0.748%

phenomenon fits the aerodynamic theory as the effects of the interference flow field to the aeronautical bomb's motion have died out and the bomb is almost in a free air flow field.

To verify the robustness of the iterative learning method w.r.t. initial estimates, a constant learning gain scheme is used. According to the above discussions, the gain $K(t)$ is chosen as −0.1. Using the same learning gain, three different initial estimates $(C_{df}(t))_0$, i.e., +0.3, 0, and −0.3, were considered. The learning iteration histories are summarized in Figure 17. Under the same exit condition $\varepsilon^* = 0.05$ (m/s), the required numbers of learning iterations are 9, 11, and 18, respectively. From aerodynamics, $(C_{df}(t))_0 = +0.3$ is a better estimate while $(C_{df}(t))_0 = -0.3$ is impractical. One may observe that the iterative learning method still works with such a wrong initial estimate while other methods, such as optimal dynamic fitting, proposed by Chen et al. [36, 38], does not work even when $(C_{df}(t))_0 = 0$.

Three proposed schemes for learning gain determination are applied for further comparison. Under the same initial estimate $(C_{df}(t))_0 = 0$ and exit condition $(\varepsilon^* = 0.05 \text{ m/s})$, extraction

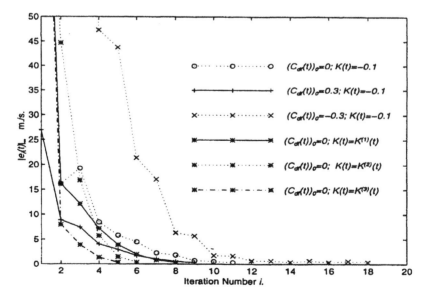

FIGURE 17
Learning iteration histories for different learning gain selection schemes.

schemes with $K^{(1)}(t)$, $K^{(2)}(t)$ and $K^{(3)}(t)$ take 8, 6, and 5 learning iterations, respectively. It can be seen from Figure 17 that $K^{(3)}(t)$ produces the fastest learning convergence. Moreover, from Figure 17, one can clearly observe that the convergence properties for learning gains varying w.r.t. time t as well as the iteration number k are better than those for the constant learning gains.

5 CONCLUSIONS

We have presented a number of developments, both theoretical and applied, of iterative learning control and direct learning control systems. As a repetition-based scheme, iterative learning control acquires the necessary control directly from previous control profiles whenever the control task is repeated. A current cycle P-type learning scheme is developed and analyzed for nonlinear servocontrol systems. It shows that the existing feedback controller is very helpful in improving the control performance. A high-order PID-type learning scheme is then developed for nonlinear uncertain systems with state delays. The tracking error bound is shown to be a class-K function of the bounds of reinitialization errors and disturbances to the systems. A dual-PID scheme in both time and iteration number is suggested, which shows the potential link with the well-established PID tuning methods. A new learning control method, direct learning control, is introduced that differs from all iterative learning control methods in that it is a pattern-based learning method in nature. Although learning from distinct patterns, direct learning control also differs from other pattern-based learning schemes in that it uses all available system structure knowledge and hence ensures exact tracking for a new trajectory by learning in a point-wise manner. We show that direct learning control is able to generate the desired control profile from previous input–output patterns with either nonuniform time scales or nonuniform magnitude scales.

Following the theoretical developments presented, three typical applications of the learning control methods are described. The first is the application of ILC methods to the temperature control of a batch chemical reactor. The second is the direct learning control of a robotic manipulator. In the last application, we show that ILC is a useful tool for solving noncontrol problems. An example is the learning-based aerodynamic curve identification.

Acknowledgment

This work is supported in part by NUS Research Grant RP-3972693.

REFERENCES

[1] J.-X. Xu, Direct learning of control efforts for trajectories with different magnitude scales, *Automatica*, Vol. 33, No. 12, pp. 2191–2195, 1997.
[2] J.-X. Xu and Y. B. Song. Direct learning control of non-uniform trajectories, in Z. Bien and J.-X. Xu (eds) *Iterative Learning Control—Analysis, Design, Integration and Application*, pp 261–284. Kluwer Academic, Boston, 1998.
[3] T. H. Lee, J. H. Nie, and W. K. Tan, Developments in learning control enhancements for nonlinear servomechanisms, *Mechatronics*, Vol. 5, No. 8, pp. 919–935, 1995.
[4] Y. Chen, Z. Gong, and C. Wen, Analysis of a high order iterative learning control algorithm for uncertain nonlinear systems, *Automatica*, Vol. 34, No. 3, pp. 345–353, 1998.
[5] K. J. Astrom, C. C. Hang, P. Persson, and W. K. Ho, Towards intelligent PID control, *Automatica*, Vol. 28, No. 1, pp. 1 –9, 1992.
[6] J.-X. Xu, C. Liu, and C. C. Hang, Tuning of fuzzy PI controllers bases on gain/phase margin specifications and ITAE, *ISA Transactions*, Vol. 35, No. 1, pp. 79–91, 1996.

[7] T. H. Lee, C. C. Hang, and W. K. Ho, Implementation of intelligent PID auto-tuning, in *Proc. IEEE Int. Symp. Circuits and Systems, Singapore*, 1991, pp 2316–2319.

[8] Y. Chen, J.-X. Xu, T. H. Lee, and S. Yamamoto, Comparative studies of iterative learning control schemes for a batch chemical process, in *Proc. IEEE Int. Symp. Control Theory and Applications (SISCTA'97), Singapore*, 1997, pp 166–170.

[9] Y. Chen, J.-X. Xu, and C. Wen, Iterative learning based extraction of aeronautical bomb drag, *AIAA: Journal of Spacecraft and Rockets*, Vol. 35, No. 1, pp. 237–240, 1998.

[10] J. J. Craig, P. Hsu, and S. S. Sastry, Adaptive control of mechanical manipulators, *Int. J. Robotics Research*, Vol. 6, No. 2, pp. 16–28, 1987.

[11] S. Arimoto, Robustness of learning control for robot manipulators, in *Proc. IEEE Int. Conf. Robotics and Automation, Cincinnati* 1990, pp. 1528–1533.

[12] S. Arimoto, S. Kawamura, and F. Miyazaki, Bettering operation of robots by learning, *J. Robotic Systems*, Vol. 1, No. 2, pp. 123–140, 1984.

[13] J. J. Craig, Adaptive control of manipulators through repeated trials, in *Proc. American Control Conference, San Diego*, 1984, pp. 1566–1573.

[14] K. L. Moore, *Iterative Learning Control for Deterministic Systems* (Advances in Industrial Control Series). Springer-Verlag, Berlin 1993.

[15] M. Uchiyama, Formulation of high-speed motion pattern of a mechanical arm by trial, *Trans. SICE (Society of Instrument and Control Engineers)*, Vol. 14, No. 6, pp. 706–712, 1978, (in Japanese).

[16] Z. Bien and K. M. Huh, High-order iterative learning control algorithm, *IEE Proc. Part D, Control Theory and Applications*, Vol. 136, No. 3, pp. 105–112, 1989.

[17] G. Heinzinger, D. Fenwick, B. Paden, and F. Miyazaki, Stability of learning control with disturbances and uncertain initial conditions, *IEEE Trans. Automatic Control*, Vol. 37, No. 1, pp. 110–114, 1992.

[18] Y. Chen, C. Wen, and M. Sun, A robust high-order P-type iterative learning controller using current iteration tracking error, *Int. J. Control*, Vol. 68, No. 2, pp. 331–342, 1997.

[19] T.-Y. Kuc, J. S. Lee, and K. Nam, An iterative learning control theory for a class of nonlinear dynamic systems, *Automatica*, Vol. 28, No. 6, pp. 1215–1221, 1992.

[20] A. De Luca and S. Panzieri, An iterative scheme for learning gravity compensation in flexible robot arms, *Automatica*, Vol. 30, No. 6, pp. 993–1002, 1994.

[21] T.-J. Jang, C.-H. Choi, and H.-S. Ahn, Iterative learning control in feedback systems, *Automatica*, Vol. 31, No. 2, pp. 243–245, 1995.

[22] G. Heinzinger, D. Fenwick, B. Paden, and F. Miyazaki, Robust learning control, in *Proc. 28th IEEE Conf. Decision and Control, Tampa, FL*, 1989, pp. 436–440.

[23] H.-S. Lee and Z. Bien, Study on robustness of iterative learning control with non-zero initial error, *Int. J. Control*, Vol. 64, No. 3, pp. 345–359, 1996.

[24] Jian-Xin Xu, Analysis of iterative learning control for a class of nonlinear discrete-time systems, *Automatica*, Vol. 33, No. 10, pp. 1905–1907, 1997.

[25] Y. Chen, J.-X. Xu, and T. H. Lee, Current iteration tracking error assisted iterative learning control of uncertain nonlinear discrete-time systems, in *Proc. 35th IEEE Conf. Decision and Control, Kobe, Japan*, 1996, pp. 3040–3045.

[26] Y. Chen, J.-X. Xu, and T. H. Lee, Feedback-assisted high-order iterative learning control of uncertain nonlinear discrete-time systems, in *Proc. Int. Conf. Control, Automation, Robotics and Vision (ICARCV), Singapore*, 1996, pp. 1785–1789.

[27] Jian-Xin Xu and Yanbin Song, Direct learning control of high-order systems for trajectories with different time scales, in *Proc. 2nd Asian Control Conference, Seoul, Korea*, 1997, Vol. 3, pp. 187–190.

[28] Jian-Xin Xu and Tao Zhu, Direct learning control of trajectory tracking with different time and magnitude scales for a class of nonlinear uncertain systems, in *Proc. 2nd Asian Control Conference, Seoul, Korea*, 1997, Vol. 3, pp 191–194.

[29] J.-X. Xu, Direct learning of control input profiles with different time scales, in *Proc. 35th IEEE Conf. Decision and Control, Kobe, Japan*, 1996, pp. 2501–2502.

[30] S. Shioya, *Batch Process Engineering* (Recent Chemical Engineering Series 36) The Society of Chemical Engineers, Japan, 1984.

[31] W. L. Luyben, *Process Modeling, Simulation, and Control for Chemical Engineers* (McGraw-Hill Chemical Engineering Series) McGraw-Hill Kogakusha, New York, 1973.

[32] C.-J. Chien and J.-S. Liu, A P-type iterative learning controller for robust output tracking of nonlinear time-varying systems, in *Proc. American Control Conference, Baltimore, MD*, 1994. pp. 2595–2599.

[33] D. H. Owens, Iterative learning control—convergence using high gain feedback, in *Proc. 31st Conf. Decision and Control, Tucson, AZ*, 1992, pp. 2545–2546.

[34] K. W. Illif, Parameter estimation for flight vehicle, *AIAA Journal of Guidance, Control and Dynamics*, Vol. 12, No. 5, pp. 609–622, 1989.

[35] D. J. Linse and R. F. Stengel, Identification of aerodynamic coefficients using computational neural networks, *AIAA Journal of Guidance, Control, and Dynamics*, Vol. 16, No. 6, pp. 1018–1025, 1994.

[36] Y. Chen, D. Lu, H. Dou, and Y. Qing, Optimal dynamic fitting and identification of aeronautical bomb's fitting drag coefficient curve, in *Proc. First IEEE Conf. Control Applications, Dayton, OH*, 1992, pp. 853–858.

[37] Y. Chen, C. Wen, H. Dou, and M. Sun, Iterative learning identification of aerodynamic drag curve from tracking radar measurements, *J. Control Engineering Practice*, Vol. 5, No. 11, pp. 1543–1554, Nov. 1997.

[38] Y. Chen, C. Wen, Z. Gong, and M. Sun, Drag coefficient curve identification of projectiles from flight tests via optimal dynamic fitting, *J. Control Engineering Practice*, Vol. 5, No. 5, pp. 627–636, May 1997.

PART II

THEORY OF SOFT COMPUTING AND INTELLIGENT CONTROL SYSTEMS

CHAPTER 11

Techniques for Genetic Adaptive Control

WILLIAM K. LENNON and KEVIN M. PASSINO

Department of Electrical Engineering, The Ohio State University, 2015 Neil Avenue, Columbus, Ohio, USA

I. INTRODUCTION

Genetic algorithms (GAs) are a parallel search technique that emulates the laws of evolution and genetics to try to find optimal solutions to complex optimization problems [1]. Some research has been conducted using genetic algorithms to help design control systems, but usually these methods involve off-line design of the control system [2–6]. GAs have also been used for off-line system identification [7]. Research on the use of GAs for on-line real-time estimation and control includes [8], where genetic algorithms are used for system identification of linear systems and coupled with pole placement-based indirect adaptive control, [9] where a direct genetic adaptive control method is introduced, and [10] where genetic adaptive observers are introduced to estimate plant states. The technique of [9] is applied to control of a brake system in [11]. Relevant general ideas on GAs and adaptive systems are in [12] and other applications and methods are studied in [13, 14].

In this chapter we investigate ways to use genetic algorithms in the on-line control of a nonlinear system and compare our results with conventional control techniques. We develop a direct genetic adaptive controller and an indirect genetic adaptive controller, and combine the two into a general genetic adaptive controller.[1] We also examine several conventional controllers including a proportional-derivative controller, a model reference adaptive controller, and two indirect adaptive controllers. To demonstrate all these control techniques, we investigate the

---

[1] Indirect adaptive control uses an "identifier" to synthesize a model of the plant dynamics and then information from this model is used to tune a controller (we say that the controller was tuned "indirectly" by first identifying a model of the plant). For "direct adaptive control", an identifier is not used for the plant; the parameters of the controller are tuned directly (some think of the direct adaptive controller as a "controller identifier"). For more details see, e.g., [15, 16].

problem of cargo ship steering. In this application, we describe the desired performance with a reference model and use our control techniques to track the output of the reference model. Overall, our goal is not to design the best possible controller for ship steering; we simply use this example to illustrate the ideas.

The direct genetic adaptive controller that we use is a type of "genetic model reference adaptive controller" (GMRAC) that was originally introduced in [9]. Here, we significantly modify the method in [9] for fitness evaluation and study the idea of initializing the population with some fixed controllers and letting these remain fixed throughout the controller's operation. We explain how this idea is related to ideas in "multiple model adaptive control" [17]. Our indirect genetic adaptive controller is most similar to one in [8] where the authors use a GA for model identification and then use the model parameters in a certainty equivalence control law based on a pole-placement method. Here, however, we use a different method for fitness evaluation and a model reference approach. Our general genetic adaptive controller is novel in that it *combines* the direct and indirect approaches. To do this, it uses genetic adaptive identification to estimate the parameters of the model that are used in the fitness function for the direct genetic adaptive controller. Essentially, the general genetic adaptive controller both identifies the plant model and tries to tune the controller at the same time, so that if the estimates are inaccurate we can still achieve good control.

While several of the genetic adaptive methods are novel, we emphasize that one of the primary contributions of this chapter lies in the comparative analysis with conventional adaptive control techniques. Overall, we feel that such comparative analysis is very important for identifying both the advantages of new intelligent control techniques and their possible disadvantages [18, 19]. The remainder of the chapter is organized as follows.

In Section 2 we define the cargo ship steering problem. In Section 3 we develop direct conventional and genetic adaptive control methods and compare their performance. In Sections 4 and 5 we do the same but for indirect adaptive methods and a combined indirect/direct genetic adaptive method. In Section 6 we provide some concluding remarks, summarize the results of the chapter, and provide an analysis of the computational complexity of the genetic adaptive controllers.

II. THE CARGO SHIP STEERING CONTROL PROBLEM

The objective in the cargo ship control problem is to control the ship heading, ψ by moving the rudder, δ. A coordinate system is fixed to the ship as shown in Figure 1. The cargo ship is described by a third-order nonlinear differential equation [16], that is used in all simulations as the truth model, and is given by

$$\dddot{\psi}(t) + \left(\frac{1}{\tau_1} + \frac{1}{\tau_2}\right)\ddot{\psi}(t) + \left(\frac{1}{\tau_1\tau_2}\right)(a\dot{\psi}^3(t) + b\dot{\psi}(t)) = \frac{k}{\tau - 1\tau_2}(\tau_3\dot{\delta}(t) + \delta(t)) \qquad (1)$$

The input, δ, and the output, ψ, are both measured in radians. The constants a and b are assigned a value of one for all simulations. The constants k, τ_1, τ_2, and τ_3 are defined as

$$k = k_0 \frac{u}{l} \qquad (2)$$

$$\tau_i = \tau_{i0} \frac{l}{u}, \qquad i = 1, 2, 3 \qquad (3)$$

where u is the forward velocity of the ship in meters/second and l is the length of the ship in meters. For the cargo ship $k_0 = -3.86$, $\tau_{10} = 5.66$, $\tau_{20} = 0.38$, $\tau_{30} = 0.89$, $l = 161$ m and $u = 5$ m/s (nominally). The maximum allowable rudder angle is ± 1.3963 radians ($\pm 80\,°$).

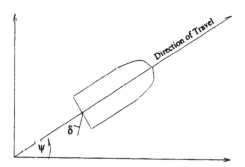

FIGURE 1
Cargo ship control problem. The input to the system is the rudder angle, δ. The output of the system is the cargo shop heading, ψ.

In all cases we set the reference model to be

$$W_m(s) = \frac{r^2}{(s+r)(s+r)}$$

with $r = 0.05$. Hence the output of the reference model is

$$\psi_m = W_m(s)\zeta$$

Here ζ is the desired cargo ship heading and ψ_m is the "ideal" response, i.e., the response we want to track. Note that this response is fairly slow, but the ship is large and hence it is not realistic to request that the rudder change its direction very fast.

In our simulation tests, the speed of the cargo ship, u, is changed every 600 seconds, beginning at the nominal 5 m/s, dropping to 3 m/s, rising back to 5 m/s and finally rising again to 7 m/s. From equations (2) and (3) it is easy to see that such speed changes significantly affect the dynamics of the ship. Intuitively, as the ship slows down, the rudder becomes less effective as a steering input. Figure 2 shows the reference input, the reference model output, and the speed of the ship used throughout all simulations to follow.

To provide an idea of how a control system will operate for this system, we show the response for the case where $\delta = -5(\zeta - \psi) - 175 \, d(\zeta - \psi)/dt$ (i.e., a manually tuned proportional-derivative (PD) controller) in Figure 3. Here we see that the PD controller is able to regulate the heading of the ship to within $\pm 2.5°$ when $u = 5$ m/s, but when $u = 3$ m/s we see that it can only regulate it to within $\pm 7.5°$. Note that the PD gains of $p = -5$ and $d = -175$ were selected because they minimize this tracking error.

III.   DIRECT ADAPTIVE CONTROL

In this section we attempt to directly adjust the parameters of a controller to make the error between the cargo ship heading and the reference model output go to zero. We begin with a conventional model reference adaptive controller from [15] and then develop a genetic model reference adaptive controller.

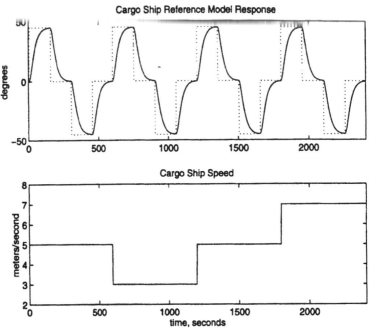

FIGURE 2

Reference input and cargo ship speed. The top plot depicts the reference input ζ (the dotted line) and the output of the reference model ψ_m (solid line). The reference input ζ changes by 0.7854 radians (45°) every 150 seconds. The bottom plot shows the speed of the cargo ship over the course of the simulation. The speed changes by 2 m/s every 600 seconds.

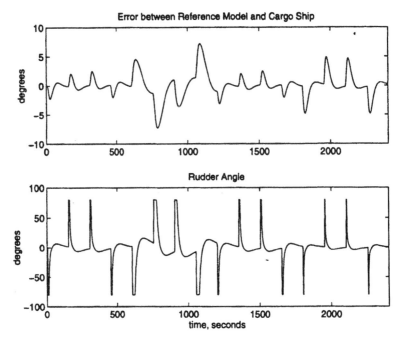

FIGURE 3

Results using a conventional proportional-derivative (PD) controller. In this simulation $p = -5$ and $d = -175$.

3.1   Model Reference Adaptive Control

In this section we develop a model reference adaptive controller (MRAC) [15] and use a gradient identification algorithm to identify the parameters of the system. We assume that the cargo ship behaves as a third-order linear system, defined by the transfer function

$$G(s) = \frac{\psi}{\delta} = \frac{k(1 + \tau_1 s)}{s(1 + \tau_2 s)(1 + \tau_3 s)} \tag{4}$$

We assume that we do not know the values of the plant parameters, but we do assume that the plant is third-order and that we know the gain $k < 0$.

Following [15], the control signal is defined as

$$\delta = \theta_1^T \alpha(s)\omega_1 = \theta_2^T \alpha(s)\omega_2 + \theta_3 \psi + c_0 \zeta \tag{5}$$

The adaptive controller will tune the scalars c_0 and θ_3 and the 2×1 vectors θ_1 and θ_2. As in [15], we assume we know an upper bound on the parameter c_0, namely $c_0 < \underline{c}_0 = -0.1$.

The terms in equation (5) are given by

$$\omega_1 = \frac{\delta}{\Lambda(s)}$$

$$\omega_2 = \frac{\psi}{\Lambda(s)}$$

$$\varepsilon = \frac{W_m(s)\delta - \hat{z}}{m^2}$$

$$\hat{z} = \theta^T \phi_p$$

$$m^2 = 1 + \phi_p^T \phi_p$$

$$\phi_p = [W_m(s)\omega_1^T \ W_m(s)\omega_2^T \ W_m(s)\psi \ \psi]^T$$

$$\theta = [\theta_1, \ \theta_2, ; \theta_3, \ c_0]^T$$

$$\alpha(s) = [s \ 1]^T$$

$$\Lambda(s) = s^2 + s + 1$$

$$g(\theta) = \underline{c}_0 + c_0$$

If $|c_0(t)| > \underline{c}_0$ or $(\Gamma \varepsilon \phi_p)^T \nabla g < 0$ $(\nabla g = dg/d\theta g = [0 \ 0 \ 0 \ 0 \ 0 \ 1]^T)$ then the controller parameter update law is

$$\dot{\theta} = \Gamma \varepsilon \phi_p$$

Otherwise we update θ using projection

$$\dot{\theta} = \Gamma \varepsilon \phi_p - \Gamma \frac{\nabla g \nabla g^T}{\nabla g^T \Gamma \nabla g} \Gamma \varepsilon \phi_p$$

We use the gradient algorithm to identify the parameters in the controller and attempt to make the error between the plant and the reference model go to zero.

The vector θ was initialized for this simulation to

$$\theta(0) = [1.3 \quad 0.9 \quad 9.9 \quad -0.1 \quad 0.4 \quad -0.3]^T$$

These values were selected because the controller will adapt to these parameters over time when the cargo ship maintains a speed of 5 m/s (i.e., we are trying to initialize the parameters as best we can). Performance degrades with other choices for initial parameters (e.g., $\theta(0) = 0$).

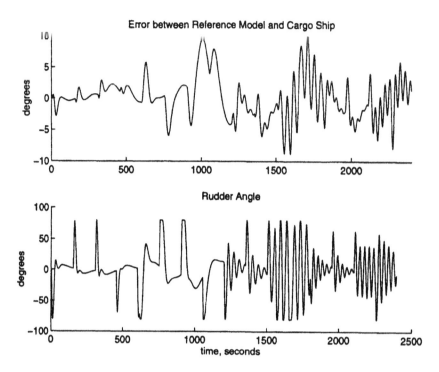

FIGURE 4
Results using MRAC with continuous-time gradient identification. The top plot shows the error between the reference model output and the cargo ship response. The bottom plot shows the rudder angle, δ.

Figure 4 shows the results using the MRAC. It is important to note that when we use the nonlinear model in simulation, the theory for the MRAC from [15] does not apply. The MRAC performed very poorly when the cargo ship speed was decreased to 3 m/s. It was unable to adapt adequately to the changing system dynamics and diverged significantly from the reference model (and we put significant efforts into tuning the controller to get even the performance shown in Figure 4). Clearly the performance is not even as good as that of the fixed PD controller shown in Figure 3.

3.2 Genetic Model Reference Adaptive Control

In this section we will use a type of genetic model reference adaptive controller (GMRAC) [9] to adjust the gains of a PD controller. The GMRAC shown in Figure 5 uses a model of the plant and a genetic algorithm to "evolve" controller parameters to minimize the error between the cargo ship heading and the reference model output. The genetic algorithm (GA) uses the principles of evolution and genetics to select and adapt the controller parameters. For our simulations, we use a set of controllers as the GA population, and evaluate each controller's potential to control the cargo ship.

First, we define the members of the population, in this case PD controllers. Each individual controller is defined by a ten-digit number, its "chromosome." The first four digits describe the proportional gain, and the last six digits describe the derivative gain. We allow the proportional and derivative gains to lie between

$$-10 < p \le 0 \quad \text{and} \quad -200 < d \le 0$$

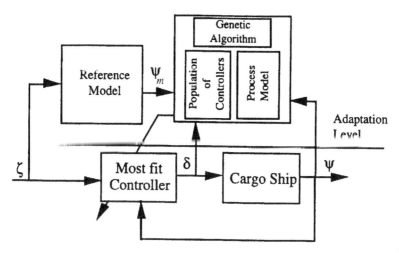

FIGURE 5
GMRAC for cargo ship steering.

For example, a possible chromosome is [1234123456]. This would translate into a proportional gain of $p = -1.234$, and a derivative gain of $d = -123.456$. Note that the negative sign is implied, as is the decimal point after one digit for the p gain and after three digits for the d gain. Also, because of the restrictions placed on d, the fifth digit in the chromosome must be either a 0 or 1 (for example, if the fifth digit were a 2, then necessarily $p \le -200$ which is outside the region we have designated).

During every time step, each member of the population is evaluated on how well it minimizes the error between the predicted closed-loop system response (using a cargo ship model) and the predicted reference model output. The cargo ship model we use is the discrete-time approxima-tion (using zero-order hold with sampling time $T = 0.5$) of the third-order continuous time plant shown in equation (4), where k, τ_1, τ_2, and τ_3 are as defined in equations (2) and (3) assuming the cargo ship is traveling at the nominal speed of 5 m/s. The discrete-time cargo ship model is

$$G(z) = \frac{\hat{\psi}}{\delta} = \frac{-0.000\,1909(z + 0.9913)(z - 0.9827)}{(z - 1)(z - 0.9972)(z - 0.9600)} \tag{6}$$

which can be written as

$$G(z) = \frac{\hat{\psi}}{\delta} = \frac{a_1 z^2 + a_2 z + a_3}{z^3 + b_1 z^2 + b_2 z + b_3} \tag{7}$$

where the values for $a_1, a_2, a_3, b_1, b_2, b_3$ can be found from equation (6).

To evaluate the controller population, the GA finds the error between the cargo ship heading ψ and the reference input ζ, $e = \zeta - \psi$, and the derivative of that error.[2] For each member of the population, the GA computes the rudder angle using e, $\dot{e}$, and the PD gains on each chromosome. Next it estimates the cargo ship heading and the reference model output $NT = 5$ seconds into the future. Using this information, the GA can determine which controllers in the population are keeping the cargo ship heading as close as possible to the reference model output.

[2] We use a continuous-time derivative. We assume it is available for the PD controller in the last section and therefore available here. We note, however that the results change very little if a backward difference approximation is used for $\dot{e}$.

The following pseudo-code more precisely defines the fitness evaluation of the GA and hence the operation of the GMRAC.

1. Compute the error and derivative of the error between the cargo ship heading and the reference input as

$$e(t) = \zeta(t) - \psi(t), \qquad \dot{e}(t) = \frac{de}{dt}$$

2. Predict the reference model output, $\hat{\psi}_m$, NT seconds into the future using a first-order approximation

$$\hat{\psi}_m(t + NT) = \psi_m(t) + NT\dot{\psi}_m(t)$$

Here $\dot{\psi}_m(t)$ is not the continuous time derivative, rather it is the discrete-time first-order approximation of the derivative,

$$\dot{\psi}_m(t) = \frac{\psi_m(t) - \psi_m(t - T)}{T}$$

(notice that we are abusing the notation for a derivative).

3. Compute the current error between the cargo ship heading and the reference model output:

$$\varepsilon(t) = \psi_m(t) - \psi(t)$$

4. Suppose that the ith candidate controller $C_i = (p_i, d_i)$. For each candidate controller, C_i, do the following:

   • Determine the rudder angle input using the p_i, d_i gains on the candidate controller chromosome

$$\delta_i = p_i\, e(t) + d_i\dot{e}(t)$$

   • Initialize the discrete-time cargo ship model (equation 7) with past samples from the cargo ship:

$$\hat{\psi}_i(k - j) = \psi(t - jT), \qquad j = 0, 1, 2$$
$$\delta_i(k - j) = \delta(t - jT), \qquad j = 0, 1, 2$$

   • Assuming the rudder angle δ_i stays constant[3] for the next N samples (i.e., $\delta_i(k + 1) = \cdots = \delta_i(k + N) = \delta_i$), predict the output of the cargo ship model, $\psi(k + N)$, N steps into the future using equation (7):
   For $j = 1$ to N,

$$\hat{\psi}_i(k + j) = a_1\delta_i(k + j - 1) + a_2\delta_i(k + j - 2) + a_3\delta_i(k + j - 3) - b_1\hat{\psi}_i(k + j - 1)$$
$$- b_2\hat{\psi}_i(k + j - 2) - b_3\hat{\psi}_i(k + j - 3)$$

   Next j
   • Using the output of the cargo ship model, estimate the error between the cargo ship heading and the reference model output NT seconds into the future.

$$\hat{\varepsilon}_i(t + NT) = \hat{\psi}_m(t + NT) - \hat{\psi}_i(k + N)$$

[3] As an alternative, one could let the controller C_i vary the rudder angle δ_i over this time interval. We chose to assume a constant control signal δ_i because it is more accurate than estimating $\delta_i(k + j)$ based on the gains of the candidate controller and an estimation of the error signal. The inherent inaccuracy of approximating the derivative of the error signal $\dot{e}(t)$ using the discrete-time cargo ship model is further amplified by the relatively large derivative gain of the PD controller.

- Estimate the derivative of the error between the cargo ship model output and the reference model output, using a first-order approximation:

$$\dot{\varepsilon}_i(t) = \frac{\hat{\varepsilon}_i(t + NT) - \varepsilon(t)}{NT}$$

Of course the $\dot{\varepsilon}$ is not a continuous-time derivative, merely a discrete time approximation.

- Assign fitness, J_i, to each controller candidate, C_i:

$$\bar{J}_i = \varepsilon(t) + \beta\dot{\varepsilon}_i(t)$$

Then

$$J_i = \frac{\alpha}{\bar{J}_i^2 + \alpha}$$

We chose $\alpha = 0.001$ and $\beta = 5$. The choices for α and β are explained below.

5. Repeat step 4 for each member of the population.
6. The maximally fit controller becomes the controller used for the next time step.

The value chosen for α sets an upper bound on the fitness J_i and its choice should be considered carefully. If α is too small, then a large disparity in fitness values will exist in the population (a small change in $\bar{J}_i$ could result in a large change in J_i), and in general only a few individuals will be selected to reproduce into the next generation (assuming roulette-wheel selection, as described below). The result could be a population of nearly identical individuals and hence eliminate the parallel-search mechanism of the GA. However, if α is chosen too large, then all members of the population will have nearly equal fitness values, and hence nearly equal chances to reproduce, thereby compromising the entire "survival of the fittest" nature of the GA. In general we select α to be about an order of magnitude smaller than the average value of $\bar{J}_i$. This appears to be a reasonable compromise value.

The value for β is chosen based on the desired performance of the system and the ability to control the plant. Heuristically speaking, β defines how quickly we would like the error ε between the cargo ship heading and the reference model to reach zero. To see this, notice that the fitness function is maximized when $\bar{J}_i^2$ is minimized, which corresponds to when $\bar{J}_i = 0$. Looking at the equation for $\bar{J}_i = \varepsilon(t) + \beta\dot{\varepsilon}_i(t)$, the fitness function is maximized when $\dot{\varepsilon}_i(t) = -\varepsilon(t)/\beta$. For example, if $\varepsilon(t) = 1.0$, then we would like $\dot{\varepsilon}_i(t)$ to be -0.2, so that the error is driven to zero in approximately $\beta = 5$ seconds. In this example, the best controller is the one that produces $\dot{\varepsilon}_i(t)$ closest to -0.2. When choosing β, we would like to make it as small as possible, but we do not wish to induce oscillations, nor can we ignore physical constraints such as rudder input saturation and slow system dynamics.

The "look ahead time window," N, was chosen to be 10 samples ($NT = 5$ seconds) as a compromise of conflicting interests. In general it is good to make N large, because often the effects of the current input signal are not readily apparent at the output of the system. The longer the time window, the better we are able to assess the effects the input has on the system. However, the error between what the cargo ship model predicts and how the actual cargo ship behaves increases as N increases, thereby degrading the accuracy of the fitness function. Also, in this application we assume the rudder angle stays constant for N seconds, an assumption that becomes less valid as N increases. In general we have found that time windows of 10–20 discrete-time samples work well.

Once each controller in the population has been assigned a fitness J_i, the GA uses the roulette-wheel selection process, as described by Goldberg [1] to pick which controllers will "reproduce" into the next generation. The individuals selected to reproduce are said to be "parents" of the next generation. In the roulette-wheel selection process, the probability of an individual reproducing into the next generation is proportional to the fitness of that individual. More specifically, the probability p_{pi} that the ith member of the population will be selected as the jth member of the parent pool is

$$p_{pi} = \frac{J_i}{\sum\limits_{k=1}^{N} J_k}$$

Note that some individuals will likely be selected to become a parent more than once (indicating that they will produce more than one offspring) while others will not be selected at all. In this manner, unfit individuals are generally removed from the population while fit individuals multiply.

Once the parents of the next generation have been selected, they are randomly paired together. Each pair of parents then has a probability, p_c of undergoing "crossover," in which some digits in the parent chromosome are exchanged with some digits of the other parent chromosome. This is most commonly done by selecting a location on the chromosome (the crossover site) and exchanging all digits past that point on the chromosome with the digits in the same locations on the mating chromosome. However, crossover is done differently in all our genetic algorithms in this chapter. Here, once two parents have been selected for crossover, each digit on the chromosome has a 0.5 probability of being exchanged for the digit in the same location on the mating chromosome. The digits that cross over maintain their original position in the chromosome, and are only exchanged with the digit in the same position on the other chromosome. For example, if two "parent" chromosomes, [1111111111] and [3333333333], undergo crossover, the resulting "children" chromosomes could be [1133313111] and [3311131333]. Note that this method of crossover is not standard, but we have found it to be more effective than the traditional method when more than two traits are encoded onto the chromosome because it allows for the possibility of two nonadjacent traits on a chromosome to remain together after crossover. Crossover is a form of local search in the p,d parameter search space. The probability of crossover, p_c, was set at 0.9.

After crossover, each digit in each child chromosome has the probability, p_m, of mutating. If a digit is selected for mutation, then that digit is replaced by a new randomly selected digit. For example, a chromosome [1111111111] may be mutated to [1115111111]. Note that a digit may be "mutated" to its original value, in effect not being mutated at all. The probability of mutation, p_m, was set at 0.1 and should take into account the possibility of these false-mutations. Mutation is a form of global search in the p,d parameter search space.

After mutation, the "children" chromosome become the next generation of controllers and the process is repeated at the next time step. One exception to this process is the elitism operator [9], which sidesteps selection, crossover, and mutation and simply places the most fit controller from the previous generation into the next generation without modification. We use elitism in all GAs in this chapter.

The results of the GMRAC are shown in Figure 6 (recall that nonadaptive PD controller results are shown in Figure 3). The controller performs very well when the cargo ship has a speed of 5 or 7 m/s. It has difficulty when the ship slows to 3 m/s, as do all of the controllers investigated in this chapter. Note that, since the GMRAC is a stochastic adaptive controller, when it is run again results may differ from those shown in Figure 6. Figure 6 shows the typical behavior of the GMRAC. In the concluding remarks we will show how an average controller will behave over a set of 100 simulations.

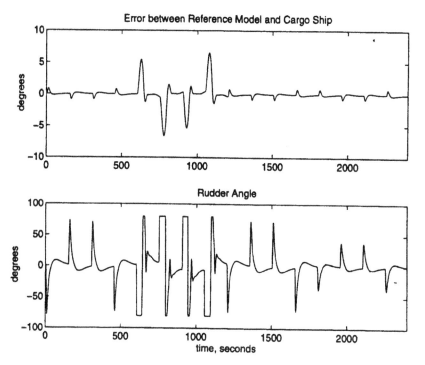

FIGURE 6

Results using GMRAC. The top plot shows the error between the reference model output and the cargo ship response. The bottom plot shows the rudder angle, δ.

3.3 GMRAC with Fixed Population Members

Because genetic algorithms are stochastic processes, there is always a small possibility that good controllers will not be found and hence performance will be degraded. While this possibility diminishes with population size, it nevertheless exists. One method to combat this possibility is to seed the population of the GA with individuals that remain unchanged in every generation. These fixed controllers can be spaced throughout the control parameter space to ensure that a reasonably good controller is always present in the population. Simulations were run for the GMRAC with 25 fixed controllers in the GA population (leaving the remaining 75 controllers to be adapted by the GA as usual). Because the controller gains were restricted to $-10 < p \leq 0$ and $-200 < d \leq 0$, the population was seeded with 25 fixed PD controllers, defined by all possible combinations of $p \in \{-10, \; -7.5, \; -5, \; -2.5, \; 0\}$ and $d \in \{ \; 200, -150, -100, -50, 0\}$.

Over the course of 100 simulations, the GMRAC with fixed population members had a smaller difference between minimum and maximum errors than did the GMRAC with no fixed population members (see Table 1). This was expected because the fixed models add a deterministic element to the inherently stochastic genetic algorithm.

Use of fixed controllers is a novel control technique that appears to decrease the variations in the performance results. The technique is similar to [17], where Narendra and Balakrishnan use fixed plant models to identify a plant and improve transient responses. Likewise, having fixed controllers in the population enables the GA to find reasonably good controllers quickly and then search nearby to find better ones.

Table 1   Results

Control Technique	Sum of the Errors Squared $e(kT)^2$	Sum of the Inputs Squared $\delta(kT)^2$
Conventional PD	29.75	3991
MRAC	79.77	8142
Genetic model reference, Adaptive control		
Minimum	9.66	5956
Average	10.06	5980
Maximum	10.25	5993
Genetic model reference, Adaptive control with fixed controllers		
Minimum	10.02	5991
Average	10.18	6002
Maximum	10.40	6014
Indirect continuous-time gradient identification	14.83	3570
Indirect discrete-time least-squares identification	27.58	3392
Indirect genetic identification		
Minimum	27.47	3776
Average	29.73	3802
Maximum	36.52	3836
General genetic adaptive control		
Minimum	8.32	5756
Average	8.73	5935
Maximum	9.21	6217
General genetic adaptive control with fixed controllers		
Minimum	8.12	5769
Average	8.66	5980
Maximum	9.09	6467

IV.   INDIRECT ADAPTIVE CONTROL

In this section we attempt to model the nonlinear cargo ship dynamics with a simple second-order linear model provided in [16] and given by

$$G(s) = \frac{k_c}{s(s + p_c)} \tag{8}$$

We will be using the parameters k_c and p_c to create proportional and derivative gains for a PD controller using the certainty equivalence principle [15]. Given the plant model $G_p(s)$ and the controller model $G_c(s) = p + ds$, the closed loop transfer function is

$$T(s) = \frac{G_c(s)G_p(s)}{1 + G_c(s)G_p(s)} = \frac{k_c p + k_c ds}{s^2 + s(p_c + k_c d) + k_c p}$$

Neglecting the closed-loop system zero and setting the closed-loop system poles equal to the reference model $W_m(s)$ poles, r, we determine the values of the proportional and derivative gains to be

$$p = \frac{r^2}{k_c}, \qquad d = \frac{2r - p_c}{k_c} \tag{9}$$

Below, we attempt to identify the plant model parameters, k_c and p_c, using a continuous-time gradient algorithm, a discrete-time least-squares algorithm, and finally a discrete-time genetic algorithm. Then equation (9) will be used to specify the PD controller gains.

4.1   Continuous-Time Gradient Identification Algorithm

Here, we are using a continuous-time gradient algorithm to identify the parameters k_c and p_c of the plant model in equation (8). Again, we vary the speed of the cargo ship and observe how well the identification algorithm can track the response of the cargo ship.
   Following [15] we define

$$z = \theta^{*T}\phi + \eta = \frac{\psi s^2}{\Lambda(s)}$$

$$\theta = [k_c \quad p_c]^T$$

$$\phi = \left[\frac{\delta}{\Lambda(s)} \quad \frac{-\psi s}{\Lambda(s)}\right]^T$$

The update law is

$$\dot{\theta} = \Gamma \varepsilon \phi$$

where

$$\Gamma = \begin{bmatrix} 200 & 0 \\ 0 & 20000 \end{bmatrix}$$

$$= \frac{z - \theta^T \phi}{m^2}$$

$$m^2 = 1 + m_s$$

$$\dot{m}_s = -\delta_0 m_s + \delta^2 + \psi^2$$

$$\Lambda(s) = s^2 + 2s + 1$$

The constant δ_0 was set to 0.001. The vector θ was initialized to $[-0.0005 \quad 0.02]$, which are the values the gradient algorithm settles on when the cargo ship is simulated at a constant speed of 5 m/s (i.e., again we are giving the algorithm an advantage by starting the values of θ close to their optimum values). The controller p and d gains were continuously adjusted using equation (9) and the current values of k_c and p_c.
   The results are shown in Figure 7. As expected, the performance degraded when the cargo ship slowed to 3 m/s. Overall, the indirect adaptive controller performed quite well. The performance is aided by using a continuous-time adaptation mechanism as opposed to the discrete-time mechanism used by the least-squares and GA-based methods studied next.

4.2   Discrete-Time Least-Squares Identification Algorithm

In this section we use the discrete-time least-squares identification algorithm to identify the linear plant model parameters. The model used is the linear, zero-order hold, discrete-time equivalent

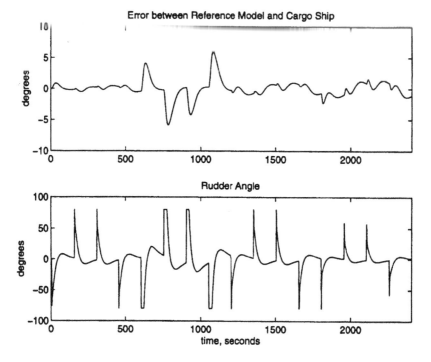

FIGURE 7
Results using indirect adaptive control with continuous-time gradient identification. The top plot shows the error between the reference model output and the cargo ship response. The bottom plot shows the rudder angle, δ.

($T = 0.5$ seconds) of the second-order linear continuous-time plant $G(s)$ as shown in equation (8):

$$G(z) = \frac{\hat{\psi}}{\delta} = \frac{k_d z^2}{(z-1)(z-p_d)} \tag{10}$$

This discrete-time equivalent cargo ship model must be written in polynomial form for the least-squares algorithm. The cargo ship model $G(z)$ can be written as

$$G(z) = \frac{a_0 z^2}{z^2 + b_1 z + b_2}$$

Because we assume from the continuous-time plant model, $G_p(s)$ that the plant contains an integrator, or $1/s$ term, we can likewise assume that the discrete-time model contains an integrator, or $1/(z-1)$ term. Therefore, when transforming the discrete-time parameters back into continuous-time parameters, we can assume that one discrete-time pole is set at 1 and therefore the second pole is simply $p_d = b_2$. Obviously the discrete-time gain, $k_d = a_0$.

The update laws for the least-squares algorithm are as follows:

$$x(k) = [-y(k-1) \quad -y(k-2) \quad u(k)]^T$$
$$\hat{\theta}(k) = [b_1 \quad b_2 \quad a_0]$$
$$\hat{y} = x^T(k)\hat{\theta}(k)$$
$$P(k) = P(k-1) - P(k-1)x(k)[1 + x^T(k)P(k-1)x(k)]x^T(k)P(k-1)$$
$$\hat{\theta}(k) = \hat{\theta}(k-1) + P(k)x(k)[y(k) - x^T(k)\hat{\theta}(k-1)]$$

If we assume some knowledge of the plant parameters, namely their relative magnitudes, we can initialize the covariance matrix, P, and parameter estimate, $\hat{\theta}$, to more quickly identify the parameters of the system and hence improve performance. The covariance matrix was initialized to

$$P(0) = \begin{bmatrix} 5 & 0 & 0 \\ 0 & 5 & 0 \\ 0 & 0 & 20 \end{bmatrix}$$

and the plant parameters estimates were initialized to

$$\hat{\theta}(0) = [-1.99 \quad 0.99 \quad -0.001]$$

The least-squares algorithm was developed with the assumption that the plant parameters remain constant. Because in our simulations we vary the speed of the cargo ship, and hence vary the nonlinear system dynamics, the least-squares algorithm has difficulty continually adjusting to the changing plant parameters. To compensate for this and improve the performance, the covariance matrix, P, was reinitialized to $P(0)$ every 150 seconds, before every change in the reference input.[4]

After each time step, we use the current estimate of the discrete-time plant parameters k_d and p_d, and use the following zero-order hold transforms to compute the continuous-time plant parameters:

$$k_c = \frac{k_d}{p_d T^2}, \qquad p_c = \frac{1 - p_d}{p_d T} \tag{11}$$

The controller p and d gains were adjusted after every sample ($T = 0.5$ seconds) using equation (9) and the current values of k_c and p_c.

The results are shown in Figure 8. The controller outperformed the nonadaptive PD controller, but it did not perform particularly well. This can mostly be attributed to the difficulty in identifying a continuous-time nonlinear system using a simple discrete-time plant with a large sampling interval.

4.3   Indirect Genetic Adaptive Control

In this section we investigate the use of a second-order linear discrete-time model of the cargo ship and use a genetic algorithm to identify the parameters of this model. The cargo ship model parameters are then used in a certainty equivalence-based adaptive controller. Using the same second-order continuous-time model as shown in equation (8), we can derive an approximate discrete-time model. Using the zero-order hold discrete-time approximation with sampling time $T = 0.5$ seconds, we get

$$G(z) = \frac{\hat{\psi}}{\delta} = \frac{k_d z^2}{(z - 1)(z - p_d)} \tag{12}$$

In this application, the genetic algorithm evolves the parameters k_d and p_d by looking at the past values for δ and ψ and attempting to minimize the error between the cargo ship heading, ψ, and the output of the cargo ship model, $\hat{\psi}$. The overall strategy is shown in Figure 9.

---

[4] That is, we perform a periodic "covariance reset," somewhat differently than in [15]. We perform the reset periodically to avoid the computational complexity of having to test the eigenvalues of P at each step.

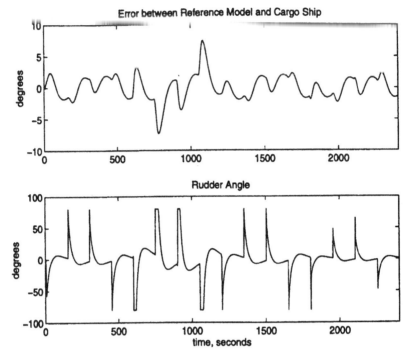

FIGURE 8
Results using indirect adaptive control with discrete-time least-squares identification. The top plot shows the error between the reference model output and the cargo ship response. The bottom plot shows the rudder angle, δ.

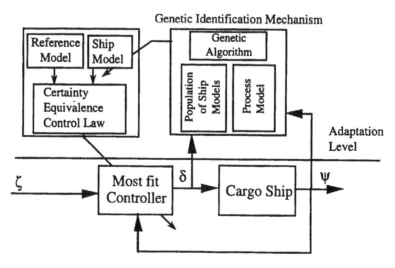

FIGURE 9
Indirect genetic adaptive control for cargo ship steering.

The individuals of the GA population are defined by 10 digits, the first 5 digits describe the k_d parameter, and the last 5 digits describe the p_d parameter. The parameter values are restricted to lie between

$$-0.001 < k_d \le -0.0001 \qquad \text{and} \qquad 0.5 \le p_d < 1.0$$

Note that both parameters are fairly restricted. While shrinking the parameter search space improves the identification performance, it also requires some a priori knowledge of the cargo ship dynamics. But for many of the techniques in this chapter we assume the existence of such knowledge. For instance, in both the gradient and least-squares algorithms, some a priori knowledge was also required to initialize the plant parameters and adaptation gains.

The following pseudo-code defines the fitness evaluation used in the genetic identification algorithm. For each plant model candidate in the population, P_i, that is characterized by $P_i = (k_{di}, p_{di})$, do the following:

1. Initialize the discrete-time model in equation (12) with the past discrete-time samples of the cargo ship heading:

$$\hat{\psi}_i(k - N - j) = \psi(t - NT - jT), \qquad j = 0, 1$$

2. Using equation (12), plant model candidate P_i, and the past $N = 200$ samples of the rudder angle input, $\delta(k)$, estimate the past N samples of the cargo ship heading, $\psi(k)$.
   For $j = 1$ to N,

$$\hat{\psi}_i(k - N + j) = k_{di}\delta(k - N + j) - (-1 - p_{di})\hat{\psi}_i(k - N + j - 1) - p_{di}\hat{\psi}_i(k - N + j - 2)$$

   Next j

3. Compute the error between the estimated output, $\hat{\psi}$, and the actual sampled cargo ship heading, ψ, using

$$\hat{e}_i = \sum_{j=1}^{N} [\psi(k - N + j) - \hat{\psi}_i(k - N + j)]^2$$

4. Assign fitness, J_i, to each plant model candidate:

$$J_i = \frac{\alpha}{\hat{e}_i + \alpha}$$

   Here $\alpha = 0.02$ and was selected for the same reasons as discussed in Section 3.2 describing the GMRAC.

5. Repeat steps 1–3 for each member of the population

6. The maximally fit cargo ship model becomes the model used for the next time step.

The model estimation window, N, was set to 200 samples (100 seconds). Large values for N obviously increase computation time, but also improve the estimation performance of the identifier. Small values for N increase the likelihood that a "bad" plant model will be selected that does not accurately estimate the long-term behavior of the actual system, thereby causing a "bad" controller to be selected that adversely affects the closed-loop system performance.

One problem with genetic adaptive identification is that the GA attempts to minimize the prediction error of the cargo ship model; it does not necessarily find the best parameters to identify the plant. Therefore the parameters the GA determines to be the best for one time instant may be far removed from the parameters the algorithm found just one time instant before. The

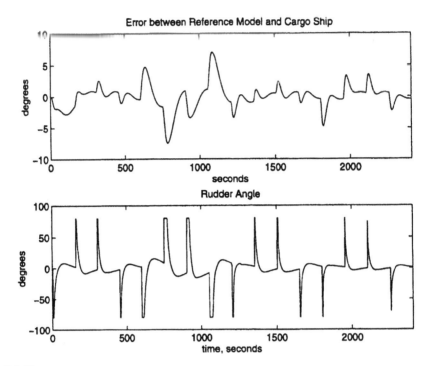

FIGURE 10
Results using indirect genetic adaptive control. The top plot shows the error between the reference model output and the cargo ship response. The bottom plot shows the rudder angle, δ.

result is that the GA switches between many plant models, and hence the parameters it identifies are somewhat erratic. Having plant parameters that move quickly causes the controller parameters also to move quickly, which results in a noisy control signal. To compensate for this, we filter the plant parameters through a low-pass filter,[5] the discrete-time (zero-order hold, $T = 0.5$) equivalent of $F(s) = 0.001/(s + 0.01)$.

Once we obtain filtered estimates of the discrete-time plant model parameters k_d and p_d, we can transform them into continuous-time plant model parameters k_c and p_c using the conversions in equation (11). The controller p and d gains are then adjusted using equation (9) and the current values of k_c and p_c.

The results are shown in Figure 10. As was the case for the least-squares adaptive controller, it is difficult to identify the parameters of a nonlinear system using a discrete-time plant with a large sampling interval. However, another problem with the genetic identification algorithm is that the GA attempts to minimize the prediction error (which it does very well); it does not attempt to find the best parameters for the cargo ship model. While it is often the case that the model with the minimum prediction error will be the model with the best parameters, it does not apply to nonlinear systems where there is not necessarily an "ideal" linear system model. The GA does very well at switching between cargo ship models to minimize the prediction error, but pays no attention to finding an "optimal" cargo ship model. Hence, using the cargo ship model parameters to define a controller is a difficult task.[6]

---

[5] An alternative to this approach would be to lower the mutation probability, but we have found this method to work better.
[6] One approach to solving this problem would be to use a parametrized feedback-linearizable model for the identifier structure and a certainty equivalence control law that is based on differential geometric methods.

V.   GENERAL GENETIC ADAPTIVE CONTROL

In this section we combine what we have developed for direct and indirect genetic model reference adaptive control into a general genetic adaptive control (GGAC). In particular, we will use a genetic algorithm to identify a cargo ship model (as used in the indirect genetic adaptive controller), and use another genetic algorithm to evolve the best controller (as used in the GMRAC). Figure 11 shows the general genetic adaptive control system.

In this control technique, we will be using the discrete-time third-order linear plant model obtained by discretizing equation (4) using the bilinear transformation:

$$G(z) = \frac{k_d(z+1)(z+1)(z-z_d)}{(z-1)(z-p_{d1})(z-p_{d2})}$$

The genetic identification algorithm identifies the parameters k_d, z_d, p_{d1}, and p_{d2}. Note that these parameters are different from those found in the indirect adaptive control technique because previously we assumed a second-order plant model and used the zero-order hold transformation to approximate the discrete time model.

The plant model chromosomes consist of 16 digits, allotting four digits for each of the four parameters. The parameters are restricted as follows:

$$-0.001 < k_d \le 0, \qquad 0.8 \le p_{d1}, p_{d2}, z_d < 1.0$$

The fitness function is identical to the one described previously for the indirect genetic adaptive controller, except that the model estimation window, N, was decreased from 200 samples to 100 samples to reduce computation time. The probability of crossover was $p_c = 0.8$ and the probability of mutation was $p_m = 0.1$.

The best cargo ship model parameters are passed directly to the genetic adaptive controller, which uses them in its fitness evaluation of the population of controllers. The genetic adaptive controller is identical to the genetic model reference adaptive controller described previously,

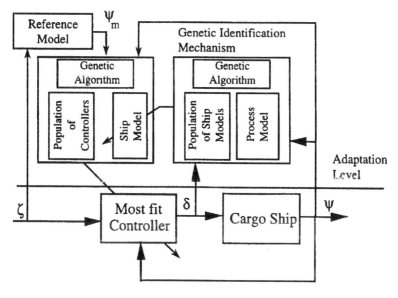

FIGURE 11
General genetic adaptive control for cargo ship steering.

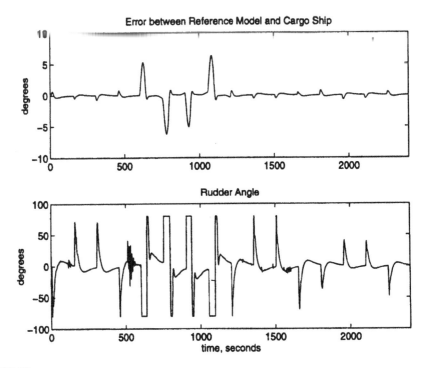

FIGURE 12
Results using GGAC. The top plot shows the error between the reference model output and the cargo ship response. The bottom plot shows the rudder angle, δ.

with the obvious exception that the plant model used in the fitness function is continually adapting.

The results using the GGAC are shown in Figure 12. The GGAC does an excellent job of tracking the reference model. In fact, the GGAC performs the best of all the control techniques investigated in this chapter at tracking. However, it should be noted that the GGAC also requires a large amount of input energy and quick movement of the rudder, which may be difficult to achieve in practice.

The GGAC was also run with fixed controllers, identical to the ones used for the GMRAC in Section 3.3. The results were not only more consistent (as measured by the variations in the tracking error), but they were also better in terms of reference model tracking (i.e., the tracking was smaller on average with fixed controller models than without them). However, the GGAC with fixed controllers required on average greater input energy than the GGAC without fixed controllers. The results for this case are summarized in Table 1.

VI. CONCLUDING REMARKS

In this chapter we have introduced several approaches to genetic adaptive control and performed a comparative analysis between several conventional and genetic adaptive controllers for a ship steering application.

6.1 Summary of Results

To see how all the controllers perform relative to each other, consider Table 1, which shows numerical results for the simulations in this chapter. We sampled the error (in degrees) between the cargo ship heading and the reference model every 0.1 seconds, squared this error, and computed the sum over the entire simulation. We did the same for the rudder angle input, δ, summing the squared error (in degrees) measured every 0.1 seconds. For the genetic adaptive controllers, we conducted 100 simulations and provided minimum, average, and maximum values of the sums of the squared errors; we did the same for the rudder inputs.

As mentioned previously, the general genetic adaptive controller performed the best on average when measured by the ability to track the reference model. However, it also required a large amount of input energy, as measured by δ^2 and shown in Table 1. While the general genetic adaptive controller performed very well, there are still many uncertainties about this technique. No proofs of stability, convergence, or robustness have been established. Moreover, we have no way to prove that the schemes will achieve a specific desired transient performance. In addition, we cannot verify that the genetic adaptive controllers will ever find an optimal controller in the space of candidate controllers.

The indirect discrete-time least-squares adaptive controller used the least control energy but achieved poor tracking. The indirect continuous-time gradient adaptive controller performed very well as a compromise between reference model tracking and minimum input energy. The indirect genetic adaptive controller did not perform particularly well. The conventional MRAC performed the worst, both in tracking performance and input energy. Finally, the genetic model reference adaptive controller tracked very well, but it too required a large amount of input energy.

6.2 Computational complexity

Perhaps the biggest concern with genetic adaptive control techniques is the computational complexity of the algorithm. To better understand the computation time of the genetic algorithms, we carefully examined our simulation program (written in the C language) and computed roughly the number of operations required per generation. Using the variables P to represent the population size, N to represent the look-ahead time window steps in the fitness function, and C to represent the length of the chromosome, we arrived at the following equation:

$$O = P(P + 40N + 20C + 60)$$

Here O represents the number of operations per generation (i.e., per time step) of the genetic algorithm, where an operation is any addition, multiplication, subtraction, division, assignment, increment, comparison, or declaration. This equation represents a rough estimate; we were careful to overestimate calculations when simplifying this equation.

Using this equation, we can see that the GMRAC of Section 3.2 requires roughly 760 000 operations per generation or 1.52 million operations per second (assuming a sampling time of $T = 0.5$ seconds). This number is less for the case with fixed population members in Section 3.3. The indirect genetic adaptive controller in Section 4.3 requires approximately 836 000 operations per generation or 1.7 million operations per second. The GGAC in Section 5 uses two genetic algorithms and requires approximately 3.2 million operations per second. Of course this computation time could be reduced with more streamlined code and a smaller population size and chromosome length. Because this research used simulations, we did not attempt to minimize the computation time. We are confident, however, that substantial improvements could be made in terms of processing time. Nevertheless, with the cheap and powerful microprocessors widely available today, a controller that requires 3.2 million operations per second is certainly implementable.

Acknowledgments

W. Lennon acknowledges the partial support of a Center for Automotive Research Fellowship. The work was supported in part by National Science Foundation Grant EEC 9315257. Please address all correspondence to K. Passino ((614) 292-5716; K. passino@osu.edu).

REFERENCES

[1] D. Goldberg, *Genetic Algorithms in Search, Optimization and Machine Learning*. Addison-Wesley, Reading, MA, 1989.

[2] M. A. Lee and H. Takagi, Integrating design stages of fuzzy systems using genetic algorithms, in *Second IEEE Int. Conf. Fuzzy Systems, San Francisco*, 1993, pp. 612–617.

[3] Alen Varšek, Tanja Urbančič, and Bodgan Filipič, Genetic algorithms in controller design and tuning, *IEEE Trans. Systems, Man and Cybernetics*, Vol. 23, No. 5, pp. 1330–1339, 1993.

[4] Daihee Park, Abraham Kandel, and Gideon Langholz, Genetic-based new fuzzy reasoning models with application to fuzzy control, *IEEE Trans. Systems, Man, and Cybernetics*, Vol. 24, No. 1, pp. 39–47, 1994.

[5] B. Porter and M. Borairi, Genetic design of linear multivariable feedback control systems using eigenstructure assignment, *Int. J. Systems Science*, Vol. 23, No. 8, pp. 1387–1390, 1992.

[6] Z. Michelewicz, et al., Genetic algorithms and optimal control problems, in *Proc. 29th Conf. Decision and Control Honolulu, Hawaii*, 1990, pp. 1664–1666.

[7] D. Maclay and R. Dorey, Applying genetic search techniques to drivetrain modeling, *IEEE Control Systems*, Vol. 13, No. 2, pp. 50–55, 1993.

[8] K. Kristinsson and G. Dumont, System identification and control using genetic algorithms, *IEEE Trans. Systems, Man, and Cybernetics*, Vol. 22, No. 5, pp. 1033–1046, 1992.

[9] L. Porter and K. Passino, Genetic model reference adaptive control, *Proc. IEEE Int. Symp. Intelligent Control, Columbus, Ohio*, 1994, pp. 219–224.

[10] L. Porter and K. M. Passino, Genetic adaptive observers, *Engineering Applications of Artificial Intelligence*, Vol. 8, No. 3, pp. 261–269, 1995.

[11] W. Lennon and K. Passino, Intelligent control for brake systems, *Proc. IEEE Int. Symp. Intelligent Control, Monterey, CA*, 1994, pp. 499–504.

[12] K. DeJong, Adaptive system design: A genetic approach, *IEEE Trans. Systems, Man, and Cybernetics*, Vol. 10, pp. 566–574, Sept. 1980.

[13] J. Renders and R. Hanus, Biological learning metaphors for adaptive process control: A general strategy, *IEEE Int. Symp. Intelligent Control, Glasgow, Scotland*, 1992, pp. 469–474.

[14] W. Zuo, Multivariable adaptive control for a space station using genetic algorithms, *IEE Proc. Control Theory and Application*, Vol. 142, pp. 81–87, Mar. 1995.

[15] Petros A. Ioannou and Jing Sun, *Robust Adaptive Control*, pp. 372–396. Prentice-Hall, Englewood Cliffs, NJ, 1996.

[16] Karl Åström and Björn Wittenmark, *Adaptive Control*, p. 356. Addison-Wesley, New York, 1989.

[17] K. S. Narendra and J. Balakrishnan, Improving transient response of adaptive control systems using multiple models and switching, *IEEE Trans. Automatic Control*, Vol. 39, No. 9, pp. 1861–1866, 1994.

[18] P. J. Antsaklis and K. M. Passino (eds.), *An Introduction to Intelligent and Autonomous Control*. Kluwer, Norwell, MA, 1993.

[19] K. M. Passino, Towards bridging the perceived gap between conventional and intelligent control, in Gupta M. M., Sinha N. K. (eds.) *Intelligent Control: Theory and Applications*, Chap. 1, pp. 1–27, IEEE Press, NJ, 1996.

CHAPTER 12

Cooperative Behavior of Intelligent Agents: Theory and Practice

BY LJUBO VLACIC and ANTHONY ENGWIRDA
Intelligent Control Systems Laboratory, Griffith University, Australia

MAKOTO KAJITANI
Kajitani-Ming Laboratory of Mechatronics, University of Electro-Communications, Japan

1 INTRODUCTION

The desire to create life in our own image and to construct intelligent agents that think like people has held us in thrall since the beginnings of civilization. Progress in this area has been slow despite this long investment, but this does not mean that realization of this goal is not possible. It may be that the solution is not quite what we first envisage.

During the past three decades there has been a resurgence of interest in the field of artificial intelligence. This has not been without problems and stagnation in the area has led to the development of advanced techniques such as neural nets, genetic algorithms, fuzzy logics, and reactive artificial intelligence, explained elsewhere in this book. Even these techniques appear to suffer the same stagnation problem that spawned their creation.

This chapter is concerned with the problem of designing useful and productive populations of intelligent machines—cooperative autonomous mobile robots that can operate in the real world. In order for a robot population to be sustainable and capable of interacting with dynamic environments in real time, it has to be considered as a society of distributed agents. Societies would enable situated robotics to be both sustainable and manageable—the attributes that are seen as key features of the ability to cooperate.

In recent years there has been an explosion in robotic knowledge and technology. It is argued here that useful and economical applications can be achieved if we make a fundamental paradigm shift toward a large-scale colony of autonomous mobile robots.

Efficient management would further enable economic task force distribution among the society members of cooperative mobile robots, which would increase productivity, reduce costs, and reduce maintenance. Each society will strive to achieve its objectives by dividing its population into task forces. Each task force would address a single task and the synergy of task solutions would enable coherent motion toward a group objective. The task forces are comprised of distributed agents. The only role filled by a human would be that of system administrator, who would intervene during system failure or goal changes.

Large scale robotic populations capable of working on useful applications in an economical manner would be of obvious benefit to humanity. Such applications would have economic value and would enable access to remote and hostile environments that would enrich the quality of our lives.

The ability of being cooperative is considered as the prime behavioral feature of the society members toward achieving the group goals. This chapter deals with both theoretical and implementational issues of cooperative work among autonomously behaving agents.

2   COOPERATIVE INTELLIGENT AGENTS

Having many agents working on tasks is useful if these agents are capable of cooperation. There are many interpretations of what constitutes cooperation between two agents and definitions include coordinated cooperation based upon explicit communication down to incidental cooperation where agents assist one another even though they lack communication and are performing different tasks. Much of this experimental work is initially performed in simulation environments [1].

A single agent can be viewed as an autonomous system, perceiving and acting on its environment, independently performing tasks and pursuing goals. Multiagent systems are suited to tasks that are too complex for any single agent. A cooperative society of agents is more than a coordinated collection of individual agents. A cooperative society is based upon commitment to a goal that is shared [2]. Some tasks require multiple agents such as group transport, while others become achievable due to the redundant nature of distributed agents.

Successful robotic research within the artificial intelligence community is directed at systems that are embedded in dynamic real-world environments. These agents continuously perceive the environment and perform actions using actuators that influence the environment so as to perform some task or achieve some goal. Such real-world environments are complex and require both reactive and goal-directed behavior [2].

To gain an understanding of the overall concept of *cooperative autonomous mobile robots* it is necessary to begin with a decomposition of these words. Having examined each individual word as it relates to this field, it should then be possible to determine the interrelationship of these ideas.

Robot. A robot is an agent that is capable of performing some task or function within the world. If we think of robots in the classical sense, then these tasks are often repetitive, exhausting, and sometimes dangerous to humans. Robots that perform these tasks are not generally considered to be intelligent.

Great advances are being made in the field of robotics to the point where robots can now operate in the real world and in real time. The major advance has been as a result of the adoption of the insect, instead of the human, as the model for intelligent agents. This has meant systems that react with the environment without trying to understand or model it. Will this insectoid model be the foundation for a new order of truly intelligent robots? This is the source of continuing debate.

Mobile. A mobile object is something that moves such that is is capable of changing its physical location or coordinates. The nature of the movement is not important and the object can drive on wheels or tracks, ambulate, slither, fly, swim, etc. An agent that is bolted to the floor in the middle of a factory and waves a mechanical arm is not sufficient to be classified as mobile. By the same token, an agent that is tethered by an umbilical cord is only partially mobile because it is not self-contained. Most of the mobile factory robots are autonomous guided vehicles that follow a predefined track or path. Such vehicles are by definition mobile but not autonomous.

There are two primary mechanisms for resolution of robot movement. First, robots can follow a hard-coded route and rely upon natural or artificial landmarks to correct odometry errors. The second option is employment of a migration decision function that enables calculation of the next hop in the journey. These solutions have different route confidence thresholds and applications [3].

Autonomy. To be considered as autonomous, a system would need some means of identifying, isolating, and correcting faults. Identification of a fault or self-diagnosis is the first step and involves knowing that a fault has occurred and the type of fault. To accomplish this, it is necessary to know how the system should be functioning.

Isolation of the fault is the ability for the system to continue to function at reduced efficiency even though part of the system is shut down or malfunctioning. Distributed systems use redundancy to automatically achieve fault isolation. Fault correction involves recovery of the part of the system that is not working properly. If the fault correction utility were also self- correcting, the system could continue until a catastrophic failure occurred.

Cooperation. Cooperation is measurable ability by which an agent works with, and aids others, so as to achieve group goals. These goals can provide benefits to the group such as greater returns for resource investment. The cost of individual agents can be reduced in a cooperative population as agents do not require every type of sensor because they can obtain information from other agents or sources.

Another form of cooperation is when two or more agents combine to perform some task that one agent alone cannot achieve. This might be moving some object that is too heavy for a single agent, or holding and bracing an object while other agent decomposes it into more manageable pieces [4].

Cooperation could take the form of agents acting as navigational landmarks for the colony or extending the sensory range of the colony beyond that of a central base. Both strategies are employed by colonial insects. The first strategy is used by ants when navigating far from the nest. The latter is used to improve colony reaction time to incoming threats and opportunities.

In order to cooperate, agents need to have some means of communication to enable information exchange and negotiation, be it explicit or implicit. In the case of a vehicle crossing an intersection, we have traffic regulations, indicators, and navigation markers that enable the process to go smoothly. This form of cooperation between agents within an environment is known as agent separation.

Communications. Communication is the act of passing information from one entity to another and is an important attribute of a cooperative agent. Humans have communication abilities that are based upon sensory perception. Communication is by voice, gesture, or physical contact. The full range of these communication options requires speech, hearing, vision, and touch. Robot communications are also limited to their sensory abilities, but they have the advantage of an enormously powerful and diverse range of abilities.

Explicit communication exists when one agent sends a message to another with the intention of causing some desired result. Implicit communication occurs when one agent that is engaged in some task is viewed by another to require some action from the watcher. Both explicit and implicit communication may result in cooperative behavior.

Explicit communication is deliberate and could use any of the available media such as radio, infrared light, odor trails, or physical connection to transmit information from one agent to another. Implicit communication is more subtle and the watcher observes the current state of the other agent to determine a cooperative action without receiving an actual transmitted message from the observed agent. Observation does not have to be a visual system but could use any available sense.

Intelligent agents could communicate using a vast number of possible technological options. Communication options are limited by the environment. Typical communication media used in robotic applications are radio signals, microwaves, infrared light, ultrasonic sound, and temporary odors. Communications can exist in a one-way direction such that the agent is able to sense the environment and broadcast a message to other agents within range. This kind of communication does not have a system of acknowledgments, so there is no way to know whether all agents within range have received the message.

Duplex communications are in a two-way direction such that the agent is able to broadcast a message to other agents and receive an acknowledgment. This form of communication enables complex cooperative behaviors.

Intelligence. Intelligence is the ability of an entity to learn from its immediate environment and to adapt its behavior to cope with an alteration within the environment. An entity is more adaptable is more intelligent. Cooperation with other intelligent agents is perceived as adaptive behavior.

Human intelligence resides not solely within the brain but throughout the entire nervous system of the body. Many of the tasks performed by an agent are processed not within the brain but locally, and they are simple reactions to stimuli. The processing performed by the brain uses concepts, grounded in reality, and gathered by the body. The implication of this line of reasoning is that you cannot have a concept of self without a body.

A great deal of work by classical artificial intelligence scientists had concentrated on issues like consciousness, but the new approach suggested that issues like understanding the concept of self were not relevant to basic intelligence [5]. The new view saw intelligence as adaptive behavior with the real world as its own best model [6].

New ways of thinking about intelligent agents produced the definition of four design requirements for such agents [5]:

1. An agent should cope with the dynamic environment in real time.
2. An agent should be robust with respect to the dynamic environment.
3. An agent should be able to maintain multiple goals.
4. An agent should have a useful purpose to its existence.

The tight coupling between perception and action enables very fast responses and real-time, real-world applications (Figure 1). The tight coupling of perception to action is also the source of the greatest drawback of reactive AI. This model is incapable of reasoning with temporal events.

A reactive agent is capable of simple reactions in response to stimuli such as closing jaws when food or prey is detected. A cooperative agent in a structured environment must typically perform a more complicated sequence of actions. Given a road intersection, for example, a cooperative agent must detect the intersection, determine whether it is clear, and cross without collision. A communication protocol with other agents and the environment may facilitate this task.

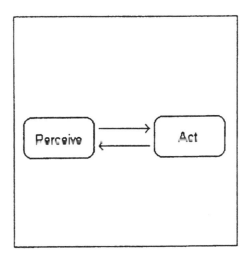

FIGURE 1
Reactive AI.

A great deal of work on cooperative agents is conducted in software stimulations. Muller and Pecchiari model agents as situated autonomous entities. Their model was extensive in that it modeled not just goals but sensors, motors, environment and agent interaction. Also, they introduced the concept of different views, Agent, Designer, and Observer [7]. These views are essentially concepts of reality.

Nakashima and Noda claimed that lack of symbolic reasoning prevents reactive agents from using communication and reduces flexibility to changes in the environment [8]. Other researches have also mentioned the limitations of a pure reactive architecture and have offered improvements such as hybrid reactive–reflective architecture [3]. One of the major goals of reactive AI and subsumption architecture was to construct robots that are sensitive to changes in the environment [9]. Kube demonstrated that reactive robots could cooperate in a coherent manner using implicit communication [1].

A much more serious flaw was identified by one of the early pioneers of reactive AI. David McFarland, a biologist, was one of the first to see issues such as autonomy and self-sufficiency as being of primary importance to robotics. Failure to address these issues is perceived to be the main reasons for the slow uptake of current robotic technology. These issues will be discussed under the topic of management.

Reasoning Agents. Reasoning agents are similar to reactive agents because of the tight coupling between stimulus and response, but they also possess the ability to reason about stimuli (Figure 2). The concept of reasoning agents was initially presented by Ray Jarvis and this figure is a modification of his research by way of avoiding directed flow from action to reasoning and from reasoning to perception [10]. The usefulness of reasoning ability was demonstrated during intersection experiments. Reasoning agents proved to be capable of using communication appropriate to the situation. Messages were precomposed and transmitted based upon temporal trigger states of specific sensors. Even simple communication mechanisms such as the presence or absence of signals are valid forms of communication [11].

A combination of elements of reactive AI and classical AI is used to produce reasoning AI. The tight coupling of perception to action is retained from reactive AI. This is necessary to

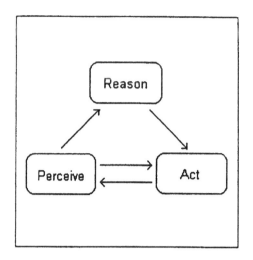

FIGURE 2
Reasoning AI.

enable real-time, real-world responses to stimuli. Added to this reactive structure are elements of planning and commitment that enable complex upper-level behaviors. The final product is a useful agent that is able to operate in the real world, in real time, make complex decisions, cooperate with other agents, reason with temporal events, and be easily understandable by humans. The ability to reason with time enables the agent to remember the past and make the correct decision about current events.

3 COOPERATIVE AGENT SYSTEMS

Multiagent Systems. Multiagent systems (MAS) involve the study of populations of agents and their mutual relationships. The field is comprised of three main areas, social, cognitive, and

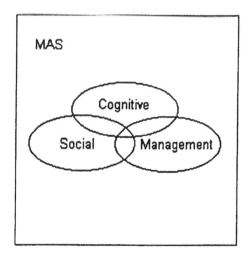

FIGURE 3
Multiagent systems.

economic management and control (Figure 3). There is significant overlap between the three main areas and there exist some related topics that are included under the same banner.

A multiagent system is defined as open when agents can be freely added or removed [12, 13]. The problem of organizational dynamics within open systems is poorly addressed in multiagent systems (MAS) literature. An organization can be modeled as having a finite number of states and transition between states due to interaction between agents and environment [12].

Removal of agents can take place due to attrition and new agents should be added to compensate for their loss. If the agents are comprised of modules and the system is automated to replace modules, then it is the module that is added or removed from the system and not the entire agent. This concept can facilitate a significant economic advantage over the conventional approach. This advantage is magnified by the knowledge that applications for this technology are suited to remote and/or hostile environments. The cost of transporting components is much less than that of entire agents but on-site repair must be possible.

A colony of robots is related to two of the topics, social and management issues, but is not related to the area of cognitive level agents. A robot colony is a complex artificial society with protocols of interaction and communication that enable social action to be simulated. While it does display emergent behavior, there is no necessity for evolution. Real-world robotic systems are also open systems when agents can be added or removed.

The robot colony uses an adaptive strategy to allocate agents to tasks, enabling satisfaction of distributed constraints. This is a form of probabilistic reasoning that attempts to provide stable and efficient solutions. Tasks are scheduled in priority order and formal specifications are used to make predictions about future returns. The intended applications for robot colonies are useful and economical industrial applications.

3.1 Learning from Biological Systems

A theory to underpin the behavior of a population of cooperative autonomous agents can be derived from five related areas, namely, reactive robotics [14], cooperative agents [1, 15], large-scale control systems theory [16], and entomology [17, 18]. Reactive robotics gives individual robots that react with the world in a cost-effective, real-time useful manner. A study of cooperative agents enables autonomous agents to work together to achieve group goals. Large-scale control systems theory enables a holistic view of the requirements for producing an autonomous dynamic system. Entomology gives real-world working examples for study so that valid questions might be asked.

Being purely reactive, ants incrementally improve the global state of the colony. This collective response from reactive individuals is an illusionary form of emergent consciousness [19]. While the typical solution to a colony problem performed by ants may not be optimal, it is certainly respectable as it permits the colony to survive and reproduce.

It has been postulated that learning is necessary for autonomy [20]. Harvester ants, *Pogonomyrmex barbatus*, appear to be capable of a limited form of learning that enhances the survival of the colony. Older ant colonies have been observed to respond to disturbances in a more routine manner than younger colonies. It appears as though younger colonies experiment with the environment on a weekly basis so as to fine-tune their reactive responses. But who or what is conducting the experiment and where is the data being stored? No single ant is aware of the entire state of the colony, so gathering results is problematic at best. The life span of an individual ant is much less than that of the colony, so how is the information passed on to new ants [17]?

Ants have several methods of short-range communication, including temporary pheromone trails, physical antenna contact, and sound [19, 21]. The incremental nature of this communication means that changes to the state of the colony take some time to ripple through the general population. This delay in communications would indicate that feedback would be received before the initial information had reached the entire colony.

The concept of distributed intelligence within an ant colony is even more amazing when considered the problem of task force distribution. Observations of ant colonies have demonstrated a standard response to disturbance: patrolling increases and foraging decreases. How many of these patrolling ants are ex-foragers and how do the ants monitor the numbers assigned to each task [17]? Ants are able to permanently switch tasks from one to another [18]. A robot should also be able to switch back to the original task An ant colony does not require human intervention, but a robot colony should retain this contingency.

The problems of AI have prevented mobile robots from operating in real time and in the dynamic real world. The solution to these problems is to construct agents, similar to insects, that react with the world. The realization of a self-sustaining adaptive population of cooperative autonomous agents is the justification for the study of a population of colonial insects. The goal is not to duplicate nature but to use nature for inspiration. The mechanics that permit a bird to fly are marvellous, but aeroplanes are more practical than ornithopters. The simple rules and incremental changes that enable an ant colony to thrive are fascinating, but a robot colony must be capable of greater functionality.

A useful robot population is comprised of a number of task forces that map to each major behavior, including a low-maintenance reserve task force. Robots are capable of moving between task forces. Each task force is comprised of the approximate number of agents required to complete the task and this number changes depending on performance in the dynamic environment. Agents not performing a task are assigned to the reserve force. The population is monitored by an administrator (a human being), who can intervene if required.

3.2   Autonomous Systems

In order for a population of robots to be considered as an autonomous system, it must meet certain conditions. These conditions are discussed in detail below. There is significant uncertainty in the environment and the system must be able to cope with this uncertainty. The system must be capable of operation for extended periods of time. It must be able to compensate for system failure without external intervention, e.g., hardware repair, tracking, regulation, and system failure. System failure identification and rectification involves the use of an FDI—a fault detection and isolation system [20].

The system must be able to plan a sequence of control actions to accomplish a complicated task. Many systems use algorithmic numeric and decision making symbolic methods to accomplish this goal. This is very similar to the classical way of thinking used in AI as it relies upon the use of mathematical models of the physical system. Such thinking leads to conventional control systems that add an intelligent level. This approach encounters the same problems as classical AI [20].

While an autonomous system needs to be tolerant of errors, it is expected to fail occasionally and, therfore, requires manual intervention and control One important requirement for an autonomous system is that the work that it produces be greater than the maintenance that it receives. Another requirement is that it deliver consistent performance so that accurate projections can be calculated [20].

Agent Interaction and Cooperation. Agent interaction is accomplished by communication and/or sensor signals. Most communication can be local in that it would have a range limited to the proximity of the agent. Longer-range communication should be used only as required.

Encoded beacons form part of the communication solution. The degree and method of cooperation would be defined and the protocols explicitly calculated. Negotiation would not be used as the agents would be modeled upon a hybrid reactive architecture. Agent knowledge would be explicitly identified. A system of navigation would also be defined.

Sustainability. Both biological and mechanical agents have needs. Biological agents require food, water and shelter in adverse environments. They have a remarkable ability to self-repairing. If biological agents do not obtain these needs, they perish. Mechanical agents require power or fuel, routine maintenance, repairs, etc. Components of mechanical agents have limited life expectancy and this may be reduced under adverse environmental conditions or as a result of accident. If mechanical agents do not obtain their needs they are unable to function. These needs of mechanical agents are referred to as sustenance functions.

Self-sustainability is the other key issue and part of the proposed solution to address this problem is to use a modular design. This approach assumes that the robots will fail due to attrition and therefore require automated repair. Modules can be replaced and only the malfunctioning piece requires replacement instead of the complete robot. It is also assumed that a modular robot would have an equal or higher chance of failure than a nonmodular design but the advantages of partial failure and ability to repair outweighs the disadvantage of increased failure.

Ability to repair is only one of the identified sustenance functions. Issues include: recharging or refuelling; reprogramming; repair, replace, calibrate or clean; recovery of lost robots; and reconfiguration of modules. The ability to automate these functions would save time, increase productivity and reduce costs.

Research by Lee on the topic of lifecycle service agents claims to enable more economical product diagnostics and repair than is currently available with standard product condition monitoring systems, and also that it will soon be technically and economically feasible to implement large-scale populations of heterogeneous products as multiagent systems. This will improve product design, service, and management and reduce costs [22].

The concept of an automated agent monitoring and repair system is very similar to the concept of a colony. Instead of having agents who are always online, it is envisaged that agents would periodically check in for routine examination and report any malfunction if detected. Agents would be fitted with a distress beacon in the event of serious failure in the field.

Minimal Viable Populations. The loss of a single member of a colony is insignificant, but when a colony has suffered attrition that results in large-scale loss of members it is reasonable to assume that there will be some performance degradation and other consequences. These consequences should affect agents, tasks, and the colony differently.

Individual agent performance should improve due to lack of obstacles that are other agents. It is less likely that tasks would be successful or that task forces would reach requested objectives. This is because there are insufficient members in specific task forces. When sufficient tasks fail, then the colony may fail. To reduce the risk of cascading failure, maintenance tasks should be listed with the highest priority.

Modules. Modules are the building blocks of the mobile robot population. Each robot is made up of a chassis and a number of interchangeable modules. Once it has been determined that a robot of a particular role is required and is not available, it is assembled from a store of modules. This approach enables the colony to reduce waste and be physically dynamic. Only failed modules are scrapped, not entire robots. If there are too many scouts and not enough transports, then a scout can be modified to become a transport.

Structures. Structures are nonmobile agents that support the mobile agents in the accomplishment of colonial goals. Structures identify the location of a colony and provide a means of interface with multiple agents. There are a number of unresolved issues with structures. What structures are required by the colony? What is their function? How does a structure perform its function? What is the intelligence requirement of a structure?

In experiments by Birk and Belpaeme [23] static agents (structures), provided information and were repaid in power. Structures have the capacity to fulfill the sustenance functional requirements of a population of mobile robots. The role of each structure needs to be identified. A level of redundancy is also required for this to work or the loss of a critical structure will disable a colony.

Roles. The roles of robots within the colon will be defined based upon needs. A number of robots will be assigned to each role. Robots will be able to change roles if required based upon hierarchy and component availability. Attributes and abilities of robots will be determined by roles and subsequent components.

Cetnarowicz introduced three interesting roles for agents, terminators, sentries and spares. Terminators disposed of other agents. Sentries acted as scouts and mobile navigation aids. Spares remained inactive until required [24]. Physical robots could use these concepts within a colony. The terminator could be viewed as a recycling structure. The sentry would remain the same and the spare would remain in low maintenance storage until required. Other roles would also be required and identified. Given the mining application, the roles of drill, transport, rescue, and maintenance would also be used.

Heterogeneous Agents. Heterogeneity is of Greek origin [*hetero* (other) and *genos* (kind)]. When considering agents, a taxonomy can be based upon some sorting criteria such as capabilities or components. Work has been done on competing heterogeneous robots within the field of artificial life. Much of this work is based upon competing species over limited resources in time and space. The main goal for these agents is self-preservation [23].

Experiments by Birk and Belpaeme revealed that there was a measured trade-off between benefit and cost of components. Vision components could help in task achievement but came at power and processing cost. It was found that costs should be kept low to achieve significant benefits. Application of the best technological solution was not always the best economical solution. These concepts of self-preservation and economical solution can be achieved with a colony approach.

Population Density. As the density of the population of physical agents in an operational area increases, this will have a detrimental effect upon performance. The two main problems are obstacle avoidance and communication. Obstacle avoidance problems may be reduced but not eliminated by separation techniques such as those used during the road intersection problem. Communication problems may be reduced by using local communication instead of global communication whenever possible.

Temporal Logic. Temporal logic can be used to predict certain results. It should be possible to find the average time for agents performing tasks. If this is combined with limits on how many robots could perform a task simultaneously, then fairly accurate predictions can be made. This could prove to be a useful management tool. This does not account for interference from other robots. As the number of robots increases above the peak amount, performance will decrease per robot. This will be demonstrated by an increase in cycle time.

Example Transport Task

Activity	Time	Limit	Peak
Journey out	15 min	5	13.3
Load truck	5 min	1	**8**
Journey return	19 min	5	10.5
Unload truck	1 min	1	40

Total cycle time = 40 min, maximum assignment limit = 12 agents.

Identification of peak: minimum (cycle time/subtask time × agent limit)

Therefore, best individual performance is achieved when 8 agents are assigned to the task of transport.

3.3 Cooperation

Agents do not just interact with each other, they also interact with the environment [25]. If an agent collides with a small obstacle, it may push it out of the way. If an agent is harvesting a resource, then the resource is diminished. If an agent is dumping waste in a pile, then the pile will grow.

Agents make local assessments and through interactions dynamically modify adaptive organizations. Interactions are sequences of actions and explicit communication may not be required. What is most important about interaction is who (agents), why (motivation) and how (protocol) [26].

Unsal demonstrated self-organizing behavior between homogeneous agents using attraction and repulsion. Agents were shown to cooperate in a material transportation task using this mechanism [27].

White and Pagurek proposed that the central idea of artificial life is the emergence of complex collective behavior from many simple agents and their interactions. This property of systems is also known as swarm intelligence. Agents are capable of observing the local environment and by the use of local processing and limited communication are able to modify the environment. These agents have no individual problem-solving knowledge or ability. Another important contribution was the interaction between mobile and stationary agents [3].

Cognitive multiagent systems use two primary forms of interaction: contract nets and negotiation. Contract nets permit limited social knowledge and do not allow persuasion. Negotiation has high social knowledge and high communication [28]. Negotiation is therefore unworkable in a large-scale population due to the high communication requirement.

There are a number of definitions for cooperation, but it might be better to take a step back and examine cooperation among people and then among machines.

3.3.1 Cooperative Examples. If you are walking down a corridor and some person steps aside for you, they are cooperating with you because they have chosen not to collide with you. This action is of mutual benefit because the cost of the side-step is much less than the cost of the collision. If you had chosen to step aside for them, it would also have enhanced your performance and theirs. Therefore, collision avoidance is a form of cooperation.

If two or more persons lift a heavy object together, they are cooperating because they have combined their individual ability to accomplish a task that could not be completed alone. Of course, they would still be cooperating if they assisted you to lift an object that was heavy but could be lifted solitaire, because they have shared your burden. Therefore, sharing a burden is a form of cooperation.

If two or more persons divide a task into a number of subtasks and then individually work on subtasks, they are cooperating because a decomposed task is accomplished more efficiency. By not competing, you are able to achieve the goal with less resource wastage. Also similar is the concept of a production line. Therefore, task decomposition is a form of cooperation.

Takeda defined cooperation as both collaboration and coordination. Collaboration was when subtasks could be assigned to an agent, and coordination enabled schedules of actions to be calculated by agents. This framework was said to be appropriate for cooperation among heterogeneous real-world agents because it was adaptive for environments and allowed implicit representation of cooperation. General tasks could be decomposed into subtasks that could be accomplished by a single agent [29].

Common Ideas Behind Cooperation
- Cooperation enhances group performance by conflict avoidance.
- Cooperation enables task accomplishment beyond individual ability.
- Cooperation enhances performance through task decomposition.

Cooperation and Conflict
- Conflict prevents personal goals from being achieved.
- Conflict prevents group goals from being achieved.
- Conflict wastes effort and is uneconomical.
- Conflict prevents achievement of tasks beyond individual ability.

Robot Cooperation. People observe others to determine their current actions, or they are informed and then make a decision that leads to action that avoids conflict, enables the task to be accomplished, or improves the task efficiency. There is no guarantee that cooperation will lead to success, but it is a more successful strategy that uncooperative individual effort. Robots perform a near-identical process in order to cooperate, but the issues are different.

Analogy with Intelligent Machines in General. People have many mediums of explicit or implicit communications based on senses. They have unpredictable behavior, unknown intentions, and unknown limitations. A mutual solution can be sought by negotiation. They have a vast array of dynamic strategies capable of dealing with uncertainty. The existence of a hidden agenda may preclude cooperation.

Agents have communication protocol based on hardware. They have predictable behavior, known intentions, and typically known or calculated limitations. A precalculated strategy with task decomposition is used and negotiation is by a system of defined rules.

Coherent Behavior. Being part of the same society does not guarantee that cooperation will have a positive effect. If we consider that one termite piles rocks into a wall and another removes them from the nest, then this behavior results in both agents wasting effort. A termite colony has redundancy in that individual members may waste effort while the colony in general achieves objectives and therefore coherent behavior [1].

Autocatalytic behavior is a self-reinforcing mechanism for achieving a coherent behavior. An example of this can be taken from colonial insects such as ants. As the number of ants following a path increases, more ants are induced to follow that path. Ants lay down a pheromone trail that attracts other ants [3]. Coherent behavior is based upon simple rules.

3.4 Communication

Coordination between agents is typically achieved by the use of a message exchange protocol. A rigid protocol prevents adaptation to changes in the environment. Sometimes messages fail to arrive or unexpected messages arrive and agents must respond to exceptions [30]. A large-scale population of agents is able to utilize redundancy and therefore message reliability is not essential. If most of the messages are transmitted and received, then the colony will continue to function efficiently.

The experiments of Ohko with Contract Net Protocol (CNP) revealed that the broadcast of task announcement messages unacceptably increased the communication load. Ohko selected a system of case-based reasoning and directed contract-return negative acknowledgements to reduce communication overheads. It is difficult to enable autonomous mobile robots to use high-speed and wideband communication lines. Also, communication is not reliable due to circumstances such as location and damage [31]. Location might include issues like terrain and range that would tend to reduce communication.

Using cooperative teams in simulation, Ye was able to demonstrate that a relationship existed between quantity of communication and cost of actions. Total ignorance of other agent activities was not acceptable because effort was wasted attempting to complete a task performed by another agent. Total knowledge of other agent activities was not acceptable due to the communication cost in time. Ye argued that there was little point in knowing the actions of another agent if interaction with that agent did not take place. Also shown was the proportional relationship between action cost and communication quantity [32].

Experiments by Sen demonstrated that increasing available information significantly increased the time to reach a desired equilibrium state. Another advantage of reducing information available to agents is which reducing contention for resources, will also enable faster convergence to stable resource usage [33]. Agents require sufficient information to make the correct decision in a real-time situation for most events but not so much information that performance is reduced.

The concept of minimal distributed communication was advocated by Ygge and Akkermans. A potential gain in reduced communication exists where information is distributed throughout a system and it is not transmitted to a central location [34]. From this and other work, two main issues began to emerge: minimize communication to required information and use a distributed system of short-range repeaters.

3.4.1 *Encoded Beacons.* An encoded beacon can be thought of as a geographically fixed device that provides an information service to agents. Agents retain autonomy as they are not controlled by the device. A beacon can be as simple as a stop line on a road to an electronic device that transmits an encoded message. Placement of communication beacons also affects energy consumption, e.g., colony entrance or exit [35]. Trials with encoded beacon technology are currently in progress for environmental information such as legal road speeds [36]. Passive encoded beacons would be used within the colony as navigation aids, while active beacons would enable periodic download of new directives to mobile agents.

3.4.2 *Ontologies.* An ontology is a predefined system of concepts that enable communication and therefore cooperation among agents by clarification of knowledge. It is reasonable to have ontologies about defined objects, spatial coordinates and legal actions. When defining a

taxonomy of objects, it is necessary to determine object attributes based upon sensors, action, or information processing. Space is defined by absolute or relative position. Actions are a list of primitive actions such as move, grasp, release, find, hold, open, or close [29]. It is worth noting that object attributes may be determined by agent primitive actions such as pushing, which would make the object attribute "movable." Space could also be defined as approximate or even unknown.

3.4.3   Stigmergy. There are two forms of indirect communication known as stigmergy. Sign-based stigmergy is the deposition of a message in the environment. The most common example of this is the pheromone trail left by ants. These messages are of no direct task benefit but influence behavior. Sematectonic stigmergy is a physical change of the environment that provides information to other agents. An example of this is found in the nest-building behavior of colonial insects. Both forms of stigmergy are examples of local communication [3].

4   POPULATION MANAGEMENT

The issues involved with the automation of a factory or plant are very similar to those in the automation of a population of intelligent agents. Much of the knowledge from the field of control theory is directly portable to the field of intelligent agents. The issue of decentralized control is particularly important.

An effective cooperative population is comprised of equal distributed autonomous agents and does not rely upon central processing. A population that is centrally controlled is limited by physical constraints. This peer-to-peer cooperative relationship between autonomous agents does not preclude times when one agent must have precedence over another. However, the complete state of the system is difficult to know for any given interval. A decentralized control system is able to bypass most of these problems [16, 20].

To make large populations of agents manageable, it is necessary to make them autonomous. One of the key criteria for such autonomy is that the agent behavior must be adaptable to a dynamic environment. If the goal is to establish a large-scale population of agents away from immediate human contact such that the population is autonomous, then it needs to be adaptable and self-sustaining. The management of an autonomous population is seen as one of the key factors for the realization of this goal.

Sustained robot operations in remote and hostile locations would become technically feasible with increased self-sufficiency. Robots designed to manage and maintain themselves with limited human involvement would be more capable and efficient. Increased productivity and cost reduction are the types of benefits that would enable industry to consider implementation of robotic workers.

A large factory or plant has interconnected subsystems that are stabilized using local inputs and outputs and must be connectively stable [16]. Populations of autonomous agents are analogous to this decentralized architecture. Instead of interconnected subsystems, there are autonomous agents. Localized communication and interaction between agents enables achievement of global goals.

A population of cooperative autonomous agents must be capable of dealing with significant uncertainty within the system and the environment. It must be able to operate without external intervention for extended periods of time and compensate for system failure. It must be able to detect, diagnose, and rectify errors. The potential for human intervention is desirable, but it should be minimized.

The centralized approach gives rise to processing problems because of the increasingly complex dynamic systems, increasingly complex design requirements, an increasingly dynamic environment, and increasing uncertainty [20]. These problems are not new and have encumbered mobile robots operating in the dynamic real world in real time. One possible solution applicable to the mobile robot problem proposed by Brooks was to construct agents, similar to insects, that react with the world [14].

If a system is centrally controlled, information resource requirements exceed system growth. A decentralized architecture offers economic and reliability advantages. Decentralized systems do not have complete state observations, so optimal decentralized control remains to be solved [16]. Natural decentralized systems are able to maintain control. It should be possible to construct an artificial system that enjoys the benefits of decentralized architecture.

Self-management is one of the key issues for the colony and the proposed solution to the problems of automated management is to implement a multitactical strategy that continually experiments with the world and monitors results.

EXAMPLE

A number of robots are harvesting a resource and performance drops unexpectedly. There are a number of reasons why this may have occurred and application of the incorrect solution will only exacerbate the problem.

Potential Problems
- Resource supply has diminished.
- Distance to resource has increased.
- Obstacle density has increased.
- Robot interference has increased.
- Current path is obstructed by damaged robot.

Each of these problems may have a different solution. Constantly assigning more robots upon the assumption that resource supply has diminished will not always improve the current situation. Implementation of a methodical and incremental experimentation process, a multitactical strategy, will identify the problem based upon results. Once the problem is identified the correct solution can be applied with greater confidence.

Management is concerned with two prime areas, performance analysis and strategic adaptation. Bouzid and Mouaddib claim that populations should maximize satisfaction of directives based on resource availability, and number, density, and utility of workers [37]. This seems rather simple when considering that economic agents within a decentralized society may have conflicting objectives [38]. From this it can be concluded that the goal is to automate direction of a population of autonomous agent while avoiding the pitfalls of reactive management.

Agents must be able to reason in order to adapt to changing resources and requirements. Agents that require assistance to achieve goals or are prevented from achieving goals because of other agents are said to be socially dependent [13]. If each agent of a vast colony knows some of the information required and there is a redundant mechanism to pass this information on to those who need to know, then the colony is a collective mind, a *Gestalt*.

A population comprised of flexible artificial agents has greater utility than a population limited to well-defined cases. The ability to adapt at both of the interdependent local and global levels will result in a more flexible system. Agent behavior is based upon agent ability, social position, and organizational structure [39].

Modular agents have the capacity to adapt physically to changes in the environment. A control system that is capable of reassigning task force members is able to adapt at the global level. The proposed system meets both of these criteria: adaption at local and at global levels. Therefore, it should be possible to produce a highly adaptive system as a result of this project

4.1 Performance Analysis

Before something can be managed, it must be measured, and therefore metrics have critical importance to the concept of a self-managing colony. It is relatively simple to measure the performance of a task force of robots harvesting a mineral resource. One solution is to measure the quantity of material removed from the mining site. Another is to measure the quantity returned to the processing plant. Another is to measure the proportion that leaves the processing plant. All of these solutions are based on the principle of quantity over time. But this method cannot be applied to all other tasks. How are the performances of scouting, rescue, or maintenance robots to be measured? A solution to performance measurement for each role will have to be identified during the analysis and design phase of the project.

The major dynamics affecting organizational reasoning of MAS are organization structure, environmental changes, agent addition and removal, and user intervention. MAS can be analyzed using population, organization time, agent behavior set, agent roles, and environment [12]. This provides a foundation for population measurement and therefore management. These dynamics affect population task achievement.

Simonin attempted to demonstrate a formal approach to performance analysis of a population of agents. However, their major contribution was to demonstrate the inappropriateness of this approach. Their motivation was a lack of formal methods applied to this discipline and studies based upon individual behavior, not global performance [40]. Several simplifications and assumptions were made, including:

1. The agent avoidance problem is totally ignored.
2. Agent speed is steady.
3. Agent behavior is known.
4. Agents perform tasks and do so independently.
5. Work time is computed from known origin and destination points.
6. Performance is solely a function of time.
7. Given agent behavior, possible events and environment then predict performance.

Given these assumptions and considering their serious nature, an error generation rate of 20% was still possible. Theoretical predictions were measured against empirical results using simulation [40]. This is perceived as an outstanding argument for nonreliance upon formal methods.

On the positive side, Simonin used discrete time, energy consumption, and a fixed base of operations. The difficult problem of exploring an unknown area to discover and transport ore samples was discussed and the exploration calculation problem was identified. The main reason for the exploration calculation problem is that the process duration and the probability of success are not known [33].

Sen approached the problem of ineffective system performance by listing the potential reasons. This list is not fully portable to a cooperative population of reactive agents as there is no conflict of interest, etc. The problem of contention for resources is identified earlier as the oscillation problem. Centralized information and control is vulnerable to system failure. Global information and control comes with a very high communication overhead. It is anticipated that the colony will also have reasons for poor performance and these should also be formally identified.

Reasons for Ineffective Performance [33]

1. Conflict of interest
2. Contention for resources
3. Asynchronicity in the decision process
4. Lack of centralized control
5. Lack of centralized information
6. Incomplete global information
7. Incorrect global information

4.2 Learning and Adaptation

One basic fact that never changes is that things change. Our world is one of these things and it changes constantly. We expect environmental conditions to remain within a range based upon previously observed conditions, but we anticipate fluctuations within this range. It is unreasonable to think that we can anticipate every single permutation of the environment. Therefore, we need to construct agents that are able to observe the current state of the world and adapt their behavior to suit prevailing conditions.

In order to achieve autonomy, a system must be capable of learning. It is not certain whether there are limits to the learning ability of biological entities, but instances of machines definitely have a limited amount of memory and require a system of finite memory management [20].

Current tools that attempt to achieve this goal of adaptation include neural nets and genetic algorithms. One of the problems these tools have is that their reasoning is not verifiable. It is not possible to look inside a neural net or a genetic algorithm and know what the machine is "thinking." It is possible to observe changes within the environment and changes within the tool and plot this as a probable cause, but it is still a best guess.

Many management systems use agents that are provided with abilities to assess the benefit they gain by interacting with each other. Positive interactions are strengthened while negative interactions are weakened [41]. Certain techniques applicable to single agents, such as reinforcement learning, grow exponentially when used with multiagent systems [42]. This makes such approaches unworkable with regard to large-scale multiagent systems. These forms of learning—neural nets, and genetic algorithms, etc.—are not examinable and the reasons for specific decisions cannot be known. The multitactical strategy is an examinable form of learning that is based upon global results and not interaction.

4.3 Standard Operating Procedure

Real-time responsiveness in dynamic real-world environments requires reductions in the decision process. A standard operating procedure can be used to regulate task coupling and minimize communication. Communication is reduced and elaborate coordination is time consuming and is not used [43]. This is possible because agents are reactive in that they perceive and act. A task is decomposed into subtasks that are organized to as to have enabling relationships. Agents search for cues/hints to migrate from one subtask to another. This can result in cascading effects based upon subtask status [40].

An incremental system based upon simple rules and minimum effort should enable a complex system to be created. Communication range is limited and messages are sent only when required. Sensors would be tailored to detect specific stimuli. Only relevant information is calculated. Even with the minimalist approach, it is certain that agents will fail and this is built into the system as acceptable.

4.4 Human Interface

Ohko claimed that a complexity-reduced human–robot interface was possible if tasks could be negotiated adaptively [31]. Although it is reasonably simple for a human operator to interact with a single mechanical agent, this task becomes much more complex as the number of agents increases. Also consider that these agents may be large machines working in a hazardous environment. It should be possible for a system administrator to communicate with the population from a remote location and using simple commands. Therefore, the interface for a large-scale population of agents should be as constant and automated as possible.

Takeda also found that environmental dynamics increased significantly when agents and humans coexisted. In their work, agents were mobile robots and computer-controlled machines. Tasks were provided by humans but mediation was automated. The mediator would decompose a task and assign an appropriate number of agents Mediation was used because agent availability in a multi- agent environment was not predictable. One of the problems of this approach is that the mediator is a centralized system and therefore vulnerable and susceptible to congestion. Another problem was that coordination scheduling was not tight enough [29]. With a colony approach it is possible to utilize a system of distributed dedicated mediators and to eliminate scheduling by using autonomous agents.

4.5 Strategy

There are many different approaches to MAS. The main area of contention is with a centralized or distributed coordination and control. One way of achieving the goal is to use the concept of global utility, which is a performance-based method. An implementation of this strategy has a range of values between lower and upper bounds [44]. Ekenberg's approach is ambiguous and does not explicitly state key issues. A lower bound is introduced but is not used in the strategy resolution. The better of two strategies with different lower bounds and the same upper bound is not identified. Global utility as an average would enable a more useful system. Large scale systems that use global utility over long periods tend to produce accurate results.

Global Utility System (Ekenberg)

Strategy	Lower	Upper
S1	0.20	0.50
S2	0.20	0.60
S3	0.40	0.60

Therefore S2 is better than S1 by 0.10 [44] and S2 and S3 are the same?

Global Utility System (Engwirda)

Strategy	Average
S1	0.35
S2	0.40
S3	0.50

Therefore S2 is better than S1 by 0.05 and S3 is the best strategy.

Fujita and Lesser examined the parallel process scheduling problem with specific attention to the problem of deadline-based multiagent task decomposition and scheduling. They used a reactive strategy called MADS and noted the degree of deviation between expected and actual results. A master agent determined task force size and subtask partition—who does what—for multiple slave agents. Prior expectations existed in that the goal was identified as explicit declaration of performance over time. Failure was dealt with by having multiple simultaneous strategies, even though this led to inefficiency problems [45].

Dynamic scheduling during execution is better than static scheduling at the beginning of execution because task performance is uncertain and cannot be predicted accurately. To determine whether rescheduling should take place, consider the cost of rescheduling and amount of quality improvement. Also note that it is difficult to achieve good-quality solutions for problems of short duration. Rescheduling of task force size was based upon the amount of standard deviation. Rescheduling of tasks was based on trigger conditions. The metrics used were rather simplistic and covered two conditions, best solution and absolute quality. An optimistic zero delay in communication and rescheduling was assumed [45]. The work on metrics needs to be expanded to cover continuous tasks and possibly other cases. A delay for communication and rescheduling should be introduced.

The strategy of Fujita and Lesser was a step in the correct direction but it is not portable to real-world agents. Rescheduling should be based upon time and performance and therefore a continuous incremental activity. A large-scale population of physical agents working in the real world experiences many more complex problems and requires a much more detailed and extensive strategy.

While this work did introduce agent limits it did not consider failure, sustenance functions, or addition or removal or agents. The environment was static, the solution relied upon plans and was limited to the field, and was not generic. There were significant problems with the strategy and, in their own words, "It is simple, extremely crude and could be significantly improved" [45]. And yet they succeeded in identification of most of the important issues.

4.6 Convergence

Simple reactive rules enable colonial insects to converge on optimal solutions that achieve global objectives. Insects are able to accomplish this by sensing the gradients of dissipative fields and selecting the option that yields higher utility. This approach can lead to dramatically reduced communication requirements, as low as 2% in some cases [46].

Sen found that deliberate limitation of information to individuals within a group of agents can enable faster convergence to a stable and optimal configuration [33].

Neiman and Lesser worked on cooperative distributed agents that have only local view of resources and tasks and are capable of incremental convergence upon an optimal solution. Their experiments tested coordination versus replanning and proactive versus retroactive replanning [47].

Convergence relies upon simple rules, distributed control, limited sensory awareness, and communication. This approach is based upon simplicity, redundancy, and economic effect. Complexity is unnecessary and repeatedly fails to achieve more reliable systems. Large-scale populations of agents are ideally suited to convergence.

5   APPLICATION ISSUES

5.1   Application Areas

Intelligent Vehicles. The application of intelligent agent technology is still in its infancy. One of the key areas of application is seen as the intelligent vehicle highway system (IVHS). As our urban population grows, our roads and highways are choking to a standstill due to the ever increasing number of vehicles. Constructing more roads and better roads is not enough to solve this problem and it is hoped that we will be able to find a more intelligent means of using our transport system [48].

Many scientists and engineers are looking to information technology to solve this problem by making vehicles and highway systems intelligent. While there are many good reasons to believe that this technology will help to alleviate some of the problems, it is unlikely that it will be able to eliminate the cause [49]. Some estimates put traffic growth at 150% over the next 15 years and within urban areas it can take several hours to travel 10 miles [48].

Service Industry. Several attempts have been made to bring intelligent agents into the service industry. So far, none of these attempts has been an outstanding success. There are a number of reasons explaining this, including economics and client resistance.

Entertainment Industry. One of the applications for intelligent agents is that of the "no-fuss pet". This pet is a physical and behavioral replicant of an animal, like the Sony dog. It looks and acts like a dog and can perform various behavior such as sitting, begging, or rolling over. Additionally, it can be put away when you are finished playing with it. While this idea is interesting, it appears to be a little superficial. Part of the charm of a real pet is that it cannot be put away and it demands your attention [50].

5.2   Current Research on Cooperative Agents

The implementation side of cooperative work among intelligent autonomous behaving agents will be addressed by presenting a population of five cooperative autonomous mobile robots developed by the Intelligent Control Systems Laboratory (ICSL), Griffith University, Australia. A case study derived from ongoing experiments with cooperative behaving agents is an intelligent vehicle and in unmanned autonomous vehicle environments will be described.

5.2.1   Road Intersection Problem. The road intersection problem is similar to the narrow bridge problem in that a number of agents must cross the same ground without collision. Past research at the ICSL has enabled two cooperative autonomous agents to successfully cross a known intersection without collision. Current research at the ICSL is aimed at building upon this success by increasing the number of agents, making the intersection pattern unknown, and optimizing the time.

The road intersection experiment deals with cooperative agents and their real-world implementation. The experiment verifies the desired behavior of two intelligent vehicles approaching an intersection. The scenario for the task decomposition of their motion uses a cooperative protocol. Communication is achieved by the use of radio equipment. The environment is semicontrolled with passive beacons, which activate event-driven behaviors by providing stimulation for the agents' sensors. These event-driven behaviors include agent communication, coordination and navigation.

Beacons. There are so many beacons within society that people have learned to filter them out of conscious thought processes and relegate them to the reactive part of the mind. If a number of typical people were removed from their native city and placed foreign cities, where they could not speak the language, they would experience greater difficulty in accomplishing simple transportation tasks. This is because they are no longer able to obtain environmental information from local beacons.

It is reasonable to suggest that people live in a dynamic environment that is somewhere between order and chaos, where information is gathered from passive and active beacons. Passive beacons are signs or devices that do not change, such as road markings that indicate lane options, or stop and give-way signs that request certain traffic behaviors. Active beacons have altered states, such as traffic lights that can request several different behavior options for given intervals of time. Within the framework of this discussion, the radio transmitter is considered an active beacon and the white line as a passive beacon.

To achieve the goal of having intelligent agents operate within society where these agents are not able to interact with current beacons, it is reasonable to modify standard beacons or to create new ones. What must be achieved is a method of making minimal modifications to the real world that will enable intelligent agents to operate as useful members of society. It is not suggested that every sign or marking within society be altered, but that civilization should be prepared to assist intelligent agents on a case-by-case basis.

Any solution to the intersection problem must permit the vehicles to pass through the intersection without collision. Vehicles must be able to identify the intersection and know whether it is blocked or clear. The solution should be real-world and operate in real time. This solution uses a cooperative protocol and passive beacons that activate event-driven behaviors by providing specific stimulation for the agents' sensors.

Solutions that are based upon simulation tend to mislead people to think of cooperative robots as perfect agents that are both omniscient and omnipotent, never malfunctioning, and having limitless power, range, and other abilities. When a solution is implemented in the real world, problems begin to emerge, such as communication issues. These include communication medium, signal strength, range, interference, additional power requirements, equipment weight, protocol robustness, interrupt generation, detection, and consequences. Solving these problems can lead to a solution that is radically different from a previous simulated solution.

The Intersection. An intersection is composed of a number of roads in a particular pattern that meet at a certain location. For example, it is possible to have three roads that meet in a "Y" or a "T" pattern. It is possible to have three to N roads that meet in any one of a number of different configurations. As the number of variables is increased—road numbers and angles—the number of combinations of possibilities is dramatically increased.

The traffic flow through the intersection used in the experiments was not governed by traffic lights, stop signs, or give-way signs. A two-lane, four-road intersection was selected for these experiments (Figure 4). Each road contains two lanes where the direction of traffic flow is opposite in each lane. It does not make any difference if agents drive on the left or right side of the road provided that it is consistent. The road lanes were non-white and marked with one white

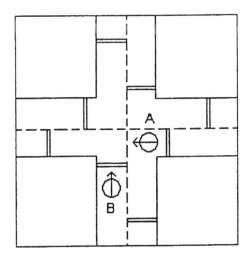

FIGURE 4
Agent crossing intersection.

strip prior to the intersection and another some distance after the intersection. The white strips act as passive navigation beacons because they do not change state.

The first white strip indicates the position where the agent should stop prior to the intersection and is referred to as the stop line. This should be placed such that the static agent will not interfere with the mobile agent. The second white strip, referred to as the clear line, indicates the position where the mobile agent is clear of the intersection such that it will not obstruct another agent.

The white strips are detected by means of a standard IR emitter and detector pair. The IR sensor will detect two state changes as it passes over a strip of white tape on a non-white surface. A counter is calculated from this state change to determine the current location of the intelligent agent with regard to the intersection. The IR line detection unit is positioned on the front underside of the vehicle.

An intelligent agent A is crossing the intersection while agent B waits at the stop line. Both of the vehicles are driving in the left lane. The stop lines are passive beacons that activate event-driven behaviors. In all cases the agents reach the stop line prior to reaching the clear line. These agents are autonomous mobile robots that carry their own power source and on-board processor. A detailed description of these agents and their components is available in [51].

Radio Communication. Communication between the agents is achieved by dual-channel UHF radio signals. The transmitter is an example of an active beacon because it is capable of multiple states. Each agent carries a transmitter and receiver that are encoded to enable multiple signal transmission on a single frequency. The signal consists of a sinusoidal carrier wave that is modulated with an agent identification code and a channel identification (Figure 5). This enables each agent to transmit two distinct signals. The signals are transmitted in conjunction with specific events. The signal is pulsed and several adjacent pulses enable an interrupt to be generated.

The signal has sufficient range that agents that are in jeopardy of collision can communicate this situation and cross the intersection in safety. The range of the signal must not be greater than the area adjacent to the intersection, otherwise agents at some other intersection will detect the signal with hazardous results. This situation could be avoided if the intersection were marked

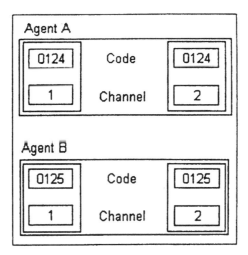

FIGURE 5
Radio signal packet options.

with a personal identification beacon or if envelope detection were used to measure the strength of the signal. Two radio signal packet options available to each agent are shown. Each packet consists of a code and a channel signal that is modulated with a sinusoidal carrier wave.

Implementation Strategies. From a logical point of view, the agents used are equal in status and can cross the intersection using the same priority as their arrival time. The agent that arrives at the stop line first will determine whether the intersection is clear. If it determines that the intersection is clear, it will transmit its intention to proceed. It will proceed across, and when it has cleared the intersection it will transmit this information. Should the other agent arrive at the stop line after the stop signal and prior to the clear signal, then it will stop and wait for the clear signal before proceeding. The transmission of stop or clear signals is determined by the recent presence of the stop or clear lines, respectively. If two agents arrive at the intersection at exactly the same time, a deadlock will occur.

Results. The agents demonstrated that the protocol functioned correctly and the navigation of an intersection was possible using this concept.

Conclusions. Two intelligent mobile agents performing in the real world have been developed that approach and cross an intersection without collision. Event-driven behaviors and active and passive beacons proved to be a workable combination that permitted an uncomplicated solution. While this design is not directly scalable into a vehicle capable of transporting human passengers, it does show that the technology and ability to create such agents are currently achievable.

Multiple Agents. This research is ongoing and attempts to improve upon the previous solution. The primary area of improvement is to increase the number of agents and simultaneously resolve the deadlock case where two agents are at the intersection at exactly the same time (Figure 6). The strategy for resolution of this problem relies upon the use of a radio packet controller (RPC)

FIGURE 6
Crossing an intersection.

and a suitable protocol that enables the agents to request permission to cross the intersection [52].

The second problem of dealing with unknown intersection layout is also addressed. The proposed solution to this problem involves the use of passive beacons. Each approach road to an intersection is equipped with a beacon that transmits a local map and current location to each agent as it passes. The final improvement relies upon reducing time wastage caused by the cautious primary solution. Local maps and standard traffic rules will enable this to be accomplished [53–55].

5.2.2 *Formation Driving.*

Formation driving is a form of cooperation and requires a complex set of rules. Formation driving typically takes the form of column, line, wedge, or echelon and might involve a translation from one formation to another. There are a number of valid reasons for platoon formations, such as resource and communication optimization.

Distance and Tracking Control. Autonomous agents that have *distance* control behaviors automatically maintain distance between two or more agents traveling in the same direction and environment. Autonomous agents that have *tracking* control behaviors automatically maintain coincident trajectories of two or more vehicles traveling in the same direction and environment (Figure 7). Intervention from humans and/or supervisory systems is not required for either *distance* or *tracking* control [56].

5.2.3 *Narrow Bridge.*

The agents approach a narrow bridge and communicate. One agent has greater priority and crosses the bridge, while the other agent remains clear. When the first agent has crossed, the second agent then proceeds across (Figure 8).

Much work on the problem of cooperative agents avoiding a collision has already been performed. In particular, there is the work from Kajitani's laboratory by Ming et al. In their paper "Cooperative Operation of Two Mobile Robots," they addressed the problem of multiple agents approaching a narrow bridge and implemented a physical experiment to demonstrate their solution. They also discussed the intersection problem but did not experiment with a solution to this problem [4].

The agents they built were distributed, autonomous and cooperative. They demonstrated collision avoidance, communication, negotiation, and cooperative motion. Explicit communica-

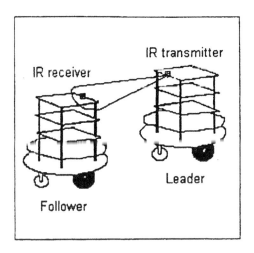

FIGURE 7
Distance and tracking control.

tion was achieved using infrared light as a medium. Cooperative motion enabled the agents to transport an object that neither agent could move alone [4].

Negotiation was implemented using a composite priority system in which the composite priority equaled the basic priority plus the dynamic priority. Their strategy for cooperative collision-free motion of multiple robots was developed by postulating the existence of a basic priority (such as traffic rules) and a dynamic priority (such as an interaction between a robot and its immediate environment). An assignment of priority among the participants involved remains to be solved [4].

5.2.4 Pipe Transportation. The joint transport problem is one of the more difficult behaviors for cooperative robots. The problem involves two or more agents jointly transporting an object such as a length of pipe. Errors arise each time a single robot moves. This is caused by servomotor errors and wheel slippage, etc. Errors are compounded when two or more robots attempt to perform a cooperative action. Incorrect position, orientation, and velocity by one robot may cause a major failure in the other robot, such as falling over.

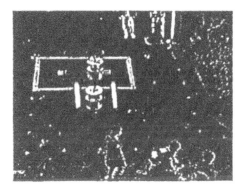

FIGURE 8
Narrow bridge experiment.

FIGURE 9
Pipe transportation.

To solve this problem it is necessary to match orientation, relative position, and velocity. This problem is even more difficult in the real world with problems of exact position. This problem was solved by the use of two passive arms with three joints and two rotary encoders each. The arm was designed to absorb some of the shock created by errors and the mechanics of normal movement. The rotary encoders enabled position, orientation and velocity information to be known. This information enabled stabilization of course, position, and velocity (Figure 9) [4].

6 CONCLUSIONS

Recent advances in technology have enabled analysis of complex multiagent systems. Issues such as management, organization, and sustainability have emerged. Strategies and tools such as performance analysis are undergoing evaluation. This progress leads inexorably toward cooperative work among autonomous behaving agents.

A large-scale population of autonomous mobile robots that perform useful work in an economical manner has not yet been achieved. Achievement of this goal will enable new applications of robot technology. These applications will be possible in remote and/or hostile environments. If a population were a society of distributed agents, then it would be capable of operating in real- time, real-world environments. A colony approach should enable the cooperative population to be self-managing, self-sustaining, and self-organizing.

A great deal has been learned from observations of biological systems including the minimalist approach. This strategy follows conventional thinking within the field. Design should be kept simple. Communication should be limited in range and quantity. Sustenance functions should be automated. The use of structures and heterogeneous modular agents enables extended useful performance and enhances coherent behavior.

A cooperative society of agents should utilize local standard operating procedures to converge upon a global solution. Learning and adaptation can be implemented at a management level to permit modification to the procedure options, thereby achieving optimization. Cooperative behavior is seen as the key to enabling current robotic technology to become useful and economic.

The field of cooperative intelligent agents offers to unlock the hidden potential of autonomous mobile robots, which is to enable them to become both useful and economic. Recent advances in the design and development of cooperative autonomous mobile robots have enabled the realization of useful applications such as intelligent transportation systems.

REFERENCES

[1] C.R. Kube, *Collective Robotics: From Local Perception to Global Action*. PhD Thesis, University of Alberta, Edmonton, 1997.

[2] L. Cavedon, A. Rao, L. Sonenberg, and G. Tidhar, Teamwork via team plans in intelligent autonomous agent systems, in *Proc. Int. Conf. WorldWide Computing and its Applications, Japan* (Lecture Notes in Computer Science Vol. 1274), pp. 106–121, 1997.

[3] T. White and B. Pagurek, Towards multi-swarm problem solving in networks, in *Proc. Third Int. Conf. Multi-Agent Systems, ICMAS'98, Paris, France*, 1998, pp. 333–340.

[4] A. Ming, V. Masek, V. Kanamori, and M. Kajitani, Cooperative operation of two mobile robots, in Asama, Fukuda, Arai, and Endo (eds.), *Proc. Distributed Autonomous Robotic Systems 2*, pp. 339–349. Springer- Verlag, Berlin, 1995.

[5] R.A. Brooks, Intelligence without representation, *Artificial Intelligence*, Vol. 47, pp. 139–159, 1991.

[6] P.M. Todd, Two approaches to machine intelligence: the Animat path to intelligent adaptive behavior, *Computer*, Vol. 25, pp. 78–81, Nov. 1992.

[7] J. Muller and P. Pecchiari, A model for systems of situated autonomous agents: an application to automated deduction, in *Proc. Second Int. Conf. Multi-Agent Systems, ICMAS'96, Kyoto, Japan*, 1996, pp. 220–227.

[8] H. Nakashima and I. Noda, Dynamic subsumption architecture for programming intelligent agents, in *Proc. Third Int. Conf. Multi-Agent Systems, ICMAS'98, Paris, France*, 1998, pp. 190–197.

[9] R.A. Brooks, Elephants don't play chess, *Robotics and Autonomous Systems*, Vol. 6, pp. 3–15, 1990.

[10] R. Jarvis, Autonomous watercraft navigation, in *Proc. Fifth Int. Conf. Autonomous Systems, IAS-5, Sapporo, Japan*, 1998, pp. 140–147.

[11] A.E. Engwirda, M.R. Hitchings, Lj.B. Vlacic, and A. Sattar, Communication among cooperative autonomous vehicles, in *Proc. Australian Conf. Artificial Intelligence, Perth, Australia*, 1997, pp. 56–61.

[12] A. Costa and Y. Demazeau, Toward a model of multi-agent systems with dynamic organizations, in *Proc. Second Int. Conf. Multi-Agent Systems, ICMAS'96, Kyoto, Japan*, 1996, p. 431.

[13] J. Sichman, On achievable goals and feasible plans in open multi-agent systems, in *Proc. Second Int. Conf. Multi-Agent Systems, ICMAS'96, Kyoto, Japan*, 1996, p. 456.

[14] R.A. Brooks, New approaches to robotics, *Science*, Vol. 253,, pp. 1227–1232, 1991.

[15] A. Agah and G.A. Bekey, Robot Colony Simulator: A research tool for studying colonies of intelligent robots, *Simulation*, pp. 82–93, August 1996.

[16] D.D. Siljak, Decentralized control and computations: status and prospects, in *Proc. Large Scale Systems: Theory and Applications*, Vol. 1, pp. 1–11.

[17] D. Gordon, Colonial memories in the ant world, *New Scientist*, Vol. 2, p. 33, July 1987.

[18] D. Gordon, Home page, http://www- leland.stanford.edu/group/biosci/faculty/gordon.html, 1998.

[19] I. Stewart, Mathematicians learn how to read the ant-trails, *Science*, Vol. 26, p. 16, June 1993.

[20] P.J. Antsaklis and K.M. Passino (eds.), Introduction to intelligent control systems with high degrees of autonomy, in *An Introduction to Intelligent and Autonomous Control*, pp. 1–26, 1993, Kluwer Academic, Boston.

[21] J. Beard, Caterpillars tap-dance for an ant audience, *New Scientist*, Vol. 30, p. 16, June 1990.

[22] B. Lee, Product populations and lifecycle services as industrial multi- agent systems in an embedded electronic commerce framework, in *Proc. Second Int. Conf. Multi-Agent Systems, ICMAS'96, Kyoto, Japan*, 1996, p. 447.

[23] A. Birk and T. Belpaeme, An overview of the extended VUB ecosystem, a MAS of heterogenous robots, in *Proc. Third Int. Conf. Multi-Agent Systems, ICMAS'98, Paris, France*, 1998, pp. 395–396.

[24] K. Cetnarowicz, G. Dobrowolski, M. Kisiel-Dorohinicki, and E. Nawarecki, Functional integrity of MAS through the dynamics of the agents' population, in *Proc. Third Int. Conf. Multi-Agent Systems, ICMAS'98, Paris, France*, 1998, pp. 405–406.

[25] B. Bouzy, An interaction-based model for situated agents, in *Proc. Third Int. Conf. Multi-Agent Systems, ICMAS'98, Paris, France, 1998, pp. 399-400.*

[26] R. Foisel, V. Chevrier, and J. Haton, Modeling adaptive organizations, in *Proc. Third Int. Conf. Multi-Agent Systems, ICMAS'98, Paris, France, 1998, pp. 427-428.*

[27] C. Unsal, *Self-Organization in Large Populations of Mobile Robots,* MSc Thesis in Electrical Engineering, Virginia Polytechnic, 1993.

[28] A. da Costa and G. Bittencourt, Dynamic social knowledge: a cognitive multi-agent system cooperation strategy, in *Proc. Third Int. Conf. Multi-Agent Systems, ICMAS'98, Paris, France,* 1998, pp. 415-416.

[29] H. Takeda, K. Iwata, M. Takaai, A. Sawada, and T. Nishida, An ontology-based cooperative environment for real-world agents, in *Proc. Second Int. Conf. Multi-Agent Systems, ICMAS'96, Kyoto, Japan,* 1996, pp. 353-360.

[30] K. Kuwabara, Meta-Level control of coordination protocols, in *Proc. Second Int. Conf. Multi-Agent Systems, ICMAS'96, Kyoto, Japan,* 1996, pp. 165-172.

[31] T. Ohko, K. Hiraki, and Y. Anzai, Reducing communication load on contract net by case-based reasoning: extension with directed contract and forgetting, in *Proc. Second Int. Conf. Multi-Agent Systems, ICMAS'96, Kyoto, Japan,* 1996, pp. 244-251.

[32] Y. Ye, How much should an agent know what other agents are doing in a cooperative team? in *Proc. Third Int. Conf. Multi-Agent Systems, ICMAS'98, Paris, France,* 1998, pp. 475-476.

[33] S. Sen, S. Roychowdhury, and N. Arora, Effects of local information on group behavior, in *Proc. Second Int. Conf. Multi-Agent Systems, ICMAS'96, Kyoto, Japan,* 1996, pp. 315-321.

[34] F. Ygge and H. Akkermans, Power load management as a computational market, in *Proc. Second Int. Conf. Multi-Agent Systems, ICMAS'96, Kyoto, Japan,* 1996, pp. 393-400.

[35] A.E. Engwirda, M.R. Hitchings, Lj.B. Vlacic, and A. Sattar, Population cooperative autonomous agents: preliminary consideration, in *Proc. 8th IFAC/IFORS/IMACS/IFIP/Symposium on Large Scale Systems: Theory and Applications, Patras, Greece,* 1998, Vol. II, pp. 1138-1143.

[36] P. Davis, Future torque, *The Road Ahead, RACQ,* Oct./Nov. 1998.

[37] M. Bouzid and A. Mouaddib, Cooperative uncertain temporal reasoning for distributed transportation scheduling, in *Proc. Third Int. Conf. Multi-Agent Systems, ICMAS'98, Paris, France,* 1998, pp. 397-398.

[38] A. Namatame and S. Ohno, Learning social behaviors in a society of economic agents, in *Proc. Second Int. Conf. Multi-Agent Systems, ICMAS'96, Kyoto, Japan,* 1996, p. 451.

[39] E. Le Strugeon and R. Mandiau, Flexible behaviors for context adaptive multi-agent organizations, in *Proc. Second Int. Conf. Multi-Agent Systems, ICMAS'96, Kyoto, Japan,* 1996, p. 458.

[40] O. Simonin, J. Ferber, and V. Decugis, Performance analysis in collective systems, in *Proc. Third Int. Conf. Multi-Agent Systems, ICMAS'98, Paris, France,* 1998, pp. 469-470.

[41] R. Foisel, V. Chevrier, and J. Haton, Improving global coherence by adaptive organization in a multi-agent system, in *Proc. Second Int. Conf. Multi-Agent Systems, ICMAS'96, Kyoto, Japan,* 1996, p. 435.

[42] N. Ono and K. Fukumoto, Multi-agent reinforcement learning: a modular approach, in *Proc. Second Int. Conf. Multi-Agent Systems, ICMAS'96, Kyoto, Japan,* 1996, pp. 252-258.

[43] J. Liu and K. Sycara, Multiagent coordination in tightly coupled task scheduling, in *Proc. Second Int. Conf. Multi-Agent Systems, ICMAS'96, Kyoto, Japan,* 1996, pp. 181-188.

[44] L. Ekenberg, Modelling decentralized decision making, in *Proc. Second Int. Conf. Multi-Agent Systems, ICMAS'96, Kyoto, Japan,* 1996, pp. 64-71.

[45] S. Fujita and V. Lesser, Centralized task distribution in the presence of uncertainty and time deadlines, in *Proc. Second Int. Conf. Multi-Agent Systems, ICMAS'96, Kyoto, Japan,* 1996, pp. 87-94..

[46] H. Parunak, A. Ward, and J. Sauter, A systematic market approach to distributed constraint problems, in *Proc. Third Int. Conf. Multi-Agent Systems, ICMAS'98, Paris, France,* 1998, pp. 455-456.

[47] D. Neiman and V. Lesser, Comparing coordination and repair strategies in a distributed scheduling system, in *Proc. Second Int. Conf. Multi-Agent Systems, ICMAS'96, Kyoto, Japan,* 1996, p. 452.

[48] G. Legg, *RFID Tags Connect Smart Cars to Smart Highways, EDN,* pp. 33-36, 1994.

[49] H. Keller, The German part in European research programmes Prometheus and Drive/ATT, in *Proc. Transportation Research, Part A, Policy and Practice,* Vol. 28A, pp. 483-493, 1994.

[50] M. Fujita and K. Kageyama, An open architecture for robot entertainment, in *Proc. Autonomous Agents 97,* pp. 435-442.

[51] M.R. Hitchings, A.E. Engwirda, Lj.B. Vlacic, and M. Kajitani, Two sensor based obstacle avoidance for autonomous vehicles, in *Proc. 3rd IFAC Symp. Intelligent Autonomous Vehicles, Spain,* 1998, Vol. I, pp. 155-160.

[52] L. Vlacic, M. Hitchings, M. Kajitani, and C. Kanamori, Cooperative autonomous road robots, in *Proc. Fifth Int. Conf. Control, Automation, Robotics and Vision, ICARCV'98, Singapore*, 1998, pp. 335–339.

[53] A. Engwirda, *ICSL Technical Report 21: Encoded Beacon Protocol*. Intelligent Control Systems Laboratory, Griffith University, 1998.

[54] A. Engwirda, *ICSL Technical Report 22: Radio Packet Controller Protocol*. Intelligent Control Systems Laboratory, Griffith University, 1998.

[55] A. Engwirda, *ICSL Technical Report 23: Multi-lane Intersection Algorithm*. Intelligent Control Systems Laboratory, Griffith University, 1998.

[56] M.R. Hitchings, Distances Tracking Control for Autonomous Vehicles, Masters thesis, to be submitted to the faculty of Griffith University, Australia, 1999.

[57] J. Doran, Social simulation, agents and artificial societies, in *Proc. Third Int. Conf. Multi-Agent Systems, ICMAS'98, Paris, France*, 1998, pp. 4–5.

CHAPTER 13

Expert Systems in Process Diagnosis and Control

D. POPOVIC
University of Bremen, Germany

1 INTRODUCTION

Artificial intelligence has been successfully applied in solving complex engineering problems that cannot be mathematically defined in a simple way. Such problems are especially found in the automated diagnosis and control of industrial plants, where numerous process parameters and external influences hinder the building of the mathematical model of the plant, so that the plant monitoring, supervision, and control are primarily based on *heuristic knowledge* and the field experience of plant operators. In the following, after describing the typical methods of applied artificial intelligence [38], their use in the design of *knowledge-based systems* for process diagnostics and control will be described, along with the software tools available.

Artificial intelligence (AI) is a relatively new science and technology as compared with the well-established engineering sciences, so that its applications are at an initial stage, at least as far as the management and control of industrial plants are concerned [37]. Initially, it was viewed as the activity area of computer scientists dealing with the knowledge acquisition, structuring, storing, processing, and retrieval required for solving cognition, classification, and other high-level problems such as speech and video data processing, scene analysis, natural language understanding, and so on. In order to solve such problems, AI borrows operational tools from such disciplines as *formal logic*, *predicate calculus*, *graph theory*, *theory of systems*, etc., shaped in the past century by Georg Boole, Gottrob Frege, Bertrand Russel, Emil Post, Alfred Tarski, and others.

Yet the most important viewpoint, accepted by the experts in the 1960s, was that intelligent problem solving should rely on the expert *domain knowledge*, stored within an AI system, and on the *search methods* used for finding the problem solution, based on some observational data. Soon, a variety of methods for the representation of knowledge and for solution search in AI systems were proposed, and a large number of application areas of AI were identified, such as

- *Natural language processing* (language analysis and language understanding)
- *Pattern recognition* (recognition of shapes and objects, based on acquired acoustic or visual patterns)
- *Computer vision* (image data processing for image analysis and image understanding)
- *Intelligent robotics* (trajectory planning for autonomous robots for avoiding obstacles based on image and scene perception and understanding, goal pursuit, etc.)
- *Expert systems* for problem solving by human expert, such as *systems monitoring*; *event prediction*; *systems diagnosis*; *systems repair and maintenance*; *plan generation*; *decision support*; *operator training and instruction*; *programming support*; *systems simulation and control*.

Due to their increasing application in the different branches of science and engineering, expert systems have become the best-known problem solving tools, offering a user-friendly interface and a transparent explanation component, as well as the possibility to automatically build, revise, and maintain large knowledge bases.

2 AI METHODS

Application of artificial intelligence in solving problems in different areas of human activity [49] relies on methods of:

- Knowledge representation
- Problem definition
- Automated reasoning
- Solution search
- Machine learning
- Knowledge acquisition

2.1 Knowledge Representation

Methods of knowledge representation deal with the way in which the facts and the rules of a specific knowledge domain are to be optimally structured and stored for *symbolic processing* [43]. For knowledge representation in artificial intelligence, generally a set of *syntactic* and *semantic* conventions is used for the description of *something*. The *syntactic conventions* specify the rules for arrangement of symbols in *expressions* belonging to the selected knowledge representation method, and the *semantic conventions* specify the way the expressions should be *interpreted*, that is, the way in which *meaning* should be extracted from the expressions. Consequently, knowledge representation is more than an automatic encoding of facts in the sense of their *encryption*. Instead, it is a *content-oriented* knowledge codification. In AI practice, by knowledge representation one primarily understands the representation of *declarative knowledge* rather than the representation of *procedural* knowledge. The knowledge is stored in the *knowledge base* using production rules, structural objects, predicate logic, and frames as knowledge representation methods.

Production rules as knowledge representation formalisms are borrowed from the *theory of formal grammar* and from the *theory of automata*. In AI the rules are known as *condition–action rules* or as *situation–action rules* because they encode the empirical associations between the patterns of facts and the related actions to be carried out. This is done by the *rule interpreter*, working on the rule set present in the *production memory*. For this reason, the resulting knowledge-based systems using the production memory are called *production systems*. In such systems, beside the domain knowledge, also the *meta-knowledge* is represented by *meta-rules* that are the *domain-free rules* required for the control of reasoning process through *reasoning about the rules*, for instance, by reasoning about the next set of rules to be interpreted.

In the early expert systems, knowledge was by preference represented using production rules. A relatively simple inference engine was sufficient for rule interpretation because the problems to be solved were relatively simple. Later, the problems became too complex to be solved using simple production rules. Structure- and function-based diagnostic reasoning was required.

Structured objects are knowledge representation forms based on *nodes* and *arcs* for structuring the knowledge. These are well known from *graph theory*. The *concepts* and the *relations* (i.e., the *objects* and the related *descriptors*) are placed in the nodes, whose *interrelationship* is traced by the interconnecting links. In this way, for example, *semantic nets* are built to represent the knowledge.

Predicate logic is a knowledge representation formalism based on *predicate calculus*, where propositions contain variables whose values determine the final (TRUE or FALSE) value of the propositions.

Due to limitations of semantic nets as knowledge representation tools, alternative structures and semantic notations have been introduced, such as *frames* that group information in terms of a record of *slots*, replacing the network nodes. Data structures represented by frames are *standard situations*. Objects, represented by frames, are *typical* objects of a *class of objects*, that is, they are the *prototypes* of an object *class*.

Structured objects and production rules are appropriate when *forward chaining* is used. Frames are more suitable for the implementation of *model-fitting approaches* that search for the *best match* of data and the current hypothesis, leading to the best decisions regarding the next steps to be made in the solution search.

Once the knowledge is stored in the knowledge base, it can be used for problem solving in the related expert domain. However, after a longer period, the initially stored knowledge may need updating by deleting invalid knowledge chunks and by adding new ones. In this way, the knowledge, once stored within the system, is maintained.

2.2 Problem Definition

In order to solve a given problem using the knowledge stored in the knowledge base, the problem itself has to be defined, that is, it has to be represented in an adequate form. In addition, an appropriate *solution method* has to be selected. The most common approach to problem definition is the use of *state-space problem representation*, which defines the problem in the *solution space* by defining

- Its *initial state*.
- The *terminal state* or the *final goal* of the problem solution.
- *State transformations*, or the operations acting on the current state stepwise forward, starting with the initial state, in order to reach the *goal state*. This is known as *data-driven strategy* or *forward chaining*. Alternatively, operations acting on the current state stepwise backward, starting with the goal state, in order to reach the initial state, are known as a *goal-driven strategy*, or *backward chaining*.

For state transformation, there is available a wide spectrum of solution search methods, known as *problem solving paradigms*. Examples of such methods are formal logic, constraint propagation, means–ends analysis, generate-and-test methods, search methods, and heuristic methods.

2.3   Automated Reasoning

Reasoning with the stored knowledge, in the sense of classical logic, is the process of inferring *conclusions* from the given *premises* [30]. Thus, the efficiency of the selected reasoning method depends strongly on the method used for knowledge representation. In any case, the methods of *automated reasoning*, because they rely on the principles of mathematical logic, are optimally implementable using *logic programming*. In knowledge-based diagnostic and control systems, the most common reasoning approaches are heuristic reasoning and fuzzy reasoning.

In automated reasoning, the process of inference is most frequently carried out by the *inference engine* or by the *rule interpreter* incorporated into the knowledge-based system.

Closely related to the nature of the stored knowledge are two basic reasoning categories:

- *Deep reasoning*, related to the representation of the *deep knowledge*, consisting of *structural* and *behavioral* system description.
- *Shallow reasoning*, related to the representation of "*shallow*" *knowledge*, consisting of system description by a set of *heuristic chunks*.

Real-time problems to be solved involve sequences of events and are thus *time related*. For representation of knowledge involving such events, *temporal logic* is used, and for the solution of time-related problems, *temporal reasoning*.

Basically, the application of problem solving paradigms is viewed as a pattern classification process in which the most probable solutions, out of a set of possible solutions, are selected, for instance, by *pattern matching* with the hypothesized patterns belonging to the set of possible solutions. To find the problem solution, hypothesized patterns at each stage of the solution search are evaluated by the *rule interpreter*, and chained as stimulus-driven (*forward chaining*), or as goal-driven (*backward chaining*). Forward chaining is appropriate when the inference is required to produce a decision based on a large set of collected observation data. Backward chaining is appropriate when less observational data is available and a conclusion is to be produced by establishing a hypothesis that has to be approved or rejected.

In rule-based systems, forward chaining triggers only the rules in which the data in the working memory of the system matches the IF parts of the rule. Each triggered rule, in turn, can generate new conditions from the conclusions deduced from its THEN parts of the rule that match the IF parts of the other rules, so that the number of conditions met steadily increases. Forward chaining proceeds recursively and terminates when the desired goal has been reached, or when the set of relevant rules is exhausted.

When the hypothesized patterns are evaluated by backward chaining, for instance, the process of chaining starts with the test of a given initial hypothesis by matching it with the available facts, and proceeds backward until the conditions necessary for its proof have been found. The recursive process, proceeding in the way described, ends with either proving or negating the initial hypothesis, or by reaching a dead-end.

In diagnostic expert systems, backward chaining is a more efficient solution search approach than is forward chaining as control strategy for problem solving. Nevertheless, a combination of both types of chaining approaches is also used for the optimization of the search procedure.

Forward and *backward reasoning* are important for the application of forward and backward chaining because the nature of reasoning characterizes the problem solving method, whereas the forward and backward chaining only shows the way in which the rules are triggered, that is, which side of the rule will be matched and which one activated.

In diagnostic expert systems the direct pattern matching approach to problem solving is used. In it, the inference engine searches for the patterns, out of a set of precompiled patterns belonging to the most frequent malfunction, that match the pattern to be diagnosed. Recently, attempts have been made to generate automatically in model-based diagnostic systems possible malfunction patterns that will speed up the search process to establish, using the *establish–refine method*, what malfunction is currently present. The method is based on establishing, at each search level, some hypothesis and refining it through the use of relevant knowledge at the neighboring lower search level.

In object- and frame-oriented expert systems, *object-oriented programming*, consists in storing in the same frame information both about the object and about the procedures associated with it. The stored procedures are triggered by incoming object-relevant data. This is especially appropriate for implementation of real-time expert systems for *on-line process diagnosis*, *plant data acquisition*, and *control*.

2.4   Solution Search Methods

Search methods are used to solve AI problems by exploring the solution space for possible solution paths leading to the goal state, whereby primarily the optimal problem solution or the optimal solution path is searched for [23]. This means that the optimal solution problem is equivalent to the path optimization problem. For this purpose various *search methods* have been proposed [20] such as blind search, brute-force search, breadth-first search, depth-first search, best-first search, bidirectional search, branch-and-bound search, A*, AO*, and B* search, and progressive deeping [35].

2.5   Machine Learning

Machine learning is the *automated learning process* of intelligent systems that enables a steady improvement of the system's behavior and problem solving efficiency [9]. The process of automated learning is required in the building phase of the system in which the system is trained how to solve the expert problems in the selected domain, as well as later, in the application phase, for learning through examples.

Learning paradigms can be classified according to their operational principles into *inductive* paradigms, *analytic* paradigms, *genetic* paradigms, and *connectionist* paradigms.

2.6   Knowledge Acquisition

Knowledge acquisition is an activity of knowledge engineering that is very important in the initial phase of system shaping for building the fundamental knowledge base, as well as in the application phase of the system for knowledge base updating [8]. To the domain knowledge to be initially acquired also belongs, in addition to the textbook knowledge of the domain, the related *heuristic* and the *meta-knowledge*, if available.

The development phase of knowledge acquisition includes the activities that precede the process of knowledge elicitation from domain experts, such as domain identification, domain knowledge conceptualization, knowledge formalization and encoding, and knowledge refinement and validation.

3 AI TECHNOLOGY

Computer technology, though originally developed for solving mathematical *routine problems*, has since its earliest development stage also been used for solving *intelligent problems*. However, entirely different computational procedures and different software tools are required for the optimal solution of these two essentially different categories of problems. For instance, in order to solve intelligent problems the computers have to support the *symbolic processing* of declarative knowledge by executing procedures written in *declarative form*. In addition, the users of such computers also like to have support for intelligent *man–machine dialog* in order to have a better internal view into the process of problem solution. Finally, for storing the voluminous knowledge on which the problem solving is based, AI-oriented computers need a large memory capacity. This was the motivation for developing new hardware and software technology that would meet the solution requirements of real-world problems in the various fields of science and engineering. For applications in engineering, the development of intelligent systems for process and production automation, in which the achievements of computer vision, pattern recognition, object tracking, robot trajectory planning, intelligent control, etc. are integrated, is of particular interest.

3.1 Expert Systems Technology

Expert systems technology is the most widely used AI technology for solving intelligent engineering problems. Expert systems, as knowledge-based systems for problem solving in specific knowledge domains, mimic the capabilities of human experts. As intelligent systems, they are capable, while solving the domain problem, of learning from the problem itself and in this way of extending their domain knowledge on-line, as the human expert is capable of doing. Fresh knowledge, learnt from the solved problems and stored in the knowledge base, does not cause any essential structural changes within the knowledge already stored, nor does it require any change in the structure of the expert system itself.

The *domain knowledge*, stored in the *knowledge base* of an expert system represents a collection of *facts*, belonging to the domain, and the *relations* between the facts. When solving a specific problem, the system primarily selects from the knowledge base the knowledge most closely related to the problem to be solved and processes it using its *inference engine*. Consequently, as shown in Figure 1, the minimal internal structure of an expert system includes two core components: the knowledge base and the inference engine. Additional system components such as the *explanation component, intelligent user interface, software interfaces, knowledge acquisition facility*, etc. only facilitate the usability of the system and extend the internal view into the system's operation.

The knowledge base is the principal part of the system and contains the domain knowledge elicited by the *knowledge engineer* from a human expert. In the majority of systems the knowledge is stored as a set of IF–THEN rules, so that the majority of knowledge-based systems are *rule-based systems* (or *production systems*). Associated with the knowledge base is the *database*, containing some supporting details, such as initial or default values, restrictions and limitations, parameter values, etc.

The *inference engine* is the executive software of the system that interprets the rules in view of the actual data collected by the observations and that controls the process of forward and/or backward rule chaining. In forward chaining, the IF part of the rule is tested and if it is TRUE the rule *fires*. In backward chaining the inference engine establishes a hypothesis on the THEN part of the rule and tests the IF part of the same rule for approval or disapproval of the established hypothesis. This is similar to the diagnostic approach of a medical doctor who first, on the basis

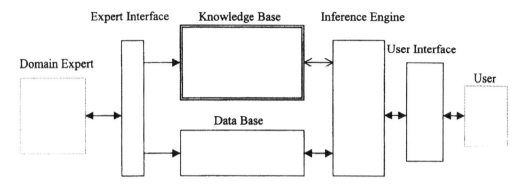

FIGURE 1
Internal expert system structure.

of observations (symptoms), establishes a disease hypothesis and then tries to approve it by taking into account additional observations.

For communication between the knowledge-based system and the user, the *user interface* is built into the system. The interface supports the man–machine dialog at a natural language level because the user is supposed to be an unskilled computer expert. A similar interface is built into the system for communication with the knowledge engineer, required in the phase of system building and during the acquisition of the initial system knowledge. This is known as the *knowledge acquisition interface.*

Expert systems technology is basically a software technology that is embedded into the basic computer software to enhance the intelligence of the computer system and to enable it to emulate the behavior and the capability of a human expert in a specific domain. For instance, when applied to monitoring and diagnosis of an industrial plant, expert system software can provide the plant supervising staff with the plant status data, optimally selected and adequately presented. Regarding process control, expert system software can establish the optimal operating conditions of the plant, even when such conditions cannot be analytically defined but must rather be estimated using the heuristic knowledge available. This situation is more frequent in industrial practice than is the situation where the optimality conditions can be analytically determined.

The wide application possibilities of expert systems in engineering sectors and their responsibility there has created the need for quality assurance of the *reliability, performance validity,* and *usability* of such systems as AI tools. The reliability aspects are of primary importance because the expert systems deal with *unreliable knowledge* about the plant and suffer from possible uncertainty in the process of reasoning.

It is much more difficult to estimate the performance validity of expert systems in the sense of knowing whether the domain knowledge stored in its knowledge base really represents the completed, conflict-free knowledge of the selected domain and whether the reasoning used in knowledge processing is adequate. O'Leary et al. [33] recommended that at least the following validation aspects should be considered:

- What should be validated?
- How is it to be validated?
- What validation procedures are to be used?
- When to validate?

- How to control the validation costs?
- How to cope with multiple results?

The best validation approach, representing *system verification*, was proposed by Jafar and Bahill [19]. This is an interactive approach in which the *validation program* interactively checks the consistency and completeness of the knowledge base. The approach points out the potential errors within the system. This, for instance, helps verify and validate the rules within a rule-based expert system.

3.2 Computing Technology

High-performance computers are needed for solving intelligent problems. Developments in single-processor computer systems and advances in communications technology, especially in high-speed bus systems, have enabled high-performance multiprocessor systems to be built. Parallel and distributed multiprocessor systems have been implemented with various internal architectures, data flow concepts, and operational principles, so that the building of *massively parallel* computer structures, known as *supercomputers*, was soon on the agenda. Developments in *parallel computer technology* have, again, had a considerable impact in intelligent image and voice data processing and in building intelligent systems for applications in industry.

At present, computer technology is rapidly approaching the theoretically possible limits of miniaturization. Further essential advances are expected from *optical computing technology*, with which higher density packages and higher computing performances are achievable. Enormous progress in this area has made optical computing technology a promising tool for building new high-performance computer architectures, high-speed computer interfaces, and high-density memories that have opened new perspectives for future artificial intelligence application. However, it will be some time before all-optical computers have been built and found their place in real applications. For the time being, the building of *hybrid optoelectronic systems* has become a technical reality in the sense that a number of modern massively parallel computers use optoelectronic architectures, at least as far as concerns data transfer within the systems. This possibility does not inhibit research in further miniaturization of electronic circuits.

Further revolutionary frontiers in computing technology are expected from *molecular computing*. Such computers mimic natural biological information processing systems and present a novel computational approach. Although the technology is in the early stage of development—only some proof-of-concept trials have been successful and no commercially available products have yet come out of research laboratories—molecular devices are increasingly maturing and promise to become the next favored technological products on the computer market. They will fundamentally change the implementation principles of intelligent systems.

The basic concept of molecular computing is more than two decades old, but its implementation seems to be taking much longer than was forecast. The most powerful encouragement has come from progress in DNA technology, which has shown how to implement some basic prototypes of computing elements. This has intensified efforts for the implementation of more advanced functional units. Apart from this, nothing technically applicable or commercially available is expected in the near future.

The computer technology that has entirely changed classical digital computing concepts is doubtless *neurocomputing technology*. Neural networks, implemented in this technology, represent versatile computational systems as intelligent systems with learning capabilities.

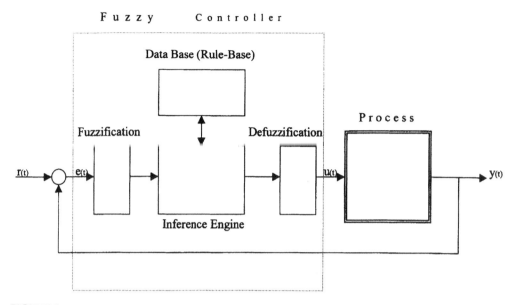

FIGURE 2
Fuzzy control.

Emulating the massive parallel neural structure of the brain, they consist of a number of simple computing elements, *artificial neurons* or *perceptrons*, mutually interconnected in a relatively extensive way with adjustable connection strengths. This is analogous to biological neural systems in which the interconnections between the *neuron bodies* are implemented as variable-resistance *dendrites*. In addition to this, the multilayer architecture adopted in building artificial neural networks represents reasonable copy of the architecture observed in biological neural systems. Such architecture enables the networks to solve complex intelligent problems, such as pattern recognition and classification, speech and speaker recognition, and image data compression. Typical of both artificial and biological neural systems is that they solve such problems in a direct way, that is, through connectionist learning rather than through involved mathematical computation. Here, the development of neural VLSI chips also opens enormous perspectives for solving real-time engineering problems using neurohardware.

Finally, the computing technology closest to the expert systems technology is the *fuzzy logic based technology* in which the fuzzy logic systems are implemented. Such systems are rule-based expert systems, mostly used in control engineering for implementation of *fuzzy logic controllers*. The core elements of these systems are like those of expert systems and include the *rule base*, the *inference engine*, and the *fuzzyfier* and *defuzzifier* as the interfacing components to the process to be controlled (Figure 2). Consequently, fuzzy logic controllers are seen as *real-time expert systems* in the control engineering domain.

3.3 System Interfacing

Intelligent systems, when employed in solving engineering problems, require at least the following interfaces:

- *Process interface*, for the collection of sensor and alarm data and for the control of external devices such as actuators, controllers, alarm announciators, digital displays, etc.

- *Software interfaces*, for data exchange between the AI software and the procedural software, for access to the internal computers and external data bases, etc
- *Man–machine interface*, required for communication in *natural language* between the user and the system.

The process interface problem is simplified when the sensor data is acquired at at higher rate than needed by the AI software. This is the case when the data is collected for plant monitoring and diagnostics. Here, the collected sensor data is stored in files that, when completed within a reading cycle, trigger the AI software for translation and processing actions, so that the problem of sensor data access becomes an internal software interface problem. A critical situation can arise when the collected sensor data is updated faster than the AI software can process it, in other words, when the dynamics of the process is faster than the processing speed of the intelligent system. In this case a *temporal database* has to be built in which individual sensor data are provided with marks of their collection times.

Interfacing to *procedural languages* is a crucial issue that involves a number of substantial difficulties. Integrating the AI software and the conventional software, however, increases the problem-solving capabilities of the intelligent system. This integration is unavoidable in intelligent control systems.

In the past, the problem of interfacing at programming language level has been solved by:

- Separation of procedural and declarative knowledge in distinct system modules.
- Building the large objects out of small ones by applying the *object-oriented approach* using frames.
- Standardization of software interfacing protocols.
- Multilevel organization of stored knowledge.
- Using the appropriate editing, debugging, and diagnostic utilities.
- Using the special functional software that establishes direct communication between two languages, for instance between the language C and the IF/Prolog [39].

An intelligent *man–machine interface* is required for greater transparency of system operation in terms of explanations to the user about how the system has achieved the proposed problem solution, as well as for *knowledge acquisition*, *updating*, and *maintenance*. In contemporary AI systems, the man–machine interface is mostly *menu-oriented*, facilitating the selection of desired functions and enabling a man–machine dialog related to the problem solution. To achieve this, it is required that:

- A *transparent* concept for consecutive selection and adequate use of menus is implemented.
- A *memo technique* for the easy formulation of requests, commands, and information is available.
- *Soft-touch* and *pen-active* graphic facilities for a comfortable dialog are provided.
- *Natural language* text and voice alternatives for printed and oral dialogue are integrated into the system.

3.4 Real-Time Expert Systems

The software requirements of real-time knowledge-based systems generally depend on the expected system response to external stimuli. Here, the system can be designed to behave like an *event-driven* system, "simultaneously" sensitive to all input signals, or like a system with a *just-in-time response* to the external real-time requirements [11]. Event-driven systems behavior is mandatory for immediate servicing of alarms, control, and other exceptional signals because asynchronous events demand asynchronous response, to be managed by parallel reasoning and parallel intelligent actions, implemented, for instance, through concurrent multitask execution. An alternative implementation would be to embed the knowledge-based system into the software of a conventional real-time system and to run the AI part of the system as a separate task under the control of the real-time operating system. The issue was discussed by Morizet-Mahoudeaux [29] in connection with the development of an on-board real-time expert system for the expert control of a vehicle. There, an alternative approach was proposed that lies between embedding the AI software in real-time software and embedding real-time software in AI software. In real-time knowledge-based systems, in addition to the *external* events, triggering by the occurrence of some internal actions may be required. Such *internal* asynchronous activation occurrences might be the so called *demons* that, when activated, have to be immediately served.

The most difficult problem to be solved when designing a real-time AI system is how to reason in real-time. Some possible answers, at least when reasoning about the collected sensor data, would be to implement one of the following approaches:

- A "snapshot" of plant data should be taken as an instant knowledge base for immediate inference by data pattern matching with a given data base.
- Instead of exact mathematical models, *heuristic models* of the process dynamics could be used, based on the "action–time-delay–expected result" principle. This allows the inference engine, after an initial response, to recommend further actions by involving new related rules and procedures, or the inference rules themselves may contain explicit directives as to which rules to apply next.
- Appropriate *meta-knowledge* should be used that, in a given situation, invokes a restricted part of the domain knowledge, strongly relevant to the required real-time reasoning.

Ingrand, Georgeff, and Rao [18] have proposed that *situated reasoning* be used for reasoning in real time. This approach is particularly successful in process supervision and control, where the AI system receives information asynchronously and, based on this information and the knowledge stored in knowledge base, assesses the regularity or the exceptionality of the process status. In order to manage the execution of AI programs under stringent real-time constraints, the following features have to be included into the system:

- *Restricted reaction time*, which is required to prevent the secondary effects of identified failures on the rest of the system.
- *Continuous operation*, which guarantees that the system is still sensitive to new failures while processing the previous one because the monitored real-time system is failure tolerant to a higher degree.
- *Procedural knowledge representation and processing*, because the sensor data are to be repeatedly collected and processed.
- *Learning and truth maintenance* facilities, in the sense that the intelligent system should be capable of learning new facts and relationships between the facts and of forgetting knowledge that has become obsolete or invalid because of changes in the monitored system and in the environment.
- *Multitasking and concurrency*, required for the proper handling of interrupt signals as asynchronous messages from the monitored system and requiring a prompt action.

- *Reactive, goal-directed response*, because the system should firmly follow the main goal (fault isolation) and still be available for further alarm messages.
- *Reflexive reasoning* that adapts the system focus in response to changes in its environment and correspondingly modifies the execution priorities of the related procedures in order to meet the changing requirements.
- *Focus of attention capability* that gives priority to the invoked response servicing procedures according to their response time in order to prevent unwanted delays.
- *Cooperation with the plant operator* to permitting that, in some defined situations, the operator may override the decisions of the system.

4 AI TOOLS

Early artificial intelligence systems were built in a straightforward way using the available high-level programming languages. The amount of programming required for this kind of system implementation, which starts from scratch, was enormous because all components of a new system to be built had to be programmed again. This was the common practice for some time, until the idea of using special *software development tools* for knowledge-based system building was born. Such tools [16] have essentially facilitated the required development work of the user and given the impetus to the AI system vendors to implement and launch on the marketplace, as support aids to the AI system developers, AI programming languages, expert systems shells, and development environments.

4.1 AI Programming Languages

The first efforts to create software tools for intelligent system building were made in improving the high-level programming languages to better meet the requirements of experts in this field. The improved languages were intended to help the direct presentation of *declarative knowledge* and the implementation of *methods of reasoning*. The first special languages introduced for this purpose were the AI languages LISP (LISt Processing) and PROLOG (PROgramming in LOGic). Later, they were joined by OPS 5 (Official Production Systems 5) and Smalltalk.

LISP was originally designed for symbolic formula translation using *lambda calculus* [46], so that the basic *syntactic elements* of LISP are symbolic expressions, appropriate to represent both *data* and *procedures*. The expressions can basically be *atoms* or *lists*, indicating that the language was originally developed for list processing. A great advantage is that in this language both numbers and symbols can be used to represent the knowledge. Currently, a large number of LISP versions (dialects) are implemented in various well-known computer systems.

PROLOG was developed for solving problems defined in terms of mathematical logic using the *proposition calculus* [6]. For knowledge representation, the concept of *objects*, belonging to defined *classes*, is used and this makes PROLOG suitable for the implementation of rule-based systems, primarily because the required inference engine is built into it. This enables the language, using backward-chaining and backtracking, to automatically draw conclusions, based on the *mathematical theory of relations*. PROLOG has also been implemented in many different computer systems and in many dialects.

OPS-5 is a programming language especially designed for building production systems [7]. For problem solving, the language uses forward-chaining and pattern matching strategy, and enables management of *files* and *default values*, manipulation of *working memory*, and generation of *actions* for new rule building in the process of program execution.

Smalltalk is an object-oriented language [15] elaborated by adapting the programming language SIMULA for the presentation and processing of declarative knowledge using:

- *Objects*, as dynamically allocated memory cells containing a collection of named and indexed instance variables designating individual objects.
- *Methods*, as preprogrammed answers to the messages sent to the objects, being analogous to the preprogrammed procedures.
- *Messages* and *control structures* that trigger the methods by specifying the destinations (*receivers*) and *message patterns* designating the program execution control to be undertaken by the *addressed receiver*.
- *Classes* and *inheritances*, as *generalized objects*, individual object being classes having the same *instances*, whereby the names, values, and methods can be inherited.
- *User interfaces* as programming features that can be exploited to operate input/output facilities of the PC using keyboard, mouse, and screen.

4.2   Expert System Shells

An expert system can solve intelligent problems in a specific domain using the specific domain knowledge stored in its knowledge base. Furthermore, the same system can solve problems in another, new specific domain after it has been provided with the knowledge of the new domain. This is because the expert capability of the system is predetermined by the domain knowledge stored in its knowledge base and not by the internal system structure. For instance, the inference engine or the rule interpreter of the system only helps interpret the stored rules when solving a given problem in any specific domain. This was decisive for initiating work on building *general* expert systems with *no* predetermined specific domain in which they should be able to solve intelligent problems. The knowledge base of such systems should simply be *empty*, and could later be filled with the required specific domain knowledge. The systems are known as *domain-free expert systems* or *expert system shells*.

Having an inference engine built in and a suitable user interface, expert system shells are of direct use as expert system developing tools, even for users unskilled in programming. Using an expert system shell, expert systems for specific knowledge domains can easily be developed as rapid prototypes. This has originally been applied in building the diagnostic expert system MYCIN, for which the expert system shell EMYCIN (*Empty MYCIN*) was used.

Because of their wide popularity, the development of expert system shells has made remarkable progress. A large number of shells, having different internal structure and based on different operating principles, are commercially available, such as rule-based shells, object-oriented shells, inductive learning shells, and domain-specific shells.

Rule-based Shells.   Rule-based shells are typical *production systems*, in which the domain knowledge is stored in terms of *production rules*. The shells, in addition to the inference engine, also contain a *working memory* and a *control structure* for guiding the *goal-finding strategy* in the process of finding a solution to the given problem. The majority of rule-based shells are small-scale (500 to 1000 rules), low-cost software packages designed to run on personal computers. Although made for nonprogrammers, a number of commercially available shells are most frequently equipped with the AI languages, preferably with LISP or PROLOG, giving skilled users the opportunity to write additional application programs.

Typical rule-based shells are:

- **ENVISAGE**, an expert system shell with the rules defined as logical assertions.

- **ES/P ADVISOR**, a shell for rapid prototyping of expert systems on PC/XT.
- **EXSYS 3.0**, a large-scale shell for handling up to 5000 rules using both forward and backward reasoning. It compiles the rules, added to the system on-line, and checks their consistency with the rules already stored in the knowledge base. The shell is a flexible, menu-oriented, and scroll-served system.
- **INSIGHT 2+**, a low-price shell for prototyping production systems with forward and backward reasoning strategy. In the shell, the facts are presented as attribute–value pairs.
- **XSYS**, a rapid prototyping shell for building rule-based systems, launched by California Intelligence.

Object-oriented Shells.   In object-oriented shells the knowledge is represented in *descriptive* form through *primary objects* and the procedures through *secondary* objects. In the shells, individual objects are encapsulated so that the shell structure is *modular*, based on frames and semantic nets. When using the shells, the user has to concentrate on description of objects and on the relationships among them, rather than on writing the rules or developing program procedures.

Typical object-oriented shells are the **KEE** and **Knowledge Kraft**.

Inductive Learning Shells.   Inductive learning shells are able to acquire knowledge by *learning from examples*. The shells directly generate the rules from given examples in a knowledge domain, so that the user, instead of writing the rules, can simply concentrate on the selection of appropriate examples to be used for teaching the shell. The main drawback of inductive learning shells, however, is the fact that such shells are restricted in the classes of problems they can solve.

Examples of inductive learning shells are:

- **EXPERT EASE**, an expert system shell that automatically generates the rules and the corresponding decision trees, defining the problem-solving procedure.
- **EXPERT ONE**, a small-scale, low-cost inductive learning shell running on the IBM PC. It is able to accept up to 1000 examples from which the shell builds internal matrices and stores there the knowledge learnt.
- **1ST CLASS**, a shell that automatically synthesizes the rules and decision trees from the given examples.
- **KDS**, an inductive learning shell that generates the rules from examples and enables direct interfacing to the external programs.
- **TIMM**, The Intelligent Machine Model, a development of General Research Corp. for personal computers and mainframes, capable of accommodating 500 to 5000 rules. The shell supports a framelike knowledge representation from which it draws conclusions and generates the rules by analogue reasoning. It is also provided with an interface facility for access to the external database files.
- **VP-EXPERT**, a small-scale advanced inductive expert shell in which the facts are represented as attribute–value pairs. The shell is able to build generalized rules from database records.

Domain-specific Shells.   Some commercially available shells are restricted in their applicability to a small number of particular expert domains. The restriction, however, is compensated by the possibility of rapid prototyping of expert systems for such domains using the domain-specific shells, this being the main reason for their wide popularity. Some typicl domain-specific shells for *systems diagnostics* and *systems control* such as **FIS**, **MIND**, **DEDALE**, etc. are presented below.

4.3 Expert System Development Environments

Expert system shells are appropriate for knowledge-based system designers having less programming experience but with expertise in engineering problem solving. However, system designers with a profound background in programming would prefer to tailor their AI application software directly using the shell services and the techniques of AI programming languages. For this purpose, *system development environments* have been developed, allowing the user to mix the programming paradigms—rules, frames, and object-oriented formations in the system under development. For instance, the expert systems shell **Personal Consultant+** enables mixing of rules with frames. A number of typical system development environments have been launched on the marketplace:

- **ART**, a versatile development tool in which the rules and frames can be combined. It is primarily a forward chaining system with an advanced user-defined pattern watching technique, based on the enhanced indexing scheme of OPS 5. ART allows the procedures to be used in association with objects in the sense of *object-oriented programming*. When solving a problem, ART considers multiple possible solutions in parallel, until the best solution is found, or, if this is not possible, until the solution constraints are violated (*hypothetical nonmonotonic reasoning*). By compiling the frame-based knowledge simultaneously with the relational knowledge into what are called *discrimination* networks, the system can generate software that can meet real-time requirements.
- **KEE**, a shell for applications in the monitoring and diagnosis of process control systems. It is provided with a reach set of graphics facilities including the possibility of *hierarchical objects modeling* and a variety of reasoning and problem search methods such as hypothetical reasoning, forward and backward chaining, etc.
- **LOOPS**, a development tool that combines procedures, rules and object-oriented and data-oriented programming. In the tool, data structures and rules are represented as hierarchically ordered objects, whereby rules can call other rules directly, or by sending messages. Using LOOPS, systems with up to 1000 rules can be generated.
- **POPLOG**, an interactive development environment that supports the mixing of PROLOG, Common LISP, and POP-11 programs.

5 APPLICATIONS

Knowledge-based systems have been widely applied at almost all levels of process and plant automation, from monitoring and single-loop control to top-end production and enterprise planning and supervision [50, 51]. The purpose of the following pages is to highlight the applications in monitoring, diagnostics, and control, primarily using real-time expert technology [40].

5.1 Systems Diagnosis

To detect the possible failures of system elements and/or malfunctions of the plant itself, industrial plants require permanent monitoring and supervision of their performance. This is usually done by plant operators, powerfully supported by automated plant monitoring and diagnostic systems. Such systems watch continuously for the normality of plant operation; discover, predict, and locate the failures within the plant; and recommend actions to be taken by operators in critical situations. For this purpose a large number of plant supervision and monitoring methods, failure detection and location techniques, and failure diagnosis strategies have been developed, based on system knowledge, heuristics, and field experience. A short survey is presented below.

5.1.1 Strategies for Diagnosis. There are two basic strategic approaches in the failure diagnosis of engineering systems: the *direct approach* and the *model-based approach*. The direct approach relies mainly on the general knowledge of the system under diagnosis and on the heuristic knowledge of the field personnel servicing the system. The model-based approach uses a model (qualitative or exact) of the system behavior to simulate its possible failures, or directly uses the *failure models* of the system [28].

Knowledge-based diagnostic and control software, superimposed on the conventional computer software, has substantially enhanced the intelligence of computer systems. Such systems, applied in industrial plant monitoring, are able to identify the operational status of the plant, to detect its failures, to predict the possible critical states of the plant, and to help the plant operator undertake the appropriate control steps to avoid them [31, 41]. Furthermore, using knowledge-based control software, known as *expert control software*, optimal plant operating conditions can be determined, based on partial mathematical models of the plant and on heuristic knowledge about the time-behavior of the plant.

The knowledge base of diagnostic expert systems most frequently consists of a collection of *pattern-to-action rules* or of *observation–hypothesis* pairs, representing the *shallow* or *surface knowledge* about the system under diagnosis. To select the observation–hypothesis pairs that best match the test situation, and to invoke the corresponding hypothesis, the precompiled knowledge about the system under observation stored in the knowledge base will be matched with the test results on the system. If no pattern stored in the knowledge base matches the results of a system test, no diagnostic hypothesis can be established, and thus no solution of the problem can be found. To avoid such situations, the "deep" knowledge related to the system to be tested is required. This knowledge is stored in the knowledge base and increases the ability of expert system to deal with even more complex problems because the "deeper" system knowledge helps to automatically generate any diagnostic pattern needed. On the other hand, the precompiled or "shallow" knowledge, although not having a complete set of diagnostic patterns needed for diagnosis, still helps to find the solution of the problem in a much shorter time than the "deep" knowledge. This is because the compiled knowledge is used directly—it does not need the extensive calculations that the "deep" knowledge needs. Consequently, the "best" diagnostic expert system should contain an optimal mix of "shallow" and "deep" knowledge of the system to be tested. This means that it should have a reasonable number of "precompiled" knowledge patterns, such as the observation–hypothesis pairs, and partial system models required for generation of missing diagnostic patterns. A similar situation is found in the activities of a human expert. When diagnosing a system, the human expert initially applies skilled knowledge (or field experience) for quick isolation of at least the most typical system failures. Only in some "special" situations, not belonging to routine work, does the human expert makes uses of "deep" system knowledge, that is, the interrelations between the system variables and system parameters.

Diagnostic expert systems with mixed "deep" and "shallow" stored knowledge are already commercially available. For instance, in **IDM** (Integrated Diagnostic Model), an expert system for the diagnosis of mechanical and electrical devices, the *experimental* ("shallow") and *fundamental* ("deep") knowledge are mixed. Experimental knowledge has been collected through empirical observations on various systems under test, and the fundamental knowledge has been picked up from the textbooks and device handbooks. It thus includes *structural* and *functional* descriptions of the devices to be tested. Typical of IDM is that it uses two inference engines, one for each type of knowledge base, integrated via an *executor* (with its own knowledge base) to a unique expert system.

Relying on the achievement of *qualitative physics* and *qualitative process theory* [13], some physical phenomena, such as mechanical movement, fluid flow, or energy transformation, can be analyzed using formal relations, such as a set of basic deductions and the rules of their utilization. In this case the use of the related differential equations is not necessary because in the qualitative theory of physical processes the *local* solutions of the exact equations in terms of inequalities in the solution space are of interest, rather than quantitative values of the exact solution. Thus, instead of equations, only *qualitative proportionalities* are used and the dynamic effects within the process are ignored. Here, the main interest is concentrated on the resulting *directional changes* in the states of process variables and not on the entire "trajectory" of the process variables.

5.1.2 Diagnostic Expert Systems.
System diagnosis from its very beginning has been the most successful application of expert systems. The earliest successful implementations of such systems, **INTERNIST** and **MYCIN**, were in this field of application. These two systems were used for patient disease diagnosis, but soon thereafter expert systems for the automated diagnosis of mechanical, electrical, electronic, and other engineering systems were produced, as well as systems for intelligent plant monitoring and supervision. Nevertheless, the widest engineering applications are in equipment testing and troubleshooting, examples of which are presented below.

FIS (Fault Isolation System) was developed for diagnosis of units under test (UUT), for which a detailed structural and functional description is available [10]. The description is used for the generation of best test recommendations, for analysis of test data, and for fault identification. For support of knowledge acquisition, FIS is provided with a *library of descriptions* containing *generic descriptions* of most common system modules to be tested. This knowledge, represented by *casual unit models*, helps to structurally and functionally describe the UUT concerned, and to reason qualitatively about the UUT, without requiring a simulation run for this purpose.

To minimize the *total test costs* for failure analysis, FIS, after some essential tests have been made on the UUT, computes the probability of each fault hypothesis. The *probabilistic reasoning* methods available within the system facilitate the optimal selection of test setups, test points, and the parameters to be measured during the test. This guarantees the maximum information gain at minimum cost. The costs can be minimized even further by storing the specific knowledge about the *a priori* failure probabilities for individual UUTs. This knowledge is to be updated by the system after every test of a unit.

MIND (Machine for Intelligent Diagnosis) is an expert system for efficient failure detection and isolation in electronic equipment and for the minimization of their *mean time to repair* (MTTR). To reduce the failure search process, MIND combines knowledge about the system to be tested with its failure statistics. In the test, MIND first hypothesizes the possible system symptoms, based on test and simulation results using the behavioristic model of the system, and subsequently tries to detect the failures using software components such as a *diagnostic rules base*, consisting of set of rules for failures isolation; *causal maps*, as structural and function descriptions of the unit under test; and an *inference engine*, for selection and interpretation of relevant rules stored.

To achieve the minimization of MTTR, MIND optimally splits up the failure isolation problems into a set of smaller subproblems to be solved separately. Based on the test results, the relevant rules in the *diagnostic rule database* are activated, and the search process is decomposed into three levels: *system level, subsystems level,* and *elements level.* At each level, for acceleration of failure detection **and failure isolation** through the selection of the most probable initial failure hypothesis, the *history* of its failure is used.

DEDALE is a troubleshooting expert system for analogue circuits in which the *functional knowledge* of the circuits under test is used, along with the *heuristic knowledge* about past tests of similar circuits. Functional knowledge of circuits includes:

- *Factual knowledge,* related to the circuit elements as generic objects and stored in a frame system, and used for diagnosis through frame instantiation.
- *Structural knowledge,* related to the most essential technological and topological aspects of the circuits.
- *Inferential knowledge,* related to the troubleshooting strategy and the strategy of selecting the most probable failure hypothesis out of a set of possible hypotheses.
- *Procedural knowledge,* consisting of (i) *influence analysis* for determining the most probable function causing the circuit faulty output; (ii) *priority analysis* based on experience gained by the diagnostic system in the course of past tests; and (iii) the *calculation algorithm for electrical parameters* that deduces certain parameter values of the circuit instead of measuring them.

The inference engine, implemented in the system, uses both backward and forward chaining strategy.

Functional knowledge can help build efficient model-based diagnostic systems relying on the functional modeling of the system under test. The model required here can be based on *generic functional primitives* as elements of functional ontology [47], or on the dynamic system behavior [1]. Model-based failure detection and isolation has been applied in complex industrial plants [52] and also in monitoring a power station control system [5].

In the past, special knowledge-based systems have been developed for the automatic testing and diagnosis of mechanical and other engineering systems. Special expert systems have also been developed for system design for reliability, where AI technology is used for increasing system safety by introducing fail-safety features into the system or by recurrent security checks. Examples of such expert systems are **ROTES** and **PUMA**, robot expert systems designed for fault isolation, symptom identification, fault classification, etc.

The repair centers of Fiat, Lancia, and Alfa Romeo have developed an Integrated Diagnostic Expert Assistant (**IDEA**). It is a large-scale model-based expert system used for fault diagnosis in a variety of automotive electronic subsystems diagnostics [44]. A mathematical model and the heuristic system model are integrated into the system. Within the first four years the system has been adopted by about 1500 Italian repair centers.

Although the same diagnostic approach can be applied for the detection of multiple system faults, the multiple fault diagnostic approach is usually based on particular *multiple fault models* and *multiple fault tests.* Such models are rather complex, so that in fault detection and diagnosis for systems permanently running under stationary conditions, single fault is assumed, and for their monitoring and testing a single-fault error model is used.

Serious obstacles in detecting individual faults are the so called *nondetectable faults.* Such faults cause simultaneous normally detectable single faults not to be distinguishable as single faults because the two faults are simultaneously present in the system. This is especially the case in redundant systems in which the faults of redundant system components are not directly detectable. In some nonredundant circuits, however, multiple faults can be detected using the *complete test sets.*

5.1.3 On-line Diagnosis. Originally, knowledge-based systems were not used for solving real-time problems. Their application was in the field of system testing and diagnosis under no severe time constraints. The increasing complexity of modern industrial plants and the growing demands for their reliability, availability, and safety increases the need for sophisticated process and production monitoring, diagnostics, and control systems [45]. Such systems are expected to guarantee steady real-time performance by managing the time-critical situations. Accordingly, the need for solving plant automation problems under real-time conditions has required some specific issues of knowledge-based systems to be addressed when knowledge-based systems are used for *on-line* plant monitoring, diagnosis, and control. For such applications a high-speed process interface and a high-speed inference engine, operating in real-time context, are required for the collection and evaluation of sensor data. The inference engine must be able to reason about the behavior of data collected over the given time and to distinguish between the past, present, and future values of data. The computational efficiency of the engine has to be enhanced, the knowledge base has to be appropriately structured, and the heuristic knowledge to be stored has to be selected carefully. To speed up the reasoning process, the inference engine of the real-time expert system must be able to use both forward and backward chaining in like manner and, to avoid wasting time following the non-critical or low-priority chains of inference, must be able to assign priorities to the various possibilities it investigates. In addition, the machine must be able to focus its attention on significant asynchronous events. Finally, for the repeated processing of control algorithms and for subsequent control actions, automatic triggering of some predetermined rules at given time instances or at the end of some time interval must be possible [11].

Because knowledge-based systems for real-time process monitoring have to deal with a large number of process sensing and alarming elements, their knowledge base may contain thousands of inference rules related to such elements. During system operation, inference rules and the accompanying procedures are invoked only when needed for diagnosing the actual problem or for undertaking the intermediate actions. When possibly significant events are detected as the result of some alarms, they will be signalled to the system, so that its inference engine can look at related process modes, as specified in associated inference rules, and can establish what alarms are present and what actions are to be taken to remove their effects. Thus, the requirements defined for knowledge-based on-line monitoring and diagnostic systems are to be extended by the following features:

- The prescribed reaction time, which could be very short because of the fast control loops to be serviced, should be guaranteed.
- Reasoning with inaccurate and incomplete sensor data must be possible, resulting in usable decisions.
- Work on temporal, time-referred databases and reasoning with such data has to be incorporated.
- Rule activation according to the sensor data contents.
- Possibility of communication with the external computer systems for the exchange of the sensor data, set-point values, and the recommended values of supervised parameters.

The diagnostic expert systems must be able to cope with unreliable data because the acquired plant data are unreliable. In addition, because some heuristic, more or less reliable facts, based on the expert's field experience, have also to be taken into account, the systems must be able to reason with uncertain facts. Such reasoning is based on:

- *Bayes' theorem*, which deals with the joint probabilities of events.
- *Plausible interference*, where the uncertainties are represented by credibility measure.
- *Belief theory*, in which the uncertainties are represented by the *degrees of belief* and the *possibility values*, and which relies on a set of mutually exclusive hypotheses over which the belief, called the *basic probability assignment*, is distributed.
- *Fuzzy set theory*, for example, a theory with partial memberships of set elements.

The main problem to be solved when building a knowledge-based system for real-time applications is the implementation of software and hardware interfaces between the system and its real-time environment. For instance, the software heterogeneity in on-line monitoring and diagnostic systems, due to the joint use of real-time and AI programming languages, creates software interfacing problems between the AI and the conventional programming paradigms, and between the structuring concepts used for building the databases and the knowledge bases. Consequently, the computer used for intelligent real-time problem solving must run programs written both in AI and in real-time languages. This suggests the following alternative solutions:

- Use of two separate computers, one for solving the AI part of the problem, and the other for solving the real-time part.
- Implementation of real-time monitoring and diagnostic systems in procedural, problem-oriented, or object-oriented languages like Pascal, FORTRAN, Ada, Language C, etc.

Reasoning strategy is a particularly sensitive issue in real-time knowledge-based systems. The reason is that a mix of at least *nonmonotonic, temporal,* and *uncertain reasoning* is required to meet the conditions found in such systems. The nonmonotonic reasoning is necessary because of changing environmental conditions and changes in the plant to be monitored. The collected sensor data are of limited duration and of steadily decreasing validity. Furthermore, the time-related values of sensor data require temporal reasoning, i.e., reasoning about the past, present, and future. Finally, because of inaccurate and incomplete plant data, reasoning with uncertainty can give the most acceptable results on which to base the counteractions to the exceptions discovered by monitoring. For instance, in the **R*Time** expert system of Talarian Corp, a real-time knowledge-based system, designed for intelligent plant monitoring and control, the inference engine analyses the acquired process data by means of objects, classes, and rules and works out the conclusions important for the plant operator using temporal reasoning.

Nevertheless, a far more efficient plant monitoring and diagnostics system and far better process control are achievable by integrating the relevant dynamic and/or heuristic models of the system, even the partial ones [14]. Using such models in situations where plant operating conditions change frequently according to various input, output, or boundary conditions, the *normality* and/or *emergency* of the instantaneous plant state can be identified by extracting the values of critical plant parameters and checking them against some given limit values. Moreover, model-based system diagnosis can help early diagnosis of critical faults [27].

An example of a model-based diagnostic system is **DISARM** (Diagnostic System with Automated Rebuilding of Models), developed by Vinson, Grantham, and Ungar [48]. Using its internal *qualitative process engine*, during the diagnosis of a chemical plant the system derives new *qualitative models* of the plant in terms of phenomena, such as heat transfer, chemical reaction, fluid flow, etc., based on *qualitative process theory*. The generalized qualitative submodels represent qualitative equations of material and energy balance, so that DISARM is directly applicable to monitoring and diagnosis of large-scale chemical plants.

The integration of model-based and heuristic features in a real-time expert system was also reported by Pfau-Wagenbauer and Nejdl [36], who integrated an alarm expert system into a

SCADA (Supervisory Control and Data Acquisition) system to build an intelligent alarm processing system for the Public Utilities Board of Singapore. The system was designed to help the operators locate and analyze network faults and detect malfunctions in the protection system based on its model. To achieve real-time performance of the entire system, a hierarchical diagnostic expert system was built in, able to use the heuristic rules and the precompiled qualitative models.

COOKER, the real-time process monitoring and operator advisory system for batch manufacturing processes, consists of four main subsystems:

- Data frames for knowledge representation in a goal/subgoal scheme.
- Data gatherer for access and transfer of real-time data.
- Inference engine for knowledge processing and problem solving.
- Operator interface for managing the windows and man–machine dialogs.

Two expert systems have been developed for the intelligent, real-time monitoring of nuclear plants:

- **CEALMON** (The Computerized Action Level Monitor), a rule-based system running in an IBM PC.
- **REACTOR**, a diagnostic and accidents treatment system that monitors the reactor facility, detects deviations from normal operating conditions and significant critical situations, and determines the appropriate response.

PREMON (The Predictive Monitoring System), presented by Doyle, Sellers, and Atkinson [12] is a model-based real-time monitoring system with the following interacting capabilities:

- Prediction of dynamic system behavior by causal simulation.
- Sensor planning and allocation for accessing the importance of device's behavior.
- Alarming based on sensor value validation and its interpretation.

Padalkar et al. [34] used the **IPCS** (Intelligent Process Control System) to develop a supervisory monitoring and diagnostics system for a congenerator plant of Osaka Gas Company. The design concept used included:

- Structural and functional modeling of faults as violations of expected plant behavior or of certain functional constraints.
- Hierarchical decomposition to support the multiple-level abstraction in structural and functional modeling, because modern industrial plants are complex and difficult to understand directly.
- Fault propagation modeling for expressing the dynamics of fault evolution in the sense that a failure in any component of a subsystem can propagate to the adjacent subsystems and generate multiple alarms.

5.2 Intelligent Control

One of the principal drawbacks of conventional analog controllers is their limited control capability, mainly restricted to the PID type of control. Introduction of microcomputers as programmable controllers has opened the possibility of implementing advanced control algorithms [4], based on modern systems theory. However, the theory has so far made only a modest impact on the practice of automatic control. The surprising observation is that, although the progress in control theory has been enormous, practical automation problems have not benefited at the same rate. This can be demonstrated with the example of an ordinary PID controller. Its behavior can be very well understood mathematically and physically, yet in practice there are many important aspects that are not captured by the PID control algorithm. To design a PID controller for plant automation it is also necessary to consider operator interfaces, possibility of switching between manual and automatic operation, transients due to parameter changes, nonlinear actuators, wind-up of the internal term, selectors, and so on. In addition, an operational industrial PID controller has to consider heuristic issues, learnt in the process instrumentation field of the plant. Such issues, unfortunately, although being of extreme importance for good control, have not attracted much interest from theoreticians. They have instead been hidden in practical designs and are rarely discussed in the control literature. It may thus be concluded that practical solutions even to such mundane problems as PID controls are not reached by theory alone and the operator/engineer experience in the form of heuristics plays an important role. Heuristics play an even more important role in multivariable and self-tuning regulation. In these cases, the control law is much more complex than that of the linear PID equation. To obtain a well-functioning adaptive control system, it is also required to provide it with a considerable amount of heuristic logic; this goes under names like *safety nets* or *safety logic*. Experience has shown that it is quite time consuming to design and test this heuristics logic.

It is clear that the future intelligent control algorithms will contain more and more heuristics. For instance, even the algorithms underlying the typical adaptive systems such as model-reference adaptive controllers or self-tuning regulators that are being currently used have a limited range in which they will operate satisfactorily. Outside of this range, they may result in unstable closed-loop systems. This is, in fact, the development that has led to the concept of *safety jackets*.

Three basic approaches are currently in use for implementation of intelligent controllers:

- Real-time expert systems for building *expert controllers.*
- Fuzzy rules based expert systems for building *fuzzy controllers.*
- Neural networks for building *neurocontrollers.*

In the following, some typical real-time expert controller implementations will be presented and some aspects of their applications discussed.

5.2.1   Expert Controllers. Expert system approach for intelligent controller implementation was originally proposed by Astrom and Anton to extend the capabilities of conventional controllers by integrating into the knowledge base of a real-time expert system the general control knowledge and the controller tuning and adaptation heuristics [2, 3]. Provided with such knowledge, the proposed expert controllers should be able to control efficiently complex, nonlinear, and time-varying systems with minimal *a priori* knowledge available. The controllers should also be able to cope simultaneously with the problems of on-line control loop diagnostics and performance monitoring and, while operating the control algorithm, to increase its knowledge about the controlled system.

Subsequently, a variety of similar proposals were made for various types of controllers and for their automated parameter tuning and adaptation [26]. Nevertheless, the most commonly used algorithm here is based on *step response analysis* in both open and closed control loop. The analysis helps determine the rise time, damping, static gain, time constant, and other loop parameters. Other proposals, such as those based on Laguerre series expansion, on correlation techniques, and on the general use of the ARMAX model have not been much used in intelligent self-tuning or adaptive systems because they require more *a priori* knowledge about the system to be controlled than the step response method. Some proposals include the possibilities of designing expert controllers that combine a wide range of algorithms with different properties. For this, efficient methods or different orchestrating algorithms are needed to achieve varying control objectives [17, 22] and for a long time this was an important research problem in the application of expert systems.

To solve a control problem using the knowledge-based system approach, it is first necessary to identify the approaches that may be appropriate to the problem. The identified design methods are then analyzed carefully to determine the conditions under which they will work and when they will fail. Next, the design criteria and the design conditions are determined, before the appropriate knowledge-based system has been built [21].

Practical experience with the knowledge-based systems for real-time applications indicates that the power of the AI approach comes to the forefront when the given control problem to be solved is relatively complex. In the majority of process plants, operators have to run systems with multiple loops, unpredictable material variations, etc. Over time and with experience, the operators generate adequate rules of thumb for a large number of exceptional plant situations that help them to deal with the complexities. This set of rules is plant-specific.

As intelligent control technology matures, increasing autonomy is conferred on local control, which is why the loop knowledge base was the strategic focus of crisis action and prevention for future systems. The central knowledge base is called upon for a broader, multiloop assessment of process perturbation when a distributed knowledge base fails to correct incipient or actual local upset. Manufacturers of distributed computer control systems, as well as process plant engineers, are commissioning distributed knowledge bases around PID algorithms, to make loops perform better and to cope with process and system faults.

The field of rule-based expert systems has been well explored. In the area of process control, fuzzy rule-based controllers have been applied successfully to the control of cement kilns and are now offered as standard equipment. Self-organizing rule-based controllers are commercially available and chips are being developed that can execute fuzzy control rules in nanoseconds. Finally, a number of expert controllers have been released to the market.

In the following the well-known intelligent controllers that have found their applications in process control are presented and briefly discussed.

Foxboro has developed **EXACT**, an expert controller for tuning of controller parameter, based on a pattern recognition approach. The approach uses direct performance feedback by monitoring the process variable to determine the action required. For parameter tuning, EXACT uses the tuning rules usually employed by skilled control engineers. Its PID algorithm (i) allows faster startup of the plant; (ii) adapts the parameters of the controller to dynamic variations within the plant and changes in setpoint values, load, and noise; and (iii) releases the plant operating personnel from the parameter tuning activities and thus reduces control operating costs. The expert controller operates so that if the sensing and the setpoint values are close to each other, the EXACT PID algorithm is in the state QUIET. However, when a disturbance appears, and is greater in amplitude than twice the noise band, the algorithm is initialized to search for possible true peaks. Once a peak occurs, its magnitude is stored and a timer records the time period. The peak is then verified and subsequently the next peak is searched for. At the end, a description of the disturbance is given in terms of overshoot, damping, I-period, and D-period. Based on this, the algorithm computes new values of the P, I, and D parameters of the controller using its ADAPT part, which contains a large number of knowledge-based rules, reflecting the long-term tuning observations of the experts.

Accol II of Bristol Babcock is the rule-based programming language of the distributed process controller DPC. It enables the embedding of control knowledge into the DPC knowledge base. DPC can be programmed to react in a manner similar to the way in which an operator or process engineer would react. The inference engine of the controller is seen as an enhancement of the language itself.

Custodian is an IBM-PC resident software package developed for building knowledge bases with up to 10 000 variables and alarms connected via programmable or process controllers. The package includes the **Superintendent Expert System**, comprising a knowledge base builder and the inference software.

PICON is a real-time expert system developed by LMI for process control. It is basically an alarm management system assisting the operators in dealing with multiple alarms. PICON can simultaneously deal with up to 20 000 process measurements and alarms using a knowledge base that may contain thousands of inference rules that are used only as needed for diagnosing a problem or for intermediate steps in a chain of inference. The knowledge acquisition interface allows the construction of complex rules and procedures for a distributed control system without requiring AI programming expertise of the engineer.

ALFA (The Automated Load Forecasting Assistant) is a rule-based forecasting expert system capable of hourly prediction of the load in an energy distribution system. By compiling the production rules, facts such as general load growth, hour of the day, day of the week and day of the year, holidays and exceptional events, seasonal and current weather conditions, etc., have been taken into account. The actual facts are used for search in a 10-yearly database.

MASTER (Monitoring and Advice on Self-Tuning with an ExpeRt) is a prototype of an intelligent system reported by Worship [53], with integrated performance monitoring functions. Knowledge is represented in the system as frames, demons, and rules. Demons are processed in forward chaining and the rules in backward chaining for better execution of control rules. Experiments with the MASTER system have shown encouraging results through the combination of the self-tuning control concept with real-time expert systems technology. Furthermore, the plant operator can benefit significantly from the intelligent self-tuning control, with no need for extensive field training.

Norman and Neveed developed a rotary cement kiln expert system supervisor for control in cement manufacturing [32]. The system runs on an IBM PC using an RS-232 interface for external units. To operating the control functions, appropriate rules are called from the knowledge base and, under changing environmental conditions, new strategies are generated for process supervision directly or through conventional control facilities.

Porter, Jones, and McKeown [42] recommend that a real-time expert tuner for PI controllers include the following components:

- *Expert signal conditioner*, a real-time program for conditioning of engineering data.
- *Intelligent PI controller*, for control of a process variable.
- *Expert supervisor*, for establishing event priorities, ensuring plant safety.
- *Expert tuner inference engine*, for tuning the controller gain.
- *Intelligent gain scheduler*, a real-time feature that identifies the open-loop step-response plant characteristics from closed-loop data.

An expert system for the on-line tuning of a PID controller was presented by Litt [25]. The controller was used in a multiple-lag process with dead time.

6 FUTURE TRENDS

The present status of knowledge-based software is characterized by a wide diversity of AI languages and systems development tools. This is expected to undergo some changes in the sense of building totally modular expert systems, compatible with conventional data processing systems, especially within the real-time computer systems. This will simplify data exchange between the AI and the procedural programming languages, including the real-time and process-oriented languages. New knowledge-based software will also support easy data exchange between AI programmes and the communication software of computer systems in which the knowledge-based systems are implemented.

It is to be expected that the future expert systems for plant automation will run in multicomputer systems and that they will share knowledge bases and databases among several related applications in plant automation. They will admit the incorporation of several types of rule bases, each rule base being employed for the diagnosis of a specific part of the system. It is also to be expected that the generation of knowledge-based software will be improved to enable a *direct translation* of the linguistic version of a diagnostic problem specification into corresponding knowledge representation method (rules, frames, etc.).

In general, it is expected that the future expert systems will include the following:

- Mixed knowledge representation by combination of production rules, frames, semantic nets, etc.
- Diversification of reasoning methods and inference techniques used by interpreters, including fuzzy reasoning and processing of heuristic knowledge.
- Simplification of knowledge base manipulation, e.g., of its on-line updating.
- Automatic check of consistency of mixed knowledge representation form.
- Increase of knowledge processing speed by exploitation of parallel and concurrent program execution.
- Total size increase of individual knowledge bases as well as the possibility of implementation for multibase systems.

In plant monitoring and fault diagnosis, classical methods based on field experience and signal evaluation are being replaced by model-based approaches combined with heuristic plant knowledge. In the meantime, however, neural network based diagnostic systems [24, 54] are strong competitors of knowledge-based diagnostic systems.

In the area of intelligent control, the use of supervisory, parameter tuning, and adaptive expert controllers, also the use of fuzzy logic controllers and neurocontrollers in the industrial plant automation is a reality.

REFERENCES

[1] A. Abu-Hanna, R. Benjamins, and W. Jansweijer, Device understanding and modeling for diagnosis, *IEE Expert*, pp. 26–32, Apr. 1991.

[2] K.-E. Arzen, An architecture for expert system-based feedback control, *Automatica*, Vol. 25, No. 6, pp. 813–827, 1989.

[3] K.J. Aström, J.J. Anton, and K.-E. Arzen, Expert control, *Automatica*, Vol. 22, No. 3, pp. 277–285, 1986.

[4] P.J. Autsaklis and K.M. Passino, *An Introduction to Intelligent and Autonomous Control*, Kluwer Academic, Boston, 1993.

[5] D.-Y. Bau and P.J. Brezillon, Model-based diagnosis of power-station control systems, *IEEE Expert*, pp. 36–44, Feb. 1992.

[6] I. Bratko, *PROLOG: Programming for Artificial Intelligence*, Addison-Wesley, Reading, MA, 1986.

[7] L. Brownston, et al., *Programming Expert Systems in OPS-5*, Addison Wesley, Reading, MA, 1986.

[8] J.F. Brule and A. Blount, *Knowledge Acquisition*, McGraw-Hill, New York, 1989.

[9] J. Carbonell (ed.), *Machine Learning*, MIT/Elsevier, Cambridge, MA, 1990.

[10] R. Davis, Diagnostic reasoning based on structure and behavior, *Artificial Intelligence*, Vol. 24, pp. 347–410, 1984.

[11] R. Dodhiawala, et al., Real-time AI systems: a definition and an architecture, *Proc. Int. Joint Conf. Artificial Intelligence (IJCAI '89)*, pp. 256–261. Morgan Kaufmann, San Matheo, CA, 1989.

[12] R.J. Doyle, S.M. Sellers, and D.J. Atkinson, Predictive monitoring based on causal simulation, *Proc. 1st Conf. AI Applications*. IEEE Computer Society Press, Washington, DC, 1987.

[13] K.D. Forbus, Qualitative process theory, *Artificial Intelligence*, Vol. 24, pp. 85–168, 1984.

[14] M.P. Frank and B. Köppen-Seliger, New developments using AI in fault diagnosis, *Engineering Applications of Artificial Intelligence*, Vol. 10, No. 1, pp. 3–14, 1997.

[15] A. Goldberg and D. Robson, *Smalltalk-80: The Language and its Implementation*. Addison-Wesley, Reading, MA, 1983.

[16] P. Harmon, R. Maus, and R. Morrissey, *Expert Systems: Tools and Applications*. Wiley, New York, 1988.

[17] B. Hayes-Roth, et al., Intelligent monitoring and control, *Proc. Int. Joint Conf. Artificial Intelligence (IJCAI '89)*, pp. 243–249. Morgan Kaufmann, San Matheo, CA, 1989.

[18] F.F. Ingrand, M.P. Georgeff, and A.S. Rao, An architecture for real-time reasoning and system control, *IEEE Expert*, pp. 34–44, Dec. 1992.

[19] M. Jafar and A.T. Bahill, Interactive verification of knowledge-based systems, *IEEE Expert*, pp. 25–32, Feb. 1993.

[20] L. Kanal and V. Kumar (eds.), *Search in Artificial Intelligence*. Springer-Verlag, Berlin, 1988.

[21] S.J. Kendra, M.R. Basila, and A. Cinar, Intelligent process control with supervisory knowledge-based systems, *IEEE Control Systems Magazine*, pp. 37–47, June 1994.

[22] T.J. Laffey, et al., Real-time knowledge-based systems, *AI Magazine*, Vol. 9, No. 1, pp. 27–45, Spring 1988.

[23] J.-L. Lauriere, *Problem Solving and Artificial Intelligence*. Prentice-Hall, New York, 1990.

[24] J.A. Leonard and M.A. Kramer, Diagnosing dynamic faults using neural modular neural nets, *IEEE Expert*, pp. 44–53, Apr. 1993.

[25] J. Litt, An expert system to perform on-line controller tuning, *IEEE Control Systems*, pp. 18–23, Apr. 1991.

[26] J. McGhee, M.J. Grimble, and P. Mowforth (eds.), *Knowledge-Based Systems for Industrial Control*. Peter Peregrinus, London, UK, 1990.

[27] U. Meyer, *Prediction of Critical States of Exotherm Chemical Reactors by Diagnostic Expert Systems*, Dissertation, University of Bremen (in German, 1988).

[28] R. Milne, Strategies for diagnosis, *IEEE Trans. Systems, Man, and Cybernetics*, Vol. 17, pp. 333–339, 1987.

[29] P. Morizet-Mahoudeaux, On-board and real-time expert control, *IEEE Expert*, pp. 71–81, Aug. 1996.

[30] M. Nagao, *Knowledge and Inference*. Academic Press, New York, 1988.

[31] N. H. Narayanan and N. Viswanhadam, A methodology for knowledge acquisition and reasoning in failure analysis, *IEEE Trans. Systems, Man, and Cybernetics*, Vol. 17, No. 2, pp. 274–288, 1987.

[32] P. Norman and S. Naveed, An expert system supervisor for a rotary cement kiln, *IEE Colloq. Real-Time Expert Systems in Process Control*, No. 107, pp. 71–79, 1985.

[33] O'Leavy, et al., Validating expert systems, *IEEE Expert*, pp. 51–58, June 1990.

[34] Padalkar, et al., Real-time fault diagnosis, *IEEE Expert*, pp. 75–85, June 1991.

[35] J. Pearl, *Heuristics: Intelligent Search Strategies for Computer Problem Solving*. Addison-Wesley, Reading, MA, 1984.

[36] M. Pfau-Wagenbauer and W. Nejdl, Integrating model-based and heuristic features in a real-time expert system, *IEEE Expert*, pp. 12–18, Aug. 1992.

[37] D.T. Pham (ed.), Expert systems is process engineering, in *Expert Systems in Engineering*. IFS Publications, Springer-Verlag, Berlin, 1988.

[38] D. Popovic and V.P. Bhatkar, *Methods and Tools for Artificial Intelligence*. Marcel Dekker, New York, 1994.

[39] D. Popovic, U. Meyer, B. Hass, and G. Berhardi, Real-time application expert systems: interfacing the AI- and real-time-languages, *IAESTED Int. Conf. Expert Systems, Geneva*, 1987, pp. 124–129.

[40] D. Popovic and I. Hofmann, A decision-support system for malfunction diagnosis of ship installations, *IASTED Int. Conf. Artificial Intelligence and Neural Networks, Zurich*, 1991, pp. 278–293.

[41] D. Popovic, I. Hofmann, and S. Andonova, A decision-support for tele-diagnosis and remote maintenance, *Proc. 8th Int. IMEKO Symp. Technical Diagnosis, Dresden*, 1992, pp. 682–692.

[42] B. Porter, A.H. Jones, and C.B. McKeown, Real-time expert tuners for PI controllers, *IEE Proc.*, Vol. 134, Pt. D, No. 4, pp. 260–263, July 1987.

[43] G.A. Ringland and D.A. Duce, *Approaches to Knowledge Representation: An Introduction*. Wiley, New York, 1988.

[44] M. Sanseverino and F. Cascio, Model-based diagnosis for automotive repair, *IEEE Expert*, pp. 33–37, Nov./Dec. 1997.

[45] S. Shum, et al., An expert system approach to malfunction diagnosis in chemical plants, *Computers and Chemical Engineering*, Vol. 12, No. 1, pp. 27–36, 1988.

[46] G.L. Steele Jr., *Common LISP: The Language (Reference Manual)*. Digital Press, Billerica, MA, 1984.

[47] J.B. Sticklen, B. Chandrasekaran, and W.E. Bond, Applying a functional approach for model-based modeling, *Proc. IJCAI Workshop Model-Based Reasoning*, pp. 165–176, 1989.

[48] J.M. Vinson, S.D. Grantham, and L.H. Ungar, Automatic rebuilding of qualitative models for diagnosis, *IEEE Expert*, pp. 23–30, Aug. 1992.

[49] K. Warwick (ed.), *Applied Artificial Intelligence*. Peter Peregrinus, London, 1991.

[50] G. Winstanley, *Artificial Intelligence in Engineering*. Wiley, New York, 1991.

[51] J.R. Quinlan, *Application of Expert Systems*. Addison-Wesley, Reading, MA, 1989.

[52] J.J. Gestler, Survey of model-based failure detection and isolation of complex plants, *IEEE Control Systems Magazine*, Vol. 8, No. 3, pp. 3–11, 1998.

[53] G.R. Worship, *Development of a self-tuning controller demonstration system incorporating an expert system monitor and advisor*, M.Eng. Thesis, Heriot-Watt University, 1998.

[54] J.C. Hoskins, K.M. Kaliyu and D.M. Himmelblau, Fault diagnosis in complex chemical plants using artificial newal networks, *AIChEJ.*, Vol. 37, pp. 137–141, 1991.

CHAPTER 14

Neural Networks for Identification of Nonlinear Systems: An Overview

PRAMOD GUPTA and NARESH K. SINHA

Department of Electrical and Computer Engineering, McMaster University, Hamilton, Ontario, Canada, L8S 4K1

1 INTRODUCTION

The problem of system modeling and identification has attracted considerable attention during the past four decades mostly because of a large number of applications in diverse fields such as chemical processes, biomedical systems, ecology, econometrics, and social sciences. In each of these cases, a model consists basically of mathematical equations that can be used for understanding the behavior of the system and, wherever possible, for prediction and control. Most processes encountered in the real world are nonlinear to some extent, and in many practical applications nonlinear models may be required to achieve an acceptable predictive accuracy. The choice of model is vitally important since it influences its usefulness in prediction and control. Practical applications have shown that nonlinear models can not only provide a better fit to the data but can also reveal rich behavior such as limit cycles and bifurcations that cannot be captured by linear models. When formulating and solving an identification problem, it is important to have the purpose of the identification in mind. Interest in this subject has various different roots: (i) definite needs by engineers in process industries to obtain better knowledge about their plants for improved control; (ii) the study of high-performance aerospace vehicles, as well as the dynamics of more down-to-earth objects like railway carriages and hydrofoils; and (iii) study of humans in tracking actions and in other types of control.

System identification consists of three steps: structure determination, parameter estimation, and model validation [74]. In the first step one tries to find the order of the model (discrete–continuous time) by which the system can be closely represented. The second step is the application of a suitable algorithm to estimate the parameters of the model as accurately as possible. The last step is the application of some criterion (e.g., the Akaike information criterion) to check how closely the fitted model represents the system under consideration.

In the past three decades, major advances have been made in adaptive identification and control of linear time-invariant plants with unknown parameters. The theory of identification and control of linear systems is well established, but very few results exist that can be applied directly to nonlinear systems. Considerable care has to be exercised in the statement of the problem and the choice of the identifier and controller structures as well as the generation of adaptive laws for adjustment of the parameters. In short, some of the problems in system identification using conventional methods are:

- Determining the order and structure of the system
- Selection of a suitable criterion for determining the "accuracy" of the model
- Designing an input signal that will maximize the accuracy of the estimates of the parameters of the model

Several nonlinear input–output model development techniques have been proposed, but they have not been widely accepted. More recently there has been great interest in "universal model-free controllers" that do not need a mathematical model of the controlled plant but mimic the functions of biological processes to learn about the systems they are controlling on-line. It is proposed that neural networks, because of their nonlinear nature, can model higher-order statistics and thus can function as an effective prediction filter for nonlinear series. It has been proven that any continuous function can be arbitrarily well approximated by a feedforward network [18]. This property can be used to implement classifiers or to represent complex nonlinear relations. The learning property, coupled with the universal approximation property of neural network structures such as the multilayer perceptron and radial basis function, has made them invaluable tools in such diverse applications as modeling, time series analysis, signal processing, and control and financial engineering. In most of these cases the neural network is trained to represent the data set using some learning algorithm. Ideally, the weights that define the strength of connections between the neurons in the network should converge to yield a neural network architecture that can emulate the mechanisms that produced the data set. This process clearly involves learning a mathematical description of the system and can therefore be studied as a system identification problem. The advantage of this interpretation is that all the fundamental results of estimation theory that have been developed over many decades [22, 55] can be employed to study rigorously both the properties and the performance of neural networks.

The main objective of the chapter is to review the research work done in neural network applications to system identification and highlight the significant aspects and recent results. It will be seen that neural networks do indeed fulfill the promise held out of providing model-free learning controllers for a class of nonlinear systems, in the sense that not even a structural or parametrized model of the system dynamics is needed. The chapter is organized as follows: A brief overview of neural networks is provided in Section 2. Section 3 deals with the application of neural networks to system identification and important results are discussed. References are provided for further detail.

2   NEURAL NETWORKS

In this section, we give a brief overview of neural networks used in system identification. For a fine collection of key papers in the development of models of neural networks see *Neurocomputing: Foundations of Research* [4]. Since the work of the PDP group [73], several well-defined architectures have been proposed to tackle a variety of problems. A neural network is made up of the interconnection of a large number of nonlinear processing units referred to as neurons. The internal structure of the neural network may involve forward paths only, or feedforward as well as feedback paths. A typical network model has a set of input patterns and a set of output patterns. The role of the network is to perform a function that associates each input pattern with an output pattern. A learning algorithm uses the statistical properties of a set of input–output pairs—called the training set—to generalize. With this model, statistical inference can be developed, which has some distinct advantages over rule-based inference. Statistical inference allows for exceptions and randomness in the association between two variables, whereas rules are deterministic. Many different networks, such as multilayer feedforward networks, recurrent and statistical networks, associative memory networks and self-organization networks, have been developed for different purposes. They have a great deal to offer when the problem of interest is made difficult by one or more of the following features:

- Lack of physical/statistical understanding of the problem
- Statistical variations in the observed data
- Nonlinear mechanism responsible for the generation of the data

From the modeling perspective, interest in neural networks is motivated by the following important properties [28]:

- They learn by experience (not by modeling or programming).
- They can generalize, i.e. they can also work successfully in situations not taught to them.
- They have inherently parallel and distributed structures.
- They can form arbitrary continuous nonlinear mappings.

2.1 Network Architectures

The architecture of a network is defined by the basic processing elements and the way in which they are connected. The neurons by themselves are not very powerful in terms of computation or representation, but their interconnection allows relation between the variables to be encoded, giving different and powerful processing capabilities. There are many paradigms available in the literature by which a network may be connected and trained. Some important forms of interconnections are discussed in the following sections.

2.2 Multilayer Feedforward Networks

A multilayer feedforward network is composed of a hierarchy of processing units, organized in a series of two or more mutually exclusive sets or layers of neurons. The first layer acts as a receiving site for the values applied to the network. At the last layer, the results of the computation are read off. Between these two layers lie (one or more) layers of hidden units. The function of the hidden neurons is to intervene between the external input and the network output. With the addition one or more hidden layers, the network is enabled to extract higher-order statistics, for (in a rather loose sense) the network acquires a global perspective despite its local connectivity by virtue of the extra set of synaptic connections and the extra dimension of neural interactions. The ability of hidden neurons to extract higher-order statistics is particularly valuable when the size of the input layer is large. The neural network is said to be *fully connected* if every node in each layer of the network is connected to every other node in the adjacent forward layer. All connections in a network are unidirectional, that is, the output of a unit, scaled by the value of a connection weight, is fed forward to provide a portion of the activation for the units in the next-higher layer. From a systems theoretic point of view, multilayer networks can be considered as versatile nonlinear maps with the elements of the weight matrices as parameters. An n-layer neural network with input $\mathbf{u}$ and output y can be described by the equation

$$y = f[\mathbf{W}_n f[\mathbf{W}_{n-1} \dots f[\mathbf{W}_1 \mathbf{u} + b_1] + \dots + b_{n-1}] + b_n] \tag{1}$$

where $\mathbf{W}_i$ is the weight matrix associated with the ith layer, the vector b_i $(i = 1, 2, \dots, n)$ represents the threshold values for each node in the ith layer, and $f[\cdot]$ is a nonlinear operator. The $\mathbf{w}_i$ and b_i are the parameters to be estimated. Equation (1) can be interpreted as a nonlinear function that represents the described n-layer feedforward neural network. This representation nests many familiar statistical models such as regression (linear and nonlinear), classification (logit, probit), latent variable models, principal component analysis, and time series analysis (ARMA, ARMAX). The basic neural network structure represented by (1) can be generalized in many different ways. For example, Poli and Jones [67] introduce a multilayer feedfoward neural network with observation noise and random connections between units. Based on some distributional assumptions of the noise and the randomness of the connections, such a neural network can be estimated by a Kalman filtering procedure, which has been shown to have a greater predictive accuracy than the Newton algorithm for a chaotic time series that was generated from a logistic gap.

2.3   Radial Basis Function (RBF) Networks

A viable alternative to the multilayer perceptron (MLP) is the radial basis function (RBF) network, which is a multilayer feedfoward network with a single layer of hidden layer nonlinear processing units, and an output layer of linear weights. The output y of an RBF network with an input vector $\mathbf{u} \in R^n$ is described by

$$y = f(\mathbf{u}) = \sum_{i=1}^{N} w_i R_i + w_0 \tag{2}$$

where w_i are the weights of the network. The functions $R_i: R^n \rightarrow R$ are termed activation functions and have the general form

$$R_i(\mathbf{u}) = \phi(\|\mathbf{u} - \mathbf{c}_i\|), \qquad \mathbf{c}_i \in R^n$$

where the function $\phi(\cdot)$ has a maximum value at the origin and drops off rapidly as its argument tends to infinity. This implies that $R_i(\mathbf{u})$ has an appreciable value only in the neighborhood of the vector $\mathbf{c}_i$, which is called the center of $R_i(\mathbf{u})$. There are many choices of the function $\phi(\cdot)$. The radial basis function is generally a Gaussian function. When the radial basis functions are specified, the only adjustable parameters of the network are the weights. Since these are linearly related to the output y and hence the output error, they can be adjusted using a straightforward least squares approach. This, in turn, has made radial basis networks attractive in identification and control.

After the assumption that neural networks are to be used, the next question that arises concerns the choice of the network to be used, i.e., whether an MLP or an RBF network should be used. RBF networks provide local approximation, whereas MLPs provide global approximation. This, in turn, means that for the approximation of a nonlinear input–output mapping, the MLP may be more parsimonious (i.e., require a smaller number of scalar coefficients) than the RBF network for a prescribed degree of accuracy. On the other hand, when continuous learning is required, as in the tracking of a time varying environment, the use of nested nonlinearities in a MLP makes it difficult to evolve the network in a dynamic fashion; that is, if we want to include a new example in the training set or enlarge the MLP by adding new weights, then the whole network must be retrained all over again. In contrast, the structure of an RBF network permits it to operate dynamically, such that the centers of the radial basis functions in the hidden layer and the linear weights in the output layer may be updated without having to recompute them from scratch. For large values of the input space, the number of radial basis functions that are needed becomes excessive. This implies that the location of the centers of the basis function should be chosen with considerable care. However, to determine precisely where to locate the centers of the RBF network, prior information is needed about magnitudes of the input signals. The MLP does not require such information. Consequently, it is preferred both when the magnitudes of the inputs are not known a priori and when the dimensionality of the input space is high.

2.4   Recurrent Neural Networks

The multilayer perceptron has been considered as providing a nonlinear mapping between an input vector and a corresponding output vector. Most of the work in this area has been devoted to obtaining this nonlinear mapping in a static setting. Many practical problems may be modeled by static models—for example, character recognition. On the other hand, many practical problems such as time series prediction, vision, speech, and motor control require dynamic modeling: the current output depends on previous inputs and outputs. There have been a number of attempts to extend the MLP architecture to encompass this class of problem [49, 61]. Waiebel et al. [80] used a time delay neural network architecture that involves successive delayed inputs to each neuron. All these attempts use only feedforward architecture, i.e., no feedback from latter layers to previous layers. There are other approaches that involve feedback from either the hidden layer or the output layer to the input layer. These define the class of recurrent networks. Recurrent or feedback networks allow information to flow from the output to the input field, so that the previous state of the network can be fed back into the input. The current input, therefore, can be processed based upon past as well as future inputs. Recurrent networks share the following distinctive features: (i) nonlinear computing units, (ii) symmetric synaptic connections, and (iii) abundant use of feedback.

Tsoi and Back [78] provide an overview of architectures of locally recurrent global feedforward (LRGF) networks introduced by a number of research groups in recent years. LRGF networks have architecture that is somewhere between a feedforward multilayer perceptron type and a fully recurrent network architecture (e.g., the Williams–Zipser model [87]). From the discussion, it appears that there are three major LRGF network architectures, one with feedback from the synapse output, one with feedback from the activation output, and one with feedback from the neuron output. They introduce a general LRGF network structure that includes most of the network architectures that have been proposed to date. These include the local synapse feedback architecture, as well as the local output feedback architecture. The transfer functions $G_1, G_2, \ldots, G_n$, and H may have both poles and zeros. They show that the different architectures behave differently when tested on the same problem and that LRGF architectures can outperform other recurrent network architectures that have global feedback, such as the Williams–Zipser architecture, on particular tasks.

2.5   Cerebellar Model Articulation Controller (CMAC)

Another network that uses the encoding system is the cerebellar model articulation controller (CMAC) [1, 2], even though CMAC does not use a competitive network to produce an encoding of the input to reach the same general objective. These networks use the concept of locally tuned overlapping receptive fields. They have the advantage that they can approximate complex nonlinear functions much faster than networks using sigmoid. Only a small subset of the parameters is adjusted at each point in the input space. This reduces sensitivity to the order in which the training data are presented.

2.6   Learning Algorithms

The real contribution of neural networks to the world of control, pattern recognition, and signal processing is learning. The new wave of neural networks (since the mid-1980s) came into being because learning could be performed at multiple levels. Neural network-based learning algorithms have allowed us to eliminate the need for hand-crafted feature extraction in hand-written recognizers.

After initialization, a neural network contains no information reflecting the system it is to approximate. Therefore, at each time instant when new observations are made available, it is desirable to incorporate the additional information into the current parameter estimate. Neural networks learn to solve a problem; they are not programmed to do so. Learning and training are thus fundamental to nearly all neural networks. Training is the procedure by which the network learns; learning is the end result of that procedure. Training is a procedure external to the network; learning is an internal process or activity. Learning is achieved not by modifying the neurons in the network but by adjustment of the synaptic weights of the neurons in the network. The adjustment of the weights is called the learning rule. To start with, when the weights are not calibrated, the network may perform badly at its task. However, after a series of learning processes that the network goes through, the weights are adjusted and the network should perform at a desired level. Typically the update to learning rules does not change, only the weights do. After the learning period, the weights are usually not changed further, unless there is a change in the operating environment.

Training of a neural network may be supervised or unsupervised. With supervised training, the network is provided with an input stimulus pattern along with the corresponding desired output pattern. The learning rule for such networks typically computes an error—that is, how far from the desired output the network's actual output really is. The error is then used to modify the synaptic weights. Unsupervised training involves presenting the data to the network until the network has discovered the emergent collective properties of the data by itself. Details of various learning algorithms have not been included as they can be found in the literature [28, 73, 87].

2.7   Neural Network Implementation and Interpretation

It is well known that several limitations may restrict the use of neural networks. First, there is no formal theory for determining the optimal network structure, and the appropriate number of layers and hidden layer units must be determined by experimentation. Second, there is no optimal algorithm to ensure the global minimum because of the multi-minima error surface. Third, statistical properties of neural networks are generally not available; thus no statistical inference can be carried out. Fourth, it is difficult to interpret a trained neural network model.

These limitations call for further studies in three broad areas outlined in [23]: (1) mathematical modeling of real cognitive processes; (2) theoretical investigations of networks and neurocomputing; (3) development of useful tools for practical prediction and pattern recognition. In this section, we outline some of the useful techniques and procedures that aim to overcome the aforementioned limitations.

Model Selection. Although neural networks can be universal approximators, the optimal network structure is not determined automatically. Failures in applications are sometimes due to a suboptimal neural structure. To develop the optimal network in any application, one needs

(1) to identify the relevant inputs and outputs; (2) to choose an appropriate network structure including the necessary number of hidden layers and hidden layer units; and (3) to use proper model evaluation criteria.

Neural Network Inputs and Outputs. The choice of network input and output variables and the quality of data are critical to the process of neural network applications. The choice depends heavily on the type of task that a neural network is expected to perform and is more or less subjective to the modeler's discretion as to the model and the scope of the study. It is common practice to use independent variables as network inputs and dependent variables as network outputs in a model. For example, in the case of inverse dynamic modeling of robots, trajectories are given as inputs to the network and the joint torques are considered as the outputs.

Sometimes, if there are more independent variables than one desires to include in the network input, dimension reduction techniques can be used. One can choose a smaller group of statistically significant variables from a regression of the dependent variable on a large group of independent variables. Principal component analysis and stepwise regression can also be used. To minimize the effect of magnitude among the inputs and outputs and increase the effectiveness of the learning algorithm, the data set is often normalized (or scaled) to be within a specific range depending on the transfer function. For example, if a neural network has a sigmoid or logistic transfer function in the output unit, the output needs to be scaled to fall in the range [0, 1]. Otherwise, a target output that falls outside that range will constantly create large back-propagation errors, and the network will be unable to learn the input–output relationship that is implied by the particular training pattern. Typically, variables will be normalized to have zero mean and unit standard deviation.

Cross-validation. The choice of the network learning paradigm depends on the pattern definition and the purpose of the network. Each paradigm must be assessed for learning ability, pattern storage capacity, training, and recalled speed. The neural network in identification must be able to generalize (i.e., generalize from a set of a sample of the pattern used to train the neural network), so that when the network is presented with a pattern on which it has not been trained, the network can respond in the same manner as with the training pattern set.

3 APPLICATION OF NEURAL NETWORKS TO SYSTEM IDENTIFICATION

This section describes a variety of neural network approaches to identifying characteristics of a nonlinear dynamical system. Both the theory and practice of nonlinear system modeling have advanced considerably in recent years. A wide class of discrete-time nonlinear systems can be represented by nonlinear autoregressive moving average with exogenous inputs (NARMAX) models [50]. The NARMAX model provides a description of system in terms of a nonlinear functional expansion of lagged inputs, outputs, and prediction errors. The mathematical function describing a real-world system can be complex and its exact form is usually unknown, so that in practice modeling of a real-world system must be based upon a chosen model set of known functions. A desirable property for this model is the ability to approximate a system to within arbitrary accuracy. Mathematically, this requires that the set be dense in the space of continuous functions. Polynomial functions are one choice that has such a completeness property. This provides the foundation for modeling nonlinear systems using the polynomial NARMAX model and several identification procedures based upon this model have been developed [8, 50]. In spite of the impressive theoretical work these methods represent, very few have found wide application in the identification of large classes of practical nonlinear systems. Because the derivation of the NARMAX model was independent of the form of the nonlinear functional, other choices of expansion can easily be investigated within this framework and neural networks are an obvious alternative. Neural networks can therefore be viewed as just another class of functional representations. From a systems theoretic point of view, artificial neural networks can be considered as a practically implementable convenient parametrization of nonlinear maps from one finite-dimensional space to another. Such networks are ideally suited to cope with all three categories of difficulties encountered in complex control systems (i.e., computational complexity, nonlinearity, and uncertainty).

Feedforward neural networks (FNN) are known to be capable of learning complex input output mapping; that is, given a set of inputs and desired outputs or targets, an adequately chosen neural network can emulate the mechanism that produced the data set through learning. This scenario can obviously be included in the framework of system identification and signal prediction and, therefore, it is not surprising that many applications of neural networks to nonlinear systems identification and prediction have been reported. The following concepts are discussed in this section:

- Nonparametric identification—developing black-box models of the input–output behavior of processes.
- Inverse modeling—developing models that predict corresponding process inputs from process outputs.
- Parametric identification—identifying structural features and parameter values for physically meaningful models.

3.1 Nonparametric Identification with Neural Networks

The supervised learning capabilities of neural networks can be used for identifying process models from input–output data. With a neural network, the process output is modeled as a nonlinear function of the past process inputs and past process or model outputs. The process data is the training set for the network, the weights of which are adjusted until the network model output accurately predicts the actual process output. Neural networks are trained to minimize the squared error between the neural network output and a plant output. In this type of identifier, the neural network output converges with the plant output after learning and the direct transfer function of the plant is composed in the neural network. Once the training process is complete, the neural network constitutes a black-box, nonparametric process model: knowledge about the process is embedded in the values of what are usually a large number of network parameters (i.e., synpatic weights). This learning structure is a classical supervised problem where the teacher (i.e., the system) provided target values (i.e., its outputs) directly in the output coordinate system of the learner (i.e., the network model).

Neural network nonparametric process models can be seen as nonlinear extensions of well-known model forms in the system identification literature [37]. For example, in the finite impulse response (FIR) structure the modeled process output $y_m(t)$ is a linear weighted sum of some number l of past input samples $u(t - i)$:

$$y_m(t) = \sum_{i=1}^{l} b_i u(t - i) \tag{3}$$

With a neural network, this weighted summation can be replaced with a more complex function, a nonlinear FIR model:

$$y_m(\mathbf{w}, t) = f_n(u(t - 1), \dots, u(t - l)) \tag{4}$$

Here f_n represents the neural network mapping mediated by the weight vector **w**. The network is thus provided as input a vector of past samples, the tapped delay line approach to modeling dynamical phenomena with algebraic model structures such as feedforward neural networks. With FIR models, a large number of terms must usually be considered: The time interval represented by the l samples must be significantly long so that no input signal prior to time $t - l$ would have any significant effect on the response at time t. An alternative to the FIR structure is the autoregressive moving average (ARMA) model, and this also has an analogous neural network extension. One advantage of ARMA-like models over FIR models is the former's parsimony. An upper bound on the number of inputs is now twice the dynamic order of the process. The work of Narendra and Parthasarthy [61] can be considered an important step in this direction. They show that neural networks can be used effectively in the identification and control of nonlinear dynamic systems. They developed generalized neural network models for both identification and control of unknown nonlinear dynamical systems. These generalized neural network models result from a unified treatment of multilayer and recurrent neural network models: for the identification of a nonlinear dynamic system, four different models, depending on how the output of the system is defined in terms of past values of the output and past values of the input. These models can be described in terms of nonlinear difference equations.

Model I. The output $y(n + 1)$ at time $n + 1$ depends linearly on N past values of the output, $y(n), \ldots, y(n - N + 1)$, and nonlinearly on M past values of the input, $u(n), \ldots, u(n - M + 1)$, as shown by

$$y(n + 1) = \sum_{i=0}^{N-1} \alpha_i y(n - i) + g(u(n), u(n - 1), \ldots, u(n - M + 1)) \tag{5}$$

where $g(\cdot, \ldots, \cdot)$ is a nonlinear function that is differentiable with respect to its arguments. It is assumed that $M \leq N$. The model is shown in Figure 1.

Model II. The output $y(n + 1)$ at time $n + 1$ depends nonlinearly on N past values of the output and linearly on M past values of the input, as shown by

$$y(n + 1) = f(y(n), y(n - 1), \ldots, y(n - N + 1)) + \sum_{i=0}^{M-1} \beta_i u(n - 1) \tag{6}$$

where $f(\cdot, \ldots, \cdot)$ is another nonlinear function that is also differentiable with respect to its arguments. The model is represented by the block diagram shown in Figure 2.

Model III. The output $y(n + 1)$ at time $n + 1$ depends nonlinearly on past values of both the output and the input in a separable manner, as shown by

$$y(n + 1) = f(y(n), y(n - 1), \ldots, y(n - N + 1)) + g(u(n), u(n - 1), \ldots, u(n - M + 1)) \tag{7}$$

Figure 3 represents the model.

Model IV. The output $y(n + 1)$ at time $n + 1$ depends nonlinearly on past values of both the output and the input in a nonseparable manner, as shown by

$$y(n + 1) = f(y(n), y(n - 1), \ldots, y(n - N + 1); u(n), u(n - 1), \ldots, u(n - M + 1)) \tag{8}$$

The model is shown in Figure 4.

Clearly, model IV is the most general, in that it includes the other three models as special cases. In the light of the universal approximation theorem, multilayer perceptrons can indeed be designed using the back-propagation algorithm to approximate the input–output mapping

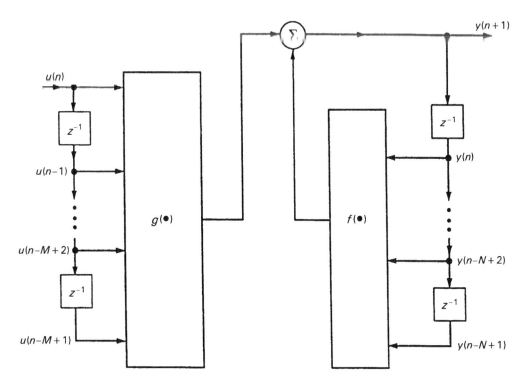

FIGURE 1
Representation of model I.

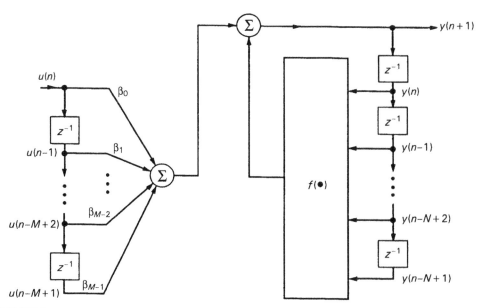

FIGURE 2
Representation of model II.

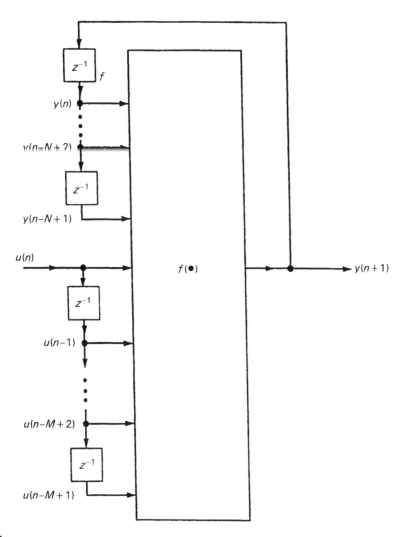

FIGURE 3
Representation of model III.

described by models I to IV over compact sets [61]. Static and dynamic back-propagation methods have been proposed to adjust the synaptic weights. The idea of dynamic back-propagation is introduced to generate the partial derivatives of a performance index with respect to adjustable parameters on line. Static or dynamic back-propagation is used, depending on the structure of the identifier. In the parallel model, past output samples are taken from the model itself and dynamic back-propagation is used,

$$\hat{y}_p(w, t) = f_w[\hat{y}_p(w, t-1), \ldots, \hat{y}_p(t-n), u(t-1), \ldots, u(t-l)] \tag{9}$$

whereas in the series parallel model, actual process outputs are taken and static back-propagation is used,

$$\hat{y}_p(w, t) = f_w(y(t-1), \ldots, y(t-n), u(t-1), \ldots, u(t-l)) \tag{10}$$

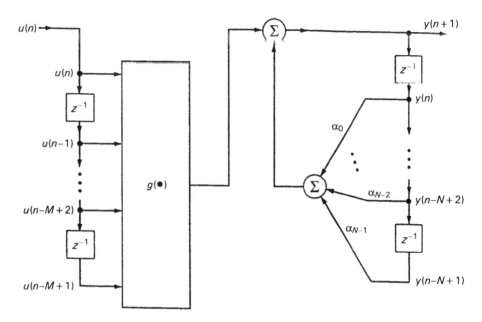

FIGURE 4
Representation of model IV.

where $n \geq l$ for physically realizable systems. Narendra and Panthasarthy [61] point out that a lot of theoretical research in the area of determining stable adaptive laws for the adjustment of the parameters, and control of unstable systems in some compact domain in state space, is needed to justify the model suggested.

Nguyen and Widrow [65] have shown how a feedforward neural network can learn on its own to control a nonlinear dynamical system. Two FNNs were used: an emulator and a controller. The emulator learnt the forward dynamics of the system, and then the controller learnt to control the emulator via error back-propagation. Thus, error back-propagation through the dynamical system was avoided. The trained controller was then used to control the actual nonlinear dynamical system. These authors have presented an example of the use of back-propagation through time to train a controller for a simulated tractor-trailer-truck that must back up to a loading dock from arbitrary initial positions.

Chen et al. [11] have developed a practical algorithm for identifying NARMAX models based on radial basis functions from noise-corrupted data. The algorithm consists of an iterative orthogonal-forward-regression (OFR) routine coupled with model validity tests. The orthogonal-forward-regression routine selects parsimonious radial-basis-function models, while the model validity tests measure the quality of fit. They have shown that the iterative identification algorithm, derived by coupling the OFR routine and the model validity tests, provides a powerful procedure for fitting parsimonious RBF models to real-world systems in the presence of correlated noise.

Kuschewski et al. [48] have reported the use of adalines, two-layer and three-layer feedforward neural networks for identification and control of dynamical systems. They discussed the application of FNNs for the identification of the system's forward and inverse dynamics. They also investigated the effect that the type of nonlinear activation functions present in the neuron and the type of nonlinear functions present in the weight adaptation algorithms have on

FNN system dynamics identification performance. They pointed out that the effect that different nonlinearities have on the identification of forward dynamics of the process is insignificant. However, the choice of the sampling period is important for good performance. In the case of identification of inverse dynamics of the system, the nonlinearities in the neurons affect the performance significantly, and therefore the choice of nonlinear function is very important for satisfactory inverse dynamics identification. In this case also, choice of sampling period was important for good performance.

Pramod and Bose [68] have investigated the system identification using ARMA modeling and neural networks. The neural network structure is utilized for identification of stochastic processes and tracks system dynamics by on-line adjustment of network parameters. Neural dynamics was based on impulse responses or the Green's functions that are the most generalized form available for investigation of nonlinear systems, and an iterative algorithm was derived using conventional principles of gradient descent and back-propagation. Exponential smoothing was used to estimate the current value from a large number of previous estimates of the Green's function. A new feedforward memory neuron was formulated and interpreted. The learning algorithms are derived by analysis of the network error equation and are found to be very similar to conventional back-propagation algorithms. Stability of convergence can also be evaluated as the iterative process develops, since the change in weights to any node follows an ARMA process depending on the current values of the estimated Green's functions. The neural identification scheme was tested for time-invariant and time-variant cases with sinusoidal and step variations in the Green's function.

Mukhopadhyay and Narendra [59] have described the use of neural networks for identification of nonlinear systems in the presence of input disturbances. Techniques, for disturbance rejection in the identification of nonlinear dynamical systems using radial basis functions as well as multilayer neural networks are reported. A large class of external disturbances are modeled as the outputs of linear or nonlinear unforced dynamic systems. The authors have discussed the case when the disturbance appears additively at the input and is the output of an unforced difference equation. They have also described the modification necessary in the identifier and controller structures to compensate for the effect of the disturbance on the plant output. The method used involves the augmentation of state space of the disturbance-free plant in an attempt to eliminate the effect of disturbance.

Wang et al. [81] have shown the use of neural networks for modeling unknown nonlinear systems subject to unmeasurable disturbances. Nonlinear modes of the disturbances were assumed to be known. A new performance function for modeling the unknown nonlinear function was selected and a gradient descent algorithm that adjusts the weights was derived.

Tsoi and Back [78] have reviewed the status of work in the area of locally recurrent globally feedforward network achitectures. They show that this class of networks provides a rich architecture for time series modeling. The simulation results reported show that the networks are capable of learning to predict nonlinear time series. The authors have pointed out that little is known about the properties of these networks. It would be of considerable interest if the relationship among these networks were studied with a view to providing a good architecture for nonlinear time series modeling, and a better understanding of their stability, convergence, and functional properties. Puskorius et al. [70] discuss the neurocontrol of nonlinear dynamical systems using recurrent networks trained with Kalman filter-based algorithm. They show how dynamic recurrent neural networks can be trained with parameter-based extended Kalman filters.

Narendra [63] has formulated a globally stable adaptive rule for nonlinear plant identification with an RBF neural network. Like the approximation theorem cited in the literature [35, 71], this adaptive rule assumes a fixed RBF hidden layer. Also, in this case the question of determining the parameters of RBF units remains open.

Mak and Sinha [57] have shown that RBF networks can be used for the identification of nonlinear systems. Their training algorithm combines the center selection by orthogonal least squares method with supervised learning of linear weights by error correction using the gradient-descent search procedure. The proposed algorithm has the ability to reduce the complexity of the RBF network with highest accuracy. The complexity is reduced by using a smaller number of RBF centers.

3.2   Inverse Models Using Neural Networks

In this approach, a neural network is trained, using supervised learning, to develop an inverse model of the plant. The network input is the process output, and the network output is the corresponding process input. The network is trained to minimize the squared error (error energy function) between the neural network output and the plant input. Figure 5 shows this type of identifier defined as an inverse transfer function identifier. In this type of identifier, the neural network output converges with the plant input after learning and the inverse transfer function of the plant is composed in the neural network. Neural network inverse models can capture a characteristic source of nonlinearity in many industrial processes, the variation of the process gain with the operating point.

Psaltis et al. [69] have used a feedfoward neural network-based controller within a general plant control system. They proposed general and specialized learning architectures that use error back-propagation methods to adjust the synaptic weights. The general architecture is suitable for learning plant inverse dynamics over the entire state space, but it can be very difficult to use it alone to provide adequate performance in a practical control application. To circumvent this problem, they introduced specialized learning. The specialized architecture uses error back-propagation through the plant as well as through the feedfoward neural network to learn plant inverse dynamics. They concluded that generalized training in conjunction with specialized training should be used to gain the advantages of both the methods.

Kawato et al. [43] have used a feedback error learning architecture to teach the inverse dynamics model of a plant to a feedforward neural network. The FNN then generates the feedforward control input for the plant. Their control architecture has the following advantages: The desired output of the inverse dynamics model is not required. Learning and controls are done on line and error back-propagation through the plant is not required. It is shown that the feedback signal reduces to zero as the learning proceeds. The authors showed that the proposed scheme has the ability to generalize learned movements.

Yamada et al. [79] have proposed a practical neural network design method for the identification of both the direct and inverse transfer function of the system. A nonlinear plant

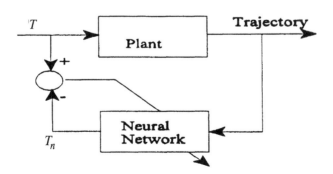

FIGURE 5
Inverse model learning.

simulator as a practical application of the direct transfer function identifier using a neural network is proposed. They show that a neural network identifer can represent nonlinear plant characteristics very well. As a practical application, the identification result of the direct transfer function was applied to a nonlinear simulator and that of the inverse transfer function was applied to a direct controller through the matrix information.

Inverse modeling suffers from two significant problems. First, many processes have transport delays that imply that any change in the input to a process will only affect the process response after a "dead time". In such cases, the process inverse is noncausal. The second problem that may arise is that the mapping from a steady-state process output to steady-state process input may be one-to-many (and thus not mathematically invertible). The least-mean-squared averaging behavior leads to control actions that will likely not be affective.

3.3   Parametric Identification with Neural Networks

While black-box modeling is the most popular approach to neural network-based process identification, other approaches have also been developed and deployed. For example, neural networks can help identify physically meaningful, non black-box models. With such models, two subproblems arise:

1. *Model structure identification*. For dynamic process models, for example, model structure refers typically to the form of (linear or nonlinear) differential or difference equations.
2. *Parameter estimation*. Given a model structure, values for the associated parameters must be determined. Relevant parameters can include "generic" ones such as time constants, gains, and delays as well as physical parameters such as diffusion rates and heat transfer coefficients.

In current practice, the model structure is usually identified either by a user or through some trial-and-error method. Parameter values are typically estimated by solving an optimization problem: values are sought for which the difference between the model output and the actual system output is minimized. When, as is often the case, the parameters depend nonlinearly on the experimental data, the optimization problem is nonlinear and iterative algorithms must be used.

Neural networks trained with supervised learning can be used for both of these problems. As structure identifiers, they can be trained to select elements of a model structure from a predetermined set [46]. These elements can then be composed to a legal structure. Structure identification with neural networks requires that the space of likely model structure be known in advance. If this condition is met, a manual, expertise-intensive aspect of system identification can be automated.

Neural network parameter estimators can generate parameter values for a given structure or set of structures, dramatically improving estimation times relative to iterative optimization algorithms. The iterative process, each iteration of which is usually computationally involved, is replaced by a feedforward one-shot operation that is computationally simple. The neural network estimator can be operated stand-alone, or as an initializer for an optimization algorithm [20].

4   CONCLUSIONS

In this chapter, application of neural networks in identification of nonlinear systems is reviewed. The study has shown that neural networks have good capabilities for representing complex nonlinear systems. Multilayer neural networks prove to be universal models for nonlinear systems. The network can learn the high-order mappings that occur in nonlinear series. Using control strategies, the network can replace the standard predictor in the internal control model and offer superior performance. The network can succeed in learning the complicated mappings of problems that are intractable to solve using standard estimation techniques. By designing the architecture to better fit the known qualities of the problem space, faster and more accurate convergence performance results.

The choice of network architectures and learning algorithm used to train the network affects the performance of the neural network. There are no set rules for determining the architecture of the neural network. Lack of sound design techniques in the development of neural networks presents difficulty for a variety of problems. This had led researchers to develop techniques for automating the design of neural network architectures to solve problems under a given design and performance constraints. The combination of neural networks and evolutionary algorithms such as genetic algorithm offers an attractive approach to solving complex problems where neither the detailed structure nor the size of solution is known in advance. The genetic algorithm introduces changes in the topology of a neural network one step at a time and measures the performance of the network in terms of reduced errors and improved training times. Topology changes that result in improved performance are retained and others are discarded. Hence, a neural network can be led to grow and perform a set of specified tasks better. There is a need to develop sound scientific principles to guide the development and application of evolutionary techniques in the design of neural network architectures.

The work done so far can be considered to be mostly experimental in nature. A firm theoretical foundation is needed. There are no set guidelines as to the type of network architecture, the number of layers, the necessary number of nodes per layer, the nonlinear transfer function to be used, and the learning rate for a particular problem. Issues such as stability, controllability, and observability of the system need to be addressed. The various neural network approaches need to be compared to conventional approaches and its needs to be determined whether neural networks provide any performance benefits. The strengths and weaknesses of neural networks must be investigated. The major drawback of the back-propagation learning rule is the long learning time and it needs to be properly justified for practical use of a neural network. These approaches will be more attractive if faster learning is used. As attempts are made to solve more complex problems using neural networks, a better understanding of the network's function is necessary. A relationship needs to be established between the system under study (i.e., the nonlinear function to be approximated) and the structure of a suitable network.

Multilayer feedfoward networks can be considered to be static mappings—each input is independent of the previous input. Introduction of feedback produces a recurrent network that can retain state information between inputs, and therefore can represent a dynamic system. While much of the work is currently being done on multilayer feedforward networks, recurrent networks are likely to play an important role in identification and control of dynamic systems. This raises questions of approximation theory and learning algorithms for dynamical networks.

A comprehensive study is required to compare the neural network model with other nonlinear models. Efficient procedures for selecting subset models have been developed for polynomial models. A parsimonious model has advantages in controller design, prediction, and other practical applications. Selection of a subset neural network model is worth investigating.

Fuzzy logic based on fuzzy set theory is being used in the identification and control of ill-defined and complex systems [53]. The fusion of neural networks and fuzzy logic would help complement the advantages that each of them possesses individually, learning can be incorporated in fuzzy logic, and a systematic structure can be incorporated in neural networks. Fuzzy neural network models tend to be easier to interpret than other types of neural network models in that the weights in the fuzzification layer determine the membership functions of the fuzzy local regions, while the weights in the function layer determine the local models in each region. In contrast, it is usually very difficult to interpet the meaning of weights in conventional neural network models. The fuzzy neural network modeling approach utilizes both system knowledge and system input–output data.

In this chapter attempt has been made to provide a survey of neural networks applied to modeling of nonlinear systems. The basic ideas and techniques of neural networks have been described. Applications of a variety of neural network architectures in modeling were surveyed. The survey is aimed at researchers currently working in the area of modeling and control. Various issues and problems are discussed. In the future, as neural networks are improved and better understood, the solutions to the problems cited in this chapter will be much more competitive with conventional approaches. The authors believe that the use of neural networks in modeling is an effective approach with great application potential and further research in this field is worth pursuing.

REFERENCES

[1] J.S. Albus, Data storage in the cerebellar model articulation controller (CMAC). *Trans. ASME, J. Dynamics Systems, Measurements, and Control*, Vol. 97, No. 3, pp. 228–233, 1975.

[2] J.S. Albus, A new approach to manipulator control: the cerebellar model articulation controller (CMAC). *Trans. ASME, J. Dynamics Systems, Measurements, and Control*, Vol. 97, No. 3, pp. 220–227, 1975.

[3] A.M. Annaswamy and S.-H. Yu, θ-adaptive neural networks: a new approach to parameter estimation, *IEEE Trans. Neural Networks*, Vol. 7, No. 4, pp. 907–918, 1996.

[4] J.A. Anderson and E. Rosenfeld, *Neurocomputing: Foundations of Research*. MIT Press, Cambridge, MA, 1988.

[5] A.D. Back and A.C. Tsoi, FIR and IIR synapses, a new neural network architecture for time series modeling, *Neural Computation*, Vol. 3, pp. 375–385, 1991.

[6] P.F. Baldi and K. Hornik, Learning linear neural networks—a survey, *IEEE Trans. Neural Networks*, Vol. 6, No. 4, pp. 837–858, 1995.

[7] A.R. Barron, Neural net approximation, *Proc. 7th Yale Workshop on Adaptive and Learning Systems*, New Haven, CT, 1992, pp. 68–72. Also, A.R. Barron, Universal approximation bounds for superposition of a sigmoidal function, *IEEE Trans. Information Theory*, Vol. 39, No. 3, pp. 930–945, 1993.

[8] S.A. Billings, Identification of nonlinear systems—a survey, *IEEE Proc.*, pp. 272–285, 1980.

[9] S.A. Billings, H.B. Jamaluddin, and S. Chen, Properties of neural networks with applications to modeling nonlinear dynamical systems, *Int. J. Control*, Vol. 55, No. 1, pp. 193–224, 1992.

[10] George E.P. Box and Gwilym M. Jenkins, *Time Series Analysis: Forecasting and Control*. Holden-Day, San Francisco, 1970.

[11] S. Chen, S.A. Billings, and P.M. Grant, Nonlinear system identification using neural networks, *Int. J. Control*, Vol. 51, No. 6, pp. 1191–1214, 1990.

[12] S. Chen, S.A. Billings, C.F.N. Cowan, and P.M. Grant, Practical identification of Narmax models using radial basis functions, *Int. J. Control*, Vol. 52, No. 6, pp. 1327–1350, 1990.

[13] S. Chen and S.A. Billings, Modeling and analysis of nonlinear time series, *Int. J. Control*, Vol. 50, No. 6, pp. 2151–2171, 1989.

[14] S. Chen and S.A. Billings, Representation of non-linear systems: the NARMAX model, *Int. J. Control*, Vol. 49, No. 3, pp. 1013–1032, 1989.

[15] B. Cheng and D. Titterington, Neural networks: a review from a statistical perspective, *Statistical Science*, Vol. 9, pp. 2–54, 1994.

[16] E.-S. Ching, S. Chen, and B. Mulgrew, Gradient radial basis function networks for nonlinear and nonstationary time series prediction, *IEEE Trans. Neural Networks*, Vol. 7, No. 2, pp. 190–194, 1996.

[17] P.S. Churchland and T.J. Sejnowski, *The Computational Brain*. MIT Press, Cambridge, MA, 1992.

[18] G. Cybenko, Approximations by superpositions of a sigmoidal function, *Mathematical Control Signal Systems*, Vol. 2, pp. 303–314, 1989.

[19] G. Cybenko, *Continous Valued Neural Networks with Two Hidden Layers are Sufficient*, Technical report, Department of Computer Science, Tufts University, Medford, MA, 1988.

[20] W. Foslien, A.F. Konar, and T. Samad, Optimization with neural memory for process parameter estimation, in S. K. Rogers (ed.), *Applications of Artificial Neural Networks III*, Proc. SPIE 1709, pp. 457–467.

[21] K. Funahasi, On the approximate realization of continuous mappings by neural networks, *Neural Networks*, Vol. 2, No. 3, pp. 183–192, 1989.

[22] G.C. Goodwin and R.L. Payne, *Dynamic System Identification: Experiment Design and Data Analysis*. Academic Press, New York, 1977.

[23] M.M. Gupta and Naresh K. Sinha, *Intelligent Control Systems*. IEEE Press, New York, 1995.

[24] Pramod Gupta and Naresh K. Sinha, A new algorithm for efficient identification of nonlinear systems using neural networks, in *Proc. Int. Conf. Trends in Industrial Measurements & Automation, TIMA- 96*, 1996, pp. 195–199.

[25] Pramod Gupta and Naresh K. Sinha, Control of robotic manipulators using neural networks—a survey, in S. Tzafestas (ed.), *Methods and Applications of Intelligent Control*, pp. 103–133, Kluwer Academic Publishers, 1997.

[26] Pramod Gupta and Naresh K. Sinha, Modeling robot dynamics using dynamic neural networks, *SYSID'97 11th IFAC Symp. System Identification, Fukuoka, Japan*, 1997, pp. 783–788.

[27] Pramod Gupta, *Neurocontrol of Robotic Manipulators*, PhD Thesis, McMaster University, 1997.

[28] S. Haykin, *Neural Networks: A Comprehensive Foundation*. Maxwell Macmillan, Canada, 1994.

[29] R. Hecht-Nielsen, Neurocomputer applications, in R. Eckmiller and Ch. V.d. Malsburg (eds.), *Neural Computers*, pp. 445–453. Springer-Verlag, Berlin, 1988.

[30] R. Hecht-Nielsen, Kolmogorov's mapping neural network existence theorem, *Proc. IEEE 1st Int. Conf. Neural Networks*, 1987, pp. 11–14.

[31] R. Hecht-Nielsen, Theory of the back-propagation neural network, *Proc. Int. Joint Conf. Neural Networks, Washington, DC*, 1989, pp. 593–606.

[32] R. Hecht-Nielsen, *Neurocomputing*. Addison-Wesley, Reading, MA, 1990.

[33] J.J. Hopfield, Neural networks and physical systems with emergent collective computation abilities, *Proc. National Academy of Sciences USA*, Vol. 79, pp. 2554–2558, 1982.

[34] J.J. Hopfield, Neurons with graded response have collective computational properties like those of two-state neurons, *Proc. National Academy of Sciences USA*, Vol. 81, pp. 3088–3092, 1984.

[35] K. Hornik, M. Stinchombe, and H. White, Multilayer feedforward networks are universal approximators, *Neural Networks*, Vol. 2, No. 5, pp. 359–366, 1989.

[36] Tomas Hryces, *Neurocontrol: Towards an Industrial Control Methodology*. Wiley, New York, 1997.

[37] IEEE, Special Issue on Neural Networks, *IEEE Control Systems Magazine*, Vol. 9, No. 3, 1989.

[38] IEEE, Special Issue on Neural Networks, *IEEE Control Systems Magazine*, Vol. 10, No. 3, 1990.

[39] Robert A. Jacobs, Increased rates of convergence through learning rate adaptation, *Neural Networks*, Vol. 1, No. 4, pp. 295–307, 1988.

[40] R.A. Jacobs and M.I. Jordan, Learning piecewise control strategies in a modular neural network architecture, *IEEE Trans. Systems, Man, and Cybernetics*, Vol. 23, No. 2, pp. 337–345, 1993.

[41] M.I. Jordan and D.E. Rumelhart, Foward models: supervised learning with a distal teacher, *Cognitive Science*, Vol. 16, pp. 307–354, 1992.

[42] L. Jin and M.M. Gupta, Globally asymptotical stability of discrete-time analog neural networks, *IEEE Trans. Neural Networks*, Vol. 7, No. 4, pp. 1024–1031, 1996.

[43] M. Kawato, Y. Uno, M. Isobe, and R. Suzuki, Hierarchical neural network model for voluntary movement with applications to robotics, *IEEE Control Systems Magazine*, pp. 8–16, 1988.

[44] T. Kohonen, *Self-Organization and Associative Memory*. Berlin: Springer-Verlag, 1987.

[45] A.N. Kolmogorov, On the representation of continuous functions of many variables by superposition of continuous functions of one variable and addition, *Doklady Akademii Nauk SSR*, Vol. 114, pp. 953–956, 1957.

[46] A.F. Konar, T. Samad, and W. Foslien, Hybrid neural network/algorithmic approaches to system identification, *Preprints of the IFAC Symposium on DYCORD 92*, College Park, MD.

[47] E.B. Kosmatopoulos, M.M. Polycorpou, M.A. Christodoulo, and P.A. Ioannou, High-order neural network structures for identification of dynamical systems, *IEEE Trans. Neural Networks*, Vol. 6, No. 4, pp. 422–431, 1995.

[48] John G. Kuschewski, Stefen Hui, and Stanislaw H. Zak, Application of feedforward neural networks to dynamical system identification and control, *IEEE Trans. Control Systems Technology*, Vol. 1, No. 1, pp. 37–49, 1993.

[49] A. Lapedes and R. Farber, *Nonlinear Signal Processing Using Neural Networks: Prediction and System Modeling*, Report LA-UR-87-2662, Los Alamos National Laboratory, 1987.

[50] I.J. Leontaritis and S.A. Billings, Input–output parametric models for nonlinear systems, *Int. J. Control*, Vol. 41, No. 2, pp. 303–344, 1985.

[51] A.U. Levin and K.S. Narendra, Control of nonlinear dynamical systems using neural networks—Part II: Observability, identification and control, *IEEE Trans. Neural Networks*, Vol. 7, No. 2, pp. 30–42, 1996.

[52] A.U. Levin and K.S. Narendra, Recursive identification using feedforward neural networks, *Int. J. Control*, Vol. 61, pp. 533–547, 1995.

[53] C.-J. Lin and C.T. Lin, Reinforcement learning for an ART-based fuzzy adaptive learning control network, *IEEE Trans. Neural Networks*, Vol. 117, No. 3, pp. 709–731, 1996.

[54] C.S. Liu and H. Kim, Selection of learning parameters for CMAC-based adaptive critic learning, *IEEE Trans. Neural Networks*, Vol. 6, No. 4, pp. 642–647, 1995.

[55] L. Ljung and T. Söderström, *Theory and Practice of Recursive Identification*, MIT Press, Cambridge, MA, 1983.

[56] G.G. Lorentz, The 13th Problem of Hilbert, *Proc. Symp. Pure Math.*, American Mathematical Society, 1976.

[57] Mak, Hung, Sing, and Naresh K. Sinha, Application of RBF neural networks for identification and control, in *Proc. Fourth Int. Conf. Control, Automation, Robotics and Vision, Singapore*, 1996, pp. 1938–1942.

[58] J.O. Moody and P.J. Antsaklis, The dependence identification neural network construction algorithm, *IEEE Trans. Neural Networks*, Vol. 7, No. 2, pp. 3–15, 1996.

[59] S. Mukhopadhyay and K.S. Narendra, Disturbance rejection in nonlinear systems using neural networks, *IEEE Trans. Neural Networks*, Vol. 4, No. 1, pp. 63–72, 1993.

[60] S. Mukhopadhyay and K.S. Narendra, Intelligent control using neural networks, in Madan M. Gupta and Naresh K. Sinha (eds.), *Intelligent Control Systems: Theory and Applications*. IEEE Press, New York, 1995, pp. 151–186.

[61] K.S. Narendra and K. Parthasarthy, Identification and control of dynamical systems using neural networks, *IEEE Trans. Neural Networks*, Vol. 1, No. 1, pp. 4–27, 1990.

[62] K.S. Narendra and A.M. Annaswamy, *Stable Adaptive Systems*. Prentice-Hall, Englewood Cliffs, NJ, 1989.

[63] K.S. Narenda, Adaptive control of dynamical systems using neural networks, in D.A. White and D.A. Sofge (eds.), *Handbook of Intelligent Control*. Van Nostrand Reinhold, New York, 1992, pp. 141–183.

[64] O. Nerrand, et al., Training recurrent neural networks: why and how? An illustration in dynamical process modeling, *IEEE Trans. Neural Networks*, Vol. 5, No. 2, pp. 178–184, 1994.

[65] D.H. Nguyen and B. Widrow, Neural networks for self-learning control systems, *IEEE Control Systems Magazine*, Vol. 10, No. 3, pp. 18–23, 1990.

[66] Fernando J. Pineda, Recurrent back-propagation and the dynamical approach to adaptive neural computation, *Neural Computation*, Vol. 1, pp. 161–172, 1989.

[67] I. Poli and R.D. Jones, A neural network model for prediction, *J. American Statistical Association*, Vol. 89, pp. 117–121, 1994.

[68] B.R. Pramod and S.C. Bose, System identification using ARMA modeling and neural networks, *J. Engineering and Industry*, Vol. 115, pp. 487–491, 1993.

[69] D. Psaltis, A. Sideris, and A.A. Yamamura, A multilayered neural network controller, *IEEE Control Systems Magazine*, Vol. 8, No. 2, pp. 17–21, 1988.

[70] G.V. Puskorius and Lee A. Feldkamp, Neurocontrol of nonlinear dynamical systems with Kalman filter trained recurrent networks, *IEEE Trans. Neural Networks*, Vol. 5, pp. 279–297, 1994.

[71] A.-P. Refenes (ed.), *Neural Networks in the Capital Markets*. Wiley, Chichester, UK, 1995.

[72] F. Rosenblatt, The perceptron: a probabilistic model for information storage and organization in the brain, *Psychological Review*, Vol. 65, pp. 386–408, 1958.

[73] J.E. Rumelhart, J.L. McClelland and the PDP Research Group, *Parallel Distributed Processing, Explorations in the Microstructure of Cognition*, Vol. I: *Foundations*. MIT Press, Cambridge, MA, 1986.

[74] N.K. Sinha and B. Kuszta, *Modeling and Identification of Dynamic Systems*. Van Nostrand Reinhold, New York, 1983.

[75] M. Stinchcombe and H. White, Universal approximation using feedforward networks with non-sigmoid hidden layer activation function, *Proc. Int. Conf. Neural Networks, San Diego*, 1989, pp. 612–617.

[76] D. Tank and J. Hopfield, Neural computation of decisions in optimization problems, *Biological Cybernetics*, Vol. 52, pp. 141–152, 1985.

[77] K. Tanak, An approach to stability criteria of neural network control systems, *IEEE Trans. Neural Networks*, Vol. 7, No. 3, pp. 629–642, 1996.

[78] Ah Chung Tsoi and Andrew D. Back, Locally recurrent globally feedforward networks: a critical review of architectures, *IEEE Trans. Neural Networks*, Vol. 5, No. 2, pp. 229–239, 1994.

[79] Takayuki Yamada and Tetsuro Yabuta, Dynamic system identification using neural networks, *IEEE Trans. Systems, Man, and Cybernetics*, Vol. 23, No. 1, pp. 204–211, 1993.

[80] A. Waibel, T. Hanazawa, G. Hinton, K. Shikano, and K. Lang, Phonemic recognition using time delay neural networks, *IEEE Trans. Acoustics, Speech, and Signal Processing*, Vol. 37, pp. 328–339, 1989.

[81] H. Wang, M. Brown, and C.J. Harris, Neural network modeling of unknown nonlinear systems subject to immeasurable disturbances, *IEEE Proc. Control Theory and Applications*, Vol. 141, No. 4, pp. 216–222, 1994.

[82] D.A. White and D.A. Sofge (eds.), *Handbook of Intelligent Control, Neural Fuzzy, and Adaptive Approaches*. Van Nostrand Reinhold, New York, 1992.

[83] H. White, Learning in artificial neural networks: a statistical perspective, *Neural Computation*, Vol. 1, pp. 425–464, 1989.

[84] H. White, Connectionist nonparametric regression: multilayer feedforward networks can learn arbitrary mapping, *Neural Networks*, Vol. 3, No. 5, pp. 535–549, 1990.

[85] H. White, A.R. Gallant, K. Hornik, M. Stinchcombe, and J. Woolridge (eds.), *Artificial Neural Networks: Approximation and Learning Theory*. Blackwell Publishers, Cambridge, 1992.

[86] B. Widrow and M.A. Lehr, 30 years of adaptive neural networks: perceptron, medaline, and backpropagation, *Proc. IEEE*, Vol. 78, pp. 1415–1441, 1990.

[87] R.J. Williams and D. Zipser, A learning algorithm for continually running fully recurrent neural networks, *Neural Computation*, Vol. 1, pp. 270–280, 1989.

[88] R.J. Williams and J. Peng, An efficient gradient-based algorithm for on-line training of recurrent neural networks, *Neural Computation*, Vol. 2, pp. 490–501, 1990.

[89] L.A. Zadeh, From circuit theory to system theory, *Proc. IRE*, Vol. 50, pp. 856–865, 1962.

[90] J. Zhang and A.J. Morris, Fuzzy neural networks for nonlinear systems modeling, *IEEE Proc. Control Theory and Applications*, Vol. 142, No. 6, pp. 551–561, 1995.

CHAPTER 15

Sensor Fusion System Using Recurrent Fuzzy Inference

FUTOSHI KOBAYASHI and FUMIHITO ARAI

Department of Micro System Engineering, Graduate School of Engineering, Nagoya University, Japan

KOJI SHIMOJIMA

National Industrial Research Institute of Nagoya, Agency of Industrial Science and Technology, MITI, Nagoya, Japan

TOSHIO FUKUDA

Center of Cooperative Research in Advanced Science & Technology, Nagoya University, Japan

1 INTRODUCTION

Robotic and manufacturing systems are becoming more and more complex in order to adapt to real environment and various fields. Measurement and control methods are very important for dealing with complex systems, and various measurement and control methods are being studied. As the states, a system must recognize become more and more complex and numerous, methods of measuring the state also become more complex because of the accuracy required or the time consumed. Various kinds of sensor have been developed and produced for measuring the state accurately and quickly. However, some states cannot be measured by existing sensors. For efficient control of the system, it must infer its state from the phenomena of the system (sensor information) [1]. Previously, the researchers have investigated sensor fusion systems for inferring the state from the phenomena—least-squares method [2], Bayesian theory [3, 4], Kalman filter [5], and so on. However, these methods cannot be applied to problems in which the relation between the phenomena and the state is not clear. For these problems, neural networks or fuzzy systems are required with a learning algorithm to construct an inference structure [6, 7]. We have also proposed a multisensor integration system applied to fuzzy inference and achieved good results [8–11]. In these systems, all the sensor information can be acquired at the same sampling time because the measuring time of each sensor is assumed to be the same. However, the measuring time is different, because each sensor has particular characteristics for measurement and the accuracy of each sensor deteriorates with time. In dynamical systems, the accuracy of the sensor information decreases with time and it is not easy to infer the state accurately from such sensor information. For this reason, the traditional multisensor fusion/integration systems cannot fuse/integrate sensor information with different measuring times. We therefore have to develop a new fuzzy inference for sensor fusion systems that cannot acquire sensor information synchronously.

Fuzzy theory and fuzzy logic were proposed by L. A. Zadeh [12] and have been applied to expert systems in various process controllers. The fuzzy inference system is based on the concept of fuzzy set theory, fuzzy rules, and fuzzy reasoning. It can represent human knowledges or experience as fuzzy rules because it implements mapping from its input space to the output space by fuzzy rules. In most fuzzy systems, the shapes of the membership functions of the antecedent and the consequent parts, and the fuzzy rules, are determined and tuned through trial and error by the operators. It takes a long time to determine and tune them, and it is very difficult to design an optimal fuzzy system in detail. These problems become more severe when the fuzzy system is applied to a more complex system. Self-tuning methods have been proposed for resolving these problems [13–20]. These self-tuning methods can be classified into three categories: (1) antecedent part learning, which optimizes the shapes of the input membership function; (2) consequent part learning, which optimizes the consequent value; (3) combined optimization. These methods can automatically acquire the shapes of membership functions by learning. However, these methods cannot construct an optimal fuzzy inference because the operators determine the number of fuzzy rules in advance. Katayama et al. proposed a new learning method [21] for optimizing the structure of the fuzzy inference system. This method consists of two processes: One is the tuning of membership functions by the gradient method for existing fuzzy rules; the other is an incremental process by which new fuzzy rules are generated in such a way that the center is located at the point where the maximum error takes place in the input space. However, this method cannot always acquire the optimal fuzzy inference because the shape of the generated membership function is determined in advance. It is also difficult to estimate the state of the system accurately by a fuzzy inference system with these learning algorithms. Because these fuzzy inference systems cannot be applied to a sensor fusion system, that cannot acquire inputs with the same sampling times, it is necessary to develop a new fuzzy inference for a sensor fusion system that acquires sensor information asynchronously.

We propose recurrent fuzzy inference (RFI) with incremental learning, which uses the outputs as recurrent inputs. The learning method is based on that proposed by Katayama et al. [21]. This learning method tunes the shapes of the membership functions by the steepest-descent method for existing fuzzy rules. New fuzzy rules are then generated in such a way that center of each membership function is located at the point where the maximum error takes place in the input space. The shape of the new membership functions is determined by the grade of the previous fuzzy rules. Accordingly, this learning method can generate the new fuzzy rules without overlapping the previous ones. Thus, this learning method can generate the optimal fuzzy inference rapidly and accurately. We apply the RFI to a sensor fusion system. The sensor fusion system uses the recurrent inputs as the virtual sensor information.

To show the effectiveness of the sensor fusion system using the RFI, we apply our sensor fusion system to some numerical simulations of a tracking moving robot and the estimation of the surface roughness in a grinding process. In the numerical simulation of the tracking moving robot, we show the result of fusing the information of sensors that have different measuring times and accuracies. In the estimation of the surface roughness in a grinding system, we show the result of estimating the state of the system in real manufacturing system.

2 RECURRENT FUZZY INFERENCE AND ITS LEARNING ALGORITHM

2.1 Recurrent Fuzzy Inference

We propose recurrent fuzzy inference (RFI) with recurrent inputs (Figure 1), where $x_1, x_2, \ldots, x_I$ and $y_{t-1}, y_{t-2}, \ldots, y_{t-O}$ are the inputs and the recurrent inputs of this fuzzy inference. We use the well-known Takagi–Sugeno fuzzy model expressed in equation (1) to infer the output of the RFI from inputs:

$$Rule_j: \quad \text{If } x_1 \text{ is } M_{1j}, \ldots, x_I \text{ is } M_{Ij} \text{ and } y_{t-1} \text{ is } M_{t-1j}, \ldots, y_{t-O} \text{ is } M_{t-Oj},$$
$$\text{then } y_t \text{ is } w_j \tag{1}$$

where $M_{1j}, \ldots, M_{t-Oj}$ are the membership functions of an input. The shape of the membership functions of the RFI is expressed by radial basis function (RBF) with dead zone and is shown in Figure 2. The membership functions based on RBF are useful for reducing the numbers of membership functions and fuzzy rules. In Figure 2, a_{nj}, b_{nj}, c_{nj} are the coefficients that determine the shape of the membership functions, I_n is the input or the recurrent input, and μ_{nj} is the grade of the jth fuzzy rule for the input or the recurrent input. The consequent part is expressed by a real number.

The membership function of the ith input for the jth fuzzy rule is expressed by equations (2) and (3):

$$f(x_i) = \begin{cases} -b_{ij}(|x_i - a_{ij}| - c_{ij})^2 & (|x_i - a_{ij}| \geq c_{ij}) \\ 0 & (|x_i - a_{ij}| < c_{ij}) \end{cases} \tag{2}$$

$$\mu_{ij} = \exp\{f(x_i)\} \tag{3}$$

where μ_{ij} is the grade of the ith input for the jth fuzzy rule.

The membership function of the oth recurrent input for the jth fuzzy rule number is expressed in equations (4) and (5):

$$f(y_{t-o}) = \begin{cases} -b_{oj}(|y_{t-o} - a_{oj}| - c_{oj})^2 & (|y_{t-o} - a_{oj}| \geq c_{oj}) \\ 0 & (|y_{t-o} - a_{oj}| < c_{oj}) \end{cases} \tag{4}$$

$$\mu_{oj} = \exp\{f(y_{t-o})\} \tag{5}$$

where μ_{oj} is the grade of the oth recurrent input for the jth fuzzy rule.

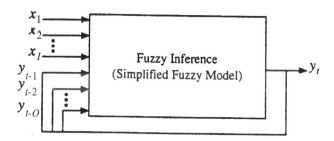

FIGURE 1
Recurrent fuzzy inference.

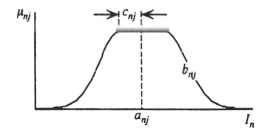

FIGURE 2
Membership function based on RBF.

The grade μ_j, for the jth fuzzy rule is expressed in equation (6) using the grade of the ith input μ_{ij} and the grade of the oth recurrent input μ_{oj}. The output y_t of the RFI is expressed by equation (7):

$$\mu_j = \prod_{i \in I} \mu_{ij} \cdot \prod_{o \in O} \mu_{oj} \tag{6}$$

$$y = \sum_{j=1}^{J} \mu_j \cdot w_j \bigg/ \sum_{j=1}^{J} \mu_j \tag{7}$$

where i is the input number, o is the recurrent input number, J is the number of the fuzzy rules, and w_j is the value of the consequent part of the jth fuzzy rule.

2.2   Learning Algorithm

The procedure of the learning method of the RFI is shown in Figure 3. This method is *incremental learning*. It is based on the steepest-descent method and can add new fuzzy rules.

The steepest-descent method is used for tuning the antecedent and consequent parts. The error function E is the mean square error of outputs expressed by equation (8):

$$E = \tfrac{1}{2}\{y - y^*\}^2 \tag{8}$$

where, y and y^* are the output of the RFI and the desired output, respectively.

The tuning formula of the consequent part of the jth fuzzy rule is expressed by equation (9):

$$w_j = w_j' - k_w \frac{\partial E}{\partial w_j} \tag{9}$$

where k_w is the coefficient of learning for the consequent part.

The coefficients a_{nj}, b_{nj}, and c_{nj} of the membership functions of the antecedent part are then tuned by equations (10), (11), and (12):

$$a_{ij} = a_{ij}' - k_a \frac{\partial E_p}{\partial a_{ij}} \tag{10}$$

$$b_{ij} = b_{ij}' - k_b \frac{\partial E_p}{\partial b_{ij}} \tag{11}$$

$$c_{ij} = c_{ij}' - k_c \frac{\partial E_p}{\partial c_{ij}} \tag{12}$$

where k_a, k_b, k_c are the coefficients of learning for the antecedent part.

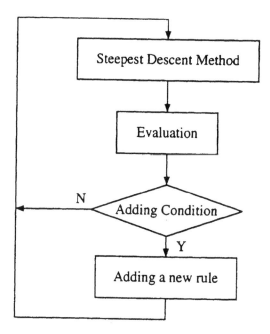

FIGURE 3
Procedure or incremental learning.

In the evaluation process, this system calculates the grade μ_j of the jth fuzzy rule at the maximum error point, and calculates the maximum grade λ at the maximum error point by equation (13):

$$\lambda = \max_{j \in J} \{\mu_j\} \tag{13}$$

When the maximum error is larger than the threshold of error, and the maximum grade λ at the maximum error point is less than the threshold of grade (equation 14), a new fuzzy rule is generated:

$$E > Th_{\text{error}}, \qquad \lambda < Th_{\text{grade}} \tag{14}$$

where Th_{error}, Th_{grade} are the thresholds, which are determined by the operator in advance.

The parameters of the new fuzzy rules are expressed by equation (15):

$$a_{ij+1} = x_i, \qquad a_{oj+1} = y_{t-o}$$
$$b_{ij+1}, \ b_{oj+1} = 100.0\lambda \tag{15}$$
$$c_{ij+1}, c_{oj+1} = \frac{1 - \lambda}{C}$$

where x_i, y_{t-o} are the values at the points where the maximum error occurs, $j + 1$ is the number of new fuzzy rules, and C is a fixed number determined by an operator.

The shape of the membership functions of the new fuzzy rules is shown in Figure 4. As shown, when the maximum grade λ at the maximum error point is large, the dead zone is narrow and the slope of new membership functions is steep. On the other hand, when the maximum grade λ at the maximum error point is small, the dead zone is wide and the slope of a new membership functions is gentle. That is, as shown in Figure 4, when the maximum grade is large, the distance between the maximum error point and the previous fuzzy rule point is small, and

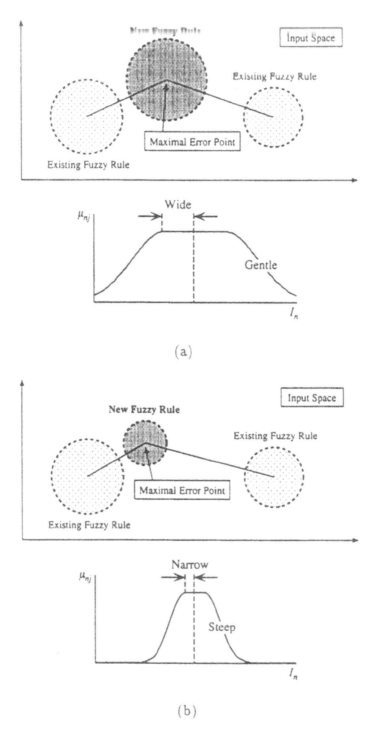

FIGURE 4
Generation of new fuzzy rules. (a) The grade of the previous rule is low. (b) The grade of the previous rule is high.

when the maximum grade is small, the distance is large. The shape of the membership functions is determined in this way.

3 SENSOR FUSION SYSTEM USING RECURRENT FUZZY INFERENCE

Robotic and manufacturing systems must recognize the various states needed for efficient control because these systems become increasingly complex. However, it is very difficult to measure some of the states because of the measuring time and the accuracy of the sensor. It is important, therefore, to develop a sensor fusion system for inferring these states. Figure 5 expresses the concept of a sensor fusion system. A sensor fusion system can extract the necessary states from environmental information. The application of soft computing methods, e.g., fuzzy logic, neural networks, evolutionary computation, and artificial intelligence, to sensor fusion systems has been proposed. We have also proposed a multisensor integration system using fuzzy inference [8–11].

There are now various kinds of sensors for measuring the phenomena of the system. The measuring time and the accuracy of the sensor information differ because each sensor has particular characteristics for measurement. In a conventional sensor fusion system, it is difficult to infer the state of a system that cannot synchronously acquire multiple sensor information using existing sensors because their measuring times are different. We therefore apply the proposed RFI to a sensor fusion system. Figure 6 shows the concept of the proposed sensor fusion system using RFI. As shown, one sensor has long measuring time and high accuracy, another sensor has average measuring time and accuracy, and the other sensor has a short measuring time and low accuracy. This system uses the outputs of each sensor as the inputs of the RFI and uses the outputs of the RFI as the recurrent inputs of the RFI. In Figure 6, the arrow from the sensor unit to the sensor fusion system expresses the quantity (measuring time) and the accuracy of sensor information. In other words, if an arrow is wide, the quantity of its sensor is greater than that of a sensor whose arrow is narrow; and if an arrow is dark, the accuracy is higher than that of a sensor whose arrow is light.

It follows from Figure 6 that the recurrent inputs of the RFI can be used as the information of virtual sensors. From these virtual sensors, the system can acquire states of the system that cannot be measured by existing sensors. However, the accuracy of the virtual sensors is determined by the condition of learning of the RFI because the recurrent inputs are the RFIs

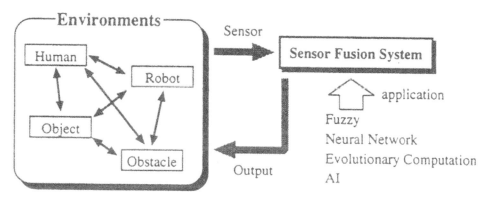

FIGURE 5
Concept of the sensor fusion system.

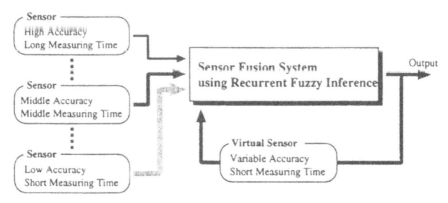

FIGURE 6
Sensor fusion system using RFI.

outputs. Then, the measuring time of the virtual sensor is determined by the measuring time of sensors mounted on the system.

4 EXPERIMENT

In this section we discuss the application of a sensor fusion system using RFI to a numerical simulation of a moving robot and to estimation of surface roughness in a grinding process. In the numerical simulation of a moving robot, we show that the sensor fusion system using the RFI can estimate the position of the robot using sensors with different measuring times. We compare the RFI to a neural network (NN) and show that the RFI can learn rapidly and accurately using the proposed learning algorithm. In estimating the surface roughness, we show that the sensor fusion system can accurately estimate the surface roughness in the grinding process.

4.1 Position Estimation of a Moving Robot

The aim of this simulation is to estimate the actual position of a moving robot at each sampling time by using sensors with different sampling times. The robot moves as shown in Figure 7, and has a velocity sensor and an acceleration sensor. The position of the robot is measured by the external position sensor (e.g., a camera).

In this simulation, the position, velocity, and acceleration sensors measure at every 10, 5 and 1 sampling times, respectively. Each sensor has the Gaussian noise shown in Table 1 as a percentage of the full scale that a sensor can measure.

We compare the RFI with a RNN (recurrent neural network) for estimating the position of a target that moves along the trajectory in straight, quadratic, oscillatory, and dissipative oscillatory ways. The RFI has a recurrent input y_{t-1} as in Figure 8 and the RNN (3 layers, 20 hidden units) has a recurrent input y_{t-1} as in Figure 9. In this simulation, the learning data sets were changed at every 2000 iterations. The number of fuzzy rules was limited to 20.

The results of each movement are shown in Figures 10 (straight), 11 (quadratic), 12 (oscillatory), and 13 (dissipative oscillatory). In each figure, (a) expresses the output values of each sensor and the actual position of the moving robot, where the value of each sensor expresses the normalized sensor output; (b) expresses the transition of the average and maximum error

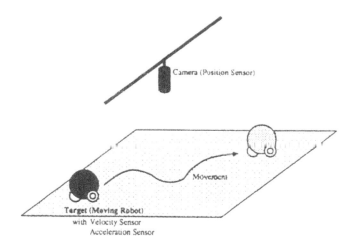

FIGURE 7
Environment of the simulation.

Table 1   Noise of Sensors

Sensor	Noise
Position sensor	0.1%
Velocity sensor	0.5%
Acceleration sensor	1%

through the learning process; and (c) expresses the actual and the estimated positions of the moving robot. Table 2 gives the average and maximum square error of the robot's position.

Figures 10–13 and Table 2 show that proposed sensor fusion system using RFI can estimate the position of moving robot using sensors with specific measuring times. By comparing the RFI with a RNN, it is seen that estimated positions of RFI are more accurate than those of a RNN. The error of the position through the learning process in the RFI converges more rapidly than that in the RNN and the error after the learning process in the RFI is smaller than that in the RNN.

4.2   Surface Roughness Estimation in a Grinding Process

Grinding processes are frequently used to produce smooth surfaces in manufacturing systems. Special whetstones such as CBN (cubic boron nitride) are frequently used in grinding systems.

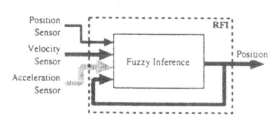

FIGURE 8
Recurrent fuzzy inference (RFI).

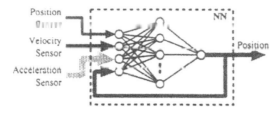

FIGURE 9
Recurrent neural network (RNN).

The life span of these whetstones is longer, but their operational costs are higher. It is important, therefore, to use them effectively. For accurate processing, operators have to dress whetstones frequently and determine the dressing intervals. The interval of dressing of the whetstones is determined by the surface roughness and the experience of the operator. It is necessary to measure the surface roughness for efficient use of the whetstones [22, 23]. However, it is difficult too measure the surface roughness during a process because the measurement takes a long time. Thus, we have to estimate surface roughness from on-line sensing information. We will apply the proposed sensor fusion system using RFI to on-line estimation of surface roughness in a grinding process.

A grinding system is a CNC internal grinder with sensors and a computer for calculating the input parameters and estimating the surface roughness, as shown in Figure 14. Table 3 shows the conditions of the grinding process. This system measures the grinding time, the grinding power, the grinding force in the normal direction, the internal diameter of the object, and the stock removal using sensors mounted on the grinding system. From this sensor information, the performance parameters of the whetstone that are used as the inputs of RFI are calculated. These performance parameters are shown in Table 4. We use these performance parameters as the inputs of the sensor fusion system using the RFI. In this experiment, the number of recurrent inputs is 1 in order to reduce the learning time of the RFI. We define the sampling time of the RFI as the time of grinding an object.

Figure 15 shows the relation of grinding power and surface roughness. Surface roughness, shown in Figure 15, is measured when we set grinding powers of 1.0 kW, 0.8 kW, 0.6 kW, 0.4 kW, and 0.2 kW. The grinding system processes 80 objects. The learning time is 10 000 times and the system executes the incremental process every 20 times. The parameters of learning the RFI are shown in Table 5. To express the effectiveness of the RFI, we compare the estimated result of RFI with that of a fuzzy inference without recurrent inputs (traditional fuzzy inference: TFI).

Table 2   Square Error of Position

		Average	Maximum
Straight	RFI	3.451×10^{-5}	5.637×10^{-4}
	NN	1.395×10^{-3}	5.848×10^{-3}
Quadric	RFI	1.690×10^{-4}	7.589×10^{-4}
	NN	1.569×10^{-4}	8.156×10^{-3}
Oscillation	RFI	1.135×10^{-4}	1.721×10^{-3}
	NN	1.823×10^{-4}	1.157×10^{-3}
Dissipative oscillation	RFI	1.245×10^{-4}	1.914×10^{-3}
	NN	2.119×10^{-4}	1.052×10^{-3}

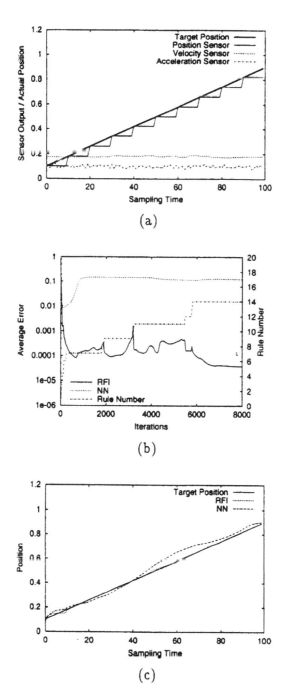

FIGURE 10

Straight movement. (a) Sensor output. (b) Learning result. (c) Estimation result.

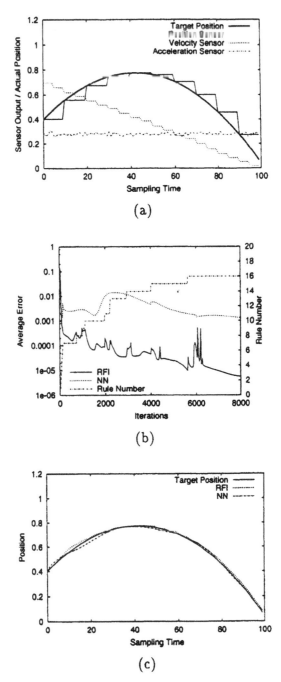

FIGURE 11

Quadratic movement. (a) Sensor output. (b) Learning result. (c) Estimation result.

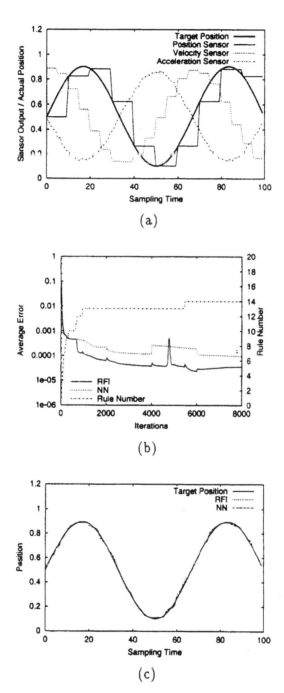

FIGURE 12

Oscillation movement. (a) Sensor output. (b) Learning result. (c) Estimation result.

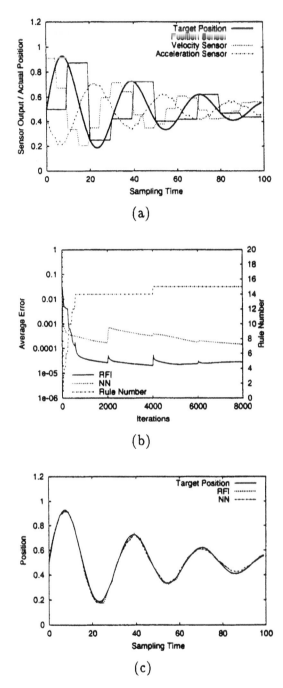

FIGURE 13
Dissipative oscillation movement. (a) Sensor output. (b) Learning result. (c) Estimation result.

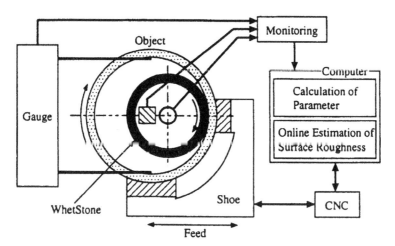

FIGURE 14
Grinding system.

Table 3 Process Conditions

CNC internal grinder		
Object:	600 rpm	
	Outside diameter	62 mm
	Inside diameter	56 mm
	Width	8 mm
Whetstone:	CBN230Q150V	
	20000 rpm	
	Outside diameter	44 mm
	Width	8.5 mm

Figures 16 and 17 show the results for TFI and the proposed RFI, respectively. In each figure, (a) shows the transformation of the average and maximum of the square error and the number of fuzzy rules, and (b) shows the estimated and measured surface roughness and the grinding power. In these figures, the fuzzy rules are generated in the early iterations of the learning process and convergent in the last iterations, and the surface roughness is expressed at the point

Table 4 Performance Parameters

Parameter	Unit
Cumulative stock removal	mm^3
Stock removal	μm
Grinding power	kW
Specific grinding power	$kW \cdot s/mm^3$
Work removal parameter	$mm^3/s \cdot N$
Grinding power ratio	F_t/F_n
Dressing lead	mm

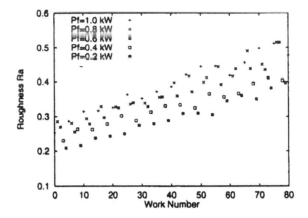

FIGURE 15
Roughness versus work number (teaching data).

Table 5 Learning Parameter

Parameter	Value
k_w	0.08
k_a	0.04
k_b	0.04
k_b	0.04
Threshold of error (Th_{error})	0.0001
Threshold of grade (Th_{grade})	0.45

where the grinding power is set at the value shown in these figures. Table 6 shows the average square error of estimating the surface roughness and the number of fuzzy rules.

Comparing Figure 16a with Figure 17a, the learning speed of the RFI is faster than that of the TFI. The number of fuzzy rules of the RFI is smaller than that of the TFI. The most likely explanation is that the RFI has more inputs than the TFI. Therefore, the RFI can estimate the surface roughness even if there are not many fuzzy rules. By comparing Figure 16b with Figure 17b, it is seen that the proposed RFI can estimate the surface roughness accurately.

5 SUMMARY

We have proposed recurrent fuzzy inference (RFI) that uses the outputs of the RFI as recurrent inputs, and have applied the RFI to a sensor fusion system for estimating surface roughness in a grinding system. The shape of the membership functions in the RFI is expressed by the radial basis function (RBF) with a dead zone. It is useful for reducing the number of fuzzy rules. The learning method of the RFI tunes the shape of the membership functions by the steepest descent method for existing fuzzy rules and generates new fuzzy rules in such a way that their centers are located at the point where the maximum error takes place in the input space. The shape of the membership functions of the new fuzzy rules is determined by the grade of the previous fuzzy

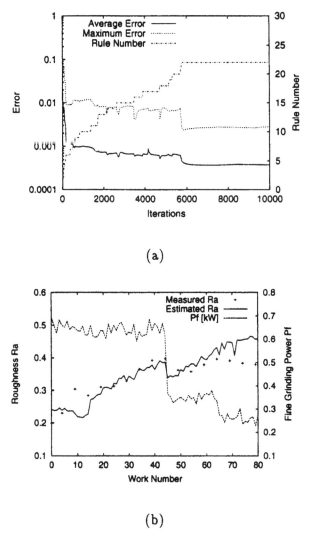

(a)

(b)

FIGURE 16
(a) Learning result and (b) estimation result without recurrent inputs.

rules. The sensor fusion system uses the recurrent inputs as the information acquired by virtual sensors. Thus, this system can measure phenomena that cannot be measured by the traditional sensor.

To show its effectiveness, we applied the sensor fusion system using the RFI to numerical simulations of a tracking moving robot and to estimating the surface roughness in a grinding system. For the tracking moving robot, we showed the result of fusing the sensor information with different measuring times and accuracies. The RFI can then learn more accurately and rapidly than a RNN (recurrent neural network). In estimating the surface roughness, we showed that this sensor fusion system can be applied to a real manufacturing system and can estimate states that the system cannot measure in real time. The RFI has fewer fuzzy rules than the usual fuzzy inference (without recurrent inputs).

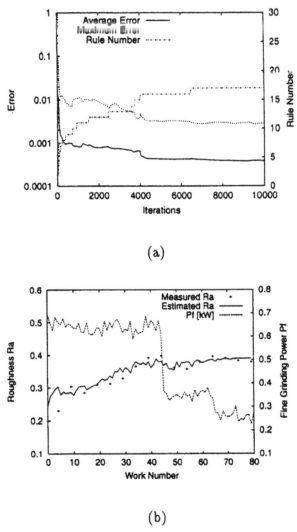

(a)

(b)

FIGURE 17
(a) Learning result and (b) estimation result with recurrent inputs.

Table 6 Square Error of Surface Roughness

	Average	Maximum	Rule Number
RFI	3.71×10^{-4}	4.05	17
TFI	1.59×10^{-2}	4.04	22

RFI, recurrent fuzzy inference; TFI, fuzzy inference without recurrent inputs.

Acknowledgments

This research was supported in part by a grant from "IMS-SIMON: Sensor Fused Intelligent Monitoring System for Machining".

REFERENCES

[1] R.C. Lou and M.G. Kay, Multisensor integration fusion in intelligent systems, *IEEE Trans. Systems, Man, and Cybernetics*, Vol. 19, No. 5, pp. 901–931, 1988.

[2] S. Shekhar, Object localization with multiple sensors, *Int. J. Robotics Research*, Vol. 7, No. 6, pp. 34–44, 1988.

[3] J. Pearl, Fusion, propagation, and structuring in bereif networks, *AI*, Vol. 29, pp. 241–248, 1986.

[4] T. Miltonberger, D. Morgan, et al., Multisensor object recognition from 3D models, *Proc. SPIE*, pp. 161–169, 1989.

[5] II.R. Hashcmlpour, 3. Roy, and A.J. Laub, Decentralized structures for parallel Kalman filtering, *IEEE Trans. Automatic Control*, Vol. 33, No. 1, pp. 88–94, 1988.

[6] I. Graham and P.L. Jones, *Expert Systems: Knowledge, Uncertainty and Decision*. Chapman and Hall, London, 1988.

[7] S.Y. Harmon, Tools for multisensor data fusion in autonomous robots, *Highly Redundant Sensing in Robotic Systems*, pp. 103–125. Springer-Verlag, Berlin, 1990.

[8] K. Shimojima, T. Fukuda, F. Arai, and H. Matsuura, Multi-sensor integration system utilizing fuzzy inference and neural network, *Robotics and Mechatronics*, Vol. 4, No. 5, pp. 416–421, 1992.

[9] T. Fukuda, K. Shimojima, F. Arai, and H. Matsuura, Multi-sensor integration system based on fuzzy inference and neural network, *Information and Science*, Vol. 71, No. 1/2, pp. 27–41, 1992.

[10] K. Shimojima, T. Fukuda, F. Arai, and H. Matsuura, Fuzzy inference integrated 3-D measuring system with LED displacement sensor and vision system, *Intelligent and Fuzzy Systems*, Vol. 1, No. 1, pp. 63–72, 1993.

[11] K. Shimojima, T. Fukuda, F. Arai, and H. Matsuura, Sensor integration system utilizing fuzzy inference with LED displacement sensor and vision system, *Proc. 2nd IEEE Int. Conf. Fuzzy Systems*, 1993, pp. 59–64.

[12] L.A. Zadeh, Fuzzy sets, *Information and Control*, Vol. 8, pp. 338–353, 1965.

[13] D.A. Linkens and J. Nie, Fuzzified RBF network-based learning control: structure and self-construction, *Proc. IEEE Int. Conf. Neural Networks*, 1993, pp. 1016–1021.

[14] K. Shimojima, T. Fukuda, F. Arai, and Y. Hasegawa, RBF-fuzzy system with GA based unsupervised/supervised learning method, *Proc. 4th IEEE Int. Conf. Fuzzy Systems/2nd Int. Fuzzy Engineering Symp.*, 1995, pp. 253–258.

[15] K. Shimojima, T. Fukuda, F. Arai, and Y. Hasegawa, Hierarchical control system based on unsupervised fuzzy-neuro system, *Proc. IEEE Int. Joint Conf. Neural Networks*, 1995, pp. 1403–1408.

[16] D. Whitley, T. Strakweather, and C. Bogard, Genetic algorithms and neural networks: optimizing connection and connectivity, *Parallel Computing*, Vol. 14, pp. 347–361, 1990.

[17] M.A. Lee and H. Takagi, Integrating design stages of fuzzy system using genetic algorithms, *Proc. 2nd IEEE Int. Conf. Fuzzy Systems*, 1993, pp. 612–617.

[18] T. Fukuda, Y. Hasegawa, and K. Shimojima, Structure optimization of hierarchical fuzzy model using by genetic algorithm, *Proc. 4th IEEE Int. Conf. Fuzzy Systems/2nd Int. Fuzzy Engineering Symp.*, 1995, pp. 295–300.

[19] H. Nomura, I. Hayashi, and N. Wakami, A self-tuning methods of fuzzy control by decent method, *Proc. 4th IFSA Congress, Engineering*, 1991, pp. 155–158.

[20] K. Shimojima, T. Fukuda, and F. Arai, Self-tuning fuzzy inference based spline function, *Proc. 3rd IEEE Int. Conf. Fuzzy Systems*, 1994, pp. 690–695.

[21] R. Katayama, Y. Kajitani, K. Kuwata, and Y. Nishida, Self generating radial basis function as neuro-fuzzy model and its application to nonlinear prediction of chaotic time series, *Proc. 2nd IEEE Int. Conf. Fuzzy Systems*, 1993, pp. 407–414.

[22] I. Inasaki, Monitoring technologies for an intelligent grinding system, *VDI Berichte*, No. 1179, pp. 31–45, 1995.

[23] R. Ivester, Optimization of cylindrical plunge grinding by recursive constraint bounding, *ASME DSC*, Vol. 1, pp. 529–537, 1995.

CHAPTER 16

Neurofuzzy State Estimators

C. J. HARRIS, X. HONG and Q. GAN

Image, Speech and Intelligent Systems Group, Department of Electronics and Computer Science, University of Southampton, Southampton UK

1   INTRODUCTION

Over the last two decades of the twentieth century there has been a strong resurgence in the field of artificial neural networks (ANNs) involving researchers from diverse disciplines. In engineering, a class of ANNs—the supervised feedforward networks—have been proven to be capable of representing a class of unknown nonlinear input–output mappings with arbitrarily small approximation capability [30], and several learning algorithms for both batch training and on-line or instantaneous training have been proposed for this class of networks [4].

Similarly, fuzzy logic (FL) systems [11] have found significant practical applications in domestic products, fuzzy logic controllers, pattern recognition, and information processing (see the 1992–1998 *EUFIT* conference proceedings for FL applications). The advantage of the FL approach is its logicality and transparency, by which it is easy to incorporate a priori knowledge about a system into an explicit fuzzy rule base. Additionally, FL represents a form of imprecision and uncertainty common in linguistics through expressions of vagueness. The main benefit of ANNs is that they are well structured for adaptive learning, have provable learning and convergence conditions (at least for linear networks in the parameters), and have the capability of parallel processing and good generalization properties for unseen data.

Fuzzy systems involve the procedures of fuzzification of a deterministic input signal with membership function, reasoning in a fuzzy rule set using a proper inference method, and a defuzzification process to produce a deterministic output. Each process, while nonunique, has an influence on the system's input–output mapping and overall performance [11]. Usually in the fuzzy system both the antecedent and consequent part of the fuzzy rules are fuzzy subsets. Also, particular choices of the membership sets, logical operators, and defuzzification scheme lead to the fuzzy logic system having an equivalence to a class of analytical ANNS [4, 28] (see also Section 2). However, generally FL systems' input–output relationships are highly nonlinear and there exist few mathematical methods for dealing with them analytically. Takagi and Sugeno have proposed a crisp type rule model in which the consequent parts of the fuzzy rules are crisp functional representation, or crisp real numbers in the simplified case, instead of fuzzy sets [27].

The Takagi–Sugeno (T–S) fuzzy model, which is usually output-linear, has found widespread application in control and local modeling due to its nice analytical properties [22] for representing input–output processes.

The class of fuzzy logic systems that have an equivalence to certain ANNs (usually linear-in-the-parameter, single larger networks such as radial basis function, B-spline, etc.) are called neurofuzzy systems. Section 2 develops their structural properties and learning attributes. A fundamental problem of neurofuzzy systems, fuzzy logic, and all other lattice-based ANNs is the curse of dimensionality, in that, as the input dimension increases, the computational cost, memory, and training data requirements increase exponentially, limiting their practical use (until recently) to input dimensions <7. Section 3 briefly describes some off-line network construction algorithms that attempt to overcome the curse of dimensionality. This is an essential requirements if the model is to be used for predictive control or estimation, as parsimonious models lead to simpler controllers and estimators. Section 4, containing the main contribution of this chapter, introduces the notion of neurofuzzy state estimators directly from input–output data, to produce analytically results that directly employ the Kalman filter. Some structural assumptions are imposed on the underlying nonlinear unknown process. A new algorithm is briefly introduced that overcomes the problem of model bias and input noise. Section 5 contains some illustrative numerical examples of this new neurofuzzy state estimator. Finally, Section 6 covers future aspects of research into neurofuzzy estimators.

2   NEUROFUZZY SYSTEM FOR MODELING

Neurofuzzy systems have emerged in recent years as researchers have tried to combine the natural linguistic/symbolic transparency of fuzzy systems with the provable learning and representation capability of linear in the weights artificial neural networks (ANN) [4, 16, 28]. A neurofuzzy algorithm can be both initialized and verified using a fuzzy algorithm; equally it can be trained via a variable rule confidence vector. However, a weight-based 3–5-layer ANN is computationally more effective in learning desired relationships. The combination of qualitatively based reasoning via fuzzy logic and quantitative adaptive numeric/data processing via ANNs is a potentially powerful concept, since it allows within a single framework intelligent qualitative and quantitative reasoning (IQ^2) to be achieved. Truly intelligent systems must make use of all available knowledge: numerical (e.g., sensory-derived) data, expert or heuristic rules (including safety jacket rules to constrain network learning or adaptability), and known functional realationship such as physical laws (so-called mechanical knowledge). Neurofuzzy systems allow all these knowledge sources to be incorporated in a single information framework. Fuzziness is introduced through the need for effective, interpretable knowledge representation (in terms of vagueness, data compression, interpretation/transparency). The architecture or topology of the class of neurofuzzy algorithms enables them to be readily assessed in terms of their modeling capability, structure, learning, construction, and numeric stability, since the results of linear optimization and algebra are directly applicable [12].

Fuzzy logic generalizes the concept of a characteristic function in Boolean logic, whereby a fuzzy membership function $\mu_A(x) \in [0, 1]$, in which A is the fuzzy label describing the variable x, is used to represent vague statements such as x is negative small. Overlapping fuzzy sets (see Figure 1) across the domain (universe of discourse) of x, give specific meaning to vague linguistic concepts. Additionally, this overlap is necessary for both learning and interpolation through generalization. A standard fuzzy logic system utilizes the logical functions of AND, OR, IF (.) and THEN (.). If the *algebraic* operators of *product* and *sum* are used, rather than the more useful truncation operators *min* and *max*, then the resultant system (i) produces smoother

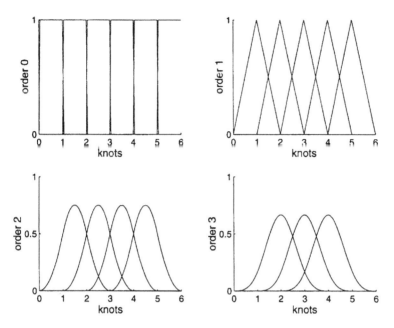

FIGURE 1
B-spline of order $m = 0, 1, 2, 3$.

interpolation, (ii) provides an equivalence between ANNs and fuzzy logic if $\mu_A(x)$ are radial basis functions or B-splines, and (iii) enables fuzzy system to be readily analyzed [4, 28]. The following result is significant in this context.

Theorem 1. When B-splines are used to implement fuzzy sets, the real-valued inputs are represented via singelton fuzzy sets, and algebraic operators are used to implement fuzzy logic function, a center of defuzzification method is used and the rule confidences are normalized, then the neurofuzzy output is given by

$$y(\mathbf{x}) = \sum_{i=1}^{p} \left(\frac{\mu_{A^i}(\mathbf{x})}{\sum_{j=1}^{p} \mu_{A^j}(\mathbf{x})} \right) w_i = \sum_{i=1}^{p} \mu_{A^i}(\mathbf{x}) w_i, \ \mathbf{x} \in R^n \tag{1}$$

where $\mu_{A^i}(\mathbf{x})$ is the ith ($i = 1, 2, \ldots, p$) fuzzy membership function of a multivariate input $\mathbf{x}$, and w_i is the ith weight.

The network weights $w_i = \sum_{j=1}^{p} c_{ij} y_j^c$, where y_j^c are centers of the jth output fuzzy membership function $\mu_{B^j}(y)$. c_{ij} is the confidence in the rule: if $\mathbf{x} \in A^i$ then $y \in B^j$ (with confidence c_{ij}, where $\sum_{j=1}^{p} c_{ij} = 1$, $c_{ij} \in [0, 1]$), where A^i and B^j are fuzzy labels defined on the input and output variables, respectively. The equivalence equation (1) is based on the constraint of a partition of unity on the input membership functions; while a restriction, this also aids generalization and regularization of the network. B-spline functions are local, compact, piecewise polynomials of a given order, for which simple recurrence relationship exist [4, 26], multivariate basis functions are formed from the tensor product of univariate basis functions

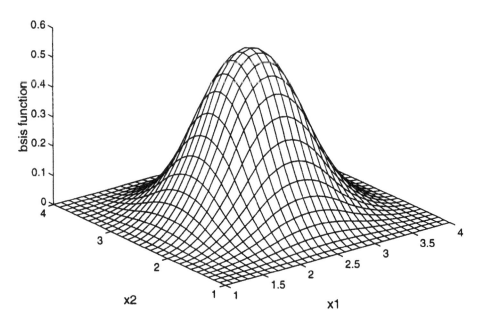

FIGURE 2
A two-dimensional quadratic multivariate B-spline basis function.

(see Figure 2). (See also Appendix A.) The jth multivariate B-spline basis function, $N_j(\mathbf{x})$, is generated by multiplying n univariate basis functions $B_i^{k_i}(x_i)$, so

$$N_j(\mathbf{x}) = \prod_{i=1}^{n} B_i^{k_i}(x_i)$$

where $j = 1, 2, \ldots, p$, $k_i = 1, 2, \ldots, m_i$, $p = \prod_{i=1}^{n} m_i$, and m_i is the number of the ith univariate basis function). Hence a multivariate function $y(\mathbf{x})$ can be expressed as

$$y(\mathbf{x}) = \sum_{j=1}^{p} N_j(\mathbf{x})\omega_j = \sum_{j=1}^{p} \prod_{i=1}^{n} B_i^{k_i}(x_i)\omega_j \tag{2}$$

The neurofuzzy structure, shown in Figure 3, also represents a wider class of lattice-based associative memory systems, including CMAC, RBF, Karneva distributed memory, and Takagi–Sugeno, networks. (Note: Generally these networks do not naturally have a partition of unity. Failure to have a partition of unity leads to input–output distortions as well as poor generalization [22]). Gaussian RBFs are very popular due to their localized spatial and frequency content and their inherent flexibility in that they can readily cluster data to make it sparse, and are infinitely differentiable and integrable, but they do not have compact support or a partition of unity, lack transparency, and are not naturally formulated for pruning redundant submodels or rules.

A neurofuzzy network must be able to learn inherent relationships contained in input–output data sets $\{\mathbf{x}(k), y(k)\}_{k=1}^{N}$ for some desired output $y(k)$. Equations (1) and (2) can be expressed as

$$\hat{y}(k) = \mathbf{N}^T(\mathbf{x}(k))\Omega(k-1) \tag{3}$$

where ˆ denotes estimates. $\Omega(k-1) = [\omega_1(k-1), \ldots, \omega_p(k-1)]^T \in \mathfrak{R}^p$, $\mathbf{N}^T(k)$ is the p-dimensional input basic (fuzzy) functions: $\mathbf{x} \in \mathfrak{R}^n \to \mathbf{N}(\mathbf{x}) \in \mathfrak{R}^p$. Typically, the network weights

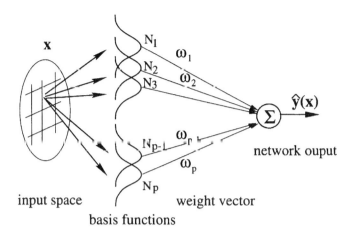

X

N_1

ω_1

N_2

ω_2

N_3

$\hat{y}(\mathbf{x})$

Σ

network ouput

N_{p-1}

ω_r

ω_p

N_p

input space

weight vector

basis functions

FIGURE 3
The B-spline neural network.

$\Omega = \{w_i\}$ are adjusted by a feedback learning law such as the *instantaneous* normalized least mean squares law (NLMS):

$$\Delta\Omega(k-1) = \delta\frac{\varepsilon_y(k)\mathbf{N}(k)}{\|\mathbf{N}(k)\|_2^2} \tag{4}$$

which minimizes the normalized mean squared error (*MSE*):

$$MSE = \frac{1}{N}\sum_{k=1}^{L}(\hat{y}(k) - y(k))^2$$

$$= \frac{1}{N}\sum_{k=1}^{L}\varepsilon_y(k)^2$$

$$= (MSE)_{\min} + (\hat{\Omega} - \Omega)^T R(\hat{\Omega} - \Omega) \tag{5}$$

where $R = E(\mathbf{N}\mathbf{N}^T)$ is the *autocorrelation* matrix of $\mathbf{N}$. It can readily be shown that the rate of convergence and stability in learning depends on the condition number $C(R)$ of R. Additionally, the $C(R)$ relates the weight vector error $\varepsilon_\Omega = (\hat{\Omega} - \Omega)$ to the network output error, $\varepsilon_y = (\hat{y}(k) - y(k))$ through

$$\frac{\|\varepsilon_\Omega\|}{\|\Omega\|} \leq \sqrt{C(R)}\frac{|\varepsilon_y|}{|y|} \tag{6}$$

So, for a poorly conditioned network, small output errors do not imply small weight errors. This is significant, since the network's ability to locally generalize depends on the parameter error, ε_Ω.

The majority of associative memory networks, like other rule-based systems, suffer from the curse of dimensionality, which has implications for the number of basis functions stored (or equivalent fuzzy rules), the training times, training data, the network's ability to generalize, and the overall resolution of the network. This in turn has serious implications for resultant neurofuzzy controller and estimation design. Parsimonious network construction is discussed in the next section.

3   NETWORK CONSTRUCTION

The curse of dimensionality occurs in neurofuzzy systems because a complete rule base is exponentially dependent on the input dimension, n. For example, for $n = 5$, with a single output and with 7 basis (fuzzy sets) functions on each variable, 16 800 weights or rules are required! Neurofuzzy construction algorithms [2] attempt to select models that minimize three criteria simultaneously: (i) MSE, (ii) complexity (through number of model parameters or degrees of freedom), and (iii) network smoothness to give good regularization by constraining the network curvature or weight values. Considerable use is made here of conventional statistical metrics such as Akaike's information criterion, structural risk minimization, or minimum description length [3]. Whatever criterion is used, the construction algorithm should embody the following principles:

- *Data reduction:* The smallest number of input variables are used to explain the maximum amount of information.
- *Network parsimony:* The best models obtained using the simplest possible structures that contain the smallest number of adjustable parameters (Occam's razor).
- *Network comprehension:* Derived input–output relationships are easy to understand and explain underlying relationships. A variety of off-line construction schemes have been derived for neurofuzzy modeling: They include:

    Adaptive network-based fuzzy inference system (ANFIS) construction algorithm [16]

    Adaptive spline modeling of observational data (ASMOD) [2, 3, 17].

    Local linear modeling tree (LOLIMOT) construction algorithm [23]

A comparsative analysis [5] of these algorithms for five data nets (for real auto car miles per gallon, a gas furnace, an engine data set, and two simulated benchmark time series) showed that generally the modified ASMOD [2] performed best, and therefore this will be described next as a precursor to neurofuzzy estimator design. A convenient framework for generating parsimonious neurofuzzy models is the generalization of the Gabor–Kolmogrov input–output analysis of variance (ANOVA) representation [2]:

$$y = f(\mathbf{x})$$

$$= f_0 + \sum_{i=1}^{n} f_i(x_i) + \sum_{i=1}^{n-1} \sum_{j=i+1}^{n} f_{ij}(x_i, x_j) + \cdots + f_{1,2,\ldots,n}(\mathbf{x}) \tag{7}$$

where $f_i(\cdot)$ etc. represent *additive* univariate, bivariate, ... components of $f(\cdot)$, in which each component is represented by a separate neurofuzzy system with reduced dimension (and rule set). So, for $n = 5$, and 7 basis functions used for each variable, and if it is known or can be determined by construction that $f(\mathbf{x}) \simeq f_1(x_1, x_2) + f_2(x_2, x_3) + f_3(x_4, x_5)$, then the number of rules required collapses from 16 800 to 100 for a complete rule base! Parsimonious neurofuzzy models are critical in both control and estimation problems, since the complexity and state dimension of the resultant controller or estimator is directly related to the process model complexity. Ideally, we seek a canonical model structure and parameterization, utilizing only input–output data. Research [2] has concentrated on the automatic iterative construction of B-spline algorithms—e.g. the adaptive spline modeling of observational data (ASMOD) procedure, which constructs models by a one-step-ahead error minimization process whereby a number of possible rule-base refinements such as the addition of univariate or bivariate functions are evaluated, retaining those that minimize the residual error. Also, regularization constrains the network weights in those input regions where there is little or no data as well as improving the network's generalization as utilizing local regularization techniques. ASMOD [17] also allows refinements through the introduction (or deletion) of bais functions and removal of redundant inputs and submodels. ASMOD in its commerical variant NeuFuz+ (see *http://www.ncs.co.uk/nfuzzy.htm*), has been applied to a wide variety of industrial applications, including modeling of gas turbines, satellites and submersible vehicles, metal fatigue, and pharmaceuticals [2]. The network structure allows *linear* learning algorithms (such as conjugate gradient or singular value decomposition) to be used to adapt weights or rule confidences, and to simultaneously extract the *internal* structure of the network (i.e., which *inputs* are important (including model orders); number and input vector for each subnetwork, and the number, position, and shape of the fuzzy input sets in each subnetwork) directly from the training data, which can be formulated as a one-step-ahead growing/pruning procedure. These algorithms repeatedly evaluate different network structures (including extended additive models to accommodate multiplicative or product-based processes). The resultant models are not only parsimonious in parameters (i.e., number of weights or rules), but also provide improved generalization and statistical significance, by *not* modeling the *inherent* noise in the data. This is significant in control and estimation design, since the model used in their design is *almost* canonical.

There are other techniques for construction algorithms, including hierarchical networks of subnet experts [22], extended additive models such as product/additive networks [3], and input space partitioning strategies such as kdtree and quad trees to produce axis orthogonal splits (see Figure 4). Unfortunately, almost all of these methods lose the transparency of interpretation that additive models such as ANOVA offer, since they remove the on-line adapatability of linear-in-the-weights structure.

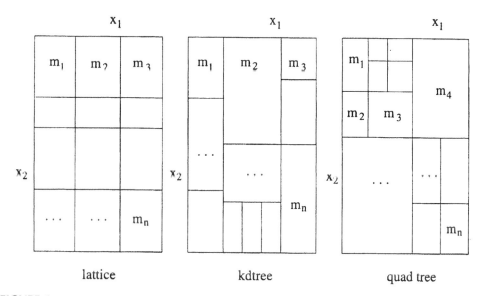

lattice   kdtree   quad tree

FIGURE 4
Different state (overlapping envelope) space decompositions.

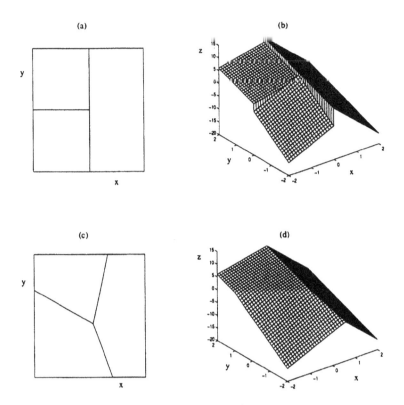

FIGURE 5
Input space partitions and the corresponding piecewise linear surfaces. (a) Orthogonal/lattice decomposition. (b) Resulting local modes. (c) Delauney partitioning. (d) Resulting mixture of expert local models.

Local linear models such as ANFIS and LOLIMOT are particularly appropriate for control and estimation, since existing linear control and estimators can be applied directly, if local conditions can be incorporated into global conditions, for, say, stability and convergence. For dynamic processes that are either concave or convex, a new local modeling method [33] automatically forms a Delaunay partition of input space, avoiding the curse of dimensionality, generating smooth, parsimonious local piecewise linear models by developing a mixture expert network (MEN) (see Figure 5).

If an unknown dynamical process can be decomposed into a series of concave/convex surfaces, the MEN algorithm is an extremely effective algorithm for automatically generating piecewise locally linear models prior to control and estimator design.

4   NEUROFUZZY STATE ESTIMATION

Given that a minimal parameter input–output process model can be generated, can a state space realization be generated from it and can its associated state be estimated? Without imposing some structure on the model, which is then amenable to state space analysis, the answer is no. The Witney–Takens theorem, however, does tell us that for a noise-free process the vector of input–output observations (see equation (17)) of appropriate dimension (the so called embedding dimension) contains the dynamics or states of the unknown process. This leaves us with two problems. What is the lag of the regressors (or embedding dimension), and how is noise appropriately represented? Assuming a priori process structure and process dimension greatly eases this problem. One obvious approach is to use nth order and autoassociative dynamic neural networks (DNN) [15] given by

$$\dot{z}_j(t) = -z_j + \sum_{i=1}^{n} w_{ij}\psi(z_i); \qquad j = 1, 2, \ldots, n \tag{8}$$

Impose on them some special adaptive observer [19] structure such as [18]

$$\dot{z} = Az + b[f(z) + g(z)u + d(t)]$$
$$y = C^T z \tag{9}$$

where $z = [z_1, \ldots, z_n]^T \in \mathfrak{R}^n$, (A, C) is in observer canonical form, $d(t)$ is unknown but bounded (e.g., represents model mismatch), $f, g: \mathfrak{R}^n \to \mathfrak{R}$ are unknown smooth functions, and (u, y) are known input/outputs. If $b = [0, \ldots, 0, 1]^T$ then equation (9) is in Brunovsky canonical form, which is *feedback linearizable*. An observer such as

$$\dot{\hat{z}} = A\hat{z} + b[\hat{f}(\hat{x}) + \hat{g}(\hat{z})u - v(t)] + K(y - C^T\hat{z})$$
$$\hat{y} = C^T\hat{z} \tag{10}$$

can be generated so that the estimation error $(z - \hat{z}) \to 0$ if $(A + KC^T)$ is strictly Hurwitz. The problem is now to find the error convergence conditions (by Lyapunov) and the estimates of $\hat{f}(\cdot)$ and $\hat{g}(\cdot)$. Appropriate approximations such as $\hat{f}(\cdot) = \hat{\Omega}_f^T N_f(\hat{x}) + \varepsilon_f$ can be used to ensure estimation convergence if the form of bounds ε_f are known a priori.

A more natural and general approach is that of Moore and Harris [21] (Figure 6) where the fuzzy mappings $f_1: u \to z, f_2: z \to y$, form an input–output transfer function $R = f_1 \circ f_2$ that can be identified by input–output data via a neurofuzzy construction algorithm such as ASMOD. $f_1(\cdot)$ is found from the relationship $f_1 = f_2^{-1} \circ R$ where $f_2(\cdot)$ is assumed known and invertible since it defines the state vector. (Note that a fuzzy relation always has an inverse, albeit nonunique.) The

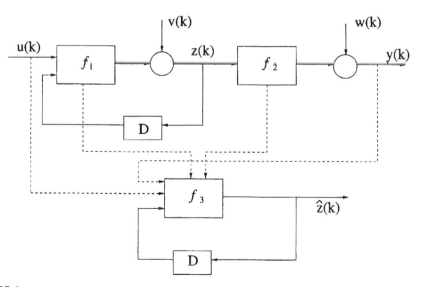

FIGURE 6
A general estimation approach.

estimation problem is now to find the fuzzy correlational mapping $f_3(\cdot)$ such that $(\hat{u}(k) \quad u(k)) > 0$. The resultant estimator is

$$\hat{z}(k) = f_3 \left[f_1 \left[\begin{array}{c} \dot{z}(k-1) \\ u(k-1) \\ f_2^{-1}(y(k)) \end{array} \right] \right] \tag{11}$$

A variety of techniques have been used for ensuring convergence, including nonlinear optimization methods such as genetic algorithms, or stability methods such as Lyapunov.

A natural extension of linear state space theory is to use *local* ARMA-type models that are applied to form global models [22, 29]. The local models can be parameterized by an operating point, O_k, a nonstate observable (e.g., Mach number and altitude for an aircraft), or a state region $\{m_i\}$ for which each model is applicable (see Figure 4). In the latter case, ASMOD-type construction algorithms can be used to determine the minimum number and average of models in the state space. Note that nonlatticed and nonorthogonal split techniques (e.g., quad trees) will lead to fewer models (and consequently estimators/controllers), and interpolation between models (regions) in the state space is achieved by imposing fuzzy overlaps for each region [11, 33].

Consider a general stochastic nonlinear system represented by the discrete time domain model

$$z(k) = f(z(k-1), \ldots, z(k-n_y), u(k-1), \ldots, u(k-n_u), \Theta) \tag{12}$$

$$yk) = z(k) + \xi(k), \qquad \text{for } k = 1, 2, \ldots, N \tag{13}$$

where (n_u, n_y), $(n_u + n_y = n)$ are positive integers representing the system known lags, $f(\cdot)$ is unknown, and $z(k)$ is an unobservable state variable that has to be estimated from the output observable $y(k)$. The observation noise $\xi(k)$ is uncorrelated, with variance σ_ξ^2. Θ is a parameter vector associated with the appropriate model structure. Model (12) can be expressed as an I–O model by substitution, so that

$$y(k) = f(z(k-1), \ldots, z(k-n_y), u(k-1), \ldots, u(k-n_u), \Theta) + \xi(k) \tag{14}$$

But, as $\{z(k-1), \ldots, z(k-n_y)\}$ contains $\{y(k-1), \ldots, y(k-n_y)\}$ and $\{\xi(k-1), \ldots, \xi(k-n_y)\}$, in order to obtain an unbiased estimate for Θ, the I–O model should incorporate noise terms into the model structure and take the modified form

$$y(k) = f(z(k-1), \ldots, z(k-n_y), u(k-1), \ldots, u(k-n_u), \xi(k-1), \ldots, \xi(k-n_\xi), \Theta) + \xi(k) \tag{15}$$

where n_ξ denotes the lag of the noise term. If a model of the form

$$y(k) = f(y(k-1), \ldots, y(k-n_y), u(k-1), \ldots, u(k-n_u), \Theta) + \xi(k) \tag{16}$$

is used for identification of the model structures $f(\cdot)$ and parameter Θ, the estimates $\hat{\Theta}$ may incorporate a bias.

Define the observational vector as

$$\mathbf{x}(k) = [x_1, x_2, \ldots, x_n]^T = [y(k-1), \ldots, y(k-n_y), u(k-1), \ldots, u(k-n_u)]^T \in \mathfrak{R}^n \tag{17}$$

Consider using a fuzzy system with functional rule to model the above system. The input to the fuzzy system is an n-dimensional vector $\mathbf{x}$, and the output of the fuzzy system is $y(k)$. The universes of discourse of x_i and y are $X_i \subset \mathfrak{R}$ $(i = 1, 2, \ldots, n)$ and $Y \subset \mathfrak{R}$, respectively. The linguistic values of x_i are $A_i^{k_i}$ $(k_i = 1, 2, \ldots, m_i$ and $i = 1, 2, \ldots, n)$. If the number of fuzzy rules is equal to $p = m_1 m_2 \cdots m_n$, the fuzzy rule base is said to be complete. In the following discussion, the fuzzy rule base is assumed to be complete. The functionally represented fuzzy rules are given in the following form:

$$j\text{th Rule: If } x_1 \text{ is } A_1^{k_1} \text{ and } x_2 \text{ is } A_2^{k_2} \text{ and } \ldots x_n \text{ is } A_n^{k_n}, \text{ then } y \text{ is } y_u(\mathbf{x}) \tag{18}$$

where $y_j(\mathbf{x}) \in Y$ ($j = 1, 2, \ldots, p$). The above rule base has been numbered by $j = 1, 2, \ldots, p$. Each j corresponds to an ordered sequence $k_1, \ldots, k_i, \ldots, k_n$, where $k_i = 1, 2, \ldots, m_i$. For system identification purposes, $y_j(\mathbf{x})$ in fuzzy rule (18) can be set to be a singleton:

$$y_j = \omega_j \qquad (j = 1, 2, \ldots, p) \tag{19}$$

or a linear combination of the components of the input vector:

$$y_j(\mathbf{x}) = \omega_{1j} x_1 + \omega_{2j} x_2 + \cdots + \omega_{nj} x_n \qquad (j = 1, 2, \ldots, p) \tag{20}$$

There currently exist many choices for the type of T-norm and S-norm operators used to implement the linguistic connectives, and it has been demonstrated that a smoother defuzzified decision surface can be obtained through the use of algebraic (product/sum) operators [11].

Let $A_i^{k_i}(x_i)$ be the membership functions of $A_i^{k_i}$. With input vector $\mathbf{x}$, using algebraic (product/sum) operators for fuzzy reasoning, the truth value of the antecedent part of the jth fuzzy rule, denoted as $\mu_j(\mathbf{x})$, is given by

$$\mu_j(\mathbf{x}) = A_1^{k_1}(x_1) A_2^{k_2}(x_2) \cdots A_n^{k_n}(x_n) = \prod_{i=1}^{n} A_i^{k_i}(x_i) \tag{21}$$

The real output of the system is given by [4]

$$y = \frac{\sum_{j=1}^{p} \mu_j(\mathbf{x}) y_j(\mathbf{x})}{\sum_{j=1}^{p} \mu_j(\mathbf{x})} \tag{22}$$

The denominator equation of (22) can be rewritten as

$$\begin{aligned}
\sum_{j=1}^{p} \mu_j(\mathbf{x}) &= \sum_{k_1=1}^{m_1} \sum_{k_2=1}^{m_2} \cdots \sum_{k_n=1}^{m_n} A_1^{k_1}(x_1) A_2^{k_2}(x_2) \ldots A_n^{k_n}(x_n) \\
&= \sum_{k_1=1}^{m_1} A_1^{k_1}(x_1) \sum_{k_2=1}^{m_2} A_2^{k_2}(x_2) \cdots \sum_{k_n=1}^{m_n} A_n^{k_n}(x_n)
\end{aligned} \tag{23}$$

Then equation (22) becomes

$$y = \frac{\sum_{j=1}^{p} \prod_{i=1}^{n} A_i^{k_i}(x_i) y_j(\mathbf{x})}{\sum_{k_1=1}^{m_1} A_1^{k_1}(x_1) \sum_{k_2=1}^{m_2} A_2^{k_2}(x_2) \cdots \sum_{k_n=1}^{m_n} A_n^{k_n}(x_n)} \tag{24}$$

Next, we can analyze the output of the above fuzzy system when the B-spline basis functions are used as the membership functions. B-spline theory can be found in [4], [26] and Appendix A.

Let $B_i^{k_i}(x_i)$ ($k_i = 1, 2, \ldots, m_i$) be the B-spline basis functions defined on input space x_i, ($i = 1, 2, \ldots, n$). Generally, the B-spline basis functions with order higher than 1 are not a normal fuzzy set: in other words, the maximum value of the B-spline membership function does not reach 1. Usually the fuzzy system requires the membership functions to be normalized; this can be resolved by normalizing the B-spline basis functions by a positive scalar λ:

$$A_i^{k_i}(x_i) = \lambda B_i^{k_i}(x_i) \qquad (i = 1, 2, \ldots, n) \tag{25}$$

It follows from equation (24) that the fuzzy system's output is given by

$$
\begin{aligned}
y &= \frac{\sum\limits_{j=1}^{p} \prod\limits_{i=1}^{n} \lambda B_i^{k_i}(x_i) y_j(\mathbf{x})}{\sum\limits_{k_1=1}^{m_1} \lambda B_1^{k_1}(x_1) \sum\limits_{k_2=1}^{m_2} \lambda B_2^{k_2}(x_2) \cdots \sum\limits_{k_n=1}^{m_n} \lambda B_n^{k_n}(x_n)} \\[2ex]
&= \frac{\lambda^n \sum\limits_{j=1}^{p} \prod\limits_{i=1}^{n} B_i^{k_i}(x_i) y_j(\mathbf{x})}{\lambda^n \sum\limits_{k_1=1}^{m_1} B_1^{k_1}(x_1) \sum\limits_{k_2=1}^{m_2} B_2^{k_2}(x_2) \cdots \sum\limits_{k_n=1}^{m_n} B_n^{k_n}(x_n)} \\[2ex]
&= \frac{\sum\limits_{j=1}^{p} \prod\limits_{i=1}^{n} B_i^{k_i}(x_i) y_j(\mathbf{x})}{\sum\limits_{k_1=1}^{m_1} B_1^{k_1}(x_1) \sum\limits_{k_2=1}^{m_2} B_2^{k_2}(x_2) \cdots \sum\limits_{k_n=1}^{m_n} B_n^{k_n}(x_n)}
\end{aligned} \tag{26}
$$

From the above equation, it can be seen that the input–output relation is independent of the normalizing factor λ.

Recall that the B-spline basis functions have a very important property in that they form a partition of unity, that is,

$$\sum_{k_i=1}^{m_i} B_n^{k_i}(x_i) = 1 \qquad (i = 1, 2, \ldots, n) \tag{27}$$

It then follows that

$$\sum_{k_1=1}^{m_1} B_1^{k_1}(x_1) \sum_{k_2=1}^{m_2} B_2^{k_2}(x_2) \cdots \sum_{k_n=1}^{m_n} B_n^{k_n}(x_n) = 1 \tag{28}$$

Thus the denominator of equation (26) vanishes.

Multidimensional B-spline basis functions are formed by the tensor product of n one-dimensional basis functions $B_i^{k_i}(x_i)$, denoted by $N_j(\mathbf{x})$:

$$N_j(\mathbf{x}) = \prod_{i=1}^{n} B_i^{k_i}(x_i) \tag{29}$$

The total number of $N_j(\mathbf{x})$ is $p = m_1 m_2 \cdots m_n$, that is, $j = 1, 2, \ldots, p$.

Therefore, the output of the fuzzy system can be written as

$$y = \sum_{j=1}^{p} \prod_{i=1}^{n} B_i^{k_i}(x_i) y_j(\mathbf{x}) = \sum_{j=1}^{p} N_j(\mathbf{x}) y_j(\mathbf{x}) \tag{30}$$

If the singleton consequent fuzzy rule is used, that is, $y_j(\mathbf{x}) = w_j$ (equation 19), the above equation become

$$\hat{y}(k) = \sum_{j=1}^{p} N_j(\mathbf{x}(k)) w_j \tag{31}$$

which is a linear combination of the multidimensional B-spline functions and can be represented by the B-spline neural network shown in Figure 3. This model canont be converted to state-space form, so it cannot be used in our filtering problem. It will be shown that if the consequent part of the fuzzy rule set takes the T S form of equation (20), the resultant model is adequate for Kalman filtering.

Substituting $y_j(\mathbf{x})$ in equation (30) with equation (20) gives

$$\hat{y}(k) = \sum_{j=1}^{p} N_i(\mathbf{x}(k))(\omega_{1i}x_1 + \omega_{2i}x_2 + \cdots + \omega_{ni}x_n)$$

$$= \left(\sum_{j=1}^{p} N_j(\mathbf{x}(k))\omega_{1j}\right)x_1 + \left(\sum_{j=1}^{p} N_j(\mathbf{x}(k))\omega_{2j}\right)x_2 + \cdots + \left(\sum_{j=1}^{p} N_j(\mathbf{x}(k))\omega_{nj}\right)x_n$$

$$= \sum_{i=1}^{n_y} \theta_i(\mathbf{x})y(k-i) + \sum_{i=n_y+1}^{n_y+n_u} \theta_i(\mathbf{x})u(k+n_y-i) \tag{32}$$

which is an ARMA-type model, for $\theta_i(\mathbf{x}) = \sum_{j=1}^{p} N_j(\mathbf{x})\omega_{ij}$ $(i = 1, 2, \ldots, n)$, if we include model mismatch noise $\varepsilon(k)$ in equation (32). As such, it is a linear combination of the multidimensional B-spline functions similar to equation (31) and so can be approximated by the sum of neural networks in Figure 3 in the structure shown in Figure 7, where

$$\mathbf{N}(\mathbf{x}) = [N_1(\mathbf{x}), N_2(\mathbf{x}), \ldots, N_p(\mathbf{x})]^T$$

$$\theta_i(\mathbf{x}(k)) = \Omega_i^T \mathbf{N}(\mathbf{x}(k)) = \sum_{j=1}^{p} \omega_{ij} N_j(\mathbf{x}(k))$$

for $\Omega_i = [\omega_{i1}, \omega_{i2}, \ldots, \omega_{ip}]^T \in \Re^p$ represents the set of adjustable parameters associated with the set of basis functions.

The local model (32) is a special case of a larger class of operating point-dependent ARMA-type models [29], where the vector $\mathbf{x}$ includes independent variables as well as dependent observables.

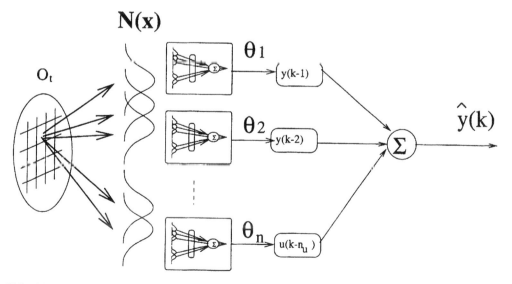

FIGURE 7
Neurofuzzy modeling network.

Returning to our state model (12), the local model for the nonlinear function $f(\cdot)$ is, from equation (32),

$$z(k) = \sum_{i=1}^{n_y} \theta_i(\mathbf{x}(k))z(k - i) + \sum_{i=n_y+1}^{n_y+n_u} \theta_i(\mathbf{x}(k))u(k + n_y - i) + \varepsilon(k) \tag{33}$$

where $\varepsilon(k)$ is an uncorrelated model residual through using B-spline expansions. Let $\mathbf{z}(k) = [z(k), z(k - 1), \ldots, z(k - n_y + 1)]^T$ be a state vector and define

$$\tilde{u}(k) = \sum_{i=n_y+1}^{n_y+n_u} \theta_i(\mathbf{x}(k))u(k + n_y - i) \tag{34}$$

Then from equations (33) and (34), model (12) can be written in canonical state space form as

$$\mathbf{z}(k) = \mathbf{A}(k)\mathbf{z}(k - 1) + \mathbf{B}\tilde{u}(k) + \mathbf{\Gamma}\varepsilon(k) \tag{35}$$

$$y(k) = \mathbf{C}\mathbf{z}(k) + \xi(k) \tag{36}$$

$$\mathbf{A}_{(k)} = \begin{bmatrix} \theta_1(\mathbf{x}(k)) & \theta_2(\mathbf{x}(k)) & \cdots & \theta_{n_y-1}(\mathbf{x}(k)) & \theta_{n_y}(\mathbf{x}(k)) \\ 1 & 0 & \cdots & 0 & 0 \\ 0 & 1 & \cdots & 0 & 0 \\ \vdots & \vdots & \cdots & \vdots & \vdots \\ 0 & 0 & \cdots & 1 & 0 \end{bmatrix} \in \mathfrak{R}^{n_y \times n_y}$$

$\mathbf{B} = [1, 0, \ldots, 0, 0]^T \in \mathfrak{R}^{n_y}$, $\mathbf{C} = [1, 0, \ldots, 0, 0] \in \mathfrak{R}^{n_y}$, and $\mathbf{\Gamma} = [1, 0, \ldots, 0, 0]^T \in \mathfrak{R}^{n_y}$. After a proper model is identified via the neurofuzzy algorithm, the Kalman filter algorithm [6] (and see Appendix B) is readily applicable if the noise terms $\{\varepsilon(k), \xi(k)\}$ are appropriately characterized. To construct the state space form (36), we only have the observation vector $\mathbf{x}(k)$. However, from equations (34) and (12), it is easy to see that

$$y(k) = \sum_{i=1}^{n_y} \theta_i(\mathbf{x}(k))z(k - i) + \sum_{i=n_y+1}^{n_y+n_u} \theta_i(\mathbf{x}(k))u(k + n_y - i) + \varepsilon(k) + \xi(k) \tag{37}$$

$$y(k) = \sum_{i=1}^{n_y} \theta_i(\mathbf{x}(k))y(k - i) + \sum_{i=n_y+1}^{n_y+n_u} \theta_i(\mathbf{x}(k))u(k + n_y - i)$$

$$- \sum_{i=1}^{n_y} \theta_i(\mathbf{x}(k))\xi(k - i) + \varepsilon(k) + \xi(k)$$

$$\approx \sum_{i=1}^{n_y} \theta_i(\mathbf{x}(k))y(k - i) + \sum_{i=n_y+1}^{n_y+n_u} \theta_i(\mathbf{x}(k))u(k + n_y - i)$$

$$- \sum_{i=1}^{n_y} \theta_i(\mathbf{x}(k))\xi(k - i) + \xi(k) \tag{38}$$

by assuming that $\sigma_{\varepsilon k}^2 \ll \sigma_{\xi k}^2$. If this assumption is weak, then it can be assumed that the model takes the form

$$y(k) = \sum_{i=1}^{n_y} \theta_i(\mathbf{x}(k))y(k - i) + \sum_{i=n_y+1}^{n_y+n_u} \theta_i(\mathbf{x}(k))u(k + n_y - i)$$

$$+ \sum_{i=n_y+n_u+1}^{n_y+n_u+n_e} \theta_i(\mathbf{x}(k))e(k + n_y + n_u - i) + e(k) \tag{39}$$

where $e(k)$ denotes the model residual, which is uncorrelated with $\{y(k-1),$ $y(k-2), \ldots, y(k-n_y)\}$. Note that the appropriate dimension of parameter vector Θ is now expanded to $(n_y + n_u + n_e)$ in equation (39).

Both equations (12) and (13) take the form of a state-dependent model that has been introduced from a quite general nonlinear background [25], but here we will call the model an operating dependent model to avoid confusion with the state variable $z(k)$, which is unobservable. This is because the system input $u(\cdot)$ and system output $y(\cdot)$ form an operating point or observation vector $\mathbf{x}(k)$.

Consider the parameter estimation based on equation (39). It is noted that noise terms are included in the model structure, and to obtain unbiased parameter estimates the extended least-squares related algorithms can be used [9]. In this model structure the free parameters Ω_i, which are in the first layer representing the set of parameters associated with the set of basis functions, may be determined by, for example, back-propagation. Equation (39) needs to be iteratively applied in training because of the included noise terms. This is a disadvantage because the model structure and training process are much more complicated. Now equation (39) can be rewritten as

$$y(k) = \sum_{i=1}^{n_y} \theta_i(\mathbf{x}(k))y(k-i) + \sum_{i=n_y+1}^{n_y+n_u} \theta_i(\mathbf{x}(k))u(k+n_y-i) + \tilde{\xi}(k) \tag{40}$$

where $\tilde{\xi}(k) = \sum_{i=n_y+n_u+1}^{n_y+n_u+n_e} \theta_i(\mathbf{x}(k))e(k+n_y+n_u-i) + e(k)$ is an assimilated noise term. If this were an independent additive noise term, the parameters could be estimated without taking into account of the noise terms based on (40) yielding $\hat{\Theta} = \arg\{\min \sum_{k=1}^{N} \tilde{\xi}(k)^2, \forall\Theta\}$, where N is the number of data samples in the estimation data set. But as $\tilde{\xi}(k)$ will in general be correlated with the past observations $\{y(k-1), y(k-2), \ldots, y(k-n_y)\}$, the parameter estimates obtained will be biased. State estimation derived from the state space model with seriously biased parameters is unlikely to be satisfactory in practice.

From the model (13), $z(k)$ may be interpreted as the noise-free part of $y(k)$, suggesting that a prefiltered $y_p(k)$ could be used for the approximation of $z(k)$ in equation (33), via

$$y(k) = \sum_{i=1}^{n_y} \theta_i(\mathbf{x}(k))y_p(k-i) + \sum_{i=n_y+1}^{n_y+n_u} \theta_i(\mathbf{x}(k))u(k+n_y-i) + \varepsilon(k) + \xi(k) \tag{41}$$

and

$$y(k) = y_p(k) + \xi(k) \tag{42}$$

respectively, where $z(k)$ is replaced by the prefiltered data $y_p(k)$. The basic idea in the new approach is that the prefiltered data $\{y_p(k)\}$ are obtained, followed by the parameter estimation performed using equation (41) via the minimization of $\sum_{k=1}^{N}[\varepsilon(k) + \xi(k)]^2$ in equation (41). If the $\{y_p(k)\}$ are the noise-free part of $y(k)$, $\varepsilon(k) + \xi(k)$ will be uncorrelated and the parameter estimates obtained will be unbiased. This is advantageous in that the iterative procedure for estimation via building a model containing noise terms in the model structure would be avoided.

The extraction of a noise-free part $y_p(k)$ from noisy observation $y(k)$ can be formulated using principal component analysis (PCA). This extraction is based on the fact that noise existing in the system output $y(k)$ is much less predictable than the noise-free part $y_p(k)$, and hence most of the system energy in system output $y(k)$ should be stored in the noise-free part $y_p(k)$. Then, the most important principal components can be used to construct the noise-free part $y_p(k)$. The significance of PCA is that it is very efficient in preserving signal energy, it is easy to include as many principal components as necessary into the noise-free part $y_p(k)$ to achieve good approximation properties, and no prior system structure information is needed.

Linear PCA is carried out directly on the covariance matrix of the output vector. When the system is nonlinear, the linear PCA may be inappropriate as a nonlinear smoother or filter may be required to effectively retrieve the noise-free part $y_p(k)$. A nonlinear optimal PCA algorithm based on neurofuzzy B-splines has been proposed by Hong [14] that provides effective prefiltering with no prior selection of the model structure (except (n_u, n_y)). This method is based on forming a regression matrix

$$\mathbf{P} = [\mathbf{N}(\mathbf{x}(1))\mathbf{N}(\mathbf{x}(2))\cdots\mathbf{N}(\mathbf{x}(N))]^T \in \mathfrak{R}^{N \times p} \tag{43}$$

and performing the singular value decomposition (SVD) of $\mathbf{P}$, so that

$$\mathbf{P} = \mathbf{V}\Lambda\mathbf{U} \tag{44}$$

where $\mathbf{V} = \{\mathbf{v}_j\} \in \mathfrak{R}^{N \times p}$ is an orthonormal matrix of the eigenvectors $\mathbf{v}_j \in \mathfrak{R}^N$ of $\mathbf{P}$, $\Lambda = \text{diag}\{\lambda_1, \lambda_2, \ldots, \lambda_p\} \in \mathfrak{R}^{p \times p}$, and $\mathbf{U} \in \mathfrak{R}^{p \times p}$.

The projection of output vector $\mathbf{y}$ on each eigenvector is

$$c_j = \langle \mathbf{y}, \mathbf{v}_j \rangle, \qquad j = 1, 2, \ldots, p \tag{45}$$

The first M of the marked (in terms of decreasing magnitude of c_j^2) $\tilde{\mathbf{v}}_j$ are used to construct

$$\mathbf{y}_p = \sum_{j=1}^{M} \tilde{c}_j \tilde{\mathbf{v}}_j \tag{46}$$

where $\tilde{\mathbf{v}}_j = \mathbf{v}_k$, $\tilde{c}_j = c_k$. M is increased incrementally until the residual $\tilde{\mathbf{e}} = \mathbf{y} - \mathbf{y}_p$ is uncorrelated.

The identification algorithms using prefiltering for nonlinear neurofuzzy Kalman filtering with neurofuzzy state space model structure can be summarized in the algorithm [14]:

1. The regression matrix $\mathbf{P}$ is constructed according to equation (43). Perform the SVD transformation defined by equation (44). Obtain the eigenvectors $\mathbf{v}_1, \mathbf{v}_2, \ldots, \mathbf{v}_p$. Set $M = 1$.

2. Using equation (46) to construct $\mathbf{y}_p$, check the residual vector $\{\tilde{e}(k)\}$ using model validity tests [1]. If the model validity tests show that the residual is decorrelated, go to step 3, otherwise increase M by 1 and repeat step 2.

3. Retrieve the noise-free part $y_p(k)$, $k = 1, 2, \ldots, N$. The noise-free parts $[y_p(k-1), y_p(k-2), \ldots, y_p(k-n_y)]$ are used to construct the regressors $\Phi(k-1)$, $k = 2, \ldots, N$, where

$$\Phi(k-1) = [N_1(\mathbf{x}(k))y_p(k-1), \ldots, N_p(\mathbf{x}(k))y_p(k-1), \ldots, N_1(\mathbf{x}(k))y_p(k-n_y), \ldots,$$

$$N_p(\mathbf{x}(k))y_p(k-n_y), N_1(\mathbf{x}(k))u(k-1), \ldots, N_p(\mathbf{x}(k))u(k-1), \ldots,$$

$$N_1(\mathbf{x}(k))u(k-n_u), \ldots, N_p(\mathbf{x}(k))u(k-n_u)]^T \tag{47}$$

4. Estimate the free parameters $\Omega(k)$ in the neurofuzzy network using NLMS algorithm (see equation (4), with $\mathbf{N}(\cdot)$ replaced by $\Phi(\cdot)$).

5. Construct the neurofuzzy state space model using equation (35).

6. Apply Kalman filter algorithms to equation (35) for on-line state vector estimation on a validation data set.

5 NUMERICAL EXAMPLES

Example 1. Consider a nonlinear system

$$z(k) = \frac{2.5z(k-1)z(k-2)}{1 + z^2(k-1) + z^2(k-2)} + 0.3 \ \cos[0.5(z(k-1) + z(k-2))] + 0.5u(k-1)$$

$$y(k) = z(k) + \xi(k)$$

(48)

where the system input $u(k) = \sin(\pi k/20)$. The noise sequence $\xi(k) \sim N(0, \sigma_\xi^2)$, where the noise level was set as $\sigma_\xi = 0.05$, was added to the state variable, generating a sequence of system output observation $y(k)$. A data sequence of 1000 samples, plotted in Figure 8, was generated. The first 500 samples $\{u(k), y(k)\}$ from $k = 1$ to $k = 500$ were used as an estimation set. The Kalman filter algorithm was applied to a validation data set of 500 samples consisting of $\{u(k), y(k)\}$ from $k = 501$ to $k = 1000$.

An order-1 ($m = 1$) B-spline neurofuzzy network was used to approximate the system. The input vector to the neurofuzzy network basis function was predetermined as $\mathbf{x}(k) = [y(k-1), y(k-2), u(k-1)]^T$, that is, $n_y = 2$, $n_u = 1$. The knot vector for the input domain was defined as

$$\{-0.5, -0.4, -0.1, 0.65, 1.4, 1.7, 1.8\}$$

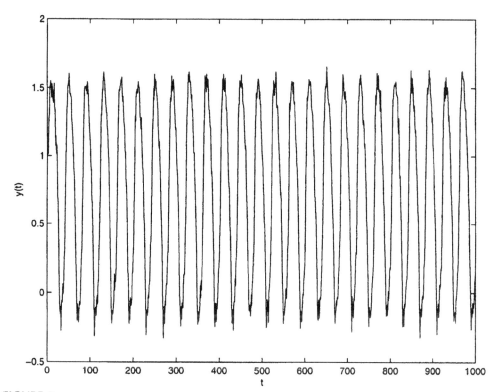

FIGURE 8
The output data $y(k)$ in Example 1.

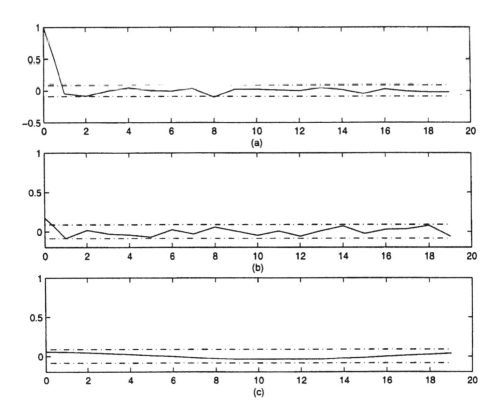

FIGURE 9
Model validity tests in Example 1. (a) Model validity test $\Phi_{\tilde{e}\tilde{e}}(\tau)$. (b) Model validity test $\Phi_{(g\tilde{e})\tilde{e}^2}(\tau)$. (c) Model validity test $\Phi_{(y\tilde{e})u^2}(\tau)$.

for system output $y(k)$, and

$$\{-1.2, -1.1, -0.9, 0, 0.9, 1.1, 1.2\}$$

for system input $u(k)$. The process was terminated as $M = 30$ by checking the residual $\tilde{e}(k)$ using the model valicity tests of [1]. The results plotted in Figure 9 indicate that the residual is uncorrelated after the prefiltering. The performance of the prefilter plotted in Figure 10 indicates that the prefilter is effective in retrieving signal from noisy observations. The prefiltered signal $y_p(k)$ was then used to construct the regressors $\Phi(k - 1)$ for training the state space model using NLMS algorithm. The learning rate selected was $\eta = 0.15$. The training process was carried out repeatedly using the estimation data. The convergence of the mean squared error of the network $(1/N)\sum_{k=1}^{N}[y(k) - \hat{z}(k)]^2$ was plotted in Figure 11, demonstrating the convergence of the network. The mean squared error was 0.0031 at epoch 50.

The Kalman filter algorithm was finally applied over the validation data set of 500 points from $k = 500$ to $k = 1000$. The initial conditions were predetermined as $z(500) = [y(500), y(499)]^T$, $\Sigma(500) = I$. The statistical information of the noise was set as $S = 0$, $Q = \sigma_{\varepsilon}^2 = 0.0004$ denoting a small number, and $R = \sigma_{\xi}^2 = 0.0031$ using the MSE of estimation data set. Note that the matrix $A(k)$ is determined using the operating point dependent neurofuzzy model at each time step. The performance of the neurofuzzy Kalman filter was plotted in Figure 12, demonstrating the excellent approximation performance of the neurofuzzy network to the real system over a validation data set. The example has been repeated for increased measurement noise to evaluate the robustness of the proposed algorithm. Similar results are reported in [14].

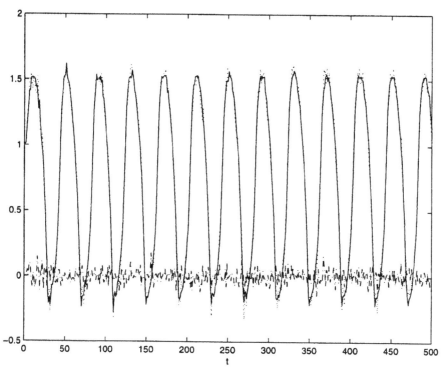

FIGURE 10
The performance of prefiltering over the estimation set in Example 1. Solid line: prefiltered signal $y_p(k)$. Dotted line: system observations $y(k)$. Dash-dot line: residual $\tilde{e}(k)$.

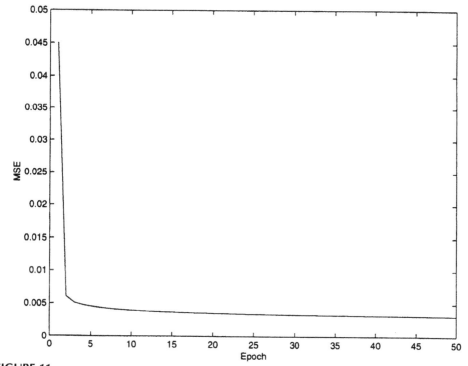

FIGURE 11
The MSE in the estimation set in Example 1.

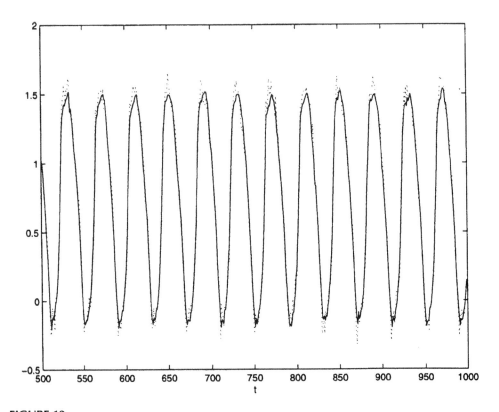

FIGURE 12
The state estimator on the validation set using Kalman filter algorithm in Example 1. Solid line: filtered state variable $z(k)$. Dotted line: system observations $y(k)$.

Example 2. Consider a nonlinear system

$$z(k) = \frac{z(k-1)z(k-2)}{1 + z(k-1)^2} - 0.2 \, \cos[\pi u(k-1)]z(k-2) + 1.2u(k-1) \tag{49}$$

$$y(k) = z(k) + \xi(k)$$

where the system input $u(k) = \sin(\pi k/50)$. A noise sequence $\xi(k) \sim N(0, 0.1^2)$ was added to the state variable generating system output observation $y(k)$. A data sequence of 1000 samples, plotted in Figure 12, was generated. The first 500 samples $\{u(k), y(k)\}$ from $k = 1$ to $k = 500$ were used as an estimation set. The Kalman filter algorithm was applied to a validation data set of 500 samples consisting of $\{u(k), y(k)\}$ from $k = 501$ to $k = 1000$.

Figures 13 and 14 illustrate the performance of the proposed neurofuzzy estimation algorithm for prefiltering and state reconstruction, respectively, again indicating the performance of the proposed algorithm.

6 DISCUSSION

The local operating point model of Figure 7, for an operating point that is the state vector $\mathbf{x}$, can be expressed as

$$\hat{y}(\mathbf{x}) = (\Omega^T \mathbf{x})^T \mathbf{N}(\mathbf{x}) \tag{50}$$

with $\Omega = \{\omega_{ij}\} \in \mathfrak{R}^{n \times p}$, $\mathbf{N}(\mathbf{x}) \in \mathfrak{R}^p$, $\mathbf{x} \in \mathfrak{R}^n$, which is a special (static) case of the generalized Hammerstein nonlinear model [10], whose state space model can be represented as

$$\begin{aligned} \mathbf{z}(k+1) &= \mathbf{A}\mathbf{z}(k) + \mathbf{B}\mathbf{\Psi}(\mathbf{x}(k)) + \mathbf{v}(k) \\ y(k) &= \mathbf{C}\mathbf{z}(k) + w(k) \end{aligned} \qquad (51)$$

where the triple $(\mathbf{A}, \mathbf{B}, \mathbf{C})$ is known or preselected (as stable, observable and controllable), but $\mathbf{\Psi}(\cdot)$ is unknown, and $\{w(k), v(k)\}$ are unknown but bounded disturbances representing system measurement noise and model mismatch terms. The unknown nonlinear term $\mathbf{\Psi}(\cdot)$ can be evaluated by a B-spline expansion via $\mathbf{\Psi}(\mathbf{x}) = \mathbf{W}^T\mathbf{N}(\mathbf{x})$, using the back-propagation algorithm for estimating the weight vector $\mathbf{W}$ and a neurofuzzy Kalman estimator that sequentially evaluates the states $\mathbf{z}(k)$ [31, 32]. The real constraint of this approach is the judicious a priori choice by the user of the triple $(\mathbf{A}, \mathbf{B}, \mathbf{C})$ when the input–output relationship is a priori unknown. In practice, some form of I–O linear model is usually known, easing this restriction. If $\mathbf{z} = \mathbf{x}$ in equation (51) and $\mathbf{\Psi}(\mathbf{x}(k)) = \Omega^T\mathbf{N}(\mathbf{x})$ then equation (51) represents a dynamic recurrent neural network with a neurofuzzy nonlinear state feedback term, which can be used as neurofuzzy observer (with proven stability/convergence condition) for system in the Brunovsky canonical form (equation 9). The Hammerstein model is simply a nonlinear static mapping followed by a linear dynamic process, and these processes if reversed yield the famous Wiener dynamic model, which is harder to model and estimate from input–output data.

Increase the nonlinear structure of equation (51) to

$$\begin{aligned} \mathbf{z}(k+1) &= \mathbf{f}(\mathbf{z}(k), \mathbf{u}(k)) + \mathbf{v}(k) \\ \mathbf{y}(k) &= \mathbf{h}(\mathbf{z}(k)) + \mathbf{w}(k) \end{aligned} \qquad (52)$$

for $\mathbf{y}(k) \in \mathfrak{R}^{n_z}$ and $\mathbf{z}(k) \in \mathfrak{R}^{n_z'}$, the unknown state vector, where n_z and n_z' are appropriate dimensions, $\{w(k), v(k)\}$ are noise terms and $\{\mathbf{u}(k), \mathbf{y}(k)\}$ are input–output observable. If $\mathbf{f}(\cdot)$, $\mathbf{h}(\cdot)$ are known a priori, and are locally differentiable, then the extended Kalman filter is applicable. If they are not a priori known and not necessarily differentiable, but are such that

$$\begin{aligned} \mathbf{f}(\mathbf{z}, \mathbf{u}) &= \mathbf{f}(\mathbf{z}') = \lfloor f_1(\mathbf{z}'^T), \ldots, f_{n_z'}(\mathbf{z}'^T) \rfloor^T \\ \mathbf{h}(\mathbf{z}) &= [h_1(\mathbf{z}^T), \ldots, h_{n_z}(\mathbf{z}^T)]^T \end{aligned} \qquad (53)$$

where $\mathbf{z}' = [\mathbf{z}^T(k), \mathbf{u}^T(k)]^T$, then the unknown nonlinear functions $(f(\cdot), g(\cdot))$ can be expanded as neurofuzzy expressions

$$f_i(\mathbf{z}') = \sum_{r=1}^{n_z'} a_{ir}(k)z_r(k) + \sum_{r=1}^{n_u} b_{ir}(k)u_r(k) \qquad (54)$$

for $i = 1, 2, \ldots, n_z'$, and

$$h_i(\mathbf{z}) = \sum_{r=1}^{n_z} c_{ir}(k)z_r(k) \qquad (55)$$

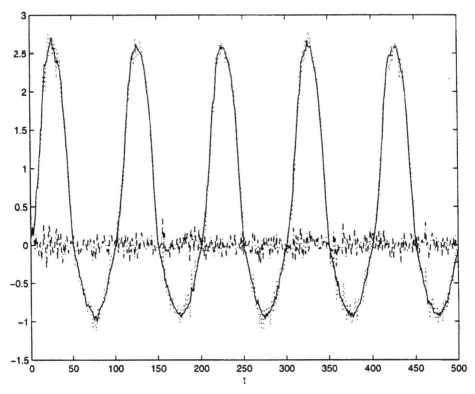

FIGURE 13
The performance of prefiltering over the estimation set in Example 2. Solid line: prefiltered signal $y_p(k)$.
Dotted line: system observations $y(k)$. Dash-dot line: residual $\tilde{e}(k)$.

for $i = 1, 2, \ldots, n_z$, where

$$a_{ir}(k) = \sum_{j'=1}^{p'} N_{j'}(\mathbf{z}')\alpha_{ir'}^{j'} \qquad r = 1, \ldots, n_z'$$

$$b_{ir}(k) = \sum_{j'=1}^{p'} N_{j'}(\mathbf{z}')\beta_{ir'}^{j'} \qquad r = 1, \ldots, n_u \qquad (56)$$

$$c_{ir}(k) = \sum_{j=1}^{p} N_j(\mathbf{z})\gamma_{ir}^{j}, \qquad r = 1, \ldots, n_z$$

where j' and j correspond to the indexes of neurofuzzy basis functions whose total numbers are p' (for $\mathbf{z}'$) and p (for $\mathbf{z}$), respectively. The unknown parameters $\{\alpha_{ir}^{j'}, \beta_{ir}^{j'}, \gamma_{ir}^{j}\}$ can be found by the conventional back-propagation algorithm. However, many of these terms may be redundant and an ASMOD expansion for each term in equations (54) and (55) will result in an increased sparsity in the following state space representation of the system (52),

$$\mathbf{z}(k+1) = \mathbf{A}(k)\mathbf{z}(k) + \mathbf{B}(k)\mathbf{u}(k) + \mathbf{v}(k)$$
$$\mathbf{y}(k) = \mathbf{C}(k)\mathbf{z}(k) + \mathbf{w}(k) \qquad (57)$$

for $\mathbf{A}(k) = \{a_{ir}(k)\}$, $\mathbf{B}(k) = \{b_{ir}(k)\}$, $\mathbf{C}(k) = \{c_{ir}(k)\}$. The state space model (57) is not in canonical form, but is directly amenable to the Kalman filter for estimating the state once the

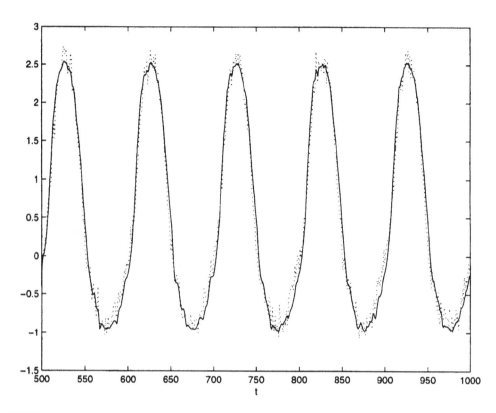

FIGURE 14

The state estimator on the validation set using Kalman filter algorithm in Example 2. Solid line: filtered state variable $z(k)$. Dotted line: system observations $y(k)$.

construction phase of evaluating from ASMOD the coefficients $\{a_{ir}(k),\ b_{ir}(k),\ c_{ir}(k)\}$ is complete. The two algorithms can be applied iteratively in a bootstrap manner.

Future research into neurofuzzy state estimators will consider additional state model structures, differentiable (B-spline) input–output models for numerically generating system states with a priori deterministic errors, and a generalized convergence theory-based neurofuzzy observer theory. Current applications by the ISIS group of the derived neurofuzzy state estimators include automobile break squeal identification, gas turbine and rotating machine condition monitoring, helicopter and ship collision avoidance data fusion systems [8] car collision avoidance algorithms [20], and missile target tracking problems [13].

APPENDIX A

A neurofuzzy network uses B-spline functions as the membership function. A general one-dimensional B-spline model is formed as a linear combination of L B-spline basis functions as

$$f(x) = \sum_{j=1}^{L} \omega_j B_m^j(x) \tag{58}$$

The coefficients ω_j represent the set of adjustable parameters associated with the set of basis functions. The set of basis functions $B_m^j(x)$ in the model is a polynomial of a given degree m and is uniquely defined by an ordered sequence of real values denoted as a knot vector $\tau = \{\tau_1, \tau_2, \ldots, \tau_{L+m+1}\}$. The knot sequence forms a partitioning of the input domain into $(L + m)$ disjoint intervals. The definition of basis functions set can be expressed as a recursion [7].

$$B_m^j(x) = \frac{x - \tau_j}{\tau_{j+m} - \tau_j} B_{m-1}^j(x) + \frac{\tau_{j+m+1} - x}{\tau_{j+m+1} - \tau_{j+1}} B_{m-1}^j(x) \tag{59}$$

with

$$B_0^j(x) = \begin{cases} 1 & \tau_j \leq x < \tau_{j+1} \\ 0 & \text{otherwise} \end{cases}$$

The multidimensional B-spline basis functions are formed by a direct multiplication of one-dimensional basis functions

$$N_j(\mathbf{x}) = \prod_{i=1}^{n} B_{i,m}^{k_i}(x_i) \tag{60}$$

for $j = 1, \ldots, p$, where $p = \prod_{i=1}^{n} L_i$, $\mathbf{x} = [x_1, x_2, \cdots, x_n]^T \in \mathfrak{R}^n$, $k_i = 1, 2, \ldots, L_i$, and L_i is the number of B-spline basis functions defined in x_i, the ith component of $\mathbf{x}$. The multidimensional B-spline basis function models are constructed as a tensor product of one-dimensional models using $p = \prod_{i=1}^{n} L_i$ basis functions as

$$f\mathbf{x}) = \sum_{j=1}^{p} \omega_j N_j(\mathbf{x})$$

$$= \sum_{j=1}^{p} \omega_j \prod_{i=1}^{n} B_{i,m}^{k_i}(x_i) \tag{61}$$

APPENDIX B

Consider the state space model of equations (35) and (36). Let $\hat{\mathbf{z}}(k)$ denote the conditional mean of $\mathbf{z}(k)$ given observations of $\{y(k)\}$ up to and including time $k - 1$. Denote

$$E\left\{\begin{bmatrix} \varepsilon(k) \\ \xi(k) \end{bmatrix} [\varepsilon(\tau)^T \xi(\tau)^T] \right\} = \begin{bmatrix} \mathbf{Q} & \mathbf{S} \\ \mathbf{S}^T & \mathbf{R} \end{bmatrix} \delta(k - \tau)$$

where $\delta(\cdot)$ denotes the Kronecker delta. Then $\hat{\mathbf{z}}(k)$ satisfies the following recursion (the Kalman filter):

$$\hat{\mathbf{z}}(k) = \mathbf{A}(k)\hat{\mathbf{z}}(k - 1) + \mathbf{K}(k)[y(k - 1) - \mathbf{C}\hat{\mathbf{z}}(k - 1)] + \mathbf{B}\tilde{u}(k) \tag{62}$$

$$\mathbf{K}(k) = [\mathbf{A}(k)\Sigma(k - 1)\mathbf{C}^T + \mathbf{S}][\mathbf{C}\Sigma(k - 1)\mathbf{C}^T + \mathbf{R}]^{-1} \tag{63}$$

$$\Sigma(k) = \mathbf{A}(k)\Sigma(k - 1)\mathbf{A}(k)^T + \Gamma\mathbf{Q}\Gamma^T - \mathbf{K}(k - 1)[\mathbf{C}\Sigma(k - 1)\mathbf{C}^T + \mathbf{R}]\mathbf{K}(k - 1)^T \tag{64}$$

with the initial conditions given as

$$\begin{aligned} \mathbf{z}(k_0) &= \mathbf{z}_0 \\ \Sigma(k_0) &= \Sigma_0 \end{aligned} \tag{65}$$

where $\mathbf{K}(k)$ is the Kalman gain. $\Sigma(k)$ is the state error variance, that is,

$$\Sigma(k) = E\{[\hat{\mathbf{z}}(k) - \mathbf{z}(k)][\hat{\mathbf{z}}(k) - \mathbf{z}(k)]^T | y(k - 1), y(k - 2), \ldots\} \tag{66}$$

REFERENCES

[1] S.A. Billings and Q.M. Zhu, Nonlinear model validation using corrrelation tests. *Int. J. Control*, Vol. 60, pp. 1107–1120, 1994.

[2] K.M. Bossley, D.J. Mills, M. Brown, and C.J. Harris, Neurofuzzy high dimensional modelling in *Adaptive Computing: Neural Networks*, pp. 297–332. Alfred Waller, Henley on Thames, 1995.

[3] K.M. Bossley, *Neurofuzzy Modelling Approaches in System Identification*. Ph.D. Thesis, Department of Electronics and Computer Science, University of Southampton, 1997.

[4] M. Brown and C.J. Harris, *Neurofuzzy Adaptive Modelling and Control*. Prentice-Hall, Hemel Hempstead, 1994.

[5] M. Brown, S.R. Gunn, C.Y. Ng, and C.J. Harris. Neurofuzzy systems modelling: a transient approach, in: K. Warwick (ed.) *Dealing with Complexity: A Neural Network Approach*. Springer-Verlag, London, 1997.

[6] Chui, C.K. and G. Chen, *Kalman Filtering with Real-Time Applications*, Springer Series in Information Science. Springer-Verlag, Berlin 1987.

[7] P. Dierckx, *Curve and Surface Fitting with Splines*, Monographs on Numerical Analysis. Clarendon Press, Oxford, 1995.

[8] R.S. Doyle and C.J. Harris, Multi-sensor data fusion for helicopter guidance using neurofuzzy estimation algorithms. *Royal Aeronautical Society Journal*, pp. 241–251, June/July 1996.

[9] G.C. Goodwin and K.S. Sin, *Adaptive Filtering Prediction and Control*, Information and System Science Series. Prentice-Hall, Englewood Cliffs, NJ, 1984.

[10] R. Haber and H. Unbehaven. Identification of nonlinear dynamical systems—a survey on input/output approaches. *Automatica*, Vol. 26, No. 4, pp. 651–677, 1990.

[11] C.J. Harris, C.G. Moore, and M. Brown. *Intelligent Control: Aspects of fuzzy Logic and Neural Nets*. World Scientific, Singapore, 1993.

[12] C.J. Harris, M. Brown, K.M. Bossley, D.J. Mills, and Feng, M., Advances in neurofuzzy algorithms for real time modelling and Control. *J. Engineering Applications, AI*, Vol. 9, No. 1, 1996, pp. 1–12.

[13] C.J. Harris, T. Dodd, and A. Bailey. Multisensor data fusion in defense and aerospace, *Royal Aeronautical Society Journal*, Vol. 102, pp. 229–244, 1998.

[14] X, Hong, C.J. Harris, and P.A. Wilson, Neurofuzzy network state space identification algorithms using prefiltering for non-linear Kalman filtering, submitted for publication.

[15] J.J. Hopfield, Neuros with graded response have connective computational properties. *Proc. National Academy of Sciences, USA*, Vol. 31, pp. 3088–3092, 1984.

[16] J.S.R. Jang, C.T. Sun, and E. Mizutani, *Neurofuzzy and Softcomputing*. Prentice-Hall, Englewood Cliffs, NJ, 1997.

[17] T. Kavli, ASMOD—an algorithm for adaptive spline modelling of observation data. *Int. J. Control*, Vol. 58, No. 4, pp. 947–967, 1993.

[18] F.L. Lewis, A. Yesildirek, and K. Liu, Neuronet robot controller with guaranteed tracking performance. *IEEE. Trans. Neural Networks*, Vol. 6, No. 3, pp. 703–715, 1995.

[19] R. Marino, Adaptive observers for SISO nonlinear systems *IEEE Trans. Automatic Control*, Vol. 35, No. 9, pp. 1054–1058, 1990.

[20] N. Mathews, E. An, J. Roberts, and C.J. Harris, A neurofuzzy approach to fuzzy intelligent driver support systems, *IME Automobile Engineering J.*, to appear.

[21] C.G. Moore and C.J. Harris, Aspects of fuzzy logic and esimation, in: C.J. Harris (ed.) *Advances in Intelligent Control*. pp. 201–242, Taylor and Francis, London, 1994.

[22] R. Murray Smith and T.A. Johnansen, *Multiple Model Approaches to Modelling and Control*. Taylor and Francis, London, 1997.

[23] O. Nelles, S. Sinsel, and R. Isermann, Local basis function networks for identification of a turbogenerator. *IEE UKACC Control Int. Conf.*, 1996, Vol. 2, pp. 7–12.

[24] A. Papoulis, *Probability, Random Variables, and Stochastic Processes*, McGraw-Hill, New York, 1965.

[25] M.B. Priestley, State-dependent models: a general approach to non-linear time series analysis. *J. Time Series Analysis*, Vol. 1, No. 1, pp. 47–71.

[26] L.L. Schumaker, *Spline Functions: Basic Theory*. Wiley, New York, 1981.

[27] T. Takagi and M. Sugeno, Fuzzy identification of fuzzy systems and its application to modelling and control. *IEEE Trans Systems, Man, and Cybernetics*, Vol. 15, pp. 116–132.

[28] L.X. Wang, *Adaptive Fuzzy Systems and Control: Design and Stability analysis*. Prentice-Hall, Englewood Cliffs, NJ, 1994.

[29] H. Wang, G.P. Liu, C.J. Harris, and M. Brown, *Advanced Adaptive Control*, Pergamon Press, Oxford 1995

[30] K. Warwick (ed.) *Dealing with Complexity: A Neural Network Approach*. Springer-Verlag, London, 1997.

[31] Z.Q. Wu and C.J. Harris, A neurofuzzy network structure for modelling and state estimation for unknown nonlinear systems. *Int. J. Systems Science*, Vol. 28, No. 4, pp. 335–345, 1997.

[32] Z.Q. Wu and C.J. Harris, *Approaches to the Application of the Standard Kalman Filter to Unknown Nonlinear Stochastic Systems*, ISIS Technical Report, University of Southampton, 1997. *http://www.isis.ecs.soton.ac.u.k*

[33] Z.Q. Wu and C.J. Harris, *A Mixture Expert Network for Piecewise Linear Modelling*, Technical Report, Department of Electronics and Computer Science, University of Southampton, 1998. *http://www.isis.ecs.soton,ac.uk*

PART III

IMPLEMENTATION AND APPLICATION OF INTELLIGENT CONTROL

CHAPTER 17

Soft Computing Paradigms for Artificial Vision

K. K. SHUKLA

Department of Computer Engineering, Institute of Technology, Banaras Hindu University, Varanasi, India

1 INTRODUCTION

Traditionally, problem-solving paradigms have been predominantly based on the concept of *programmed* computing. However, humanlike computing is characterized not by a preprogrammed algorithm follower, but by massive asynchronous parallelism and learning by example. Despite an exponential growth in available computing power, a 4-year-old can still beat the mightiest of traditional computers in many perceptual and pattern recognition tasks. This fact reinforces the belief that artificial intelligence techniques cannot get very far by pursuing the symbol manipulator metaphor put forth by Turing, but must look toward biologically motivated soft computing paradigms [1].

Soft computing emulates the flexible knowledge representation and processing capabilities exhibited by humans. Current research in this direction points to a synergy of methodologies aimed at exploiting the tolerance for imprecision in real-life problems [11–14]. It offers the robustness of humanlike problem solving in AI-oriented applications where a fast approximate solution to a vaguely formulated problem is the prime concern and exact solutions are intractable by traditional computing [2].

Computational vision is an emerging field in artificial intelligence. Its goal is to develop image-understanding systems that can provide scene descriptions from digitized images. Computational vision is confronted with the inverse problem of recovering features from images. Vision problems are often ill-conditioned in traditional formulation, and can benefit from a fuzzy interpretation of the images and associate operators [3]. This chapter considers possible synergies between neural networks (NN), fuzzy logic (FL), and genetic algorithms (GA) and then presents a new soft computing-based algorithm for a computational vision problem. This algorithm exploits NN, FL, and GA to achieve superior performance with respect to traditional algorithms.

2 SOFT COMPUTING COMPONENTS

The three principal components of soft computing are fuzzy logic (FL), artificial neural networks (ANN), and genetic algorithms (GA). FL provides a framework for expressing imprecision and nonstatistical uncertainty in real-world problems; ANN provides machinery for learning from examples; and GA is a global optimizer successfully used by nature for the evolution of species. There has been a surge of research activities in recent times aimed at developing a plethora of intelligent systems applications using soft computing technologies. These applications span a very wide spectrum including electric motor control, process control, power systems, security assessment, medical diagnosis, image processing, character recognition, speech synthesis, financial forecasting, natural language processing, remote sensing, quality inspection, navigation, and many more aspects.

3 SYNERGY OF THE COMPONENTS

Synergy of the three components of soft computing, viz. NN, FL and GA, is an active research area. The possible fusion alternatives are shown in Figure 1 and discussed in the following sections.

3.1 NN Inference Engine for Fuzzy Reasoning

Takagi [11] first used NN to generate nonlinear multidimensional membership functions in a fuzzy system (FS). The advantage of this synergy is that it is more general than the conventional FS because the membership combination operators are absorbed by the NN, which learns by examples provided by an expert. The design of NN-driven fuzzy reasoning is accomplished by first clustering the given training data, then fuzzy partitioning the input space by NN, and finally designing the consequent part for each partitioned space. The initial clustering of the training data partitions the input space such that the number of clusters discovered gives the number of

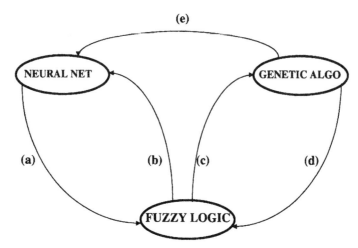

FIGURE 1
Synergy between soft computing components. (a) Learn fuzzy rules/membership functions. (b) Fuzzify NN/training set. (c) Fuzzy crossover. (d) Tune memberships. (e) Global optimization for supervised training.

rules to be used in the FS. The membership generator NN is then trained in the supervised mode using the training data derived from the clustering process in the previous step. The designer may modify the training data if she feels that some membership assignments based on clustering are not realistic. The consequent parts can also be implemented using NN, or, alternatively, conventional implementation using fuzzy variables can be employed.

3.2 Fuzzifying NN and Training Sets

Stadter et al. [12] have introduced a fuzzy Vornoi neural network (FVNet) for automatic pattern classification. FVNet has sub-networks that can learn fuzzy logic constructs from empirical data. The first layer computes fuzzy proximity values that are propagated to the second layer where memberships of the feature vector to various fuzzy partitions are estimated. This model has been successfully applied to many synthetic and real-world data, including Fisher's Iris data, medical diagnosis, and discrete event identification.

A neural fuzzy system learning with fuzzy training data has been proposed by Chin-Teng Lin et al. [13]. A fuzzy supervised learning algorithm has been developed using interval arithmetic. This algorithm can train the proposed system with fuzzy input–output pairs. This model has also been used to minimize the number of rules in a fuzzy knowledge base. It can be applied to fuzzy-input–fuzzy-output systems, as well as crisp-input–fuzzy-output systems.

3.3 Fuzzy Logic Applied to GA

F. Herrera et al. [14] have introduced a new concept of crossover operators based on fuzzy connectives for real-coded genetic algorithms. This approach reduces the premature convergence in GA due to lack of diversity in the population. The fuzzy crossover operators allow controlled degrees of exploration (broad search) and exploitation (refinement), inducing different levels of diversity in the population. The action interval of genes is subdivided into three intervals that bound regions to which offspring may belong. Various functions that allow recombination of genes are defined using fuzzy connectives like t-norms, t-conorms, averaging functions, and generalized compensation operators. This results in four families of fuzzy crossover operators and corresponding families of GAs. The monotone property of fuzzy connectives guarantees that the fuzzy GAs fit their action range depending on the convergence level of the population using specific information held by the parents. Further, there is a possibility of using a fuzzy knowledge base to tune the GA parameters dynamically based on certain population characteristics.

3.4 Application of GA to Fuzzy Systems

The fusion of GA with FL requires parametrized representation of the membership functions. These parameters are then encoded as chromosomes and the GA is run to optimize a matching function between the desired and actual outputs. Researchers have used triangular, sigmoidal, and Gaussian membership functions. Fuzzy rules proposed by Takagi and Sugeno [15] have the structure:

$$\text{IF } \theta \text{ is } small \text{ AND } d\theta/dt \text{ is } big \text{ THEN } force = w_0 + w_1\theta + w_2 d\theta/dt$$

To optimize this type of fuzzy system genetically, Takagi has suggested three steps:

1. Represent the membership functions as left and right base widths, and center distance from the previous membership.

2. Represent the number of rules by considering the boundary conditions and the centers of membership functions.

3. Represent consequent parts.

These three representations have to be suitably encoded as chromosomes. The GA can then optimize a fitness function that is related to the goodness of a solution. A priori knowledge can be used to initialize the population.

3.5 GA Applied to NN Training

The supervised learning capability of feedforward NNs can be significantly improved by genetically optimizing a performance criterion. The simplest fitness function is the inverse of the mean square output error over the training set. However, more sophisticated fitness functions that encourage generalization and fault tolerance in the resulting NNs are possible. The main problem in genetically training NNs is to select an appropriate encoding scheme for the weight matrix as chromosomes. Here, two possibilities exist. One can use the *strong specification scheme*, which is a direct encoding in which each connection of the network is specified by its binary representation. Alternatively, one may use a *weak specification scheme*, which is an indirect encoding in which exact connectivity is not specified but is estimated based on information encoded in the string. There is no definite view in the literature about the suitability of strong or weak schemes, with various researchers being in favor of one scheme or the other. Our work presented as a case study in this chapter demonstrates successful application of the strong scheme to artificial soft vision.

4 CASE STUDY—EDGE DETECTION USING A GENETICALLY TRAINED FUZZY NEURAL NETWORK

Soft computing paradigms are ideally suited to perceptual tasks like vision. Kerr and Bezdek [9] proposed the use of a fuzzified basis set of Sobel windows to train a neural network in an *image-independent* manner. This case study identifies convergence difficulties in their method and demonstrates better learning ability by genetically evolving the neural weights using a novel reproduction operator—the MRX crossover—introduced by us. Simulations with a natural scene against a textured background show considerable advantages in solving the edge detection problem with the new method. Further research directions using this methodology are identified.

Machine vision uses an array of intensity values obtained through a digital camera. The raw image data so obtained is processed in stages (low, medium, and high levels) to understand a scene. *Edges* are one of the most important features in an image since they represent object boundaries, changes in surface orientation, or changes in material properties.

An edge is the *perceived boundary* between two pixels when their brightness values are *significantly* different. The actual value of what is *significant* depends upon the distribution of brightness values around each pixel. The array of intensities representing the image is created by sampling a real-valued function f—defined on the domain of the image that is a bounded and connected subset of the real plane $\mathbb{R}^2$. A numerical approximation of the first spatial derivative of intensity is usually based on the assumption that f is linear. Edge detection is then mathematically equivalent to fitting a function to sample values.

Conventional edge detectors in the literature by Haralick [4], Watson [5], Rosenfeld [6], Zucker [7], and Morgenthaler [8] are based on the surface fit concept. The sequential nature of these algorithms and their lack of robustness make them unsuitable for many real-world problems. Progress in medium and high-level vision tasks is hampered by the lack of a fast, reliable edge detector.

In this case study we show that the generalization power of a feedforward neural network can be used to learn the edge detection task in an *image-independent* manner using a synergy of the three soft computing components.

4.1 ANN as Edge Detector

An artificial neural network can be used as a classifier to segregate edge pixels from non-edge pixels based on the intensity values in the neighborhood of pixels. The ANN must learn the *inherent mapping* required for the edge detection process so that it may give good performance on *any* image, not just on a particular image that may be used for training. Kerr and Bezdek [9] have achieved this by using a training set that is not dependent on any specific image data. Our approach differs from [9] in that we demonstrate improved generalization and edge detection performance by genetically training the neural network to minimize the mean square output error over the training set.

4.2 Training Set Formulation

Let a set of window vectors $e \in \mathbb{R}^9$ be derived from (3×3) subimage:

$$\mathbf{W}_{3\times3} = \begin{bmatrix} f_1 & f_2 & f_3 \\ f_4 & f_5 & f_6 \\ f_7 & f_8 & f_9 \end{bmatrix} \tag{1}$$

$$\leftrightarrow \boldsymbol{E} = [f_1 \ \ f_2 \ \ f_3 \ \ f_4 \ \ f_5 \ \ f_6 \ \ f_7 \ \ f_8 \ \ f_9] \tag{2}$$

where, f_i is the intensity at location i.

For example, if the number of bits per pixel is 1, then we may have [9]

$$\mathbf{W}_{3\times3} = \begin{bmatrix} 0 & 0 & 1 \\ 0 & 1 & 1 \\ 1 & 1 & 1 \end{bmatrix} \tag{3}$$

$$\leftrightarrow \boldsymbol{E} = [0 \ \ 0 \ \ 1 \ \ 0 \ \ 1 \ \ 1 \ \ 1 \ \ 1 \ \ 1] \tag{4}$$

Approximations to the partial derivatives at the center pixel are

$$\frac{\partial f}{\partial x} = G_x = (f_7 + 2f_8 + f_9) - (f_1 + 2f_2 + f_3) \tag{5}$$

and

$$\frac{\partial f}{\partial y} = G_y = (f_3 + 2f_6 + f_9) - (f_1 + 2f_4 + f_7) \tag{6}$$

Hence, the gradient of the image intensity function $f(x, y)$ is the 2-dimensional vector

$$\boldsymbol{G}[f(x, y)] = \begin{bmatrix} G_x \\ G_y \end{bmatrix} = \begin{bmatrix} \dfrac{\partial f}{\partial x} \\ \dfrac{\partial f}{\partial y} \end{bmatrix} \tag{7}$$

Sobel approximated the length of the gradient vector G by the L_1 norm:

$$|G_x| + |G_y| \tag{8}$$

In the example given above, the value of Sobel operator is

$$S(e) = (4 - 1) + (4 - 1) = 3 + 3 = 6 \tag{9}$$

Clearly, there are $2^8 = 256$ Sobel windows for any given pixel. The set of vectors $E_8 = \{0, 1\}^8$ contains the 256 window vectors and forms an edge detector basis set.

We can obtain a *crisply labeled set of training data* by taking positive and negative examples of edges:

$$E \in E_8 \text{ is an edge iff } S(e) = 6 \text{ and is not an edge iff } S(e) = 0$$

This training set could be used in the learning phase of the neural edge detector. However, as reported in [9], this does not give a very robust system.

4.3   Fuzzifying the Training Set

A *fuzzy subset* of a set of objects $x \in X$ is characterized by the membership function $\mu: X \rightarrow [0, 1]$. The value of $\mu(x)$ is the degree to which x is compatible with the concept of X. In the present context we define E *as the fuzzy set of edge vectors* E_8 *such that*:

$$\mu_E(e) = \frac{S(e)}{S_{\max}} = \frac{S(e)}{6} \tag{10}$$

Applying this formula to the members of E_8 gives the membership function values to each Sobel window of the basis set. This gives rise to the notion of a *fuzzy edge*, or partial edge as in [9]. This gives the advantages of larger training set as well as a more *humanlike* definition of edge in a scene.

We now have the labeled training data for supervised learning:

Input vectors:

$$E_8 = \{e_1, e_2, \ldots, e_{256}\} = \{0, 1\}^8 \tag{11}$$

Output values:

$$E = \{\mu(e_1), \mu(e_2), \ldots, \mu(e_{256})\} \tag{12}$$

Bezdek used the training set in the back-propagation learning procedure with some success [9], but we found that the method is very sensitive to weight initializations and the choice of learning parameters and fails to converge in many cases. We therefore tried using the genetic approach to train the fuzzy neural network as described in the next section.

4.4   Genetic Training of ANN

The gradient-directed back-propagation used in [9] does not perform very well in detecting edges in natural scenes, since it is not robust with respect to weight initialization. Very often, it is stranded in local minima of the error function. In addition, because it does not converge very well, it produces unacceptable results in some cases, e.g. with textured background. We encoded

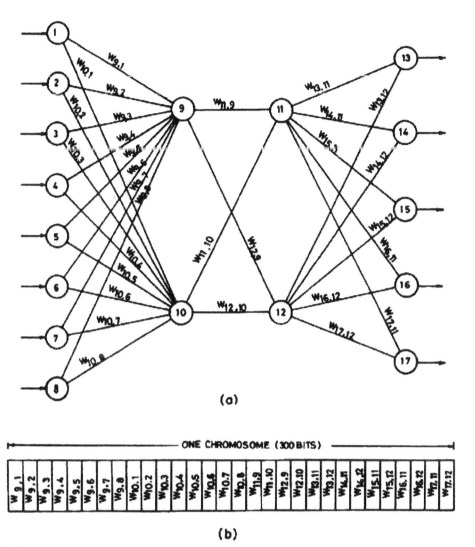

(a)

(b)

FIGURE 2
A neural network encoded as a chromosome. (a) Example NN. (b) Genetic representation.

the weights of the neural networks into chromosomes using 10 bits per weight as shown in Figure 2. Since the standard genetic algorithm *maximizes* the fitness function, we take

$$fitness = \frac{1}{MSE + t} \tag{13}$$

where, *MSE* is the mean square output error of the neural network *over the fuzzy training set* formulated in the previous section, and *t* is a small positive number used to avoid arithmetic overflows in computation of *fitness* as $MSE \rightarrow 0$.

The simple genetic algorithm given below is used to evolve the neural network weights to learn the fuzzy edge detection:

[1] Randomly create an initial population of neural networks.

[2] Perform the following sub-steps iteratively for each generation until a termination condition is fulfilled:

    (a) Evaluate the fitness of each individual in the population, save the best individuals.

    (b) Create a new population by applying the genetic operators SELECTION, CROSS-OVER, and MUTATION.

    (c) Replace population the current population by new the population

[3] Report the neural network with the best fitness as the solution.

4.5 Simulation Results

In order to evaluate the improvement in performance resulting from our method vis-à-vis Bezdek's method, we used the same neural network configuration as in [9], i.e., three hidden layers, (7–2–3 configuration), and one output neuron that produced the membership values. Each node computed the standard scalar product between its input and weight vectors, and had a sigmoid activation function with unit gain. In the genetic algorithm, we used the *roulette wheel selection* [10], and a new *multipoint restricted crossover* (MRX) operator introduced by us. *Mutation* with very low probability was used. We found that the standard crossover often resulted in the destruction of the *good* weights, leading to poor convergence of the algorithm. Based on the study of a large number of simulation runs, we introduced the MRX operator where multiple random crossover sites *restricted within corresponding weight boundaries in the*

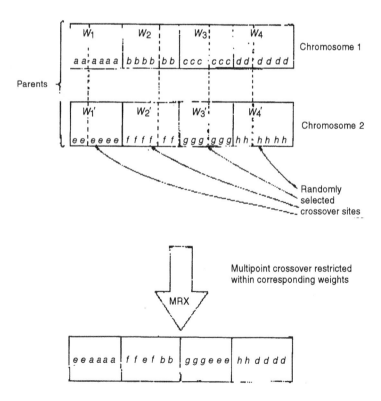

FIGURE 3
The MRX genetic operator.

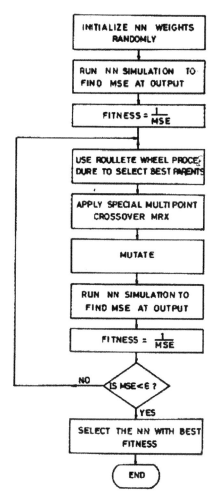

FIGURE 4
Flowchart for genetically training a neural network.

chromosomes, as shown in Figure 3, was used. This improved the GA convergence remarkably. The simulation flowchart for the genetic training of the fuzzy neural network is given in Figure 4.

Our simulations showed that Bezdek's BP base method [9] is very sensitive to the weight initialization. The best learning curve we could obtain with this method is shown in Figure 5. The trained neural network was used on a natural scene comprising a bunch of keys against a textured (cloth) background (Figure 6). the resulting defuzzified output showing crisp edges is given in Figure 7. Notice that, owing to the poor convergence of the NN during training, the edges were seriously distorted with the background texture.

We repeated the experiment with our genetic training on the same NN with the same fuzzy training set. One of the learning curves is shown in Figure 8. We obtained more or less the same performance with different initial populations. This NN was then used as an edge detector on the same natural scene with a textured background, Figure 6. The resulting edges after defuzzification are shown in Figure 9, which shows considerable improvement over the edges in Figure 7.

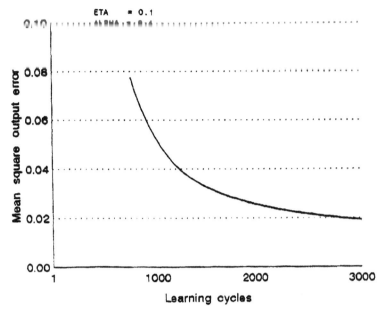

FIGURE 5
Best-case learning curve using back-propagation (edge detection).

This case study thus demonstrates that efficient edge detectors can be implemented using a synergy of the three components of the soft computing paradigm. Using a basis set of Sobel windows, a neural network can be trained independently of any specific image. Fuzzification of the edge set gives rise to a larger training set that results in better generalization ability. Genetically training the neural network gives superior performance compared with Bezdek's neural edge detector.

FIGURE 6
Test image—a bunch of keys against textured background.

FIGURE 7
Edges detected using BP-trained neural network (fuzzy training set).

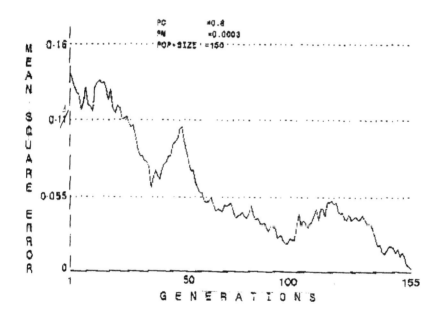

FIGURE 8
Learning curve—genetically trained neural network.

5 CONCLUSIONS

Soft computing is an alternative computing methodology based on a consortium of NN, FL, and GA. It offers the superiority of humanlike problem solving in AI-oriented applications where a fast approximate solution to a vaguely formulated problem is the prime concern and exact solutions may be intractable by traditional computing. Various alternative synergistic combinations of the soft computing components exist. The case study of a machine vision problem amply

FIGURE 9
Edges detected using genetically trained NN (fuzzy training set).

demonstrates the power of soft computing in perceptual tasks. As the knowledge-based approach used by traditional AI approaches saturation, AI-oriented problem solving will increasingly rely on soft computing. Many vision-related problems can benefit from the fuzzification of the digital image and image processing operators. Design and analysis of fuzzy morphological algorithms for vision is an open research area. In the near future, soft computing-based mobile intelligent agents [16] will become a reality for the management of computer and communication systems. These agents will tackle the perceptual and AI-oriented tasks in a heterogeneous distributed environment, while numeric intensive tasks will be handled conventionally.

REFERENCES

[1] S. K., Pal, P. K. Srimani (eds.), *IEEE Computer*, Special Issue on Neural Networks, Vol. 29, No. 3, 1996.

[2] L. A. Zadeh, Fuzzy logic, neural networks, and soft computing;. *Commun. ACM*, Vol. 37, pp. 77–84, 1994.

[3] D. Sinha, P. Sinha, E. R. Doughterty, and S. Batman, Design and analysis of fuzzy morphological algorithms for image processing, *IEEE Trans. Fuzzy Systems*, Vol. 5, No. 4, pp. 570–584, Nov. 1997.

[4] R. M. Haralick, Edge and region analysis for digital image data, *Computer Vision Graphics and Image Processing*, Vol. 12, pp. 60–73, 1980.

[5] R. M. Haralick, and L. Watson. A facet model for image data, *Computer Graphics and Image Processing*, Vol. 15, pp. 113–129, 1981.

[6] A. Rosenfeld, Multi-dimensional edge detection by hypersurface fitting, *IEEE Trans. Pattern Analysis and Machine Intelligence*, Vol. PAMI-3, pp. 482–486, 1981.

[7] S. W. Zucker. et al. A three dimensional edge operator, *IEEE Trans. Pattern Analysis and Machine Intelligence*. Vol. PAMI-3, pp. 324–331, 1981.

[8] D. G. Morgenthaler, A new hybrid edge detector, *Computer Graphics and Image Processing*, Vol. 16, pp. 166–176, 1981.

[9] D. A. Kerr, and J. C. Bezdek, Edge detection using a fuzzy neural network, *SPIE*, Vol. 1710, pp. 510–521, 1992.

[10] L. Davis, *Handbook of Genetic Algorithms*, Van Nostrand Reinhold, New York, 1991.

[11] H. Takagi and I. Hayashi, ANN driven fuzzy reasoning, *Proc. Int. Workshop on Fuzzy System Applications* 1988, pp. 217–218.

[12] P. A. Stadter, and N. K. Bose, Neuro-fuzzy computing: structure performance measure and applications, *Proc. Int. Workshop on Soft Computing & Intelligent Systems, Calcutta, India*, 1998, pp. 97–114.

[13] Chin-Teng Lin and Ya-Ching Lu, A neural fuzzy system with fuzzy supervised learning, *IEEE Trans. Systems, Man, and Cybernetics*, Vol. 26, No. 5, Oct. 1996, pp. 744–763.

[14] F. Herrera, M. Lozano, and J. L. Verdegay, Dynamic and heuristic fuzzy connectives based crossover operators for controlling the diversity and convergence of real-coded genetic algorithms, *International Journal of Intelligent Systems*, Vol. II, pp. 1013–1040, 1996.

[15] T. Takagi, and M. Sugeno, Fuzzy identification of systems and its applications to modelling and control, *IEEE Trans. Systems, Man, and Cybernetics*, Vol. SMC 15-1, pp. 116–132.

[16] S. Nwana Hyacynth, and Nader Azcrmi (eds.), *Software Agents and Soft Computing: Towards Enhancing Machine Intelligence*, Springer-Verlag, Berlin, 1997.

CHAPTER 18

Intelligent Control with Neural Networks

D. POPOVIC

University of Bremen, Germany

1 INTRODUCTION AND MOTIVATION

The invention of neural network technology was an attempt to mimic the information processing system of the human brain, in which a huge number of elementary information processing units, the *neurons*, are organized in structures capable of processing sensory data in an intelligent way. In a similar manner, neural networks consist of a large number of elementary information processing units—*artificial neurons* or *perceptrons*—and are organized into structures capable of processing the information content of input signals acquired from the real world.

The general estimate is that the human brain could have around 10^{10} brain cells (neurons) highly interconnected for intelligent information processing. Each neuron consists of a *cell body* or *soma* with a nucleus that contains the information to be processed. The *dendrites* provide the soma with information from other neurons, and the *axon* distributes the information of the neuron to other neurons (Figure 1a). As basic building blocks of a neural system, the neurons receive, process, and send the information within the nervous system.

Rosenblatt extended the idea of the *computing neuron* to the *perceptron* (Figure 1b), the artificial neuron representing an element of the network capable of learning by structural adaptation [50]. This has enabled neural networks to become intelligent information processing systems, capable of mimicking the human brain, learning the features of the sensed data at their input and adapting to the variations of such data. The concept of the perceptron was widely accepted because of its simplicity in representing the "information storage and organization in the brain" [51, 69]. The extensive theory of perceptrons, however, was first published by Minsky and Papert in 1969, who proved that a *single* perceptron has serious limitations in solving computational problems in *pattern recognition* and *pattern classification* [36]. This, in their opinion, would only be possible if multiperceptron configurations were used, similar to those present in the human brain, for learning and cognition. This was done later by introducing various multiperceptron architectures—the neural networks—that have become massively

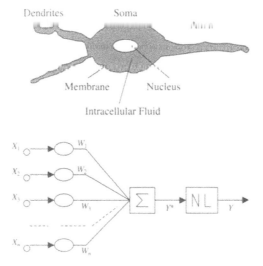

FIGURE 1
(a) Neuron structure; (b) Perceptron structure.

parallel and distributed information processing systems, capable of learning, adapting themselves to the problems they have to solve, and generalizing the recognized facts.

2   PERCEPTRON-BASED CONFIGURATIONS

Widrow and Holf [68] proposed to model the perceptron as an adaptive linear element, the
Adeline (Figure 2), that sums the weighted inputs $X_1, X_2, \ldots, X_n$ with the weights $W_1, W_2, \ldots,$
W_n, and a reference value $x_0 = 1$ with the weight W_0 and sends the result through a nonlinear
element $f(\cdot)$ to build the output signal of the perceptron,

$$Y = f(X_1 W_1 + X_2 W_2 + \cdots + X_n W_n + X_0 W_0)$$

where the non-linearity $f(\cdot)$ is usually the sigmoid function

$$f(\cdot) = [1 + \exp(-ax)]^{-1}$$

The main characteristic of the perceptron is that it *fires*, that is, it produces an output signal,
when the sum of all the weighted inputs meets the condition

$$X_1 W_1 + X_2 W_2 + \cdots + X_n W_n \geq 0$$

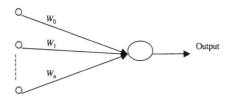

FIGURE 2
ADALINE.

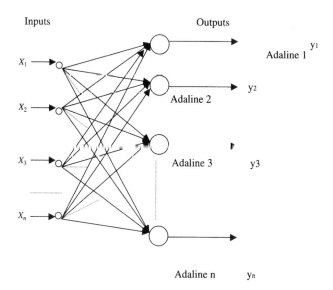

FIGURE 3
ADALINE layer as MADALINE.

where $W_1, W_2, \ldots, W_n$ represent the connection weights. Otherwise, when

$$X_1 W_1 + X_2 W_2 + \cdots + X_n W_n < 0$$

the perceptron is *inhibited*. As pointed out by Widrow, the ADALINE model was expected to become a powerful tool for *adaptive signal processing* and for *adaptive control* [66].

Combining the Adaline units, the Adaline *neural layer* can be built, implementing a complex multivalued binary function (Figure 3). Moreover, by combining the ADALINE layers, MADA-LINE (many-ADALINE) networks (Figure 4) can be built [68].

ADALINE and MADALINE belong to the early neural network architectures. Later, a multilayer network architecture, the *back-propagation* architecture (Figure 4), was proposed [62] that became the best-known and most widely applied neural net option. The architecture includes, apart from the input and output layers, at least one *hidden layer* and uses the general delta rule for learning. The basic theory of networks was very well explained by Hecht-Nielsen [22].

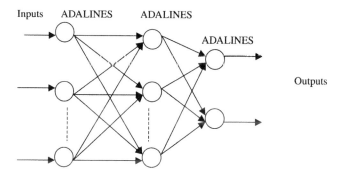

FIGURE 4
MADALINE.

3   LEARNING LAWS

Along with the architectural development of neural networks, their learning capabilities have also been developed, mainly by using different variations of the basic learning law, *Hebb's rule* [21]. The rule defines the *biological law* of learning, i.e., the learning process of the brain at the cellular level: "When an axon of cell A is near enough to excite a cell B, and repeatedly or persistently takes part in firing it, some growth process of metabolic change takes place in one or both cells such that A's efficiency, as one of the cells firing B, is increased." In terms of neural networks this can be formulated so that if a processing element of the network is excited by another processing element, and if both are highly active, the interconnection between them should be strengthened, i.e., its weight increased. The corresponding mathematical definition was given by Sutton and Barto as

$$W(k + 1) = W(k) + cX(k)y(k)$$

where c is a selected constant influencing the rate of learning [57].

Working on the ADALINE network, Widrow and Hoff formulated the *delta rule*, known as the Widrow–Hoff method or the Widrow learning law [68]. The rule was generalized by Widrow [65].

Applied to a perceptron-based network in its training phase, in which the network learns by adjusting the connection weights to produce a certain function at its output, the delta rule represents the general weight modification law

$$W_{\text{new}} = W_{\text{old}} + \Delta W$$

with

$$\Delta W = \alpha(y_d - y)x$$

Here, x represents the perceptron input value, y_d and y the desired and the actual output values, and α the learning constant selected for training that determines the speed of the learning process. This is the LMS (least mean square) learning rule because it is based on the minimization of the difference between the desired output value and the instantaneous output value of the network.

4   NETWORK ARCHITECTURES

The concept of the perceptron actually emerged as an alternative to the classical computational concept of John von Neumann. It was realized that, when solving complex problems, a large number of high-speed interconnections among the simple fragments of knowledge would be required for an accelerated solution process because the massive interconnections would significantly reduce the total number of calculations required, even if the individual calculations were very simple.

Understanding the brain as a highly parallel and distributed computing system, with the neurons as basic computational elements, attempts have been made to mimic it by the interconnection of a huge set of artificial neurons (perceptrons). However, for the implementation of behavioral similarity between natural and artificial brains, complex multilayer perceptron interconnections have been built with learning and cognition capabilities. McClelland, Rumelhart, and the PDP Research Group (1986) formulated the connectionist system capable of learning and solving intelligent problems [35]. Thereafter, various connectionist models were proposed and their learning capabilities on application examples were demonstrated.

Knowledge stored in a connectionist network can be local, each unit storing a fragment of the knowledge, or it can be distributed, stored as a collection of knowledge patterns over all the units or over a large number of them. The *localist* approach tends to create hierarchical layers of units and, consequently, a hierarchical problem space, requiring an appropriate search algorithm for pursuing the final goal or problem solution. In the distributed connectionism approach, each unit represents a microfeature of the system's knowledge. Similar knowledge concepts share a number of microfeatures because similar concepts have similar patterns. In this way, the total number of units for representation of certain concepts is also reduced. In addition to this, distributing the concepts over a large number of units decreases their sensitivity to the failure of individual units and, accordingly, the reliability or the robustness of the connectionist net is increased.

The perceptron was chosen as the basic element of a connectionist net built as a layered structure of a collection of units (Figure 5), many of them being in the hidden layers, situated behind the front layer, interconnected to the external sensors. As a rule, in the layered perceptron net each classification result is associated with a single output unit. The results obtained in this way are local.

Hopfield [23, 23a] introduced a multiperceptron network architecture, a single-layer binary network analogue to a *state machine* (Figure 6), known as the *Hopfield network*, and demonstrated its associative memory features such as:

- Distributed knowledge concepts representation.
- Distributed, asynchronous control with autonomous, local decision power for each unit of the network.
- Content-addressability.
- Fault tolerance.

He also demonstrated the optimization and pattern classification problems that can be solved with the network.

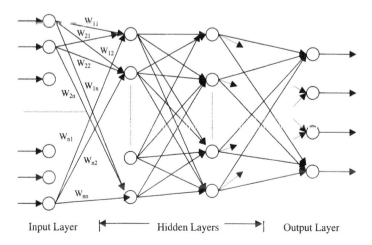

FIGURE 5
Multilayer perceptron.

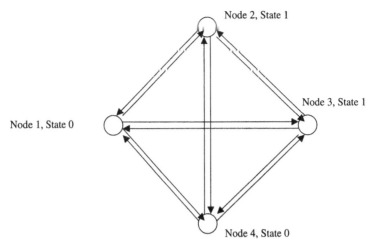

FIGURE 6
Hopfield network as a binary state machine $\{0,1,1,0\}$.

As a state machine, the network starts the processing with an initial pattern of states, forced by the external input vector. From the connections to the other units, each unit then computes its local energy function, which is lowered stepwise during the process of computation. At the end of the process, the global state achieved represents a local minimum configuration corresponding to the acting input. This configuration, which is not necessarily global, masks the actual problem solution lying in the global minimum configuration.

Neural network research on real-world problems has increased exponentially since the 1990s. Presently, neural networks are viewed as new computers and as versatile powerful tools for solving problems in the fields of signal processing, pattern recognition, process control, robotics and manufacturing, medical engineering and bio-engineering, financial engineering, etc. In control engineering, neural networks have been accepted as a tool for modeling, identification, and adaptive control of nonlinear systems, where conventional digital computers frequently fail. The main reason for the wide acceptance of neural networks, apart for their parallelism and increased computational power, lies in their ability to solve cognitive problems directly, i.e., by learning, feature extraction, pattern classification, and association, rather than by using complex identification algorithms as conventional computers do. Their suitability for solving nonlinear problems, again, is due to their capability to implement nonlinear mapping.

Currently a wide variety of neural network architectures are being studied and used in various application areas. From the mathematical systems theory and control engineering points of view, the most important ones are:

- Back-propagation networks
- Recurrent networks
- Hopfield networks
- Radial basis function networks
- Adaptive resonance theory networks
- Restricted Coulomb energy networks
- Probabilistic networks
- Modular networks

4.1 Back-propagation Networks

The concept of back-propagation networks, or multilayer perceptron networks, was first presented by Werbos [62] and described by McClelland and Rumelhart [35]. The concept is based on a multilayer architecture in which each layer is fully connected to the adjacent layers. Within the network the signals are propagated in one direction, from the input to the output of the network. No lateral interconnections are present and no lateral signals flow. A typical back-propagation network, a three-layer network containing the input, output, and the hidden layers, is shown in Figure 7. The outstanding characteristic of the network is that it maps the input stimuli, based on the features of their patterns, to a set of output patterns. This characteristic is due to the hidden layer of the network, which is capable of identifying the features present in the input stimuli. Moreover, when trained on many examples with similar features, the layer is capable of *generalizing* the features learnt from the examples and of recognizing later any feature belonging to the feature class generalized from the examples. Owing to such basic characteristics, the back-propagation network architecture was the first one used for pattern recognition and pattern classification. For this purpose, the network was trained by the *supervised learning* approach. To achieve good recognition and classification results, the *data base*, i.e. the collection of training examples as input stimuli, selected for learning phase of the network, should be as complete as possible (i.e., *statistically significant* and *consistent*) and made up of functional pairs of values (x, y)—the *input feature vectors* and the *expected* output vectors. After being trained, the network is validated on new *unknown* input patterns to check whether it produces acceptable classification results at its output [34].

The hidden layer of the network enables the solving of much more complex problems than it would be possible to solve without such a layer. It introduces a new innovative component into the back-propagation networks, their ability to extract the characteristic features from the input patterns. This capability is due to the internal mappings of input patterns on the hidden layer during the training phase of the network so that, in its application phase, it automatically recognizes the previously mapped features of the input pattern classes. The hidden layer, however, because of the additional operations required for tuning of its connection weights, slows down the learning process both by decreasing the learning rate and by increasing the number of learning steps required.

Generally speaking, back-propagation neural networks are *nonlinear pattern discriminators* that map an n-dimensional input vector into an m-dimensional output vector by adjusting the weights of the network interconnection links during the learning phase. The adjustment is carried out by minimizing the error present at the output, defined as the difference between the *desired*

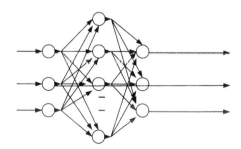

Input Layer   Hidden Layer   Output Layer

FIGURE 7
A typical 3-layer back-propagation network.

and the *actual* output vector, usually based on a *gradient descent algorithm* and the *mean-squared error* as the *performance index*. The mapping itself is performed in two steps. The input vector is first mapped onto the hidden layer of the network, which, in sequence, is mapped onto the network output layer. The hidden layer is thus equivalent to a *data concentrator* (i.e., to a lumped network that internally encodes the essential pattern features in a compressed form and sets the values of the weights that represent its distributed memory).

The problem addressed by functional mapping using neural networks is the approximation of a bounded mapping function $f: A \subset \mathbf{R}^n \to \mathbf{R}^m$ from a bounded subset A of an n-dimensional Euclidean space, to a bounded subset $f[A]$ of an m-dimensional space by means of training on examples (X_k, Y_k), $k = 1, 2, 3, \ldots$, where $Y_k = f(X_k)$.

Back-propagation networks have proven to be very suitable for the identification of nonlinear systems using the *regressive* input/output system model, as well as using the *state space* system model [60].

4.2   Recurrent Networks

Back-propagation networks, as described above, are *feedforward networks* in which the signals propagate in only one direction, from the inputs of the input layer to the outputs of the output layer. No feedback links are present within the network. However if any feedback link is present in the network, the network is called a *recurrent network* [27]. The signals in such a network can propagate in either direction from all and to all the layers (Figure 8), and also in the lateral directions within the same layer. The network behavior is *dynamic*, similar to the behavior of a *state machine*. The output states of neurons depend not only on their inputs but also on the previous state of the network. In this way the past events can be retained by the network and used in further processing that gives increased computational power over the feedforward networks. For instance, recurrent networks can perform mappings that are functions of time, can learn temporal pattern sequences, and so on. However, owing to the feedback links, the network can become unstable which is the main concern in their design and application.

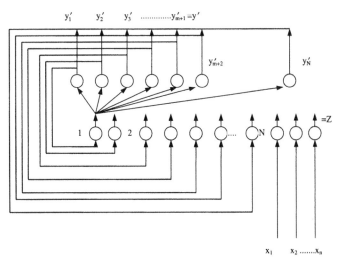

FIGURE 8
Recurrent back-propagation network.

4.3 Hopfield Networks

The Hopfield network is a typical recurrent *fully interconnected* network in which every processing unit is connected to all other units (Figure 9). It is represented by a vector

$$S = (s_1, s_2, \ldots, s_n)$$

that describes the instantaneous *state* of the network. The components of the state vector are binary variables and can have either the value 0 or the value 1. Furthermore, the weights of the interconnections between the nodes, called the *connection strengths*, are elements of the symmetric matrix

$$W_{ij} = W_{ji}$$

Each node is excited by the resulting input signal

$$X_j = \sum S_i W_{ij}$$

where the S_i is the binary output value of the processing unit i. Here, if the neuron of the processing unit fires its output has the value 1, i.e.,

$$X_j \geq 0,$$

and if it is inhibited its output is 0.

4.4 Radial Basis Function Networks

A number of comparative studies have shown that back-propagation networks, although being *universal* approximators, are still far from being the *best* pattern classifiers [71]. This is because they produce *separating surfaces* strictly based on patterns used for their training. This has the consequence that new patterns, not present in the training set, will be arbitrarily classified. Such networks behavior is due to the dot product of w and x, selected as its *distance metrics*, and to the *sigmoidal* transfer function of neurons. This is understandable from the following mathematical point of view. Each signal pattern at the network input represents a multidimensional function defined in a number of points, say n, where n is the number of network inputs. The network should "smoothly" approximate the function using sigmoids as a basic set of functions. The

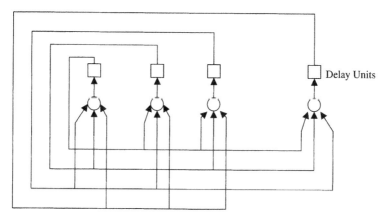

FIGURE 9
Hopfield network architecture.

approximation should be *exact* in the sampled points of the function represented by the individual network inputs, and *as exact as possible* elsewhere.

A function approximation relying on a set of monotonic basis functions like sigmoids cannot be optimal because the sigmoids have nonzero, slowly decaying values in a large area of their argument. A much better approximation can be achieved by using a set of basis functions that are nonmonotone in the sense that each function of the set *exactly* reproduces the given points of the input pattern and rapidly decays even in the close neighborhood of the point. Much better approximation results are obtained with different functions used as a set of basis functions for implementation of the *improved approximators*. It is expected that such approximators will also be *improved pattern classifiers*. Following this expectation, radial basis functions relying on the *Euclidean distance* $\| x - c \|$, the difference between the input vector x of the neuron and the center c of the radial basis function belonging to the same neuron, have been proposed for neural network implementation instead of sigmoids based on the *dot product* $w^T x$.

In the *radial basis function networks* proposed by Moody and Darken [36a] the *sigmoid transfer function* is replaced by the transfer function

$$F_{ai} = \exp(-\|x_i - c_i\|^2 / \sigma_i^2)$$

similar to the *Gaussian density function*, where x_i is the input pattern vector of the neuron in the hidden layer of the network and c_i is the position of the *radial unit center* of the same neuron. The parameter σ_i quantifies the *spread* around the center c_i or the radius of influence of the ith basis function. Similarly to the *standard deviation* in the normal probability distribution it determines how fast the basis function decays with the increasing distance from the center.

The network structure (Figure 10) is slightly different from the structure of a back-propagation network [20]. The neurons of the input layer are connected directly (i.e., not via any weighting elements) to the radial basis units in the hidden layer of the network. However, the radial basis units are connected with the neurons of the output layer via the weighting elements. Both interconnections are full. The neurons in the output layer are simple linear summing elements.

Radial basis function networks *always* have a three-layer structure, not only in some applications as do the back-propagation networks. Thus, the training of radial basis function networks is significantly different from that of back-propagation networks. The training here includes the selection, for each neuron in the hidden layer, of the center c_i and the radius r_i.

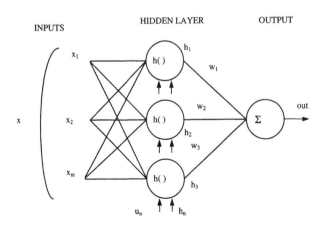

FIGURE 10
Radial basis fuction network.

When applying the network, the *optimal position of* radial unit centers can be selected *at random* using the *k-means clustering algorithm* or, in supervisory mode of network training, using an appropriate cost function to be minimized. The values of the parameters σ_i can then be estimated in a *heuristic way*, taking into account the following *heuristic way*, taking into account the following opposing requirements:

(1) The selection should be made so that the parameters σ_i, defining the sphere of influence of the radial basis function around its center, should be *as small as possible* to prevent a large spreading of the activation area of the unit, and to guarantee the unambiguous identification of patterns belonging to the cluster represented by the same center.

(2) On the other hand, the sphere of influence should be *large enough* to influence the neighboring centers in order that the desired network output becomes smooth, and it should be *small enough* in order *not* to influence the distance units, or not all of them as the sigmoid function does in the back-propagation network.

The optimal values of the weighted connections of the output layer are determined by *multiple linear regression* in the network training phase. Here, each training pattern is passed through the hidden layer of the network to generate a hidden node *activation vector* so as to minimize the *squared norm of residuals* as the performance index for estimation of weight values. This training is an order of magnitude faster than the training of an equivalent back-propagation network because the two layers of the radial basis function network are decoupled. In addition, the *classification robustness* of the radial basis function networks is far better than that of back-propagation networks [32]. However, radial basis networks suffer from the effect of the *curse of dimensionality*, i.e., the number of required hidden layer units increases exponentially with the dimensional increase of the input space.

Radial basis function networks have been successfully applied to the identification of nonlinear systems using the recursive, ARMA model-based technique as well as to the failure diagnosis of a continuous stirred-tank reactor as an alternative to the use of modular networks [12, 32, 33].

4.5 Adaptive Resonance Theory (ART) Networks

ART networks are based on the principle of *competitive learning*, which does not involve any supervision in the training phase of the network (i.e., the pattern classifications are based on unsupervised learning [8]. An ART network is a *two-layer network* (Figure 11) with two *short-term memories*, STM1 and STM2. The first belongs to the *feature extraction layer*, and the second one to the classes or *categories identification layer*, individual classes being represented by individual neurons.

Competition in the process of learning within the ART network is possible owing to the *lateral connections* between the neurons in the STM2 layer. In addition, as compared with the alternative neural networks, the adaptive resonance theory networks have at least the following advantages:

- Extremely fast learning capability when nonstationary feature vectors are to be classified in real-time mode
- Robust convergence of the learning process
- Self-organizing operation with nonsupervisory learning capacity

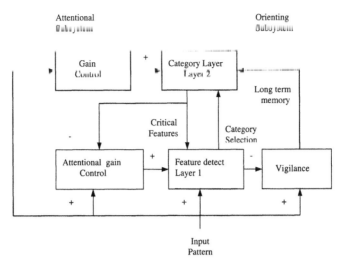

FIGURE 11
ART network architecture.

ART networks were developed with the objective of mimicking the human ability to learn relatively quickly the objects and the rules of their behavior even in a noise-contaminated environment. This natural adaptability of intelligent systems has been artificially implemented using neural networks designed according to the so-called *stability–plasticity dilemma* and *adaptive resonance theory.* The theory helps in the design of a *plastic* or *adaptive learning system* using a network architecture that self-organizes stable recognition codes in real-time in response to arbitrary input pattern sequences. This is actually the principle of adaptive pattern recognition implemented as competitive learning.

4.6 Restricted Coulomb Energy Networks

Restricted Coulomb energy networks, or RCE networks [49], although having three (*and only three*) neuron layers (Figure 12), differ in their architectural details in the sense that each neuron in the input layer is excited by a specific feature of the pattern to be classified. In the case of signal analysis for quality inspection, the input values of the network might be the values of the signal power spectrum at different frequencies.

The output layer of the network contains as many neurons as required to represent the number of classes into which the signal records are to be classified (i.e., there should be an exact, one-to-one correspondence between a class of signals and the pertinent output neuron). In the case of an unequivocal classification of the signal concerned, only one neuron in the output layer of the network should "fire". The network is said to be an *unambiguous classifier.* In the case of simultaneous "firing" of more than one neuron, the classification is not unambiguous but is rather dispersed around the most likely class, and the network is said to be an *ambiguous classifier.* This can be understood in terms of *class delimiters* of the network. Whereas back-propagation networks mutually separate the individual classes by *hyperplanes* as class delimiters, RCE networks accomplish the same objective using *hyperspheres* (Figure 13) as class delimiters. They are stored in the hidden layer of the network and are responsible for the "firing" of the neurons in the output layer. In RCE networks the pattern classes are viewed as separate collections of points in a high-dimensional feature space of the signal under classification that excite the input neurons of the network. During the training phase, the network determines, in

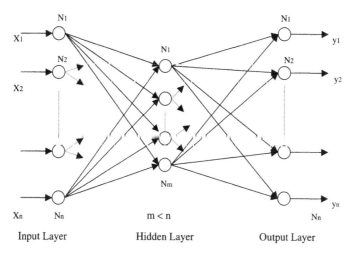

FIGURE 12
RCA network as data processor.

only a few training steps, the final number of neurons required in the hidden layer. This is an advantage of the network. Thus, the circumstantial network adaptation procedure, unavoidable in the training phase of back-propagation networks, is considerably simplified when RCE networks are adapted to the problem to be solved.

The hidden layer of a RCE network is completely interconnected with the input layer (Figure 14). Each neuron of this layer is connected to every neuron of the input layer, so that each neuron of the hidden layer is provided with the full information carried by the feature vector at the network input. The interconnection of the hidden layer with the output layer is relatively poor, however. The output of each of its neurons is connected to *only one* neuron of the output layer, providing the neuron with the information required for its activation. The information stored in each neuron of the hidden layer is a particular mapping of the feature vector at the network input to the neuron representing the *particular pattern class* to which the feature vector belongs. There is, therefore, a direct correspondence between the pattern class at the network input and the

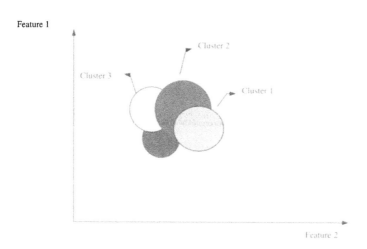

FIGURE 13
Hyperspheres class clustering of RCE network.

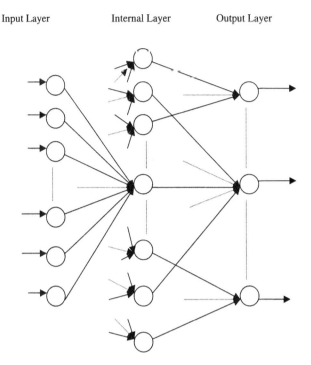

FIGURE 14
Restricted coulomb energy network.

activated neuron in the hidden layer. This way of storing information learnt during the network training phase makes the neurons of the hidden layer mutually independent in the sense that information stored in the individual neurons of the layer does not influence the information stored in other neurons of the same layer. The network can be considered as a *distributed knowledge system* capable of storing new knowledge by adding new neurons in its hidden layer without disturbing the knowledge already stored in other neurons of the layer. That is, by extending the number of neurons in the hidden layer and by training the network on new examples, the network will be able to identify new pattern classes without "forgetting" the classes it has once learnt. This is known as *dynamic class learning*.

The neurons of the hidden layer belonging to the same pattern category are connected to the same neuron in the output layer. Each neuron of this layer has an OR transfer function. Consequently, each neuron of the output layer "fires" when any of the neurons in the hidden layer belonging to the same category and connected to it is activated in response to the input pattern.

The input–output behavior of the hidden-layer neurons is mathematically described as

$$y_i = \theta\lambda(W_i^T x)$$

where y_i is the output of the ith neutron in the hidden layer, W_i the weight vector of the neuron, x the network input vector or the pattern feature vector, and $\theta\lambda$ an appropriately chosen *threshold function*, usually with zero as the threshold value. The dot product of vectors W_i and x is used because the normalized pattern vectors are expected on the network input, so that the *distance metrics* between the two vectors is defined as their *inner product*.

Defined in this way, the output of each hidden layer neuron is associated with a pattern class defined in feature space at the network input. The *location* of the class in the region is defined by the vector W_i and its field of influence by the threshold constant λ_i of the neuron. Finally, the *geometrical shape* of the region is defined by the selected distance metrics. For example, for Cartesian distance metrics the regions have the shape of multidimensional spheres.

A general comparison of the two networks described above reveals the following:

- *Back-propagation networks*
  - Have a variable, freely selectable network topology.
  - Work with a fixed length hidden layer.
  - Have required storage capacity that *can* be precalculated.
  - Require a relatively long period of training time.
- *Restricted Coulomb energy networks*
  - Have a fixed network topology.
  - Work with self-determined hidden layer length.
  - Have required storage capacity *cannot* be precalculated.
  - Have an extremely short training phase.

4.7 Probabilistic Networks

Specht introduced probabilistic networks for the classification of sonar signals [54, 55]. The sampled signals were preprocessed using smoothing algorithms and Fourier transformed to generate their equivalent spatial pattern. The patterns were then sent to a probabilistic neural network for feature extraction and pattern classification. After being trained on a large number of sonar signals, the network was capable of classifying surface ship patterns with 100 % accuracy and submarine patterns with 70 % accuracy.

Probabilistic networks are *feedforward networks* (Figure 15) with one input layer, one *pattern unit layer*, one *summation unit layer*, and one *output layer*. Although the networks have no feedback path in the application phase, feedback can still be used in the training phase of the network for learning the statistics of the training set of patterns.

The input layer of the network contains only *passive elements* that distribute the components of the input pattern vector x to the units in the second layer of the network. Each unit of this layer (i.e., each *pattern unit*) forms at its input the dot product $W_i^T x$ with its particular weighting vector W_i and subsequently calculates the value of the exponential function

$$y_i = \exp\{-(W - x)^T (W - x)/2\sigma^2\}$$

representing its *activation function*. The activation output y_i of each unit is forwarded to only one unit of the next network layer, which simply sums the input signals y_i to construct the categories present in the pattern vector at the network input. The summing results are sent to the output units of the network that have two inputs and one output and the binary response.

The probabilistic neural network paradigm is based on *Bayes' decision strategy*, a strategy that minimizes the expected risk. The decision rule used, *Bayes' decision rule*, extendable to any numbers of categories to be classified, can easily be explained for the two-dimensional case, when the two categories, C_1 and C_2, are to be classified using the measurement data sets represented by n-dimensional vectors x. For this, the *probability density functions* $p_1(x)$ and $p_2(x)$ of the categories are first calculated. If the a priori probability p_{a1} and p_{a2} of the occurrence

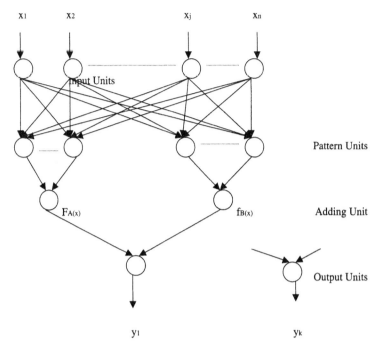

FIGURE 15
Probabilistic network architecture.

of patterns of category c_1 and c_2 are known, or can be estimated using the collected data, the Bayes' decision rule to be used is

$$C = C_1 \quad \text{if} \quad l_1 p_{a1} p(x) > l_2 p_{a2} p_2(x)$$

$$C = C_2 \quad \text{if} \quad l_2 p_{a2} p_2(x) > l_1 p_{a1} p_1(x)$$

where l_1 and l_2 are *losses* caused by making the decision C_1 or C_2. The *decision boundary* defined by the above decision rule is

$$p_1(x) = (l_2 p_{a2}/l_1 p_{a1}) p_2(x)$$

It could be a nonlinear decision surface of arbitrary complexity, which is taken into account when only two categories are present in the input data by selecting for the output units of the network a binary transfer function defined as the equivalent weight

$$W_o = (l_2 p_{a2}/l_1 p_{a1}) R_N$$

where R_N is the ratio between the number of training patterns of the category 1 and of the category 2.

The probabilistic networks are trained in one step. A separate neuron in the pattern units layer is assigned to each training pattern x and the corresponding weighting vector W_i is tuned to activate the output of the assigned neuron for this pattern. The neuron is then connected to the appropriate summation unit. This can be seen as an advantage because each neuron is trained in one step, or as a disadvantage because for each training pattern one separate neuron is required in the network application phase.

A typical probabilistic network uses a back-propagation network in which the sigmoidal activation functions are replaced by exponential activation functions. The modification enables the network to be *asymptotically convergent* to the behavior of a *Bayes' optimal decision strategy* and to be immune against being trapped in a local minimum. At the same time, the network is orders of magnitude faster than the equivalent back-propagation network. The advantage, however, is "offset" by the extended computational effort required in the application phase of the network.

4.8 Modular Networks

Comparison of radial basis function (RBF) networks and back-propagation (BP) networks suggests two contradictory statements:

- RBF networks, as local approximation networks using a Gaussian type of activation function, generally need more storage units than BP networks as global approximation networks using a sigmoid-like activation function.
- RBF networks need less time to be trained on a set of input patterns than do BP networks.

This leads to the idea of combining the two network types, accumulating their advantages, and resulting in an optimal network structure. This concept has been implemented in *modular networks* that are basically networks with a heterogeneous architecture in which supervised learning and unsupervised learning are used in the different modules of the network [26]. The modules are coordinated by a common central network that assigns the "credits", i.e., distributes the "jobs" to the modules (Figure 16). This gives the network the ability to learn different parts of knowledge from the input patterns using different modules. In the network, each module is provided the quantity of information that makes it capable of learning. This is carried out as unsupervised learning within the entire network, so that the "winner" modules get more knowledge to learn than the "losing" modules. Thus, if the given input pattern to be learnt is

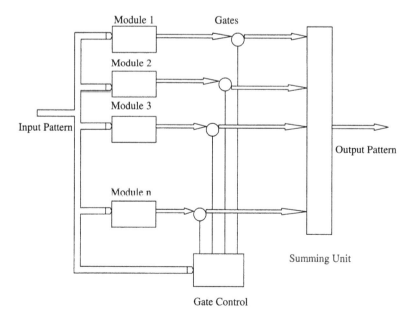

FIGURE 16
Modular network architecture.

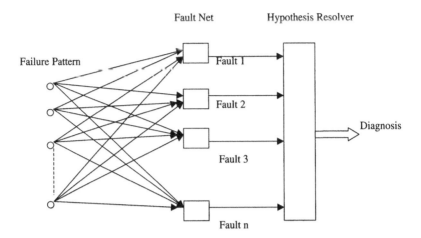

FIGURE 17
Plant monitoring and diagnosis using modular network.

separable into a set of simple patterns, the individual simple patterns will be distributed to individual network modules for learning, which will considerably speed up the entire learning process. The learning of a piecewise linear function by a modular network is taken as an example, where individual linear pieces will be learnt very quickly by individual network modules. This can be used in the implementation of fast nonlinear control configurations based on the *gain scheduling strategy* [26a].

As a practical example, we consider the implementation of an on-line plant monitoring and diagnostic system using a modular network [33] called the Rho-Net (Figure 17). The network was used for the monitoring and failure diagnosis of a continuous stirred-tank reactor based on 16 sensors on the reactor, the values of which are fed into the network. In the network, 36 diagnostic sub-nets with varying numbers of hidden neurons are incorporated, each assigned to a specific failure class. This has reduced the total training time for the entire network by a factor of 100 and considerably increased the accuracy of failure identification and classification compared with the application of a RBF network. In addition, the modular structure of the network facilitates the addition of new failure classes or updating of the existing ones without retraining the already trained modules.

5   NETWORK TRAINING APPROACHES

The approaches used in training neural networks are essentially supervised learning, unsupervised learning, or combined (supervised/unsupervised) learning.

Supervised learning is learning through comparison—for given patterns at network inputs—of the expected (correct) output patterns and the actual output patterns of the network. The interconnection weights within the network are then adjusted so that the actual output becomes as close as possible to the expected output. Thus, supervised learning actually trains the networks to behave properly in the sense of mapping the correct pattern at the output for each input pattern. For this the network needs a *trainer* that controls the correctness of output patterns and a set of training examples on which during the training phase the network learns to recognize the individual patterns or the class of patterns. After being trained, the network should be able, with no trainer help, to recognize any new pattern belonging to the same class as the training examples.

The supervised learning approach is the standard learning approach implemented in back-propagation networks [35,62]. In these networks, the tuning of weights is carried out layer by layer, starting in each tuning cycle with the output layer and ending with the input layer. This is repeated until a performance index, usually the sum of the squared errors (i.e., of differences between the expected correct output pattern and the actual network output pattern), is minimized. This backward, layer-by-layer tuning of the network parameters is the reason for calling the networks *back-propagation networks*, although, as far as the signal propagation is concerned, there is no internal back-propagation within the network.

For tuning the interconnecting weights, the gradient (or the *steepest descent*) method is most frequently used. The tuning of weights based on such calculations is known as the *generalized delta law* because, like the originally proposed delta law of learning, it is applicable to network structures with hidden layers [52]. The tuning is performed, at least formally, in two alternating phases:

(1) *Forward phase*, in which the network input signals are propagated *forward* through the network. The output signals are generated and their values are compared with the expected accurate output values.

(2) *Backward phase*, in which the tuning increment and/or decrement values are calculated and the weights are readjusted *backward* starting with the output layer.

Training a multilayer perceptron to solve specific problems using the back-propagation learning approach has serious disadvantages because it is based on a rigid, randomly or very generally selected network structure that retains its original shape to the end of the training phase of the network and also in the application phase. Also, because of the free selection of the network structure, usually containing more neurons than really required for optimal problem solution, the parameter tuning process is slowed down, requiring hundreds or thousands of iteration steps for the minimization of the square-error performance index. This calls for improved training strategies.

Unsupervised learning, in contrast to supervised learning, does not directly compare the actual with the expected output pattern of the network. It does not even know what the correct output should be but simply feeds back the information whether the output is correct or not. No care is taken about the degree of correctness or incorrectness. The network is simply rewarded when its output is correct and punished when it is incorrect. This is generally known as *reinforcement through graded training*.

Unsupervised learning requires no trainer for its implementation. Instead, a set of input patterns is used to discover regularities and/or relationships between the different members of the set. To this end, the network steadily organizes itself, with the objective of building an internal model that helps recognize the regularities of the input patterns, for example, building and clustering the corresponding feature vectors. In this way, learning can progress by the recognition of more and more features typical for the class of patterns to be learned and fewer and fewer features that are not typical for the same class of patterns. Discrimination between the input patterns can be achieved by discovering the similarities, regularities, and/or correlations between the output feature vectors generated by the different input patterns. The learning is thus seen as *self-supervised learning*.

The *competitive learning model* is used for the implementation of unsupervised learning. In this model, all inputs are connected in an *excitatory* way to the output units, but the output units are also connected to each other in an *inhibitory* way (Figure 18), so that the output unit initially having the highest excitation at its input inhibits all other output units in the strongest way. As a consequence, all other units inhibit the unit with the highest initial excitation less and less

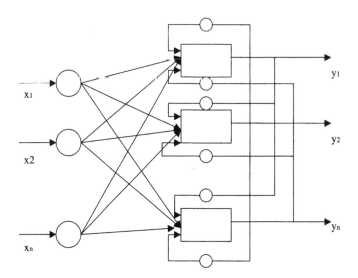

FIGURE 18
Competitive learning network.

strongly. This process continues, with the strongest unit becoming steadily stronger until it overwhelms all other units and becomes the "winner" of the learning process. This is known as the *winner-takes-all* principle.

The competitive learning algorithm described above generally gives good practical results. However, it can be inefficient if the pattern classes to be recognized are close to each other, so that their clustering is ambiguous or fuzzy. This is particularly the case when the input patterns used for network training are contaminated by noise. For managing such situations, an extended version of competitive learning that efficiently discriminates between the signal and the noise was proposed by Grossberg [19]. Called *competitive–cooperative* learning, it was implemented by modifying the activation dynamics of the competitive learning networks to better discriminate against noise.

Combined learning is implemented through the functional-link concept that embodies an enhanced representation of input patterns. This, in turn, enables the input–output pairs to be learnt with flat net structures, i.e., with nets without hidden layers and with a nonlinear response [40]. In such networks, some or all of the inputs are fed through a nonlinear function before being attached to the network. This is viewed as being equivalent to Fourier synthesis or polynomial curve-fitting, which substantially increases the learning rate of the network. A flat net modified in this way can be used for supervised as well as unsupervised learning. An appropriate algorithm, ART2, capable of efficiently clustering two closely related pattern classes was proposed by Carpenter and Grossberg [7].

6 IMPROVED LEARNING PROCESS

A factor of importance when training a back-propagation network is the learning rate achievable with the selected learning. This rate is directly influenced by the size of the increments and/or decrements by which the interconnection weights are readjusted in the individual training cycles.

The selection of the learning rate is generally a matter of trade-off between the convergence of the tuning process and the final achievable accuracy in the sense that slower learning (i.e., learning with smaller decrement values) might guarantee a higher degree of discrimination. Thus, the question arises of how fast the learning should be, or what learning rate should be used.

Originally a constant learning rate over all the training cycles was adopted for network training; that is, it was supposed that the rate does not change during the entire process of network training. In improved training methods a variable rate—i,e, an *adaptive learning rate*—was proposed, mainly relying on adaptive filter theory [70].

Generally, the network learning speed depends strongly on the *character* of the problem to be solved and on the internal network factors, such as network architecture, activation functions, and the interconnections used [16]. For instance, training a network on a large number of pattern classes takes more time than training it on a smaller number of pattern classes. Since the character of the problem to be solved cannot be changed in this way in order to speed up the process of learning, the internal network factors and the learning law used need to be appropriately selected [77, 78].

The learning rate can be improved directly by modification of the parameter tuning algorithm used in the training phase of the network. For instance, in back-propagation networks, the minimization of the sum of the squared errors

$$J(W) = \frac{1}{2} \sum_{k=1}^{N} e^T(k) e(k)$$

is used for updating the network weight parameters, where N is the number of training patterns, $e(k) = Y_k - Y(X_k, W)$ is the output error of the network, $Y(X_k, W)$ is the network output vector, and W is the row vector of the network parameters. The updating is carried out using the relation

$$W^{new} = W - \eta \frac{\partial J(W)}{\partial W}$$

where η is the learning rate of the proposed updating law and the gradient of $J(W)$ related to the parameter vector W:

$$\frac{\partial J(W)}{\partial W} = \frac{1}{2} \sum_{k=1}^{N} \frac{\partial e^T(k) e(k)}{\partial W}$$

The above updating, based on the gradient vector of $J(W)$, moves the weight parameter vector W in the direction of the steepest descent of $J(W)$, so that the larger the norm of the gradient $\partial e^T(k) e(k)/\partial W$ the stronger is its influence on the size of the moving step of the parameter vector W. This, however, is not necessarily optimal. For instance, it would be better if the following rule holds: The larger the error $e^T(k) e(k)$, the stronger the influence of its gradient $\partial e^T(k) e(k)/\partial W$ on the size of the moving step of the parameter vector W. However, from the fact that if, for the error $e^T(k) e(k)$, the relation

$$e^T(i) e(i) > e^T(j) e(j)$$

holds, it is not guaranteed that the relation

$$\left\| \frac{\partial e^T(i) e(i)}{\partial W} \right\| > \left\| \frac{\partial e^T(j) e(j)}{\partial W} \right\|$$

also holds. Consequently, the standard delta learning rule, based on the minimization of the squared error index, does not guarantee that the large errors receive much greater attention than the small errors, which would be desired. Such a learning rule is not optimally efficient. To increase its learning efficiency, an improved error index should be used, as proposed below [15, 72].

Let the output changing rate for the mapping function f be defined as

$$\Delta f(X_i, X_j) = f(X_i) - f(X_j)$$

and the output changing rate for the neural network as

$$\Delta Y(i, j) = \Delta Y(X_i, X_j, W)$$
$$= Y(X_i, W) - Y(X_j, W)$$

so that the modified error index is defined as

$$E(W) = \frac{1}{2}\sum_{k=1}^{N} e^T(k)e(k) + \mu\frac{1}{2}\sum_{k=1}^{N}\sum_{h=k}^{N}(\Delta f(k, h) - \Delta Y(k, h))^T(\Delta f(k, h) - \Delta Y(k, h))$$

with $e(k) = Y_k - Y(X_k, W)$. Here μ is the parameter that evaluates the influence of the second term in the above equation on the extended error measurement. Generally, $\mu > 1$ and, consequently, the modified delta updating law with the extended error measurement becomes

$$W^{\text{new}} = W - \eta\frac{\partial E(W)}{\partial W}$$

Now, taking into account that

$$e^*(k) = Y_k - Y_n(X_k, W)$$

we can write

$$e^*(k, h) = \Delta f(W_k, X_h, W) - \Delta Y(X_k, X_h, W)$$
$$= e^*(k) - e^*(h)$$

and

$$(\Delta f(k, h) - \Delta Y(k, h))^T(\Delta f(k, h) - \Delta Y(k, h) = e^{*T}(k, h)e^*(k, h)$$

so that the new error index $E(W)$ can be expressed as ·

$$E(W) = \frac{1}{2}\sum_{k=1}^{N} e^T(k)e(k) + \mu\frac{1}{2}\sum_{k=1}^{N}\sum_{h=k}^{N} e^{*T}(k, h)e^*(k, h)$$

Correspondingly, the gradient $\partial E(W)/\partial W$ takes the form

$$\frac{\partial E(W)}{\partial W} = \sum_{k=1}^{N} e^T(k)\frac{\partial e(k)}{\partial W} + \mu\sum_{k=1}^{N}\sum_{h=k}^{N}(e(k) - e(h))^T\left(\frac{\partial e(k)}{\partial W} - \frac{\partial e(h)}{\partial W}\right)$$

which can be transformed into

$$\frac{\partial E(W)}{\partial W} = \sum_{k=1}^{N}(e(k) + \mu N(e(k) - \tilde{e}))^T\frac{\partial e(k)}{\partial W}$$

where $\tilde{e} = (1/N)\sum_{k=1}^{N} e(k)$ is the average value of the error $e(k)$ on the N training data of the network.

Finally, the modified updating law becomes

$$W^{\text{new}} = W - \eta \sum_{k=1}^{N} (e(k) + \mu N(e(k) - \tilde{e})) \frac{\partial e(k)}{\partial W}$$

From the last equation, it is evident that the parameter vector is tuned by two terms,

$$-\eta \sum_{k=1}^{N} e(k) \frac{\partial e(k)}{\partial W} \quad \text{and} \quad -\eta \sum_{k=1}^{N} \mu N(e(k) - \tilde{e})^T \frac{\partial e(k)}{\partial W}$$

the second term being the gradient of an error index

$$E_m(W) = \mu N \frac{1}{2} \sum_{k=1}^{N} (e(k) - \tilde{e})^T (e(k) - \tilde{e})$$

that can play an essential role in training the network.

The efficiency of the modified updating law was tested on the dynamic system described by

$$y(k) = \frac{y^2(k-1)}{1 + y^2(k-1)} + u^2(k-1)$$

For comparison of the modified with the standard back-propagation error index, the sum of squared errors J of every 100 training steps is used, i.e.,

$$J = \sum_{k=n_k}^{n_k+100} \left| e(k) \right|^2$$

where the training period $n_k = 1, 2, 3, \ldots$. Having only one hidden layer with 6 neurons on the 2–6–1 structure, the network was trained both with the standard and the new learning error index. Its training performances are shown in Figure 19 and Figure 20 where N is the number of training data that have been taken in each training step. The system input training data $u(k-1)$ was randomly chosen in the range [0,1].

Figure 19 shows not only the slow convergence but also the oscillation of the training process when the standard learning algorithm is used. From Figure 20, however, it is obvious that with the extended error index the network had a smoother training performance than that in Figure 19 and that its convergence was about 30 times faster than when the standard error index was used. We consequently conclude that training the network with the extended error index algorithm

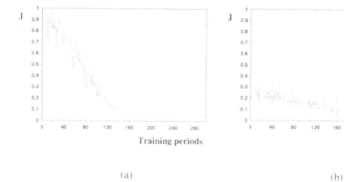

(a)   (b)

FIGURE 19

Training performance with standard algorithm. (a) $\eta = 0.05$ and $N = 4$. (b) $\eta = 0.02$, and $N = 30$.

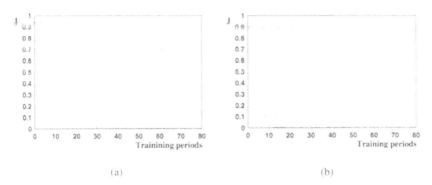

FIGURE 20

Training performance with the new algorithm. (a) $\eta = 0.02$, $\mu = 9$, and $N = 4$. (b) $\eta = 0.001$, $\mu = 10$, and $N = 30$.

- realizes the requirement that large errors receive more attention than small errors in a better way than does the standard back-propagation learning algorithm;
- ensures a smoother error surface than the training with the standard error index, so that the oscillations in the learning process can be resisted and the speed of learning of the neural network is increased;
- can avoid the local minima at a higher energy level and converge to minima at lower energy level.

7 CONTROL APPLICATIONS

The increasing complexity of control tasks in modern processing industries [43] and in manufacturing [45] calls for ever-improving control technology capable of executing such tasks in real-time. Neurotechnology promises to open qualitatively new perspectives in this sense because neural networks, as massively parallel processing systems with learning capability, represent a powerful new tool for solving complex control problems that have previously been very difficult to solve using conventional computing technology [39]. For instance, because of the nonlinearity of their processing elements (the neurons), neural networks represent *universal* nonlinear approximators [24] capable of modeling complex industrial processes, especially those that can hardly be described in a direct mathematical way. Moreover, the learning capability of the networks [42] allows their adaptation to the problems they are solving and improved performance when solving similar problems. This makes networks appropriate for implementation in advanced control configurations [63] such as the following:

- *Supervisory control*, where the controller, trained on examples showing the correct controller behavior in specific selected situations, learns the mapping from sensed input values to adequate control actions at output.
- *Direct inverse control*, where the underlying neural network learns the inverse dynamic of the system to be controlled and generates the input signals that produce the desired actions at the controller output. (For instance, the network can learn the mapping from the desired trajectory that the system should follow to the corresponding input signals that enable the tracking of such a trajectory, like the network implemented by Miller, Sutton, and Werbos [35a] for a Puma robot.)

- *Adaptive control*, mostly implemented as *model-reference adaptive control* [38], or a *self-tuning regulator* [30] in which the neural networks are used to replace the standard mappings required by the classical theory of adaptive systems.
- *Back-propagation of utility*, where an optimal controller is adapted by solving a calculus of variations problem.
- *Adaptive critic methods*-based controller—in fact a controller based on approximate dynamic programming.

7.1 Connectionist Learning and Systems Modeling

In mathematical systems theory, modeling of the behavior of dynamic systems is one of the chief goals. The mathematical models are built using the theory underlying the nature of the systems and the system parameters are determined using the observation data collected at the input and output of the system to be modeled. Also, when using neural networks for model building, the network parameters selected to represent the system model should be determined by training of the network on observation data acquired from the system to be modeled. The basic functional capability of neural networks to map the observation data from one domain into another one that was originally used only for pattern classification is generally applicable to model building and system identification [38, 48, 59]. The networks' ability to approximate arbitrary nonlinear patterns qualifies them for modeling of the complex dynamic processes that has proven to be extremely difficult using conventional digital computers.

Model building is the major problem the control engineer has to solve before designing advanced control schemes for a plant to be automated because modern methods and techniques of advanced controller design are based on a mathematical model of the system to be controlled. To solve the model building problem the control engineer has to solve the two-stage problem known as the *system identification* problem:

(1) Selection of *model structure* based on the character of the system to be modeled
(2) Collection of the observation data from the system, which is required for the *estimation of the system parameters*

When using neural networks for model building and system identification, the selection of the model structure is equivalent to the selection of the network structure. This problem is easier to solve than in the classical systems theory because there the problem has to be solved of selection of equations that represent the behavior of the complex system "well enough". Numerous case studies in many different fields of application show that for this purpose, apart from back-propagation and recursive networks, the Hopfield and the adaptive resonance networks have been used. Although the problem solution is not always optimal—and not even unique—when selected for model representation the redundant architectures can also give good identification results. Thus, for the time being any selected network structure giving a "good enough" problem solution is acceptable. The problem of optimal network structure, however, is still on the agenda.

Once one has the neural network structure to model the system, the problem of system parameter estimation remains. This is equivalent to the problem of finding the values of the adjustable network parameters for which the selected network matches the input and the corresponding output data collected from the system to be modeled; that is, the values for which the network mapping corresponds to the input–output behavior of the system.

Identification of nonlinear systems is a much more difficult task than the identification of linear systems [5, 10, 60]. This is primarily because of the mathematical difficulties that accompany the handling of the nonlinear differential and/or difference equations. The underlying difficulties can be resolved using neural networks as universal nonlinear approximators. For the building of nonlinear system models for control purposes, two basic approaches are available:

(1) The direct *state-variable approach*, relying on the representation of the nonlinear system in the state space using the system equations

$$x(t+1) = \psi(x(t), u(t))$$

$$y(t) = \phi(x(t))$$

(2) The *regressive model approach*, relying on the approximation of nonlinear system representation by

$$y^*(t+1) = f(y^*(t), y^*(t-1), \ldots, y^*(t-n), u(t), u(t-1), \ldots, u(t-m))$$

where $y^*(\cdot)$ indicates the observed values at the system output.

The corresponding neural network implementation of the approaches is shown in Figures 21a and 21b, respectively. Simulation results have shown that both approaches are sufficiently general for model building using back-propagation networks [60]. The state-variable approach, however, gave more exact results and was more robust than the regressive model approach.

The problem of identification of nonlinear systems using the state-space representation has also been studied by Pham and Lice [41], who used two separate back-propagation networks for model building (Figure 22).

Tan, Hao, and Vanderwalle [59] have solved the nonlinear system identification problem using radial basis function networks, implementing the equivalent ARMA model of the system. They demonstrated that the convergence of the implementation is higher than when using other network architectures. This, however, is at the cost of a larger number of neurons required for the implementation than when using back-propagation networks.

7.2 Application to Real-time Identification

In applications of the back-propagation networks to modeling and identification of dynamic systems based on observation data collected from the system itself, a large set of input–output data pairs is required on which the network is to be trained. This makes the training relatively long lasting [46], and decreases the network's ability to meet real-time requirements. In real industrial environments it is very difficult, or nearly impossible, to obtain many input–output data pairs of the process to be modeled or identified that are uniformly distributed in time and state space. This makes the model built or the identification carried out ultimately invalid, particularly when the process has such time-variable parameters that the model built using a neural network cannot follow their rate of change. The only solution is to increase the speed of the training process of the network by improving its learning performance [28, 46]. However, when on-line modeling and identification is required, the increase of learning speed demanded by the reduced network training time causes the set of training data pairs collected to become less representative because they are not uniformly distributed in the entire state space range required. Thus, the learning process becomes inadequate. It is therefore proposed to use a modified network structure that will strongly decouple the interdependency of the network parameters and enable acceptable on-line system modeling and identification. For this, the activation functions of the neurons in the hidden layer of the network need to be modified by a limiting function that makes the modified neural network become content-addressable and

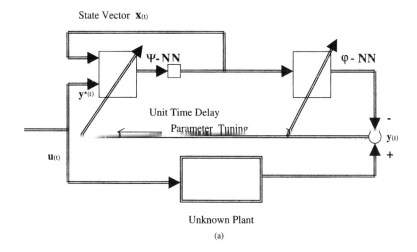

State Vector $\mathbf{x}_{(t)}$

Ψ-NN

φ-NN

$\mathbf{y}^*_{(t)}$

Unit Time Delay

Parameter Tuning

$\mathbf{y}_{(t)}$

$\mathbf{u}_{(t)}$

Unknown Plant

(a)

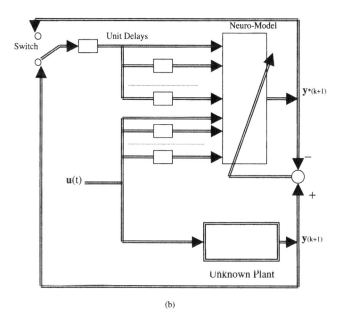

Neuro-Model

Switch

Unit Delays

$\mathbf{y}^*_{(k+1)}$

$\mathbf{u}(t)$

$\mathbf{y}_{(k+1)}$

Unknown Plant

(b)

FIGURE 21
(a) State-space neuro-identifier; (b) Regression-based neuro-identifier.

capable, when learning in a new range of state space, of retaining the knowledge learnt in another range of state space. This is what the unmodified back-propagation networks with a purely sigmoidal activation function cannot do. For instance, the network trained in one range of training data "forgets" the majority of knowledge learnt when it is trained in another range of input data. Thus, a network modification is required that enables learning of the patterns in the new domains without loss of the knowledge learnt in earlier domains. Such a network would be closer to the learning capability of the human brain [75].

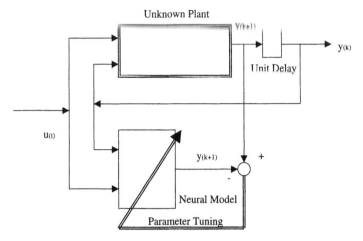

FIGURE 22
State-space neural identification.

The general structure of a back-propagation network with only one hidden layer and the linear activation functions in the output layer is shown in Figure 23, where γ is the activation function for the hidden layer. It is generally chosen as the sigmoid function $\gamma(x) = 1/(1 + e^{-x})$. The outputs of the network are the weighted sums of the hidden-layer outputs. If, for simplicity, we assume that the network has only two inputs and one output, i.e., that $n = 2$ and $m = 1$, the output of each neuron in the hidden layer will be given by

$$V(u_1, u_2) = \gamma(u_1, u_2) = \frac{1}{1 + e^{-(w_1 u_1 + w_2 u_2 + b)}}$$

If $w_1 = -7.5$, $W_2 = 7.5$, $b = 10.5$, and the range of the network inputs is in $(0, 1)$, its form will be as shown graphically in Figure 24. In this case the output of the network is the weighted sum of p such nonlinear surfaces.

From Figure 24 it is apparent that this type of nonlinear surface influences the network output not only for a few of the training data, but for the whole range of the network inputs. The optimization problem becomes more difficult as the number of neurons increases. The problem of strong coupling between all neurons of the network can be resolved by multiplying the sigmoid function by a limiting function that restrains the behavior of each neuron to a very small range. In this way, the memory of the network is divided into many smoothly connected

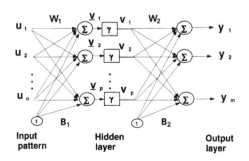

FIGURE 23
The structure of a single hidden layer back-propagation network.

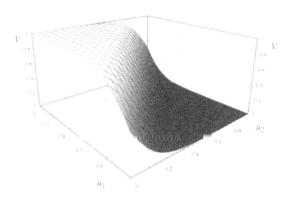

FIGURE 24
The output of neurons in the hidden layer.

independent areas. The new activation function proposed for the back-propagation network is expressed as [47]

$$V(u_1, u_2) = \gamma(u_1, u_2)e^{-\alpha_1(u_1 - \beta_1)^2 - \alpha_2(u_2 - \beta_2)^2}$$

Its structure is shown in Figure 25. For $w_1 = -7.5$, $w_2 = -7.5$, $b = 10.5$, $\alpha_1 = 15$, $\beta_1 = 0.5$, $\alpha_2 = 10$, and $\beta_2 = 0.5$, the output of the neurons in the hidden layer will have the form shown in Figure 26.

In Figure 26 the center of the limiting range for the neuron considered is (0.5, 0.5). The connecting weights to this neuron are only responsible for storing the behavior of the identified

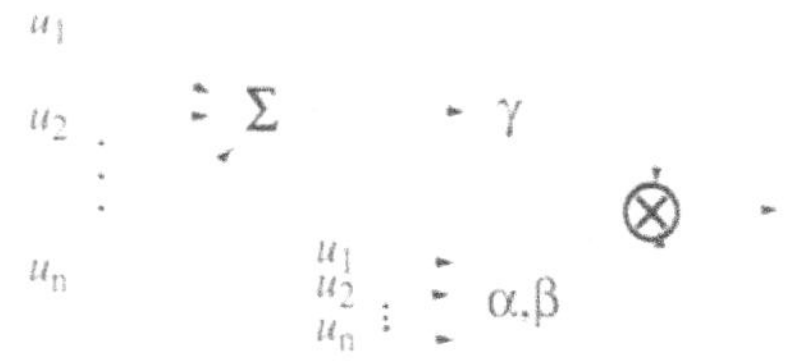

FIGURE 25
The structure of the new activation function.

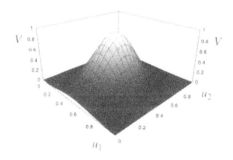

FIGURE 26
The output of neurons in the hidden layer at the new activation function.

process in a small range around (0.5, 0.5). The weights of the other neurons are for the other ranges of the training data. If the current training data is far away from the center (0.5, 0.5), the connecting weights to this neuron will almost be unchanged, i e , the knowledge of the network stored in this small range will not be forgotten. For modification of the sigmoid-like activation function of the neurons, transfer functions can be selected with fixed or with adjustable parameters for each neuron. In the first case, the parameters of the selected functions remain constant during the network training process, whereas in the second case they should be readjusted to learn according to an adaptive algorithm to be developed.

We now refer to the theorem of Stinchcombe and White [56], according to which a sufficiently complex single-hidden-layer back-propagation network with arbitrary activation functions of the neurons in this layer can, under certain conditions, approximate an *arbitrary* function. In our case, the nonlinear approximation capability of the modified network is guaranteed, because the modification of the sigmoid-like activation functions of the neurons in the hidden layer using an exponential transfer function meets the conditions specified in the theorem.

In the following example, modification functions are selected that have fixed parameters homogeneously distributed in the identification domain. Figure 27 schematically illustrates the network with two inputs in which the distribution of the limiting functions in the identification range has been partitioned into 25 sub-ranges as individual memory area. In this figure, each circle denotes a center of the modification function, whereby—depending on the complexity of the identification problem—one or more than one neuron can be assigned to each modification function, taking care that the number of neurons in the hidden layer is not smaller than the number of modification functions.

It should be noted that the knowledge learnt during the system identification is memorized by the neurons of the network and not by the modification functions. The functions merely decouple the mutual dependency of neurons so as to increase the learning capability of the network. For instance, if during the training process it is detected that the range of the training examples is larger than expected, as shown by the crosses in Figure 28a, the network can simply be expanded as shown in Figure 28b with only slight loss of memorized information. Such expansion is not permitted in the network in which the hidden-layer neurons have the unmodified sigmoidal activation functions, because in this case the new neurons may severely influence the knowledge already learnt.

As an example, the on-line identification of the dynamic system described by

$$y_d(k) = \frac{y_d^2(k-1)}{1+y_d^2(k-1)} + u^2(k-1)$$

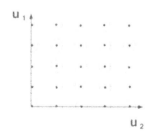

FIGURE 27
The distribution of limiting functions.

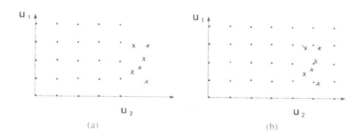

FIGURE 28
Network expansion. (a) Training data out of supposed input range. (b) Adequate network expansion.

is used with the input range $u_1 = (0.1)$ and $u_2 = (0, 1.5)$, as shown in Figure 28. For system modeling, a 2–36–1 network structure was used and for its training the *oscillation-resisting learning law* [74]; this law significantly accelerates the convergence speed of the training process. For on-line identification purposes, the training examples are supposed to be nonuniformly distributed in the input range in the following way. The input ranges of u_1 and u_2 were divided into the sub-ranges (0, 0.5), (0.5, 1) and (0, 0.5), (0.5, 0.5) and the training data for 5 training periods were randomly chosen from the first sub-ranges and for another 5 training periods from the second ones. This was repeated for 50 training periods. The resulting training performance, i.e., the learning convergence achieved, is presented in Figure 29a and compared with the training performance achievable with the standard back-propagation learning in Figure 29b.

The inability of the standard back-propagation network in on-line identification can be clearly seen in Figure 29a. The network, after learning the system behavior in one input sub-range, will forget the knowledge learnt when being trained in another sub-range. This is characterized by the oscillation of its training performance. However, if the dynamic system is modeled with the new-structured back-propagation network, the oscillations in the training process disappear, as shown in Figure 29b, and the trained network can predict the system output accurately in the entire range of input signals, as shown in Figure 30.

The responses of the simulated system to be identified and of the trained network for a step input signal are shown in Figure 30, from which it is evident that the network, after being successively trained using the standard learning law in both sub-ranges, has lost the training knowledge of the first sub-range, so its reproduction of the system behavior in this range is erroneous. This is not the case with the reproduction shown in Figure 30b when the oscillation-resisting learning law was used for training.

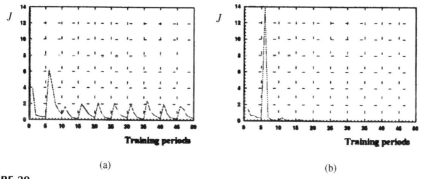

(a)   (b)

FIGURE 29
The learning convergence: (a) using the standard learning law, (b) using the modified learning law.

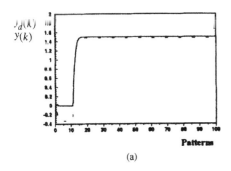
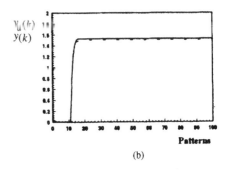

(a) (b)

FIGURE 30
Step response of the trained network ($\cdots$) and of the simulated system (—) using (a) the standard learning law, (b) oscillation-resisting learning law.

7.3 Neural network-based Controllers

The advantages of neural networks when applied to implementation of control configurations, are seen in the following [3]:

- Universal nonlinear pattern approximators capable of modeling complex input–output mapping required for control purposes.
- Adaptive systems, enabling implementation of advanced control schemes.
- Robustness and failure-tolerances due to internal redundancy.
- Massively parallel and distributed systems enabling the fast processing of a huge number of data.

Although a nonlinear or an adaptive neurocontroller executes the same operations as does a conventional controller, it is still expected that the neurocontroller will execute them better and with greater flexibility owing to its ability to learn and to generalize the facts learnt [64].

Two types of basic controllers using neural networks have most frequently been considered: *feedforward controllers* and *feedback controllers*. The feedforward controller accepts at its input the set-point value $r(t)$ and delivers at its output the process control variable $u(t)$, whereas the feedback controller accepts the difference between the set point value $r(t)$ and the actual value of the process output $y(t)$ and delivers to the process input the control signal $u(t)$. In Figure 31 the process control architecture is shown containing both controllers.

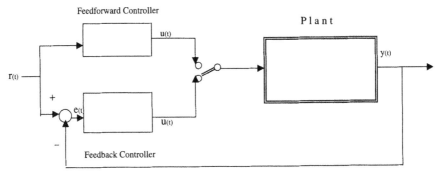

FIGURE 31
Process control architecture.

Modern control concepts can incorporate into the control configuration the mathematical model of the system to be controlled. When implemented using neural networks technology, the model can be a *direct system model* or an *inverse system model*. The *direct* or *parallel system model* is implemented, as shown in Figure 32a, using the difference between the model output variable $y_m(t)$ and the process output variable $y(t)$ for tuning the model parameters during the learning phase, whereby both the model and the process are excited by the same input signal $r(t)$. The *inverse* or *serial system model* is implemented, as shown in Figure 32b using the difference between the set-point value $r(t)$ and the output value of the controlled process. The process control variable $u(t)$ is generated by the preceding model, driven by the operating set-point value. Using the inverse model, the system can be controlled as shown in Figure 33, where the inverse model of the system compensates the system nonlinearity so that the real control can be performed by any linear controller, so long as the inverse model of the plant is physically realizable. However, far better control results are achieved if both the parallel and serial models are used simultaneously in the control scheme (Figure 34), implementing the *internal model control*.

Nguyen and Widrow [39a] have proposed that the neural network controller be incorporated into the control loop and that it be taught on-line (Figure 35). Kuntanapreeda, Gundersen, and Fullmer [28a] improved the control concept by introducing a reference model into the control loop configuration (Figure 36) that can control even unstable nonlinear systems such as the inverted pendulum.

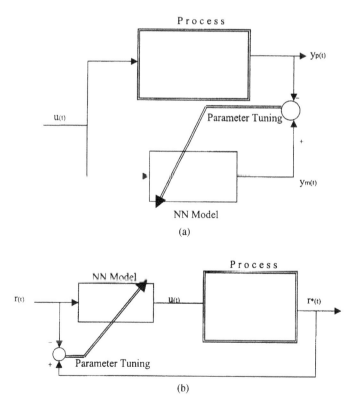

FIGURE 32
(a) Training of a parallel NN model; (b) Training of a serial NN model.

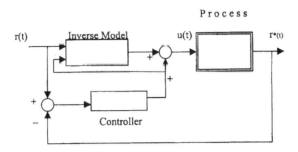

FIGURE 33
Inverse model-based control.

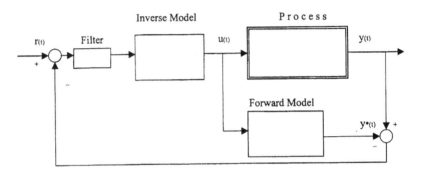

FIGURE 34
Internal model control.

Sorensen has proposed a back-propagation network for building an *innovation state space model* using the plant input–output [53]. The model is trained to be applied as a parallel model for plant parameter extraction. It is a *nonlinear parametric model,*

$$x^*(t) - f(x^*(t-1), u(t-1), e(t-1))$$

$$y^*(t) = Hx(t)$$

$$y(t) = y^*(t) + e(t)$$

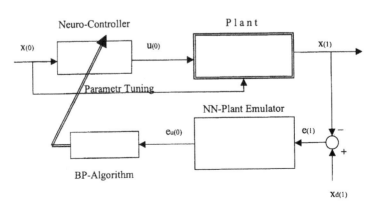

FIGURE 35
Neutral network incorporated controller.

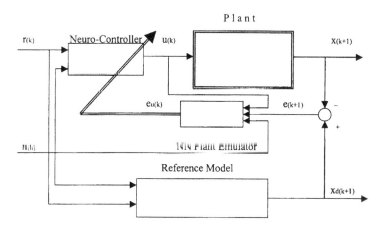

FIGURE 36
Reference model-based neuro-controller.

that helps calculate directly the optimal controller parameters, where x is the state vector, u is the input vector, y is the output vector x^* and y^* are the estimated values of x and y, e is the external noise effecting the system, and H is a constant matrix. The configuration of the model is shown in Figure 37, where it is used for the implementation of a nonlinear state controller.

Antony and Acar [2] have simplified the problem by supposing that the system to be controlled is described in state space by

$$x(t+1) = f(x(t)) + Bu(t)$$

with a constant control matrix B. For system modeling and identification, only the nonlinear term of the state space equation $f(x(t))$ was considered (Figure 38) and used for the implementation of an optimal controller.

The model building, learning, and adaptation abilities of neural networks enable the implementation of a number of advanced control configurations such as self-adjusting, adaptive, and predictive control as described below [11]. For instance, a parallel plant model, trained with the delayed plant input signal at its input (Figure 39), will be able to predict the plant behavior

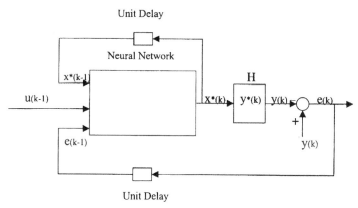

FIGURE 37
Innovation state space model-based controller.

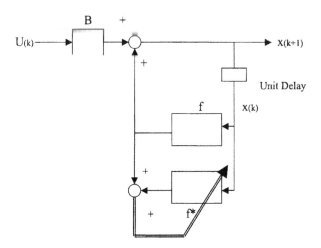

FIGURE 38
Neural network-based non-linear system modeling.

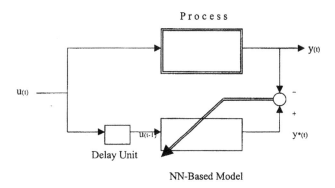

FIGURE 39
NN training for predictive control.

when fed with the same signal at its input as in the plant. This can be used for implementation of *model predictive control* of the plant.

External system disturbances and internal system drifts due to material wear, aging of system components, poor adjustment of system parameters, etc., prevents a mathematical model of the system being valid for all time. As a consequence, the controllers associated with the system and optimally tuned to the system model also do not remain optimal for all time. They have to be retuned regularly. If the retuning has to follow the system parameter drifts automatically, the control should be designed as a *self-tuning* or *self-adjusting* control. A number of proposals have been made for the design of such controllers, including those based on the use of neural networks. For instance, Chen and Khalil [11] proposed using the approximation capability of back-propagation neural networks for the implementation of a nonlinear self-tuning control for a single-input–single-output system described by

$$y(t+1) = f(y(t)) + g(y(t))u(t)$$

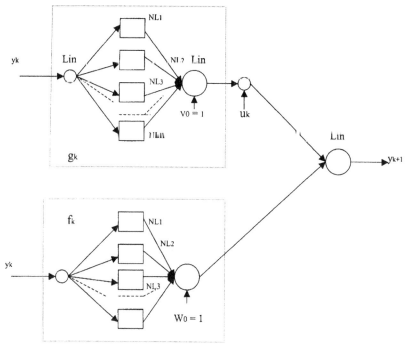

FIGURE 40
Neural network model of a non-linear system.

It can be modeled by two separate neural networks (Figure 40):

$$y^*(t+1) = f^*(y(t), W(t)) + g^*(y(t), V(t))u(t)$$

where $W(t)$ and $V(t)$ are the network weight matrices. In Figure 41 the implementation structure of the controller is given, where $u(t)$ is calculated from the above model equation by setting $y(t) = s(t)$, and $s(t)$ is the set-point value to be followed by $y(t)$. From the same equation, $y^*(t)$ is also calculated using the controller output $u(t)$

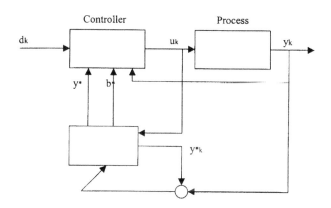

FIGURE 41
Neural network based self-tuning control.

7.4 Reinforcement Learning and Control

Reinforcement learning is a general learning approach not requiring a network trainer or a supervisor. This kind of learning is recommended when the knowledge needed for supervised learning is not available, because it does not directly compare the *actual* with the correct pattern at the system output. No attention is paid to the exact *degree* of the correctness or incorrectness. Instead, the network is simply rewarded when the output is acceptable and punished when it is not [4, 67].

Sutton, Barto, and Williams [58] defined reinforcement learning as a learning approach based on the *common sense* idea that if an action is followed by a satisfactory state of affairs then the tendency to produce that action is strengthened, i.e., reinforced. Otherwise, the tendency of the system to produce that action is weakened [44].

Reinforcement learning networks have found application in solving nonlinear control problems, exploiting the *actor–critic* or *Q-learning* algorithm. A learning system based on the actor–critic algorithm consists of two modules: one for the estimation of long-term utility for each system state, and one for learning to choose the optimal actions in each state. A learning system based the Q-learning algorithm estimates the utilities for the entire set of the state–action pairs and considers them by selecting the actions.

The difference between supervised learning and reinforced learning is shown in Figure 42. Whereas in supervised learning (Figure 42a), the neural network under training is tuned according to the exact and the actual values of the output pattern, in enforcement learning (Figure 42b) the network under training receives the output signal from the system whose input–output behavior it has to learn. On the basis of some criteria and on the critics or reinforcement used for learning, the network generates an output that is forwarded as a stimulating signal to the

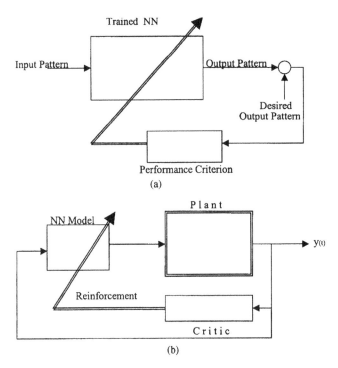

FIGURE 42
(a) Supervised learning; (b) Reinforcement learning.

plant. The final objective is to tune the network so that its input–output mapping minimizes the reinforcement.

8 APPLICATIONS TO PROCESS CONTROL

The problem of model building and system identification of mechanical, thermal, and electrical systems is relatively easy because the mathematical models of such systems are relatively simple in the majority of cases. They mainly rely on Newton's laws of motion, heat transfer, and circuit and/or electromagnetic theory. However, serious difficulties arise when mathematical models of chemical plants are to be developed because the related chemical processes are complex, nonlinear, distributed, and possibly time-variable and contaminated by noise. Chemical processes involve complex reactions and energy transformations of which the mathematical description may not be known exactly. Additionally, the mathematical formulation of related physical and chemical law, the physical size and geometry of the reactors play an important role. All of this calls for an approach that can resolve the modeling difficulties in a relatively direct manner and facilitate the subsequent design and implementation of an appropriate optimal controller. Neural networks promise to be the appropriate technology because they can help in direct implementation of nonlinear learning models [2, 6] and because they are less noise-sensitive and have a high fault tolerance. This has made these networks widely applicable in model building, process identification, supervisory control, and so on [17]. This will be demonstrated using some practical examples.

Modern strategies of complex plant automation rely on the use of nonlinear controllers for the control of nonlinear systems such as continuous stirred-tank reactors [1]. However, nonlinear controllers can be avoided when there is available a global transformation that transforms a nonlinear system to be controlled into an equivalent linear system. In this case equivalent *linear* controllers are to be designed, for instance by pole placement or by other design techniques.

The application of neural network technology in solving nonlinear control problems will be demonstrated using the example of a continuous stirred-tank reactor (CSTR). In this example the network is used for the on-line identification of the *inverse inherent model* of the reactor and, in an alternating switching mode, for the temperature and concentration control of the reactor. The reactor modeling is based on the material and energy balance equations of the reaction taking place in the reactor,

$$V\frac{dC}{dt} = G(C_0 - C) - VkC$$
$$V\rho c_p \frac{dT}{dt} = -\Delta HVkC - G\rho c_p(T - T_0) - \chi F(T - T_c)$$
$$k = k_0 e^{-E/RT}$$

where T and C are the temperature and the concentration in the reactor, T_0 and C_0 are inlet-temperature and the inlet-concentration of the reactants G is the volume flow rate of the inlet reactants, and T_c is the coolant temperature.

The control problem here is to maintain the temperature T and the concentration C constant around the selected operating point, despite the disturbances by manipulating the volume flow rate G and the coolant temperature T_c as control variables. It will be shown that a neurocontroller designed for the simultaneous control of two reactor variables can maintain the temperature and the concentration in the reactor stable around the stationary operating point in spite of strong external disturbances.

In practice, it is preferred to use the normalized model equations [73]:

$$\frac{dX}{dt} = g(1 - X) - kX$$

$$\frac{dY}{dt} = \Delta T_{ad}kX - g(Y - T_0) - u_m(Y - T_c)$$

$$k = k_0 e^{-E/RT}$$

with

$$x = \frac{c}{c_0}, \quad Y = T, \quad g = \frac{G}{V}, \quad \text{and} \quad u_m = \frac{\chi F}{V \rho c_p}$$

The corresponding control strategy is presented schematically in Figure 43, where the block Reference is a setting unit, giving the desired concentration X^* and temperature T^* in the reactor. The control objective is to minimize the error $E(i + 1)$ between the actual values $[X(i + 1), Y(i + 1)]$ in the reactor and the reference values. This can be achieved using the conditions of global asymptotic stability [70] based on the corresponding Ljapunov function $V(i)$. The neural network block N-Net is the core part of the nonlinear controller, which operates as follows:

- When the switch is in the position 1–3–4, the network learns on-line the reactor model and the inherent relations between the control variables and the states of the reactor.
- When the switch is in the position 2–4–5, the network serves as a predictor of the control variables for the desired states in the reactor.

Before actually using a nonlinear controller its stability should be verified [79]. This can be done when the nonlinear system to be controlled is defined by the state space equation

$$\mathbf{X}(i + 1) = \mathbf{f}[\mathbf{X}(i), \mathbf{u}(i)]$$

by defining its *inverse inherent relation*

$$\mathbf{u}(i) = \mathbf{f}^{-1}[\mathbf{X}(i), \mathbf{X}(i + 1)]$$

if it exists. In the equations, $X \in R^n$ is the state vector and $u \in R^n$ is the control vector. The objective is to develop a nonlinear controller that will force the nonlinear system to behave like the linear system represented by the reference model

$$\mathbf{X}_R(i + 1) = \mathbf{A}\mathbf{X}_R(i) + \mathbf{B}\mathbf{U}_R(i)$$

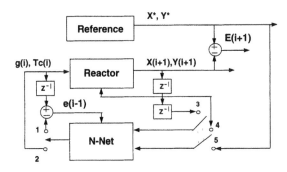

FIGURE 43
The schematic illustration of the control problem.

with the state vector $\mathbf{X}_R \in R^n$, input vector $\mathbf{U}_R \in R^n$ and constant matrices $\mathbf{A}_{n \times n}$ and $\mathbf{B}_{n \times n}$. By definition, a *proper* control law should minimize the state *error vector* $\mathbf{E}(i) = \mathbf{X}_R(i) - \mathbf{X}(i)$, i.e., it should force the nonlinear system to follow the dynamic behavior of linear reference model. This will be the case when the positive-definite form of $\mathbf{E}(i)$ with a $n \times n$ matrix $\mathbf{P}$ meets the condition

$$\lim_{i \geq \Gamma} \mathbf{E}^T(i)\mathbf{P}\mathbf{E}(i) \leq \delta$$

where Γ is the maximal regulating time allowed by the nonlinear system and δ is the acceptable output error of the nonlinear system.

According to *Liapunov's Second Method* a nonlinear system is asymptotically stable if the relation

$$\mathbf{E}^T(i+1)\mathbf{P}\mathbf{E}(i+1) \leq \mathbf{E}^T(i)\mathbf{P}\mathbf{E}(i)$$

holds. The control law $\mathbf{u}^*(i) = \mathbf{N}[\mathbf{X}_R(i+1), \mathbf{X}(i)]$ is called proper, if $\mathbf{N}[*]$ can precisely predict the inverse model $\mathbf{f}^{-1}[*]$ of the nonlinear system in the sense that $\mathbf{e}^T(i)\mathbf{Q}\mathbf{e}(i) \leq \varepsilon$, for $i \geq \Gamma$, where

$$\mathbf{e}(i) = \mathbf{F}^{-1}[\mathbf{X}(i), \mathbf{X}(i+1)] - \mathbf{N}[\mathbf{X}(i), \mathbf{X}(i+1)]$$

ε is an acceptable error index, and $\mathbf{Q}$ is a $n \times n$ positive-definite matrix.

The predictor $\mathbf{N}[*]$ of the inverse nonlinear model $f^{-1}[*]$ plays a very important role. In Figure 43 it is realized using a generalized back-propagation net, the N-Net, with an enhanced training algorithm [46] having an improved convergence property and relying on the extended error index

$$J(W(i-1)) = \frac{1}{2}\sum_{l=i-m}^{i}\sum_{k=1}^{2}[e_k(l)] + \mu\frac{1}{2}\sum_{l=i-m}^{i}\sum_{h=1}^{i}\sum_{k=1}^{2}[e_k(l) - e_k(h)]^2$$

where W is the connecting weights vector of the neural network, i is the ith step of learning, m is the number of errors already considered in the ith learning step, μ is a selectable parameter related to the learning index extension, and $e_k(i) = [e_1(i)\ e_2(i)]^T$ the predicting error vector. The updating rule of the network weight vector is

$$W(i) = W(i-1) - \eta\frac{\partial J[W(i-1)]}{\partial W(i-1)}$$

where η is the learning rate of the neural network.

The reaction taking place in the CSTR presented here is the decomposition of hydrogen peroxide into water and free oxygen [14]:

$$H_2O_2 \xrightarrow{Fe^{3+}} H_2O + \tfrac{1}{2}O_2 \uparrow$$

The following reactor parameters were taken for simulation purposes: volume $V = 0.5$ (L), concentration $c_0 = 7.49$ (mol L^{-1}) and temperature $T_0 = 293$ (K). The value of the Arrhenius constant $R = 0.00831$ (KJ mol k^{-1}), was used and the values of other relate reaction constants were taken as $k_0 = 1.6 \times 10^{18}$ (S^{-1}), $\Delta T_{ad} = 173.2(K)$, $\rho c_{cp} = 4.10$ (kJ K^{-1} L^{-1}), $\chi F = 0.01139$ (kJ K^{-1} s^{-1}), $E_0 = 116.34$ (KJ mol^{-1}), and the concentration of the catalyst Fe^{3+} as 0.02 (mol L^{-1}). The inlet flow rate g of the reactant H_2O_2 and the coolant temperature T_c were selected as the control variables, and the periodic oscillating point was determined using $c_s = 3.745$ (mol^{-1}/l), $T_s = 282.185$ (K), $g_s = 0.00045$ (L s^{-1}) and $T_{c,s} = 274.22$ (K) as the desired reactor stationary operating state.

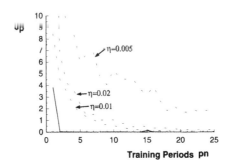

FIGURE 44
Convergence property in modeled CSTR.

To test the convergence of the learning algorithm used for system simulation, the CSTR was modeled with both the enhanced and the standard back-propagation learning rule.

The simulation results obtained are shown in Figure 44 where g is supposed to be white noise in the range (0.000255, 0.00055), T_c is white noise within the range (264.0, 284.0), $C(i)$ is randomly chosen in the range (2.247, 5.243), and $T(i)$ is random variable in the range (275.0, 295.0). The concentration and the temperature in the reactor are sampled every 6 seconds. From Figure 44, the advantages of the *enhanced* learning over the *standard* back-propagation learning can be seen quite clearly.

The control problem is now that of maintaining the concentration C and the temperature T at the desired stationary values c_s and T_s. The control variables are within the range $0.00055 > g > 0.00035$ and $264.0 > T_c > 284.0$. Figure 45 shows the time-behavior of C and T in the absence of control and disturbances with the original states $C(0) = 3.745 \,(\text{mol L}^{-1})$, $T(0) = 283.5 \,(\text{K})$, $g = 0.00045 \,(\text{L s}^{-1})$ and $T_c = 274.22 \,(\text{K})$. From Figure 45 it follows that because of a very small error in the initial state $T(0)$, the concentration and the temperature in the reactor begin to oscillate and after about 165 minutes the system becomes unstable.

When the reactor is controlled in our case using a neurocontroller, the responses of C and T are as shown in Figure 46, in which the states of the reactor within the first 2 minutes of time were randomly chosen in the range $2.5 \,(\text{mol L}^{-1}) < C < 5.0 \,(\text{mol L}^{-1})$ and $275 \,(\text{K}) < T < 295 \,(\text{K})$, and g and T_c were also randomly chosen in the bounded control ranges. After 2 minutes, the neural controller began to control the system.

For simulation purposes, the neural network was first trained off-line to learn the characteristics of the reactor around the desired stationary point. Subsequently at time $t = 0$, the reactor was switched on to work at the desired stationary points and at the same time a disturbance of the inlet temperature or of the inlet concentration was added to the dynamics of the reactor. At $t = 2$

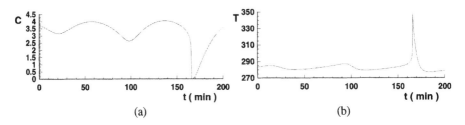

(a)   (b)

FIGURE 45
Non-controlled behavior of C and T.

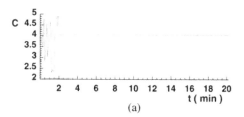

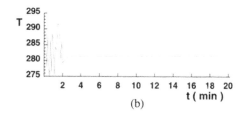

FIGURE 46
Neural network-controlled behavior of C and T.

minutes, the trained neural network was switched onto the control the reactor. Thereafter, the neural network was trained on-line to follow the structural changes of the reactor.

Figure 47 shows the responses of the state and the control to a +20% and a −10% step change in the inlet temperature of the reactants and Figure 48 shows the responses of the same variables to a +10% and a −10% step change in the inlet concentration of the reactants.

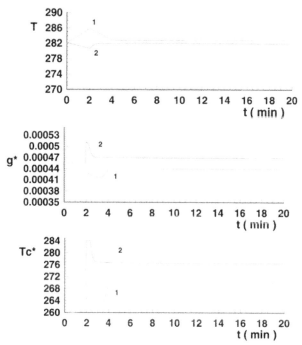

FIGURE 47
State and control response to inlet temperature step.

FIGURE 48
State and control response to the inlet concentration step.

9 IMPLEMENTATION TECHNOLOGIES

The majority of contemporary neural networks applications are implemented on conventional computers using neurosoftware or *neuroware*. This is the most straightforward method of implementation, but the run-time of neurosoftware is generally not applicable to real-time problems. However, it has advantages:

- Configuration flexibility in the sense of easy selection and reselection of any arbitrary network type, network structure, and network elements, including the type of neuron activation function.
- Availability of low-priced PC-based development tools with the capability of software interfacing to different real-time programming languages, such as Language C, Real-Time Fortran, etc., so that the final version of the developed neuroware is generated in languages to run on real-time computers.

In the early development phase, neural networks were implemented using transputers as parallel processing units and used for building special acceleration boards as coprocessors of microcomputers or PCs. Later, special VLSI implementations were launched, usually as dedicated neural network hardware for solving specific types of applications [76]. Here, two basic technologies are available: *electronic* and *optical*. Progress has also been made in *opto-electronic technology*. Integrated circuit-based implementation of neural networks, because of its hardware parallelism, is indicated for real-time applications. However, a crucial issue related to the development of VLSI chips is their accuracy. Because signal and weight values can be represented in this technology with limited range, the convergence rate of the learning algorithm might be reduced considerably. This is noticeable, for instance, when processing the back-propagation algorithm with an accuracy below 16 bits.

Work has been done on the appropriate modification of the learning algorithms so that they retain their high learning efficiency in spite of the lower accuracy of the processing elements. To achieve this, the training algorithms have to operate on a user-selected network structure that is usually not optimal for solving the given problem. In the meantime, attempts been made to structure optimally the network to be trained with *on-chip learning* as implemented by Lehmann, Viredaz, and Blayo [31].

From an economic point of view, there is a great advantage when the neural networks are implemented in analog technology because such networks are capable of carrying out the arithmetic operations using relatively inexpensive linear computing elements such as operational amplifiers for the implementation of addition, along with some nonlinear elements such as MOS transistors for the implementation of multiplication, etc. Nevertheless, analog nonlinear elements have poor accuracy, are sources of noise, are thermally unstable, and are cross-talk sensitive.

Analog networks are therefore appropriate for the implementation of relatively simple, small-scale neurocomputing devices.

The key issue of the analog implementation of neural networks is still the implementation of the variable synaptic weights that have to be adjusted to follow the learning law. Here, resistors are used that change their values according to the values of some internal analog signals. For instance, Mitsubishi has fabricated a 336-neuron analog chip with 28 000 self-learning synapses in CMOS technology with a training speed of 28 giga connection updates per second and 1 TCPS (tera connections per second). In the network, the weight values learnt in the training phase are electrically stored and updated in capacitors. In the largest configuration, up to 200 chips can be integrated, giving a large-scale circuit with 3000 neurons and 5.6 million connections and with performance of 200 TCPS and 5.6 TCPS in the learning and operational phase, respectively.

Nevertheless, noise immunity and the capacity for reliable data transfer make digital circuits appropriate for hardware implementation of neural networks because in such implementations a huge number of calculations per second and a high computational accuracy are achievable. However, silicon implementation of high-precision floating-point multiplication and the precise calculation of the activation functions of neurons requires much of the space on the chip. The problem has been solved using the time-multiplexing principle, in which millions of connection updates per second (MCUPS) are achievable.

Finally, advances in optical computing have made optical technology a competitive substitute for electronics, particularly in special applications such as neural networks [9,29]. Because neural networks merge *computation* and *communication* in their operations, the optical implementation of networks is homogeneous, based on optical elements only. Additionally, optical network implementation avoids the problem of electrical insulation in the interconnection of neurons because light beams are used instead of electron flow, and this also holds for interconnections between the individual chips. Furthermore, the possible density of optical interconnections is much higher than that of electrical interconnections. Finally, the operational speed and the bandwidth of optical elements are considerably higher and the noise sensitivity and heat generation are lower than those of electronic elements. For instance, the operational speed can be 1000 times faster than in VSL implementation, and the packing density can reach 250 000, interconnections per square inch. Nonetheless, the optical elements are more limited in computation.

We are now coming to the final trend of neural network implementation in which the neural network learning paradigm and fuzzy systems rule-based reasoning are combined to give neuro-fuzzy systems. This is known as *synergetic artificial intelligence*. New generations of controllers combine both techniques to improve performance and to widen the areas of application.

Fuzzy control, being a model-free control approach and not requiring a mathematical model of the system to be controlled, is becoming attractive for applications in the control of nonlinear and complex systems, the mathematical models of which are extremely difficult to build. This is particularly true for industrial plants, the mathematical models of which are extremely involved. Combining the advantages of fuzzy controllers with the capacity for neural network learning opens enormous possibilities, such as solving the intelligent control problem of difficult real systems with unknown internal structures and parameter values. Neurofuzzy control systems, based on data collected in the real world, can have neural networks' learning capability incorporated into the fuzzy part of the system to generate the fuzzy rules that match the observation data [25,61]. This could be of immense importance for the elicitation of knowledge distributed in observation data with the fuzzy control rules intuitively compiled by an expert based on heuristic knowledge. Another approach, based on input–output data pairs collected and on the set of the proposed IF–THEN rules, would be to generate the membership functions most appropriate for the control problems to be solved [61].

A number of different ways of building synergetic neurofuzzy systems [18] have been explored such as

- *Combination*, through a straightforward sequential interconnection of neural networks and fuzzy logic systems
- *Integration*, through implementation of hybrid architectures
- *Fusion*, through merging (fusion) of different intelligent techniques to optimize the capabilities of the basic hybrid system
- *Association*, through building distributed multi-agent systems of optimal configuration for specific dedicated applications

Chiaberge and Reyneri [13] presented a neurofuzzy real-time controller, based on the pulse stream computational technique, designed for applications in the control of nonlinear systems. Furthermore, a number of control strategies have been examined using the neurofuzzy approach in which the network was trained on different fuzzy controllers previously defined, tested, and optimally tuned off-line. For optimal network training, *genetic algorithms* and *simulated annealing* are available within the system.

A direct fusion of a fuzzy system and a neural network creates a hybrid system that can be better tailored to specific applications and optimized by learning. The fusion of the two technologies has been applied to create an elementary fuzzy-neuro system, the *fuzzy neuron*. A silicon implementation of a fuzzy neuron, as a modification of an ordinary neuron model by fuzzy logic, was reported by Yamakawa [76]. As a further alternative, NeuraLogix has designed the fuzzy controller NLX230 with an integrated neural network to accelerate the inference process of the controller. In addition, the neural network helps the fuzzy controller to adapt optimally to the basic membership functions and the control strategy to give the optimal control results in spite of the changing environmental conditions.

REFERENCES AND FURTHER READING

[1] J. Alvarez. Global nonlinear control of a continuous stirred tank reactor, *Chem. Eng. Sci.*, Vol. 44, No. 5, pp. 1147–1160, 1989.

[2] J.K. Antony and L. Acar, Real-time non-linear optimal control using neural networks, *Proc. American Control Conf.*, pp. 2926–2930, 1994.

[3] P. Antsalkis (ed.), Special issue on neural networks in control systems, *IEEE Control Systems Magazine*, Vol. 10, No. 3, Apr. 1990.

[4] A. Barto, R. Sutton and C. Anderson, Neuron-like adaptive elements that can solve difficult learning control problems, *IEEE Trans. Systems, Man and Cybernetics*, Vol. 13, No. 5, pp. 834–846, 1983.

[5] S.A. Billings et al. Properties of neural network with application to modeling non-linear dynamic systems, *Int. J. Control*, Vol. 55, No. 1, pp. 193–224, 1992.

[6] S.A. Billings, H.B. Jamaluddin and S. Chen, Properties of neural networks with applications to modeling non-linear dynamical systems, *Int. J. Control*, Vol. 55, No. 1, pp. 193–224, 1992.

[7] G. Carpenter and G. Grossberg, ART 2: Self-organization of stable category recognition codes for analog input patterns, *IEEE Trans. Systems, Man and Cybernetics*, Vol. 13, pp. 815–825, 1987.

[8] G. Carpenter and G. Grossberg, *Pattern Recognition by Self-Organizing Neural Networks*. MIT Press, Cambridge, MA, 1991.

[9] D. Casasent. Optical processing in neural networks, *IEEE Expert*, pp. 55–61, Oct. 1992.

[10] S. Chen, S.A. Billings and P.M. Grant, Nonlinear system identification using neural networks. *Int. J. Control*, Vol. 51, No. 6, pp. 1192–1214, 1990.

[11] F.C. Chen and H.K. Khalil, Adaptive control of nonlinear systems using neural networks, *Intl. J. Control*. Vol. 55, No. 6, pp, 1299–1317, 1992.

[12] S. Chen et al. Recursive hybrid algorithm for nonlinear system identification using radial basis function networks, *Intl. J. Control.* Vol. 55, No. 3, pp. 493–497, 1992.

[13] M. Chiaberge and L.M. Reyneri, Cintia: A neuro-fuzzy real-time controller for low-power embedded systems, *IEEE Micro*, pp. 40–47, June 1995.

[14] X.S. Deng, D. Popovic and G. Schulz-Ekloff, Real-time identification and control of a continuous stirred tank reactor with neural network, *IEEE/IAS Int. Conf. Industrial Automation and Contol, Hyderabad, India*, 1995, pp. 67–70.

[15] X.S. Deng, D. Popovic and G. Schulz-Ekloff, Oscillation-resisting in the learning of back-propagation networks, *3rd IFAC/IFIP Workshop on Algorithms and Architectures for Real-time Control Ostend, Belgium*, 1995, pp. 21–25,

[16] S. Ergezinger and E. Thomasen, An accelerated learning algorithm for multilayer perceptron: optimization layer by layer, *IEEE Trans. Neural Networks*, Vol. 6, No. 1, pp. 31–42, 1995.

[17] T. Fukuda and T. Shibata, Theory and applications of neural networks for industrial control systems, *IEEE Trans. Industrial Electronics*, Vol. 39, No. 6, pp. 472–489, 1992.

[18] M. Funabashi, et al. Fuzzy and neural hybrid systems: synergetic AI, *IEEE Expert*, pp. 32–40, Aug. 1995.

[19] S. Grossberg, *Studies of Mind and Brain: Neural Principles of Learning Perceptron, Cognition and Motor Control*, Reidel, Boston, MA.

[20] S. Haykin, *Neural Networks: A Comprehensive Foundation*, Macmillan College Publishing, New York, 1994.

[21] D.O. Hebb, *The Organization of Behavior.* Wiley, New York, 1949.

[22] R. Hecht-Nielsen, Theory of the back-propagation neural networks, *Int. Joint Conf. Neural Networks, Washington D.C.* 1989, Vol. 1, pp. I-251–I-256.

[23] J.J. Hopfield, Neural networks and physical systems with emergent collective computational abilities *Proc. Natl. Acad. Sci.*, Vol. **79**, pp. 2554–2558, 1982.

[23a] J.J. Hopfield, Neutrons with graded response have collective computational properties like those of two-state neurons, *Proc. Natl. Acad. Sci.*, Vol. 81, pp. 3088–3092, 1984.

[24] K. Hornik, M. Stinchcombe and H. White, Multi-layer feed-forward networks are universal approximators, *Neural Networks*, No. 2, pp. 183–192, 1989.

[25] H. Ishibuchi, R. Fujioka and H. Tanaka, Neural networks that learn from fuzzy IF–THEN rules, *IEEE Trans. Fuzzy Systems*, Vol. 1, No. 2, pp. 85–97, May 1993.

[26] R.A. Jacobs and M. Jordan, A competitive modular connectionist architecture, in *Advances in Neural Information Processing Systems*, R.P. Lippmann, J.E. Moody and D.J. Touretzky (eds.), pp. 767–773, Morgan Kaufmann, San Mateo, CA, 1991.

[26a] R.A. Jacobs and M.I. Jordan, Linear precewise control strategies in a modular neural network architecture, *IEEE Trans. Systems, Man, and Cybernetics*, p.. 337–345, 1993.

[27] M. Jordan, Generic constraints and underspecified target trajectories, *Proc. IJCNN-89*, New York, 1989, pp. I 217–225.

[28] N.B. Karayiannis and A.N. Venetsanopoulos, Efficient learning algorithms for neural networks, *IEEE Trans. Systems, Man and Cybernetics.* Vol. 23, No. 5, pp. 1372–1383, 1993.

[28a] J. Katunapreeda R.W. Gundersen and R.R. Fullmer, Neural network model reference control at nonlinear systems, *IJCNN-92*, Baltimore, 1992, pp. II 94–99.

[29] E. Lange, Y. Nitta and K. Kyuma, Optical neural chips, *IEEE Micro*, No. 12, pp. 29–41, 1994.

[30] M. Lee, S.-Y. Lee and C.H. Park, Self-tuning control by neural networks, *IEEE Int. Conf. Neural Networks, ICNN '94*, 1994, Vol. IV, pp. 2411–2414.

[31] Ch. Lehmann, M. Viredaz and F. Blayo, A generic systolic array building block for neural networks with on-chip learning, *IEEE Trans. Neural Computing*, Vol. 4, No. 3, pp. 400–407, May 1993.

[32] E.A. Leonard, M.A. Kramer and L.H. Ungar, Using radial basis functions to approximate a function and its error bounds, *IEEE Trans. Neural Networks*, Vol. 3, No. 4, pp. 624–627, 1991.

[33] E.A. Leonard and M. Kramer, Diagnosis dynamic faults using modular neural network, *IEEE Expert*, pp. 44–53, Apr. 1993.

[34] A.J. Maren, C.T. Harston and R.M. Pap, *Handbook of Neural Computing Applications*, Academic Press, New York, 1990.

[35] J.L. McClelland and D.E. Rumelhart (eds.), *Parallel Distributed Processing: Explorations in the Microstructure of Cognition*, PDP Research Group, Vols. 1 & 2, MIT Press, Cambridge, MA, 1986.

[35a] W.T. Miller, R.S. Sutlon, and P.J. Werbos (eds.), *Neural Networks for Control*, MIT Press, MA., 1990.

[36] M. Minsky and S. Papert, *Perceptrons*, MIT Press, Cambridge, MA, 1969.

[36a] J.E. Moody and C.J. Darken, Fast learning in networks of locally-tuned processing units, *Neural Computing*, Vol. 1, pp. 281–294, 1989.

[37] K.S. Narendra, Adaptive control using neural networks, in W.T. Miller III, R.S. Sutton and P.J. Werbos, (eds.) *Neural Networks for* pp. 115–142. MIT Press, Cambridge, MA, 1990.

[38] K S Narendra and K. Parthasarathy, Identification and control of dynamic systems using neural networks, *IEEE Trans. Neural Networks*, Vol. 1, No. 1, pp. 4–27, 1990.

[39] K.S. Narendra and S. Mukhopadhyay, Adaptive control of nonlinear systems using neural networks, *Neural Networks*, Vol. 7, No. 5, pp. 737–752, 1994.

[39a] Ngugen and Widrow, The truck backer-upper: An example of self-learning in neural networks, in *Neural Networks for Control*, W.T. Miller, R.S. Sutton and P.J. Webos (eds.), MIT Press, MA, 1990.

[40] Y.-H. Pao, *Adaptive Pattern Recognition and Neural Networks*. Addison-Wesley, Reading, MA, 1989.

[41] D.T. Pham and X. Liu, *Engineering Applications AAI*, State-space identification of dynamic systems using neural networks, Vol. 3, No. 1, pp. 198–203, 1990.

[42] T. Poggio and F. Girosi, Networks for approximation and learning, *Proc. IEEE*, Vol. 78, No. 9, 1481–1497, 1990.

[43] D. Popovic and V.P. Bhatkar, *Distributed Computer Control for Industrial Control*. Marcel Dekker, New York, 1990.

[44] D. Popovic and V.P. Bhatkar, *Methods and Tools of Applied Artificial Intelligence* Marcel Dekker, New York, 1994.

[45] D. Popovic and L. Vlacic, *Mechatronics in Engineering Design and Product Development*, Marcel Dekker, New York, 1998.

[46] D. Popovic and D. Xiasong, An approach of on-line modeling of dynamic systems with neural networks, *Preprints of ASCC*, Tokyo, Japan, July 1994, Paper SP-10-2.

[47] D. Popovic and D. Xiaosong, Structural optimization of neural networks for systems modeling, *IFAC Symp. Systems Identification, SYSID '97, Fukuoka*, July 1997, pp. 771–775.

[48] D. Popovic and S. Zhou, Application of a neural identification of kinetic parameters of chemical processes, *Application of Artificial Intelligence in Engineering IX*, 1994, pp. 65–72.

[49] D.L. Reilly, L.N. Cooper and C. Elbaum, A neural model for category learning, *Biological Cybernetics*, Vol. 45, pp. 35–41, 1982.

[50] F. Rosenblatt, *The perceptron: A perceiving and recognizing automation (project PARA)* Cornell Aeronautical Lab. Rep. 85-460-1, 1957.

[51] F. Rosenblatt, The perceptron: A probabilistic model for information storage and organization of the brain, *Psychological Review*, Vol. 65, No. 6, pp. 386–408, 1958.

[52] D.E. Rumelhart, G.E. Hinton and R.J. Williams, Learning internal representations by back-propagation errors, *Nature*, Vol. 23, pp. 533–536, 1986.

[53] O. Sorensen, Neural networks for nonlinear control, *3rd IEEE CCA*, 1994, pp. 161–166.

[54] D.F. Specht, Probabilistic neural networks for classification, or associative memory, *Proc. IEEE Int. Conf. Neural Networks, San Diego*, 1988, Vol. 1, 525–532.

[55] D.F. Specht, Probabilistic neural networks and the polynomial adaline as complementary techniques for classification, *IEEE Trans. Neural Networks*, Vol. 1, pp. 111–121, 1990.

[56] M. Stinchcombe, H. White, Universal approximation using feed-forward networks with non-sigmoid hidden-layer activation functions, *Int. Joint Conf. Neural Networks, Washington D.C.*, 1989, Vol. 1, pp. 1613–1617.

[57] R.S. Sutton and A. Barto, Toward a modern theory of adaptive networks: expectation and prediction, *Psychological Review*, Vol. 88, No. 2, pp. 135–170, 1981.

[58] R.S. Sutton, A.G. Barto and R.J. Williams, Reinforcement learning in direct adaptive optimal control, *Proc. Am. Control Conf., Boston*, 1992, pp. 2143–2146.

[59] S. Tan, J. Hao and J. Vanderwalle, Nonlinear systems identification using RBF neural networks, *Proc. 1993 Int. Joint Conf. Neural Networks*, 1993, pp. 1833–1836.

[60] J. Tanomaru, Comparative study of two neural network approaches for nonlinear identification, *1994 Int. Symp. Speech, Image Processing and Neural Networks, Hong Kong*, 1994, pp. 487–490.

[61] S. Wang, Generating fuzzy membership function: a monotonic neural network model, *Fuzzy Sets and Systems*, Vol. 61, pp. 71–81, 1994.

[62] P.J. Werbos, *Beyond regression: New tools for prediction and analysis in the behavioral Sciences*, Ph.D. Dissertation, Harvard University, 1974.

[63] P.J. Werbos, Back-propagation through time: What it does and how to do it, *Proc. IEEE*, Vol. 78, pp. 1550–1560, 1990.

[64] P.J. Werbos, An overview of neural networks for control, *IEEE Control Systems Magazine*, pp. 40–41, Jan. 1991.

[65] B. Widrow, Generalization and information storage in networks of adaline "Neurons," in M.C. Yovich et al. (eds.), *Self-Organizing Systems*. Sparton Book, Washington D.C., 1962.

[66] B. Widrow, The original adaptive neural net broom-balancer, *Int. Symp. Circuits and Systems, IEEE, New York*, 1987, pp. 351–357.

[67] B. Widrow, N. Gupta and S. Maitra, Punish/reward: Learning with a critic in adaptive threshold systems, *IEEE Trans. Systems, Man and Cybernetics*, Vol. SMC-5, pp. 455–465, 1973.

[68] B. Widrow and M.E. Hoff, Adaptive switching circuits, *IRE WESCON Convention Records*, Pt. 4, pp. 96–104, 1960.

[69] B. Widrow and M.A. Lehr, 30 years of adaptive neural networks: Perceptron, Madaline and back-propagation, *Proc. IEEE*, Vol. 78, No. 9, pp. 1415–1442, 1990.

[70] B. Widrow and S.D. Stearns, *Adaptive Signal Processing*. Prentice-Hall, Englewood Cliffs, NJ, 1985.

[71] R.C. Williamson and U. Helmke, Existence and uniqueness results for neural network approximations, *IEEE Trans. Neural Networks*, Vol. 6, No. 1, pp. 2–13, 1995.

[72] D. Xiasong, *Improved back-propagation neural networks for application to real-time modeling and control of continuous stirred tank Reactor*, Ph.D. Thesis, University of Bremen, 1995.

[73] D. Xiasong, D. Popovic and G. Schulz-Ekloff, Real-time identification and control of a continuous stirred tank reactor with neural networks, *IEEE/IAS Int. Conf. Industrial Automation and Control, Hyderabad, India*, 1995, pp. 67–70.

[74] D. Xiasong, D. Popovic and G. Schulz-Ekloff, Oscillation-resisting in the learning of back-propagation neural networks, *3rd IFAC/IFIP Workshop on Algorithms and Architectures for Real-Time Control, Ostende, Belgium*, 1995, pp. 21–25.

[75] D. Xiasong, D. Popovic and G. Schulz-Ekloff, The back-propagation neural network being capable of real-time identification, *4th IEEE Conf. Control Applications, Albany, New York*, 1995, pp. 572–577.

[76] T. Yamakawa, Silicon implementation of a fuzzy neuron, *IEEE Trans. Neural Systems*, Vol. 4, No. 4, pp. 488–505, Nov. 1996.

[77] S. Zhou, D. Popovic and G. Schulz-Ekloff, An improved learning law for back-propagation networks, *IEEE IJCNN, San Francisco*, Mar. 1993, pp. 573–579.

[78] S. Zhou, D. Popovic and G. Schulz-Ekloff, A motivation-following learning, *IEEE IJCNN, Nagoya, Japan*, Oct. 1993, pp. 573–579.

[79] S. Zhou, G. Schulz-Ekloff and D. Popovic, A direct criterion for stability analysis of steady-state of CSTR, *Chemical Engineering Science*, Vol. 46, No. 11, pp. 2961–2964, 1991.

CHAPTER 19

Knowledge-based Adaptation of Neurofuzzy Models in Predictive Control of a Heat Exchanger

MARTIN FISCHER[†]
[†]Siemens AG, Automotive Systems, Regensburg, Germany

OLIVER NELLES AND ROLF ISERMANN
Darmstadt University of Technology, Institute of Automatic Control Laboratory of Control Systems and Process Automation, Darmstadt, Germany

1 INTRODUCTION

Heat exchangers are standard components in the chemical and process industry. Temperature control is still a major challenge if the heat exchanger is used over a wide range of operating conditions (see e.g. [2, 6, 8, 19]. The nonlinear behavior depends strongly on the flow rates and on the temperatures of the media. Here, a cross-flow water/air heat exchanger is considered. The goal is to control the water outlet temperature by manipulating the flow rate of the air.

A novel strategy for adaptive predictive control of nonlinear processes based on local linear fuzzy models is introduced and applied to a heat exchanger pilot plant. Model predictive control is well established in applications [28]. Originally, the concept was introduced for linear models [5, 29], but the extension of the basic ideas to nonlinear processes is straightforward [31, 36]. The process model provided to the controller plays a crucial role in terms of control performance. As a consequence, a great portion of the implementation effort has to be spent on system modeling. In principle, different types of system models can be used for prediction. Here, Takagi–Sugeno type fuzzy models are employed [33]. On the one hand, prior knowledge can be used to build the fuzzy model or at least to determine the structure of the rule premises and consequents. On the other hand, these models can be interpreted as generalized radial basis function networks [11], and training algorithms from the field of neural networks can be applied for identification from measurement data. The modeling of the heat exchanger will be performed very carefully in order to demonstrate the power of this approach. Information from different sources such as qualitative expert knowledge, theoretical modeling, and data-driven identification can be integrated because of the highly transparent model structure.

If the process is subject to unmeasurable or unmodeled disturbances or if it reveals time-variant behavior, on-line adaptation of the fuzzy model becomes necessary. As for off-line identification, this can be data-driven or knowledge-based. While a data-driven approach is presented by Fischer et al. [10], a knowledge-based technique is proposed here that avoids the disadvantages of data-driven adaptation, such as the requirement for persistent excitation and possibly diverging parameter estimates. Insights from physical modeling will be used for scheduling the fuzzy model. Again, this highlights the interpretability of the chosen model type.

The chapter is organized as follows. In section 2, the thermal plant comprising the cross-flow heat exchanger is presented. Section 3 reviews dynamic Takagi–Sugeno fuzzy models and a suitable off-line identification algorithm. After a few general comments on modeling, dynamic Takagi–Sugeno fuzzy models are reviewed. Then, various approaches to data-driven and knowledge-based modeling are presented and the integration of both types of modeling is discussed. The resulting modeling scheme is applied to the heat exchanger. The knowledge-based adaptation that utilizes information from theoretical modeling is explained in section 4. The nonlinear predictive controller as well as the results from control experiments are shown in section 5. Finally, a summary and the conclusions are given in section 6.

2   THERMAL PLANT

The pilot plant depicted in Figure 1 comprises two heat exchangers. W1 is a tubular steam/water heat exchanger, and W2 is the cross-flow water/air heat exchanger under investigation In the primary circuit, the electric steam generator D1 ($P = 54\,\text{kW}$) produces saturated steam at a pressure of 6 bar. The steam flow rate F_s is manipulated by a motor-driven valve whose position is controlled by an inner control loop. The steam condenses in the tubular heat exchanger W1 and the liquid condensate is pumped back to the steam generator. The water in the secondary circuit is heated by means of W1. A predictive functional controller (PFC) based on semiphysical modeling regulates the water temperature T'_{wi} by sending reference values to the inner control loop of the steam valve (see [6]).

On the left side of the secondary circuit, the water is cooled in the cross-flow water/air heat exchanger W2. Cold air from the environment (temperature T_{ai}) is sucked in by the fan. After passing the heat exchanger and the fan, the air is blown out back to the environment. The water temperature T_{wo} is to be controlled by manipulating the fan speed S_f. As well as depending on the manipulated variable S_f, the control variable T_{wo} also depends on the measurable disturbances: inlet temperature T_{wi} air temperature T_{ai}, and water flow rate F_w. The last of these is regulated by a PI-controlled pneumatic valve and it strongly influences the static behavior of the heat exchanger W2, as can be seen from the static mapping in Figure 2 ($T'_{wi} = 45\,°\text{C}$, $T_{ai} = 5\,°\text{C}$). It is a major challenge to design a temperature controller for T_{wo} when the flow rates vary in a wide range. Figure 3 shows the gain $K_{sf} = \Delta T_{wo}/\Delta S_f$ versus the fan speed S depending on the flow rate F_w, which changes by a factor of about 4 ($T'_{wi} = 45\,°\text{C}$, $T_{ai} = 5\,°\text{C}$). Moreover, different water flow rates induce varying time constants (see Figure 4) and varying dead times between T_{wi} and T_{wo}.

The signal processing is performed on a P-133 PC under MATLAB®/Simulink™. A self-made Simulink block addresses an AD/DA converter board and the predictive controller is implemented as a C-coded S-function.

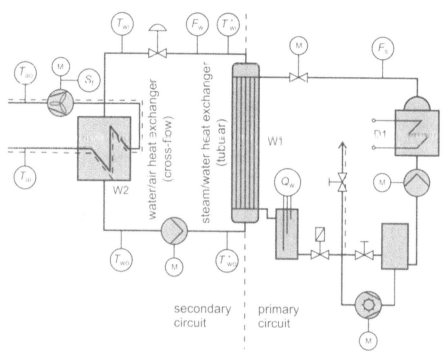

FIGURE 1
Scheme of the thermal pilot plant.

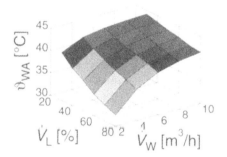

FIGURE 2
Static mapping, $T_{wi} = 45°C$, $T_{ai} = 8°C$.

3 MODELING AND IDENTIFICATION

Figure 5 gives an overview of different categories of modeling and the respective types of models. In theoretical modeling, first principles are utilized to establish a system of algebraic and differential equations. Owing to their transparency, the resulting process description is called a *white-box* model. All parameters possess a physical meaning and are known a priori. In contrast, in the case of experimental modeling, only a model class is assumed. Both structure and parameters are determined from measurement data. Since the structure and the parameters cannot be interpreted physically, this strategy is referred to as *black-box* modeling. So-called *grey-box* models represent a compromise between white-box and black-box models [37]. They

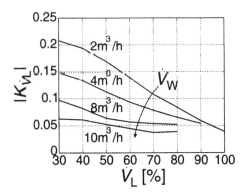

FIGURE 3
Static gain $K_{Sf} = \Delta T_{wo}/\Delta S_f$, $T_{wi} = 45°C$, $T_{ai} = 8°C$.

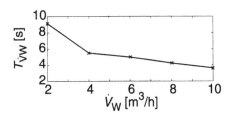

FIGURE 4
Major time constant of the transfer function T_{wo}/S_f, $T_{wi} = 45°C$, $T_{ai} = 8°C$, $S_f = 50\%$.

are based on information gathered from both first principles and measurement data. Furthermore, Figure 5 distinguishes between *light-grey-box* and *dark grey-box* models depending on the availability of structural knowledge. Fuzzy models belong to the latter model category because they are capable of integrating different information sources. In the following, Takagi–Sugeno type fuzzy models are used that are equivalent to a local linear modeling

3.1 Approaches to Fuzzy Modeling

The application of fuzzy models for modeling nonlinear dynamic systems is described. A large class of single-input–single-output nonlinear dynamic processes with measurable disturbances can be described in the discrete-time domain by (see [21])

$$y(k) = f(\phi(k)) \tag{1}$$

where the regression vector

$$\phi(k) = [u(k - d - 1)\ldots u(k - d_1 - nu)\, n_1(k - d - 1)\ldots n_1(k - d_1 - nn_1)\ldots$$

$$n_m(k - d_m - 1)\ldots n_m(k - d_m - nn_m)\, y(k - 1)\ldots y(k - ny)]^T \tag{2}$$

is composed out of previous process inputs u, previous process outputs y, and m measurable disturbances $n_i(i = 1, \ldots, m)$. The dead times of the input and the disturbances are denoted by d and d_i, respectively. nu, nn and ny are the dynamic orders of u, n, and y. The restriction to single-

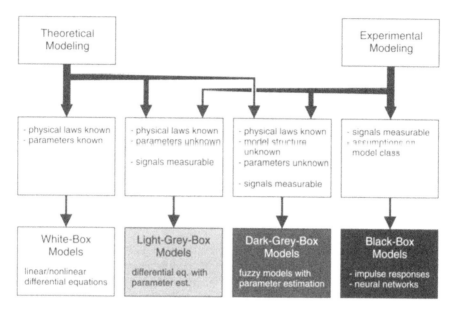

FIGURE 5
Classification of modeling approaches.

input–single-output systems in (1) and (2) is made with respect to the application. An extension to multivariable systems is straightforward.

Throughout this chapter, the unknown function $f(\cdot)$ is approximated by a Takagi–Sugeno fuzzy model that is characterized by rule consequents that are linear functions of the input variables [4, 38]. The rule base comprises M rules of the form

$$R_j: \quad \text{IF } z_1 \text{ is } A_{j,1} \text{ AND } z_2 \text{ is } A_{j,2} \text{ AND } \ldots \text{ AND } z_{nz} \text{ is } A_{j,nz}$$

$$\text{THEN } y_j(k) = w_{j,0} + w_{j,1}x_1 + \cdots + w_{j,nx}x_{nx}, \quad j = 1, \ldots, M \tag{3}$$

where $A_{j,i}$ are fuzzy sets defined on the universe of discourse of input i. Both the nz dimensional vector $z(k) = [z_1 \, z_2 \ldots z_{nz}]^T$ in the rule premise and the nx-dimensional vector $x(k) = [x_1 \, x_2 \ldots x_{nx}]^T$ in the consequent contain subsets of the elements of $\phi(k)$. The rule consequents represent linear difference equations that are linear in the parameters $w_{j,i}$. The additional constants $w_{j,0}$ define the operating points.

Choosing the product-operator for the t-norm, the output of the fuzzy system with M rules is aggregated as

$$y(k) = \sum_{j=1}^{M} (w_{j,0} + w_{j,1}x_1 + \cdots + w_{j,n}x_{nx}) \cdot \Phi_j(z, c_j, \sigma_j) \tag{4}$$

where Φ_j denote the normalized validity functions

$$\Phi_j(z, c_j, \sigma_j) = \frac{\mu_j}{\sum\limits_{i=1}^{M} \mu_i} \tag{5}$$

The membership functions μ_i are chosen as Gaussians with centers c_j and standard deviations σ_j:

$$\mu_i = \exp\left(-\frac{1}{2}\frac{(z_1 - c_{i,1})^2}{\sigma_{i,1}^2}\right) \cdot \ldots \cdot \exp\left(\frac{1}{2}\frac{(z_{nz} - c_{i,nz})^2}{\sigma_{i,nz}^2}\right) \tag{6}$$

Murray-Smith refers to this type of model as local model network interpolating local linear models by overlapping local basis functions [25]. The equivalence of generalized radial basis function networks (RBF) and Takagi–Sugeno models was proven by Hunt et al. [12]. Subsequent normalized radial basis function networks [23] are a special case of the proposed fuzzy system if the linear coefficients are set to $w_{j,i} = 0$ for $i \neq 0$ [20].

The task of fuzzy modeling is to determine the regressors x and z, the rule base as well as the premise and consequent parameters. In addition to pure data-driven or knowledge-based modeling, an integration of both information sources is also possible.

3.1.1 Data-driven Modeling.

Fuzzy model identification algorithms can determine both the linear parameters $w_{j,i}$ in the rule consequents and the nonlinear consequents and the nonlinear parameters c_j and σ_j in the rule premises. While the parameters $w_{j,i}$ are estimated by means of linear regression, the nonlinear parameters can be identified by fuzzy clustering [1], tree construction algorithms [16, 26, 32] or other neurofuzzy approaches [15].

The linear regression for estimation of the $w_{j,i}$ can be carried out globally or locally. As demonstrated by Murray-Smith [25], the local estimation approach offers some important advantages in computational complexity, robustness against noise, and interpretability. When the premise structure has been determined, M linear optimization problems are solved separately. The nonweighted output of the jth rule can be written as

$$y_j = \boldsymbol{\psi}_j^T \cdot \boldsymbol{w}_j \tag{7}$$

with parameter and regression vectors

$$\boldsymbol{w}_j = [w_{j,0} \ w_{j,1} \ w_{j,2} \ldots w_{j,nx}]^T, \tag{8}$$

$$\boldsymbol{\psi}_j = [\psi_1 \ \psi_2 \psi_3 \ldots \psi_{nx+1}]^T = [1 \ x_1 \ x_2 \ldots x_{nx}]^T \tag{9}$$

Consequently, the parameters $\boldsymbol{w}_j$ are computed from N data samples as

$$\boldsymbol{w}_j = (\boldsymbol{\Psi}_j^T \boldsymbol{Q}_j \boldsymbol{\Psi}_j)^{-1} \boldsymbol{\Psi}_j^T \boldsymbol{Q}_j \boldsymbol{y}_d \tag{10}$$

where $\boldsymbol{y}_d = [y_d(1) \ y_d(2) \ldots y_d(N)]^T$ is the vector of desired model outputs and $\boldsymbol{\Psi} = [\boldsymbol{\psi}_j(1) \ \boldsymbol{\psi}_j(2) \ldots \boldsymbol{\psi}_j(N)]^T$ is the regression matrix. The weighting matrix $\boldsymbol{Q}_j = \text{diag}(\Phi_j(z(1), c_j, \sigma_j), \Phi_j(z(2), c_j, \sigma_j), \ldots, \Phi_j(z(N), c_j, \sigma_j))$ contains the values of the validity function. Data samples located close to the center of the respective validity function have a higher influence on the parameter estimates than data points that are far away in the input space. Hence, in contrast to the global model estimation, it can be guaranteed that the local models represent the local behavior of the nonlinear system and that they do not suffer from compensation effects. One should notice that the overlap of the local models is neglected by this estimation scheme, which might degrade the model's accuracy if the standard deviations of the Gaussian membership functions are chosen too large. The local parameter estimation can be seen as a special form of regularization [25].

3.1.2 Knowledge-based Modeling.

In this section, different information sources and a suitable procedure for fuzzy model construction are presented.

(a) Information Sources. Basically, one can distinguish between the three following information sources:

- *Expert knowledge:* Fundamental knowledge about the process behavior and experiences of operators can be exploited to describe the process characteristics qualitatively. This can be formulated effectively as if–then fuzzy rules.
- *Theoretical modeling*: First principles are utilized to establish a set of balance equations for storage of mass, energy, and momentum; constitutive equations for sources transformators, and converters; and phenomenological equations for irreversible processes such as dissipative elements or sinks. Such a complete theoretical modeling is typically time-consuming and expensive. Moreover, it is only possible for processes of small or moderate complexity. Nevertheless, a rough theoretical analysis may yield important structural information that can be exploited for the construction of fuzzy models. For example, knowledge about the model inputs or the static behavior can be gained.
- *Prior experiments*: Simple experiments can provide information about the process characteristics. Step responses at different operating points allow evaluation of the nonlinearity, gains, and time constants.

Usually, some of the knowledge described above is available in practice. Theoretical modeling is typically performed in the design stage of a process. In the start-up stage, the process is put into operation with the help of simple experiments. During operation, the users gather experience with the process that can be used to further build the model.

(b) Fuzzy-model Construction. The structure and parameter determination for a Takagi–Sugeno fuzzy model can be split into the following three parts:

- *Determination of model inputs*: First, the relevant physical model inputs u_i and disturbances n_i have to be deduced with the help of a basic understanding of the process or by theoretical modeling. Second, the elements of the regression vector ϕ must be determined. The number of energy-storing elements obtained by theoretical modeling yields the dynamic order of the process. The dead times can be concluded from the physical quantities characterizing transport mechanisms.
- *Determination of rule premises*: The premise vector z should contain those regressors from ϕ that influence the nonlinear characteristics of the process. This information can be derived either from theoretical modeling or from prior experiments. Next, the premise structure, that is the partitioning of the input space, has to be selected. Here, the linguistic formulation of if–then rules is especially suitable for capturing expert knowledge. The parameters of the fuzzy sets are harder to choose because this requires quantitative considerations. Because the premises define operating regimes in which the process is approximately linear, theoretical modeling and prior knowledge can be employed.
- *Determination of rule consequents*: The consequent vector x can be specified at least partially according to theoretical modeling. Alternatively, simple step response experiments reveal the dynamic properties of the process, so that the dynamic orders and dead times of the local linear models can be defined individually. Next, rule consequent parameters can be interpreted as the numerator and denominator coefficients of a linear transfer function in the z-domain. If gains, time constants, and damping factors can be obtained from step response experiments, these continuous-time quantities can be mapped to the z-domain coefficients. Finally, the offset parameters can be concluded from the static characteristics of the process, which often can either be measured or be taken from the literature.

3.1.3 Integration of Various Information Sources. A major advantage of fuzzy models is the integration of knowledge-based and data-driven modeling because in this way a maximum amount of information can be utilized. The two approaches for modeling can be combined in three different ways as illustrated in Figure 6.

- *Parameter dependent*: As discussed in section 3.1.2(b), the model inputs and the rule premises can be reasonably determined from process knowledge, while the rule consequent parameters should be estimated from measurement data. This can be efficiently done with linear regression techniques as pointed out in section 3.1.1.
- *Operating point dependent*: When either process knowledge or data are available for distinct operating regimes, they can be modeled separately and merged into one overall model afterward. This approach is helpful in coping with process conditions in which measurements are not possible owing to safety restrictions but in which theoretical or qualitative modeling can be applied.
- *Knowledge-based initialization with subsequent data-driven fine-tuning*: Process knowledge is used to roughly specify the initial model structure and parameters; subsequently, the complete model is optimized by the means of measurement data. To preserve the prior knowledge, regularization techniques or parameter constraints are applied during the optimization phase [17, 22].

3.2 Fuzzy Modeling of a heat Exchanger

This section presents an integrated approach for modeling and identification of the heat exchanger introduced in Section 2.

3.2.1 Knowledge Acquisition. In the following, different information sources are discussed that can be utilized for modeling and identification of the heat exchanger.

(a) Expert Knowledge. From the description of the thermal plant in section 2 the model inputs fan speed S_f, water flow rate F_w, water inlet temperature T_{wi}, air inlet temperature T_{ai}, and the

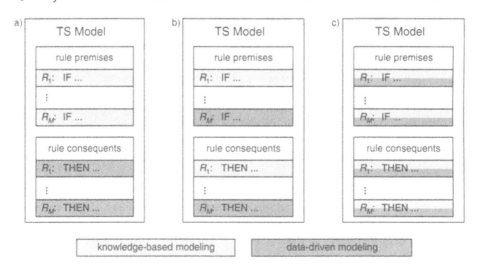

FIGURE 6
Integration of knowledge-based and data-driven modeling: (a) parameter dependent, (b) operating point dependent, (c) knowledge-based initialization with subsequent data-driven fine-tuning.

model output water outlet temperature T_{wo} are known. The transfer behavior between these four inputs and the output can be qualitatively described even by nonexperts with the following four simple rules (see Figure 7):

$$\text{IF } S_f \text{ grows THEN } T_{wo} \text{ decreases} \Rightarrow \text{negative gain}$$

$$\text{IF } F_w \text{ grows THEN } T_{wo} \text{ increases} \Rightarrow \text{positive gain}$$

$$\text{IF } T_{wi} \text{ grows THEN } T_{wo} \text{ increases} \Rightarrow \text{positive gain}$$

$$\text{IF } T_{ai} \text{ grows THEN } T_{wo} \text{ increases} \Rightarrow \text{positive gain}$$

(b) Theoretical Modeling. A *dynamic* model of the heat exchanger is difficult to derive by theoretical modeling since the underlying physical effects are quite complex and a huge number of physical parameters e.g., heat transfer coefficients, are unknown. Consequently, here only a *static* model will be built, based on the catalogued standard models in the "VDI-Wärmeatlas" [35]. Thus, the effort of static theoretical modeling is minimized: first, the structure of the nonlinearity is looked up; then, its effective parameters are estimated from steady-state measurements.

According to "VDI-Wärmeatlas" [35], the static nonlinearity of any heat exchanger can be described by

$$T_{wo} = T_{wi} + \Phi_w(\cdot) \cdot (T_{ai} - T_{wi}) \tag{11}$$

where

$$\Phi_w = f(S_f, F_w, k, A, c_{p,a}, c_{p,w}, \rho_a, \rho_w) \tag{12}$$

is a function that depends on the flow rates, the spatially averaged heat transfer coefficient k, the exchange surface A, the two constant-pressure specific heat capacities c_p, and the densities ρ. In addition to the flow rates, the function $\Phi_w(\cdot)$ depends on only five effective parameters because some physical parameters enter (12) as ratios rather than directly. The identification of these parameters is illustrated in Figure 8. Data points (+) from the gray-shaded area are taken for estimation. As Figure 8 shows, the static model exhibits excellent extrapolation properties because the structure of the nonlinearity is provided by (11) and (12).

Additionally to the static nonlinear process characteristics, the dead times between T_{wi} and T_{wo}, which are caused by the water flow, can easily be deduced from theoretical considerations:

$$t_d(F_w) = \frac{lA_T}{F_w} \tag{13}$$

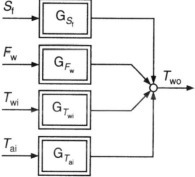

FIGURE 7
Transfer behavior of the heat exchanger.

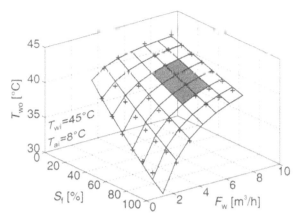

FIGURE 8
Static mapping: measurements (+) and output of the physical model.

where l is the length of the tube between the temperature sensors for T_{wi} and T_{wo} and A_T is the cross-section of the pipe.

(c) Knowledge from Prior Experiments. Simple experiments like the recording of step responses show the principal behavior of the heat exchanger. First-order time-lag models are sufficient to describe the dynamics of the function G_{S_f} (cf. Figure 7). Characteristic quantities such as gains and dominant time constants can be extracted from the step responses. Figure 3 and 4, respectively, show their operating point dependency. The dead time of G_{S_f} decreases with increasing water flow rate F_w and its minimum value is $t_d = 5$ s.

(d) Generation of Identification Data. Figure 9 shows the identification data. Their design takes the following aspects into account in order to gain a maximum amount of information from a given number of data samples [9]:

- *Purpose of modeling*: The model of the heat exchanger will be used for predictive control. Since the performance of the controller is determined by the model accuracy to a great extent, a relatively large effort in the design of the signal can be justified.
- *Maximum length of the training data set*: In order to obtain a reasonably sized data set, the maximum measurement time is restricted to 6000 samples. This is equivalent to a time of 100 min at a sample time of $T_0 = 1$ s.
- *Characteristics of different input signals*: The fan speed S_f is the manipulated variable. Since highly dynamic control behavior is desired, dynamic excitation is also needed for identification. The remaining input variables are interpreted as measurable disturbances. The water inlet temperature T_{wi} is assumed to be nearly constant because it is controlled by the steam flow in the primary circuit. The water flow rate F_w changes slowly. Hence, quasi-static excitation is sufficient. The environmental temperature T_{ai} cannot be manipulated. It is subject to slow changes depending on season, weather, and time.
- *Range of input signals*: The following signal ranges are used: $S_f = 20\text{--}100\%$, $T_{wi} = 45 \pm 2\,°C$ (control accuracy of the primary loop), $F_w = 2\text{--}10\,\text{m}^3/\text{h}$.
- *Equal data distribution*: To capture the process behavior equally in all operating regimes, a balanced data distribution at the process output is required. The static mapping from Figure 8 is utilized for this purpose. Roughly speaking, the relationship between the water outlet temperature T_{wo} and the flow rate F_w is hyperbolic ($T_{wo} \sim 1/F_w$) with large gain at small

flows. Therefore, equally distributed output data should be obtained for the input signal shown in Figure 9. The slope of the ramp increases with increasing flow rate. The same idea will be pursued for generation of the speed signal S_f, which is described in the next paragraph. The data distribution in Figure 9 is also advantageous with respect to the fuzzy modeling in the next section. The strong nonlinearity at low flow rates can only be properly approximated by a relatively high number of local linear models. Hence, a high data density is required at low flow rates.

- *Dynamic properties*: For different amplitude ranges of the flow rate F_w (see Figure 9), an individual dynamic excitation for the control variable S_f must be designed. This becomes clear from Figure 4, which shows that the dominant time constant of the transfer behavior from S_f to T_{wo} decreases with increasing F_w. There is only a weak dependency of the time constant on S_f, which need not to be considered.

3.2.2 Modeling and Identification.
The fuzzy modeling is carried out with regard to section 3.1.3. The information from the previous section is utilized by following the parameter-dependent integration strategy.

- *Model inputs*: In comparison to Figure 7, only the fan speed S_f, water flow rate F_w, water inlet temperature T_{wi} are used as model inputs. The fan speed $u = S_f$ is the manipulated variable, while $n_1 = F_w$ and $n_2 = T_{wi}$ are modeled disturbances. The air inlet temperature T_{ai} cannot be excited and thus acts as a measurable, nonmodeled disturbance.
- *Rule premises*: The theoretical modeling in section 3.2.1(b) has shown that the nonlinearity of the process depends on both flow rates. This behavior can be described by the following premise input vector:

$$z(k) = [S_f(k-5)F_w(k-1)]^T \tag{14}$$

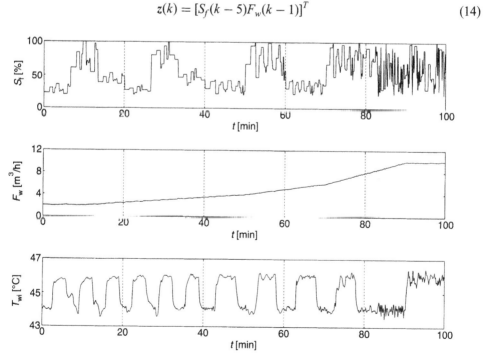

FIGURE 9
Excitation signals.

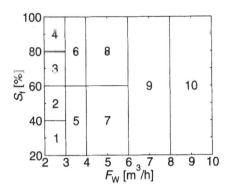

FIGURE 10
Approximately linear operating regimes.

The delay $d = 5$ is the minimum dead time of S_f. Strictly speaking, $z(k)$ must also include the larger dead times. However, they can be neglected in the rule premises without a significant loss in model quality. The static nonlinearity in Figure 8 suggests the premise structure shown in Figure 10, which possesses many local linear models in regions of strongly nonlinear behavior. This premise input space partitioning corresponds to the membership functions depicted in Figure 11 and to the following rule premises:

$$R_1: \quad \text{IF } F_w(k-1) \text{ VS AND } S_f(k-5) \text{ S}^-$$
$$R_2: \quad \text{IF } F_w(k-1) \text{ VS AND } S_f(k-5) \text{ S}^+$$
$$R_3: \quad \text{IF } F_w(k-1) \text{ VS AND } S_f(k-5) \text{ L}^+$$
$$R_4: \quad \text{IF } F_w(k-1) \text{ VS AND } S_f(k-5) \text{ LS}^+$$
$$R_5: \quad \text{IF } F_w(k-1) \text{ S} \quad \text{AND } S_f(k-5) \text{ S}$$
$$R_6: \quad \text{IF } F_w(k-1) \text{ S} \quad \text{AND } S_f(k-5) \text{ L}$$
$$R_7: \quad \text{IF } F_w(k-1) \text{ M} \quad \text{AND } S_f(k-5) \text{ S}$$
$$R_8: \quad \text{IF } F_w(k-1) \text{ M} \quad \text{AND } S_f(k-5) \text{ L}$$
$$R_9: \quad \text{IF } F_w(k-1) \text{ L} \quad \text{AND } S_f(k-5) \text{ DC}$$
$$R_{10}: \quad \text{IF } F_w(k-1) \text{ VL AND } S_f(k-5) \text{ DC}$$

- *Rule consequents*: The following regressors are chosen for the consequent input vector:

$$x(k) = [S_f(k-5) \ S_f(k-7) \ldots S_f(k-17) \ F_w(k-1) \ T_{wi}(k-4)$$
$$T_{wi}(k-5) \ldots T_{wi}(k-14) \ T_{wo}(k-1)]^T \tag{15}$$

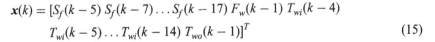

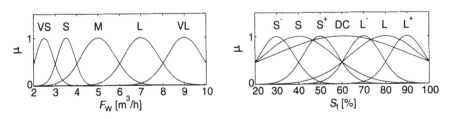

FIGURE 11
Membership functions for the premise inputs S_f and F_w.

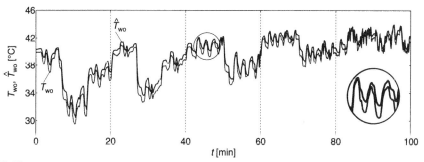

FIGURE 12
Fuzzy model validation (F_w, see Figure 9; $T_{wi} = 45°C$; $T_{ai} = 7°C$).

Since first-order dynamics are to be modeled, it is sufficient to include the previous model output $T_{wo}(k-1)$ in x. The dead time in the transfer function $G_{T_{wi}}$ varies from $d = 4$ to 14 s. Only two of these regressors are supplied to each local linear model, depending on the water flow rate F_w in the operating range of the corresponding rule. If, for example, according to (13), a dead time of $d = 6.8$ s is calculated, the regressors $T_{wi}(k-6)$ and $T_{wi}(k-7)$ are chosen. The water flow rate F_w influences the output directly without any delay. Because the dead time of G_{S_f} cannot be determined explicitly, x is provided with several delayed inputs S_f. Thus, the model's flexibility is increased since the moving-average filter in the numerator of G_{S_f} can compensate for the deficiencies of the simplified first-order time-lag approach. The resulting high model accuracy with regard to the transfer function G_{S_f} allows a good control performance. Finally, the parameters of the local linear models in the rule consequents are locally estimated from the identification shown in Figure 9.

Figure 12 shows the model performance on validation data. For this purpose, the model output is simulated in parallel configuration. While the model dynamics fit the process dynamics quite well, the statics reveal larger deviations. The latter effect is caused by a change of the air temperature T_{ai} that is three degrees lower than in the identification experiment. The next section proposes a knowledge-based adaptation strategy as a remedy for the shortcomings of the model.

4 KNOWLEDGE-BASED ADAPTATION

In Fischer et al. [10] a data-driven approach to fuzzy model adaptation is presented for the heat exchanger. It is based on a local recursive least-squares on-line identification of the rule consequent parameters keeping the premises fixed. The advantage of this method is its applicability to a great variety of processes. On the other hand, this technique suffers from the following two drawbacks. The time required for convergence of the estimation of tracking of changing process behavior causes a temporary plant–model mismatch. Moreover, persistent excitation must be guaranteed in order to avoid divergence of the parameter estimates. Since the latter demand usually cannot be met in practice, a supervisory level has to be established. Its task is to make the on-line adaptation more robust, e.g., by introducing excitation-controlled variable forgetting factors.

Another feature of the data-driven identification is to select a subset of parameters to be updated. Instead of adapting all parameters, only those are chosen for whose estimation the data contains enough information. For example, if the process operates in steady-state, the parameters related to the related to the plant's dynamics cannot be estimated. However, the offset parameters

$w_{j,0}$ can still be updated to adjust the operating points of the local models. Such a simple offset adaptation does not require supervision and can be implemented with little computational effort.

The adaptation of all parameters is very complex and the adaptation of the offsets cannot cope with changing process gains and dynamics. These drawbacks can be overcome by a knowledge-based adaptation that utilized prior knowledge. The basic idea is illustrated in Figure 13. The measurable but nonmodeled disturbances $\tilde{n}$ are used for scheduling parameters of the fuzzy model.

Here, the air temperature T_{ai} is used as the scheduling variable. Based on the static theoretical model in (11) the following derivation yields the gains of all transfer functions (cf. Figure 7):

$$K_{S_f} = \frac{\partial T_{wo}}{\partial S_f} = (T_{ai} - T_{wi}) \cdot \frac{\partial \phi(\cdot)}{\partial S_f}, \qquad K_{F_w} = \frac{\partial T_{wo}}{\partial F_w} = (T_{ai} - T_{wi}) \cdot \frac{\partial \phi(\cdot)}{\partial F_w}$$

$$K_{T_{wi}} = \frac{\partial T_{wo}}{\partial T_{wi}} = 1 - \phi(\cdot), \qquad K_{T_{ai}} = \frac{\partial T_{wo}}{\partial T_{ai}} = \phi(\cdot) \tag{16}$$

Thus, only the local transfer functions G_{S_f} and G_{F_w} are influenced by T_{ai}. This dependency can be incorporated into the model by adapting the numerator coefficients $b_{j,l}$ of the respective local transfer functions:

$$b_{j,l}^{(S_f)} = \frac{T_{ai} - T_{wi}}{T_{ai}^{(0)} - T_{wi}^{(0)}} \cdot b_{j,l}^{(S_f,0)}, \qquad b_{j,l}^{(F_w)} = \frac{T_{ai} - T_{wi}}{T_{ai}^{(0)} - T_{wi}^{(0)}} \cdot b_{j,l}^{(F_w,0)} \tag{17}$$

The parameters are proportional to the difference of the inlet temperatures, while the upper index '0' denotes the quantities from the original identification experiment.

There are two major advantages of this idea in comparison to data-driven identification. The convergence time of the parameters and the gains, respectively, tend to zero and the method does not require any excitation of the system. Moreover, the calculation of the new parameters requires only little computational effort.

Since the adapted model gains influence the static behavior of the fuzzy model, the offset parameters $w_{j,0}$ must also be updated. Here, the approach of data-driven adaptation is pursued because only one parameter per local model is to be adapted. As mentioned above, in this case there is no risk of diverging parameters even if persistent excitation cannot be guaranteed. In analogy to (7)–(10), a *local* recursive least-squares estimator (RLS) is implemented for the experiments [14].

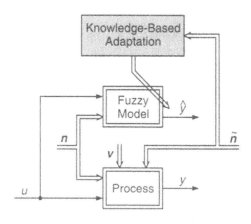

FIGURE 13
Knowledge-based adaptation.

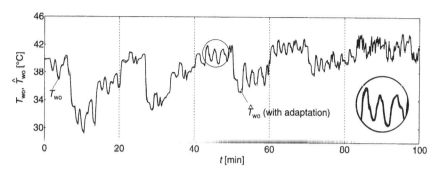

FIGURE 14
Fuzz model validation with knowledge-based adaptation (F_w see Figure 9; $T_{wi} = 45°C$; $T_{ai} = 7°C$).

In Figure 14, the validation experiment from Figure 12 is repeated with the knowledge-based adaptation of the gains and the data-driven adaptation of the offset parameters. The model accuracy has been significantly improved. The magnified excerpt shows that both the gains and the operating points of the model match the process characteristics very well. Thus, a high control performance can be expected for the predictive controller presented in the next section.

5   CONTROL

In this section, a nonlinear predictive control scheme for temperature control of the heat exchanger is introduced that utilizes the fuzzy model presented and its knowledge-based adaptation. In general, predictive controllers can operate with any kind of process model, and the control performance depends strongly on the model accuracy. Thus, powerful modeling tools, such as fuzzy models or neural networks, open new fields for the application of predictive control [3, 12, 34].

5.1   Nonlinear Predictive Control

The local linear fuzzy model and the knowledge-based adaptation strategy described in the previous sections can be used in combination with any kind of fuzzy model-based controller. Here, the adaptive nonlinear model predictive controller (ANMPC) depicted in Figure 15 is utilized. A SISO (single-input–single-output) process with the manipulated variable u, m measurable disturbances $n = [n_1 \ldots n_m]^T$, an arbitrary number of unmeasurable disturbances v, and system output y is considered.

The optimizer determines the new actuation signal $u(k) = u(k-1) + \Delta u(k)$. At the current time instant k, the sequence of N_u future accuation increments $\Delta u(k+j)$ is obtained by minimization of the quadratic cost function

$$J = \sum_{j=N_1}^{N_2} (\hat{y}(k+j) - r(k+j))^2 + \beta(k) \sum_{j=0}^{N_u-1} (\Delta u(k+j))^2 \qquad (18)$$

N_1 and N_2 denote minimum and maximum prediction horizons, and $\beta(k)$ is the penalty factor for future changes of the manipulated variable $\Delta u(k+j)$. The first sum in (18) penalizes the control error, which is calculated as the difference between the predicted process outputs $\hat{y}(k+j)$ and the reference values $r(k+j)$ taken from the reference vector $r = [r(k+N_1) \ldots r(k+N_2)]^T$. If the reference signal is not known in advance, r is assumed to keep its current value over the

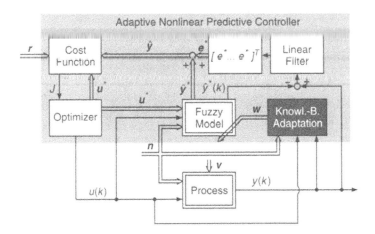

FIGURE 15
Fuzzy model-based nonlinear predictive controller with knowledge-based on-line adaptation.

complete prediction horizon, i.e., $r(k + j) = r(k)$. The fuzzy process model is used for calculating the predicted values $\hat{y}(k + j)$, process model is utilized. The prediction vector $\hat{y}^* = [\hat{y}^*(k + N_1) \ldots \hat{y}^*(k + N_2)]^T$ is generated from the inference equation (4) with the regression vector (2) rewritten as

$$\phi(k) = [u(k - d - 1) \ldots u(k - d - nu) \, n_1(k - d_1 - 1) \ldots$$

$$n_m(k - d_m - nn_m) \, \hat{y}^*(k - 1) \ldots \hat{y}^*(k - ny)]^T \qquad (19)$$

Previously simulated values $\hat{y}^*$ are fed back in what is called a parallel model configuration. In contrast, when the measured outputs y are used in the predictor, this is called series–parallel mode. For future time instants, the actuation signals $u^* = [u^*(k) \ldots u^*(k + N_u - 1)]^T$ derived by the optimizer are substituted in the regression vector and the measurable disturbances are assumed to keep their current values $n(k + j) = n(k)$.

The standard formulation of the cost function is extended by the time-dependent penalty factor $\beta(k)$, see equation (18). While for linear processes a constant $\beta(k) = \beta_0$ is usually sufficient, for nonlinear processes the changing process gain must be taken into consideration. In operating points of relatively low process gain, larger changes in the actuation signal can be accepted. In contrast, aggressive control actions are not desirable in regimes of high gains [13]. Accordingly, the following equation is recommended for nonlinear processes:

$$\beta(k) = K_p^2(k) \cdot \beta_0 \qquad (20)$$

The current process gain $K_p(k)$ can be determined by dynamic linearization of the fuzzy model [7].

For linear processes without any imposed constraints, the optimization problem can be solved analytically because then the cost function J depends linearly on the actuation increments Δu (see e.g. [30]). If nonlinear process models are utilized or nonlinear constraints on any of the variables are to be considered, nonlinear optimization routines must be applied, for example, search algorithms or gradient-based techniques. Here, a combination of a one-dimensional grid search, a subsequent Hooke–Jeeves search, and an optimization with Newton's method is used [27].

The unmeasurable disturbances v effect only the real process and cause a plant/model mismatch that cannot be avoided by the knowledge-based adaptation, which considers only measurable disturbances. Because of the deviations between plant and model output signals, the prediction vector $\hat{y}^*$ should not be used directly for the calculation of the cost function. Instead, a feedback component is added to the predictive controller. The current model error

$$e(k) = y(k) - \hat{y}^*(k) \tag{21}$$

is calculated, low-pass filtered with a linear filter $F(q^{-1})$ and used for the correction of the simulated outputs $\hat{y}^*$:

$$\hat{y}(k+j) = \hat{y}^*(k+j) + F(q^{-1})e(k) = \hat{y}^*(k+j) + e^*(k) \quad j = N_1, \ldots, N_2 \tag{22}$$

The most obvious improvement is the cancelation of steady-state control errors in the case of offset errors in the fuzzy model. The linear filter suppresses measurement noise and it can be heuristically tuned to ensure stability of the feedback loop. This feedback structure is equivalent to the well-known internal model control (IMC); see, e.g., Morari and Zafiriou [24].

5.2 Control of the Heat Exchanger

The nonlinear predictive controller from the previous section as well as the fuzzy model, together with the knowledge-based adaptation, are applied to temperature control of the cross-flow heat exchanger. The values of the fixed parameters N_u, N_1, and N_2 are given in Table 1. The penalty factor $\beta(k)$ for changes of the manipulated variable is chosen as proposed in equation (20). For optimization, only grid search and Hooke–Jeeves search are performed. Since the offset parameters of the local models are numerically updated on the basis of measurement data, the feedback for the correction of the prediction in (22) can be omitted.

Figure 16 shows a representative control experiment. The water flow rate F_w covers the whole operating range and thereby causes strong nonlinear behavior of the plant. Since the adaptation capabilities will be demonstrated and the air temperature T_{ai} cannot be manipulated, the water temperature T_{wi} is increased at $t = 30$ min. Figure 17 reveals that the absolute values of the local gains, which are calculated from the physical steady-state model, increase. In order to prevent measurement disturbances and temperature oscillations from entering the model parameters, the fuzzy model is updated only if the local gains change by more than 3%. If the knowledge-based adaptation is applied, good control performance is achieved during the complete experiment (see Figure 16). Changes of the reference signal are quickly tracked, and the control variable S_f shows highly dynamic behavior. The magnified excerpt ($t = 2850$–3150 s) contains a comparison with an experiment in which the fuzzy model is not adapted to changing gains caused by temperature deviations. Without adaptation, the control variable suffers from large overshoots on reference steps. Since the model pretends a relatively low process gain, the controller acts too aggressively. Hence the necessity and the effectiveness of knowledge-based fuzzy model adaptation have been demonstrated.

Table 1 Parameters of the nonlinear predictive controller

N_1	5
N_2	25
N_u	1
β_0	1
N_{grid}	20
$N_{Hooke-Jeeves}$	30
λ	0.98

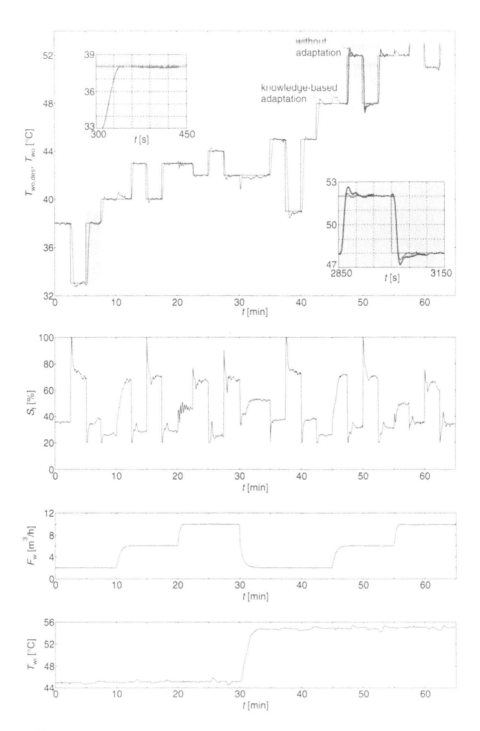

FIGURE 16
Nonlinear predictive controller with knowledge-based adaptation ($T_{ai} = 10°$C).

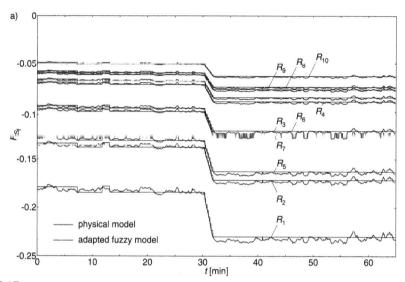

FIGURE 17
Gains of the local models with knowledge-based adaptation.

6   CONCLUSIONS

An adaptive nonlinear predictive controller for a heat exchanger based on a neurofuzzy model has been developed. The focus was on the integration of various knowledge sources in designing the model and on a suitable adaptation strategy. Takagi–Sugeno type neurofuzzy models offer some distinct advantages in this respect because they allow differentiation between the model structure in the rule premises that the operation regimes and the local linear models in the rule consequents. The premise structure can be favorably determined by theoretical modeling of the static process behavior which is typically quite simple to obtain and often can be looked up in modeling catalogs. Owing to the inherent extrapolation capabilities of first-principles models, the structure of a wide-envelope neurofuzzy model can be determined even without good coverage of the input space with data.

In contrast to the rule premise, the rule consequent parameters are advantageously estimated from data. Accordingly, good excitation training data set can be designed with the help of rough local process gains and time constants determined from simple prior experiments like step responses. Such an integration of theoretical modeling, simple prior experiments, and measurement data for the development of a neurofuzzy model is much more robust with respect to the quality of the data than is a black-box approach and much easier and less time-consuming than is complete theoretical modeling.

The knowledge-based adaptation strategy utilizes information about the influence of measurable but unmodeled disturbances on the process acquired by theoretical modeling. With this knowledge it is possible to schedule the local linear model parameters in the Takagi–Sugeno neurofuzzy model according to the disturbances. This strategy offers two major advantages compared to a data-driven adaptation by a recursive least-squares algorithm: it requires no excitation of the process, and it adjusts the model immediately, without delay.

These concepts for modeling and adaptation have been successfully applied to temperature control of a cross-flow heat exchanger with a nonlinear predictive controller. Both control performance and robustness against changing environmental temperatures were improved compared to previous results without knowledge integration. The application of these concepts is beneficial whenever neither theoretical modeling nor a black-box approach alone is feasible or yields sufficiently good results.

REFERENCES

[1] R. Babuška and H.B. Verbruggen. An overview of fuzzy modelling for control, *Control Engineering Practice*, Vol. 4, No. 11, pp. 1593–1606, 1996.

[2] S. Bittanti and L. Piroddi, Nonlinear identification and control of a heat exchanger: A neural network approach, *Journal of the Franklin Institute*, Vol. 334B, No. 1, pp. 135–153, 1997.

[3] H.A.B. Braake, R. Babuška and E.v. Can, Fuzzy and neural models in predictive control, Journal A, Vol. 35, No. 3, pp. 44–51, 1994.

[4] S.G. Cao, N.W. Rees and G. Feng, Analysis and design for a class of complex control systems, Part I: Fuzzy modelling and identification, *Automatica*, Vol. 33, No. 6, pp. 1017–1028, 1997.

[5] C.R. Cutler, B.L. Ramaker, Dynamic matrix control. A computer control algorithm, in *Proc. JACC, San Francisco*, 1980.

[6] E.-J. Ernst and O. Hecker, Predictive control of a heat exchanger, in *Theory and Applications of Model Based Predictive Control (MBPC)*, Brussels, Belgium, 1996.

[7] M. Fischer and O. Nelles, Fuzzy model-based predictive control of processes with fast dynamics, in *2nd Int. Symp. Fuzzy Logic and Applications, Zürich*, 1997, pp. 359–365.

[8] M. Fischer, O. Nelles and R. Isermann, Fuzzy model-based predictive control of a heat exchanger, in *IFAC Int. Symp. Artificial Intelligence in Real-Time Control, Kuala Lumpur*, 1997, pp. 463–468.

[9] M. Fischer, O. Nelles and R. Isermann, Exploiting prior knowledge in fuzzy model identification of a heat exchanger, in *IFAC Intl. Symp. Artificial Intelligence in Real-Time Control, Kuala Lumpur*, 1997, pp. 445–450.

[10] M. Fischer, O. Nelles and R. Isermann, Adaptive predictive control of a heat exchanger based on a fuzzy model, *Control Engineering Practice*, Vol. 6 No. 6, pp. 259–269, 1998.

[11] K.J. Hunt, R. Haas and R. Murray-Smith, Extending the functional equivalence of radial basis function networks and fuzzy inference systems, *IEEE Trans. Neural Networks*, Vol. 7, No. 3, pp. 776–781, 1996.

[12] K.J. Hunt, D. Sbarbaro, R. Zbikowski and P.J. Gawthrop, Neural networks for control systems—a survey, *Automatica*, Vol. 28, No. 6, pp. 1082–1112, 1992.

[13] R. Isermann, *Digital Control Systems*, Springer-Verlag, Berlin, 1981.

[14] R. Isermann, K.-H. Lachmann and D. Matko, *Adaptive Control Systems*, Prentice-Hall, Englewood Cliffs, NJ, 1992.

[15] J.S. R. Jang, ANFIS: Adaptive-network-based fuzzy inference system. *IEEE Trans. Systems, Man and Cybernetics*, Vol. 23, No. 3, pp. 665–685, 1993.

[16] T.A. Johansen, *Operating regime based process modeling and identification*, Ph.D. Thesis, Norwegian Institute of Technology, University of Trondheim, 1994.

[17] T.A. Johansen, Identification of non-linear systems using empirical data and prior knowledge—an optimization approach, *Automatica*, Vol. 32, No. 3, pp. S. 337–3546, 1996.

[18] T.A. Johansen and B.A. Foss, Constructing NARMAX models using ARMAX models, *Int. J. Control*, Vol. 58, No. 5, pp. 1125–1153, 1993.

[19] N.V. Joshi, P. Murugan and R.R. Rhinehart, Experimental comparison of control strategies. *Control Engineering Practice*, Vol. 5, No. 7, pp. 885–896, 1997.

[20] V. Kecman and B.-M. Pfeiffer, Exploiting the structural equivalence of learning fuzzy systems and radial basis function neural networks, in *Second European Congress on Fuzzy and Intelligent Technologies, Aachen*, 1994, pp. 58–66.

[21] I.J. Leontaritis and S.A. Billings, Input–output parametric models for nonlinear systems, Part 1: Deterministic nonlinear systems. *Int. J. Control*, Vol. 41, No. 2, pp. 303–328, 1985.

[22] P. Lindskog, *Methods, algorithms and tools for system identification based on prior knowledge*, Dissertation, Linköping University, Sweden, 1996.

[23] J. Moody and C. Darken, Fast learning in networks of locally-tuned processing units, *Neural Computation*, Vol. 1, No. 2, pp. 281–294, 1989.

[24] M. Morari and E. Zafiriou, *Robust Process Control*, Prentice-Hall, Englewood Cliffs, NJ, 1989.

[25] R. Murray-Smith, *A local model approach to nonlinear modeling*, Ph.D. Thesis, University of Strathclyde, UK, 1994.

[26] O. Nelles and R. Isermann, Basis function networks for interpolation of local linear models. *IEEE Conf. Decision and Control, Kobe*, 1996, pp. 470–475.

[27] G.V. Reklaitis, A. Ravindran and K.M. Ragsdell, *Engineering Optimization, Methods and Applications*. Wiley, Chichester, UK, 1983.

[28] J. Richalet, Industrial applications of model based predictive control, *Automatica*, Vol. 29, No. 5, pp. 1251–1274, 1993.

[29] J. Richalet, A. Rault, J.L. Testud and J. Papon, Model predictive heuristic control: applications to industrial processes, *Automatica*, Vol. 14, No. 5, pp. 413–428, 1978.

[30] R. Soeterboek, 1992, *Predictive Control—A Unified Approach*, Prentice-Hall, Englewood Cliffs, NJ, 1992.

[31] A.R. M. Soeterboek. H. B. Verbruggen and J.M. Wissing, Predictive control of nonlinear processes, in R. Devanathan (ed.), *Selected Papers from the IFAC Symposium, Singapore*, 1991.

[32] M. Sugeno and G.T. Kang, Structure identification of fuzzy model, *Fuzzy Sets and Systems*, Vol. 28, No. 1, pp. 15–33, 1988.

[33] T. Takagi and M. Sugeno, Fuzzy identification of systems and its application to modeling and control, *IEEE Trans. Systems, Man and Cybernetics*, Vol. 15, No. 1, pp. 116–132, 1985.

[34] H. Tolle and E. Ersu, *Neurocontrol*, Springer-Verlag, Heidelberg, 1992.

[35] VDI-Wärmeatlas (1994). Berechnungsblätter für den Wärmeübergang, VDI-Gesellschaft Verfahrenstechnik und Chemieingenieurwesen, VDI-Verlag, Dusseldorf, 1994.

[36] M.J. Willis, M.T. Tham, G.A. Montague and A.J. Morris, Non-linear predictive control, in R. Devanathan (ed.), *Selected Papers from the IFAC Symposium, Singapore*, 1991.

[37] H.J.A.F. Tulleken, Grey-box modelling and identification using physical knowledge and Bayesian techniques, *Automatica*, Vol. 29, No. 2, pp. 285–308, 1993.

CHAPTER 20

Neural Network Approximation of Piecewise Continuous Functions: Application to Friction Compensation

RASTKO R. ŠELMIĆ and FRANK L. LEWIS

Automation and Robotics Research Institute, The University of Texas at Arlington, Fort Worth, Texas, USA

1 INTRODUCTION

Neural nets (NNs) have been used extensively in feedback control systems [21, 24, 25, 37]. When stability proofs are provided, they rely almost invariably on the universal approximation property for NNs [8, 9, 19, 20, 30, 32–34]. However, in most real industrial control systems there are nonsmooth functions (piecewise continuous) for which approximation results in the literature are sparse [28, 29]. Examples include friction, deadzones, backlash, and so on. It is found (see subsequent example), that attempts to approximate piecewise continuous functions using smooth activation functions require many NN nodes and many training iterations, and still do not yield very good results. Sontag has shown [38] that nonlinear control systems can be stabilized using two-hidden-layer NNs, but not in general using one-layer NNs, due to the requirement for inverting discontinuous mappings in the control law.

Our main result is an approximation theorem for piecewise continuous functions or functions with jumps. It is found that, to approximate such functions suitably, it is necessary to augment the standard NN that uses smooth activation functions with extra nodes containing a certain *jump function approximation basis set* of nonsmooth activation functions. Applications of this augmented NN are given in friction compensation of industrial motion devices.

Friction is a nonlinear effect that can limit the performance of industrial control systems; it occurs in all mechanical systems and therefore is unavoidable in control systems. It can cause tracking errors, limit cycles, and other undesirable effects. In order to design accurate control systems it is necessary to analyze the model of friction and techniques for its compensation.

Friction modeling has been studied by many researchers. Models of Coulomb friction have been widely used, and there are various techniques for its compensation [5, 13, 22]. On the other hand, more general friction models given in [1, 2, 5, 6] are more accurate, but it is much harder to design compensators for them. Often, inexact friction compensation is used with standard adaptive techniques that require models that are linear in the unknown parameters [5]. A dynamic friction model is presented in [6]. Observer-based friction compensation for a dynamical friction model is given in [7, 27].

Robust adaptive friction compensation of the static friction model is given in [16], and using reinforcement adaptive learning neural networks in [15]. Identification and compensation of the static friction model using neural networks is given in [11, 39], but without any closed-loop stability proof or guarantee of bounded weights.

It is shown here how a certain class of augmented NN, capable of approximating piecewise continuous functions, can be used for friction compensation. The general friction model given in [2, 5] is used. It is not required for the model to be linear in the unknown parameters. We show how to design the friction compensator, and provide a *rigorous closed-loop system stability proof* that guarantees small tracking error and bounded NN weights.

2   BACKGROUND

Let S be a compact simply connected set of $\mathfrak{R}^n$. With map $f: S \to \mathfrak{R}^m$, define $C(S)$ as the space such that f is continuous. The space of functions whose rth derivative is continuous is dentoed by $C^r(S)$, and the space of smooth functions is $C^\infty(S)$.

By $\| \ \|$ is denoted any suitable vector norm. When it is required to be specific, we denote the p-norm by $\| \ \|_p$. The supremum norm of $f(x)$, over S, is defined as [4]

$$\sup_{x \in S} \|f(x)\|, \qquad f: S \to \mathfrak{R}^m \tag{1}$$

Given $A = [a_{ij}]$, $B \in \mathfrak{R}^{m \times n}$, the Frobenius norm is defined by

$$\|A\|_F^2 = \text{tr}(A^T A) = \sum_{i,j} a_{ij}^2 \tag{2}$$

with tr( ) the trace. The associated inner product is $\langle A, B \rangle_F = \text{tr}(A^T B)$. The Frobenius norm is compatible with the 2-norm so that $\|Ax\|_2 \leq \|A\|_F \|x\|_2$.

When $x(t) \in \mathfrak{R}^n$ is a function of time, we use the standard L_p norms. It is said that $x(t)$ is bounded if its L_∞ norm is bounded. Matrix $A(t) \in \mathfrak{R}^{m \times n}$ is bounded if its induced matrix ∞-norm is bounded.

2.1   Stability

Consider the nonlinear system

$$\dot{x} = g(x, u, t), \qquad y = h(x, t) \tag{3}$$

with state $x(t) \in \mathfrak{R}^n$. The equilibrium point x_e is said to be uniformly ultimately bounded (UUB) if there exists a compact set $S \subset \mathfrak{R}^n$, so that for all $x_0 \in S$ there exist an $\varepsilon > 0$, and a number $T(\varepsilon, x_0)$ such that $\|x(t) - x_e\| \leq \varepsilon$ for all $t \geq t_0 + T$. That is, after a transition period T, the state $x(t)$ remains within the ball of radius ε around x_e.

2.2 Robot Arm Dynamics

The dynamics of an n-link robot manipulator may be expressed in the Lagrange form [17, 35]

$$M(\dot{q})\ddot{q} + V_m(q, \dot{q})\dot{q} + G(q) + F(\dot{q}) + \tau_d = \tau \qquad (4)$$

with $q(t) \in \Re^n$ the joint variable vector, $M(q)$ the inertia matrix, $V_m(q, \dot{q})$ the coriolis/centripetal matrix, $G(q)$ the gravity vector, and $F(\dot{q})$ the friction. Bounded unknown disturbances (including unstructured, unmodeled dynamics) are denoted by τ_d and the control input torque is $\tau(t)$.

Given a desired arm trajectory $q_d(t) \in \Re^n$, the tracking error is

$$e(t) = q_d(t) - q(t) \qquad (5)$$

and the filtered tracking error is

$$r = \dot{e} + \Lambda e \qquad (6)$$

where $\Lambda = \Lambda^T > 0$ is a design parameter matrix. Differentiating $r(t)$, the arm dynamics may be written in terms of the filtered tracking error as

$$M\dot{r} = -V_m r - \tau + f + \tau_d \qquad (7)$$

where the nonlinear robot function is

$$f(x) = M(\dot{q})\ddot{q}_d + V_m(q, \dot{q})(\dot{q}_d + \Lambda e) + G(q) + F(\dot{q}) \qquad (8)$$

where

$$x \equiv [q^T \quad \dot{q}^T \quad q_d^T \quad \dot{q}_d^T \quad \ddot{q}_d^T]^T \qquad (9)$$

Functions $f(x)$ is generally unknown or incompletely known. Define a control input torque as

$$\tau_0 = \hat{f} + K_v r \qquad (10)$$

with gain matrix $K_v = K_v^T > 0$ and $\hat{f}(x)$ and estimate of $f(x)$. The closed-loop dynamics is given by

$$M\dot{r} = -(K_v + V_m)r + \tilde{f} + \tau_d \qquad (11)$$

where the functional estimation error is

$$\tilde{f} = f - \hat{f} \qquad (12)$$

Note that, according to equation (6), one has

$$\frac{e}{r} = (sI + \Lambda)^{-1}, \qquad \frac{\dot{e}}{r} = s(sI + \Lambda)^{-1} \qquad (13)$$

$$\|e\| \le \|(sI + \Lambda)^{-1}\| \|r\|, \qquad \|\dot{e}\| \le \|s(sI + \Lambda)^{-1}\| \|r\| \qquad (14)$$

Using operator gain properties, it follows that

$$\|e\| \le \frac{\|r\|}{\sigma_{\min}(\Lambda)}, \qquad \|\dot{e}\| \le \|r\| \qquad (15)$$

with $\sigma_{\min}(\Lambda)$ the minimum singular value of Λ [17, 36].

There are several properties of the robot arm dynamics [17] important in control:

Property 1. $M(q)$ is a positive definite symmetric matrix bounded by $m_1 I \le M(q) \le m_2 I$, where m_1, m_2 are known positive constants.

Property 2. $V_m(q, \dot{q})$ is bounded by $|V_m(q, \dot{q})| \leq v_b(q)\|\dot{q}\|$, with $v_b(q)$: $S \to \Re^1$ a known bound.

Property 3. The matrix $\dot{M} - 2V_m$ is skew-symmetric.

Property 4. The unknown disturbance satisfies $\|\tau_d\| < b_d$, where b_d is a known positive constant.

3 FRICTION

Friction is a nonlinear effect that can limit the performance of industrial control systems; it occurs in all mechanical systems and therefore is unavoidable in control systems. It can cause tracking errors, limit cycles, and other undesirable effects.

In order to design accurate control systems it is necessary to study models of friction and techniques for its compensation. Many researchers have studied friction modeling. Models of Coulomb friction have been widely used, and there are various techniques for its compensation [5, 13, 22]. On the other hand, more general friction models [1, 2, 5, 6] are more accurate, but it is much harder to design compensators for them. Often, inexact friction compensation is used with standard adaptive techniques that require a model linear in the unknown parameters [5]. This linearity in the parameters (LIP) requirement is a severe restriction for practical systems.

A dynamic friction model has been recently introduced [6] that models static and dynamic behavior of the friction effect. Observer-based adaptive friction compensation for a dynamical friction model is given in [7]. The observer-based controller for dynamical friction compensation is given in [27].

Robust adaptive friction compensation of the static friction model is given in [16], and using reinforcement adaptive learning neural networks in [15]. Identification and compensation of the static friction model using neural networks is given in [11, 39], but without any closed-loop stability proof of guarantee of bounded weights. We consider here the static complex friction model introduced in [5, 23]. We do not need the LIP condition. In Section 6 we show how to design the friction compensator, with *rigorous* closed-loop system stability proofs.

3.1 Friction Model

There are several ways to model friction effects. Static friction models are studied in [2]. From the simplest case to more general cases one has following models: Coulomb friction (Figure 1a}, Coulomb and viscous friction (Figure 1b), static and Coulomb and viscous friction (Figure 1c).

A detailed friction model suitable for an industrial controller design is given in [5] as

$$F(\dot{q}) = [\alpha_0 + \alpha_1 e^{-\beta_1|\dot{q}|} + \alpha_2(1 - e^{-\beta_2|\dot{q}|})]\mathrm{sgn}(\dot{q}) \qquad (16)$$

where Coulomb friction is given by α_0 [N · m], static friction is $(\alpha_0 + \alpha_1)$ [N · m], and α_2 [N · m · s/rad] represents the viscous friction model. The Stribeck effect is modeled with an exponential second term in the model (16). Figure 2 shows the dependence of the friction force on velocity.

The model given by (16) includes Coulomb friction, viscous friction, static friction, and negative viscous friction. Justification for using (16) is provided by Armstrong's experimental results [1]. A static model similar to (16) is given in [23], where dynamic effects are included as well.

One can see that model (16) is highly nonlinear and discontinuous at zero. This makes accurate friction compensation a difficult problem. Note specially that (16) is not linear in the

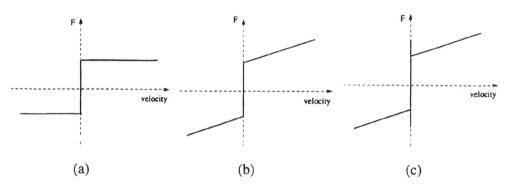

FIGURE 1
Friction models: (a) Coulomb friction model. (b) Coulomb and viscous friction model. (c) Static, Coulomb and viscous friction model.

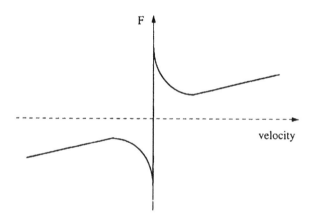

FIGURE 2
Stribeck effect; static, Coulomb and viscous friction model.

parameters, so that standard adaptive robot control approach cannot be used. In the given friction model, friction depends only on velocity. Friction can also depend on position, but this dependence is negligible [1], and is neglected here.

In the n-link robot manipulator dynamics, the friction term $F(\dot{q})$ is a function: $S \to R^n$. Since friction is a local effect, it is assumed that $F(\dot{q})$ is uncoupled among the joints, so that

$$F(\dot{q}) = [f_1(\dot{q}_1) \quad \cdots \quad f_n(\dot{q}_n)]^T \tag{17}$$

with functions f_i that represent friction terms for each joint given by (16).

4 NEURAL NETWORK APPROXIMATION OF PIECEWISE CONTINUOUS FUNCTIONS

Neural nets have been used extensively in feedback control systems. Most applications are ad hoc with no demonstrations of stability. The stability proofs that do exist rely almost invariably on the universal approximation property for NNs [8, 19, 20, 30, 32–34]. However, in most real industrial control systems there are nonsmooth functions with jumps for which approximation results in the literature are sparse [28, 29]. Examples include friction, deadzone, backlash, and so on. Although there do exists some results for piecewise continuous functions, it is found (see subsequent example) that attempts to approximate jump functions using smooth activation functions require many NN nodes and many training iterations, and still do not yield very good results.

Therefore, in this section we present our main result: an approximation theorem for piecewise continuous functions. It is found that to approximate such functions suitably, it is necessary to augment the standard NN that uses smooth activation functions with extra nodes containing a certain *jump function approximation basis set* of nonsmooth activation functions.

4.1   Background on Neural Networks

The two-layer NN in Figure 3 consists of two layers of tunable weights and has a hidden layer and an output layer. The hidden layer has L neurons, and the output layer has m neurons. The multilayer NN is a nonlinear mapping from input space $\Re^n$ into output space $\Re^m$.

The NN output y is a vector with m components that are determined in terms of the n components of the input vector x by the equation

$$y_i = \rho\left(\sum_{l-1}^{L} w_{il}\sigma\left(\sum_{j=1}^{n} v_{lj}x_j + v_{l0}\right) + w_{i0}\right), \qquad i = 1, 2, \ldots, m \tag{18}$$

where $\sigma(\cdot)$ are the hidden-layer activation functions, $\rho(\cdot)$ are the output layer activation functions, and L is the number of hidden-layer neurons. The first-layer interconnection weights are denoted v_{lj} and the second-layer interconnection weights by w_{il}. The threshold offsets are denoted by v_{l0}, w_{i0}.

By collecting all the NN weights v_{lj}, w_{il} into matrices V^T, W^T, the NN equation with linear output activation function $\rho(\cdot)$, may be written in terms of vectors as

$$y = W^T\sigma(V^Tx) \tag{19}$$

The thresholds are included as the first column of the weight matrices W^T, V^T; to accommodate this, the vector x and $\sigma(\cdot)$ need to be augmented by placing a '1' as their first element (e.g. $x = [1\, x_1\, x_2 \ldots x_n]^T$). In this equation, to represent (18) one has sufficient generality if $\sigma(\cdot)$ is

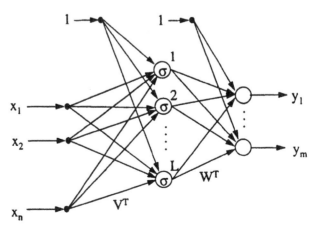

FIGURE 3
Two-layer neural net.

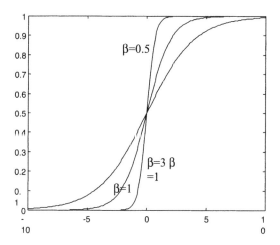

FIGURE 4
Sigmoid function for $\beta = 0.5, 1, 3$.

taken as a diagonal function from $\Re^L$ to $\Re^L$, that is, $\sigma(z) = \text{diag}\{\sigma(z_l)\}$ for a vector $z = [z_1 \ z_2 \ldots z_L]^T \in \Re^L$.

There are many different ways to choose the activation functions $\sigma(\cdot)$, including sigmoid, hyperbolic tangent, etc. Figure 4 shows the sigmoid activation function,

$$\sigma(x) = \frac{1}{1 + e^{-\beta x}} \tag{20}$$

for different parameters β.

4.2   NN Approximation of Continuous Functions

Many well-known results say that any sufficiently smooth function can be approximated arbitrarily closely on a compact set using a two-layer NN with appropriate weights [10, 12, 14]. For instance, Cybenko's result [10] for continuous function approximation says that given any function $f \in C(S)$, with S a compact subset of $\Re^n$, and any $\varepsilon > 0$, there exists a sum $G(x)$ of the form

$$G(x) \quad \sum_{k=0}^{L} \alpha_k \sigma(m_k^T x + n_k) \tag{?1}$$

for some $m_k \in \Re^n$, $n_k \in \Re$, $\alpha_k \in \Re$, such that

$$|G(x) - f(x)| < \varepsilon \tag{22}$$

for all $x \in S$. Function $\sigma(\cdot)$ could be any continuous sigmoidal function [10]. This result shows that any continuous function can be approximated arbitrarily well using a linear combination of sigmoidal functions. This is known as the NN *universal approximation property*.

4.3 NN Approximation of Jump Functions

There are few results for approximation of nonsmooth functions [28, 29]. Here are presented our main results for approximation of piecewise continuous functions or functions with jumps. It is found that to approximate such functions suitably, it is necessary to augment the set of functions $\sigma(\cdot)$ used for approximation. In addition to continuous sigmoidal functions, one requires a set of discontinuous basis functions. We propose two suitable sets: the "polynomial jump approximation functions," and the "sigmoidal jump approximation functions."

Theorem 1 (*Approximation of Piecewise Continuous Functions*). Let there be given any bounded function $f\colon S \to \Re$ that is continuous and analytic on a compact set $S \subset \Re$, except at $x = c$ where the function f has a finite jump and is continuous from the right. Then, given any $\varepsilon > 0$, there exists a sum F of the form

$$F(x) = g(x) + \sum_{k=0}^{N} a_k f_k(x - c) \tag{23}$$

such that

$$|F(x) - f(x)| < \varepsilon \tag{24}$$

for every x in S, where g is a function in $C^{\infty}(S)$, and the *polynomial jump approximation basis functions* f_k are defined as

$$f_k(x) = \begin{cases} 0, & \text{for } x < 0 \\ \dfrac{x^k}{k!}, & \text{for } x \geq 0 \end{cases} \tag{25}$$

Proof. Let f be a smooth bounded function on S, except at $x = c$, where the function has a finite discontinuity. Let g be an analytic function in $C^{\infty}(S)$, such that $f(x) = g(x)$ for all $x < c$ as shown in Figure 5.

Then for $a \geq c$ and $x \geq c$, expand f and g into Taylor series as

$$f(x) = f(a) + \frac{f'(a)}{1!}(x - a) + \frac{f''(a)}{2!}(x - a)^2 + \cdots + \frac{f^{(N)}(a)}{n!}(x - a)^N + R_f^N(x, a) \tag{26}$$

$$g(x) = g(a) + \frac{g'(a)}{1!}(x - a) + \frac{g''(a)}{2!}(x - a)^2 + \cdots + \frac{g^{(N)}(a)}{n!}(x - a)^N + R_g^N(x, a) \tag{27}$$

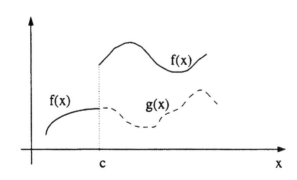

FIGURE 5
Functions f and g.

Combining these two equations yields

$$f(x) = g(x) + f(a) - g(a) + \frac{f'(a) - g'(a)}{1!}(x - a) + \frac{f''(a) - g''(a)}{2!}(x - a)^2 + \cdots$$

$$+ \frac{f^{(N)}(a) - g^{(N)}(a)}{N!}(x - a)^N + R_f^N(x, a) - R_g^N(x, a) \tag{28}$$

Letting $a \to c$, and knowing that the first N derivatives of g are continuous and that f is continuous from the right, results in

$$f(x) = g(x) + f(c) - g(c) + \frac{f'(c) - g'(c)}{1!}(x - c) + \frac{f''(c) - g''(c)}{2!}(x - c)^2 + \cdots$$

$$+ \frac{f^{(N)}(c) - g^{(N)}(c)}{N!}(x - c)^N + R_f^N(x, c) - R_g^N(x, c) \tag{29}$$

for $x \geq c$. Therefore, one has

$$f(x) = g(x) + a_0 f_0(x - c) + a_1 f_1(x - c) + \cdots + a_N f_N(x - c) + R_f^N(x, c) - R_g^N(x, c) \tag{30}$$

Since $R_f^N(x, c)$ and $R_g^N(x, c)$ go to zero as N approaches infinity, the proof is complete. ∎

Remark. We use the terminology "basis set" for (25) somewhat loosely. Note that $f_k(x - c)$ is a basis set for approximation of functions with discontinuities at a specified valueu $x = c$.

The next results follow directly from the foregoing proof.

Corollary 1. Given the hypotheses of Theorem 1, define the *jump approximation error* as $E = |F(x) - f(x)|$. Then,

$$E = R_f^N(x, c) - R_g^N(x, c) = \frac{f^{(N+1)}(d)}{(N+1)!}(x - c)^{N+1} \frac{g^{(N+1)}(d)}{(N+1)!}(x - c)^{N+1} \tag{31}$$

where d is between c and x. Therefore, the error is bounded by

$$E \leq \frac{(x - c)^{(N+1)}}{(N+1)!} \sup_d |f^{(N+1)}(d) - g^{(N+1)}(d)| \tag{32}$$

where d is between c and x.

Corollary 2. If the function f is continuous from the left, then f_k is defined as

$$f_k(x) = \begin{cases} 0, & \text{for } x \leq 0 \\ \dfrac{x^k}{k!}, & \text{for } x > 0 \end{cases} \tag{33}$$

It is desired now to replace the polynomial jump approximation basis functions f_k by another set of basis functions that are bounded. This yields a result more useful for closed-loop feedback control purposes. To accomplish this, some technical lemmas are needed.

Lemma 1

$$\sum_{i=0}^{m} \binom{m}{i} (-1)^i (-i)^k = 0 \tag{34}$$

for every $m > k$, where $\binom{m}{i}$ is defined as usual,

$$\binom{m}{i} = \frac{m!}{i!(m-i)!}$$

Proof. We will prove this expression using regressive mathematical induction.
(a) For $k = 1$ (34) is simplified to

$$\sum_{i=0}^{m}\binom{m}{i}(-1)^i(-i) = m\sum_{i=1}^{m}\binom{m-1}{i}(-1)^i(-i)$$

$$= -m\sum_{i=1}^{m}\binom{m-1}{i-1}(-1)^i$$

$$= m\sum_{j=0}^{m-1}\binom{m-1}{j}(-1)^j$$

$$= m(1-1)^{m-1} = 0 \tag{35}$$

where $j = i - 1$. Therefore, for $k = 1$ expression (34) is true.

(b) Assume expression (34) is true for some $k = p$, $k = p - 1$, $k = p - 2, \ldots, k = 1$. One needs to show that it is true for $k = p + 1$.
For $k = p + 1$,

$$\sum_{i=0}^{m}\binom{m}{i}(-1)^i(-i)^{p+1} = \sum_{i=0}^{m}\frac{m(m-1)\cdots(m-i+1)}{i!}(-1)^i(-i)^p(-i)$$

$$= -\sum_{i=0}^{m}\frac{m(m-1)\cdots(m-i+1)}{(i-1)!}(-1)^i(-i)^p \tag{36}$$

Putting $j = i - 1$ and knowing that the term for $i = 0$ is equal to zero, using binomial formula one can transform a (36) into

$$-m\sum_{j=0}^{m-1}\frac{(m-1)\cdots(m-j)}{j!}(-1)^{j-1}(-j+1)^p = m\sum_{j=0}^{m-1}\binom{m-1}{j}(-1)^j\sum_{k=0}^{p}\binom{p}{k}(-j)^k$$

$$= m\sum_{k=0}^{p}\binom{p}{k}\left[\sum_{j=0}^{m-1}\binom{m-1}{j}(-1)^j(-j)^k\right] = 0 \tag{37}$$

Expression (37) is equal to zero for every $m - 1 > k$, $k = 0, 1, \ldots, p$ because of the induction assumption. Therefore, (34) is true for $k = p + 1$.

Lemma 2. Any linear combination of polynomial jump approximation functions f_k, $\sum_{k=0}^{N} a_k f_k(x)$, can be represented as

$$\sum_{k=0}^{N} a_k f_k(x) = z(x) + \sum_{k=0}^{N} b_k \varphi_k(x) \tag{38}$$

where the φ_k (*sigmoid jump approximation functions*) are defined as

$$\varphi_k(x) = \begin{cases} 0, & \text{for } x < 0 \\ (1 - e^{-x})^k, & \text{for } x \geq 0 \end{cases} \tag{39}$$

and where $z(x)$ is a function that belongs to $C^N(S)$.

Proof. It is enough to prove that there exist coefficients b_k, such that the first N derivatives of the expression

$$\sum_{k=0}^{N} a_k f_k(x) - \sum_{k=0}^{N} b_k \varphi_k(x) \tag{40}$$

are continuous.

For $x < 0$, expression (40) has the constant value 0. Therefore, one must show that there exist coefficients b_i, such that for $x > 0$, the first N derivatives of the expression (40) are equal to zero. For $x > 0$, one has

$$z(x) = \sum_{k=0}^{N} a_k f_k(x) - \sum_{k=0}^{N} b_k \varphi_k(x) \tag{41}$$

$$= \sum_{k=0}^{N} a_k \frac{x^k}{k!} - \sum_{k=0}^{N} b_k (1 - e^{-x})^k \tag{42}$$

Using the binomial formula, one can expand expressions (42) into

$$\sum_{k=0}^{N} a_k \frac{x^k}{k!} - \sum_{k=0}^{N} b_k \left[\sum_{i=0}^{k} \binom{k}{i} (-e^{-x})^i \right] \tag{43}$$

$$= \sum_{k=0}^{N} a_k \frac{x^k}{k!} - \sum_{k=0}^{N} b_k \left[\sum_{i=0}^{k} \binom{k}{i} (-1)^i (e^{-ix}) \right] \tag{44}$$

$$= \sum_{k=0}^{N} a_k \frac{x^k}{k!} - \sum_{k=0}^{N} b_k \left[\sum_{i=0}^{k} \binom{k}{i} (-1)^i \sum_{j=0}^{\infty} \frac{(-ix)^j}{j!} \right] \tag{45}$$

$$= \sum_{k=0}^{N} a_k \frac{x^k}{k!} - \sum_{k=0}^{N} \sum_{i=0}^{k} b_k \binom{k}{i} (-1)^i \sum_{j=0}^{\infty} (-1)^j \frac{x^j}{j!} \tag{46}$$

$$= \sum_{k=0}^{N} a_k \frac{x^k}{k!} - \sum_{k=0}^{N} \sum_{i=0}^{k} \sum_{j=0}^{\infty} b_k \binom{k}{i} (-1)^i (-i)^j \frac{x^j}{j!} \tag{47}$$

$$= \sum_{k=0}^{N} a_k \frac{x^k}{k!} - \sum_{j=0}^{\infty} \sum_{k=0}^{N} \sum_{i=0}^{k} b_k \binom{k}{i} (-1)^i (-i)^j \frac{x^j}{j!} \tag{48}$$

$$= \sum_{k=0}^{N} a_k \frac{x^k}{k!} - \sum_{k=0}^{\infty} \sum_{m=0}^{N} \sum_{i=0}^{m} b_m \binom{m}{i} (-1)^i (-i)^k \frac{x^k}{k!} \tag{49}$$

In order that first n derivatives of expression (40) be zero, the coefficients of (49) of x^k for $k = 0, 1, \ldots, N$ should be zero. Therefore, one requires

$$a_k - \sum_{m=0}^{N} \sum_{i=0}^{m} b_m \binom{m}{i} (-1)^i (-i)^k = 0 \tag{50}$$

$$a_k - \sum_{m=0}^{N} b_m \sum_{i=0}^{m} \binom{m}{i} (-1)^i (-i)^k = 0 \tag{51}$$

Using Lemma 1, which says that $\sum_{i=0}^{m} \binom{m}{i} (-1)^i (-1)^k = 0$, for every $m > k$, one obtains

$$a_k - \sum_{m=0}^{k} b_m \sum_{i=0}^{m} \binom{m}{i} (-1)^i (-i)^k = 0 \tag{52}$$

for $k = 1, 2, \ldots, N$, or

$$a_k - b_k \sum_{i=0}^{k} \binom{k}{i} (-1)^i (-i)^k - \sum_{m=0}^{k-1} b_m \sum_{i=0}^{m} \binom{m}{i} (-1)^i (-i)^k = 0 \tag{53}$$

for $k = 1, 2, \ldots, N$. Therefore, one obtains the recurrent relation for coefficients b_k,

$$b_k = \frac{a_k - \sum_{m=0}^{k-1} b_m \sum_{i=0}^{m} \binom{m}{i} (-1)^i (-i)^k}{\sum_{i=0}^{k} \binom{k}{i} (-1)^i (-i)^k} \tag{54}$$

for $k = 1, 2, \ldots N$, and with $b_0 = a_0$.   ■

The next main result provides a set of bounded jump approximation basis functions that is extremely useful for feedback control purposes.

Theorem 2 (*Approximation Using Sigmoid Basis Functions*). Let there be given any bounded function $f: S \to \Re$ that is continuous and analytic on a compact set S, except at $x = c$ where function f has a finite jump and is continuous from the right. Then, given any $\varepsilon > 0$, there exists a sum F of the form

$$F(x) = g(x) + \sum_{k=0}^{N} a_k \varphi_k (x - c) \tag{55}$$

such that

$$|F(x) - f(x)| < \varepsilon \tag{56}$$

for every x in S, where g is a function in $C^N(S)$, and the *sigmoid jump approximation basis functions* φ_k are defined as

$$\varphi_k(x) = \begin{cases} 0, & \text{for } x < 0 \\ (1 - e^{-x})^k, & \text{for } x \geq 0 \end{cases} \tag{57}$$

Proof. According to Theorem 1, there exists a sum F of the form

$$F(x) = g(x) + \sum_{k=0}^{N} a_k f_k (x - c) \tag{58}$$

such that

$$|F(x) - f(x)| < \varepsilon \tag{59}$$

Using Lemma 2,

$$\sum_{k=0}^{N} a_k f_k(x) = z(x) + \sum_{k=0}^{N} b_k \varphi_k(x) \tag{60}$$

one obtains the result.   ■

Theorem 2 says that any bounded function with a finite jump can be approximated arbitrary well by a sum of a function with continuous first N derivatives, and a linear combination of jump basis functions φ_k. Functions φ_k for $k = 0, 1, 2, 3$ are shown in Figure 6.

Using the known result of Cybenko for continuous function approximation, one can formulate the following result for approximation of functions with a finite jump.

Theorem 3 (*General Approximation Result*). Let there be given bounded function $f\colon S \to \Re$ that is continuous and analytic on a compact set S, except at $x = c$ where function f has a finite jump and is continuous from the right. Given any $\varepsilon > 0$, there exists a sum F of the form

$$F(x) = \sum_{k=0}^{L} \alpha_k \sigma(m_k x + n_k) + \sum_{k=0}^{N} a_k \varphi_k(x - c) \tag{61}$$

such that

$$|F(x) - f(x)| < \varepsilon \tag{62}$$

for every x in S, where $\sigma(x)$ is a sigmoid function, e.g., (20), and the sigmoidal jump approximation functions φ_k are defined as (57).

Proof. Using Theorem 2 and applying Cybenko's result to function $g \in C^N(S)$, one obtains expression (61). ∎

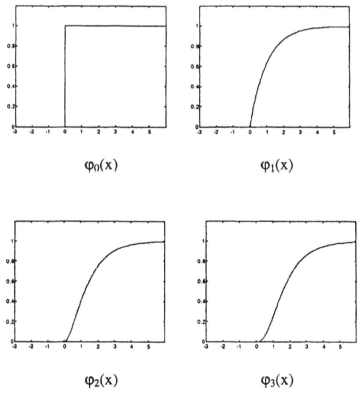

$$\varphi_0(x) \qquad\qquad \varphi_1(x)$$

$$\varphi_2(x) \qquad\qquad \varphi_3(x)$$

FIGURE 6
Sigmoid jump approximation functions.

In a similar manner as in Theorem 2, it can be shown that instead of the sigmoidal jump approximation functions, one can use either

$$
\varphi_k(x) = \begin{cases} 0, & \text{for } x < 0 \\ \left(\dfrac{1 - e^{-x}}{1 + e^{-x}}\right)^k, & \text{for } x \geq 0 \end{cases}
\tag{63}
$$

or jump basis functions based on the hyperbolic tangent

$$
\varphi_k(x) = \begin{cases} 0, & \text{for } x < 0 \\ \left(\dfrac{e^x - e^{-x}}{e^x + e^{-x}}\right)^k, & \text{for } x \geq 0 \end{cases}
\tag{64}
$$

5 AUGMENTED MULTILAYER NN FOR JUMP FUNCTION APPROXIMATION

Here are presented the structure and training algorithms for an augmented multilayer NN that is capable of approximating functions with jumps, provided that the points of discontinuity are known. Since the points of discontinuity are known in many nonlinear characteristics in industrial motion systems (e.g., the friction model is discontinuous at zero, the deadzone inverse is discontinuous at zero, etc.), this augmented NN is a useful tool for compensation of parasitic effects and actuator nonlinearities in industrial control systems.

5.1 Structure of Augmented Multilayer NN

The augmented multilayer NN shown in Figure 7 is capable of approximating any piecewise continuous function $f: S \subset \Re \rightarrow \Re$, provided that the points of discontinuity are known.

Comparing with the standard NN given in Figure 3, one can see that the augmented NN has two sets of hidden activation functions, σ and φ_i; two sets of weights for the first layer, V_1^T and V_2^T; and two sets of weights for the second layer, W_1^T and W_2^T. With this structure of NN, one has

$$
y = \sum_{l=1}^{L} w_{1l}^1 \sigma(v_{l1}^1 x_1 + v_{l0}^1) + \sum_{l=1}^{N} w_{1l}^2 \varphi_l(v_{l1}^2 x_1 + v_{l0}^2) + w_{10}
\tag{65}
$$

If the hidden layer activation functions σ are defined as the sigmoids (20), and one takes the jump basis functions φ_i in (57), then using Theorem 3 for approximation of jump functions one can see that the augmented NN is capable of approximating any continuous function with a finite jump, provided that the jump location is known.

The standard NN tuning algorithms must be modified since the structure of the NN is changed. The set of second-layer weights, W_1^T and W_2^T are trained as in the usual multilayer NN. Both of them are treated the same way, including threshold weights. The first-layer weights V_1^T are updated as in the usual NN (e.g., by a back-propagation approach). Weights V_2^T and the threshold c are fixed, and correspond to the known point of discontinuity.

5.2 Augmented NN for Friction Compensation

In order to apply the augmented NN for friction compensation, it is necessary to estimate functions like (17), which is a map from $\Re^n$ to $\Re^n$. Since the friction terms in most industrial motion systems are uncoupled among the joints and can be presented as (17), the augmented

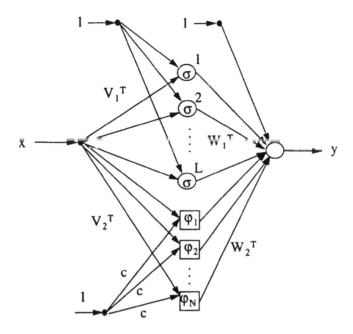

FIGURE 7
Augmented multilayer neural net.

multilayer NN in Figure 8 can be used for friction compensation in multivariable systems. The augmented NN is capable of approximating vector functions like (8).

The upper part of the NN in Figure 8 is the standard NN for approximating continuous vector functions. In addition, there are M additional sets of nodes for jump approximation. The number M depends on the number of points where the function has jumps and the number of inputs n. In fact,

$$M = \sum_{i=1}^{n} v_i \tag{66}$$

where n is the number of inputs, and v_i is the number of discontinuities in the ith input (coordinate). For instance, for the two-link robot arm one has $M = 2$ because of friction discontinuities at zero velocities in each of the two links. The fixed values of the bias weights c_i are the locations of the jump points. In a similar manner as in the standard NN case, the output of the NN is given in matrix form as

$$y = W_1^T \sigma(V_1^T x) + W_2^T \varphi(V_2^T x) \tag{67}$$

where

$$W_1^T = [w_{il}^1], \qquad W_2^T = [w_{il}^2], \qquad V_1^T = [v_{lj}^1], \qquad V_2^T = [v_{lj}^2]$$

In order to include thresholds in the matrix form, matrices W_1^T, W_2^T, V_1^T, V_2^T are augmented in the same manner as in Section 4.1, so that vector functions are defined as

$$\sigma(\omega) = [1 \quad \sigma(\omega_1) \quad \sigma(\omega_2) \quad \cdots \quad \sigma(\omega_L)]^T,$$

$$\varphi(\omega) = [1 \quad \varphi_1(\omega_1) \quad \varphi_2(\omega_2) \quad \cdots \quad \varphi_N(\omega_N) \quad \varphi_1(\omega_{N+1}) \quad \varphi_2(\omega_{N+2}) \quad \cdots \quad \varphi_N(\omega_{2N}) \quad \cdots \quad \varphi_N(\omega_{NM})]^T.$$

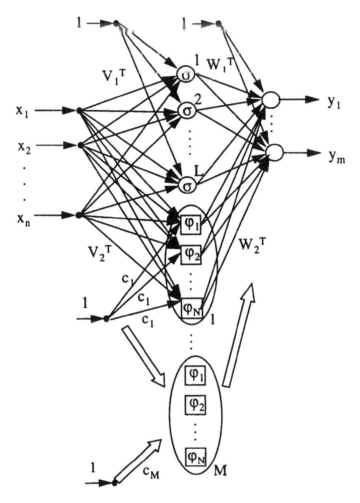

FIGURE 8
Augmented multilayer NN used for friction compensation.

For friction compensation, for instance in a robot arm with two joints, a function (8) that includes the friction term (17) needs to be approximated. Function f maps a simply connected set of R^{10} to R^{10}, and depends on q_1, $\dot{q}_1$, q_2, $\dot{q}_2$, q_{1d}, q_{2d}, $\dot{q}_{1d}$, $\dot{q}_{2d}$, $\ddot{q}_{1d}$, $\ddot{q}_{2d}$, and is discontinuous at $\dot{q}_1 = 0$ and at $\dot{q}_2 = 0$. Therefore, in Figure 8 one has $M = 2$, and values of weights V_2^T should be selected such that the weights between $\dot{q}_1$ input and the first N activation functions $\varphi_1(\omega_1)$, $\varphi_2(\omega_2), \ldots, \varphi_N(\omega_N)$ are set to one. The same applies to weights V_2^T between $\dot{q}_2$ input and next N activation functions $\varphi_1(\omega_{N+1})$, $\varphi_2(\omega_{N+2}), \ldots, \varphi_N(\omega_{2N})$. All other weights in V_2^T are set to zero. Threshold weights in V_2^T are set to zero, since discontinuity occurs in zero.

5.3 Simulation of the Augmented Multilayer NN

Here are presented some simulation results that compare the approximation capabilities of the standard NN in Figure 7 and our augmented NN in Figure 8. Both NNs had $L = 20$ hidden nodes, both were trained for the same number of iterations, and the augmented NN had two

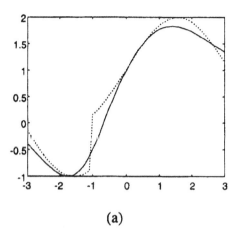 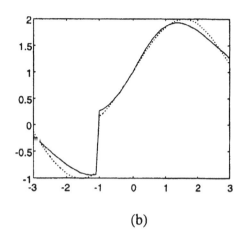

(a)   (b)

FIGURE 9
Approximation of jump functions using standard NN (a), and using augmented NN (b). full line, NN function; dashed line, desired function.

additional jump approximation nodes. Two samples of jump functions were chosen. Both NN were first trained to approximate the discontinuous function defined as $y = \sin(x)$ for $x < -1$, else $y = 1 + \sin(x)$. The results are shown in Figures 9a and 9b. Next, the function defined as $y = x$ for $x < 0$, else $y = 0.5x + 1$ was approximated. The results are shown in Figures 10a and 10b.

From this simulation it is obvious that the NN augmented by jump approximation functions has significantly better performance in approximating discontinuous functions, and that it should be a very powerful tool for friction compensation. In this simulation, the modified NN has only two jump nodes. Two or three jump nodes are usually enough in practical industrial applications.

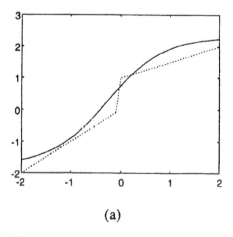 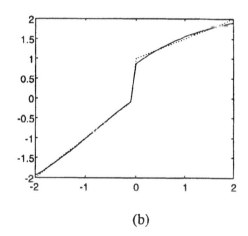

(a)   (b)

FIGURE 10
Approximation of jump functions using standard NN (a), and using augmented NN (b). full line, NN function; dashed line, desired function.

6 NN CONTROLLER

There are numerous papers employing NN in robot control, but for the most part stability proofs are omitted and they rely on ad hoc design and simulation studies. Several researchers have studied NN control and managed to prove stability [8, 19, 26, 30–33]. Here is presented a NN robot controller based on a filtered-error approach and employing a NN to approximate the unknown nonlinear function (8) in the robot arm dynamics. A serious problem in using adaptive controllers in robotics, the requirement for *linearity in the unknown system parameters*, is overcome here using the *universal approximation property of NN* [3, 10, 12, 13]. In Sections 4 and 5 it has been shown how augmented NN can be used for approximation of piecewise continuous functions. The main result of this section is the controller presented in Figure 11, based on the results of Lewis and Yesildirek [17–20] but modified for friction compensation. Instead of requiring knowledge of the system structure, as in adaptive control, a NN is used to approximate the unmodeled dynamics. The use of the augmented NN in Figure 8 gives the controller much better performance if there is significant unknown friction, since friction is discontinuous at zero.

In order to prove stability of the overall system, some mild assumptions are required.

Assumption 1 (*Bounded Reference Trajectory*). The desired trajectory is bounded so that

$$
\left\| \begin{matrix} q_d(t) \\ \dot{q}_d(t) \\ \ddot{q}_d(t) \end{matrix} \right\| \le q_B \tag{68}
$$

with q_B a know scalar bound.

Lemma 3 (*Bound on NN Input x*). For each time t, $x(t)$ is bounded by

$$
\|x\| \le c_1 + c_2\|r\| \le 2q_B + c_0\|r(0)\| + c_2\|r\| \tag{69}
$$

for computable positive constants c_0, c_1, c_2.

Proof. The solution of LTI system (6) with the initial value vector $q(t_0)$ is

$$
e(t) = e_0 \varepsilon^{-\Lambda(t-t_0)} + \int_{t_0}^{t} \varepsilon^{-\Lambda(t-\tau)} r(\tau)\, d\tau, \qquad \forall t \ge t_0 \tag{70}
$$

where $e_0 = q_d(t_0) - q(t_0)$. Thus,

$$
\|e\| \le \|e_0\| + \frac{\|r\|}{\sigma_{\min}(\Lambda)} \tag{71}
$$

with $\sigma_{\min}(\Lambda)$ the minimum singular value of Λ. The NN input can be written as

$$
x = \begin{bmatrix} q \\ \dot{q} \\ q_d \\ \dot{q}_d \\ \ddot{q}_d \end{bmatrix} = \begin{bmatrix} -e \\ -r + \Lambda e \\ q_d \\ \dot{q}_d \\ \ddot{q}_d \end{bmatrix} + \begin{bmatrix} q_d \\ \dot{q}_d \\ 0 \\ 0 \\ 0 \end{bmatrix} \tag{72}
$$

Then a bound can be given as

$$
\begin{aligned}
\|x\| &\le (1 + \sigma_{\max}(\Lambda))\|e\| + 2q_B + \|r\| \\
&\le \{[1 + \sigma_{\max}(\Lambda)]\|e_0\| + 2q_B\} + \left\{ 1 + \frac{1}{\sigma_{\min}(\Lambda)} + \frac{\sigma_{\max}(\Lambda)}{\sigma_{\min}(\Lambda)} \right\} \|r\| \\
&= c_1 + c_2\|r\|
\end{aligned}
\tag{73}
$$

with

$$
c_1 = [1 + \sigma_{\max}(\Lambda)]|e_0| + 2q_B
\tag{74}
$$

$$
c_2 = 1 + \frac{1}{\sigma_{\min}(\Lambda)} + \frac{\sigma_{\max}(\Lambda)}{\sigma_{\min}(\Lambda)}
\tag{75}
$$

Now from (6) one has $\|e\| < \|r\|/\sigma_{\min}(\Lambda)$ for all t, whence one obtains that

$$
c_0 = \frac{1 + \sigma_{\max}(\Lambda)}{\sigma_{\min}(\Lambda)}
\tag{76}
$$

■

6.1   NN Approximation and the Nonlinearity in the Parameters Problem

Nonlinear robot function (8) is a discontinuous function due to friction. Using the universal approximation property of NN, and our Theorem 3 for approximation of jump functions, there is a two-layer NN such that

$$
f(x) = W_1^T \sigma(V_1^T x) + W_2^T \varphi(V_2^T x) + \varepsilon
\tag{77}
$$

with the approximation error bounded on a compact set by $\|\varepsilon\| < \varepsilon_N$, with ε_N a known bound. W_1, W_2, V_1, V_2 are ideal target weights that give good approximation to $f(x)$; they are unknown. All that is required here is that they exist; it is not even required for them to be unique.

Define $\hat{W}_1, \hat{W}_2, \hat{V}_1, \hat{V}_2$ as estimates of the ideal NN weights, which are given by the NN tuning algorithms. Since the weights V_2^T are given by the designer depending on the location of the jumps, then $V_2^T = \hat{V}_2^T$. Define estimation error as

$$
\tilde{W}_1 = W_1 - \hat{W}_1, \qquad \tilde{W}_2 = W_2 - \hat{W}_2, \qquad \tilde{V}_1 = V_1 - \hat{V}_1
\tag{78}
$$

and the approximation of nonlinear function (8) as

$$
\hat{f}(x) = \hat{W}_1^T \sigma(\hat{V}_1^T x) + \hat{W}_2^T \varphi(V_2^T x)
\tag{79}
$$

Let Z be the matrix of all the NN weights:

$$
Z = \begin{bmatrix} W_1 & 0 & 0 \\ 0 & W_2 & 0 \\ 0 & 0 & V_1 \end{bmatrix}
\tag{80}
$$

Note that weights V_2 are not included in (8), since they are known.

Assumption 2 (*Bounded Ideal Target NN Weights*). On any compact subset of $\mathfrak{R}^n$, the ideal NN weights are bounded so that

$$
\|Z\|_F \le Z_B
\tag{81}
$$

with Z_B known.

Proceeding as in [20], one can define the hidden-layer output error for a given x as

$$\tilde{\sigma} = \sigma(V_1^T x) - \sigma(\hat{V}_1^T x) \tag{82}$$

Using a Taylor series one has

$$\sigma(V_1^T x) = \sigma(\hat{V}_1^T x) + \sigma'(\hat{V}_1^T x)\tilde{V}_1^T x + O(\tilde{O}_1^T x)^2 \tag{83}$$

where σ' denotes the first derivative, and $O(\tilde{V}_1^T x)^2$ represents higher-order terms. The importance of this equation is that it replaces $\tilde{\sigma}$, which is nonlinear in $\tilde{V}_1$, by an expression linear in $\tilde{V}_1$ plus higher-order terms. The Jacobian $\sigma'(\hat{V}_1^T x)$ is easily computable in terms of measured signals $x(t)$ and the current weights $\hat{V}_1$.

It can be shown (see [20]) that the higher-order terms in equation (83) are bounded by

$$\|O(\tilde{V}_1^T x)^2\| \le c_3 + c_4 q_B \|\tilde{V}_1\|_F + c_5 \|\tilde{V}_1\|_F \|r\| \tag{84}$$

for some constants c_2, c_4, c_5.

6.2   Controller Structure and Error System Dynamics

The structure of the NN controller is shown in Figure 11. Using (81), control input is

$$\tau = \tau_0 - v = \hat{W}_1^T \sigma(\hat{V}_1^T x) + \hat{W}_2^T \varphi(V_2^T x) + K_v r - v \tag{85}$$

where v is robustifying term, and τ_0 is defined by (10). The closed-loop error dynamics is given by

$$M\dot{r} = -(K_v + V_m)r + W_1^T \sigma(V_1^T x) + W_2^T \varphi(V_2^T x)$$
$$- \hat{W}_1^T \sigma(\hat{V}_1^T x) - \hat{W}_2^T \varphi(V_2^T x) + \varepsilon + \tau_d + v \tag{86}$$

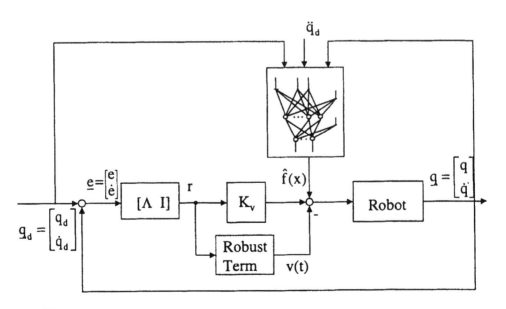

FIGURE 11
NN controller.

Using (80) one has

$$M\dot{r} = -(K_v + V_m)r + \tilde{W}_1^T\sigma + W_1^T\tilde{\sigma} + \tilde{W}_2^T\varphi + \varepsilon + \tau_d + v \tag{87}$$

Applying Taylor series approximation for $\tilde{\sigma}$, one can obtain the expression for closed-loop error dynamics [20]:

$$M\dot{r} = -(K_v + V_m)r + \tilde{W}_1^T(\hat{\sigma} - \hat{\sigma}'\hat{V}_1^T x) + \hat{W}_1^T\hat{\sigma}'V_1^T x + \tilde{W}_2^T\varphi + w + v \tag{88}$$

with disturbance term given by

$$w = \tilde{W}_1^T\hat{\sigma}'\hat{V}_1^T x + W_1^T O(\tilde{V}_1^T x)^2 + \varepsilon + \tau_d \tag{89}$$

It is shown in [19, 20] that the disturbance term is bounded by

$$\|w(t)\| \le C_0 + C_1\|\tilde{Z}\|_F + C_2\|\tilde{Z}\|_F\|r\| \tag{90}$$

with C_i known positive constants.

6.3 Weight Tuning and Stability Proof

Here are presented NN weight tuning laws, derived from Lyapunov theory, that guarantee stable tracking with internal stability. It is shown that the tracking error is suitably small, the NN weights are bounded, and the control $\tau(t)$ is bounded. The NN weights are adjusted on-line in real-time with no preliminary off-line learning required.

Initial Tracking Error Requirement. The next assumption specifies the region of convergence of the two-layer NN controller.

Assumption 3 (*Initial Condition Requirement*). Suppose the desired trajectory $q_d, \dot{q}_d, \ddot{q}_d$ is bounded by q_B as in Assumption 1. Define known constants c_0, c_2 by Lemma 3. Let the NN approximation property (79) hold for the function $f(x)$ given in (8) with a given accuracy ε_N for all x in the compact set $S_x = \{x | \|x\| < b_x\}$ with $b_x > q_B$. Define $S_r = \{r | \|r\| < (b_x - q_B)/(c_0 + c_2)\}$. Let $r(0) \in S_r$.

The set S_r specifies the set of *allowed initial tracking errors* $r(0)$. Note that the approximation accuracy of the NN determines the allowed magnitude of the initial tracking error $r(0)$. For a larger NN (i.e., more hidden-layer units), ε_N is small for a larger radius b_x; thus, the allowed initial condition set S_r is larger. The key role of the initial condition requirement is in showing the dependence of the allowed initial condition set S_r on design parameters. The constants q_B, c_0, c_2, b_x need not be explicitly determined.

A key feature of the initial condition requirement is its *independence of the NN initial weights*. This is in stark contrast to other techniques in the literature where the proofs of stability depend on selecting some initial stabilizing NN weights, which is very difficult to do.

Theorem 4 (*Augmented Backprop Weight Tuning*). Let the desired trajectory be bounded by q_B as in Assumption 1, and the initial tracking error $r(0)$ satisfy initial condition Assumptioin (3). Let the ideal target weights be bounded as in Assumption 2. Take the control input for the robot dynamics (87) with gain satisfying

$$K_{v_{\min}} > \frac{(C_0 + kC_3^2/4)(c_0 + c_2)}{b_x - q_B} \tag{91}$$

where C_3 is defined in the proof and C_0 and C_2 are defined in (90). Let the robustifying term be

$$v(t) = -K_z(\|\hat{Z}\|_F + Z_B r) \tag{92}$$

with gain

$$K_z > C_2 \tag{93}$$

Let the NN weight tuning be provided by

$$\dot{\hat{W}}_1 = S\hat{\sigma}r^T - S\hat{\sigma}'\hat{V}_1^T x r^T - kS|r|\hat{W}_1 \tag{94}$$

$$\dot{\hat{V}}_1 = Txr^T\hat{W}_1^T\hat{\sigma}' - kT\|r\|\hat{V}_1 \tag{95}$$

$$\dot{\hat{W}}_2 = E\varphi r^T - kE|r|\hat{W}_2 \tag{96}$$

with any constant matrices $S = S^T > 0$, $T = T^T > 0$, $E = E^T > 0$, and let $k > 0$ a small scalar design parameter. Then the filtered tracking error $r(t)$ and NN weight estimates $\hat{V}_1$, $\hat{W}_1$, $\hat{W}_2$ are UUB, with bounds given by (101) and (102). Moreover, the tracking error may be kept as small as desired by increasing the gains K_v in (87).

Proof. Select a Lyapunov function as

$$L = \tfrac{1}{2}r^T M r + \tfrac{1}{2}\text{tr}(\tilde{W}_1^T S^{-1}\tilde{W}_1) + \tfrac{1}{2}\text{tr}(\tilde{V}_1^T T^{-1}\tilde{V}_1) + \tfrac{1}{2}\text{tr}(\tilde{W}_2^T E^{-1}\tilde{W}_2) \tag{97}$$

One has derivative

$$\dot{L} = r^T M\dot{r} + \tfrac{1}{2}r^T \dot{M} r + \text{tr}(\tilde{W}_1^T S^{-1}\dot{\tilde{W}}_1) + \text{tr}(\tilde{V}_1^T T^{-1}\dot{\tilde{V}}_1) + \text{tr}(\tilde{W}_2^T E^{-1}\dot{\tilde{W}}_2) \tag{98}$$

Assuming that the initial tracking error satisfies initial condition Assumption 3, including the system error dynamics (88), one has

$$\dot{L} = -r^T(K_v + V_m)r + r^T\tilde{W}_1^T(\hat{\sigma} - \hat{\sigma}'\hat{V}_1^T x) + r^T\hat{W}_1^T\hat{\sigma}/\hat{V}_1^T x + r^T\tilde{W}_2^T\varphi + r^T w + r^T v$$
$$+ \tfrac{1}{2}r^T\dot{M}r + \text{tr}(\tilde{W}_1^T S^{-1}\dot{\tilde{W}}_1) + \text{tr}(\tilde{V}_1^T T^{-1}\dot{\tilde{V}}_1) + \text{tr}(\tilde{W}_2^T E^{-1}\dot{\tilde{W}}_2) \tag{99}$$

Using Property 3 and tuning rules yields

$$\dot{L} = -r^T K_v r + k\|r\|\text{tr}\{\tilde{W}_1^T(W_1 - \tilde{W}_1)\} + k\|r\|\text{tr}\{\tilde{V}_1^T(V_1 - \tilde{V}_1)\}$$
$$+ k\|r\|\text{tr}\{\tilde{W}_2^T(W_2 - \tilde{W}_2)\} + r^T(w + v)$$
$$= -r^T K_v r + k\|r\|\text{tr}\{\tilde{Z}^T(Z - \tilde{Z})\} + r^T(w + v) \tag{100}$$

Proceeding as in [20], one obtains that $\dot{L}$ is negative as long as either

$$\|r\| > \frac{C_0 + kC_3^2/4}{K_{v_{\min}}} \equiv b_r \tag{101}$$

or

$$\|\tilde{Z}\|_F > \frac{C_3}{2} + \sqrt{(C_0/k) + (C_3^2/4)} \equiv b_z \tag{102}$$

Therefore, $\dot{L}$ is negative outside a compact set, and $\|r\|$ and $\|\tilde{Z}\|_F$ are UUB as long as the control remains valid within this set. However, the PD gain (91) shows that the compact set defined by $\|r\| \leq b_r$ is contained in S_r so that the approximation property holds throughout. ∎

The following remarks are relevant.

Weight Initialization and On-line Training. No preliminary off-line learning phase is required. The hidden-layer weights V_1 are initialized randomly, as in [15]. The output-layer weights W_1 and W_2 are initialized at zero. In that way, the stability of the system is not affected. Weight training occurs on-line in real time.

Unsupervised Back-propagation through Time with Extra Terms. The first terms of (94), (95), (96) are modified versions of the standard back-propagation algorithm. The last terms correspond to the e-modification [22], to guarantee bounded parameter estimates.

Bounds on the Tracking Error and NN Weight Estimation Errors. The right-hand side of (101) can be taken as a practical bound on the tracking error in the sense that $r(t)$ will never stray far above it. It is important to note from this equation that the tracking error increases with the NN reconstruction error ε_N and robot disturbances b_d (both appear in C_0), yet arbitrarily small tracking errors may be achieved by selecting large gains K_v. On the other hand, the NN weight errors are fundamentally bounded by Z_B. The tuning parameter k offers a design trade-off between the relative eventual magnitudes of $\|r\|$ and $\|\tilde{Z}\|_F$.

Design Trade-off of NN Size versus Tracking Accuracy. Note that there is design freedom in the degree of complexity (e.g., size) of the NN. For a more complex NN (e.g., more hidden units), the NN estimation error ε_N decreases, so the bounding constant C_0 will decrease, resulting in smaller tracking errors. On the other hand, a simplified NN with fewer hidden units will result in larger error bounds; this degradation can be compensated for by selecting a larger value for the PD gain K_v.

7 SIMULATION OF NN CONTROLLER

To illustrate the performance of the augmented NN controller used for friction compensation, the two-link robot arm (Figure 12) is used. The model of the system shown in Figure 12 is given by [17]

$$\tau_1 = [(m_1 + m_2)a_1^2 + m_2 a_2^2 + 2m_2 a_1 a_2 \cos \theta_2]\ddot{\theta}_1$$
$$+ [m_2 a_2^2 + m_2 a_1 a_2 \cos \theta_2]\ddot{\theta}_2 - m_2 a_1 a_2(2\dot{\theta}_1\dot{\theta}_2 + \dot{\theta}_2^2) \sin \theta_2 \qquad (103)$$
$$+ (m_1 + m_2)ga_1 \cos \theta_1 + m_2 ga_2 \cos(\theta_1 + \theta_2)$$

$$\tau_2 = [m_2 a_2^2 + m_2 a_1 a_2 \cos \theta_2]\ddot{\theta}_1 + m_2 a_2^2 \ddot{\theta}_2 + m_2 a_1 a_2 \dot{\theta}_1^2 \sin \theta_2 + m_2 ga_2 \cos(\theta_1 + \theta_2) \qquad (104)$$

The system parameters are chosen as $a_1 = 1.1$, $a_2 = 1$, $m_1 = 3$, $m_2 = 2.3$. The nonlinear, discontinuous at zero friction model is included for both joints. The friction model parameters for the first joint are $\alpha_0 = 35$, $\alpha_1 = 1.1$, $\alpha_2 = 0.9$, $\beta_1 = 50$, $\beta_2 = 65$, and for the second joint are $\alpha_0 = 38$, $\alpha_1 = 1$, $\alpha_2 = 0.95$, $\beta_1 = 55$, $\beta_2 = 60$. It is assumed that the model of the robot arm as well as friction model are unknown. Note that the friction is discontinuous at zero.

The NN weight tuning parameters are chosen as $S = \text{diag}\{10, 10\}$, $T = \text{diag}\{10, 10\}$, $E = \text{diag}\{35, 35\}$, $k = 0.01$. The NN controller parameters are chosen as $\Lambda = \text{diag}\{5, 5\}$, $K_v = \{20, 20\}$. The input to the NN is given by (9). The NN has $L = 10$ hidden-layer units with sigmoidal activation functions, and four additional nodes with jump approximation activation functions (three for each joint). According to the notation shown in Figure 8, $N = 2$, $M = 2$.

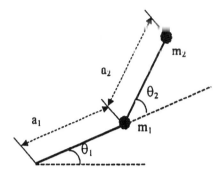

FIGURE 12
Two-link robot arm.

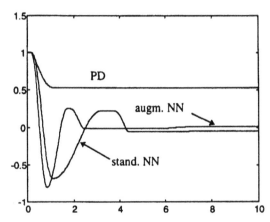

FIGURE 13
Position error for the first joint: PD controller, standard NN, and augmented NN.

We compared the PD controller, the standard NN controller, and the augmented NN controller. Figure 13 shows the position error for the first joint; Figure 14 the position error for the second joint. The step input is applied to the system. Notice that there is the steady-state error when PD is used because of the presence of unknown dynamics as well as unknown friction. The standard NN controller reduces the steady-state error, but it is still noticeable. The augmented NN controller shows superior performance. The NN controller does not require preliminary off-line training.

8   CONCLUSION

A new NN structure is presented for approximating piecewise continuous functions. A standard NN with continuous activation functions is augmented with an additional set of nodes with piecewise continuous activation functions. It is proved that such a NN can approximate arbitrarily well any piecewise continuous function provided that the points of discontinuity are known. Since this is the case in many nonlinearities in industrial motion systems (friction,

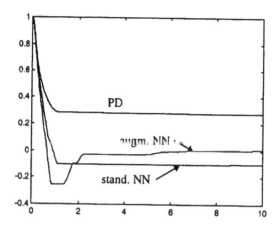

FIGURE 14
Position error for the second joint: PD controller, standard NN, and augmented NN.

deadzone inverse, etc.), such a NN is a powerful tool for compensation of systems with such nonlinearities.

A NN controller with friction compensation is designed based on the new augmented NN. Based on the feedback linearization method, the NN controller approximates unmodeled dynamics including the unknown friction. A general complicated friction model can be approximated, based on the new NN. It is not required for the friction model to be linear in unknown parameters. The NN controller does not require preliminary off-line training. A stability proof is given without any need for selecting initial stabilizing NN weights.

Acknowledgements

This research is supported by NSF Grant ECS-9521673, Texas ATP Grant 003656-027, and ARO Grant 39657-MA.

REFERENCES

[1] B. Armstrong, Friction: experimental determination, modeling and compensation, *IEEE Int. Conf. Robotics and Automation, Philadelphia* 1988, pp.1422–1427.
[2] B. Armstrong-Hélouvry, P. Dupont, and C. Canudas de Wit, A survey of models, analysis tools and compensation methods for the control of machines with friction, *Automatica*, Vol. 30, No. 7, pp. 1083–1138, 1994.
[3] R. Barron, Universal approximation bounds for superpositions of a sigmoidal function, *IEEE Trans. Information Theory*, Vol. 39, No. 3, pp. 930–945, May 1993.
[4] R.G. Bartle, *The Elements of Real Analysis*, Wiley, New York, 1964.
[5] C. Canudas de Wit, P. Noël, A. Aubin, and B. Brogliato, Adaptive friction compensation in robot manipulators: low velocities, *Int. J. Robotic Research*, Vol. 10, No. 3, June 1991.
[6] C. Canudas de Wit, H. Olsson, K.J. Åström, and P. Lischinsky, A new model for control of systems with friction, *IEEE Trans. Automatic Control*, Vol. 40, No. 3, pp. 419–425, Mar. 1995.
[7] C. Canudas de Wit and S.S. Ge, Adaptive friction compensation for systems with generalized velocity/position friction dependency, *Proc. 36th IEEE Conf. Decision and Controls, San Diego*, Dec. 1997, pp. 2465–2470.

[8] F.C. Chen and H.K. Khalil, Adaptive control of nonlinear systems using neural networks, *Int. J. Control*, Vol. 66, No. 6, pp. 1299–1317, 1992.

[9] S. Commuri and F.L. Lewis, CMAC neural networks for control of nonlinear dynamical systems: structure, stability and passivity, *Proc. IEEE Int. Symp. Intelligent Control, Monterey*, 1995, pp. 123–129.

[10] G. Cybenko, Approximation by superpositions of a sigmoidal function, *Mathematical Control, Signals and Systems*, Vol. 2, No. 4, pp. 303–314, 1989.

[11] H. Du and S.S. Nair, Low velocity friction compensation, *IEEE Control Systems Magazine*, Vol. 18, No. 2, pp. 61–69, Apl. 1998.

[12] K. Funahashi, On the approximate realization of continuous mappings by neural networks, *Neural Networks*, Vol. 2, pp. 183–192, 1989.

[13] J.W. Gilbart and G.C. Winston, Adaptive compensation for an optical tracking telescope, *Automatica*, Vol. 10, pp. 125–131, 1974.

[14] K. Hornik, M. Stinchombe, and H. White, Multilayer feedforward networks are universal approximators, *Neural Networks*, Vol. 2, pp. 359–366, 1989.

[15] Y.H. Kim and F.L. Lewis, Reinforcement adaptive learning neural network based friction compensation for high speed and precision, *Proc. 37th IEEE Conf. Decision and Control, Tampa, FL*, 1998 pp. 1064–1069.

[16] S.-W. Lee and J.-H. Kim, Robust adaptive stick-slip friction compensation, *IEEE Trans. Industrial Electronics* Vol. 42, No. 5, pp. 474–479, Oct. 1995.

[17] F.L. Lewis, C.T. Abdallah, and D.M. Dawson, *Control of Robot Manipulators*. Macmillan, New York, 1993.

[18] F.L. Lewis, K. Liu, and S. Commuri, Neural networks and fuzzy logic systems for robot control, in F. Wang (ed.) *Fuzzy Logic and Neural Network Applications*. Intelligent Control and Automation Series. World Scientific, Singapore.

[19] F.L. Lewis, K. Liu, and A. Yesilidrek, *Neural Network Control of Robot Manipulators and Nonlinear Systems*. Taylor and Francis, Philadelphia, 1999.

[20] F.L. Lewis, A. Yesilidrek, and K. Liu, Multilayer neural net robot controller: structure and stability proofs, *IEEE Trans. Neural Networks*, Vol. 7, No. 2, pp. 388–399, Mar. 1996.

[21] F.L. Lewis, Neural network control of robot manipulators, in K. Passino and Ü. Özgüner (eds.) *IEEE Expert Special Track on Intelligent Control*, pp. 64–75, Jun. 1996.

[22] W. Li and X. Cheng, Adaptive high-precision control of positioning tables—theory and experiments, *IEEE Trans. Control Systems Technology*, Vol. 2, No. 3, Sept. 1994.

[23] P. Lischinsky, C. Canudas de Wit, and G. Morel, "Friction compensation for an industrial hydraulic robot," *IEEE Control Systems Magazine*, Vol. 19, No. 1, pp. 25–32, Feb. 1999.

[24] K.S. Narendra, Adaptive control using neural networks, in W.T. Miller, R.S. Sutton, P. J. Werbos (eds.) *Neural Networks for Control*, pp. 115–142. MIT Press, Cambridge, MA, 1991.

[25] K.S. Narendra and A.M. Annaswamy, A new adaptive law for robust adaptation without persistent excitation, *IEEE Trans. Automatic Control*, Vol. AC-32, No. 2, pp. 134–145, Feb. 1987.

[26] K.S. Narendra and K. Parthasarathy, Identification and control of dynamical systems using neural networks, *IEEE Trans. Neural Networks*, Vol. 1, pp. 4–27, Mar. 1990.

[27] H. Olsson and K.J. Åström, "Observer-based friction compensation," *Proc. 35th IEEE Conf. Decision and Control, Kobe, Japan*, 1996, pp. 4345–4350.

[28] J. Park and I.W. Sandberg, Criteria for the approximation of nonlinear systems, *IEEE Trans. Circuits and Systems*, Vol. 39, No. 8, pp. 673–676, Aug. 1992.

[29] J. Park and I.W. Sandberg, Nonlinear approximations using elliptic basis function networks, *Circuits, Systems, and Signal Processing*, Vol. 13, No. 1, pp. 99–113, 1993.

[30] M.M. Polycarpou, Stable adaptive neural control scheme for nonlinear systems, *IEEE Trans. Automatic Control*, Vol. 41, No. 3, pp. 447–451, Mar. 1996.

[31] M.M. Polycarpou and P.A. Ioannou, Modeling, identification and stable adaptive control of continuous-time nonlinear dynamical systems using neural networks, *Proc. Am. Control Conf.*, 1992, Vol. 1, pp. 36–40.

[32] G.A. Rovithakis and M.A. Christodoulou, Adaptive control of unknown plants using dynamical neural networks, *IEEE Trans. Systems, Man, and Cybernetics*, Vol. 24, No. 3, pp. 400–412, 1994.

[33] N. Sadegh, A perceptron network for functional identification and control of nonlinear systems, *IEEE Trans. Neural Networks*, Vol. 4, No. 6, pp. 982–988, Nov. 1993.

[34] R.M. Sanner and J.-J.E. Slotine, Stable recursive identification using radial basis function networks, *American Control Conference, Chicago, IL*, 1992, pp. 1829–1833.

[35] J.R. Schilling, *Fundamentals of Robotics Analysis and Control*. Prentice-Hall, Englewood Cliffs, NJ, 1990.

[36] J.-J.E. Slotine and W. Li, *Applied Nonlinear Control*. Prentice-Hall, Englewood Cliffs, NJ, 1991.

[37] E.D. Sontag, Neural networks for control, in H.L. Trentelman and J.C. Willems (eds.) *Essays on Control: Perspectives in the Theory and Its Applications*, pp. 339–380. Birkhauser, Boston, 1993.

[38] E.D. Sontag, Feedback stabilization using two-hidden-layer nets, *IEEE Trans. Neural Networks*, Vol. 3, pp. 981–990, 1992.

[39] A. Tzes, P.-Y. Peng, and C.-C. Houng, Neural network control for DC motor micromaneuvering, *IEEE Trans. Industrial Electronics*, Vol. 42, No. 5, pp. 516–523, Oct. 1995.

CHAPTER 21

Fuzzy Adaptive and Predictive Control of a Thermic Process

IGOR ŠKRJANC and DRAGO MATKO
Faculty of Electrical and Computer Engineering, University of Ljubljana, Slovenia

1 INTRODUCTION

The use of adaptive control techniques is generally required to obtain a high-performance control system in the case of unknown or poorly known parameters of a controlled process which might be also time-varying. Similarly to conventional adaptive controllers, adaptive fuzzy controllers can also be categorized into direct and indirect types. The direct type of fuzzy controller can be designed as a self-tuning (self-regulating, self-adjusting) controller. A typical scheme of a direct type fuzzy adaptive controller consists of an auxiliary part that can be a reference model, an auxiliary controller, and a monitor or a parameter adjuster that is designed to adjust the fuzzy controller in a direct loop. The indirect type of fuzzy adaptive controller is usually based on recursive fuzzy identification. Our approach is of the indirect type based on a fuzzy model. The first one is called fuzzy adaptive cancelation control. This approach is based on the Sugeno zero-order fuzzy input model. The fuzzy input model is used to cancel the plant dynamics. After cancelation of the plant dynamic, new prescribed dynamics are incorporated into the block by the reference model. According to dynamic cancelation this approach can be used only in the case of stable and phase-minimal systems.

The second scheme is called fuzzy predictive control. In this case the fuzzy model is given as the output error model. The form of the fuzzy model is the same as in the case of cancelation control. On basis of the model, a predictive control law is given using the dynamic matrix control approach.

Both algorithms have been tested on a heat exchanger pilot plant that exhibits strong nonlinear dynamics and time-varying characteristics. The heart of the thermic plant is a plate heat exchanger serviced by primary (heating water) and secondary (cold water) circuit. In the primary circuit, the water in the electrically heated reservoir is kept at a constant temperature by a simple on–off controller that is used in the local control loop. The flow rate in the primary circuit is controlled by a servo valve. In the secondary water circuit, water from the main water supply enters the heat exchanger with a certain flow rate, which is very changeable and can cause an additional disturbance in the system. After being heated in the plate exchanger, it flows to the drain. The output variable of the process is the temperature of the secondary circuit water at the outlet of the exchanger and the manipulated variable is the positioning signal to the servo valve. The dynamic behavior of the plant strongly depends on the operating point and consequently is strongly nonlinear. Both applied algorithms exhibit very good performance in tracking the reference trajectory and also good disturbance rejection properties.

This chapter is organized as follows: First the fuzzy models are reviewed. Four types of models are discussed, representing an extension of the classical linear model error representation to nonlinear models. In Sections 2 and 3, types of fuzzy model-based controllers, the adaptive cancelation and the predictive controller, and their applications are given.

2   FUZZY MODELING

In terms of classical modeling the basic approach in building fuzzy models is called theoretical modeling. Quantitative knowledge about the object to be modeled is formulated in the form of if–then rules. The number of rules and their form correspond to the model structure, while the shape and number of membership functions, the choice of fuzzy-logic operators, and the defuzzification method correspond to the fuzzy model parameters. Initially, the fuzzy models used for control were models of the controllers. The knowledge gathered in the mind of experienced plant operators was used as the knowledge base in the fuzzy inference engine. The benefit of such an approach is the direct applicability of the resulting controller. The same procedure can be used to design a model of the controlled plant. However, such models have seldom been used because there is no direct mapping between the model and the controller. The relationship between the model and controller is the main part of this chapter.

The proposed approach can be treated as universal approximator that can approximate continuous functions to an arbitrary precision [1, 3]. In general, fuzzy logic universal approximators (denoted UA) have several inputs and outputs. Without loss of generality, only one output will be treated here. Approximators with more than one output can be treated as several approximators in parallel.

A typical Sugeno-type rule can be written as

$$R^j: \quad \text{if } x_1 \text{ is } A_1^j \text{ and} \ldots \text{and } x_N \text{ is } A_N^j \text{ then } y = f^j(x_1 \ldots x_N) \tag{1}$$

where $x_1 \ldots x_N$ are the inputs, A_1^j is a subset of the input space, y is the output and f^j is a function (in general nonlinear, usually linear).

However, even with the Mamdani-type rules where the consequence is symbolic (fuzzy set):

$$R^j: \quad \text{if } x_1 \text{ is } A_1^j \text{ and} \ldots \text{and } x_N \text{ is } A_N^j \text{ then } y \text{ is } B^j \tag{2}$$

the fuzzy system (fuzzyfication–inference–defuzzyfication) can be treated as a nonlinear mapping between the inputs and outputs.

2.1   Dynamic Models

The input–output relations of industrial processes and controllers are dynamic. The dynamics are introduced into the fuzzy logic models by introducing the derivatives (integrals) and/or time shifted inputs of the UA.

A common approach to dynamic fuzzy logic models is to use time-shifted signals in what results in discrete-time models. The usage of derivatives, integrals or other transfer functions results in continuous-time models. Mixed continuous–discrete time models are also possible. In this chapter the discrete-time models will be treated and tapped lines will be used to generate the time-shifted signals. If only the (tapped) input signal of the model is used as the input of the UA, the resulting model is nonrecursive and has a finite impulse response. If (tapped) inputs and (tapped) outputs of the model are used as the inputs of the UA, the resulting model is recursive and may have an infinite impulse response.

The dynamic fuzzy logic models described above are a class of NARX (nonlinear autoregresive with exogenous variable) [8] models and will be denoted by FNARX (fuzzy logic/neural net autoregresive with exogenous variable) in what follows.

2.2 Experimental Modeling

Contrary to theoretical modeling based on mathematical formulation of human experience, experimental modeling or identification is based on the observation of input–output data. In the sequel it will be supposed that the unknown plant that produced the input–output data can be described by a FNARX model written in the mathematical form

$$y(k) = f(u(k), \ldots, u(k - N_p), y(k - 1), \ldots, y(k - N_p) + n(k)) \tag{3}$$

where $f(\ )$ is an unknown nonlinear function, N_p is the order of the model, and $n(k)$ is the measurement noise. The resulting model is obtained by the best fit of the model response to the identified process response if the same input signal is applied to both of them. The identification problem is formulated, therefore, as an optimization problem utilizing a criterion in the form of a functional, e.g., the sum of squared errors

$$E(y, y_M) = \sum_{k=0}^{N} \varepsilon^2(k) \tag{4}$$

where y is the observed signal, y_M is the model output, and ε is the error.

The case

$$\varepsilon(k) = y(k) - y_M(k) \tag{5}$$

where

$$y_M(k) = f_o(u(k), \ldots, u(k - N), y_M(k - 1), \ldots, y_M(k - N)) \tag{6}$$

is the output of the recursive model and the input is $u(k)$, is referred to as the *output error model*. In the ideal case, where the plant is identified perfectly and no noise is present, the nonlinear function in equation (6) is equal to the nonlinear function in equation (3) $(f(\ ) = f_o(\ ))$.

The case

$$\varepsilon(k) = u(k) - u_M(k) \tag{7}$$

where

$$u_M(k) = f_i(y(k), \ldots, y(k - N), u_M(k - 1), \ldots, u_M(k - N)) \tag{8}$$

is the output of a recursive model with the input $y(k)$, is known as the *input error model*.

It should be noted that the function $f_i(\ )$ represents an inverse of the function $f(\ )$ in the sense that if the signal $y(k)$ is produced by equation (7) and no noise is present $(n(k) = 0)$, then the signal $u_M(k)$ produced by equation (8) is identical to the signal $u(k)$. There are also some limitations of application of the input error model with regard to the time delay of the process and the nature of the modeled process.

If in the right-hand side of equation (6) the output of the model $y_M(k)$ is replaced by the measured output of the process, i.e.,

$$y_M(k) = f_{go}(u(k), \ldots, u(k-N), y(k-1), \ldots, y(k-N)) \tag{9}$$

the error defined by equation (5) becomes a *generalized output error model*. It has two inputs, namely, the plant input signal $u(k)$ and the plant output signal $y(k)$, and one output signal $y_M(k)$. In the ideal case, where no noise is present and the plant is identified perfectly, the nonlinear function $f_{go}(\ )$ in equation (9) is equal to the nonlinear function $f(\ )$ in Eq. (3).

If in the right-hand side of (8) $u_M(k)$ is replaced by the input of the process, i.e.,

$$u_M(k) = f_{gi}(y(k), \ldots, y(k-N), u(K-1), \ldots, u(k-N)) \tag{10}$$

the error defined by equation (7) becomes a *generalized input error model*. It has two inputs, namely, the plant output signal $y(k)$ and the plant input signal $u(k)$, and one output signal $u_M(k)$. In the ideal case, where no noise is present and the plant is identified perfectly, the nonlinear function $f_{gi}(\ )$ in equation (10), represents an inverse of the function $f(\ )$ in the sense that if the signal $y(k)$ is produced by equation (7) and no noise is present ($n(k) = 0$), then the signal $u_M(k)$ produced by equation (10) is identical to the signal $u(k)$.

Figure 1 represents all four cases—the output, the input and both generalized error identification models.

All four forms of the error models are closely related. The input error and the generalized input error models are inverse to the output error and the generalized output error models, respectively, in the sense described above. The output and input models are complementary, respectively, to the generalized output and the generalized input models in the sense that generalized models are suitable for identification since the estimation of the unknown parameters becomes a linear problem, and the output/input models are applicable in prediction They are also called prediction or simulation models. The four models described by equations (6), (8), (9) and (10) can be treated as universal dynamic approximators (UDA) where the nonlinear function is realized by fuzzy logic universal approximators (UA). According to the topology of the models in Figure 1, the input, the output, and both generalized models can also be called parallel, series, and series-parallel models, respectively. It should be noted that there are two kinds of generalized error (series-parallel) models, originating in the output and input error models, respectively.

The identification procedure involves the structure identification of the plant and the estimation of the unknown parameters. In the case of the FNARX models, the structure is usually chosen ad hoc (by engineering "feeling") and then improved by some optimization procedure. Optimization is also used for the determination of parameters. In the case of Sugeno-type models with Center of Singletons defuzzification, and of the generalized error models, the estimation is especially simple since the problem is linear in unknown parameters and the least-squares technique can be used.

In this case the output of the UA with n inputs can be written in the form

$$y(k) = \frac{\sum_{i1}, \sum_{i2}, \ldots, \sum_{in} S_{i1,i2,\ldots,in}(\mathbf{u}) r_{i1,i2,\ldots,in}}{\sum_{i1}, \sum_{i2}, \ldots, \sum_{in} S_{i1,i2,\ldots,in}} \tag{11}$$

where $S_{i1,i2,\ldots,in}$ is the element of the multidimensional structure (tensor)

$$S = \mu_1 \otimes \mu_2 \otimes \cdots \otimes \mu_n \tag{12}$$

which is obtained by the composition of the fulfillment grade vectors (of dimensions mi) of the membership functions on the universe of discourse

$$\mu_i = [\mu_i^1, \mu_i^2, \ldots, \mu_i^{mi}]^T \tag{13}$$

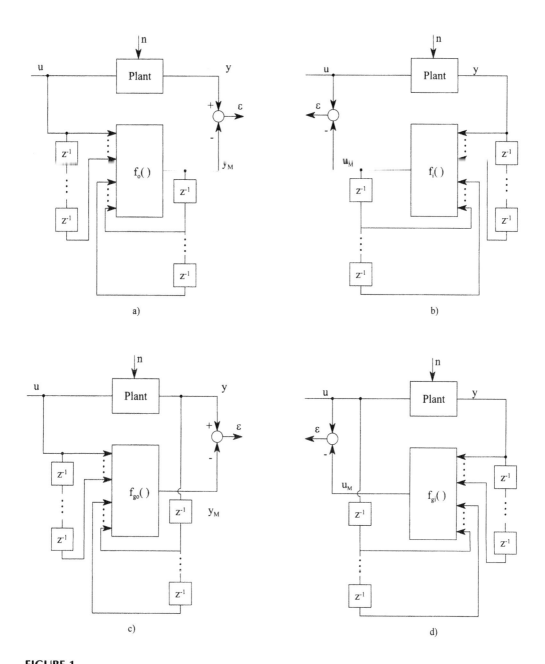

FIGURE 1

(a) The output, (b) the input, (c) the generalized output, and (d) the generalized input error identification models.

where $r_{i1,i2,...,in}$ are consequences of the Sugeno-type model according to equation (1). In the simplest case they are constants.

If the membership functions of all the input variables form a complete set, i.e., their sum on the universe of discourse of all input variables equals 1, the denominator of equation (11) becomes 1.

It is well known that the convergence of the identification procedure is assured only if the plant is persistently excited. The same is true also for the identification of ГГ1.^ПХ models by fuzzy logic UDA. However, in this case another condition for the convergence of UDA is necessary; namely, excitation throughout. This is excitation in all ranges of the variables entering the UA. The convergence of identification is assured, therefore, only by throughout persistent excitation.

Another important point of identification is convergence in the presence of noise. Since white noise has minimal variance, all optimization procedures seek the minimum of the criterion function (4) in the sense that the residuals $\varepsilon(k)$ become white noise. An unbiased estimation is possible only in cases where the noise has the special character that is illustrated in Figure 2.

The estimation is unbiased if the structure of the model is the same as the structure of the plant and the white noise enters the plant in a special location depending on the type of model used in the identification. With the output error model, this is the output of the UDA. The plant output is, in this case, the sum of the uncorrupted signal of the UDA and the white noise. With the input error model this is the input of the plant. The input signal of the UDA is the sum of the

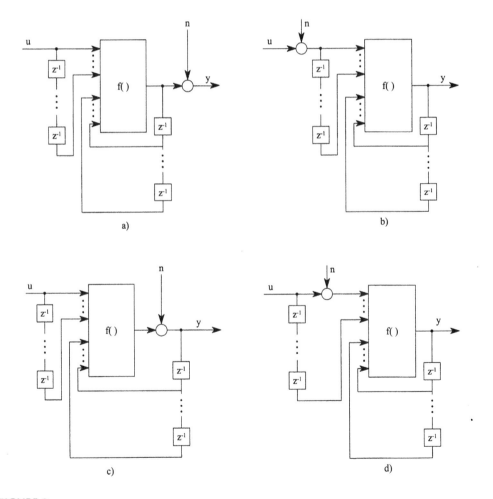

FIGURE 2
The representation of noise that results in an unbiased estimation for (a) the output, (b) the input, (c) the generalized output, and (d) the generalized input error models.

uncorrupted input signal and the white noise. With the generalized output error model the white noise enters the plant at the output of the UA. The corrupted output signal is fed back and represents the input of the UA. With the generalized input error model the white noise enters the plant only at the first input of the UA.

3 FUZZY ADAPTIVE CANCELATION CONTROL

When the process parameters of a controlled process are either poorly known or vary during operation, the use of the adaptive control technique is necessary to obtain a high-performance control system. Many solutions have been proposed to make the control systems adaptive. One of these solutions the model-reference adaptive system, evolved in the late 1950s. The main innovation of this system was the presence of a reference model that specifies the desired dynamics of the closed-loop system. The reference model can also be implicitly included in the closed-loop system as a cancelation principle. The cancelation principle of model-reference control has been used to develop a fuzzy adaptive system.

In this chapter a fuzzy adaptive cancelation controller that is based on the inverse fuzzy model is investigated. The adaptive scheme is tested on a real, mutable process with single dynamics, i.e., a highly nonlinear heat exchanger pilot plant whose parameters vary during the operation time. The nature of the process requires an adaptive scheme. The fuzzy adaptive scheme is based on the recursive fuzzy identification of the inverse model. The algorithm requires on-line identification developed and discussed in this chapter. A fuzzy Takagi–Sugeno zero-order model is obtained on the basis of fuzzified process input and output variables. The fuzzy model actually represents the relationship between those fuzzified variables.

3.1 Fuzzy Identification

In this subsection Takagi–Sugeno fuzzy identification is discussed. Suppose the rule base of a fuzzy system is as follows:

$$R_i: \quad \text{if } x_i \text{ is } A_i \text{ and } x_2 \text{ is } B_i \text{ then } y = f_i(x_1, x_2), \quad i = 1, \ldots, N \tag{14}$$

where x_1 and x_2 are the input variables of the fuzzy system, y is an output variable, and A_i, B_i are fuzzy sets characterized by their membership functions. The if-parts (antecedents) of the rules describe fuzzy regions in the space of input variables and the then-parts (consequent) are functions of the inputs; usually defined as

$$f_i(x_1, x_2) = a_i x_i + b_i x_2 + r_i \tag{15}$$

where a_i, b_i are the consequent parameters. For $a_i = b_i = 0$ the model becomes a Takagi–Sugeno fuzzy model of the zeroth order. Such a very simplified fuzzy model can be regarded as a collection of several linear models applied locally in the fuzzy regions defined by the rule antecedents. The smooth transition from one subspace to another is assured by the overlapping of the fuzzy regions.

Fuzzy identification based on the fuzzy Sugeno model of the zeroth order is concerned with fuzzy rules of the following form:

$$R_i: \quad \text{if } x_1 \text{ is } A_i \text{ and } x_2 \text{ is } B_i \text{ then } y = r_i, \quad i = 1, \ldots, N \tag{16}$$

This is a singleton fuzzy model where f_i is a constant.

Rule premises are formulated as fuzzy AND relations on the Cartesian product set $X = X_1 \times X_2$, and several rules are connected by logical OR. Fuzzification of a crisp input value x_1 produces a column fuzzy set

$$\mu(x_1) = [\mu_{A_1}(x_1), \mu_{A_2}(x_1), \ldots, \mu_{A_m}(x_1)]^T \tag{17}$$

and similarly for a crisp value x_2. The degrees of fulfilment for all possible AND combinations of rule premises are calculated and written into a matrix S. If the algebraic product is used as an AND operator, this matrix can be directly obtained by the multiplication

$$S = \mu_1 \otimes \mu_2^T = \mu_1 \cdot \mu_2^T \tag{18}$$

where $\mu_1(m \times 1)$ and $\mu_2(n \times 1)$ are the input fuzzy sets.

A crisp output value y is computed by a simplified algorithm for singletons as a weighted mean value (Center of Singletons):

$$y = \frac{\sum_{i=1}^{n} \sum_{j=1}^{m} s_{ij} r_{ij}}{\sum_{i=1}^{n} \sum_{j=1}^{m} s_{ij}} \tag{19}$$

The dimension of the matrix $S(m \times n)$, which actually represents the structure of the model, depends on the dimensions of the input fuzzy sets $\mu_1(m \times 1)$ and $\mu_2(n \times 1)$. The fuzzy relational matrix R consists of the elements r_{ij}.

In order to apply a standard least-squares method to estimate the parameters r_{ij} the vectors s and r are formed from S and R, respectively

$$
\begin{aligned}
s &= (s_{11} \quad s_{12} \quad s_{1n} \quad \cdots \quad s_{m1} \quad s_{m2} \quad \cdots \quad s_{mn})^T \\
r &= (r_{11} \quad r_{12} \quad \cdots \quad r_{1n} \quad \cdots \quad r_{m1} \quad r_{m2} \quad \cdots \quad r_{mn})^T
\end{aligned} \tag{20}
$$

Using these vectors, equation (19) is rewritten as

$$y = \frac{s^T \cdot r}{s^T \cdot I} = \frac{s^T(x_1, x_2) \cdot r}{s^T(x_1, x_2) \cdot I} \tag{21}$$

where I defines the vector of ones of the same dimension ($n \cdot m \times 1$) as s and r. The elements r_{ij} are estimated on the basis of the observations, which are obtained in equidistant time intervals by measuring the process input and output. A system of linear equations is constructed from the above equations for the time points $t = t_i, t = t_2, \ldots, t = t_N$

$$
\begin{bmatrix}
s^T(t_1) \\
s^T(t_2) \\
\vdots \\
s^T(t_N)
\end{bmatrix} \cdot r =
\begin{bmatrix}
s^T(t_1) \cdot Iy(t_1) \\
s^T(t_2) \cdot Iy(t_2) \\
\vdots \\
s^T(t_N) \cdot Iy(t_N)
\end{bmatrix} \tag{22}
$$

The system is of the form

$$\Psi \cdot r = \Omega \tag{23}$$

with a known nonsquare matrix Ψ and a known vector Ω. The solution of this overdetermined system is obtained by taking the pseudo-inverse as an optimal solution of the vector r in a least-squares sense

$$r = (\Psi^T \Psi)^{-1} \Psi^T \Omega \tag{24}$$

where Ψ stands for the fuzzified data matrix with dimension $N \times (n \cdot m)$ and Ω has the dimension $N \times 1$.

In the case of more than two input variables (MISQ: multi-input–single-output fuzzy system), S and R are no longer matrices, but become tensors, defined on the total product space of the inputs.

When the observations are obtained sequentially, the recursive equation can be derived. The procedure is known as recursive identification. The acquisition of new data at certain time instants gives information on the current behavior of the process. Each observation, each pair of input–output data, contributes a new equation that gives information on the process parameters. The whole algorithm should be calculated in the time between two samples. This restriction can be a serious problem. The identification procedure in recursive form saves some computing time and is suitable when the process parameters are time-varying. When the process parameters are changing during the operation, it is necessary to eliminate the influence of old data. This can be done using a method with exponential weighting. The old data are forgotten exponentially because the new samples give more adequate information on the current behavior of the process. The method of recursive fuzzy identification with exponential weighting is based on the loss function

$$J(\hat{\mathbf{r}}_c) = \sum_{k=1}^{N} \lambda^{N-k} \left(y(k) - \frac{\mathbf{s}^T(k)}{\mathbf{s}(k)\mathbf{I}} \hat{\mathbf{r}}_c(k) \right)^2 \tag{25}$$

where $y(k)$ is the current value of the process output, $\mathbf{s}^T(k)$ is the fuzzy data vector in the transposed form, $\hat{\mathbf{r}}_c(k)$ is the current value of the estimated fuzzy relational vector, and λ is the forgetting factor. The proper value of the forgetting factor is chosen between 0.95 and 0.98 as proposed by Isermann, Lachmann, and Matko [14].

Optimizing the loss function (25) and expressing the normalized fuzzy data vector as

$$\mathbf{s}_n(k) = \frac{\mathbf{s}^T(k)}{\mathbf{s}(k)\mathbf{I}} \tag{26}$$

the recursive fuzzy identification with exponential weighting is obtained in the following form:

$$\hat{\mathbf{r}}_c(k+1) = \hat{\mathbf{r}}_c(k) + \mathbf{K}(k)(y(k+1) = \mathbf{s}_n^T(k)\hat{\mathbf{r}}_c(k)) \tag{27}$$

$$\mathbf{K}(k) = \mathbf{P}(k)\mathbf{s}_n(k+1)[\lambda + \mathbf{s}_n^T(k+1)\mathbf{P}(k)\mathbf{s}_n(k)]^{-1} \tag{28}$$

$$\mathbf{P}(k+1) = \frac{1}{\lambda}[\mathbf{I} - \mathbf{K}(k)\mathbf{s}_n^t(k+1)]\mathbf{P}(k) \tag{29}$$

Equation (27) expresses the new estimate $\hat{\mathbf{r}}_c(k+1)$ of the process parameters as a correction of the previous estimate $\hat{\mathbf{r}}_c(k)$. The correction is proportional to the error between the observed value of y at time $k+1$ and the prediction of $y(k+1)$ which is based on the preceding estimates of the parameters.

The initial value of the matrix is chosen as the covariance of the initial values of the estimated fuzzy relational vector parameters $\hat{\mathbf{r}}_c$ as follows:

$$\mathbf{P}(0) = \text{cov}(\hat{\mathbf{r}}_c - \mathbf{r}). \tag{30}$$

When there is no a priori information on the initial values of the estimated parameters, the initial values of the matrix $\mathbf{P}(0)$ have to be chosen sufficiently large,

$$\mathbf{P}(0) = \alpha\mathbf{I}, \qquad \alpha \gg 1 \tag{31}$$

and the initial values of the estimated fuzzy relational vector parameters are set to

$$\hat{\mathbf{r}}_c(0) = \mathbf{0} \tag{32}$$

The application of recursive fuzzy identification requires continuous monitoring and supervision of several parameters. The identification algorithm can be started in a closed loop after specifying free parameters and setting the initial conditions for parameter estimation. These problems are connected with the start-up procedure or preidentification. Another problem is persistent excitation in the closed loop. All these problems are discussed in the subsection on supervision and coordination.

3.2 Fuzzy Adaptive Cancelation Controller Based on Fuzzy Relational Matrix

Fuzzy models give some advantage in comparison to the conventional models, and this justifies the introduction of the fuzzy adaptive system shown in Figure 3.

The fuzzy adaptive system consists of the recursive identification of the fuzzy model and the fuzzy controller. In our case, the fuzzy model of the process is given in the form of the relational matrix representation of the process inverse. This model is used by the cancelation fuzzy controller. In the next two subsections, the relational matrix identification and the fuzzy cancelation controller will be given.

The conventional cancelation control is used for tracking control problems and the model-reference control. The basic idea of the cancelation control is to design a controller that ensures the desired closed-loop response. Basically, this is the controller that can be encountered in model-reference adaptive control. The closed-loop transfer function, consisting of a conventional cancelation controller and the process, is supposed to be equal to the prescribed reference model,

$$G_m(z) = \frac{Y(z)}{W(z)} = \frac{G_r(z)G_p(z)}{1 + G_r(z)G_p(z)} \tag{33}$$

where $G_m(z)$ is the reference model, $G_r(z)$ is the transfer function of the controller in the direct loop, and $G_p(z)$ is the transfer function of the process. To obtain the closed-loop response defined with the reference model as in equation (33), the controller transfer function is equal to

$$G_r(z) = \frac{1}{G_p(z)} \cdot \frac{G_m(z)}{1 - G_m(z)} \tag{34}$$

The goal of the cancelation controllers is to cancel the process dynamic with the cancelation part of the controller and to implement the model-reference dynamic with the model-reference part of the controller. Mathematically, this can be described as follows:

$$G_{comp} = \frac{1}{G_p(z)} \tag{35}$$

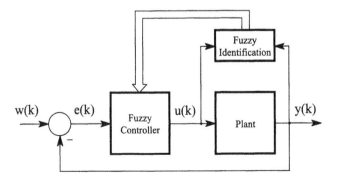

FIGURE 3
The scheme of the fuzzy adaptive system.

This equation expresses the cancelation part and the following equation expresses noncancelation part:

$$G_{\text{noncomp}}(z) = \frac{G_m(z)}{1 - G_m(z)} - \frac{B_m(z)z^{-d}}{A_m(z) - B_m(z)z^{-d}} \tag{36}$$

where $B_m(z)z^{-d}$ is the numerator and $A_m(z)$ the denominator of the reference-model transfer function.

The cancelation characteristic involves some constraints. The first problem is the realization of a controller connected with the time delay of the process. The transport time delay of the process cannot be compensated and should be incorporated into the closed-loop system as the delay of the reference model. So the delay of the reference-model should be chosen equal to or greater than the delay of the controlled process. A detailed explanation is to be found in [13] and [14]. Other constraints are related to the cancelation of the zeros and poles that lie outside the unit circle. The cancelation implies that all poles and zeros must lie inside the unit circle, and so the cancelation controller in its original form is applicable only to the stable minimum-phase processes. This drawback can be eliminated by appropriate measures. The cancelation can be avoided if the desired polynomial $B_m(z)$ includes all of the zeros of the process outside the unit circle. The polynomial $A_m(z) - B_m(z)z^{-d}$ must include all of the unstable poles of the process.

The fuzzy cancelation controller is designed with the same considerations as the conventional cancelation controller. It also consists of a cancelation and a noncancelation part. The cancelation part in the case of fuzzy cancelation controllers is realized as the fuzzy inverse model of the process. The fuzzy inverse model of a mutable single dynamic process has two inputs, $y(k)$ and $y(k - 1)$, and one output, $u_m(k)$. The fuzzy inverse model is obtained using the input error model shown in Figure 4 and described by the fuzzy relational equation.

$$U_{k+1} = Y_k \circ Y_{k-1} \circ \mathbf{R}_0 \tag{37}$$

The noncancelation part of the controller is the same as for the conventional cancelation controller,

$$\frac{U_{\text{aux}}(z)}{E(z)} = \frac{G_m(z)}{1 - G_m(z)}, \tag{38}$$

where $E(z)$ is the Z-transform of the error signal $e(k)$, and $U_{\text{aux}}(z)$ is the Z-transform of auxiliary control signal $u_{\text{aux}}(k)$, which is the input of the inverse fuzzy model. The fuzzy data matrix of the controller's inverse model is composed of the actual value of the auxiliary control signal $u_{\text{aux}}(k)$ and of the one-time sample delayed auxiliary control signal $u_{\text{aux}}(k - 1)$. The output of the inverse model is the current control signal $u(k)$. Figure 5 shows the fuzzy cancelation controller in the closed loop.

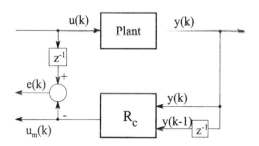

FIGURE 4
The input error model.

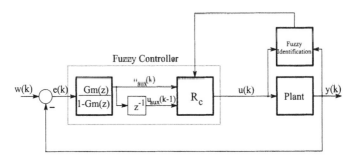

FIGURE 5
The scheme of fuzzy cancelation adaptive system.

The relation between the auxiliary control signal and the control signal is described by

$$u(k) = \frac{\mathbf{s}^T(\mu(u_{\text{aux}}(k)), \mu(u_{\text{aux}}(k-1))) \cdot \hat{\mathbf{r}}_c(k)}{\mathbf{s}^T(\mu(u_{\text{aux}}(k)), \mu(u_{\text{aux}}(k-1))) \cdot \mathbf{I}} \tag{39}$$

where $\mathbf{s}^T(\mu(u_{\text{aux}}(k)), \mu(u_{\text{aux}}(k-1)))$ is the fuzzy data vector and $\hat{\mathbf{r}}_c$ is the current estimate of the fuzzy relational vector of the inverse process.

The described algorithm of the fuzzy cancelation adaptive controller exhibits some advantages over the conventional adaptive technique. These advantages are based on fuzzy identification, which enables the identification of nonlinear process dynamics and also implicitly describes the operating point of the process.

3.3 Supervision and Coordination

The implementation of fuzzy adaptive control requires an additional supervision and coordination system to eliminate and avoid all expected or unexpected changes in the operating conditions of the controlled process in the adaptive control loop. These changes may result in unacceptable or unstable control behavior of the fuzzy adaptive system. Therefore, continuous monitoring and supervision of the fuzzy adaptive control loop functions are required.

A very important part of supervision is the P-controller which controls the difference between the variable on the inverse model input $u_{\text{aux}}(k)$ and the process output $y(k)$. In the ideal case, both variables should be equal. When the controller action of the implemented fuzzy cancelation controller is too weak or too strong, an additional supervision controller is needed. The input into the P-supervisory controller is the difference between the variables $y(k)$ and $u_{\text{aux}}(k)$ and the output is $u_p(k)$ which, together with the output from the fuzzy cancelation controller $u_f(k)$, forms the control signal $u(k)$ of the process. Figure 6 shows the fuzzy cancelation controller with the P-supervisory controller in the closed loop.

3.4 Fuzzy Adaptive Control of the Heat Exchanger Pilot Plant

The adaptive approach discussed has been implemented in a real temperature plant, which consists of a plate heat exchanger through which hot water from an electrically heated reservoir is continuously circulated in countercurrent flow to cold process fluid (cold water). The thermocouples are located in the inlet and outlet flows of the exchanger: both flow rates can be monitored visually. Power to the heater is controlled by time-proportional control using the external control loop. The flow of the heating fluid is controlled by the proportional motor-driven valve. A schematic diagram of the plant is shown in Figure 7.

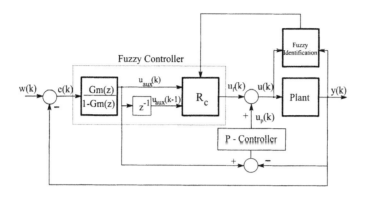

FIGURE 6
The scheme of the fuzzy cancelation adaptive system with supervision system.

The temperature plant is a process wherein the variables are significantly dependent on the spatial coordinates at a given moment in time, so the dynamics of the heart of the process, the heat exchanger, can be represented by the following set of partial diferential equations:

$$\frac{\partial T_1(z, t)}{\partial t} + B_1 \frac{\partial T_1(z, t)}{\partial z} = k_1[T_s(t) - T_1(z, t)]$$

$$\frac{\partial T_s(t)}{\partial t} = k_2[T_2(z, t) - T_s(t)] - k_2[T_s(t) - T_1(z, t)] \tag{40}$$

$$\frac{\partial T_2(z, t)}{\partial t} - v_2(t)\frac{\partial T_2(z, t)}{\partial z} = k_1[T_s(t) - T_2(z, t)]$$

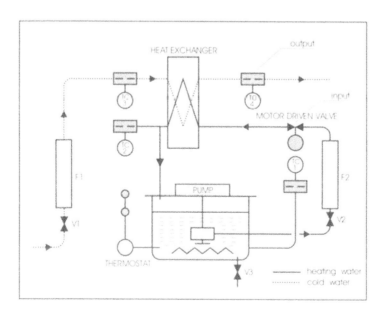

FIGURE 7
The heat exchanger pilot plant.

where $T_1(z, t)$ is measured by the temperature sensor TC4, $T_2(z, t)$ is measured by the temperature sensor TC1, and $T_s(t)$ represent the temperatures of the cold water, heating water and the iron wall, respectively; $v_1(t)$, measured by the flow sensor F1, and $v_2(t)$ measured by the flow sensor F2, are the velocities of the cold and heating water; and k_1 and k_2 are constants that include the heat transfer coefficients and the physical dimensions of the heat exchanger.

The solution of the set of equation (40) yields the mathematical model of the heat exchanger with the input defined by the current velocity $v_2(t)$ of the heating water and the output defined as the outlet temperature T_1 of the cold water. To obtain the simple model of the heat exchanger, theoretical modeling would be very difficult because of the nonlinear character of the third equation from the set (40). Furthermore, the heat exchanger is just one part of the plant, so the sensors and the actuators should also be modeled. The motor-driven valve exhibits a strong nonlinear and time-varying behavior.

System modeling based on the conservation laws and first principles would be a very difficult, expensive, and time-consuming task. Instead, fuzzy identification of the process is used. Although the process is very complex, it could be presented as a model with approximately first-order dynamics with small time delay, with significantly time-carrying parameters and nonlinearities according to the operating point.

During the experiments, some values of the physical parameters (velocity v_1 of the outlet and the temperature T_2 at the inlet of the exchanger) that are supposed to be constant were changing. The time course of the changing outlet flow v_1 is presented in Figure 8. The inlet temperature of the heated water T_2 is controlled using a simple on–off controller and varies between 60°C and 65°C. These variations have a great influence on the gain and on the dominant time constant of the process. A period of initially 2500 s was been used for the preidentification in the closed loop. During this period, the robust PI-controller was used to control the inlet temperature T_2. Afterwards, the fuzzy adaptive controller was switched on.

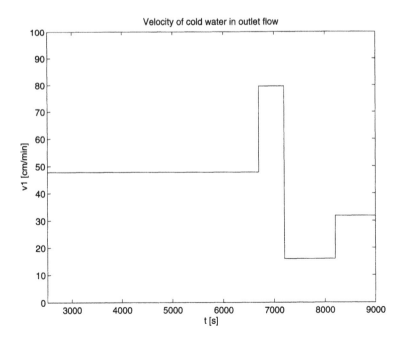

FIGURE 8
Velocity of cold water in outlet flow.

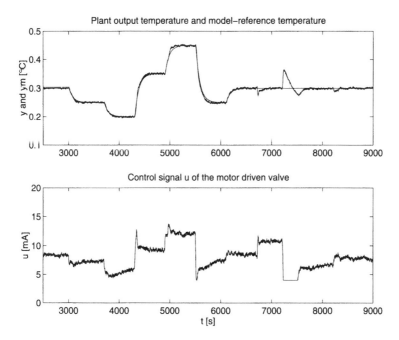

FIGURE 9
Plant output temperature and model-reference temperature.

The output of the closed-loop $y(t)$ and the reference model output $y_m(t)$ are shown in Figure 9. In this figure only the period of the fuzzy adaptive control is shown. In spite of changing conditions (changing outlet velocity v_1 and inlet temperature T_1) and the nonlinear system dynamics, the closed-loop response obtained using the proposed fuzzy adaptive algorithm exhibits a very good performance in both modes, in the model following mode and in the disturbance rejection mode.

4   FUZZY MODEL-BASED PREDICTIVE CONTROL

Predictive control has become a very important area of research in recent years. It is based on the forecast of the output signal y at each sampling instant. The forecast is made implicitly or explicitly according to the model of the controlled process. In the next step the control is selected that brings the predicted process output signal back to the reference signal so as to minimize the area between the reference and the output signal. The fundamental methods that are essentially based on the principle of predictive control are Richalet's method [23] (model algorithmic control), Cutler's method (dynamic matrix control), De Keyser's method (extended prediction self-adaptive control), and Ydstie's method (extended horizon adaptive control).

According to the process model, two main approaches have been developed in the area of predictive control. The first is based on the parametric model of the controlled process. The parametric model could be described in the form of a transfer function, or in the state-space domain. An important disadvantage of using the parametric model is that it represents a linearized model of the process. The control of strong nonlinear processes could be unsatisfactory. The second approach proposed is based on the nonparametric model. The advantage of this approach is that the model coefficient can be obtained directly from samples of the input and output responses without assuming the model structure. Predictive control based on fuzzy models represents a combination of the nonparametric and parametric approaches to predictive control.

Predictive control based on a fuzzy model is capable of controlling very difficult processes, such as nonlinear processes, processes with long time delays and nonminimum phase. The controllers based on the prediction strategy also exhibit remarkable robustness with respect to model mismatch and unmodeled dynamics.

Model-based predictive control (MBPC) is a control strategy based on the explicit use of a dynamic model of the process to predict the future behavior of the process output signal over a certain (finite) horizon and to evaluate control actions to minimize a certain cost function. MBPC stands for a collection of several different techniques all based on the same principles. Originally, the algorithms were developed in the linear domain, but the basic idea of prediction has been extended to nonlinear systems. The direct approach, based on optimization of the proposed cost function, is accompanied by a major drawback. Due to the nonlinear nature of the models (fuzzy models, neural network models, or any other nonlinear models), a nonlinear and nonconvex optimization problem has to be solved in each sampling period. It cannot be guaranteed in real-time applications that the global optimum is found within one sampling period. To overcome this disadvantage, some attempts at using approximate local linear models for each operating domain and the linear MBPC algorithm have been reported in the literature [22, 23].

4.1 Dynamic Matrix Control Algorithm

In this subsection the basics of predictive control based on the convolution theorem are introduced. The convolution model is described using

$$y(k) = \sum_{i=1}^{\infty} g_i\, \Delta u_{k-i} + n(k) \tag{41}$$

where $y(k)$ represents the output signal, $\Delta u(k)$ is the input signal, g_i are the coefficients of the process step response, and $n(k)$ describes the unmodeled dynamics.

The control signal in the case of the model-reference predictive control is obtained optimizing the criterion function according to the variable $\Delta u(k + j)$:

$$J = \sum_{j=N_1}^{N_2} (\hat{y}(k+j) - y_m(k+j))^2 + \lambda \sum_{j=0}^{N_u-1} (\Delta u(k+j))^2 \tag{42}$$

where $\Delta u(k + j) = 0$ for $j \geq N_u$ is assumed. The variable $y_m(k + j)$ represents j-steps-ahead prediction of the reference signal; $\hat{y}(k + j)$ describes the prediction of the output signal obtained using the process model; and $\Delta u(k + j)$ stands for the prediction of the control signal. The values N_1 and N_2 are the lower and upper prediction horizon and N_u denotes the control prediction horizon. The parameter λ represents the weight of the control signal.

The output signal prediction can be divided into the free response of the process $y_p(k + j)$ and the forced response $y_v(k + j)$ as follows:

$$\hat{y}(k+j) = y_p(k+j) + y_v(k+j) + n(k) \tag{43}$$

The free response of the process denotes the behavior where $\Delta u(k + j) = 0$ for $j = 1, \ldots, N_u$ is assumed. The forced response describes the behavior in the case of the input signal $\Delta u(k + j)$ for $j > 0$.

Output signal prediction is according to the superposition described in the following form:

$$\hat{y}(k+j) = \sum_{i=1}^{j} g_i \, \Delta u(k+j-i) + \sum_{i=j+1}^{\infty} g_i \, \Delta u(k+j-i) + n(k) \tag{44}$$

$$= y(k) + \sum_{i=1}^{j} g_i \, \Delta u(k+j-i) + \sum_{i=j+1}^{\infty} g_i \, \Delta u(k+j-i) - \sum_{i=1}^{\infty} g_i \, \Delta u(k-i) \tag{45}$$

The previous equation can also be described in the compact form

$$\hat{y}(k+j) - \mathbf{g}_j \, \Delta u(k+j) + p_j \tag{46}$$

where

$$\mathbf{g}_j = [g_1 \quad g_2, \dots, g_j] \tag{47}$$

denotes the vector of the step response coefficients, and p_j represents the free response of the system given by equation

$$p_j = y(k) + \sum_{i=j+1}^{\infty} g_i \, \Delta u(k+j-i) - \sum_{i=1}^{\infty} g_i \, \Delta u(k-i) \tag{48}$$

$$p_j = y(k) + \sum_{i=1}^{\infty} (g_{j+i} - g_i) \, \Delta u(k-i) \tag{49}$$

In the case of asymptoticaly stable processes, the upper equation can be given in the form

$$p_j = y(k) + \sum_{i=1}^{N} (g_{j+i} - g_i) \, \Delta u(k-i) \tag{50}$$

where the maximum prediction horizon N is chosen to fulfill the equation

$$g_{j+i} - g_i \cong 0 \tag{51}$$

for $i > N$ and $j = N_1, \dots, N_2$. Equation (51) can be fulfilled only for asymptoticaly stable processes.

Equation (42) can be described in the compact matrix form

$$J = (\mathbf{y} - \mathbf{y}_m)(\mathbf{y} - \mathbf{y}_m)^T + \lambda \, \Delta \mathbf{u} \, \Delta \mathbf{u}^T \tag{52}$$

where

$$\mathbf{y} = [\hat{y}(k+N_1), \dots, \hat{y}(k+N_2)]^T \tag{53}$$

denotes the vector of output signal prediction and $\mathbf{y}_m$ is vector of reference signal prediction between the lower and upper prediction horizon described as follows.

$$\mathbf{y}_m = [y_m(k+N_1), \dots, y_m(k+N_2)]^T \tag{54}$$

Vector $\Delta \mathbf{u}$ is vector of the control signal sequence, described as follows:

$$\Delta \mathbf{u} = [\Delta u(k), \dots, \Delta u(k+N_u-1)]^T \tag{55}$$

The prediction of the output signal in the compact matrix form is given as

$$\mathbf{y} = \mathbf{G} \, \Delta \mathbf{u} + \mathbf{p} \tag{56}$$

where

$$
\mathbf{G} = \begin{bmatrix} g_{N_1} & \cdots & g_1 & 0 & \cdots & 0 \\ g_{N_1+1} & \cdots & g_2 & g_1 & 0 & \vdots \\ \vdots & \vdots & \vdots & \vdots & \vdots & \vdots \\ g_{N_2} & g_{N_2-1} & \cdots & \cdots & \cdots & g_{N_2-N_u+1} \end{bmatrix} \tag{57}
$$

and the vector $\mathbf{p}$ represents the sequence of the process free response

$$
\mathbf{p} = [p_{N_1}, \ldots, p_{N_2}]. \tag{58}
$$

Considering the previous equations, the criterion function can be described as

$$
J = (\mathbf{G}\,\Delta\mathbf{u} + \mathbf{p} - \mathbf{y}_m)(\mathbf{G}\,\Delta\mathbf{u} + \mathbf{p} - \mathbf{y}_m)^T + \lambda\,\Delta\mathbf{u}\,\Delta\mathbf{u}^T \tag{59}
$$

The optimal solution of the criterion function gives the control law of the DMC algorithm in the form

$$
\Delta\mathbf{u} = (\mathbf{G}^T\mathbf{G} + \lambda\mathbf{I})^{-1}\mathbf{G}^T(\mathbf{y}_m - \mathbf{p}) \tag{60}
$$

The solution is given in vector form and provides the calculation of the input signal for N_u values in advance where only the first value is applied to the process. In the next sampling period the solution is computed again and another set of N_u values of the control is obtained according to a receding horizon strategy.

4.2 Calculation of the Dynamic Matrix Based on the Fuzzy Model

The main idea of fuzzy predictive control using the dynamic matrix is to combine the advantages of fuzzy modeling and predictive control. The idea is based on *on-line* computing of the dynamic matrix $\mathbf{G}$. The method described offers some advantages in the case of nonlinear processes where the dynamics depend on the operating point and can be presented as $\mathbf{G}(u, y)$. The dynamic matrix is calculated on the basis of the fuzzy model $\mathbf{r}$ and the fuzzy inverse model $\mathbf{r}_{inv}$ of the process whenever the operating point of the system is changed. The vector $\mathbf{g}_j$ consists of the j normalized step response coefficients. These coefficient are calculated using the algorithm given below. First, the N-step-ahead prediction of the control signal $u_{pred}(k+N)$ is calculated:

$$
u_{pred}(k+N) = \frac{\mathbf{s}^T(y_m(k+N), y_m(k+N)) \cdot \mathbf{r}_{inv}}{\mathbf{s}^T(y_m(k+N), y_m(k+N)) \cdot \mathbf{I}} \tag{61}
$$

The predicted control action in the future is then given as the difference between the current control signal value $u(k)$ and the predicted control value $u_{pred}(k+N)$:

$$
\Delta u_{pred} = u_{pred}(k+N) - u(k) \tag{62}
$$

The predicted control signal $u_{pred}(k+N)$ is than used to calculate the future behavior of the system in the sense of predicted step response:

$$
g_1 = y(k) \tag{63}
$$

$$
g_j = \frac{\mathbf{s}^T(g_{j-1}, u_{pred}(k+N)) \cdot \mathbf{r}}{\mathbf{s}^T(g_{j-1}, u_{pred}(k+N)) \cdot \mathbf{I}}, \qquad j = 1, \ldots, N_2 \tag{64}
$$

The vector $\mathbf{g}_j$ is then normalized in the following manner:

$$\mathbf{g}_j = \frac{|\mathbf{g}_j - g_1|}{|\Delta u_{\text{pred}}|} \tag{65}$$

The dynamic matrix $\mathbf{G}$ is then formed of the coefficient vectors $\mathbf{g}_j$ for $j = N_1, \ldots, N_2$.

A new dynamic matrix $\mathbf{G}$ of the system is calculated when the reference signal $w(k)$ is changed, or the difference between the process output $y(k)$ and the model-reference signal $y_m(k)$ becomes significant.

4.3   Application of Predictive Control Based on the Fuzzy Model to a Simulated Process

This subsection shows the behavior of the proposed predictive control algorithm applied to a nonlinear process. Application to the simulated nonlinear process of liquid level control is discussed. The simulation of the problem may give a very transparent insight into how predictive control based on the fuzzy model actually works. The almost complete compensation of the nonlinearity of the process by the proposed control algorithm can be seen due to the almost perfect model-reference matching at all operating points. Generally, it can be said that nonlinear algorithms that are designed on the basis of the nonlinear process model describing the nonlinear process behavior sufficiently accurately show acceptable and adequate control performance. Predictive control based on the fuzzy model is also robust with respect to process–model mismatch.

4.3.1 Modeling of Liquid Level Process.
The structure of a highly nonlinear liquid level process used as an example of predictive control consists of a spherical tank, a valve, and a motor-driven valve. The liquid level in the closed spherical tank is manipulated by the incoming flow rate $\Phi_{\text{in}}(t)$. The flow rate of the stream is controlled by the motor-driven valve. The system is disturbed by the outlet flow rate $\Phi_{\text{out}}(t)$.

The nonlinear dynamics of the system are mainly caused by the spherical shape of the tank, the inner pressure p_i, and the valve characteristics.

The process can be theoretically determined on the basis of the equilibrium equation, which describes the known volume balance,

$$\Phi_{\text{in}}(t) - \Phi_{\text{out}}(t) = S(h(t)) \frac{dh(t)}{dt} \tag{66}$$

In equation (66) $h(t)$ denotes the liquid level and $S(h(t))$ is the transverse section of the tank, which changes according to the liquid level as

$$S(h(t)) = \pi(2Rh(t) - h^2(t)) \tag{67}$$

where R stands for the radius of the spherical tank.

The manipulated or input variable in this case is the incoming flow rate $\Phi_{\text{in}}(t)$. The controlled or output variable is the liquid level in the tank $h(t)$. The disturbance by the outlet flow rate $\Phi_{\text{out}}(t)$ can be described as

$$\Phi_{\text{out}}(t) = c_p \sqrt{2gh(t)} \tag{68}$$

where g is the gravitational acceleration and c_p is the constant of the outlet valve and denotes the transverse section of the outlet valve.

The nonlinear model of the liquid level process can be described by

$$\frac{dh(t)}{dt} = \frac{\Phi_{in}(t)}{\pi(2Rh(t) - h^2(t))} - \frac{c_p\sqrt{2gh(t)}}{\pi(2Rh(t) - h^2(t))} \tag{69}$$

$$\frac{dh(t)}{dt} = f(\Phi_{in}(t), h(t)) \tag{70}$$

where the process parameters have the values $R = 1\,\text{m}$, $c_p = 0.05\,\text{m}^2$ and $g = 9.81\,\text{m}/2^2$.

Linearization of the nonlinear model is give in the following to represent the behavior of the plant in a conventional way and for greater clarity. The linearized process dynamics are of first order and can be described by the following differential equation of first order:

$$\frac{dh(t)}{dt} = A(\Phi_{in_0}, h_0)h(t) + B(\Phi_{in_0}, h_0)\Phi_{in}(t) \tag{71}$$

The linearization is developed around the equilibrium or operating point which is given by

$$f(\Phi_{in_0}(t), h_0(t)) = 0 \tag{72}$$

$$\frac{dh(t)}{dt} = \frac{\Phi_{in_0}(t)}{(2Rh_0(t) - h_0^2(t))} - \frac{c_p\sqrt{2gh_0(t)}}{\pi(2Rh_0(t) - h_0^2(t))} = 0 \tag{73}$$

In equation (73) the operating point is denoted by the values $h_0(t)$ and Φ_{in_0}, which related by

$$\Phi_{in_0}(t) = c_p\sqrt{2gh(t)} \tag{74}$$

The constants $A(\Phi_{in_0}, h_0)$ and $B(\Phi_{in_0}, h_0)$ of the linear process model are then given by the partial derivatives

$$A(\Phi_{in_0}, h_0) = \frac{\partial f(\Phi_{in}(t))}{\partial h(t)}\Big|_{h_0(t), \Phi_{in_0}(t)} \tag{75}$$

$$B(\Phi_{in_0}, h_0) = \frac{\partial f(\Phi_{in}(t))}{\partial \Phi_{in_0}(t)}\Big|_{h_0(t), \Phi_{in_0}(t)} \tag{76}$$

and have the given values

$$A(\Phi_{in_0}, h_0) = \frac{-c_p g(2Rh_0(t) - h_0^2(t))}{\pi\sqrt{2gh_0(t)}(2Rh_0(t) - h_0^2(t))^2} \tag{77}$$

$$B(\Phi_{in_0}, h_0) = \frac{1}{\pi(2Rh_0(t) - h_0^2(t))} \tag{78}$$

For the classical representation of the process behavior the time constant T and process gain K are given, both of which are strongly dependent on the current operating point $h_0(t)$ and $\Phi_{in_0}(t)$. The time constant of the process is given as a function of operating point by

$$T(h_0(t)) = \frac{\pi\sqrt{2gh_0(t)}(2Rh_0(t) - h_0^2(t))}{c_p g} \tag{79}$$

and the process gain as

$$K(h_0(t)) = \frac{\sqrt{2gh_0(t)}}{c_p g} \tag{80}$$

Figures 10 and 11 represent the time courses of the process gain and process time constant, respectively, according to the operating point. The figures show transparently the strong

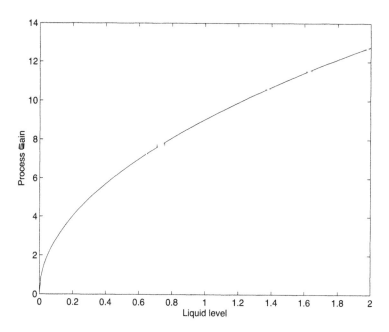

FIGURE 10
The process gain as a function of liquid level.

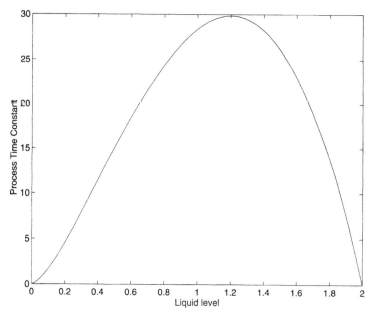

FIGURE 11
The process time constant as a function of liquid level.

nonlinear behavior of the process. The nonlinear analytical model is used to simulate the actual process. The sampling period, $T_s - 1 s$ used to obtain the simulated measurement data.

4.3.2. Fuzzy Modeling of the Process.

The Takagi–Sugeno fuzzy model of zeroth order has been constructed from only the input–output simulated data measurements. This procedure is the so-called parametric identification, because the structure of the model is known and only the parameters of the model are estimated. A step input excitation was used to obtain the input–output data. The dynamics of the process can be represented as a first-order NARX output model:

$$h(k + 1) = \mathscr{F}(\Phi_{in}(k), h(k)) \tag{81}$$

where $\mathscr{F}$ is an unknown nonlinear function approximated by the fuzzy model. The fuzzy model of the nonlinear function approximation is given in the form of the fuzzy matrix $\mathbf{R}$. To apply the predictive control algorithm based on the fuzzy model, the inverse process model must be obtained. The inverse dynamics of the process can be described using a first-order NARX input model:

$$\Phi_{in}(k) = \mathscr{G}(h(k - 1), h(k)) \tag{82}$$

where $\mathscr{G}$ stands for the unknown nonlinear function approximated by the fuzzy model. The fuzzy model of the nonlinear function approximation is given in the form of the fuzzy matrix $\mathbf{R}_{inv}$.

The domains of the fuzzy model and the fuzzy inverse model variables are divided on the membership sets, which represent the partition of the operating domain into the subdomains. In our simulation problem each variable has been divided into three membership sets. The upper part of Figure 12 represents the fuzzy variable of the signal Φ_{in}. The lower part of Figure 12 represents the fuzzy variable of the signal h. In general, the number, positions, and shapes of the membership functions are chosen based on the system behavior and can be chosen using several methods (clustering techniques, neural network approach, genetic algorithms approach). The

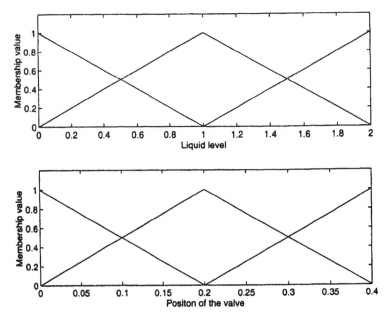

FIGURE 12
Membership functions for Φ_{in} and h.

resulting parameters of the fuzzy model and the fuzzy inverse model have been determinated by the ordinary least-squares algorithm.

The fuzzy model of the liquid level process in the fuzzy matrix form is then

$$\mathbf{R} = \begin{bmatrix} -0.0015 & 0.8978 & 0.0000 \\ 0.0296 & 0.9942 & 1.9448 \\ -0.0116 & 1.0575 & 2.0460 \end{bmatrix} \tag{83}$$

and can be reshaped column by column into the vector form **r**:

$$\mathbf{r} = (-0.0015 \quad 0.0296 \quad -0.0116 \quad 0.8978 \quad 0.9942 \quad 1.0575 \quad 0.000 \quad 1.9448 \quad 2.046)^T \tag{84}$$

The inverse fuzzy model of the liquid level process in the fuzzy matrix form has the following parameters:

$$\mathbf{R}_{inv} = \begin{bmatrix} -0.0150 & -0.8468 & 0.0000 \\ 1.4088 & 0.1774 & -1.1082 \\ 0.0013 & 1.7615 & 0.2903 \end{bmatrix} \tag{85}$$

and can similarly be reshaped column by column into the vector form $\mathbf{r}_{inv}$

$$\mathbf{r}_{inv} = $$
$$(-0.0150 \quad 1.4088 \quad 0.0013 \quad -0.8468 \quad 0.1774 \quad 1.7615 \quad 0.000 \quad -1.1082 \quad 0.2903)^T \tag{86}$$

Validation of the fuzzy model that is presented in Figure 13 was done using the input–output data for different excitation signals. A better approximation of the process output would be obtained using more membership functions for both input model variables. Additionally, the

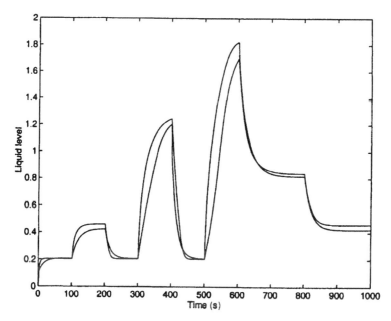

FIGURE 13
Validation of fuzzy model **R**.

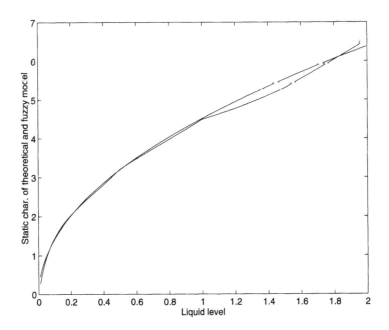

FIGURE 14
Comparison of steady-state characteristics of the fuzzy model and simulated process.

steady-state characteristic of the fuzzy model is compared with the steady-state characteristic of the simulated process in Figure 14.

4.4   Dynamic Matrix Control Based on the Fuzzy Model for the Liquid Level Process

The identified fuzzy model is integrated into a DMC predictive control scheme in the manner described earlier. The values of the lower and upper prediction horizons were chosen to be $N_1 = 1$ and $N_2 = 6$, respectively. The control horizon is chosen as $N_u = 3$, and the maximum prediction horizon as $N = 100$. The penalty of the control effort was chosen as $\lambda = 0.25$. The reference model transfer function was to be

$$G_m(z) = \frac{0.0952z^{-1}}{1 - 0.9048z^{-1}} \tag{87}$$

at the sampling time $T_s = 1$ s, which is the discrete equivalent of the continuous transfer function

$$G_m(s) = \frac{1}{10s + 1} \tag{88}$$

Figures 15 and 16 show the simulation results of the proposed fuzzy predictive control applied to the spherical tank output and the model-reference control signals, respectively. The effectiveness of the control scheme is confirmed by the perfect reference model tracking in the entire control domain despite the strong nonlinearity of the simulated process, shown in Figure 15 where the output signals $y(k)$ and $y_m(k)$ are presented. The control signal $u(k)$ is shown in Figure 16. The proposed novel fuzzy model-based dynamics matrix control algorithm exhibits very good tracking properties and also good disturbance rejection properties.

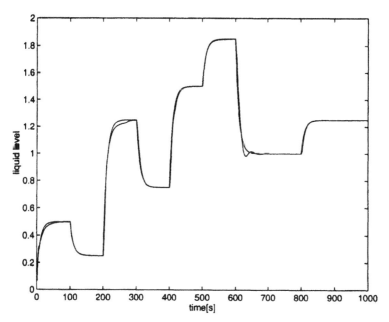

FIGURE 15
Simulation results of fuzzy predictive control for a spherical tank.

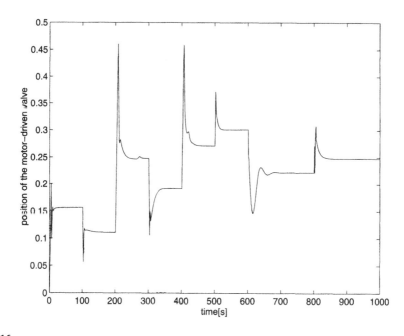

FIGURE 16
The control signal for fuzzy predictive control of a spherical tank.

4.5 Fuzzy Model-based Predictive Control of a Laboratory-Scale Heat Exchanger

The proposed fuzzy model-based predictive control was tested on a laboratory-scale heat exchanger. The equipment, depicted schematically in Figure 7, consists of a plate heat exchanger, through which hot water from an electrically heated reservoir is continuously circulated in countercurrent flow to cold process fluid (cold water). Thermocouples are located in the inlet and the outlet streams of the exchanger. The primary and secondary flow rates can be monitored visually. Power to the heater is controlled by an external control loop The flow of the heating fluid can be controlled by a proportional motor-driven value. The control variable is the control current of the valve (4–20 mA). The controlled variable is the temperature of the water in the secondary circuit at the heat exchanger outlet.

The plant was identified off-line on the basis of signals that assure a throughout excitation. The used sampling time was 4 s.

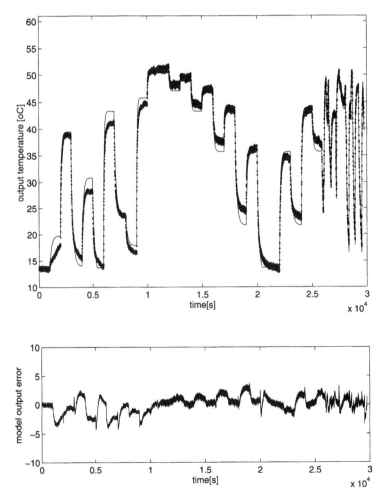

FIGURE 17
The validation of the fuzzy model.

As input to the neurofuzzy UA, the three-step-delayed control variable and the one-step-delayed controlled variable were used:

$$y_m(k) = f(u(k-3), y(k-1)) \tag{89}$$

Using three steps delay of the control variable, a dead time of 8 s was realized. The universes of discourse of the control and controlled variables was divided into five membership functions and the zero-order Sugeno model was used. Twenty-five parameters were estimated by the least-squares method. Analysis of the nonlinear model identified showed that the gains of the linearized first-order models varied in the range 0.49 to 6.5°C/mA, and the time constant in the range 30 to 278 s.

The uncertainty of the nonlinear fuzzy model was then evaluated. Figure 17 shows the validation of the nonlinear fuzzy model. It was assumed that the contribution of each linear model to the error, i.e., the difference between the simulated and the measured response, is proportional to the corresponding element of the matrix **S**, as is the control signal. The design parameters of the model-based predictive control, the control, and the prediction horizon, respectively, and the weight factor r were determined next with respect to the set of models, and the worst-case complementary sensitivity function, which must be below that used in the frequency response shaping. The resulting parameters were $N_1 = 2$, $N_2 = 30$, $N_u = 3$ and $r = 0.002$.

Figure 18 depicts the closed-loop response of the fuzzy model-based predictive control. It can be seen that the closed-loop response remained approximately the same over the entire range of the controlled variable and that the response was stable and adequate.

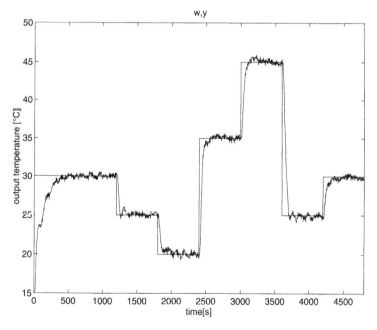

FIGURE 18
The closed loop response of the neurofuzzy model-based predictive control.

5   CONCLUSIONS

In this chapter the fuzzy adaptive cancelation control scheme was presented. The development of a new fuzzy adaptive scheme was motivated by the unsatisfactory results obtained using conventional adaptive techniques. The real-time experiments on the heat-exchanger plant showed that the novel algorithm introduces faster convergence and better performance in the presence of nonlinearity and unmeasured dynamics. The main disadvantages of this algorithm are the stability analysis, which is still unsolved, and the very complicated fuzzy model in the case of a higher-order system. The proposed approach seems to be usable for time-varying or nonlinear systems with simple dynamics. In such cases, the proposed algorithm gives some advantages over other conventional model-reference adaptive techniques. Fuzzy model-based predictive control was also discussed with respect to fuzzy logic as universal approximators, yielding the possibility of modeling nonlinear autoregressive models with exogenous variables. An application of the proposed design techniques to a laboratory-scale heat exchanger illustrated the practicability of the proposed design techniques.

REFERENCES

[1] J. Castro, Fuzzy logic controllers are universal approximators. *IEEE Trans. Systems, Man and Cybernetics*, pp. 629—635, 1995.

[2] C.R. Cutler, Dynamic matrix control—a computer control algorithm. *Pro. JACC, San Francisco*, 1982.

[3] F. Girosi, and T. Poggio, Networks and the best approximation property, *C.B.I.P.*, 45, 1994.

[4] R. Jager, H.B. Verbruggen, and P.M. Bruijn, Demystification of fuzzy control, in S.G. Tzalestas and A.N. Venestanopoulos (eds.) *Fuzzy Reasoning in Information, Decision and Control Systems*, Kluwer Academic, Dordrecht, 1994, pp. 165–197.

[5] V. Kecman, and B.M. Pfeiffer, Learning fuzzy rules equals radial basis function neural network training, *IEEE World Congress on Computational Intelligence, Orlando*, 1994.

[6] R. Lozano, and I.D. Landau, Redesign and explicit and implicit discrete time model reference adaptive control schemes. *Int. J. Control*, Vol. 33, pp. 247–268, 1981.

[7] J.R. Ragazzini, and G.F. Franklin, *Sampling Data Control Systems*. McGraw-Hill, New York, 1958.

[8] J. Sjöberg, Q. Zhang, L. Liung, A. Benveniste, B. Delyon, P-Y. Glorennec, H. Hjalmarsson, and A. Juditsky, Nonlinear black-box modeling in system identification: a unified overview. *Automatica*, Vol. 31, No. 12, pp. 1691–1724, 1995.

[9] I. Škrjanc, K. Kavšek-Biasizzo, and D. Matko, Real-time fuzzy adaptive control, *Engineering Applications of Artificial Intelligence*, Vol. 10, No. 1, pp. 53–61, 1997.

[10] T. Takagi, and M. Sugeno, Fuzzy identification of systems and its applications to modelling and control, *IEEE Trans. Systems, Man, and Cybernetics*, Vol. 15, pp. 116–132, 1985.

[11] B.P. Graham, and R.B. Newell, Fuzzy identification and control, first-order process, *Fuzzy Sets and Systems*, Vol. 26, pp. 255–273. North Holland, Amsterdam, 1988.

[12] C.G. Moore, and C.J. Harris, Indirect adaptive fuzzy control, *Int. J. Control*, Vol. 56, No. 2, pp. 441–468, 1992.

[13] K.J. Aström, and B. Wittenmark, *Computer-controlled systems, Theory and Design*. Prentice-Hall International, Englewood Cliffs, NJ, 1984.

[14] R. Isermann, K.H. Lachmann, and D. Matko, *Adaptive Control Systems*. Prentice-Hall, Englewood Cliffs, NJ, 1992.

[15] P. Eykhoff, *System Identification*. Wiley, New York, 1979.

[16] M. Sugeno, and K. Tanaka, Successive identification of a fuzzy model and its application to prediction of a complex system. *Fuzzy Sets and Systems*, Vol. 42, pp. 315–334, 1991.

[17] R.M. Tong, The evaluation of fuzzy models derived from experimental data. *Fuzzy Sets and Systems*, Vol. 4, pp. 1–12, 1980.

[18] D. Clarke, *Advances in Model-Based Predictive Control*. Oxford Science, Oxford, 1994.

[19] J. L., Marchetti, D.A. Mellicamp, and D.E. Seborg, Predictive control based on discrete convolution models. *Industrial and Engineering Chemistry, Process Design and Development*, Vol. 22, pp. 488–495, 1983.

[20] R. De Keyser, P.G.A. Van de Valde, and F.A.G. Dumortier, A Comparative study of self-adaptive long-range predictive control methods, *Automatica*, Vol. 24, No. 2, pp. 149–163, 1988.

[21] M. Ayala-Botto, T.J.J. van den Boom, A. Krjgsman, and J.S. da Costa, Constrained nonlinear predictive control based on input–output linearization using a neural network, *IFAC World Congress '96, San Francisco*, 1996, pp. 175–180.

[22] H.M. Ritt, P. Krauss, and H. Rake, Predictive control of pH-plant using gain scheduling, *IMACS CESA '96 Multiconference, Lille, France*, 1996, pp. 473–478.

[23] J. Richalet, A. Rault, J.L. Tertud, and J. Papon, Model predictive heuristic control: Application to industrial process, *Automatica*, Vol. 14, pp. 413–428.

CHAPTER 22

An Intelligent Approach to Positive Target Identification

RAM-NANDAN P. SINGH

Department of the Navy, Naval Air Warfare Center, Patuxent River, Maryland, USA

1 INTRODUCTION

Positive identification of friends, foes, and noncombatants at maximum detection ranges plays a major role in the utilization of advanced weapon systems for both offensive and defensive scenarios. Major goals and objectives of positive target identification are to reduce fratricides and improve combat effectiveness by enabling the most efficient use of our long-range weapon systems. Hence, in a rapidly changing battle space typical of joint operations, positive target identification capability for use in modern fighter aircraft is essential to enhance the destruction of hostile targets while reducing incidents of fratricide. This capability is currently achieved by performing either signature pattern matching or specialized processing of the radar signature. Desert Storm has clearly revealed the inadequacy of existing target identification systems aboard fighter aircraft [6]. Since positive target identification is an essential element of the rule-of-engagements (ROE), this inadequacy in positive target identification limits the use of long-range, accurate weapons systems in operations. It has also demonstrated the critical need to positively identify air and surface targets. This chapter presents a new approach to address this complex problem. It enables the intelligent fusing of images of an object received from diverse sensors into a single composite (synthetic) picture in real time beyond visible range. In practice, this provides fighter aircraft with a long eye in the sky.

Image fusion is currently an active field of research. This research may be broadly classified into three categories: (a) fusion of multiple cues from a single image sensor, (b) fusion of images from different views with the same modality, and (c) fusion of images from multiple modalities. In general, computer vision research based on multiresolution techniques has been dominating this field. Now there are many new techniques available including wavelet transform, quadtree, and pyramid processing for image fusion. The wavelet transform fuses transform coefficients rather than spatial image pixels, and reconstructs a fused imaged from fused transform coefficients [10, 12, 20, 22]. Li, Manjunath, and Mitra [10] have applied wavelet transform for multisensor image fusion, and used an integration rule that selects the larger (absolute value)

549

of the two wavelet coefficients at each point. Wilson, Rogers, and Kabrisky [22] have performed perceptual-based hyperspectral image fusion using multispectral analysis. They have fused wavelet coefficients from each image using a perceptual-based weighting. Burt and Lolczynski [4] have applied pyramid processing to fuse images. Pyramid image decomposition methods include mathematical morphology and steerable pyramid decomposition. The steerable pyramid is a multiscale, multiorientation image decomposition that uses "wavelet transfom." Queiroz, Florencio, and Schaefer [14] have used a nonlinear filterbank for pyramid image coding. These methods are mathematically elegant, but usually prove poor in handling complex real life spatiotemporal image fusion.

Multisource image fusion generates a single image by fusing images received from disparate sources. A human operator cannot obtain such information by viewing the images sequentially. Further, the integration of images across multiple human operators is nearly impossible. An image fusion system that fuses images received from multiple sensors into a single composite image is, therefore, of great practical value. In defense applications, targets that are hard to detect in a visual image can sometimes easily be noticed in a thermal image. In practice, aircraft fighter pilots need target area imagery in real time; commanders require tactical reconnaissance in near-real time. To realize these goals, collection, fusion and dissemination of reconnaissance and surveillance images are required. Multisensor image fusion will play a key role in accomplishing these goals. The objective of multisensor image fusion is to intelligently fuse images received from diverse sources into a composite image. This will increase the amount of information required to be absorbed visually, while reducing nonvisual cues. In addition, an image fusion system can take full advantage of the complementary capabilities of individual sensors to increase overlapping coverage for higher accuracy and resolution, as well as enhanced target recognition in real time.

Many surveillance aircraft have missions oriented to search for, detect, classify, and track targets. Active and passive imaging sensors include radar, infrared detection set (IRDS), CCD cameras, and visual-view optical systems. Presently, these image sensors are optimized for different ranges and missions, and operate independently. Thus we have image sensors for short, medium, and long range. When all the image sensors start operating synergistically, the entire image sensor suite will provide a continuous, consistent picture of a scene (or target area) to the operator in a timely fashion. Furthermore, target detection and classification is dependent upon the strengths and weaknesses associated with each sensor. If these image sensors were made to operate synergistically, gains achieved through integrating images from multiple sensors could be significant in terms of reducing workload and uncertainty, increasing the confidence of target detection, and enhancing classification and tracking accuracy. Moreover, in a hostile environment, where operators are often required to make a decision on target classification in a short time, this decision aid would reduce operator stress and increase efficiency.

Recently, there has been a new trend in the defense modernization industry to achieve a multimission capability for aircraft by adding more image sensors and data links. Further, it may be noted that multiple dissimilar image sensors provide spatial, temporal, spectral, polarimetric, and other observable characteristics of an image field, and combine high intelligibility with high contrast for interesting objects or phenomena. These image characteristics greatly enhance discrimination as well as tracking of targets, including small targets and extended targets, using shape, size, color, temperature, spectral response, texture, and other attributes of these objects in imaged scenes. Currently image sensor processing produces mainly two types of data for target identification and tracking: (a) *digitized imagery* (b) *processed data*. The processed data consists of the target attributes, and the target classification result associated with its confidence level. These two types of data are transmitted to a display unit for operator evaluation. At present these individual image sensors aboard the aircraft operate independently. As a result, human operators do not get a single composite picture of a target scene. If we make these image sensors operate synergistically, it will generate a single, composite picture providing a continuous, consistent image of a target area to human operators. Hence, there is a need for the development of real-time image fusion technology to meet the Fleet operational requirements. This technology would provide the ability to fuse imagery data from diverse sensors and produce a composite picture in a timely fashion for positive target identification in a combat environment, which would also enhance the ability to resolve friendly fire concerns (i.e., an antifratricide system) and to identify targets beyond the visual range (thereby not limiting long-range anti-air missile use).

This research presents a new framework for multisensor image fusion in the area of digital image fusion. It enables the intelligent use of image field characteristics to generate a composite picture with high fidelity and high intelligibility. A composite database has been developed. This consists of sensor-level digitized data and sensor-level processed data. This new image fusion framework applies this composite database to digitally merge corresponding images into a composite (synthetic) picture.

1.2   Complementarity and Redundancy

In a surveillance mission an object can be viewed by a number of image sensors simultaneously (e.g., radar, IRDS, CCD camera). What is the technical approach when classifiers designed and optimized for each sensor yield contradictory results when focused on the same object? These results are partly due to the fragmentary or poor-quality images derived from the sensors. Fusion of the images, which combines the visible and nonvisible spectrum with the radar spectrum, will yield an enhanced image and avoid confusion. Under these circumstances one would match (or register) these images with one another, or match some given pattern (i.e., piece of image) with another with a view to identifying the object. If we bring them into registration with one another, we can determine the characteristics of each pixel with respect to all of the image sensors [2,11]. As a result, the unique information gained through registration of these images can enhance the systems's ability to classify the pixels. This illustrates one of the benefits derived from using different sensor images together.

Image information can be obtained at several levels. There are three important levels. Pixel level is the lowest possible level of data that contains original information from all sensors. Feature level provides quantitative information on the characteristics of an object. Decision level is a high level of abstraction of a knowledge source (e.g., a sensor) and provides qualitative information. At what level should the information derived from different image sensors be merged, and how should this merger be accomplished? Technically, image fusion can be performed using different levels of image abstraction [18]. It is best to fuse image data at the lowest level (pixel level). However, image fusion at pixel level demands very high computation power. Artificial neural networks can be applied to feature level extraction for image fusion but cannot use domain expertise in the form of linguistic information. At a high level, hierarchical knowledge structure can be applied to image fusion, but is limited by its numerical data character. To maximize the amount of data that can be analyzed for enhanced visibility and identification of an object, it will be necessary to combine the images from several sensors to bring out the subtle differences that may be recorded in different parts of the electromagnetic spectrum. This correlation and fusion of multisensor imagery data in an intelligent way is the purpose and thrust of this research.

First, we provide a theoretical foundation for understanding the structure of an image using continuous formulations of image pyramids and for correlation and fusion of images This reveals the deep structure of an image and its relationship to discrete pyramid construction. A new image fusion paradigm through fuzzy pattern combination is presented Based on the theory and fuzzy pattern combinations, an image fusion scheme has been developed to fuse images into a composite image.

2 IMAGE FUSION BASICS

This section discusses the basic nature of an image and the image field characteristics.

2.1 Basic Structures of Images

An image could represent luminance of objects in a scene (picture by an ordinary camera), absorption characteristics of body tissues (X-ray imaging), the radar cross-section (radar imaging), temperature profile of a region (infrared imaging), and much more. In practice, these images often have imprecise boundaries and broad description of details. J.K. Hawkin echoed this in his statement:

> In reality, in our normal visual environments, no two objects are exactly alike. An organism that wants to *survive* or a device that has to act *intelligently* in such an environment, must be able to disregard variations which are unimportant at a particular instant. Only then can the visual environments become describable in terms of rather loosely defined sets of objects, sets of actions which the object is capable of or which it is useful for.

This is the primary guideline that provides a basis for a meaningful image fusion.

The basic structure of a human visual perception model provides a basis for understanding the image fusion processing of diverse images by human beings. The brain samples and represents the optic array at many resolution scales simultaneously. As a result, the visual system represents retina images at all levels of resolution simultaneously, and deals with contrast, spatial frequencies, and color. This reveals the hierarchical architecture of this model with links between the different levels of resolution. This structure fits into existing theories of the visual system as a continuous stack of homogeneous layers characterized by iterated local processing schemes which, in turn, point to pyramid processing. The three different formulations that define the deep structure of an image are the diffusion of an image characterized by a parabolic linear partial differential equation of the second order, the convolution of an image with a family of Gaussian point spread functions, and the iterated blurrings of an image (which asymptotically leads to diffusion) in an apparently ad hoc fashion.

2.2 Image Field Characteristics

The development of new imaging sensors has opened up new areas for image processing. These include the intelligent use of spatial, spectral, polarimetric, and temporal characteristics of an image field to "synthesize" images which combine high intelligibility with high contrast for interesting objects of phenomena. Since we can measure the polarization state, the phase, and the amplitude, we can take advantage of these three attributes together for object recognition by machines, whereas the human eye only sees amplitudes.

2.3   Complexity

Since images very often have imprecise boundaries and broad descriptions of details, fusing images into a composite image in a timely fashion is a problem intrinsically incapable of precise mathematical formulation. In practice, we have to deal with imperfect measurements. These measurements may be both imprecise and uncertain. In this context, Albert Einstein observed, "So far as the laws of mathematics refer to reality, they are not certain; and so far as they are certain, they do not refer to reality." Further, L.A. Zadeh has remarked, "As the complexity of a system increases, our ability to make precise and yet significant statements about its behavior diminishes until a threshold is reached beyond which precision and significance (or relevance) become almost mutually exclusive characteristics" [23]. In a nutshell, high precision is incompatible with high complexity. However, human operators can tolerate some degree of inprecision in detail. As a result, the conceptual structure of the theory of fuzzy sets and fuzzy logic may well provide a natural setting for the formulation and approximate solution of complex, nonlinear problems in image fusion.

2.4   Requirements for Fusion

There are two essential requirements for image fusion: (1) pattern conservation: important details of the component images must be preserved in the composite image; and (2) avoidance of spurious elements it must not introduce any new pattern elements or artifacts that could interfere with subsequent image analysis. Because spatial information is essential in reconstructing a composite image, it cannot be sacrificed while decomposing an image into a set of primitive patterns. This is key to putting a successful image fusion scheme into practice. Keeping this in mind, an intelligent image fusion theory has been developed based on diffusing images with respect to contrast, spatial frequencies, and color into a set of diffused images; and molding the diffused images into a composite image. This involves generating a set of diffused images from a given set of candidate images, combining them into a composite set of diffused images, and, finally, compacting them into a composite image. Based on this theory, the design of the image fusion paradigm involves decomposing each source image into primitive pattern elements; fuzzifying each element; combining them into a composite set of fuzzy primitives; dufuzzifying each composite primitive; and reconstructing a composite image from the set of composite primitives.

2.5   Problem Definition

Multisensor image fusion is a complex task. As a final product, fused images may portray the specific mission needs and objectives. This research presents a general framework for fusing intelligently diverse and imprecise images from multiple dissimilar image sources into a single composite (synthetic) image in a timely fashion. The state-of-the-art technology in image processing and analysis by a single image sensor uses the frame grabber to digitize the video and to send it to the internal image analyzer of a sensor. Second, the sensor image processor derives target attributes and classification information associated with its confidence level, and outputs those processed data. Finally, these output data go to the display along with the original digitized image data for operator evaluation. In a nutshell, a single image sensor, currently outputs two types of data:

- Processed data (target attributes, classification result, confidence level)
- Digitized image

Figure 1 presents this configuration.

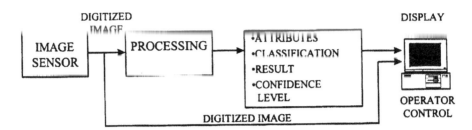

FIGURE 1
Single-sensor image processing (current technology).

In this research we propose a new scheme for fusing images received from two or more image sensors. Figure 2 depicts a new scheme for fusing imagery from two image sensors. Here we store processed data in a database called the "knowledge-base" and digitized image data in "digital imagery." This scheme gives rise to several new problems. The first and foremost is sensor registration. Images received from two separate sensors need to be registered. There are

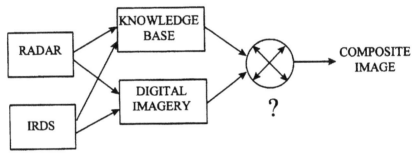

FIGURE 2
Proposed fusion of two image sensors.

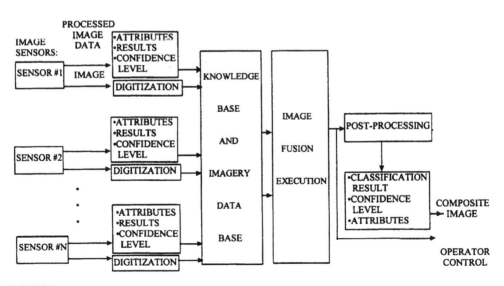

FIGURE 3
Intelligent image fusion architecture for positive target identification.

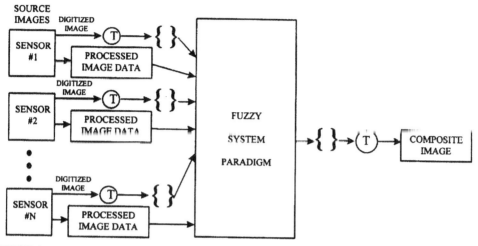

FIGURE 4
Generic image fusion data flow.

two types of registration: temporal registration and spatial registration. These align the imagery data both in space and in time. The spatial registration of the images corrects for relative translation shifts and rotational shifts as well as geometrical and intensity distortions of each image [2]. Given two or more pictures of the same object from different sensors and their registration, we can determine the characteristics of each pixel with respect to all of sensors. We assume here that the images to be combined are already perfectly registered.

Figure 3 presents an intelligent image fusion architecture for target identification. How do we realize this scheme? Figure 4 depicts a generic image fusion paradigm. The theoretical foundation for this realization is presented in Section 3, and the methodology to implement this scheme is presented in Section 4.

3   THEORETICAL FOUNDATION

In this section we develop a theoretical framework for understanding the deep structure of an image with a view to developing a sound basis for intelligent image fusion in the sequel. The simplest method of fusing images is accomplished by computing their average. Although the features from each candidate image, to a varying degree, are present in a fused image, the contrast of the original feature can be significantly reduced and blurred. This can render the fused image useless for practical applications. Another simple method is to use the maximum values to generate a fused image. Even though this method is analytically tractable, it can miss the minimum values (which may be critical to the mission) submerged in the processing. To overcome this deficiency, we can use max-min techniques for fusion. In reality, both bright areas and shades of an image are required to a varying degree to fuse with other images [5,13]. More sophisticated techniques rely on multiscale representations, such as pyramid [3] and wavelet transform [12]. Pyramid image decomposition methods include mathematical morphology and steerable pyramid decomposition. The steerable pyramid is a multiscale, multiorientation image decomposition that uses "wavelet transform." Wavelet transforms fuse transform coefficients rather than spatial image pixels, and reconstruct a fused image from fused transform coefficients. Here we first provide a theoretical framework for constructing various types of pyramids and then reconstructing an original image from various levels of the pyramid.

3.1 Basic Structure of Pyramid

In practice, pyramid architectures for image processing usually consist of discrete grids and discrete levels. However, we can also represent pyramid architectures by their continuous formulation for analysis, stability, and accuracy of image fusion results.

Let t be a continuous resolution variable and (x, y) be continuous domain variables. Let $f(x, y)$ represent the image data and t the pyramid level. Then, the continuous analog of the pyramid data will be

$$u(x, y, t); \quad (x, y) \in \mathfrak{R}^2, t \geq 0$$

The value $t = 0$ represents the base of the pyramid, and for the Gaussian pyramid the condition becomes

$$u(x, y, 0) = f(x, y)$$

It may be noted the number of levels in a discrete pyramid is always finite, whereas for the continuous version we may have an unbounded scale $0 \leq t < \infty$, or a bounded scale $0 \leq t \leq T$.

3.1.1 Gaussian Pyramid.
In the Gaussian pyramid, each level represents a coarser resolution of the original data. The base of the pyramid contains the original data at full resolution, and high levels typically contain blurred and subsampled versions of the immediately lower level. The subsampling that is most commonly applied is to select every other pixel or every other row, for a reduction factor of 2 in each dimension. Other sampling methodologies are also possible, but it is always true that each level contains fewer points than the preceding level. We define the Gaussian pyramid as

$$u(x, y, t) = \iint_{\mathfrak{R}^2} G(x', y', t) f(x - x', y - y') \, dx' \, dy' \tag{1}$$

where

$$G(x, y, t) = \frac{1}{\sqrt{4\pi t}} e^{\frac{-(x^3 + y^2)}{(4t)}} \tag{2}$$

For any fixed value of $t > 0$, $G(x, y, t)$ is a Gaussian distribution centered at $(0,0)$ with standard deviation $\sigma = \sqrt{2t}$.

For $t = 0$, $G(x, y, t)$ is a delta-function centered at $(0,0)$. Hence, we have the initial image as $u(x, y, 0) = f(x, y)$. Thus $f(x, y)$ is a base pyramid that represents the original image.

Alternatively, for $t > 0$, we can rewrite equation (1) as

$$u(x, y, t) = G(x, y, t) * f(x, y) \tag{3}$$

where the star ($*$) denotes convolution.

A natural framework with which we can study Gaussian pyramids on a continuous domain is by means of the heat diffusion equation [9]. This equation is a parabolic partial differential equation:

$$\frac{\partial u(x, y, t)}{\partial t} = \Delta u(x, y, t); \quad u(x, y, 0) = f(x, y) \tag{4}$$

where

$$\Delta u = \frac{\partial^2 u}{\partial x^2} + \frac{\partial^2 u}{\partial y^2}$$

For every initial bounded image $f(x, y)$, the output image $u(x, y, t)$ is a solution of the heat equation given by equation (1). This means that all linear "low pass" iterated filters are equivalent to the heat equation (and to the convolution with Gaussians with increasing width). Since a coarser image can be derived from a finer one without any dependence upon the original image, the pyramid structure can be computed at scale t from the output at scale $t - h$ for very small h. In practice, the solution of a partial differential requires the definition of boundary-value conditions. However, a well-posed boundary-value problem can generally be transformed into a discrete pyramid construction procedure. In this sense, the heat equation explicitly defines the deep structure of the image [16, 21].

3.1.2 Laplacian Pyramid.

In discrete settings, the Laplacian pyramid is obtained by taking the difference between adjacent layers in the Gaussian pyramid. Since the levels have different sizes, they must first be made commensurate. This can be done by expanding the smaller level by an interpolating procedure [3]. Thus, each level contains something approximating a difference-of-Gaussian filter of the original data, which can be replaced as a band-pass filter on the data. Burt [3] has shown that the original image can be reconstructed by essentially adding together all levels, from small levels to larger, expanding the result at each stage.

The continuous analog is obtained by substituting a difference quotient for a difference in levels. Let $u(x, y, t)$ represent a Gaussian pyramid. Then the difference of levels is $u(x, y, t_1) - u(x, y, t_2)$.

The Laplacian pyramid will be formed from the relation

$$V(x, y, t) = \lim_{t_2 \to t_1} \frac{u(x, y, t_2) - u(x, y, t_1)}{t_2 - t_2} = \frac{\partial u(x, y, t)}{\partial t} \tag{5}$$

Since the Gaussian pyramid function $u(x, y, t)$ is a solution to the heat diffusion equation, we can relate the Laplacian pyramid function $u(x, y, t)$ to it by

$$V(x, y, t) = \frac{\partial u(x, y, t)}{\partial t} = \Delta u(x, y, t) \tag{6}$$

Thus, the Laplacian pyramid contains imagery data which is simply the Laplacian of values in the Gaussian pyramid. Using the properties of convolution in conjunction with equations (4) and (5), we can write the Laplacian function as

$$V(x, y, t) - \frac{\partial u}{\partial t} - \Delta G * f - G * \Delta f \tag{7}$$

This equation shows that $V(x, y, t)$ itself is a solution to the heat equation

$$\frac{\partial V}{\partial t} = \Delta V \qquad \text{with initial data } \Delta f \tag{8}$$

This implies a rapid method of constructing V by blurring Δf data. However, it is much simpler to evaluate the Laplacian of the data in the Gaussian with difference adjacent levels. Using the definition of V by equation (5) we can reconstruct the original image $f(x, y)$ as

$$f(x, y) = -\int_0^T V(x, y, t)\, dt + u(x, y, T) \tag{9}$$

where $0 \le t \le T$ and T is the height of the finite resolution length. This shows that the image $f(x, y)$ can be reconstructed from $V(x, y, t)$ by adding together all levels, and then adding in a simple function. Thus, as long as the Gaussian pyramid data $V(x, y, t)$ is supplemented with the data $u(x, y, T)$ (which may be zero, harmonic, or a constant), the information supplies a complete representation of the original image $f(x, y)$ [21].

3.1.3   Contrast Pyramid. According to Weber's law, human visual perception is sensitive to luminance contrast rather than the absolute luminance values [19]. This can be stated as

$$\frac{\Delta f}{f} \approx d(\log_2 f)$$

In a ratio pyramid, every layer is the ratio of two successive levels in the Gaussian pyramid. This concept can be extended to contrast pyramids. Here we employ different discrimination functions depending upon their applications. Let μ_{L_1} and μ_{L_2} denote two statistical mean values for two layers. Then we have discrimination functions defined as

$$(1) \quad J_1(h) = \frac{\mu_{L_1}}{\mu_{L_2}} \qquad \text{(mean ratio)} \tag{10}$$

$$(2) \quad J_2(h) = \frac{(\mu_{L_1} - \mu_{L_2})^2}{\sigma_1^2 + \sigma_2^2} \quad \text{(Fisher criterion)} \tag{11}$$

where σ_1 and σ_2 denote the standard deviations [8] for two levels of a contrast pyramid.

Following the procedures described in Sections 3.1.1 and 3.1.2, a continuous formulation can also be obtained for a ratio pyramid.

3.2   Combining Methodologies for Different Images

Here we present different methods for combining images.

3.2.1   Partial Differential Representations. The partial differential equation (PDE) formulation allows us to combine algorithms. If two different image processing schemes are given by

$$\frac{\partial I}{\partial t} = F_1(x, y, t) \qquad \frac{\partial I}{\partial t} = F_2(x, y, t) \tag{12}$$

we can combine them as

$$\frac{\partial I}{\partial t} = \alpha F_1 + F_2 \quad \text{(linear combination)}$$

where α is a scalar; $\alpha \in R$. Alvarez and Mazorra [1] successfully used this where F_1 was a smoothing operator and F_2 the shocks filter. There are other ways to combine these schemes in practice.

In this section we have presented partial differential equations in image processing to understand the deep structure of an image for image fusion. In practice, continuous formulations enable us to analyze the system behavior over time and space, and to determine an estimate of stability and accuracy of the results.

3.2.2   Fuzzy Logic for Merging Patterns. In image fusion, the central problem is how to combine the set of imprecise image pattern elements into a single pattern element. Fuzzy sets and fuzzy logic techniques provide a methodology to handle such complex problems [7, 23].

3.2.2.1   Basic Fuzzy Paradigm. A fuzzy system paradigm contains four basic elements: fuzzification interface, fuzzy knowledge-base, fuzzy inference engine, and defuzzification. Figure 5 provides a functional paradigm for fuzzy systems. These elements are described below.

Fuzzification Interface. The fuzzification interface transforms the numerical data received from sensor measurements into fuzzy variables. The number of fuzzy sets defined in the input discourse and their specific membership functions define the fuzzification interface design. It is a

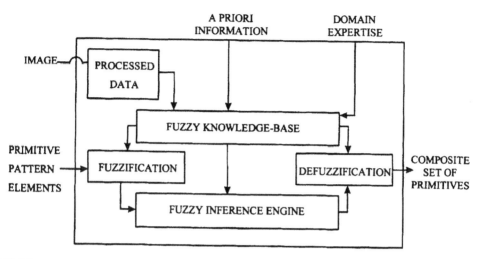

FIGURE 5
Fuzzy systems paradigm.

fact of life that much of the evidence on which human decisions are based is both fuzzy and granular [24]. With this motivation, the fuzzification of numerical data from sensor measurements requires the division of an optimal (or empirical) membership X into a number of fuzzy subsets (or term sets). This may also be considered a fuzzy partitioning of a fuzzy set X. The main requirement is to come up with fuzzy subsets that ensure a uniform activation of the original membership function of a fuzzy set X.

Fuzzy Knowledge-Based. This contains IF–THEN rules and simple fuzzy statements, postprocessed data and fuzzy primitives, domain expertise and a priori knowledge, and provides a methodology to represent human knowledge and reasoning. We specify the meaning of fuzzy rules using linguistic terms defined by their membership functions.

Fuzzy Inference Engine. The fuzzy inference engine employs a particular kind of fuzzy logic. It simulates human decision making procedures, and employs a fuzzy knowledge base and fuzzy input to generate fuzzy decisions (output).

There are two common methods for performing fuzzy logic inferences: the max-min method and the max-product method. In the max-min method the final output membership function for each output is the union of the fuzzy sets assigned to that output, and the degree-of-membership values are clipped at the degree-of-membership for the corresponding premise. In the max-product inference method, the final output membership function for each output is the union of the fuzzy sets assigned to that output in a conclusion, and their degree-of-membership values are scaled to peak at the degree-of-membership for the corresponding premise [7].

Defuzzification Interface. All fuzzy logic inference methods result in fuzzy values for all output information. The defuzzification interface transforms the fuzzy output into crisp (nonfuzzy) data for use. There are several defuzzification methods including the centroid method (also known as center of gravity method) and the height method. The centroid method is the most common in use. This method selects the output value corresponding to the centroid of the output membership function as the crisp value for an output.

3.2.2.2 Fuzzy Strategies. The fuzzy paradigm, as discussed above, provides a powerful mechanism for applying fuzzy sets and fuzzy logic to solve complex image fusion problems. In practice the information may be imprecise, incomplete, and conflicting. To combine imperfect images, the fuzzy paradigm may employ various fuzzy combination strategies. Some of them are discussed below.

Let A_1 and A_2 be fuzzy image patterns. Given their possibility distributions

$$\pi_1 = \mu A_1 \qquad \text{(membership function)}$$

$$\pi_2 = \mu A_2 \qquad \text{(membership function)}$$

Depending upon the nature of given situations, we may employ fuzzy set union and/or intersection to combine these fuzzy image patterns as follows.

(i) When two fuzzy image patterns are reliable,

$$\pi_{12} = \frac{\pi_1(s) \wedge \pi_2(s)}{\sup_{s \in S} \int \pi_1(s) \wedge \pi_2(s)}; \qquad \forall s \in S$$

(ii) When two fuzzy image patterns are in severe conflict,

$$\pi_{12} = \pi_1(s) \vee \pi_2(s)$$

where $\wedge$ denotes an intersection operation between fuzzy sets and $\vee$ a union operation.

Primitive pattern elements are first transformed into fuzzy patterns. Then fuzzy inference is applied to the fuzzy primitives and knowledge-base for decision making Finally the fuzzy output is defuzzified. Fuzzy if–then rules provide a very powerful, flexible mechanism for combining very different classes of attributes easily [7, 15].

3.2.3 Combining Linguistic with Numeric Attributes.
In practice, linguistic information such as shape, size, orientation, or curvature can describe image patterns which, in turn, can provide information about the structure of an image pattern. Numeric attributes of an image provide information about the granularity of a pattern. The fuzzy system paradigm enables conversion of numeric attributes into fuzzy membership functions for combining fuzzy image pattern elements. Combining linguistic with numeric information provides a powerful tool for fusing imprecise information.

4   IMAGE FUSION METHODOLOGY

This section presents the construction of an intelligent image fusion scheme.

4.1   Image Pyramid Construction

An image pyramid construction may be viewed as a transformation that decomposes an input image into various sizes and amplitudes [3, 16]. Using the discrete formulation of an image, the decomposition transformation (T) can be written as

$$G_l(i,j) = \sum_{m,n=-2}^{+2} W(m,n) G_{l-1}(2i+m, 2j+n) \tag{14}$$

Here, the weighting function W is called the generating kernel. For a Gaussian pyramid, this will be a Gaussian weighting function.

Inversely, given the pyramid of an input image, we may reconstruct the input image. The reconstructing transformation (T^{-1}) reconstructs an image by adding the levels of the pyramid. This is given as

$$G_{l,k}(i,j) - 4 \sum_{m,n=-2}^{+2} W(m,n) G_{l,k-1} \left(\frac{i+m}{2}, \frac{j+n}{2} \right) \tag{15}$$

Theoretically, the reconstructed image should be identical to the original image.

4.1.1 *Gaussian Pyramid.*

To generate a Gaussian pyramid, one can apply formula (1) to an input image. This convolves the input image with a Gaussian weighting function. In practice, this · is equivalent to applying a low-pass filter to an image. The Gaussian pyramid construction generates a set of low-pass filtered copies of the image each with a band limit of one octave lower than its predecessor. Thus, an image pyramid is a sequence of images in which each image is a filtered and subsampled copy of its predecessor. In general, these successive levels are reduced-resolution versions of the input image. Hence, this is also called a multiresolution representation. In addition, this representation may also consist of descriptive information about certain image features (points, lines, edges, contours, etc.). In this case, successive levels of the pyramid represent increasingly coarse approximations of the object features. Pyramids also convert local image features into global features. As a result, hierarchical operations can be more computationally efficient than operations performed at a single level of resolution. Since these pyramids are hierarchically organized and locally interconnected through level-to-level inter-connections, they provide a bridge between pixel-level processing and more global-level (i.e., object-level) processing. Hence, a pyramid representation may serve as a unifying structure in which to perform image fusion.

4.1.2 *Laplacian Pyramid.*

Humans are relatively insensitive to errors in high-frequency image components, and are more sensitive to errors in low-frequency components. A Laplacian pyramid provides an elegant solution to a more practical problem in image combination.

The Laplacian pyramid is obtained by taking the difference between adjacent layers in the Gaussian pyramid. It tends to enhance image features. It is a compact representation that is robust in the presence of noise. The changes in image scales correspond to simple shifts in the representation to higher or lower pyramid levels. The Laplacian pyramid levels represent an image with many scales. Its local operators of many scales but identical shapes serve as the basis functions. The Laplacian pyramid requires relatively simple computations. These computations are local, and may be performed in parallel, and iterated to build each pyramid level from its predecessors. We may envision performing Laplacian pyramid processing in real time using array processors and a pipeline architecture.

4.2 Application to Image Fusion

Given a number of source images of an object obtained from diverse image sensors, one can decompose each source image into a Gaussian pyramid. Next, using some merging rules, these pyramids may be combined into a single composite pyramid. Finally, by applying the inverse transformation (2) to this composite pyramid, a composite picture may be generated. In order for this methodology to work in practice, it is implicitly assumed that the source images are *crisp* (not fuzzy) with high contrast. In real-life situations, images are not crisp; they are very often less than perfect, ambiguous, incomplete, and blurred in many details to varying degrees. The SNR level is often so low that does not permit an application of the inverse transformation. Hence, we need a methodology to overcome this difficulty in practice.

In a generic image fusion architecture for intelligent image fusion, each image sensor outputs two type of data: (a) raw digitized image data and (b) processed image data (target attributes, classification result, and confidence level). All these data go to a *composite knowledge base* consisting of digitized and processed data. In addition, it also contains domain expertise, sensor characteristics, and fuzzy rule-base. Clearly this composite knowledge-base contains both numeric as well as linguistic information. The data flow and the processing mechanism to process these data at different stages of image fusion processing involve various transformations and combinations. Digitized data from each input image undergo a decomposition transformation that decomposes the input image into a number of pyramid levels. For the purpose of image fusion, each resolution level may be considered as single or multiple pattern elements. Next, it goes through a fuzzy system paradigm that performs fuzzification, combination, and defuzzi-fication of the composite set of primitives. Finally, an inverse pyramid transformation is used to reconstruct a composite image.

5 IMPLEMENTATION

Primary difficulties in fusing diverse images arise from the fact that scene information gathered using various image sensors (ISAR/SAR radar, IRDS, EO, etc.) possess imprecise boundaries and varying resolutions derived from uncertain, dynamic environments. In addition, an image understanding task becomes difficult because of complex shapes, uneven illuminations, shadows, and complex textures. As a result, all these factors make it difficult to design general algorithms to solve real-life image fusion problems.

This image fusion paradigm provides a generic image fusion procedure. Each candidate image is transformed into primitive pattern elements. Merging of primitive patterns takes place in a transformation domain. Fuzzy merging rules are applied to merge fuzzy primitive patterns into a set of composite patterns. These rules ensure that pattern elements that are important perceptually, or which will be used in subsequent analysis, are conserved. Valid patterns are retained while no distortions or artifacts are introduced that may interfere with perception or analysis. Both numeric data and linguistic information are used to generate a composite picture. The resolution, accuracy, and perspective of sensor-derived information tends to vary from sensor to sensor. Because emulation of human-level reasoning can require the use of both absolute and relative values, the system should ideally support both crisp and fuzzy data.

5.1 Generic Pyramid-based Image Fusion

A pyramid representation provides a structure for merging primitive elements/attributes on a local level, and subsequently on a global (i.e., object) basis. A generic image fusion method is a four-stage process to accomplish this goal. It consist of th following:

1. Decompose each source image into primitive elements.
2. Determine suitable criteria to merge primitive pattern at each pyramid level.
3. Combine source pyramids to form a composite pyramid.
4. Regenerate the composite image through an application of the inverse pyramid transformation.

This methodology requires crisp images for processing.

5.2 Composite Database Construction

In practice, there is no crisp hierarchy of layers in a pyramid. There is always some degree of overlap between adjacent layers, with gradual transitions into one another. Thus, each layer can be modeled with one or more fuzzy membership functions. Sometimes each layer can represent separate attributes. Using fuzzy rules, these attributes/primitives can be combined. It consists of the following processing:

1. Decompose each source image into a set of primitive pattern elements.
2. Fuzzify attributes and/or pattern elements.
3. Develop fuzzy rules to merge fuzzy pattern elements at each pyramid level.
   - Apply these rules to merge the set of fuzzy primitives to form a single set of fuzzy primitives for the composite image at each pyramid level.
   - Defuzzify each element of the composite pyramid. This will produce a composite pyramid of crisp elements.
   - Reconstruct a composite image from the composite pyramid using an inverse pyramid transform.

5.3 Levels of Image Fusion

There are three important levels of image fusion:

- *Element-level fusion*—employs pixels or primitive image patterns. This is low-level fusion that uses basic information.
  Attribute-level fusion—intermediate level fusion that uses derived information from pixels or image primitives.
- *Decision-level fusion*—high-level fusion that uses merging rules.

It may be noted that single-level fusion ignores some of the information that is available at other levels. Multilevel fusion uses most of the available information across the three levels of fusion (see Figures 6 and 7). There are two image sensors generating images IMAGEA and IMAGEB. The first step requires constructing pyramids for each sensor image. The fuzzy system paradigm is then used to accomplish fuzzy pattern fusion into a composite set of patterns. The reconstruction transformation (T^{-1}) to reconstruct a composite image. Implementation of this paradigm using real data is under way.

5.4 Basis for Merging Rules

Detecting objects in imagery can be accomplished by the analysis of amplitude, spatial, spectral, and temporal characteristics of two-dimensional images. Rules for merging primitive pattern elements/attributes may be based on the following structures:

- *Hierarchical Reasoning*—uses image structures to frame merging rules. This implies a ranking or ordering process. Human perception involves a hierarchical reasoning process that relies on both bottom-up and top-down reasoning. Situation awareness often demands both bottom-up and top-down reasoning.
  Spatial reasoning—exploits spatial frequencies and relationships between elements of different images. It implies a three-dimensional character of the physical world.

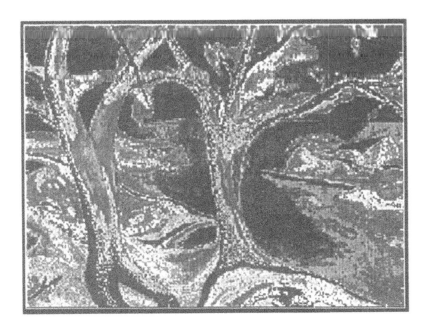

FIGURE 6
(a) Image source #1. (b) Gaussian pyramid #1.

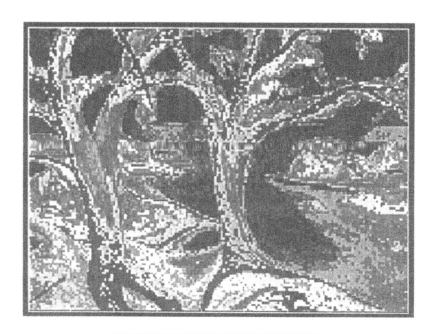

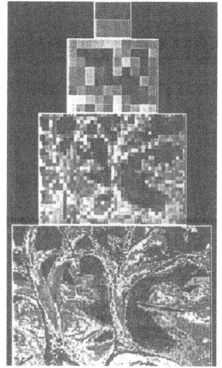

FIGURE 7
(a) Image source #2. (b) Gaussian pyramid #2.

- *Temporal reasoning*—deals with motion images. It involves dynamic and evolving situations in space and time.

Using the fuzzy rule, the confidence levels associated with different target IDs determined independently by individual sensors can be combined into a composite pattern confidence event.

5.5   Implementation Centers

There are three ways to make the image fusion results available to the users. In a cockpit an image fusion center can provide a direct access to the pilot. An image fusion center can send a fused image over a data-link in real time to a pilot. An off-line image fusion center can transmit the processed results of image fusion for target identification to a pilot over a data-link.

6   EXAMPLE

There are four critical components of multisensor image fusion processing: (a) image registration, (b) image normalization, (c) image correlation, and (d) image fusion (or update). For the purpose of demonstrating the intelligent image fusion theory, it is *assumed* that all data are properly registered and normalized. An example is provided for illustration.

Given two source images, obtain a composite picture. The following steps are involved:

Step 1   Perform convolution with a source image using a Gaussian function as a weighting function. (equation 1). This will generate Gaussian pyramid #1 for the input image #1.

Step 2   Derive Laplacian pyramid #1 from Gaussian pyramid #1 following the methodology as outlined in Section 2.2.

Step 3   Repeat the above two steps for source image #2. This will generate Gaussian pyramid #2 and Laplacian pyramid #2.

Step 4   Fuzzify each level in both Laplacian pyramids.

Step 5   Develop a set of fuzzy rules to determine the degree of correlation between two images.

Step 6   Apply fuzzy logic to compute the correlation values for each level.

Step 7   Merge the primitives into a composite set of primitives. Construct a fuzzy composite Laplacian pyramid.

Step 8   Defuzzify each fuzzy primitive in the fuzzy Laplacian pyramid. This will generate a crisp composite Laplacian pyramid.

Step 9   Regenerate a composite image from the composite Laplacian pyramid.

To fuzzify each level in a crisp Laplacian pyramid, one can model it with a single or multiple fuzzy membership functions [15, 24]. Two key fuzzy variables for deriving fuzzy rules are intensity differences and intensity gradients. Fuzzy rules have been developed to provide various combinations of these two fuzzy variables with varying degrees of fuzziness [15, 17].

The two input images of the same object are selected. The image source #1 is shown in Figure 6a and the image source #2 in Figure 7a. Figure 6a shows that the image #1 has more detail, whereas the input image #2 is more blurred. Figures 6b and 7b depict their pyramid representations. Figure 8 presents their Gaussian pyramids in a compact form. Figure 9 depicts the Laplacian pyramid #1 derived from the Gaussian pyramid #1, and similarly Figure 10 shows the Laplacian pyramid #2 for the Gaussian pyramid #2. Figure 11 depicts the composite

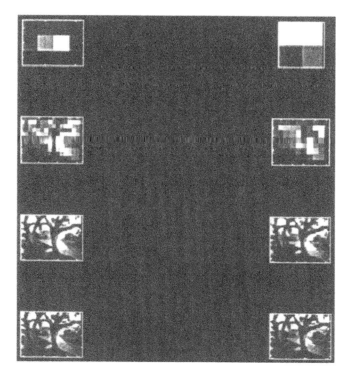

FIGURE 8
(a) Gaussian pyramid #1. (b) Gaussian pyramid #2.

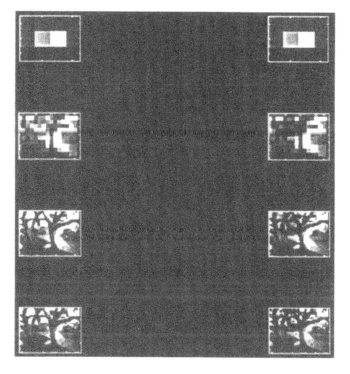

FIGURE 9
(a) Gaussian pyramid #1. (b) Laplacian pyramid #1.

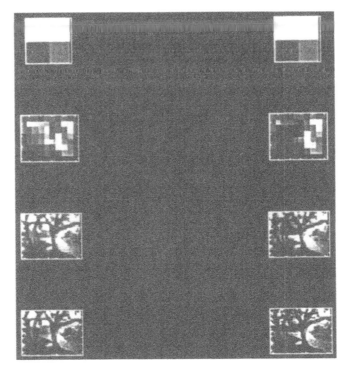

FIGURE 10
(a) Gaussian pyramid #2. (b) Laplacian pyramid #2.

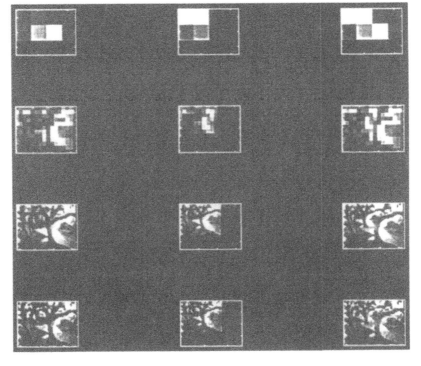

FIGURE 11
(a) Laplacian pyramid #1. (b) Laplacian pyramid #2. (c) Composite Laplacian.

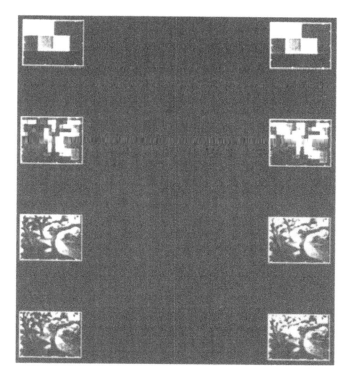

FIGURE 12
(a) Composite Laplacian pyramid. (b) Reconstructed image.

Laplacian pyramid after the two Laplacian pyramids #1 and Laplacian pyramid #2 have been combined. Figure 12 presents the composite image obtained from the composite Laplacian pyramid.

7   DISCUSSION

A theoretical foundation for the understanding of the deep structure of an image has been presented. Different types of pyramid generation provide a mechanism to generate image patterns for image fusion. Fuzzy logic as an enabling technology helped to obtain a complete result in a very natural way. This is a natural setting for combining operator's expertise with sensor measurements. Thus, intelligent image fusion has the technical potential to become operationally viable to provide direct combat identification in real time. An intelligent image fusion paradigm based on the theoretical framework developed has been implemented. Fuzzy system techniques provide a powerful methodology for merging image primitives in real situations. It has been demonstrated that the composite image contains more detail about the object than any single input image. Potential applications for defense include direct combat target identification in real time and underwater mine detection, classification, and identification.

REFERENCES

[1] L. Alvarez, and L. Mazorra, Signal and image restoration using shock filters and anisotropic diffusion, *SIAM J. Numerical Analysis*, Vol. 31, pp. 590–605, 1994.

[2] P.J. Burt, The pyramid as a structure for efficient computation, A. Rosenfield (ed.) in *Multi-Resolution Image Processing and Analysis*, pp. 6–35. Springer-Verlag, Berlin, 1984.

[3] P.J. Burt and R.J. Lolczynski, Enhanced image capture through fusion, in *Proc. Fourth Int. Conf. Computer Vision*, Berlin, Germany, 1993, pp. 909–960.

[4] J.J. Clark, and A.L. Yuille, *Data Fusion for Sensory Information Processing Systems*. Kluwer Academic, Boston, 1990.

[5] Andrew Dichter, A balanced approach to combat ID, *Proc. DoD Joint-Service Combat Identification Systems Conference (CISC-95)*. 1995, Vol. II (SECRET), pp. 1–29.

[6] D. Dubois and H. Prade, *Fuzzy Sets and Systems: Theory and Applications*. Academic Press, New York, 1980.

[7] K. Fukunaga, *Statistical Pattern Recognition*, 2d ed. Academic Press, New York, 1990.

[8] F. John, *Partial Differential Equations*, 2d ed. Springer-Verlag, Berlin, 1975.

[9] H. Li, B.S. Manjunath, and S.K. Mitra, Multi-sensor image fusion using the wavelet transform, *Graphics Models and Image Processing*, Vol. 57, No. 3, pp. 235–245, 1995.

[10] R. Luo, and M. Kay, Data fusion and sensor registration: state-of-the-art in 1990s, in M. Abidi and R. Gonzaloz, (eds.) *Data Fusion in Robotics and Machine Intelligence*, pp. 7–136, Academic Press, San Diego, 1992.

[11] S.G. Mallat, A survey of multiresolution signal decomposition: wavelet representation, *IEEE Trans Pattern Analysis and Machine Intelligence*, Vol. PAMI-11, pp. 674–693, July 1989.

[12] D. Marr, and E.C. Hildreth, Theory of edge detection, *M.I.T. Artificial Intelligence Laboratory Memo. No. 518*, Cambridge, Mass, Apr. 1979.

[13] R.L. de, Queiroz, D.A.F. Florencio, and R.W. Schaefer, Nonexpensive pyramid for image coding using a nonlinear filterbank, *IEEE Trans. Image Processing*, Vol. 7, No. 2, pp. 246–252, Feb. 1998.

[14] Ram-Nandan P. Singh and William H. Bailey, Fuzzy logic applications to multisensor multitarget correlation, *IEEE Trans. Aerospace and Electronic Systems*, Vol. 33, No. 3, pp. 752–769, July, 1997.

[15] Ram-Nandan P. Singh, Multisensor image fusion for positive target identification, *Proc. U.S. DoD Joint-Service Combat Identification Systems Conference (CISC-95)*, 1995, Vol. I, pp. 163–180.

[16] P. Ram-Nandan Singh, Intelligent image fusion for positive target identification, *Proc. U.S. DoD Joint-Service Combat Identification Systems Conference (CISC-97)*, 1997, Vol. I, pp. 387–399.

[17] A. Toet, Hierarchical image fusion, *Machine Vision Applications*, Vol. 3, pp. 1–11, Mar. 1990.

[18] M.I. Trifonov, and D.A. Ugolev, Uncertain principle in human visual perception, *SPIE*, Vol. 2179, pp. 60–69, 1994.

[19] M.V. Wickerhauser, *Adapted Wavelet Analysis from Theory to Software*. IEEE Press, New York, 1994.

[20] D.V. Widder, *The Heat Equation*. Academic Press, New York, 1975.

[21] A.T. Wilson, S.K. Rogers, and M. Kibrinski, Perceptual-based image fusion for hyperspectral data, *IEEE Trans Geoscience and Remote Sensing*, Vol. 35, No. 4, pp. 1007–1017, July 1997.

[22] L.A. Zadeh, Outline of a new approach to the analysis of complex systems and decision processes, *IEEE Trans. Systems Man, and Cybernetics*, Vol. 1, pp. 28–44, 1973.

[23] L.A. Zadeh, Fuzzy sets and information granularity, in M.M. Gupta, R.K. Ragade, R.R. Yager, (eds.), *Advances in Fuzzy Set Theory and Application*. pp. 3–18. North-Holland, Amsterdam, 1979.

CHAPTER 23

Adaptive Agents and Artificial Life: Insights for the Power Industry

STEVEN ALEX HARP and TARIQ SAMAD

Honeywell Technology Center, Minneapolis, Minnesota, USA

INTRODUCTION

Changes in the power industry in the United States and other parts of the world have fostered an urgent need to better understand how this extremely complex system will behave. Deregulation, competition, and environmental and land-use restrictions complicate the planning process. Power markets, unbundling, wholesale and retail wheeling and real-time pricing have proceeded from abstract concepts to real operations in many places today. Misjudgments of these new markets have already led to substantial difficulties for some participants.

One potential source of insight is simulation—artificial worlds with the same driving forces as the real one. But to approach realism, we cannot assume that participants in these artificial economies will blindly follow a single preprogrammed strategy. Rather, we must accommodate the possibility that they will learn and adapt to pursue their own interests. This chapter describes highlights from a series of computer experiments conducted to explore the capabilities of adaptive autonomous agents. We have used an abstract version of a real problem from the electric power industry as a test case. We believe that eventually observations gleaned from these artificial worlds will provide insights to make better decisions, or improve regulations in the real world.

The problem we have examined involves an experimental pricing method for electricity, *spot pricing*, also known as *real-time pricing* (RTP). Although it departs from the current practice of electric utilities, the spot-pricing framework presents an interesting set of problems for study of adaptive agent-based techniques. The application has a natural decomposition into a set of semi-autonomous agents—the consumers and producers on a power grid. Some details of the problem are included in the first section of the chapter. A defining characteristic of the agents discussed here is the ability to learn, evolve, and adapt to their environment. We have explored two different mechanisms for learning, with different characteristics. These are discussed in the central sections of the chapter. The final section describes an ongoing research and development program to provide an advanced tool for building such simulations.

Other researchers have been studying diverse uses of adaptive agents in the power industry. Ygge & Akkermans [51] have pursued a computational market approach similar to that of Wellman [49] They present a decentralized approach to the problem power load management by modeling direct load management as a computational market. Sheblé [38] describes the use of a genetic algorithm for adaptive agents in electric power auctions. He simulates a double auction market in which power buyers and sellers make transactions. Ostrov and Rucker [31] look at evolving cellular automata that model electrical properties of the power grid. Talukdar et al. [43] look at agents for real-time operation of power networks.

2   SPOT PRICING DOMAIN

Spot pricing of electricity is a pricing scheme in which the cost of electric power may fluctuate on a rapid basis, perhaps hourly. In our rendition of this scheme, the price of electricity for a given hour as seen by the consumer reflects the *actual cost* during that hour to produce the electricity, transmit it, and maintain the generating system, etc. Utilities can be most efficient, in terms of cost per kWh, if the demand is nearly constant from hour to hour. Variations in demand require fast-acting generators that use expensive fuel, more maintenance etc. (Figure 1). Designing power grids to handle large peak loads is likewise expensive, since it demands more high-tension cables, and the overhead of excess capacity.

Thus, system-wide optimization is a plausible generating company objective. In theory, a progressive generating company could set its rates to minimize peak expected load, and hence maximize its efficiency and profitability. Smart customers would shift at least some of their demands to hours when electricity ought to be inexpensive. They might also buy and store energy at such times for later use.

We describe a slightly richer version of the problem framework than was actually used for conducting experiments. Our simulation of the energy marketplace is nonetheless both highly simplified and in some respects (to be discussed) significantly different from current practice by electric utilities. However, this marketplace offers several interesting problems to explore with adaptive agents. We have focused on the system-wide dynamics of consumers, i.e., the collective behavior of a large number of the utility's customers. We note in passing some alternative problems: the internal dynamics of individual consumers or individual utilities, and the relation between groups of utilities.

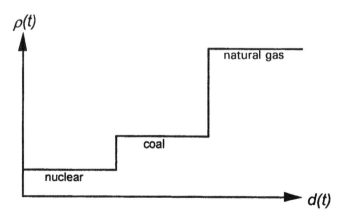

FIGURE 1
Cost as a function of demand.

In the simulated environment, all of the *J adaptive* agents are consumers of electricity. The supplier here is a nonadaptive entity, responding to demand according to a fixed formula. The focus of our experiments has been the evolution of effective energy management strategies among consumers. During a given period of the day, a consumer is obliged to expend a certain amount of energy to cover the loads that must run during that hour, e.g. building elevators, lights, computers. This may vary from one period to another, but for a given period is essentially the same from day to day. Unlike real power grids, there are neither weekly nor seasonal variations in our simulation. This *fixed load profile* may differ from one class of consumers to another, e.g. commercial versus domestic. We further assume that each consumer has another load that can be run during any hour of the day, but must be run exactly once each day. This "shiftable load" might be an appliance like a dishwasher. Figure 2a illustrates this situation in the case where there are four pricing periods per day.

In some of our experiments, we allow agents to buy a limited amount of energy for storage. Stored energy can be used in lieu of or in addition to energy supplied directly from the power grid. We will refer to this as a *battery*, but in a real application it is more likely to be an apparatus such as a pump or icemaker (cooling is major use of electric power). Using storage, a shrewd agent might hedge, reducing risk by buying energy now in order to defray costs at a later time when energy might be more expensive. The simulation allows that the storage devices are imperfect, and stored energy leaks away at a fixed hourly rate.

The *period* is the smallest time resolution of the system. At the beginning of each period, consumers must decide whether to (1) run the shiftable load, or (2) charge, hold, or discharge

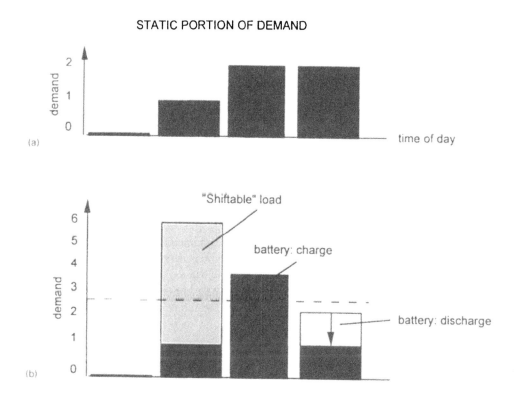

FIGURE 2
Demand of a single agent over the four-period day. (a) Fixed demand profile. (b) Net effect of fixed demand plus battery and shiftable load.

FIGURE 3
Period activities for consumers.

storage. The consumer agents make their decisions independently. When all consumers have made their decisions for the period, the total demand can be calculated by the utility, and used to compute the spot price and period bills. This cycle repeats for the $h = 4$ periods of every epoch (nominal day) as shown in Figure 3.

The simulation runs for a predetermined number of epochs, M. Consumers evaluate themselves according to their average energy costs, relative to the population at large. After every epoch, consumers may use their self-assessed performance to alter their internal decision-making apparatus (Figure 4). Agents are nominally selfish—they only attempt to optimize their own long-term utility. A consumer that did relatively poorly will tend to make alterations to avoid the same mistakes. A consumer that did relatively well might reinforce the responsible decision elements.

2.1 Comments on the Problem

It is useful to consider this problem as a multiplayer game. The loss function is defined in a purely selfish manner by consumer agents as their individual cost of operation. The agents are designed to pursue their own interests, which may not necessarily coincide with those of the supplier or fellow consumers. The nature of the payoff function (the spot pricing formula) will influence the sort of strategies that develop and survive.

This is not a game with perfect information. All of the agents make their moves simultaneously, and a given agent does not know what usage decisions all the other agents will make in the next period.

This is not a zero sum game. It does not necessarily follow that the gain of one agent is the loss of the others. However, in the experiments reported herein, we have set the parameters of the simulation so that the population could just achieve maximal generation efficiency (hence the lowest average price) through cooperation. In other words, under such conditions there is an incentive to cooperate if the bulk of the population is willing to cooperate.

This version of spot pricing differs substantially from the real-time pricing schemes currently being evaluated by utilities. The phrase "real time pricing" encompasses a variety of contracts in the dozen or so electric utilities in the United States experimenting with spot-pricing [23]. A basic difference is that current experiments are much more conservative in conception, and are best seen as an evolutionary change in the form of the contract between utility and customer. Commonly the utility forecasts the hourly marginal cost-based prices for the next 24-hour period based on previous demand trends, weather forecast, etc. The forecast price is then honored for 24 hours, regardless of the demand.

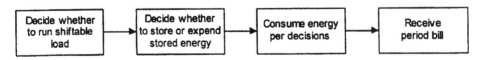

FIGURE 4
Epoch activities for consumers.

The current trials involve only a modest number of customers with quite limited ability to either store energy or to reschedule their loads. Consequently, generation companies can expect little change to the prevailing load dynamics—about 10% reduction in usage during peak periods has been observed in successful cases. The dynamics would change if the utility had a large number of customers with significant storage and rescheduling ability. Honoring a 24-hour price contract in this market would disadvantage the producer. Customers would happily mob the projected low-price periods and the utility would suffer substantial losses. Attempts to stabilize behavior by adjusting price forecasts could be undermined by customers conspiring to fool the projections. A flat price would be the utility's only resort, and this defeats the purpose of an adaptive pricing scheme.

The pricing policy that inspired our simulated experiments is the extreme version of those outlined by Schweppe et al. [37]. The utility gets a fixed margin above cost—no more, no less. From the (public) producer's standpoint this might be considered a fair system. Would consumers happily subscribe to this set of rules? At this date, probably not—the uncertainty about the actual prices for the next day would present an unfamiliar risk. Moreover, the technology for energy storage and load scheduling is still fairly primitive, and is unlikely to give small consumers the sort of leverage required for the highly volatile market described here. This risk is familiar to speculators in other markets, however, and risk reduction mechanisms such as futures and options markets have been proposed. Electrical power futures markets are in operation in New York and California; descriptions of these are available on the Internet (e.g. http://www.calpx.com, http://www.nymex.com/contract/cinergy.html).

One of the motivations for studying systems such as the one described here is that it allows us to examine the consequences of hypothetical policies where it is difficult to obtain analytical solutions. This use is analogous to some of the economic studies described above. We may ask several interesting questions: Is there a stationary equilibrium for consumers in this game? Is it unique? Is it optimal? Can these techniques reliably find such an equilibrium? With a large number of players with differing capabilities, complicated strategies, and the possibility of cooperation, these questions do not have simple solutions. The approach should yield some insight into the behavior of such systems.

3 PROBLEM FORMULATION

This subsection offers a brief formalization of the problem. In general, we follow the notation of Schweppe et al. [37].

The decision made by customer i whether to run the load for the coming period t is

$$\delta_i(t) = \begin{cases} 1 & \text{run load during hour } t \\ 0 & \text{don't run load in hour } t \end{cases}$$

The decision made by customer i whether to store energy or expend stored energy (or neither) is

$$\beta_i(t) = \begin{cases} 1 & \text{charge battery} \\ 0 & \text{hold} \\ -1 & \text{discharge battery} \end{cases}$$

The amount of energy that customer i is obliged to consume during period t (the fixed part of the demand) is

$$\kappa_i(t) = f_i(t \bmod h)$$

where h is the number of periods per epoch, e.g., 4. The function f_i is a static lookup table.

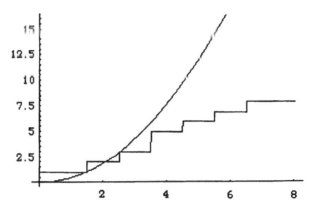

FIGURE 5
Two forms of the function γ: a smooth quadratic and a step function.

The total demand of customer i during period t is

$$d_i(t) = \delta_i(t) + \beta_i(t) + \kappa_i(t)$$

The total demand made by all n customers is thus

$$d(t) = \sum_{i=1}^{n} d_i(t)$$

The total generation during hour t is

$$g(t) = d(t) + L(t)$$

where the loss, $L(t)$, is the amount of energy dissipated as waste heat, etc. The spot price assessed for period t is

$$\rho(t) = \gamma_F(t) + \gamma_M(t) + \gamma_R(t)$$

where the various γ terms correspond to fuel costs, maintenance costs, and return on investment (profit). We have experimented with two forms of this function. One is a step function, the other a quadratic (Figure 5).

The cost billed to customer i at the end of period t is

$$c_i(t) = \rho(t)d_i(t)$$

A set of constants needs to be determined prior to running the simulation. Except where otherwise specified, the parameter values of Table 1 were used, and apply to all agents. These include constants for the price function and the fixed and shiftable components of demand. Energy units are nominal. Although they are experimental parameters of system, we have not done much systematic manipulation of them.

Table 1 Default Parameters

Periods per epoch:	4
Shiftable load size:	5
Fixed load profile:	0, 1, 2, 2
Battery capacity:	2
Battery charge rate:	2/period (when enabled)
Battery carryover:	0—energy must be used in the same epoch as stored.

3.1   Agent Structure

The job of an agent is to make a sequences of decisions that will minimize its energy costs. An agent has two sorts of internal control actions available to it (Figure 6). The total load consists of a fixed portion and, optionally, a shiftable portion (here resistors). The fixed load is switched automatically by the clock each period; one of the four resistors is always in the circuit. Switch SW2 controls when the shiftable load is engaged ("run"). The shiftable load is constrained to run in exactly one period of a day.

Switch SW1 controls whether the battery is to be charged, discharged or kept offline. If the battery is fully charged, it will consume no further energy even if SW2 is put in the "charge" position. In the "discharge" position, the battery will be applied to the load, and the agent will draw from the generating company only as required to finish the job. If the battery is attached to the load but has no charge, or if SW2 is placed in the "hold" position, the line voltage (Vcc) from the utility will run the load by itself.

At the beginning of each period, the switches are set by the agent to some position. During the period, the two switches remain in the chosen position. The extended sets of inputs and outputs to the agent are summarized in Table 2.

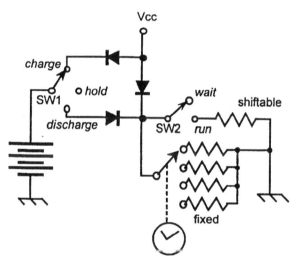

FIGURE 6
Schematic diagram of an agent (decision mechanisms not shown).

Table 2   Agent Inputs and Outputs

Variable	Description	Domain
B	Battery mode	$\{-1, 0 + 1\}$
D	Run load	$\{0, 1\}$
C	Control outputs	$B \times D$
S	Storage status	$\{0, 1, 2\}$
L	Load status	$\{0, 1\}$
P	Last price input	$\{1, 2, 3, 4, 5, 6, 7, 8\}$
T	Time remaining	$\{1, 2, 3, 4\}$
E	Environment in	$S \times L \times I \times P \times T$

In these terms, the agent must select some control action $c \in C$ when presented with an environment $e \in E$. Agents may adopt a deterministic (*pure*) strategy, or a mixed strategy. In the latter case, each $e \in E$ specifies a probability distribution P_e on all the possible elements of C, i.e.,

$$P_e(c) = \Pr\{c \in C | e \in E\}$$

Given a state of the environment e, the agent will make the decision c with probability $P_e(c)$. As the agent learns, the probabilities are altered to make better decisions more likely and foolish decisions less likely. Under fairly general conditions, there will always exist at least one Nash equilibrium if players are allowed to employ mixed strategies.

3.2   Implementation

Our experiments to date have been restricted to subsets of the model described. In particular:

- All consumers are identical in terms of their loads and capabilities. This makes the game homogeneous—no player holds an advantageous position.
  Energy leakage was ignored; the agents had either perfect batteries, or no storage capability at all.
- Experiments reported were run with the smooth (quadratic) cost function.

The software was programmed in Common Lisp and runs on Symbolics and Sun computers. Current work (see the section below on Complex Adaptive Strategies Tool) focuses on an open binary standard (ActiveX) that allows agents to be programmed in nearly any computer language.

4   REINFORCEMENT LEARNING TECHNIQUES

The basic challenge facing a consumer in this environment is deciding what to do next based only on what it has tried in the past and how that paid off. The task of learning from only scalar performance feedback (payoff here) is known as *reinforcement learning* [41]. It is generally more challenging than learning situations where a teacher is present during training to give the right answers in each situation, i.e., supervised learning. The task of deciding which of your past actions should get the credit or blame for the state in which you now find yourself is the *temporal credit assignment problem*. Reinforcement learning and temporal credit assignment are both difficult problems. Some readers may recognize the situation as similar to direct adaptive optimal control [42]. Others may recognize this as a common paradigm in animal learning experiments (e.g., Pavlovian and operant conditioning). The learning algorithms that try to solve these problems can be discussed independently from the mechanism they use for association and generalization, and we will mention several memory mechanisms.

Q-Learning [47,48] offers another approach to this problem. It is a technique related to the temporal difference methods of Sutton [39] and may also be viewed as an incremental realization of dynamic programming [5]. It is a "direct" or model-free method, using the environment as a model. The framework for Q-learning is illustrated in Figure 7.

A measurable state of the world, x, appears at the agent's sensors. The agent assesses (as best as it can) the utility of the various actions open to it, selects one, and activates the appropriate effector, a. Q-learning uses its memory to approximate the utility function $util(x,a)$, the expected

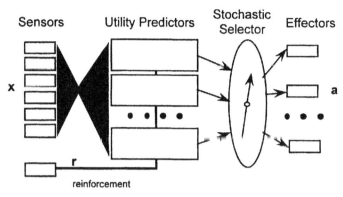

FIGURE 7
Framework for Q-learning.

discounted cumulative reinforcement that will follow from the agent choosing action a in situation x. (We adopt the notation of Lin [52]). util(x,a) may be split into two pieces: an immediate payoff for the action a, plus the best utility that can be had from the next state y, will arise from taking action a in state x leads to state y. Then

$$\text{util}(x,a) = r + \gamma \, \text{Max}\{\text{util}(y, k)\}$$

r is the immediate reinforcement; γ is the discount factor, discounting the value of long-term consequences. The maximization is taken over all possible actions, k, available from state y.

When the agent is in a given state, x, as dictated by its sensors (and any internal state variables), the utility predictors attempt to estimate the utility of each possible action a. If the estimate were perfect, the agent would simply select the action with the highest utility. However, the estimate will generally be imperfect; indeed, at first it will be quite poor. To force the agent to explore alternatives, a stochastic selector (based on the Boltzmann distribution) is used to pick one of the actions at random. This selector introduces a new parameter, temperature T, which controls the variance of the pick. At very low temperatures, the selector almost always picks the action with highest expected utility. At high temperatures, the choice becomes nearly uniform over the possible actions.

4.1 Memory Mechanisms

We have experimented with four different memory mechanisms for associating actions and their consequences: multilayer perceptrons, CMACs, SDMs, and hash tables. All of them may be viewed as essentially trainable function approximators or as artificial neural networks.

Multilayer perceptrons are networks made by composing simple threshold functions. The inputs to each threshold "unit/neuron" are "weighted" in a manner that approximates the desired function. This sort of network is commonly trained by the back-propagation of error (see [53] for a review). We used a variant (Fahlman's Quickprop) for our experiments.

CMAC, the Cerebellar Model Articulation Controller, was proposed by Albus [2] as a means for motor tasks such as controlling robotic arms. It is arguably one of the most successful sorts of artificial neural network, with its popularity due to its computational efficiency. Some of the ideas in it are inspired by simple models of the cerebellum, a region of the vertebrate brain responsible for fine motor control. Briefly, a CMAC has a set of association cells with overlapping receptive fields in the input space. A set of learned weights map the cells activated by a given input with the desired output. The CMAC was used by Watkins [47] in his original work on Q-Learning.

Kanerva's [15] sparse distributed memory (SDM) is somewhat reminiscent of the CMAC, also patterned after neural structures. It writes information for a new association at many scattered memory addresses simultaneously. Because memory is finite, each new piece of information will be superimposed on some previously stored associations, and will partially erase them. SDM uses statistical properties of recall to reconstruct an accurate memory from multiple distributed memory locations.

Sparse matrices may also be stored in hash tables. The numerical inputs are bit-field coded to produce an integer that serves as a key to a hash table. In this scheme, any given input pattern addresses a unique cell; however, we are obliged to maintain storage only for cells that are actually used. The content of a cell is a number that is adapted to the desired output with a Widrow–Hoff style rule. A parameter, $0 < \alpha < 1$, serves to moderate the learning rate. Unlike the other techniques, hash tables are not biologically plausible.

CMACs, SDMs, and multilayer perceptions (MLPs) are all potentially more efficient than tables from a storage standpoint. They make varying assumptions about the regularity of the function to be approximated, and, to the degree that these are met, offer both a compact representation and a useful means for generalization. Our experience suggests that they are comparatively time-consuming to train, particularly the MLPs. To compare the algorithms, we applied them to a static problem: learning to play the game of tic-tac-toe (noughts & crosses). The details will not be reported here, but of our various mechanisms, only the hash table (sparse table lookup) could be described as efficient at learning a strong game from online play against a skillful opponent. This is consistent with other results that have shown that explicit tabular encoding, coupled with some other conditions, guarantees that Q-learning will learn an optimal policy if it exists.

4.2 Experimental Results

We have created a species of *Q-agents* for experiments in the spot-pricing problem. Q-Agents are structured much like the diagram of Figure 7. They have six actions at their disposal, corresponding to the combinations of the load switch (offline, online) and the battery switch (charge, discharge, hold). Each action has a separate table associating the inputs with the estimated utility of the action.

We will refer to the *performance* of an agent as its average daily energy cost relative to a perfectly balanced load. Since an agent is obliged to consume 10 units of energy a day, it is easy to see from a symmetry argument that an optimal scheme (for a smooth, monotone cost function) would be to expend 2.5 units during each of the four periods. This we define as a performance of 1.0. Under the rules, it is clearly impossible for an agent to spend exactly 2.5 energy units, so a performance of 1 is only possible for an ensemble of agents.

There were some questions as to how this form of reinforcement learning would be able to handle the nonstationary environment posed by a population of adaptive agents. The simplest case is a population with a single Q-agent playing against the fixed strategy of the utility. Figure 8 shows the performance of such an individual as it learned to minimize its cost.

In about 200 epochs of training, the initially uninformed agent has learned to do as well as a single agent can. It charges its battery in the first period when there is no fixed portion of demand. It runs its load and discharges the battery in the second period, where the fixed demand is only 1. The battery and load are offline for the remainder of the day. The optimal solution gives a demand profile of 2–4–2–2 and performance 0.710.

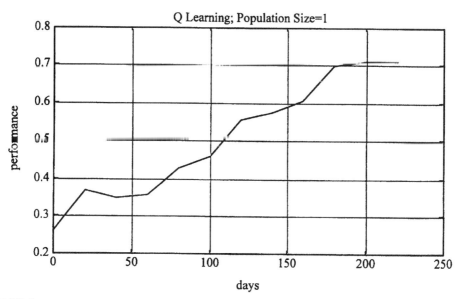

FIGURE 8
Q-learning by a single individual over epochs (days).

Figure 8 shows the speediest learner discovered. In this case, the learning rate parameter α was 0.1. The discount factor, γ, was 0.99. The initial temperature was 0.5, and it was cooled by a factor of 0.8 every 20 epochs. We have done some experimentation with the parameters and found that they are somewhat sensitive. For example, an agent with a higher learning rate, $\alpha = 0.5$, fails to converge to the solution on this cooling schedule. Similarly, a faster cooling schedule, such as 0.8 by every 10 days, also fails to reliably converge to the optimal solution.

We had initially employed a slightly lower discount factor (0.8) and were perplexed at why the agent always settled on a suboptimal demand profile, 2–1–2–5: running the load in the final period. It seems the discounting of the future profit (loss) in the final period was sufficiently great to convince the agent to take the short term profit of a period-2 with only a single unit of energy.

The next simplest configuration consists of two individuals simultaneously adapting to balance the load on the grid. Figure 9 shows typical performance in this situation. Learning in this competitive environment is slower. To allow for a longer exploration period, the action selection temperature was reduced by a factor of 0.8 every 100 epochs. The other parameters are as before. The two agents improve until a constraint is reached. In the case of two agents, it is impossible for either to achieve optimal performance (1). They can nonetheless do better than a single agent. The two agents would continue to oscillate between 0.8 and 0.9, except that the temperature at 2000 days is already quite cold, so under this simple cooling schedule the agents are essentially frozen at the performance levels shown. We will return to this difficulty shortly.

Figure 10 shows results from a larger scale study with a population of 16 agents. The graph shows average performance as well as the performance of the best and worst agents. The more agents in the population, the more closely a perfect score may be approximated. Note that a performance figure *above* 1.0 is possible for a minority of agents. They achieve this by consuming energy in periods that are slightly less favored by the rest of the population; this strategy is not sustainable when the agents are allowed to continually adapt—others will readily invade these periods.

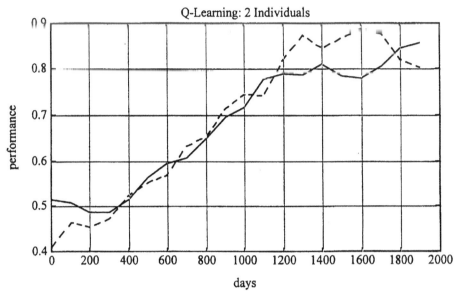

FIGURE 9
Q-learning by a pair of agents of 2000 epochs (days).

4.3 Conclusions about Q-Agents

Autonomous agents with Q-Learning were able to find near optimal equilibria in each of the situations tested. They did so without central control and without even any direct communication. Their reinforcement learning scheme was designed to maximize the profit of the individual,

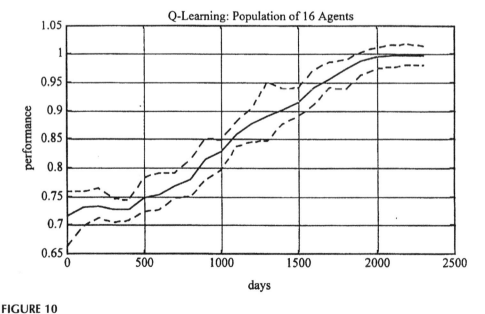

FIGURE 10
Q-learning by a population of 16 agents. The solid line is the average performance. Dashed lines are the performances of the best and worst agent at any given time. $\alpha = 0.1$, $\gamma = 0.99$. Cooling by a factor of 0.8 every 100 days.

not the community. In the context of this problem, an implicit form of cooperation emerged to achieve this.

By contrast to static problems like tic-tac-toe or mazes, Q-learning proved slow in the dynamic situation of our spot pricing environment. Thousands of epochs of were required in the cases examined. The need for prolonged exploration in this changing environment led to a slow rate of learning. Others have also commented on the difficulty of adapting rapidly to changes in the problem [32]. Higher learning rates may be possible if somewhat greater capabilities are awarded to the agents. We explore one possibility in the next section.

We have not explored adjustments of Q-agent learning capabilities, e.g. extending the input space with memories of recent events, or lengthening the exploration schedule. These strategies have been explored somewhat by Sandholm and Crites [34] in the context of Q-Learners competing in an iterated prisoners dilemma problem. Their tentative conclusion was that agents with more memory and longer exploration periods fare better.

There is a further shortcoming in the adaptability of Q-agents: they inevitably cool into a rigid pattern of behavior. As shown, this can yield reasonable results. But the lack of flexibility means that the system could not adapt to unexpected outside disturbances. Thus our Q-agents are not quite complete. A future design should incorporate a "motivational" circuit to adapt their temperature according to circumstance. Some researchers have begun looking at cases like this; for example, how does the robot that has learned one path through the maze adapt when that path is suddenly blocked by a new wall? The stability of a community of agents with adaptable motivation is an open question. For instance, would it be possible for a clever agent to destabilize the grid to its advantage?

5   EVOLUTIONARY TECHNIQUES

Q-Learning has two disadvantages in the general formulation of the spot pricing problem: It learns slowly and there is no simple way to make it respond to a changing environment. These difficulties are partly attributable to the complexity of Q-Learning and partly to the very limited information available in the environment. To address these, we have explored agents that employ an even simpler learning mechanism and have provided them with a means to share information.

There are a number of possible ways to let agents communicate, including direct agent-to-agent messaging, posting messages in particular places in the environment (e.g., pheromone marking), "applause meter" broadcasts, or a common exchange or blackboard. We have settled on a restricted form of direct exchange. One motivation for this is the practical constraint common in large distributed systems—the communications load implied by unrestricted message traffic. To limit this, the simulation allows agents to share information only with other agents in the same physical neighborhood. This could be viewed either as a mandated disclosure or as a form of intelligence gathering, such as that in which businesses engage when they monitor their local competitors.

We have explored this idea by situating the agents in 20-by-20 toroidal grid. Each of the 400 agents has 8 connected neighbors: above, below, left, right, and corners (Figure 11).

The evolutionary grid agents, *G-agents*, use a much simpler sort of strategy than Q-agents. Each G-agent selects a fixed plan for the day, which completely specifies actions in each period of the day. The structure of this plan is shown in Figure 12. The first four fields specify how to set the battery switch during the four periods of the day. The final field indicates in which period to run the load. At the end of the day, each agent evaluates its performance relative to its neighbors, and may decide to abandon its current strategy or retain it. If it abandons the strategy, it replaces

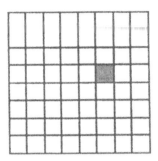

FIGURE 11
Typical grid world of agents. Left and right edges are connected, as are top and bottom, forming a torus. The 8 neighbors of the black position are shaded gray.

it by means of a genetic algorithm operating on the population of its local neighborhood (excluding the agent itself).

G-Agents adapt via a genetic algorithm [26]. Genetic algorithms (GAs) are stochastic optimizers that manipulate strings in a manner analogous to the operations on chromosomes in natural evolution. The string illustrated in Figure 12 is the effective chromosome of the agent used by our GA. With one exception, the results reported here use a GA that employs tournament selection with a tournament of size 2. Briefly, two neighbors are selected at random from the 8 adjacent neighbors. The selected neighbor with the higher fitness becomes a parent for the next strategy; ties are broken at random. Two parents selected this way undergo crossover: a random dividing line is placed across the pair and the first segment from one parent is concatenated to the second segment of the other. Random mutation is applied to the product of the crossover (at a rate of 0.01) to produce the new strategy.

Each agent decides at the end of every epoch whether it will retain its strategy or abandon it for a new one. This is done based on relative performance in its neighborhood. G-Agents measure the performance of a strategy as the average efficiency of that strategy over all consecutive days it has been employed. The current strategy will be abandoned unless any of the following conditions holds:

C1 The current strategy has been held for less than L epochs, where L is a discrete uniform random number distributed as $[0, \ldots, \lambda]$. We refer to λ as the breeding latency parameter.

C2 Fewer than α agents in its neighborhood are performing as well or better.

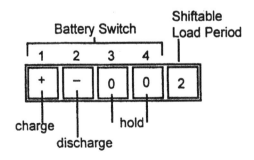

FIGURE 12
The structure of a G-agents's daily strategy, and chromosome.

C3 More than β other agents in its neighborhood are performing only just as well or worse.

C4 γ or fewer other agents in its neighborhood performed as well or worse on the *last* epoch.

Manipulation of these *breeding criteria* is discussed below. With suitable settings, agents will tend to borrow strategies from neighbors who have discovered better ones. Balancing the grid thus becomes a cooperative learning exercise.

Cellular genetic algorithms like this have been used for optimization problems (e.g. [54]), but are seldom cast as a mechanism of communication, essentially the role the GA plays here. Note that while agent strategies are transitory, individual G-agents are permanent—they are never removed from the grid, no matter how badly they perform. It is reasonable to cast these agents as specialized stochastic cellular automata [30].

The results reported here impose one further restriction, a prohibition on the use of energy storage. With the battery switch disabled, the only decision that the agent makes is when to run the shiftable load. In the problem as formulated, storage is not required to achieve optimal collective performance. This restriction has the added benefit that it enables easy visualization of the distribution of strategies over the grid.

Given the no-storage restriction, there are only four effective strategies in the simulation. For the load profiles of Table 1, a given distribution of the four strategies over the 400 agents in the grid will yield a total load profile (seen by the power provider) varying over the four periods of an epoch. The total for an epoch will, of course, be a constant. There are over 10 million different feasible mixtures of the strategies. *There is, however a unique optimum mixture, yielding a completely flat load of 1000 across the four periods.* In this configuration, 200 run their shiftable load in period 1, 120 in period 2, and 40 each in periods 3 and 4. This optimum is also a Nash equilibrium for the game, i.e., no agent has an incentive to switch to a different strategy given that others do not switch. Can the G-agents find this configuration, and if so, under what circumstances?

5.1 Experimental Results

Thousands of simulations of the grid world have demonstrated that, for various settings of the agent breeding criteria $(\alpha, \beta, \gamma, \lambda)$, G-agents can find the optimal strategy mixture, and indeed can do so fairly quickly. Figure 13 shows an example of the grid's evolution from the perspective of total system demand. The two curves plot the demand in the highest and lowest of the four periods. The strategies are initially assigned at random in epoch 0. Over 43 epochs, the curves converge to the optimum value and remain there indefinitely as long as no external disturbance is applied.

The number of epochs required to stabilize is a function of initial conditions and the agent breeding criteria. It is an obvious measure of system performance, but we do not have an analytic model that fully explains all the observed phenomena with this simulation. However, several reliable effects can be empirically demonstrated. First, it is important for the agents to look not only at the mean performance of their neighbors' strategies (the focus of criteria C2 and C3), but also at the performance on the most recent epoch. This is the role of γ in criterion C4. By inhibiting strategy switching when γ or fewer neighbors performed as well or worse on the last epoch, the optimal configuration becomes a fixed point. This is not the case for the mean performance, because the mean depends on the tenure of the strategy, which at any given time past the first few epochs can vary significantly from agent to agent over the population. Without a criterion like C4, the population wanders in the near vicinity of the optimum indefinitely, but never rests there. However, performance on the last epoch is not a substitute for mean

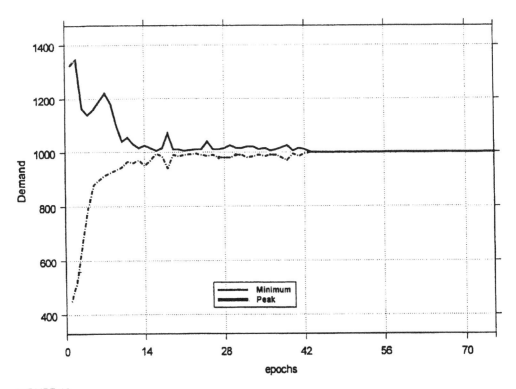

FIGURE 13
Demand range by simulation epochs. Convergence to equilibrium is obtained in this simulation run in epoch 43.

performance. It is too volatile; attempts to use this as the sole measure of performance yield worse global performance (higher variance) than simulations without C4.

The G-agents are not irrevocably frozen after arriving at equilibrium. This can be demonstrated by introducing a disturbance into the system. Figure 14 shows a system in which we have allowed the population to stabilize for 100 days, and then added a large fixed demand to period 0 (the equivalent of a smelter moving into the neighborhood and starting up at midnight every night.) The peak demand (lower graph) initially surges up, but within about 50 days, it is stabilized at a new plateau. Removal of the disturbance at 300 epochs lets the system return to its former peak level.

Extensive competitions between algorithms have been held in the study of iterated Prisoner's Dilemma problems [3]. In summarizing the results of these competitions as advice for contestants, Axelrod suggests:

1. Don't be envious.
2. Don't be the first to defect.
3. Reciprocate both cooperation and defection.
4. Don't be too clever.

At least the first two of these seem to have bearing on the problem faced in the grid world. The issue of "envy" is addressed by criteria C2–C4. G-Agents decide whether to switch strategies based on examining their performance relative to their immediate neighbors. We have already

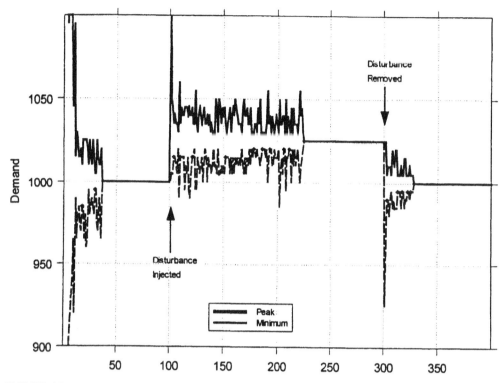

FIGURE 14

Peak demand as managed by a population of G-agents. A disturbance is introduced at time 100, and removed at time 300. The initial demand range (time < 10) had been trimmed to show later details.

mentioned the importance of C4 in establishing a fixed point. Manipulations of parameters (α, β) can be summarized by the rule:

- Switch strategies only if no neighbor is doing worse.

This corresponds to $(\alpha - 8)$. For this setting of α, β appears to be irrelevant to the time required by the system to reach equilibrium. More "envious" strategies, corresponding to values of α less than 8, take significantly longer to stabilize, when they do so at all.

As to the second part of Axelrod's advice (don't be the first to defect), this is witnessed by apparent benefits to delaying breeding. The breeding latency parameter λ controls a coin-toss that effectively inhibits strategy switching when a strategy has been held for a short time. The inhibition gradually disappears as the strategy has been evaluated for a number of epochs approaching λ. This criterion (C1) can be disabled ($\lambda = 0$), but this is not an optimal choice, as illustrated by Figure 15. This shows median epochs required for convergence to equilibrium. The optimal value appears to be approximately 20 (given $\alpha = 4$, $\beta = 8$).

Examination of the update method used to generate a new agent strategy yields one further observation pertaining to envy (or perhaps being too clever). In the experiments described, a genetic algorithm using tournament selection, crossover, and mutation was used to pick a new strategy. Because of the storage restriction, the chromosome consists effectively of a single gene, so, unlike a traditional GA, crossover is not doing the work here—the burden of picking a better strategy is being carried by the selection algorithm. Would a "greedy" algorithm that always

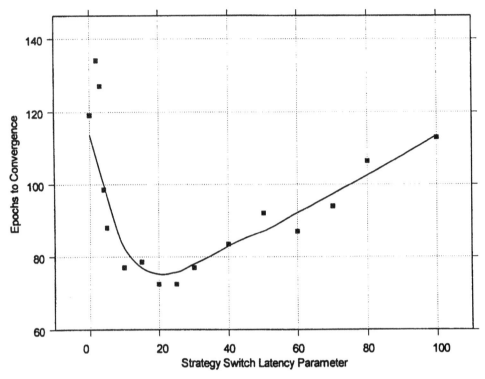

FIGURE 15

Effect of latency to switch strategy on the number of epochs required for convergence. Each point is the median on the convergence times for 100 simulations. The line is a smoothing of the data by the Loess algorithm.

elected to duplicate the strategy of best-performing neighbor be an improvement over the probabilistic algorithm used in the GA? In the cases we have examined, the answer appears to be no. On the contrary, the greedy update scheme seems to retard convergence (Figure 16).

Because of the local nature of the strategy exchange mechanism, the distribution of strategies tends to exhibit some spatial coherence. By assigning each strategy a color, the strategy distribution over the grid can be visualized, as in Figure 17. The spatial coherence is most striking if breeding criteria allow the agents to adjust continually over a large number of epochs; this situation can yield a map with only four homogenous color regions.

Conclusions about G-Agents

The updating scheme used by G-agents proved to be surprisingly capable with the spot pricing problem. It was able to find and maintain optimal equilibrium rapidly and restore it under changing conditions. This was achieved in a purely local fashion without resort to global control or global communications. There are open questions with respect to scaling of the approach to more difficult problems where the simple representations used may be inadequate. The fact that others have had success with more complicated automata leads us to think that this is a most promising direction for research (e.g. [27]).

Several extensions are suggested. Just as the temperature schedule for Q-agents was contrived, so is the decision strategy for evolutionary agents to abandon a strategy. We speculate that this strategy could also become part of the agent's genetic makeup. Changing the rule to

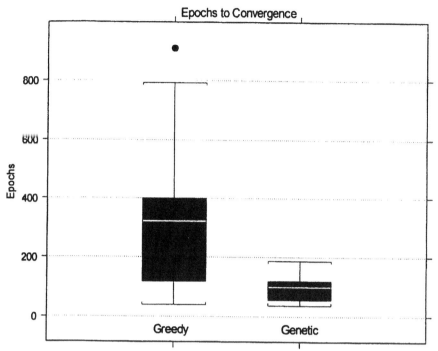

FIGURE 16

Effect of update strategy on the number of epochs required for convergence. Left: greedy update; Right: genetic algorithm (tournament selection). Boxplots summarize distribution of 100 simulations in each condition. The box borders show the first and third population quartiles with the light bisecting line at the median. Whiskers indicate population tails. The dot is an outlier.

abandon strategies can have dramatic effects. It is possible, for example, to make the equilibrium state absorbing, so that once the system attains this state, it does not change at all until further perturbed. (We have been able to demonstrate this behavior with a fairly simple abandonment rule.)

G-agents seem to find the optimal load distribution faster than Q-agents, e.g. 100 versus 2000 periods. However, direct comparison is inappropriate for two reasons. First, the Q-agents were given a finer-grained control problem to solve. Second, the G-agents had the advantage of learning from their neighbors' strategies, whereas Q-agents were isolated. There are several possible ways to couple reinforcement learning with evolutionary adaptation. This was not attempted, but would be a logical avenue to explore.

6 FUTURE DIRECTIONS

The work described above was carried out with custom Lisp programs that embed the learning algorithms used by the agents as well as specific details of the scenario. The implementation of this software represents an unavoidable compromise between the physical and marketplace realism of the scenario explored and the sophistication of the adaptive techniques. We would of course have preferred to build on a testbed for adaptive agents that embedded a flexible yet high-fidelity modeling environment for the power market. Unfortunately, no such testbed was available when this work was initiated.

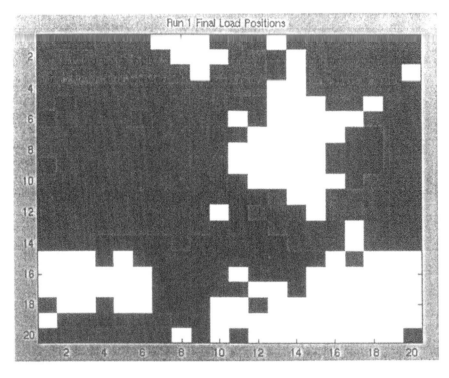

FIGURE 17
Final distribution of strategies from a converged population of G-agents.

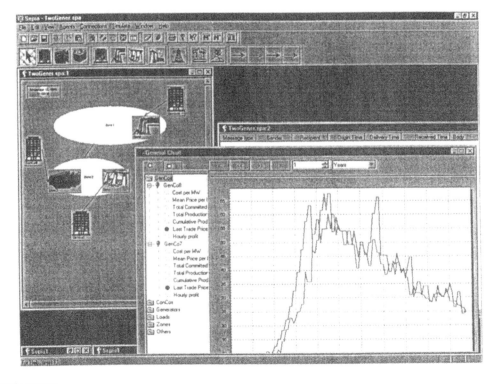

FIGURE 18
The SEPIA simulating environment.

Now, some steps are being taken to realize this long-term vision. In our current EPRI-supported effort (jointly with the University of Minnesota) we have developed a first version of a program called SEPIA—Simulator for Electric Power Industry Agents [50]. The first prototype version of SEPIA allows the simulation of a wide variety of open-access transmission scenarios. The scenario structure can be defined by a user at run time with graphical icons, creating zones, generators, loads, and business entities that own these physical systems. SEPIA is based on Microsoft ActiveX technology to allow agents to be built in a variety of languages and then plugged into the SEPIA shell environment. These agents can avail themselves of standard code modules implementing adaptive techniques including Q-Learning and genetic classifier systems.

REFERENCES

[1] D. Ackley and M. Littman, Interactions between learning, and evolution, in C. Langton et al. (eds.) *Artificial Life II*, pp. 487–509, Addison-Wesley, Redwood City, CA, 1992.

[2] J.S. Albus, A new approach to manipulator control: the cerebellar model articulation controller. *J. Dynamic Systems, Measurement, and Control, Trans. ASME* Vol. 97, pp. 220–227, 1975.

[3] R. Axelrod, *The Evolution of Cooperation*. Basic Books, New York, 1984.

[4] A.G. Barto, R.S. Sutton and C.J.C.H. Watkins, *Learning, and sequential decision making*. COINS Technical Report 89–95. Dept. Computer and Information Science, University of Massachusetts, Amherst, 1989.

[5] D.P. Bertsekas, *Dynamic Programming: Deterministic, and Stochastic Models*. Prentice Hall, Englewood Cliffs, NJ, 1987.

[6] A.W. Burks (ed.), *Essays on Cellular Automata*. University of Illinois Press, Urbana, IL, 1970.

[7] L.D. David, *The Handbook of Genetic Algorithms*. Van Nostrand Reinhold, New York, 1991.

[8] W. Fontana, Algorithmic chemistry, in C. Langton et al. (eds.) *Artificial Life II*, pp. 159–209, Addison-Wesley, Redwood City, CA, 1992.

[9] D. Goldberg, *Genetic Algorithms in Search Optimization, and Machine Learning* Addison-Wesley, Reading, MA, 1989.

[10] J. Hertz, A. Krogh and R.G. Palmer, *Introduction to the Theory of Neural Computation*. Addison-Wesley, Reading, MA, 1991.

[11] D. Hillis, Co-evolving parasites improve simulated evolution as an optimization procedure, in Langton et al. (eds.) *Artificial Life II*, pp. 313–324, Addison-Wesley, Redwood City, CA, 1992.

[12] Hinton, G. E. and S.J. Nowlan, How learning can guide evolution, *Complex Systems*, Vol. 1, pp. 495–502, 1987.

[13] J. Hoffbauer and K. Sigmund, *The Theory of Evolution, and Dynamical Systems*. Cambridge University Press, Cambridge, UK, 1988.

[14] J. Holland, Escaping brittleness: The possibilities of general-purpose learning algorithms applied to parallel rule-based systems. In R.S. Michalski, J.G. Carbonell and T.M. Mitchell (eds.) *Machine Learning 2*, pp. 593–624. Morgan Kaufmann, San Mateo, CA 1986.

[15] P. Kanerva, *Sparse Distributed Memory*. MIT Press, Cambridge, MA, 1988.

[16] S. Kauffman and S. Johnsen, Co-evolution to the edge of chaos: coupled fitness landscapes, poised states and co-evolutionary avalanches, In Langton et al. (eds.) *Artificial Life II*, pp. 325–369, Addison-Wesley, Redwood City, CA, 1992.

[17] J. Kephart, T. Hogg, and A. Huberman, Dynamics of computational ecosystems, *Physical Review A*, Vol. 40, p. 404, 1989.

[18] N. Kiyotaki, and R. Wright, On money as a medium of exchange, *J. Political Economy*, Vol. 97, pp. 927–954, 1989.

[19] D.E. Knuth, *The Art of Computer Programming*, Volume 3. Addison-Wesley, Reading, MA, 1973.

[20] J. Koza, Genetic evolution, and co-evolution of computer programs. In Langton et al. (eds.) *Artificial Life II*, pp. 603–629, Addison-Wesley, Redwood City, CA, 1992.

[21] J. Koza, *Genetic Programming*. MIT Press, Cambridge, MA, 1993.

[22] C. Langton, C. Taylor, J. Farmer and S. Rasmussen, (eds.) *Artificial Life II*. Addison-Wesley, Redwood City, CA, (1992).

[23] J. Mak, and B. Chapman, A survey of current real-time pricing programs, *The Electricity Journal*, Aug./Sept. pp. 54–65.

[24] O. Maler, Why should we build artificial worms, and how? in J.A. Meyer et al. (eds.) *From Animals to Animats 2*, p. 519. MIT Press, Cambridge, MA, 1993.

[25] R. Marimon, R. McGrattan and T. Sargent, Money as a medium of exchange in an economy with artificially intelligent agents, *J. Economic Dynamics and Control*, Vol. 14, pp. 329–373, 1990.

[26] M. Mitchell, *An Introduction to Genetic Algorithms*. MIT Press, Cambridge, MA, 1996.

[27] M. Mitchell, J.P. Crutchfield and P.T. Hraber, *Evolving cellular automata to perform computations: mechanisms and impediments*. Santa Fe Institute working paper 93-11-071, 1993.

[28] M. Mitchell and S. Forrest, Genetic algorithms, and artificial life. Santa Fe Institute working paper 93-11-072.

[29] J-A. Meyer, H. Roitblat, and S. Wilson. (eds.) *From Animals to Animats 2*. MIT Press, Cambridge, MA, 1993.

[30] K.S. Narendra and M.A.L. Thathachar, Learning automata: a survey, *IEEE Trans. Systems, Man, and Cybernetics*, Vol. 4, pp. 323–334, 1974.

[31] D.N. Ostrov and R. Rucker, Continuous valued cellular automata for nonlinear wave equations, *Complex Systems* 10 (1196) 91–119.

[32] J. Peng and R. Williams, Efficient learning, and planning within the Dyna framework, in J.A, Myer et al. (eds.) *Animals to Animats 2*, MIT Press, Cambridge, MA, pp. 281–290; 1993.

[33] T. Ray, An approach to the synthesis of life, in C. Langton et al. (eds.), *Artificial Life II*, pp. 371–408, Addison-Wesley, Redwood City, CA, 1992.

[34] T.W. Sandholm and R.H. Crites, Multiagent reinforcement learning in the iterated Prisoner's Dilemma, *Biosystems* special issue on Prisoner's Dilemma, Vol. 37, pp. 147–166.

[35] A.V. Sannier and E.D. Goodman, Midgard: a genetic approach to adaptive load balancing for distributed systems, in *Proc. Fifth Int. Conf. Machine Learning, Ann Arbor*, Morgan Kauffman, San Mateo, CA, 1988.

[36] H.E. Scarf and J.B. Shoven, (eds.) *Applied General Equilibrium Analysis*. Cambridge University Press, Cambridge, UK, 1984.

[37] P.C. Schweppe, M.C. Caraminis, R.D. Tabors and R.E. Bohn, *Spot Pricing of Electricity*. Kluwer Academic, Boston, 1988.

[38] G. Sheblé, *Computer Simulation of Adaptive Agents for an Electric Power Auction*. EPRI Technical Report TR-107975. Electric Power Research Institute, Palo Alto, CA, 1997.

[39] R.S. Sutton, Learning to predict by the methods of temporal differences, *Machine Learning*, Vol. 3, pp. 9–44, 1989.

[40] R.S. Sutton, Planning by incremental dynamic programming, in *Proc. 8th Int. Machine Learning Workshop*, Morgan Kaufmann, pp. 353–357, 1991.

[41] R.S. Sutton and A.G. Barto, *Reinforcement Learning: An introduction*, MIT Press, Cambridge, MA, 1998.

[42] R.S. Sutton, A.G. Barto and R.J. Williams, Reinforcement learning is direct adaptive optimal control, *IEEE Control Systems Magazine*, Vol. 12, pp. 19–22, 1992.

[43] S. Talukdar, V.C. Ramesh, R. Quadrel and R. Christie, Multiagent organizations for real-time operations, *Proc IEEE* Vol. 80, No. 5, pp. 765–778, 1992.

[44] K. Thearling, Putting artificial life to work, in R. Manner and B. Manderick (eds.) *Parallel Problem Solving from Nature, 2*. Elsevier Science, Amsterdam, 1992.

[45] T. Toffoli and N. Marrgolus, *Cellular Automata Machines*. MIT Press, Cambridge, MA, 1987.

[46] M.D. Vose, Generalizing the notion of schema in genetic algorithms, *Artificial Intelligence*, Vol. 50, No. 3, pp. 385–396, 1991.

[47] C.J.C.H. Watkins, *Learning from delayed rewards*. Ph.D. Dissertation, Cambridge University, 1909.

[48] C.J.C.H. Watkins and P. Dayan, Q-Learning, *Machine Learning*, Vol. 8, pp. 279–292, 1992.

[49] M.P. Wellman, A market-oriented programming environment, and its application to distributed multicommodity flow problems. *J. AI Research*, Vol. 1, pp. 1–23, 1993.

[50] M. Wildberger and M. Amin, Simulating the evolution of the electric enterprise with autonomous adaptive agents, Submitted to: *32nd Annual Hawaii Int. Conf. System Sciences*, 1999, unpublished manuscript.

[51] F. Ygge and H. Akkermans, Power load management as a computational market, *Proc. 2nd Int. Conf. Multi-Agent Systems (ICMASI'96), Kyoto, Japan*, AAAI Press, pp. 393–400, 1996.

[52] L.-J. Lin, Self-improving reactive agents based on reinforcement learning, planning and teaching, *Machine Learning*, Vol. 8, pp. 293–321, 1992.

[53] D.E. Ruaelhart, J.L. McClelland, *Parallel distributed processing: Explorations in the microstructure of cognition, Vol. I, foundations*. Bradford/MIT Press, Cambridge, MA, 1986.

[54] D. Whitley, Cellular genetic algorithms, In Stephanie Forrest (ed.) *Proceedings of the Fifth International Conference on Genetic Algorithms*, Morgan Kaufmann, p. 258, 1993.

CHAPTER 24

Truck Backer-Upper Control Using Dynamic Neural Network

MADAN M. GUPTA

Intelligent Systems Research Laboratory, College of Engineering,
University of Saskatchewan, Saskatoon, Saskatchewan, Canada

DANDINA H. RAO

Department of Electronics and Communication Engineering, Gogte Institute of Technology,
Udyambag, Belgaum, Karnataka, India

1   INTRODUCTION

Conventional control systems design methods involve the construction of a mathematical model describing the dynamic behavior of the plant to be controlled and the application of analytical techniques to this model to derive a control law. Usually, such a mathematical model consists of a set of linear or nonlinear differential/difference equations, most of which are derived using some forms of approximation and simplification. These conventional techniques break down, however, when a representative model is difficult to obtain due to uncertainty or sheer complexity, or when the model thus produced violates the underlying assumptions of the control law design techniques. Also, modeling of a physical system for feedback control involves a trade-off between the simplicity of the model and its accuracy in matching the behavior of the physical system. This technique of developing controllers becomes much more complex, or sometimes impossible, if the system under control is uncertain and nonlinear with unknown dynamics [1, 2].

On the other hand, the recent emergence of neurocontrol systems has made it possible to circumvent many of the limitations of conventional controllers developed on the concept of mathematical modeling. This is primarily due to the fact that neurocontrol systems exhibit learning and adaptive capabilities in addition to features such as nonlinear functional approximation, fault-tolerance, and parallelism. A neurocontrol system is defined as the use of neural networks as *controllers* that generate a vector of control signals as a function of time [2]. In this endeavor of developing neurocontrol techniques for complex systems, a host of neural network structures and learning algorithms have been reported in the literature, which are summarized in [3]. The most commonly used neural structures in the control paradigm are the static (feedforward) and the recurrent neural networks. The major concern in using these traditional neural structures, which represent a very simple approximation of their biological counterparts, is that they are very slow in learning to perform a given task.

The purpose of this paper is to describe a dynamic neural structure called the *dynamic neural processor* (DNP) and to use this structure to arrive at feasible solutions to a complex nonlinear control problem such as backing a trailer truck to the loading dock. The DNP is developed based on the neurophysiological hypothesis that neural activities of any complexity are dependent upon the interaction of antagonistic neural subpopulations, namely excitatory and inhibitory. The remaining part of this chapter is organized as follows. The architectural details of the DNP and the learning algorithm to update the DNP weights are presented in Section 2. The problem of truck backer-upper control and computer simulations are discussed in Section 3, followed by the conclusions in the last sections.

2   THE DYNAMIC NEURAL NETWORK

2.1   Architectural Details

A large number of neural network structures described in the existing literature often consider the behavior of a single idealized static neuron as the basic *processing (computing) element*. The ideal neuron is mathematically modeled as a simple summation circuit followed by a nonlinear activation operator. Furthermore, this type of processing element is assumed to respond in an optimal fashion to the applied inputs. However, experimental studies in neurophysiology show that the response of a biological neuron is a random process, and only by an ensemble of many observations is it possible to obtain predictable resutls [4, 5]. It is postulated, therefore, that the collective activity generated by large numbers of locally redundant neurons is more significant in a computational context than the activity of a single neuron. Thus, an alternative to the concept of an ideal neuron is to model the processing elements based upon underlying dynamic properties of an assembly of spatially localized neurons [4].

The neural activity of any complexity arises from a spatially localized assembly of neurons called a *neural population* or a *neural mass* [4, 5]. Each neural population may be further divided into several coexisting *subpopulations*. A single subpopulation is assumed to contain a large class of similarly acting neurons that lie in close proximity. For analytical simplicity, only two subpopulations are assumed to coexist within a neural population. The first subpopulation is assumed to contain only excitatory neurons that project a positive influence when they are active. The second subpopulation contains only inhibitory neurons that project a negative influence when they are active. Such a neural mass can be modeled by a structure that contains excitatory (positive), inhibitory (negative), excitatory-inhibitory (synaptic connections from excitatory to inhibitory), and inhibitory–excitatory (synaptic connection from inhibitory to excitatory) feedback loops.

A simplified model, called the *dynamic neural processor* (DNP), of the neural activity exhibited by a localized population of antagonistic excitatory and inhibitory nerve cells was proposed in [6, 7]. The focus of this model was not to emulate experimentally observed biological phenomena, but rather to investigate the computation role being performed by such coupled nonlinear dynamic systems composed of excitatory and inhibitory neurons. The general topology of the DNP is shown in Figure 1.

The functional dynamics of the antagonistic subpopulations are represented by [Neural Dynamics]$_E$ and [Neural Dynamics]$_I$ respectively. The responses u_E and u_I generated

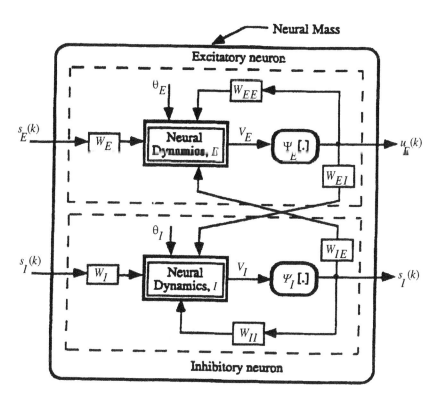

FIGURE 1

The dynamic neural processor with antagonistic neural units, namely, excitatory and inhibitory neurons. w_{EE}, w_{II} represent the strengths of self-synaptic connections, while w_{IE}, w_{EI} represent the inter-subpopulation connections. w_E and w_I are the input weights for excitatory and inhibitory neural inputs $s_E(k)$ and $s_I(k)$, respectively. v_E and v_I are the internal states, and $u_E(k)$, and $u_I(k)$ represent the responses of the excitatory and inhibitory neural subpopulations. θ_E and θ_I represent the thresholds of excitatory and inhibitory neurons, respectively.

at time $(k + 1)$ by the excitatory and inhibitory neural units of the DNP are modeled by the following nonlinear functional relationships:

$$u_E(k + 1) = \mathbf{E}[u_E(k), v_E(k)] \tag{1a}$$

$$u_I(k + 1) = \mathbf{I}[u_I(k), v_I(k)] \tag{1b}$$

where $v_E(k)$ and $v_I(k)$ denote the internal states that represent the proportion of neurons in the neural units that receive inputs greater than an intrinsic threshold, and $\mathbf{E}$ and $\mathbf{I}$ represent the nonlinear excitatory and inhibitory actions of the neurons. The neurons that receive inputs greater than a threshold value are represented by a nonlinear function of $v_\lambda(k)$ (the subscript λ indicates either an excitatory, E, or an inhibitory, I, state). This nonlinear function, $\Psi[v_\lambda(k)]$, is related to the distribution of neural threshold within the neural unit [4, 8]. The states v_λ of the DNP are governed by the following difference equations:

$$v_E(k + 1) = -\alpha_E v_E(k) + (\gamma_E - \beta_E v_E(k))(w_E s_E(k) - \theta_E + w_{EE} u_E(k) - w_{IE} u_I(k)) \tag{2a}$$

$$v_I(k + 1) = -\alpha_I v_I(k) + (\gamma_I - \beta_I v_I(k))(w_I s_I(k) - \theta_I + w_{II} u_I(k) - w_{EI} u_I(k)) \tag{2b}$$

and

$$u_E(k) = \Psi_E[v_E] \tag{3a}$$

$$u_I(k) = \Psi_I[v_I] \tag{3b}$$

In equations (2) and (3), w_{EE}, w_{II} represent the strengths of self-synaptic connections; w_{IE}, w_{EI} represent the inter-subpopulation connections; w_E and w_I are the input weights for the excitatory and inhibitory neural inputs $s_E(k)$ and $s_I(k)$, respectively; θ_E and θ_I represent the thresholds of excitatory and inhibitory neurons, respectively; $\Psi_E[\cdot]$ and $\Psi_E[\cdot]$ denote nonlinear activation operators; and α, β, and γ are constants that affect the dynamic properties of the DNP as described below.

(i) The proportion of neurons active at time $(k + 1)$ that were active during the previous sampling period at time k is given by the term $\alpha_\lambda v_\lambda(k)$ in equations (2a) and (2b), and $\alpha < 1$ is the rate of decay in the proportion of neurons that are still active after one sampling period.

(ii) The proportion of neurons that are refractory but still receive inputs greater than an intrinsic threshold is given by the term $(\gamma_\lambda - \beta_\lambda v_\lambda(k))$. The rate of growth in neural activity is often assumed to be $\beta = (1 - \alpha)$.

The simplified DNP model of the neural mass is achieved by assuming $\alpha_E = \alpha_I = 1$, $\gamma = 1$, and $\beta = 0$, thus simplifying equations (2) and (3) to

$$v_E(k + 1) = -v_E(k) + w_E s_E(k) - \theta_E + w_{EE} u_{EE}(k) - w_{IE} u_I(k) \tag{4a}$$

$$v_I(k + 1) = -v_I(k) + w_I s_I(k) - \theta_I + w_{II} u_I(k) - w_{EI} u_I(k) \tag{4b}$$

and

$$u_E(k) = \Psi_E[v_E] \tag{5a}$$

$$u_I(k) = \Psi_I[v_I] \tag{5b}$$

The neural dynamics of the excitatory and inhibitory neural subpopulations in the DNP are assumed to be identical and are described by the difference equation.

$$v_1(k) = -b_1 v_1(k - 1) - b_2 v_1(k - 2) + a_0 s(k) + a_1 s(k - 1) + a_2 s(k - 2) \tag{6}$$

where $\mathbf{a}_{ff} = [a_0, a_1, a_2]^T$ and $\mathbf{b}_{fb} = [b_1, b_2]^T$ are adaptable feedforward and feedback weights, respectively. Equation (6) represents a second-order linear structure whose output forms an argument to the nonlinear activation operator assumed to be a unimodal sigmoidal function. This neural model, called the dynamic neural unit (DNU) and shown in Figure 2, was proposed in [9]. We now define the vectors of the signals and adaptable weights of the neural dynamics as

$$\Gamma(k, v_1, s) = [v_1(k - 1) v_1(k - 2) s(k) s(k - 1) s(k - 2)]^T \tag{7a}$$

$$\zeta_{(\mathbf{a}_{ff}, \mathbf{b}_{fb})} = [-b_1, -b_2, a_0, a_1, a_2]^T \tag{7b}$$

where the subscript T in the above equations denotes transpose operation. Using (7a) and (7b), equation (6) is written as

$$\mathbf{v}_1(k) = \zeta_{(\mathbf{a}_{ff}, \mathbf{b}_{fb})}^T \Gamma(k, v_1, s) \tag{8}$$

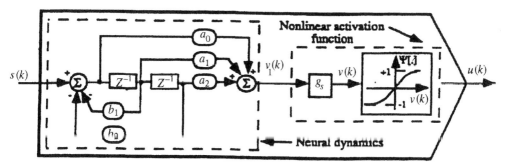

FIGURE 2

The basic structures of dynamic neural unit (DNU). z^{-1} is the unit delay operator, and $\mathbf{a}_{ff} = [a_0, a_1, a_2]^T$ and $\mathbf{b}_{fb} = [b_1, b_2]^T$ are the adjustable feedforward and feedback weights contributing to the forward and feedback dynamics, respectively. The output $v_1(k)$ of this dynamic structure is passed through the somatic gain (slope) g_s and a nonlinear activation function $\Psi[\cdot]$ which produces the neural output $u(k) \in \Re^1$ in response to an input signal $s(k)$.

As discussed above, the nonlinear mapping operation on $v_1(k)$ yields a neural output $u(k)$ given by

$$u(k) = \Psi[g_s v_1(k)] \tag{9}$$

where g_s is the parameter called the somatic gain that controls the slope of the sigmoidal function. Many different forms of mathematical functions can be used to model the nonlinear behavior of the biological neuron. We use a bounded, monotonically increasing and differentiable sigmoidal activation function. To extend the mathematical operations to both the excitatory and inhibitory inputs, the activation (sigmoidal) function is defined over $[-1, 1]$ as

$$\Psi[v(k)] = \frac{[e^{(g_s v_1)} - e^{-(g_s v_1)}]}{[e^{(g_s v_1)} + e^{-(g_s v_1)}]} = \tanh[g_s v_1(k)] = \tanh[v(k)] \tag{10}$$

where $v(k) = g_s v_1(k)$.

The DNP consists of two such DNUs coupled in a flip-flop configuration to function as antagonistic neural units as depicted in Figure 3. In this structure, $s_\lambda(k)$ and $u_\lambda(k)$ represent, respectively, the neural stimulus (input) and neural output of the computing unit, where the subscript λ indicates either an excitatory, E, or inhibitory, I, state; $s_{t\lambda}(k)$ denotes the total input to the neural unit; $w_{\lambda\lambda}$ represent the strength of self-synaptic connections w_{EE}, w_{II} in Figure 3); and $w_{\lambda\lambda'}$ represent the strength of cross synaptic connections from one neural unit to another (w_{IE}, w_{EI} in Figure 3). The z^{-1} elements in Figure 3 denote the communication delays in the self- and the intersynaptic paths.

The total inputs incident on the excitatory and inhibitory neural units are, respectively,

$$s_{tE}(k) = w_E s_E(k) + w_{EE} u_E(k-1) - w_{IE} u_I(k-1) - \theta_E \tag{11a}$$

$$s_{tI}(k) = w_I s_I(k) + w_{II} u_I(k-1) - w_{EI} u_I(k-1) - \theta_I \tag{11b}$$

Equations (11a) and (11b) may be written in a matrix form as

$$\begin{bmatrix} s_{tE}(k) \\ s_{tI}(k) \end{bmatrix} = \begin{bmatrix} w_E & 0 \\ 0 & w_I \end{bmatrix} \begin{bmatrix} s_E(k) \\ s_I(k) \end{bmatrix} + \begin{bmatrix} w_{EE} & -w_{IE} \\ w_{EI} & -w_{II} \end{bmatrix} \begin{bmatrix} u_E(k-1) \\ u_I(k-1) \end{bmatrix} - \begin{bmatrix} \theta_E \\ \theta_I \end{bmatrix} \tag{12}$$

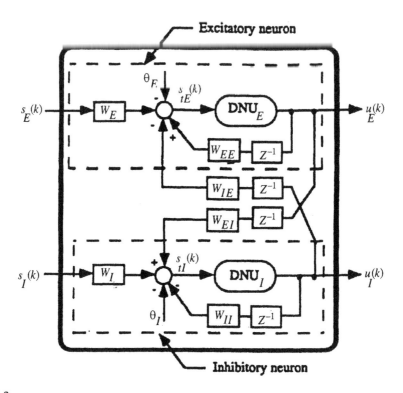

FIGURE 3
The dynamic neural processor with two dynamic neural units coupled as excitatory and inhibitory neurons represented as DNU_E and DNU_I, respectively.

The general expression for the dynamic neural activity of the DNP can be represented in a compact form by the equation

$$S_{t\lambda}(k) = W_{\lambda'}^{\lambda} S_\lambda + W_{\lambda\lambda'}^{\lambda\lambda} U_\lambda - \theta_\lambda \qquad (13)$$

where

$$S_{t\lambda}(k) = \begin{bmatrix} s_{tE}(k) \\ s_{tI}(k) \end{bmatrix} \text{ (input incident vector)} \qquad S_\lambda(k) = \begin{bmatrix} s_E(k) \\ s_I(k) \end{bmatrix} \text{ (stimulus (input) vector)}$$

$$W_{\lambda'}^{\lambda} = \begin{bmatrix} w_E & 0 \\ 0 & w_I \end{bmatrix} \text{ (input scale matrix)} \qquad W_{\lambda\lambda'}^{\lambda\lambda} = \begin{bmatrix} w_{EE} & -w_{IE} \\ w_{EI} & -w_{II} \end{bmatrix} \text{ (synaptic weight matrix)}$$

$$U_\lambda = \begin{bmatrix} u_E(k-1) \\ u_I(k-1) \end{bmatrix} \text{ (response (output) vector)} \qquad \theta_\lambda \begin{bmatrix} \theta_E \\ \theta_I \end{bmatrix} \text{ (threshold vector)}$$

In equation (13) it is assumed that $W_{\lambda\lambda'}^{\lambda\lambda}$ is a nonsingular matrix. From this equation, the responses of the neural units, $u_\lambda(k)$, in terms of the stimulus (inputs) $s_\lambda(k)$, the input $s_{t\lambda}(k)$, and the strength of the synaptic connections $w_{\lambda\lambda}$ and $w_{\lambda\lambda'}$ may be obtained as

$$U_\lambda = [W_{\lambda\lambda'}^{\lambda\lambda}]^{-1}[S_{t\lambda} - W_{\lambda'}^{\lambda} S_\lambda(k) + \theta_\lambda] \qquad (14)$$

The transient behavior and the applications of the DNP are discussed in [6, 7]. In the next subsection, a learning algorithm for the adjustable parameters of the DNP, namely, the feedforward and feedback, the sigmoidal gain g_s, and the connection strength of the self- and inter-subpopulation feedback paths, is briefly described.

2.2 The Learning Algorithm

It is believed that the connectivity strengths, that is, the weights between the neurons, change as the brain learns. Due to the complexity and the incomplete knowledge of the biological learning process, many concepts and algorithms have been developed in the area of neural networks in order to mimic the learning process in artificial neural networks. One method involves minimizing a certain performance index with respect to the weights of the neural network. In such a learning scheme, the weights of the neural network are modified in each iteration to cause the neural output $u(k)$ to approach the desired state $u_d(k)$. For arbitrary initial conditions, if the error between the targeted and the observed responses can be reduced to an acceptable tolerance limit, that is, $u(k) \rightarrow u_d(d)$ as $k \rightarrow \infty$, the learning scheme is said to be convergent. The detailed learning algorithm for the DNP parameters is derived in [7]. For completeness, this algorithm is discussed briefly in the following paragraphs.

Let the parameter vector of the generalized model be defined as

$$\mathbf{\Omega} \underline{\Delta} [\mathbf{a}_{f\!f}, \mathbf{b}_{fb}, g_s, \mathbf{W}^{\lambda\lambda}_{\lambda\lambda}]^T \tag{15}$$

The components of the parameter vector $\mathbf{\Omega}$ and error $e(k)$ vary with every learning trail k. To obtain $\mathbf{\Omega}(k+1)$ requires only the information set $\{\mathbf{\Omega}(k), e(k-m), e(k)\}$, where $m = 1, 2, \ldots$ determines the size of the window. As the number of learning trails increases, the information set reduces to only $\{\mathbf{\Omega}^*(k), e^*(k)\}$, which indicates that the parameters and the error have converged to the optimal values. To achieve this, a performance index, which has to be optimized with respect to the parameter vector, is defined as

$$J = E\{F[e(k; \mathbf{\Omega}]\} \tag{16}$$

where E is the expectation operator. A commonly used form of $F[e(k; \mathbf{\Omega})]$ in equation (16) is an even function of the error, that is,

$$J = \tfrac{1}{2} E\{e^2(k; \mathbf{\Omega})\} \tag{17}$$

Each component of the vector $\mathbf{\Omega}$ is adapted in such a way so as to minimize J using the steepest-descent algorithm. This adaptive rule may be then written as

$$\mathbf{\Omega}(k+1) = \mathbf{\Omega}(k) + \delta\mathbf{\Omega}(k) \tag{18}$$

where $\mathbf{\Omega}(k+1)$ is the new parameter vector, $\mathbf{\Omega}(k)$ is the present parameter vector, and $\delta\mathbf{\Omega}(k)$ is an adaptive adjustment in the parameter vector. In the steepest-descent method, the adjustment of the parameter vector is made proportional to the negative of the gradient of the performance index J, that is,

$$\delta\mathbf{\Omega}(k) \propto (-\nabla J), \qquad \text{where } \nabla J = \frac{\partial J}{\partial \mathbf{\Omega}}$$

Thus,

$$\delta\mathbf{\Omega}(k) = -\text{dia}[\mu] \frac{\partial J}{\partial \mathbf{\Omega}} = -\text{dia}[\mu] \nabla J \tag{19}$$

where dia[μ] is the matrix of individual adaptive gains. In the above equation, dia[μ] is defined as

$$
\text{dia}[\mu] = \begin{vmatrix} \mu_{a_i} & 0 & 0 & 0 \\ 0 & \mu_{b_j} & 0 & 0 \\ 0 & 0 & \mu_{g_s} & 0 \\ 0 & 0 & 0 & \mu_{\lambda\lambda'} \end{vmatrix} \tag{20}
$$

In equation (20), μ_{a_i}, $i = 0, 1, 2$; μ_{b_j}, $j = 1, 2$; μ_{g_s} are the individual learning gains of the adaptable parameters of the DNU; and $\mu_{\lambda\lambda'}$ denote the learning gains for the self- and inter-neuron synaptic connections. From equations (17–20), the following learning rules to update the DNP parameters can be derived (see Appendix for details):

$$
a_{ff_i}(k + 1) = a_{ff_i}(k) + \mu_{a_i} E[e(k) \operatorname{sech}^2[v(k)] \mathbf{P}_{\phi_{a_{ff,i}}}(k)], \qquad i = 0, 1, 2 \tag{21a}
$$

$$
b_{fb_j}(k + 1) = b_{fb_j}(k) + \mu_{b_j} E[e(k) \operatorname{sech}^2[v(k)] \mathbf{P}_{\phi_{b_{fb,j}}}(k)], \qquad j = 1, 2 \tag{21b}
$$

$$
g_s(k + 1) = g_s(k) + \mu_{g_s} E[e(k) \operatorname{sech}^2[v(k)] v_1(k)] \tag{21c}
$$

$$
w_{\lambda\lambda'}(k + 1) = w_{\lambda\lambda'}(k) + \mu_{\lambda\lambda'} E[e(k)\{\operatorname{sech}^2[v(k)] g_s u_\lambda(k - 1)\}] \tag{21d}
$$

For clarity, equation (21d) is written for the individual synaptic weights as

$$
w_{EE}(k + 1) = w_{EE}(k) + \mu_{EE} E[e(k) \{\operatorname{sech}^2[v(k)] g_s u_E(k - 1)\}] \tag{22a}
$$

$$
w_{IE}(k + 1) = w_{IE}(k) + \mu_{IE} E[e(k) \{\operatorname{sech}^2[v(k)] g_s u_I(k - 1)\}] \tag{22b}
$$

$$
w_{EI}(k + 1) = w_{EI}(k) + \mu_{EI} E[e(k) \{\operatorname{sech}^2[v(k)] g_s u_E(k - 1)\}] \tag{22c}
$$

$$
w_{II}(k + 1) = w_{II}(k) + \mu_{II} E[e(k) \{\operatorname{sech}^2[v(k)] g_s u_I(k - 1)\}] \tag{22d}
$$

Equations (21a) and (21b) provide adaptation in the synaptic weights, while equation (21c) does so in the sigmoidal gain of the DNU, and equation (21d) provides adaptation in the external synaptic weights. Using these learning rules, computer simulation studies have been carried out to study the DNP performance as applied to the truck backer-upper control problem. This control problem and the computer simulation studies are discussed in the next section.

3 TRUCK BACKER-UPPER CONTROL PROBLEM AND COMPUTER SIMULATION STUDIES

Backing a trailer truck to the loading dock can be a challenging task even to experienced drivers. This control problem, also referred to as the truck "backer-upper" control, was originally proposed by Nguyen and Widrow [1]. Backing a truck to the loading dock is a difficult nonlinear control problem for which no traditional control system design methods exist [10]. This control problem is being used as a benchmark to evaluate the performance of neural and fuzzy controllers. Nguyen and Widrow used two static neural networks, one as an emulator and the second one as a controller, to guide the truck to the loading zone. The controller network produced the appropriate steering angle of the truck from any given initial position. The emulator network computed the next position of the truck. The inputs to the emulator network were the previous truck position and the current steering angle output computed by the controller network. As reported in [1], the neural network was trained for about 1000 truck backups per lesson during the early lessons, and about 2000 truck backups per lesson during the last few. The number of backups required to train the controller was about 20 000. Kong and Kosko [11] proposed a fuzzy control strategy for the same problem. Wang and Mendel [10] developed a "numerical-fuzzy approach" for the problem. In this approach, they determined the control angle θ based on "common sense," and after some trails they chose the desired input–output pairs corresponding to the smoothest successful trajectory. However, here we use the DNP in the direct-control mode to generate the proper steering angles, which avoids training the neural network or generating the fuzzy rules.

The simulated truck and loading zone are shown in Figure 4. The truck position is exactly determined by variables x, y, and ϕ, where ϕ is the angle of the truck with the horizontal. The control signal to the truck is the steering angle θ. Only backing up was considered in the simulation studies presented here. The truck moved backward a fixed unit distance at each time interval. For simplicity, enough clearance between the truck and the loading dock was assumed such that y did not have to be considered as an input. The task was to generate proper steering angles of the truck for the input variables $x \in [0, 20]$ and $\phi \in [-90°, 270°]$ such that the final truck position was $(x_f, \phi_f) = (10, 90°)$. The following dynamic equations of the truck backer-upper control system [10] were used during the simulation studies:

$$x(k + 1) = x(k) + \cos[\phi(k) + \theta(k)] + \sin[\theta(k)] \sin[[\phi(k)] \tag{23a}$$

$$y(k + 1) = y(k) + \cos[\phi(k) + \theta(k)] + \sin[\theta(k)] \sin[[\phi(k)] \tag{23b}$$

$$\theta(k + 1) = \phi(k) - \sin^{-1}\left[\frac{2 \sin \theta(k)}{L}\right] \tag{23c}$$

where L is the length of the truck, which was assumed to be 4 in the simulation studies. Equations (23a–c) were used to obtain the next state when the present state and control are given. Since y was not considered, a state, only equations (23a) and (23c) were used in the simulations. The initial values of the synaptic connections of the DNP were arbitrarily set to $w_{EE} = 1$, $w_{EI} = 0.5$, $w_{IE} = -0.5$, $w_{II} = 1$, and the components of the scaling vector $w = [w_E \ w_I]^T$ to 1. The parameters of the DNP, namely, the feedforward weights $\mathbf{a}_{ff}$, the feedback weights $\mathbf{b}_{fb}$, the somatic gain g_s, and the self- and inter-subpopulation feedback weights $w_{\lambda\lambda'}$ were adapted based on the learning algorithm described in the preceding section.

Figure 5 shows the simulation results for backing up the truck to the loading dock from a given initial position $(x_i, \phi_i) = (5, 220°)$. The x, ϕ, and θ trajectories of the truck for this starting

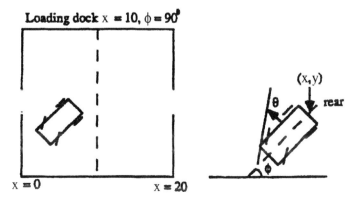

FIGURE 4
Diagram of the simulated truck and loading zone.

position are shown in Figures 5a and 5b. In order to compare the performance of the DNP with
that of the recurrent neural network (RNN), a two layer RNN was used to steer the truck to the
loading zone. The weights of the RNN were updated using the standard error back-propagation
algorithm. The docking-error, defined as the Euclidean distance from the actual final position
(x, ϕ) to the desired final position (x_f, ϕ_f) [11], obtained from the DNP and the RNN was
compared for 300 learning iterations as respectively shown in Figures 5c and 5d. The RNN was
able to steer the truck to the desired position only after about 7000 iterations.

Figure 6 shows the x and ϕ trajectories using the DNP and the RNN from an initial position
$(x_i, \phi_i) = (0, -90°)$. The DNP used fewer than 200 iterations while the RNN required more than
8000 iterations for the truck to reach the target position. Figure 7a shows the x and ϕ trajectories
from an initial position $(x_i, \phi_i) = (3, -30°)$, and Figure 7b compares the docking-error obtained
from the DNP and RNN. The latter required about 7500 iterations to steer the truck to the
loading dock. These simulations were carried out from the different initial positions of the truck.
Some of the results obtained using the DNP are given in Table 1.

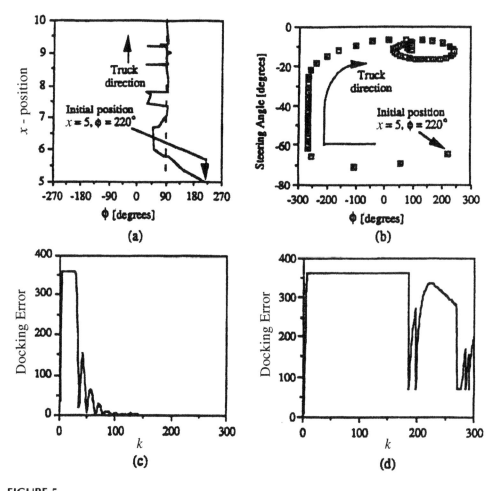

FIGURE 5
Truck trajectories from an initial position $(x_i, \phi_i) = (5, 220°)$. (a, b, c) Truck trajectories using the DNP.
(d) Truck trajectory using the RNN.

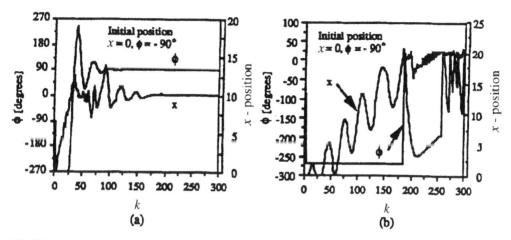

FIGURE 6
Truck trajectories from an initial position $(x_i, \phi_i) = (0, -90°)$. (a) Using the DNP. (b) Using the RNN.

From these simulation studies, it is clear that the DNP could steer the truck to the target position much more quickly than the RNN. In some cases, the RNN did not converge. On the other hand, the DNP could coerce the truck from any initial position to the target position. As the DNP was used in the direct control mode, off-line training was not necessary, which is in sharp contrast with the methodology involving conventional neural structures. It was found necessary for the conventional neural networks, with error back-propagation learning algorithm, to be trained off-line for different initial positions and to use the trained network to drive the truck to the target position.

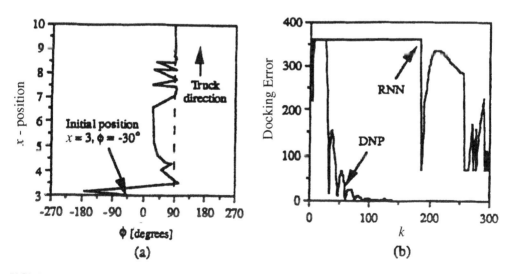

FIGURE 7
Truck trajectories from an initial position $(x_i, \phi_i) = (3, -30°)$.

Table 1   Dynamic Neural Processor (DNP) in Positioning the truck

Desired Position: $x_d = 10$ and $\phi_d = 90°$

Truck Initial Positions		Final Position of the Truck Using DNP			
x_i	$\Phi_i°$	x	$\phi°$	$\theta°$	Number of Iterations
1.00	0	10.08	90.42	−18.56	436
3.00	−30	9.97	88.54	−11.3	308
5.00	−90	9.97	88.95	−11.01	383
20.00	90	10.06	89.3	−10.87	421
10.00	120	9.91	88.66	−11.41	386
0.00	270	9.9	89.06	−11.86	248
10.00	220	9.95	89.01	−9.0	274
13.00	30	10.01	91.45	−11.28	333
20.00	270	9.91	91.63	−11.12	382
20.00	−90	9.92	91.19	−10.49	381
0.00	−90	9.99	90.71	10.55	315
10.00	−90	10.01	89.51	−10.82	261
5.00	90	10.02	90.18	−8.45	156
9.88	89.44	10.01	90.01	−2.14	11

4   CONCLUSIONS

A dynamic neural processor (DNP) that emphasizes the dynamic properties of a subpopulation of neurons has been described. The basic motivation for this neuronal model has been the observations in neurophysiology that neural activity of any complexity is dependent upon the interaction between the antagonistic (excitatory and inhibitory) neural subpopulations. Dynamic neural units (DNUs), which are coupled as excitatory and inhibitory neurons, have been used as the basic computing elements in the DNP architecture. The mathematical model and the algorithm to modify the parameters of DNP were briefly discussed. The commonly used dynamic neural structure is the recurrent neural network (RNN) consisting of feedforward (static) networks included in a feedback configuration with a time delay. Except for the delay operator, these neural networks do not employ any dynamic elements in the forward path. The feedback paths are also nonadaptable. On the other hand, the DNP consists of a dynamic structure in the forward path, and adaptable feedback connections. The DNP functionally mimics an ensemble of the dynamic properties of a neural population. Thus, the structure of the DNP is different from the conventionally assumed structures of neural networks in that the former uses two second-order nonlinear dynamic systems coupled in a flip-flop configuration, while the latter are developed based on the concept of an idealized single static neuron.

It was demonstrated through the stimulation studies in the preceding section that the DNP could steer the truck from different initial positions to the desired position very quickly compared to the recurrent neural network. The dynamic learning feature of the DNP made it unnecessary for the off-line training of the network which is normally used in the conventional neural and fuzzy controllers.

APPENDIX: LEARNING ALGORITHM

In this appendix, the learning rules for modifying the DNP parameters are derived. For the DNU's synaptic weight vector $\phi_{(a_{ff}, b_{fb})}$, the gradient of performance index with respect to $\phi_{(a_{ff}, b_{fb})}$ is obtained as

$$
\frac{\partial J}{\partial \phi_{(a_{ff}, b_{fb})}} = \frac{1}{2} E\left[\frac{\partial [u_d(k) - u(k)]^2}{\partial \phi_{(a_{ff}, b_{fb})}} \right] = E\left[e(k)\left\{ -\frac{\partial \Psi(v)}{\partial \phi_{(a_{ff}, b_{fb})}} \right\} \right]
$$

$$
= E\left[-e(k)\left\{ g_s \frac{4}{[e^{(g_s v_1)} - e^{-(g_s v_1)}]^2} \frac{\partial v}{\partial \phi_{(a_{ff}, b_{fb})}} \right\} \right]
$$

$$
= E\left[-e(k)\{ \text{sech}^2[v(k)] \mathbf{P}_{\phi_{a_{ff}, b_{ff}}}(k) \} \right] \tag{A1}
$$

where

$$
\mathbf{P}_{\phi_{(a_{ff}, b_{fb})}}(k) = \frac{\partial v}{\partial \phi_{(a_{ff}, b_{fb})}} = g_s \frac{\partial v_1(k)}{\partial \phi_{(a_{ff}, b_{fb})}}
$$

represents a vector of the parameter-state (or sensitivity signals). The parameter-state signals for the feedforward and feedback weights are respectively given by the relations

$$
\mathbf{P}_{\phi_{a_{ff_i}}}(k) = g_s[s(k-i)], \qquad i = 0, 1, 2 \tag{A2a}
$$

$$
\mathbf{P}_{\phi_{b_{fb_j}}}(k) = -g_s[v_1(k-j)], \qquad j = 1, 2 \tag{A2b}
$$

Proofs of Equation (A2) and (A2b)

From equation (8) one can write

$$
\mathbf{P}_{\phi_{ff_i}}(k) = g_s \frac{\partial}{\partial a_{ff_i}(k)} \left\{ [-b_1 \ -b_2 \ a_0 \ a_1 \ a_2] \begin{bmatrix} (v_1(k-1)) \\ (v_2(k-2) \\ (s(k)) \\ (s(k-1)) \\ (s(k-2)) \end{bmatrix} \right\}
$$

$$
= g_s \frac{\partial}{\partial a_{ff}(k)} \left\{ [a_0 \ a_1 \ a_2] \begin{bmatrix} (s(k)) \\ (s(k-1)) \\ s(k-2)) \end{bmatrix} \right\}, \qquad i = 0, 1, 2
$$

Thus, the individual parameter-state signals for the feedforward weights are:

For $i = 0$, $\qquad\qquad \mathbf{P}_{a_0}(k) = g_s[s(k)]$

For $i = 1$, $\qquad\qquad \mathbf{P}_{a_1}(k) = g_s[s(k-1)]$

For $i = 2$, $\qquad\qquad \mathbf{P}_{a_2}(k) = g_s[s(k-2)]$

Therefore, the parameter-state signals for the feedforward weights are

$$
\mathbf{P}_{\phi_{a_{ff_i}}}(k) = g_s[s(k-i)], \qquad i = 0, 1, 2 \tag{A3}
$$

Similarly, the parameter-state signals for feedback weights can be obtained as briefly described

$$\mathbf{P}_{\phi_{a_{fb_j}}}(k) = g_s \frac{\partial}{\partial b_{ff_j}(k)} \left\{ [-b_1 \ -b_2 \ a_0 \ a_1 \ a_2] \begin{bmatrix} (v_1(k-1)) \\ (v_2(k-2) \\ (s(k)) \\ (s(k-1)) \\ (s(k-2)) \end{bmatrix} \right\}$$

Thus, the individual parameter state signals for the feedback weights are

For $j = 1$, $\qquad\qquad \mathbf{P}_{b_1}(k) = -g_s[v_1(k-1)]$

For $j = 2$, $\qquad\qquad \mathbf{P}_{b_2}(k) = -g_s[v_1(k-2)]$

Therefore, the parameter state signals for the feedback weights may be written as

$$\mathbf{P}_{\phi_{a_{fb_j}}}(k) = -g_s[v_1(k-j)], \qquad j = 1, 2 \tag{A4}$$

As seen from equations (A3) and (A4), the parameter-state signals for the feedforward weights may be obtained by tapping the node signals from the controller structure, while the generation of the parameter-state signals for the feedback weights requires an additional sensitivity structure with only feedback weights [7].

Similarly, the gradient of the performance index with respect to the somatic gain g_s is given by

$$\frac{\partial J}{\partial g_s} = \frac{1}{2} E \left[\frac{\partial u_d(k) - u(k)]^2}{\partial g_s} \right] = E[-e(k)\{\text{sech}^2[v(k)]v_1(k)\}] \tag{A5}$$

The adaptation in self- and inter-neuron synaptic connections may be obtained as follows:

$$\frac{\partial J}{\partial w_{\lambda\lambda'}} = \frac{1}{2} E \left[\frac{\partial u_d(k) - u(k)]^2}{\partial w_{\lambda\lambda'}} \right] = E \left[-e(k) \left\{ \frac{\partial \Psi(v)}{\partial v} \frac{\partial v}{\partial w_{\lambda\lambda'}} \right\} \right]$$

$$= E[-e(k)\{\text{sech}^2[v(k)]g_s u_\lambda(k-1)\}] \tag{A6}$$

REFERENCES

[1] D. Nguyen and B. Widrow, Neural networks for self-learning control systems, *IEEE Control System Magazine*, Vol. 10, No. 3, pp. 18–23, 1990.

[2] P.J. Werbos, Neurocontrol and elastic fuzzy logic: capabilities, concepts and applications, *IEEE Trans. Industrial Electronics*, Vol. 40, No. 2, pp. 170–180, Apr. 1992.

[3] M.M. Gupta and D.H. Rao, Neuro-control systems: a tutorial, in M.M. Gupta and D.H. Rao (eds.) *Neuro-Control Systems: Theory and Applications*, pp. 1–44, IEEE Press, New York, 1990.

[4] H.R. Wilson and J.D. Cowan, Excitatory and inhibitory interactions in localized populations of model neurons, *Biophysical J.*, Vol. 12, pp. 1–24, 1972.

[5] W.J. Freeman, Linear analysis of the dynamics of neural masses, *Biophysical J.*, Vol. 1, pp. 225–256, 1972.

[6] D.H. Rao and M.M. Gupta, A multi-functional dynamic neural processor for control applications, in *Proc. American Control Conference, San Francisco*, 1993, pp. 2902–2906.

[7] D.H. Rao, M.M. Gupta, and P.N. Nikiforuk, Performance comparison of dynamic neural processor and recurrent neural networks, *J. Neural, Parallel and Scientific Computation*, Vol. 2, No. 1, pp. 55–80, Mar. 1994.

[8] G.K. Knopf and M.M. Gupta, A multipurpose neural processor for machine vision systems, *IEEE Trans. Neural Networks*, Vol. 4, No. 5, pp. 762–777, Sept. 1993.

[9] M.M. Gupta and D.H. Rao, Dynamic neural units with applications to the control of unknown nonlinear systems, *J. Intelligent and Fuzzy Systems*, *J. Intelligent and Fuzzy Systems*, Vol. 1, No. 1, pp. 73–92, Jan. 1993.

[10] L.X. Wang and J.M. Mendel, Generating fuzzy rules by learning through examples. *IEEE Trans. Systems, Man, and Cybernetics*, Vol. 22, No. 6, pp. 1414–1427, Nov./Dec. 1992.

[11] S.G. Kong and B. Kosko, Comparison of fuzzy and neural truck backer-upper control systems, in B. Kosko (ed.) *Neural Networks and Fuzzy Systems*. Prentice-Hall, Englewood Cliffs, NJ, pp. 368–380, 1992.

PART IV

FUTURE PERSPECTIVES

CHAPTER 25

Toward Intelligent Systems: Future Perspectives

MADAN M. GUPTA

Intelligent Systems Research Laboratory, College of Engineering, University of Saskatchewan, Saskatoon, Saskatchewan, Canada

NARESH K. SINHA

Department of Electrical and Computer Engineering, McMaster University, Hamilton, Ontario, Canada

1 INTRODUCTION

Over the last decade or so, several parallel advances have been made in two distinct disciplines: *fuzzy logic* and *neural networks*. As the names imply, fuzzy logic provides mathematical strength to the process of emulation of certain perceptual and linguistic attributes associated with human cognition, whereas the mathematics of neural networks provides new computing morphologies with learning and adaptive capabilities.

A marriage between these two distinct disciplines has the potential for producing offsprings with the capability of generating a new discipline—*intelligence*—with a new generation of computing systems—*cognitive systems*. Such cognitive systems will, hopefully, capture certain aspects of human cognition. The integration of these two fields, neural networks and fuzzy logic, has the potential of producing robust sensors and robust control mechanisms. Scientists and engineers are exploring the possibility of creating new paradigms that seem to have the potential for creating a new class of computing systems—*soft computing.*

---

[1] Man has always dreamed of creating machines with humanlike attributes. In this technological world, there are machines that have emulated several human functions with tremendous capacity and capabilities. Some examples of these are: transportation systems versus human locomotion, communication systems versus human speech and vision, and computers versus human cognition (of course, a very low level of cognition).

2 HUMAN COGNITION

Modern neural science has evolved from the research studies of many individuals working in a wide class of disciplines over a relatively large time span. These studies have extended from philosophical dialogue on the *cognitive* (thought processes) and *affective* (emotional processes) aspects of the brain to the basic understanding of the neuron, the elementary building block of our central nervous system (CNS). Indeed, the neuronal morphology of the human central nervous system is too complex to analyze, although we certain speculative analogies have been presented, and, based upon this superficial understanding, some computational networks have been developed—known in the literature as *neural networks* (NN).

Given basic knowledge of the mathematics of digital logic such as *OR, AND, NOT,* and *NAND* gates, the human mind is capable of synthesizing a super digital computing system. However, if we are presented with a supercomputer with a superficial knowledge of its computing functions, we can only speculate on the morphology and organizational aspects of its behavior. If this problem is given to specialists in different fields, they will come up with different speculative responses based upon their observations and their fields of specialization. A synthesis of these speculative responses, it is hoped, may provide some clues as to the working of digital machines. It is reminiscent of the story of six blind people who were asked to examine the morphology of an elephant. Based upon their own individual experiences and observations, each blind person gave a correct narration of his findings. However, a synthesis of these findings did not make sense to a person examining the elephant with full vision.

Nature has given us a beautiful and robust cognitive and affective faculty—the brain—and we have no choice but to examine its working from various angles embodied in various disciplines, and then to provide a synthesis. As system scientists, our ultimate objective is that, based upon this superficial understanding of the brain, we can create an intelligent cognitive system that can aid humans in their various decision-making tasks.[1]

The discipline of neural science has evolved over the centuries through the understanding of the basic functions of neurons and the neuronal morphology of the central nervous system. Essentially, the central nervous system acquires information from the external environment through the natural sensors, and stores past experiences. It also processes new information in conjunction with the past experiences, and provides new decision signals. Although many aspects of the biological features of neuronal morphologies are still not well understood, on a speculative basis they have led to various morphologies of artificial neural networks with learning and adaptive capabilities. A host of these neural networks have been proven to provide efficient computational tools for many information processing and decision-making tasks. [1, 2, 3,9, 14–20, 25, 26].

3 THE NEURON

Nature has developed a very complex neuronal morphology in biological species (Figure 1). Biological neurons, over one hundred billion in number, in the central nervous systems (CNS) of humans play a very important role in the various complex sensory, control, affective, and cognitive aspects of information processing and decision making. In neuronal information processing, there are a variety of complex mathematical operations and mapping functions involved that, in synergism, act in a parallel-cascade structure forming a complex pattern of neuronal layers evolving into a sort of pyramidal pattern. The information flows from one neuronal layer to another in the forward direction, with a continuous feedback evolving into a dynamic pyramidal structure. The structure is pyramidal in the sense of the extraction and

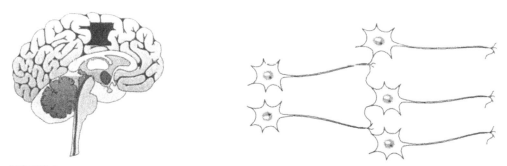

FIGURE 1
(a) Biological neural computing system: the cognitive faculty. (b) Biological neural network.

convergence of information at each point in the forward direction. A study of biological neuronal morphology provides not only a clue but also a challenge in the design of a realistic cognitive computing machine—an intelligent system.

From the neurobiological as well as the neural-mathematical point of view, we identify two key neuronal elements in a biological neuron: the synapse and the soma, which are responsible for providing neuronal attributes such as learning, adaptation, knowledge (storage or memory of past experience), aggregation, and nonlinear mapping operations on neuronal information (Figure 2). We now give a brief description of neuronal morphology [23, 24].

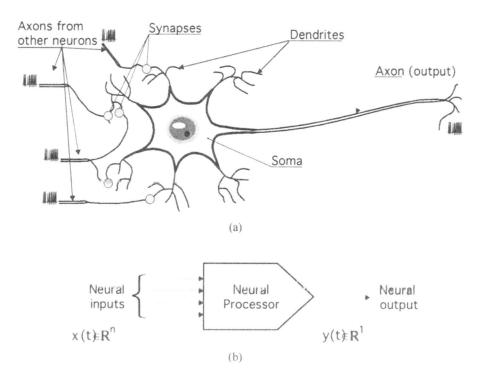

FIGURE 2
(a) A schematic view of the biological neuron. The soma of each neuron receives parallel inputs through its synapses and dendrites, and transmits a common output via the axon to other neurons. (b) Model representation of a biological neuron with multiple inputs $\mathbf{x}(t) \in \Re^n$, and a single output, $y(t) \in \Re^1$.

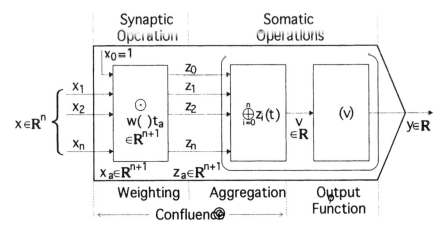

FIGURE 3

Mathematical representation of a generalized neuron. The confluence operation, $\copyright$, compares new neural information $x_a(t)$ with the past experience stored in the synaptic weights $w_a(t)$, and the nonlinear activation operation, $\phi(v)$, provides a bounded neural output $y(t)$.

Synapse. The synapse is a storage element of past experience (knowledge). It learns from the neuronal environment and continuously adapts its strength. Past experience appears in the form of synaptic strength, which we also call *synaptic weight*. There are over one hundred billion neurons in our central nervous systems and, on the average, there are over 1000 synapses (the input terminals), per neuron. Mathematically, a synapse provides a confluence operation between the new neuronal inputs (information) and the past experience stored in the form of synaptic weights, and sends signals to the dendrite—the input node to the main body (soma) of the neuron. We will refer to the mathematical operation in a synapse as the *synaptic operation* or *synaptic confluence operation*.

Soma. The soma (neural cell) refers to the main body of the neuron. It receives signals from a very few to over 1000 synapses through its dendrites and provides an *aggregation* operation. If the aggregated value of the dendritic inputs exceeds a certain *threshold*, it fires, providing an axonal (output) signal that is a sort of nonlinear function of the aggregated value. We refer to this mathematical operation in the soma as *somatic operation*. Thus, in somatic operation one can identify three distinct mathematical operations: (i) *aggregation*, (ii) *thresholding*, and (iii) *nonlinear transformation (mapping)*. Figure 2 shows the morphology of a biological neuron, and Figure 3 depicts the mathematical morphology of a neuron.

Biological neuronal processes generate some interesting mathematical mapping properties because of their nonlinear operations combined with thresholding in the soma. In fact, if the neuron carried out only linear operations, the mathematical attractiveness and the robustness of neural circuits for most applications would disappear.

4 NEURONAL-FUZZY LOGIC

The theory of fuzzy logic [26] has been developed in order to capture the uncertainties associated with human cognitive processes such as in thinking, reasoning, perception, and so on, For example, consider the statement, "Driving conditions in Saskatoon in January, when it is *extremely* cold, are *not so bad* compared to what they are in *late* February or *early* March, especially when there is a *large* temperature variation between day time (snow is melting) and night time (freezing cold)". Here, the words in italics express various vague notions that can be modeled using the concept of graded membership inherent in the mathematics of fuzzy sets [19–22]. The theory of fuzzy logic, unlike that of binary logic, is developed using the notion of *graded membership* distributed over the closed unit interval [0,1].

The basic mathematical notion of graded membership was introduced in 1965 by Professor Lotfi A. Zadeh [26]; however, the recent marriage between the two mathematical fields of fuzzy logic and neural networks has led to the development of a new field, called "fuzzy-neural systems." It combines the attribute of graded membership in fuzzy logic with those of learning and adaptation strength found in neuronal morphology. This new and rapidly developing field promises to provide emulation of some aspects of the cognitive faculty and adds strength to the field of intelligent systems.

5   NEURONAL LEARNING

Biological species have adopted strategies that are based upon learning, adaptation, and self-organization in an uncertain environment. "Learning while functioning" is the most important attribute that makes these species so robust and flexible. It is natural, therefore, that we adopt a similar strategy in the design of intelligent systems.

Certainly, the process of neuronal learning and adaptation in biological species is enormously complex, and the progress made in the understanding of the field through experimental observations in such fields as neurophysiology and psychology during the last century is limited and crude compared to the achievements made in the physical sciences during the same period. Nevertheless, it is true that neurophysiological and psychological understanding of the biological process has provided a tremendous impetus to the emulation of certain neurological morphologies and their learning behavior through the fields of mathematics and systems science. We have a long way to go before we can speak of understanding the principles of cognition (learning, thinking, reasoning, and perception) and, thus, of the field of cognitive computing to the degree that we understand the principles of the electrochemical, biochemical and ionic behaviors of neuronal populations in biological species.

We have emphasized some of the difficulties in the understanding of neurophysiology. Still, biology has inspired the work of system scientists in the past, and at an accelerated pace during more recent years. There has been an exponentially increasing number of attempts to develop neuronal paradigms for application to problems such as machine vision and control systems [11, 12, 15, 16]. Indeed, the neuronal learning paradigms developed during recent years combined with the cognitive strength of the notion of graded membership promise to provide robust solutions to problems in pattern recognition, decision making, control of complex dynamic flexible structures in space, and, in general, in intelligent robotic systems for applications to manufacturing and medical sciences.

6   INTELLIGENT SYSTEMS

One of the tenets of recent research in robotics and systems science is that intelligence can be cast into a machine. The thought of creating virtual intelligence on a silicon chip (machine), unlike the thought of creating a mighty (powerful) machine, engenders strange feelings.

Intelligence implies the ability to comprehend, reason, learn, and memorize, or, in general, refers to the human mentation and cognition processes. One of the last frontiers of science, perhaps its ultimate challenge, is understanding the biological basis of mentation and cognition.

Can this process be described by known physical laws, or does it lie within the domain of metaphysical principles? What are the processes of comprehending, reasoning, learning and remembering, and perceiving? We still do not understand how the brain can perceive a dangerous situation and act instantaneously while it usually takes several seconds to multiply two three-digit numbers. How do genes contribute to the process of mentation and cognition, and how do they adapt to the environment?

Recent technological advances in computer hardware (including optoelectronics, programmable lasers, molecular computing, and the like) have made it possible to carry a very powerful and ultrafast computer in a briefcase. Such computers are very efficient for numerical computation. However, *cognitive information*, the information that our natural sensors acquire and process. is not numerical. While the human brain is very efficient and fast in the processing of such cognitive information, present-day computers still fail to process such nonnumerical information. The following questions arise: "Can the mathematical functions and attributes of the human sensory systems, mentation, and cognitive processes be emulated for the creation of an intelligent machine? Do we have the appropriate mathematical tools to emulate such cognitive functions, and do we have the hardware to implement such processes?"

For such an emulation to be successful, it is necessary to understand the biological, physiological and metaphysical functions of the brain and develop a new type of mathematics. The mathematics that we know today was developed for the understanding of physical processes, whereas the process of cognition does not necessarily follow these mathematical laws. Then what is *cognitive mathematics*? This is a difficult and a challenging question to answer. However, scientists have realized that if we reexamine some of the "mathematical aspects" of our thinking process and "hardware aspects" of the "neurons", the principal element of the brain, we may succeed to some extent in the emulation process.

The mentation and cognitive functions of the brain, unlike the computation functions of the binary computer, are based upon the *relative grades* of the information acquired by the natural sensory systems. The conventional mathematical tools, whether deterministic or probabilistic, are based upon some absolute measure of information. Our natural sensors acquire information in the form of relative grades rather than in absolute numbers. The "perceptions" and "actions" of the cognitive process also appear in the form of relative grades. While driving on an icy road, for example, we perceive the driving environment in a relatively graded sense and act accordingly. The attributes of elasticity and robustness are inherent in our cognitive functions.

The processes of mentation and cognition thus act upon the graded information. Information may appear in a numerical form (the normal temperature of the human body is $39.012°C$). However, during the process of cognition, a physician perceives this temperature as *near normal*, in the form of a relative grade. Thus, the cognitive process acts upon the different forms of information and this leads to "formless" uncertainty: *temperature is near normal*.

The theory of fuzzy logic (soft logic), founded by Zadeh in 1965, is based upon the notion of graded membership, and so are the functions of the cognition and mentation processes. In the past, studies of *cognitive uncertainty* and its cognate, the *cognitive information*, were hindered by the lack of suitable tools for modeling such information. However, with the introduction of the theory of fuzzy logic and soft computing, it seems possible to extend these studies to the important field of cognitive information. A marriage between the cognitive information aspects and the neuronal morphology in the design of information systems may provide better computational tools in the years to come.

The emerging paradigms based upon cognitive-neural computing have potential uses in the development of new research studies such as cognitive information processing, cognitive feedback controllers and neurovision systems with promising applications to intelligent robotic systems and health sciences.

7 SOME REMARKS

Recent progress in information-based technology has significantly broadened the capabilities and application of computers. Today's computers, however, are merely being used for the storage and processing of numerical data (hard uncertainty and hard information). Should we not reexamine the functions of these computing tools in view of the increasing interest in subjects such as knowledge-based systems, expert systems, and intelligent robotic systems, as well as for solving problems related to decision and control? Human mentation acts upon cognitive information and cognitive information is characterized using relative grades. Human mentation and cognition functions use fresh information (acquired from the environment by our natural sensors) together with the information (experience, knowledge-base) stored in the biological memory.

Shannon's definition of "information" was based upon certain physical measurements of random activities in physical systems, in particular, in communication channels. This definition was restricted, however, to a class of information arising from physical systems.

If we wish to emulate in a machine, some of the cognitive functions (learning, remembering, reasoning, intelligence, perceiving, etc.) of humans, we have to generalize the definition of information and develop new mathematical tools and hardware. These new mathematical tools and hardware must deal with the simulation and processing of cognitive information and soft logic. Many new notions, although still in primitive stages, are emerging around the mathematics of fuzzy neural logic and, it is hoped, we will be able to nurture some interesting studies in the not too distant future. Indeed, biological processes have much to offer to engineers, system scientists, and mathematicians for solving many practical problems of the world in which we live today.

After we finish some initial studies on an intelligent machine, the next natural stage for us would be to embark upon the design of a robotic machine that could play a game of ping-pong with us with the same degree of emotion, enthusiasm, and pleasure that we receive when we are playing with our students, friends, and family members. Such studies would also, of course, need basic understanding of the theory of metaphysics.

8 CONCLUSIONS

The major reason that the subject of intelligent systems is in such an exciting state of research is the wealth of information that we researchers are able to extract from the carbon-based computer—the neuronal morphology of the brain, biological sensory systems such as vision systems, and the human cognition and decision-making processes that form the elements of soft computing.

Humans have been learning from nature. They have imitated the birds and have created super flying machines. Now we are trying to imitate some of the attributes of cognition and intelligence of the brain, and are in the process of creating intelligent systems. Some of the recent work in the field of intelligent systems has led us to a strong belief that our efforts should focus on the understanding of neurophysiological principles and the development of new morphologies of intelligent control systems encompassing the various disciplines of system science.

At this stage, we bring out an analogy from the field of aviation. Until the Wright brothers invented the airplane, the basic scientific thinking had been to develop a flying machine in a way that would mimic a bird. Most scientists of those days thought that the crucial component of flying was the flapping of wings. It took the genius of the Wright brothers to understand that, although wings were required to increase the buoyancy in the air, they also needed power from the propeller to make the flight possible. In the same way, although there is a great emphasis in

BIOLOGICAL SYSTEMS   ARTIFICIAL SYSTEMS

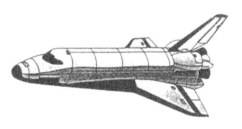

(a1) Biological bird with flapping wings   (a2) Flying machine with fixed wings:
                                            an artificial flying bird

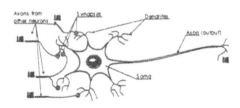

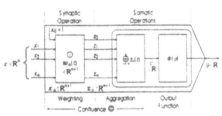

(b1) Biological neuron: (b2) Artificial neuron:
a biological computing element   an artificial computing element

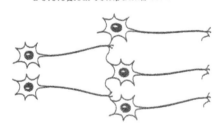

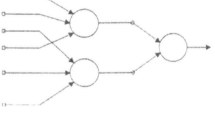

(c1) Biological neural network   (c2) Artificial neural network
(morphological similarity between biological and artificial neural network)

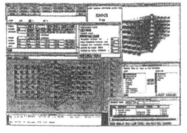

(d1) Biological neural computing system: (d2) Artificial neural computing system:
the cognitive faculty   the cognitive computer

FIGURE 4
From biological systems to artificial systems.

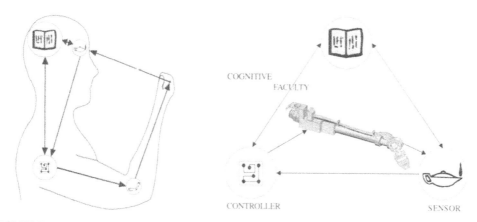

FIGURE 5
From human cognitive and control functions to robotics cognitive and control function: an intelligent robot.

the current scientific community on the understanding of the working of the human brain, and developing the theory of soft computing that mimics the human linguistic expressions, the feelings and the functioning of the brain, there is a great danger in trying to mimic without a thorough understanding of the functions of this carbon-based cognitive computer and of human expression.

Thus, today's flying machines, in many ways, emulate the aerodynamic behavior of a flying bird, but they are not replicas of the natural bird. For many centuries we have attempted to understand the neuronal computing aspect of biological sensory and control mechanisms. This basic understanding, combined with the strength of the new computing technology (optical computing, molecular computing, etc.) and the thinking of the systems scientist, can create artificial sensory and intelligent control mechanisms. These concepts may also lead us in the development of a new type of computing machine—a cognitive computing machine.

Figure 4a shows that an artificial flying machine with fixed wings evolved from the biological bird with flapping wings. Likewise, Figures 4b, 4c and 4d show the evolution of computing elements—the neuron, a neural network, and a cognitive computing system—that are in the process of evolving from their respective biological counterparts.

We system scientists would like to see an intelligent system using the elements of the mathematics of soft computing.

Although it is very difficult, and often unwise, to make predictions about the future, we nevertheless feel that further research in neurosensory systems (such as neurovision systems) and neurocontrol systems will be the key to the development of truly intelligent control systems and, in general, intelligent systems. We also believe that we are slowly progressing in that direction, and early in the 21st century, may be able to see versions of *intelligent systems*. To continue our analogy with aviation, most scientists in the 19th century did not believe that it was possible to have flying machines that were heavier than air, and a great deal of work was devoted to developing lighter-than-air flying machines, such as balloons and Zeppelins. On the other hand, today we have heavy flying machines (airplanes) that are much faster and more versatile than biological birds. In the same way, it appears quite probable that, as our understanding of cognitive faculty improves, we may be able to develop intelligent control systems that may even surpass the human brain in some respects [1–14]. In particular, we can expect the evolution of intelligent robots that will be able to perform most routine household and industrial work (Figure 5).

REFERENCES

[1] S.I. Amari, and M.A. Arbib, (eds.) *Competition and Cooperation in Neural Nets, Lecture Notes in Biomathematics*, Vol. 45, Springer-Verlag, New York, 1982.

[2] D.J. Amit, H. Gutfreund, and Y. Sompolinsky, Spin-glass model of neural networks, *Physical Review A*, Vol. 32, pp. 1007–1018, 1985.

[3] J.A. Anderson, Cognitive and psychological computation with neural models, *IEEE Trans. Systems, Man, and Cybernetics*, Vol. SMC-13, pp. 799–815, 1983.

[4] M. Black, Vagueness: an exercise in logical analysis, *Philosophy of Science*, Vol. 4, pp. 427–455, 1937.

[5] L. Brillouin *Science and Information Theory*. Academic Press, New York, 1956.

[6] S.R.Y. Cajal, Les preuves objectives de l'unite anatomique de cellules nerveuses. *Trob. Lab. Inest. Biol. Univ. Madrid*, Vol. 29, pp. 1–37, 1934.

[7] R.C. Conant, Laws of information which govern systems, *IEEE Trans. Systems, Man and Cybernetics*, Vol. 6, pp. 334–338, 1976.

[8] M.M. Gupta, *Fuzzy Automata and Decision Processes: The First Decade*, Sixth Triennial World IFAC Congress, Boston, Cambridge, 1975.

[9] M.M. Gupta, On the cognitive computing: perspectives, in M.M. Gupta, T. Yamakawa (eds.) *Fuzzy Logic in Knowledge-based System, Decision and Contols*. North Holland, Amsterdam, pp. 7–10, 1988. Also in *Fuzzy Computing: Theory, Hardware and Applications*, pp. 7–10.

[10] M.M. Gupta, Cognition, perception and uncertainty, in M.M. Gupta, T. Yamakawa (eds.) *Fuzzy Computing: Theory, Hardware and Applications*, North Holland, Amsterdam, pp. 3–6, 1988. Also in *Fuzzy Logic in Knowledge-based Systems*, North Holland, Amsterdam, pp. 3–6.

[11] M.M. Gupta, Biological basis for computer vision: some perspective, *SPIE Conf. Intelligent Robots and Computer Vision*, Philadelphia, 1988, Paper #1192-49, pp. 811–823.

[12] M.M. Gupta, Fusion of fuzzy logic and neural networks with applications to decision and control problems, *Automatic Control Conference, Boston*, 1991, pp. 30–31.

[13] M.M. Gupta, Uncertainty and information: the merging paradigms, *Int. J. Neuro and Mass-Parallel Computing and Information Systems*, Vol. 2, pp. 65–70, 1991.

[14] M.M. Gupta, *Adaptive Methods for Control Systems Design*. IEEE Press, sponsored by the IEEE-SMC Society, New York, 1986.

[15] M.M. Gupta, and D.H. Rao, *Neuro-Control Systems: Theory and Applications*. IEEE Neural Network Council, IEEE-Press, New York, 1994.

[16] M.M. Gupta, and G.K. Knopf (eds.), *Neuro-Vision Systems: Principles and Applications*, IEEE-Neural Networks Council, IEEE-Press, New York, 1994.

[17] M.M. Gupta, and N.K. Sinha (eds.), *Intelligent Control Systems: Theory and Applications*, IEEE Neural Networks Council, IEEE Control Systems Society, IEEE-Press, New York, 1995.

[18] D.O. Hebb, *The Organization of Behavior*. Wiley, New York, 1949.

[19] A. Kaufmann, *Introduction to the Theory of Fuzzy Subsets*, Volume 1. Academic Press, New York, 1975.

[20] A. Kaufmann, and M.M. Gupta, *Introduction to Fuzzy Arithmetic: Theory and Applications*, Van Nostrand Reinhold, New York, 1991.

[21] A. Kaufmann, and M.M. Gupta, *Fuzzy Mathematical Models in Engineering and Management Science*, North Holland, Amsterdam, 1988 (also, Japanese translation, Ohmsha Publication, Tokyo, 1991).

[22] G.J. Klir, Where do we stand on measure of uncertainty, ambiguity, fuzziness and the like?, *Fuzzy Sets and Systems*, Special Issue on Measure of Uncertainty, Vol. 24, No. 2, pp. 141–160, 1977.

[23] W.S. McCulloch, and W. Pitts, A logical calculus of the ideas immanent in nervous activity, *Bulletin of Mathematical Biophysics*, Vol. 5, pp. 115–133, 1943.

[24] W.S. McCulloch, *Embodiments of Minds*, p. 20 of Introduction by S. Papert. MIT Press, Cambridge, MA, 1965.

[25] N. Wiener, *Cybernetics*. Wiley, New York, 1948.

[26] L.A. Zadeh, Fuzzy Sets, *Information and Control*, Vol. 8, pp. 338–353, 1965.

Major Current Bibliographical Sources on Neural Networks, Fuzzy Logic, and Applications

1 SOCIETIES

Canadian Society for Fuzzy Information and Neural Systems (CANS-FINS)
Canadian Society for Computational Studies of Intelligence (CSCSI)
Dutch Foundation for Neural Networks (SNN)
European Neural Network Society (ENNS)
IEEE Neural Networks for Signal Processing Committee
International Fuzzy Systems Association (IFSA)
Italian Neural Network Society (SIREN)
Japanese Neural Network Society (JNNS)
North American Fuzzy Information Processing Society (NAFIPS)
Neural Computing Applications Forum (NCAF)
Stimulation Initiative for European Neural Applications (SIENA)
Swedish Neural Network Society (SNNS)
The International Neural Network Society (INNS)

2 JOURNALS

Adaptive Behaviour
Behavioural and Brain Sciences
Biological Cybernetics
Biophysical Journal
Connection Science
Fuzzy Sets and Systems
IEEE Transactions on Fuzzy Systems
IEEE Transactions on Image Processing
IEEE Transactions on Neural Networks

IEEE Transactions on Signal Processing
IEEE Transactions on Systems, Man and Cybernetics
International Journal of Approximate Reasoning
International Journal of Neural Systems
Journal of Artificial Intelligence Research
Journal of Cognitive Neuroscience
Journal of Fuzzy Sets and Systems
Journal of Uncertain, Fuzziness and Knowledge-Based Systems
Journal of Intelligent and Fuzzy Systems
Network: Computation in Neural Systems
Neural Computation
Neural Networks
Neural Network World
Neural Processing Letters
Neurocomputing

3 CONFERENCES

Artificiall Neural Networks in Engineering (ANNIE)
Annual Conference on Evolutionary Programming
Annual Meeting on Neural Control of Movement
European Congress on Intelligent Techniques and Soft Computing (EUFIT)
European Meeting on Cybernetics and Systems Research
From Animals to Animate – International Conference on Simulation of Adaptive Behaviour (SAB)
Genetic Programming Conference
IEEE International Conference on Fuzzy Systems (FUZZ IEEE)
IEEE International Conference on Neural Networks (IEEE ICNN)
IEEE International Conference on Systems, Man, and Cybernetics
IEEE International Conference on Tools with Artificial Intelligence (ICTAI)
IEEE Workshop on Neural Networks for Signal Processing
IFAC Symposium on Intelligent Autonomous Vehicles
Industrial Fuzzy control and Intelligent Systems Conference (IFIS)
Intelligent Systems and Control (ISC)
International Conference on Artificial Neural Networks (ICANN)
International Conference on Evolutionary Computation
International Conference on Evolvable systems: From Biology to Hardware (ICES)
International Conference on Intelligent Robots and Systems (IROS)
International Conference on Neural Networks and Brain
International Conference on Simulation of Adaptive Behavior
International Fuzzy Systems and Intelligent Control Conference (IFSIC)
International ICSC/IFAC Symposium on Neural Computation
International Symposium on Intelligent Systems (AMSE-ISIS)
International Symposium on Soft Computing (SOCO)
International Symposium on Robotics with Applications (ISORA)
International Workshop on Neural Networks for Identification, Control
Joint Conference on Information Sciences (JCIS)
Neural Information Processing Systems – Natural and Synthetic (NIPS)

Robotics, and Signal/Image Processing (NICROSP)
World Congress on Computational Intelligence (IJCNN, FUZZ-IEEE, ICEC)
World Congress on Neural Networks (WCNN)

4 INTERNET RESOURCES

IEEE Neural Network council: *http://engine.ieee.org/ncc/*
International Fuzzy Systems Association: *http://www.abo.fi/~rfuller/ifsa.html*
North American Fuzzy Information Processing Society: *http://seraphim./csee.usf.edu/nafips.html*
NeuroNet European Network of Excellence: *http://www.ph.kcl.ac.uk/neuronet/index.html*
Fuzzy Logic and Fuzzy Expert Systems FAQ: *http://www.cs.cmu.edu.Groups.AI/html/faqs/ai/fuzzypart1/faq.html*
Neural Network FAQ: *ftp://ftp.sas.com/pub/neural/FAQ.html*
Fuzzy Logic and Neuro fuzzy resources: *http://www.isis.ecs.soton.ac.uk/research/nfinfo/fuzzy.html*

About the Editors

Madan Mohan Gupta (Fellow: IEEE and SPIE) received the B.E. (Hons.) in Electronics – Communication Engineering from the Birla Institute of Technology and Science (formerly Birla Engineering College) Pilani, India, and was the recipient of that Institute's Gold Medal. In 1962, he received the M.E. degree from this same Institute. He received the Commonwealth Research Fellowship for his studies in the United Kingdom and spent the first year at the Queen's University of Belfast (1964–65), and then at the University of Warwick (1965–67). He received the Ph.D. degree from the University of Warwick in 1967 for his research in the field of Adaptive Control Systems. In 1998, Dr. Gupta received the additional honor of earned Doctor of Science (D.Sc.) degree from the University of Saskatchewan for his work on neurocontrol systems, neurovision systems, fuzzy-neural systems, and early detection of ischemic heart disease.

Dr. Gupta was a lecturer in the Department of Electronics and Communication Engineering at the University of Roorkee, India during 1962–64. He joined the University of Saskatchewan in 1967 as a Lecturer. He was promoted to Assistant Professor in 1968, Associate Professor in 1971, and Professor in 1978. He has carried out a wide range of research since 1967. His initial focus was on dynamic sensitivity methods and adaptive control systems, and he was one of the first to report results in this important area. In the early 1970s, Dr. Gupta extended his research to fuzzy logic and fuzzy control systems. His work in this area led to the coauthorship of two textbooks on fuzzy logic and its applications, which were translated into Japanese.

In the mid-1980s, Dr. Gupta turned some of his efforts to the area of neural systems, particularly neurovision systems and neurocontrol systems. He also extended his early work on dynamic sensitivity methods to incipient failure detection in cyclic machines and the early diagnosis of ischemic heart disease. He has supervised or cosupervised over 35 post-doctoral fellows and visiting professors, and 36 Ph.D and M.Sc. students. He has also coauthored two textbooks and been editor or coeditor of 20 press books, a nine-volume Encyclopedia on Control Systems, and has been the author or coauthor of more than 650 research publications. All these publications are in the field of adaptive control systems, fuzzy logic/computing, neurovision, neurocontrol systems, and early diagnosis of ischemic heart disease.

Dr. Gupta has contributed intensively to his fields of research in other ways as well. He has been a Keynote Speaker at conferences around the world. He is a Founding Member of a number of national and international associations, including the North American Fuzzy Information Processing Society (NAFIPS), the International Fuzzy Systems Association (IFSA), and the Canadian Society for Fuzzy Information and Neural Systems (CANS-FINS). He is an Honorary

Member of the Japanese, Korean, Chinese, and Indian Fuzzy Information Processing Societies. For his contributions to the theory of fuzzy sets and adaptive control systems. Dr. Gupta was elected Fellow of the Institute of Electrical and Electronics Engineers (IEEE) in 1990, and Fellow of the International Society for Optical Engineering (SPIE) for his contributions to neurovision, neurocontrol, and fuzzy-neural systems. In 1991 he was the corecipient of the Institution of Electrical Engineering Kelvin Premium. Dr. Gupta has also served as a Special Advisor to the United Nations Industrial Development Organization (UNIDO) in the area of industrial automation. In June 1998, Dr. Gupta was honoured once again by the award of the very prestigious Kaufmann Prize Gold Medal for Research in the field of fuzzy logic, which was presented to him at a special meeting in Reus, Spain.

Dr. Gupta's present research interests have expanded to the areas of neurovision, neurocontrol and integration of fuzzy-neural systems, neuronal morphology of biological vision systems, intelligent and cognitive robotic systems, cognitive information, new paradigms in information processing, and chaos in neural systems. He is also developing new architectures of computational neural networks (CNNs), and computational fuzzy neural networks (CFNNs) for applications to advanced robotic systems.

Naresh K. Sinha was born at Gaya (India) in 1927. He obtained the B.Sc. (Engineering) degree from Banaras Hindu University in 1948 and the Ph.D. degree in Electrical Engineering from the University of Manchester in 1955.

Dr. Sinha taught at Bihar Institute of Technology at Sindri in India and the University of Tennessee at Knoxville (U.S.A.) before joining the Faculty of Engineering of McMaster University in 1965, where he is currently Professor Emeritus as well as Adjunct Professor, after serving as Professor in the Department of Electrical and Computer Engineering until retirement in July 1993. He has served as the Chairman of that Department from July 1982 to June 1988 and Director of Instructional Computing in the Faculty of Engineering from July 1988 to June 1992. He has also been Visiting Professor at Stanford University, the Institute of Control Sciences in Moscow, Tianjin University and the Beijing University of Science and Technology in China, Delhi Institute of Technology in India, and Nanyang Technological University in Singapore. He has been the author or coauthor of over 450 technical papers and author, coauthor, or editor of 13 books.

His current research interests are in the areas of adaptive control, system modeling and identification, robotics, intelligent control systems, and industrial applications of modern control theory.

Dr. Sinha was the Founder Chairman of the Hamilton Section IEEE Chapter on Circuits, Computers, Communications, and Control. He is a Fellow of the Institution of Electrical Engineers (London), Life Fellow of the Institute of Electrical and Electronics Engineers (New York) and a Registered Professional Engineer in the Province of Ontario. He has been active in the International Federation of Automatic Control and has organized several sessions in the Symposia and Congresses of the IFAC in addition to serving on the International Program Committees of many IFAC Symposia. From January 1982 to January 1987, he was an Associate Editor of the IEEE magazine *Technology and Society.*

Lotfi A. Zadeh is a Professor in the Graduate School, Computer Science Division, Department of EECS, University of California, Berkeley. In addition, he is serving as the Director of BISC (Berkeley Initiative in Soft Computing).

Lotfi Zadeh is an alumnus of the University of Teheran, MIT and Columbia University. He held visiting appointments at the Institute for Advanced Study, Princeton, NJ; MIT; IBM Research Laboratory, San Jose, CA; SRI International, Menlo Park, CA; and the Center for the

Study of Language and Information, Stanford University. His earlier work was concerned in the main with systems analysis, decision analysis and information systems. His current research is focused on fuzzy logic, computing with words and soft computing, which is a coalition of fuzzy logic, neurocomputing, evolutionary computing, probabilistic computing and parts of machine learning. The guiding principle of soft computing is that, in general, better solutions can be obtained by employing the constituent methodologies of soft computing in combination rather than in stand-alone mode.

Lotfi Zadeh is a Fellow of the IEEE, AAAS, ACM and AAAI. He is a member of the National Academy of Engineering and a Foreign Member of the Russian Academy of Natural Sciences. He is a recipient of the IEEE Education Medal, the IEEE Richard W. Hamming Medal, the IEEE Medal of Honor, the ASME Rufus Oldenburger Medal, the B. Bolzano Medal of the Czech Academy of Sciences, the Kampe de Feriet Medal, the AACC Richard E. Bellman Central Heritage Award, the Grigore Moisil Prize, the Honda Prize, the Okawa Prize, the AIM Information Science Award, the IEEE-SMC J. P. Wohl Career Acheivement Award, the SOFT Scientific Contribution Memorial Award of the Japan Society for Fuzzy Theory, and other awards and honorary doctorates. He has published extensively on a wide variety of subjects relating to the conception, design and analysis of information/intelligent systems, and is serving on the editorial boards of over fifty journals.

INDEX

Printed and bound by CPI Group (UK) Ltd, Croydon, CR0 4YY

03/10/2024

01040323-0014